READING, THEN WRITING

From Source to Essay

READING, THEN WRITING
From Source to Essay

Thayle Anderson
Kent Forrester
Murray State University

McGRAW-HILL, INC.

New York St. Louis San Francisco Auckland Bogotá Caracas
Hamburg Lisbon London Madrid Mexico Milan Montreal
New Delhi Paris San Juan São Paulo
Singapore Sydney Tokyo Toronto

This book was developed by STEVEN PENSINGER, Inc.

Reading, Then Writing: From Source to Essay

1 2 3 4 5 6 7 8 9 0   HAL HAL   9 0 9 8 7 6 5 4 3 2 1

ISBN 0-07-001957-6

This book was set in Melior by Monotype Composition Company.
The editors were Steve Pensinger and James R. Belser;
the designer was Amy Becker;
the cover illustrator was Ric Del Rossy;
the production supervisor was Louise Karam.
Arcata Graphics/Halliday was printer and binder.

Acknowledgments appear on pages 515-517, and on this page by reference.

Library of Congress Cataloging-in-Publication Data

Anderson, Thayle K.
    Reading, then writing: from source to essay / Thayle Anderson, Kent Forrester.
        p.   cm.
    Includes index.
    ISBN 0-07-001957-6
    1. English language—Rhetoric.   2. College readers.
I. Forrester, Kent.   II. Title.
PE1408.A593   1992
808'.0427—dc20
                                                    91-6844

About the Authors

Thayle Anderson, who earned a B.A. and an M.A. at Brigham Young University and a Ph.D. at Purdue University, is a professor of English at Murray State University, where he has taught graduate and undergraduate courses for over 20 years. He served as editor of *The Kentucky Philological Bulletin* for 9 years, and he also served as Director of Composition in MSU's English Department. Currently he is director of the department's graduate program. He is coauthor (with Kent Forrester) of *Point Counterpoint: Eight Cases for Composition* (1987), a text which is currently going into its second edition.

Kent Forrester, who has taught at Murray State University for 19 years, earned his B.A. and M.A. from the University of Oregon and a Ph.D. (1971) from the University of Utah. He has served as Director of Humanities at Murray State University and as president of the Kentucky Philological Association. He is the coauthor of two books: *The Freshman Reader: Essay and Casebook*, 1983 (with Jerry Herndon) and *Point Counterpoint: Eight Cases for Composition*, 1987 (with Thayle Anderson). He has published essays on composition and eighteenth-century literature.

For our wives and children

Patricia Anderson
Nicole
Elise
Raina
Ashley
Keri

Marie Forrester
Kelly
Annie
Alan

Contents

Preface

Reading, Then Writing is based on a few ideas that have grown with us as the years have passed: The personal essay, that traditional vehicle for prose, has outlived its usefulness; students need to learn how to incorporate other people's ideas—in particular those from essays and books—into their own writing, and writing classes should be full of reading so that students will have interesting, significant things to write about.

The personal essay, where the focus is on subjective prose and personal experiences, doesn't move our students forward to the common college tasks of writing reports, critiques, and reviews, but instead moves them backward to their high school English classes. Indeed, when we assign personal essays, we only reinforce the common notion among students that college writing classes lack significant content, resembling nothing so much as the English classes our students have been sitting through since they started school, where writing was almost always self-focused and reading was almost always peripheral to that writing.

No doubt *because* they have been asked to focus on *their* ideas almost exclusively, students come to us lacking higher-level writing skills—skills like introducing and punctuating quotations and summaries, critiquing an idea in a book or essay, and paraphrasing passages. That's why we begin the book with six chapters on those neglected skills. We've filled these chapters with a wealth of short, lively, and informative readings on which the students can practice their skills. Indeed, we hope your students will find that even the passages they are asked to summarize will be appealing enough for the class to linger over for a moment or two.

In Chapter 7 the book turns into a reader—but a reader with a difference: Each of the last six chapters contains eight or so tightly focused essays. In fact, they're so tightly focused that you can use them as the raw material for source papers of one sort or another.

We realize that no teacher is going to cover all six reading chapters in a semester. That's why we have tried to provide a variety of topics that cross the college curriculum. Chapter 7 deals with the history of science and medicine (*Medicine before Science: The Treatment Was Successful, But the Patient Died*). Chapter 8 deals with a political-social issue (*The Jonestown Massacre: How Could It Happen?*) Chapter 9 deals with a literary work (*Flannery O'Connor's "Good Country People": What Is the Author Up To?*). Chapter 10 deals with a scientific-ethical controversy (*Animal Rights: Where Do We Draw the Line?*). Chapter 11 deals with a social-feminist issue (*Sexist Language: Is the Cure Worse Than the Disease?*). Chapter 12 deals with a historical event that hinged on an ethical decision (*Hiroshima and Nagasaki: Did We Have to Drop the Bomb?*).

This book can serve as a text for either semester of first-year composition. You might, for instance, want to use it in the first semester of a year-long writing program. If that's the case, you can focus on the first six skills chapters (remember, even those chapters contain plenty of readings), and then end up with a couple of the "mini-casebook" chapters. Or you might want to use the book in the second semester, typically a research-oriented semester. If that's the case, you can select assignments from the first six chapters, but focus much of your students' attention on Chapter 6. Then you can use Chapters 7 to 12 as raw material for source papers.

McGraw-Hill and the authors would like to thank Michael Hennessy, Southwest Texas State University; Judith Stanford, Rivier College; and Tom Zaniello, Northern Kentucky University, for their careful review of this manuscript.

We're especially grateful to three people from McGraw-Hill: James Belser, who supervised the editing of our manuscript; Martha Cameron, who caught numerous errors and smoothed out our prose; and Steve Pensinger, our developing editor, who helped shape our book from its very inception.

Thayle Anderson
Kent Forrester

READING, THEN WRITING
From Source to Essay

PART ONE

Starting Up: How to Handle Your Sources

— 1 —

The Shape of Things to Come

If you've already heard more than you need to about what goes into an essay, you might want to simply browse through this chapter, slowing down only when you come across an idea that seems new. But if you've been away from school for a few years, or forgotten over the course of a long summer what you once knew from a high school English class, or were listening with only half a mind when your English teachers started talking about main ideas and topic sentences, then this chapter is for you.

Although this book is mainly about how to use other people's ideas in your own writing, we begin with this short chapter on that classic college writer's medium, the short essay, because most of your reading in this book will come in the shape of essays and your writing will almost always take that same shape. Let's start from the top.

AN ESSAY'S TITLE

Writers of books and essays need to come up with an idea *about* something when they set out to write. When they have those two things, a subject and an idea about that subject, they have what's commonly known as a thesis, or a main idea. The subject "Okra," for instance, just can't serve as the thesis of an essay. But "The History of Okra" or "The Influence of Okra on Southern Politics" or "Is Okra Fuzzy or Slimy?" or "Elvis Presley's Relationship with Okra" all make fine essay titles.

Since most titles contain a subject and an idea, most titles are miniature theses, like this one:

"The Full Circle: In Praise of the Bicycle" by Stefan Kanfer

Even before reading that essay, you could probably give it a very general summary, something like this:

3

Stefan Kanfer argues that even in this day and age, bicycling is a pleasurable and practical means of transportation.

Here are other titles that are, in effect, miniature theses:

"Terrorism Can Be Eliminated" by Benjamin Netanyahu
"Where College Fails Us" by Caroline Bird
"Why English Should Be Our Official Language" by S. I. Hayakawa
"Hiroshima Was a War Crime" by Shigetoshi Iwamatsu
"Why Mothers Should Stay Home" by Deborah Fallows

If you were writing a paper on *Moby Dick*, then, you wouldn't want to title your paper "*Moby Dick*." Moby Dick is only a subject; it lacks an idea. But you might title your paper "The Character of Ahab in *Moby Dick*" or "A Study of Personal Names in *Moby Dick*" or even "A Review of *Moby Dick*."

Most titles aren't so easy to decipher. In fact, the main idea of an essay sometimes lies hidden behind a title's puns and clever phrases. Consider, for instance, the title of Stephen King's essay, "Now You Take *Bambi* or *Snow White*—That's Scary!" If you had a mother in your past who read you fairy tales, you no doubt already have a strong suspicion of King's thesis. But even without such a mother, you could probably, after a little thought, come up with King's thesis without going past his title. (Can you make an intelligent guess as to King's thesis? If there is a comparison in his essay, what do you suppose it is?) Occasionally, however, a title will be so cryptic that it can do no more for you than confirm your understanding of an essay after you've finished reading it—as you can see in the following titles:

"Viable Solutions": In this essay, Edwin Newman bemoans the trend toward stilted and jargon-laden language. His title, "Viable Solutions," is an example of the kind of bureaucratic buzzwords that Newman attacks in his essay.
"The Hard Sell": This essay, by Ron Rosenbaum, is an attack on the advertising industry. The word "hard" in the title conveys Rosenbaum's idea that the advertising industry is cold and callous.
"The Bier Barons": Al Morgan satirizes the greed and tastelessness of Forest Lawn cemetery. (You'll have to understand the pun to figure out this one.)

AN ESSAY'S INTRODUCTION

Like a title, the thesis of an essay (or a book, for that matter) consists of a subject and an idea about that subject. Here's how Sir Edmund Hillary, the famed conqueror of Mount Everest, makes his thesis clear in his introduction to "Epitaph to the Elusive Abominable Snowman":

Does the Yeti, or "abominable snowman," really exist? Or is it just a myth without practical foundation? For the last four months our Himalayan scientific and mountaineering expedition has been trying to find out—and now we think we know the answer.

In fact, a thesis can be seen as an expanded form of a title, as you see by the relationship between Hillary's title and his thesis.

Hillary's title	**A summary of Hillary's thesis**
"Epitaph to the Elusive Abominable Snowman"	We think we know the answer to the question of the abominable snowman's existence.

There's a word in the title that contains Hillary's idea about his subject. In fact, that word gives away the answer to the question of the existence of the abominable snowman. What is that word and what is that answer?

Although writers often like to wait until the last sentence in their introduction before stating their thesis, a thesis can appear anywhere in an introduction. For instance, the preamble of the Declaration of Independence contains its thesis.

> When in the course of human events, it becomes necessary for one people to dissolve the political bands which have connected them with another . . . a decent respect to the opinions of mankind requires that they should declare the causes which impel them to the separation.

So the Declaration *begins* by contending that when a group of people decide to form a new nation, they ought to explain why they are doing so.

AN ESSAY'S BODY

The body of an essay consists of a series of paragraphs in which you do what you promised you were going to do when you wrote your thesis. To help the reader move through the body, writers almost always begin their paragraphs with topic sentences. Just as a thesis statement tells what an essay is going to be about, a topic sentence tells what the paragraph is going to be about, as you see in this example from Ernest Sackville Turner's book, "*Call the Doctor.*"

> **No doubt there was a certain amount of exhibitionism in the operating theatre.** Yet a surgeon aware of the torture he was inflicting on an unanaesthetised patient could hardly be blamed for working with utmost speed and taking pride in saying to his audience, like Robert Liston, "Now, gentlemen, time me." Liston, who was said to have had a wrist strong enough to screw off a man's head, could amputate a leg at the thigh, single-handed, compressing the artery with his left hand, "in as

few seconds as a first-class sprinter takes to run a hundred
yards." Another surgeon was reputed to have taken off an arm
at the shoulder while his colleague turned for a pinch of snuff.

And that's the shape of a typical paragraph. It begins with a topic sentence,
which is simply a suggestion of what is to follow (in this case, exhibitionism
among surgeons), and then supports that topic sentence with an argument
or an illustration. If you'll shape your own paragraphs that way, you'll likely
write better paragraphs.

Many topic sentences do more than suggest the main idea of a paragraph:
Often they provide a transition that helps a reader move from one paragraph
to the next. These transitions can be as simple as a single word, like the
words in boldface that follow:

- **Furthermore**, the same technique can be used to kill a pig.
- Don't believe, **however**, that aerobic exercise will allow you to live
  forever.

Words like "however" and "furthermore" are general-purpose transitions.
Most transitions don't rely on single words or short phrases; most are built
into the flow of the meaning. For instance, some transitions ask a question
of an idea in the previous paragraph; some link an idea in the topic sentence
with an idea in the last sentence of the previous paragraph; some comment
on an idea in the previous paragraph.

But enough of that: it's time to move on. Writers learn to use transitions
by writing, not by reading about them. You'll have a chance at the end of
this chapter to write paragraphs with good transitions.

AN ESSAY'S CONCLUSION

Really, conclusions don't deserve the worry that writers give to them. They're
almost as easy as saying good-bye to your friends. You don't want to walk
away without a word, and you don't want to bore them with a belabored
farewell. In a paper, all you need to do is either restate your thesis or make
a recommendation based on points you've made in the paper. Here, for
instance, is a perfectly adequate two-sentence conclusion to an essay called
"How We Listen," in which Aaron Copland argues that we can improve our
enjoyment of music by listening to it with an active and alive mind.

What the reader should strive for, then, is a more *active* kind
of listening. Whether you listen to Mozart or Duke Ellington,
you can deepen your understanding of old music only by being
a more conscious and aware listener—not someone who is just
listening, but someone who is listening *for* something.

If you have something good, of course, go with it. In an essay called
"Can You Afford to Die?" an attack on the greed of the funeral industry, Roul

Tunley ends with a lengthy story of a mortician who admitted that he could embalm an elephant for $1.50. Now that's worth a reader's time.

> One of the most passionate critics of morticians was the late W. W. Chambers, a Washington, D.C. funeral director. The firm that bears his name conducts more funerals in the nation's capital than does any other firm and has handled five of them in the White House. Testifying before a congressional committee in 1948 against a proposal to license undertakers, the late Mr. Chambers said, "The business is a mighty sweet racket." He said he got into it when he was working in a livery stable and saw a "poor broken widow" being sold a seventeen-dollar casket for $250. "It has the horse business beat a mile," he declared. During his testimony, Mr. Chambers made coast-to-coast headlines by insisting he could embalm an elephant for $1.50.

And in "On the Trail of the Curly Cows," an essay that describes the rigors of nineteenth-century buffalo hunters, John Madson plays back an old song to end his essay.

> Oh, it's now we've crossed Pease River, and homeward we are bound.
> No more in that hell-fired country shall e'er we be found.
> Go home to our wives and sweethearts, tell others not to go.
> For God's forsaken the buffalo range and the darned old buffalo!

But as we say, don't belabor your conclusion unless you have something worth the time.

It's now time to put some of this knowledge about the structure of an essay into practice, but before we turn you loose we want to offer two more bits of advice. First, when you *read* an essay, try to recreate the author's plan. (You can be sure that professional writers plan their essays.) If you can see the essay as a whole, you won't get lost in the forest of details. Then once you see its general shape, focus your vision to see how the essay's details support its main points. And second, plan *your* essay before you write it. Yes, we know that's the same dreary advice English teachers have been giving out since kids wrote their lessons on slate tablets, but that fact doesn't undermine its validity. You don't have to write a formal outline—or even a detailed one—but you *should* sit down and think through your paper. At the very least, set down a clear main idea and write out the main points you want to make.

Now it's your turn.

EXERCISE 1-1: *Analyzing Structure*

Read the following short essay. Look for the author's thesis, topic sentences, and conclusion. Then answer the questions that follow.

Simplicity

Clutter is the disease of American writing. We are a society strangling in unnecessary words, **1.**
circular constructions, pompous frills and meaningless jargon.

Who can understand the viscous language of everyday American commerce and enterprise: **2.**
the business letter, the interoffice memo, the corporation report, the notice from the bank
explaining its latest "simplified" statement? What member of an insurance or medical plan can
decipher the brochure that tells him what his costs and benefits are? What father or mother can
put together a child's toy—on Christmas Eve or any other eve—from the instructions on the
box? Our national tendency is to inflate and thereby sound important. The airline pilot who
announces that he is presently anticipating experiencing considerable precipitation wouldn't
dream of saying that it may rain. The sentence is too simple—there must be something wrong
with it.

But the secret of good writing is to strip every sentence to its cleanest components. Every **3.**
word that serves no function, every long word that could be a short word, every adverb that
carries the same meaning that's already in the verb, every passive construction that leaves the
reader unsure of who is doing what—these are the thousand and one adulterants that weaken
the strength of a sentence. And they usually occur, ironically, in proportion to education and
rank.

During the late 1960s the president of a major university wrote a letter to mollify the **4.**
alumni after a spell of campus unrest. "You are probably aware," he began, "that we have been
experiencing very considerable potentially explosive expressions of dissatisfaction on issues
only partially related." He meant that the students had been hassling them about different things.
I was far more upset by the president's English than by the students' potentially explosive
expressions of dissatisfaction. I would have preferred the presidential approach taken by Franklin
D. Roosevelt when he tried to convert into English his own government's memos, such as this
blackout order of 1942:

> Such preparations shall be made as will completely obscure all Federal build-
> ings and non-Federal buildings occupied by the Federal government during an
> air raid for any period of time from visibility by reason of internal or external
> illumination.

"Tell them," Roosevelt said, "that in buildings where they have to keep the work going **5.**
to put something across the windows."

Simplify, simplify. Thoreau said it, as we are so often reminded, and no American writer **6.**
more consistently practiced what he preached. Open *Walden* to any page and you will find a
man saying in a plain and orderly way what is on his mind:

> I love to be alone. I never found the companion that was so companionable as
> solitude. We are for the most part more lonely when we go abroad among men
> than when we stay in our chambers. A man thinking or working is always
> alone, let him be where he will. Solitude is not measured by the miles of space
> that intervene between a man and his fellows. The really diligent student in
> one of the crowded hives of Cambridge College is as solitary as a dervish in
> the desert.

How can the rest of us achieve such enviable freedom from clutter? The answer is to clear **7.**
our heads of clutter. Clear thinking becomes clear writing: one can't exist without the other. It
is impossible for a muddy thinker to write good English. He may get away with it for a paragraph
or two, but soon the reader will be lost, and there is no sin so grave, for he will not easily be
lured back.

Who is this elusive creature the reader? He is a person with an attention span of about **8.** twenty seconds. He is assailed on every side by forces competing for his time: by newspapers and magazines, by television and radio, by his stereo and videocassettes, by his wife and children and pets, by his house and his yard and all the gadgets that he has bought to keep them spruce, and by that most potent of competitors, sleep. The man snoozing in his chair with an unfinished magazine open on his lap is a man who was being given too much unnecessary trouble by the writer.

It won't do to say that the snoozing reader is too dumb or too lazy to keep pace with the **9.** train of thought. My sympathies are with him. If the reader is lost, it is generally because the writer has not been careful enough to keep him on the path.

This carelessness can take any number of forms. Perhaps a sentence is so excessively **10.** cluttered that the reader, hacking his way through the verbiage, simply doesn't know what it means. Perhaps a sentence has been so shoddily constructed that the reader could read it in any of several ways. Perhaps the writer has switched pronouns in mid-sentence, or has switched tenses, so the reader loses track of who is talking or when the action took place. Perhaps Sentence B is not a logical sequel to Sentence A—the writer, in whose head the connection is clear, has not bothered to provide the missing link. Perhaps the writer has used an important word incorrectly by not taking the trouble to look it up. He may think that "sanguine" and "sanguinary" mean the same thing, but the difference is a bloody big one. The reader can only infer (speaking of big differences) what the writer is trying to imply.

Faced with these obstacles, the reader is at first a remarkably tenacious bird. He blames **11.** himself—he obviously missed something, and he goes back over the mystifying sentence, or over the whole paragraph, piecing it out like an ancient rune, making guesses and moving on. But he won't do this for long. The writer is making him work too hard, and the reader will look for one who is better at his craft.

The writer must therefore constantly ask himself: What am I trying to say? Surprisingly **12.** often, he doesn't know. Then he must look at what he has written and ask: Have I said it? Is it clear to someone encountering the subject for the first time? If it's not, it is because some fuzz has worked its way into the machinery. The clear writer is a person clear-headed enough to see this stuff for what it is: fuzz.

William Zinsser

QUESTIONS ON *SIMPLICITY*

1. Is the author arguing, or is he merely clarifying a point?
2. Does the title reveal the author's attitude toward his subject? Or does the author only reveal his subject in his title?
3. Write down the sentence in which Zinsser most clearly expresses his thesis.
4. Write Zinsser's thesis in your own words.
5. Which paragraphs, if any, do not have a reasonably clear topic sentence?
6. What is the precise transitional expression in paragraph 3?
7. How does Zinsser move from paragraph 6 to paragraph 7?
8. What is the precise transitional expression in paragraph 12?

9. Which of the two types of conclusions does the essay contain, the restatement of the thesis or the recommendation?

EXERCISE 1-2: *Writing Assignment*

Now we want you to write an analysis of the structure of "Simplicity." Here's how to go about it: In your introduction, identify the author and the title of the essay, summarize its main idea, and let your reader know, in one way or another, that you're going to analyze its structure. In the body of *your* paper, show how Zinsser develops his thesis by using alternating examples and advice. Illustrate your thesis by summarizing some of the examples and advice. Remember to write good topic sentences in this section of your paper, and provide transitions between paragraphs. Finally, close up your essay with a short conclusion that comes back to *your* thesis. One more suggestion: Focus your attention on the essay, not on Zinsser. In fact, leave Zinsser's name out of it after you have identified him in the first paragraph. Keep your verbs in the present tense.

2

Summarizing and Paraphrasing

Coming out of church one Sunday morning, Calvin Coolidge—Silent Cal they called him—was confronted by an eager reporter, who wanted to know what the president thought of the preacher's sermon on sin. "He said he was against it," Coolidge replied. Now *that* is a summary.

You will probably never need to summarize a sermon, but you will certainly need to summarize the central idea of a paragraph, an essay, or a book. In fact, when you come to think of it, much of the writing in what goes on in school and on the job consists of summaries of other people's ideas. You can be sure of one thing: Employers and professors won't ask you to write personal essays. ("Alice, write me a nice little essay on a traumatic experience that has increased your self-awareness—and have it on my desk by Monday!") But they will ask you to perform writing tasks—reports, reviews, studies, critiques, essay exams, and so forth—that involve summarizing.

By the way, summarizing and paraphrasing are basically the same thing. In both the writer puts someone else's ideas into his or her own words. A paraphrase is simply a more detailed summary. In fact, however, at some point on a continuum, a summary shades into and becomes a paraphrase. For the sake of simplicity, we'll often use the word "summary" as a generic term to represent both broad and detailed "translations" of someone else's ideas.

Let's begin by listing a few important points about summarizing and paraphrasing. Although we'll touch on each of these points later in the chapter, this is a good place to get them all down in a bunch. In fact, you might want to come back and review these every now and then as you work your way through the chapter.

EARLY ADVICE

1.   Search out theses and topic sentences. These are the authors' own summaries. Outside of narratives and heavily descriptive essays, the vast majority of all other kinds of writing have clearly identifiable theses and topic sentences, and that fact makes it worth your while to look for them. For a discussion of theses and topic sentences, see Chapter 1.

2.   Begin your summary with a good introduction that includes the author's name. If there is no author, include the title of the essay or the name of the magazine or book from which your summary is taken. If you can, identify the author and use a verb that conveys the author's intent. Here are two common patterns for summary introductions. Notice that the first introduction is a dependent clause, attached to the main clause (the summary) by a comma. In the second example, the introduction flows into the summary without any punctuation.

> **According to Jane Addams, the founder of Hull House**, private charities could not keep up with the vast numbers of Chicago's needy families.

> **Jane Addams, the founder of Hull House, claimed that** private charities could not keep up with the vast numbers of Chicago's needy families.

There are other kinds of summary introductions, but for the time being you can use the above two as models. When you are comfortable with them, go on to expand your repertoire of introductions. You'll have plenty of practice in this chapter.

3.   Begin paragraph-length summaries and paraphrases with a topic sentence. Usually the paragraph you are summarizing will already have a topic sentence. Your job, then, will merely be to put that topic sentence in your own words and then fill out your paragraph by elaborating on what is now *your* topic sentence. That is, begin with an overview and then fill in the details. Occasionally you'll come across a paragraph that lacks a topic sentence—or has a cryptic one; then you'll have to come up with a clear topic sentence of your own.

4.   When your summary is a paragraph or more in length, break into it every now and then to remind your reader that these are someone else's ideas. These little interruptions are hardly noticeable, yet they perform a valuable service by reminding readers whose ideas they are reading. Notice these little reminders (in boldface) in the paragraph below:

> In *The American Way of Death* Jessica Mitford pokes fun at the crassness and greed of America's funeral industry. The funeral industry, **Mitford argues**, seems to be drawn to the sentimental, the tasteless, and the gaudy, and greedy morticians exploit the living by selling overpriced coffins, by pushing useless products like coffin vaults, and by encouraging open coffin services in order to sell "death clothes" and facial makeovers. People can bypass morticians, **Mitford notes**, by joining burial societies that offer cheap funerals.

Keep these suggestions in mind as you go through the remainder of this chapter, and come back every now and again to review them. Before you go on, however, it might be a good idea to practice a few of these suggestions.

Exercise 2-1: *Writing a Summary*

Using the suggestions above, write a brief summary (three to five sentences) of the following paragraph.

Call the Doctor

In the main remedies were esteemed according to whether they were rare, complex, or unpleasant. A drug which combined all three qualities was irresistible. Certain specifics were so rare that they didn't exist, and therefore had to be counterfeited. Among these was unicorn's horn, for which the horn of a rhinoceros or the tusk of a narwhal was often substituted. A king of France jealously clung to what he fancied to be a real unicorn's horn and valued it at more than 100,000 crowns. Nearly as elusive as unicorn's horn was genuine Egyptian mummy. Abroise Paré explains that the rich Egyptians were embalmed in myrrh, aloes, saffron, spices and other drugs with or without therapeutic value; the poorer Egyptians were fobbed off with asphalt. Paré was doubtful whether any good could be derived from consuming powder even from a genuine mummy. He was certain that no good was to be derived from the bogus mummy in which many French apothecaries, "men wondrous audacious and covetous," had set up a profane but profitable trade. They had taken to seizing the bodies of the hanged, embalming them in salt and drugs, drying them in an oven and selling the results as genuine old Egyptian mummy. The only effect on the patient, said Paré, was "vomiting and stink of the mouth."

Ernest Sackville Turner

HONESTY AND ACCURACY

The next two lessons depend on the paragraph below written by J. H. Plumb. Because the paragraph appears out of context, let us say a few things about the essay it comes from. In that essay, "De Mortuis," Plumb claims that modern burial practices, which may seem a bit bizarre at times, are really not all that different in their intent from funeral practices of the past. (By the way, the "refrigerators at Phoenix" mentioned in the first sentence are cylinders filled with supercold gas, which are used to preserve corpses until the time when they can be thawed and, so some people believe, cured of the disease that killed the person in the first place; "Chanel" in the last line is a famous perfume company.) Here, then, is the source.

> Seen in the context of history, Forest Lawn is neither very vulgar nor very remarkable, and the refrigerators at Phoenix are no more surprising than a pyramid in Palenque or Cairo. If life has been good, we, like the rich Etruscans, want it to go on and on, or at the very least to be remembered. Only a few civilizations have evaded expansive funerary habits for their illustrious rich, and these usually poverty-stricken ones. For all their austerity,

the Hindus, burning bodies and throwing the ashes into the Ganges, have maintained distinction in their pyres. Not only were widows coaxed or thrown onto the flames, but rare and perfumed woods were burned to sweeten the spirit of the rich Brahman as it escaped from its corrupt carapace. Cremation à la Chanel!

Avoid Plagiarism

When you summarize or paraphrase, you are, in effect, making an unstated claim that you are "translating" the original passage into your own idiom or style. When you pick up too much of the source's idiom, then you are, technically speaking, plagiarizing. That kind of plagiarism is not as serious as the kind in which a writer tries to pass off someone else's writing as his or her own. That is *rank* dishonesty. Nevertheless, stealing phrases from a source you're supposed to be paraphrasing is a variety of plagiarism, and good writers try hard to avoid it.

In the following paraphrase of the "De Mortuis" passage, the paraphraser stuck too close to the source—and thus plagiarized. We have boldfaced the passages that were lifted directly from the original.

> According to J. H. Plumb, Forest Lawn is really **neither especially vulgar nor remarkable** if it is **seen in the context of history**. Viewing a pyramid in Palenque or Cairo should prepare one for refrigerators at Phoenix. If we have loved life, we **want it to go on and on**—or at least we want to dwell in the memories of our survivors. Only a few, relatively poverty-stricken civilizations have avoided **expansive funerary habits for their illustrious rich**. The Hindus, despite their poverty, were extravagant and expensive when it came to their burial methods. Widows, for instance, were often **coaxed or forced to join** the corpses of their husbands in the flames, and often **rare and perfumed woods** were thrown on the pyres to **sweeten the spirit** of the wealthy Hindu as it ascended from its **corrupt carapace. Eau de cremation!**

What makes this a plagiarized version is the fact that it is larded with phrases lifted intact from the original. As you can see by the boldfaced words above, the paraphraser stayed too close to the source. Such pilfered phrases should not appear in a paraphrase unless they are enclosed in quotation marks. And of course a paraphrase freighted down with that many quoted passages would collapse of its own weight.

Of course, you *have* to use some of the words of your source. There are, for instance, words without synonyms like "and" and "therefore" and "wood" that you can use without fear. Indeed, what is a person supposed to use as a substitute for "pyramid"? ("When we visited Egypt, we climbed the magnificent polyhedron with a polygonal base.") What you have to avoid, really, is the duplication of distinctive words like "carapace" and, *especially,* whole phrases like "expansive funerary habits" and "rare and perfumed woods."

Part of the problem in the paraphrase above is that the writer probably didn't clearly understand the rather subtle train of ideas in Plumb's paragraph. To substitute for that lack of understanding, the writer used the source's words. Remember, if you don't have a thorough grasp of your source's ideas, you will inevitably cling to the diction and the sentence structure of your source—and therefore plagiarize. What you will also be doing is dumping what was Greek to you onto the laps of your even less informed and hapless reader.

Make Your Summary Accurate

Language is a fuzzy and unwieldy thing, and a hundred things can go wrong when you're trying to capture the ideas of someone else. Most of those problems can be traced to a faulty reading of the source. Can you see what went wrong with this paraphrase of our model passage?

> According to J. H. Plumb, viewed from a historical perspective, the vulgarity of Forest Lawn pales by comparison with a pyramid in Palenque or Cairo. If we have clung to a good life, we strive to imitate the Etruscans, who made every effort to perpetuate themselves in their survivors' memories. Only three or four civilizations oppressed with abject poverty have ever avoided ostentation in their funerals. The Hindus were a good case in point: They cremated their deceased and spread the ashes in the Ganges. The only inconsistency in their Spartan funeral rites was their insistence that the pyre's flames be perfumed with the scent of rare wood and that the corpse of the deceased be joined in the flames by the widow. What a way to go!

As you've probably noticed, not all writings—even those done by professionals—are crystal clear. In fact, there is at least one ambiguous idea in the original passage by Plumb. That makes your job more difficult, of course, but it doesn't change your job. You are still obligated to make the original clear, even when you have to make an intelligent guess about your source's intent.

Now to our analysis of the above paraphrase. Plumb does not contend that the pyramids of Palenque or Cairo are *more* vulgar than the monuments at Forest Lawn. Plumb actually contends that they are basically the same. Plumb doesn't say that we consciously *strive* to imitate the Etruscans. He merely says that we may resemble them. Yet another problem: Plumb doesn't say that all civilizations that have avoided ostentation in their funeral rites have been impoverished. Nor does he say that the Hindus had "Spartan funeral rites." He says that their lives were Spartan, but that they lavished money on their funerals. Finally, the paraphraser's short exclamatory conclusion is not close enough in meaning to the source for the reader to discern exactly what Plumb's concluding idea is.

You see the problem here, don't you? The paraphraser simply has not read the source carefully enough to understand its ideas clearly. When it comes time to paraphrase a passage, take your time.

Here is a good paraphrase of Plumb's paragraph.

> J. H. Plumb argues that the elaborate and tasteless burial practices at Forest Lawn cemetery are not all that different in their intent from burial practices of the past. Like ancient peoples, we moderns too want to somehow escape death—or at least achieve a type of immortality by leaving something behind in the memories of our survivors. According to Plumb, very few ancient peoples, even poverty-stricken ones, have not buried their dead in fantastic, often expensive, ways. Even the Hindus of India, for instance, practiced costly and elaborate burials: Widows, along with expensive perfumed woods, were thrown into the very fires that consumed their husbands' corpses. Plumb concludes with a kicker: "Cremation à la Chanel!"

EXERCISE 2-2: *Writing a Summary*

Write a summary of the following passage that is both accurate and in your own idiom. Be sure to follow the suggestions outlined earlier in this chapter.

A Distant Mirror: The Calamitous 14th Century

"A terrible worm in an iron cocoon," as he was called in an anonymous poem, the knight rode on a saddle rising in a high ridge above the horse's backbone with his feet resting in very long stirrups so that he was virtually standing up and able to deliver tremendous swinging blows from side to side with any one of his armory of weapons. He began battle with the lance used for unhorsing the enemy, while from his belt hung a two-handed sword at one side and an eighteen-inch dagger on the other. He also had available, either attached to his saddle or carried by his squire, a longer sword for thrusting like a lance, a battle-ax fitted with a spike behind the curved blade, and a club-headed mace with sharpened, ridged edges, a weapon favored by martial bishops and abbots on the theory that it did not come under the rule forbidding clerics "to smite with the edge of the sword." The war-horse carrying this burden was itself armored by plates protecting nose, chest, and rump and caparisoned with draperies that got in the way of its legs. When his horse was felled, the knight, weighed down by his armor and tangled in weapons, shield, and spurs, was likely to be captured before he could manage to rise.

                                                                    Barbara Tuchman

DEEPER INTO THE ESSAY

As we move away from the analysis of short passages and toward longer pieces, we need to slow down for a moment and discuss some matters that have to do with essays as a whole.

First of all, as you read, don't get bogged down in details before you understand the big picture, the author's main idea. Bad summarizers focus on individual sentences and lose their way. Good summarizers keep their minds focused on the essay's thesis, or main idea, even when they're involved in individual sentences. Once you have the author's thesis firmly in mind, you might ask questions like these as you move your way through a piece of writing: Where is the writer going? What are these details accomplishing? How do these examples support the thesis of the essay?

Obviously, good summaries are the result of good reading—and only *then* of good writing. Unfortunately, a writer's thesis—which is what you're trying to put in your own words when you summarize—is sometimes obscured by a sprawl of words as they tumble down the page. You can get lost in that dark sprawl and fail to recognize the essay's main idea. As we pointed out in Chapter 1, to help readers find their way, writers usually shine a beam of light on their thesis (which you may know as the main idea) in three special spots in an essay: the title, the introduction, and the conclusion. In other words, most writers—at least good-hearted ones—leave behind well-lighted signposts for the reader.

Authors almost always begin a piece of writing with one of two broad intentions in mind: They either want to clarify something, or they want to argue a point. So the first question you should ask of a piece of writing is this: Is the author trying to clarify or argue a point? Once you understand which the author is doing, you're off to a solid start.

Of course, you'll often need to summarize more than the author's broad intention (and the main idea). Often you'll need to summarize the points that support an argument or clarify an idea. And that leads us to a second important point: When you are asked to summarize more than an essay's main idea, you need to see into the essay's heart. In fact, unless you can do that, you'll likely get lost in a forest of seemingly random sentences—and then end up summarizing minor points and seemingly random ideas.

Seeing into the heart of a piece of writing is, in effect, recreating the author's thought processes when he or she wrote the piece, and that's not an easy task. Indeed, it's the hardest kind of reading there is—one might call it *deep* reading—but good summarizers *have* to learn the skill.

Fortunately, there are a few common designs that appear again and again in essays. Once you learn to spot those designs, your job of understanding—and then summarizing—a passage or an essay is made much easier. That's why the rest of this chapter focuses on common organizational designs. Once you learn to see into the heart of these designs, you'll be able, we hope, to see into the heart of all kinds of writing.

Summarizing an Essay That Clarifies

The purpose of many books, essays, chapters, and paragraphs is merely to describe, or explain, something to the reader. For instance, a writer may want to explain what the gargoyles on Notre Dame Cathedral mean, or what it was like to ride in the rumble seat of a Ford coupe, or how the spadefoot toad survives while it hibernates at the bottom of a dry mud hole.

If the author is simply explaining or clarifying, then, be sure to let your reader know that in your introduction. Here is a typical introduction to a summary of an essay that simply describes something.

> In "The Kandy-Kolored Tangerine-Flake Streamline Baby," Tom Wolfe **describes** [shows, reveals, etc.] the world of custom cars.

Of course, there are a variety of methods that an author uses to explain something. He or she might, for instance, explain it by using examples, by comparing it to something else, or by grouping it with others. To summarize a clarification passage, you need to understand what method an author is using: example, description, comparison, or classification.

Clarification through Examples

One of the most common ways that authors have of making a point is by using examples. For instance, an author will often begin a paragraph with a topic sentence, as in these examples from H. S. Glasscheib's *The March of Medicine.*

> We can hardly envisage today the bloody horrors that took place at the scene of the birth and the uncertain hideous fate that often awaited a pregnant woman.

Then the author will simply fill in the paragraph with examples of the "bloody horrors" and "hideous fate."

> She was completely in the hands of these ragged old harridans, who travelled from house to house like tinkers with their old-fashioned labour chair and filthy hooks hanging at their belts. Woe to the pregnant woman when the birth did not run smoothly. It meant the certain death of the child and often the death of the mother, for there were no means of overcoming the slightest difficulty at the birth. In a long travail the child suffocated in the womb and then the so-called "child breaking" took place, i.e., the child was hacked to pieces with instruments and the individual parts torn from the mother's body with hooks and forceps.

That's enough examples of "bloody horror," don't you think?

EXERCISE 2-3: *Writing a Summary*

Write a paragraph-length summary of the essay below. Your first sentence should be an overview of your source; only then do you elaborate on that topic sentence. You might open your summary with words like these: "In 'Here is New York,' E. B. White describes . . ."

Here Is New York

It is a miracle that New York works at all. The whole thing is implausible. Every time the residents brush their teeth, millions of gallons of water must be drawn from the Catskills and the hills of Westchester. When a young man in Manhattan writes a letter to his girl in Brooklyn, the love message gets blown to her through a pneumatic tube—pfft—just like that. The subterranean system of telephone cables, power lines, steam pipes, gas mains and sewer pipes is reason enough to abandon the island to the gods and the weevils. Every time an incision is made in the pavement, the noisy surgeons expose ganglia that are tangled beyond belief. By rights New York should have destroyed itself long ago, from panic or fire or rioting or failure of some vital supply line in its circulatory system or from some deep labyrinthine short circuit. Long ago the city should have experienced an insoluble traffic snarl at some impossible bottleneck. It would have perished of hunger when food lines failed for a few days. It should have been wiped out by a plague starting in its slums or carried in by ships' rats. It should have been overwhelmed by the sea that licks at it on every side. The workers in its myriad cells should have succumbed to nerves, from the fearful pall of smoke-fog that drifts over every few days from Jersey, blotting out all light at noon and leaving the high offices suspended, men groping and depressed, and the sense of world's end. It should have been touched in the head by the August heat and gone off its rocker.

E. B. White

Clarification through Description

Writers often clarify a complex idea by breaking it down into a series of steps. For instance, a writer might describe how a wood mill works by describing the stages a tree goes through as it becomes a board. Or the writer might describe the stages in the development of eighteenth-century satire, or the steps that led to the founding of the Roman Empire, or the process that led to a courtship ritual among South Sea Islanders.

If you were summarizing these ideas, you would certainly want to communicate the idea that a process—a *series* of steps that leads to a particular result—is being described. Here are the kinds of introductions you might use:

In "The Preying Tree," Joseph Wheelwright describes, step by step, how he transformed a tree into a piece of living sculpture.
In "The Railroad Century," Guy Flores describes the process of putting together a railroad engine.

When your summary is a paragraph or more in length, break into it every now and again to remind your reader that these are someone else's ideas. Without these reminders, your reader won't know who is speaking: you or your source. So every now and then, interrupt your summary with a "Carla Hernandez then describes" or "Hernandez claims." Here is what one of those reminders (in boldface) looks like in a sentence:

Women have always been used, **Virginia Woolf says,** as reflections for men—reflections that have the "delicious power" of casting back men's images at twice their original size.

EXERCISE 2–4: *Writing a Summary*

Choose an introductory verb that emphasizes that you are describing a process. Here are some examples:

The author shows the steps that . . .
The author describes the process of . . . from [this point] to [this point].
The author shows, in three easy steps, how . . .

Write a one-paragraph summary of the following essay. The topic sentence by itself should serve as a concise overall summary. After you have written a one-sentence summary, elaborate on that summary by writing additional sentences. One more thing: A summary should get across not just *what* the author says, but the *way* he or she says it. If you merely describe what happens in the essay below, your reader will miss a good part of what goes on in that essay, so you'll have to convey more than just what goes on. You'll have to convey the tone of the essay.

Legs

When I was about twelve, I saw, to my huge sorrow, that I was growing hair on my legs. No one else but boys had hair on their legs. And I sure as heck didn't want it on *my* legs. But I also saw that there was a solution to my problem. According to the advertisements on television, I could transform my hirsute legs into silky smooth legs with hardly any trouble at all. So all you young girls out there, listen up while I tell you how to become mature, sophisticated women—well, a hairless young girl, anyway.

First, realize that this shaving business is done behind a locked bathroom door. For reasons beyond my understanding, mothers want their young daughters to have hairy legs. So lock the door and find your dad's shaving cream and safety razor. Now turn on the hot water in the bathtub—the hotter the better.

When the tub is full of hot water, get settled into it and rest one leg on the side of the tub. After shaking the shaving cream can, squirt some lather onto your hand and then spread it on your legs. Now take the razor and begin at your ankle. (You don't need to shave your foot unless you're a *very* hairy young girl.) Take long strokes. That way you won't gouge yourself as often or as deep. Watch out for your knee. It's bony and easy to cut. After your legs are glistening, rinse off and count the gashes. Get an equivalent number of band-aids and cover each injury.

You've just become a mature, sophisticated American woman.

Carla Hernandez

Clarification through Comparison

A writer also clarifies by comparing two things. For instance, a writer might want to clarify the difference between Golden hamsters and Teddy Bear hamsters by comparing the characteristics of the two animals. Or the writer might want to compare Ford and Chevy pickups to clarify their features and driving characteristics. (By the way, the word "comparison" is a generic term for both comparisons and contrasts.)

Looking at two objects or ideas side by side illuminates both sides. When you see a comparison being made in an essay, let your reader know that. For example, your summary of an article in *Family Computing* might look like this.

The author **contrasts** IBM XT computers and Apple Macintoshes to help prospective buyers decide which computer is best for their needs.

Reminders: As you summarize the passage in Exercise 2-5, try to see into the heart of the passage by understanding its structure, the way it's put together. Back off and see how the parts make up the whole. Also, use your own idiom or style. That doesn't mean, of course, that you can't use *some* of the words that the author, Jacob Bronowski, uses. You just can't use "special" words or strings of words. For instance, you would want to avoid using the words "singular" and "ubiquitous," which Bronowski uses in his first paragraph. (Of course, you could quote them without hesitation.) And you would not want to use a string of words, like "gifts which make him unique," unless you put them in quotation marks.

EXERCISE 2-5 *Writing a Summary*

The essay below analyzes a topic through comparison. After reading it, write a paragraph length summary, and introduce your summary with words that indicate that the author is comparing. If you sense that the author is arguing as well as comparing, you might let your reader know that as well.

Man and the Grunion

Man is a singular creature. He has a set of gifts which make him unique among the animals: so that, unlike them, he is not a figure in the landscape—he is a shaper of the landscape. In body and in mind he is the explorer of nature, the ubiquitous animal, who did not find but has made his home in every continent.

It is reported that when the Spaniards arrived overland at the Pacific Ocean in 1769 the California Indians used to say that at full moon the fish came and danced on these beaches. And it is true that there is a local variety of fish, the grunion, that comes up out of the water and lays its eggs above the normal high-tide mark. The females bury themselves tail first in the sand and the males gyrate round them and fertilize the eggs as they are being laid. The full moon is important, because it gives the time needed for the eggs to incubate undisturbed in the sand, nine or ten days, between these very high tides and the next ones that will wash the hatched fish out to sea again.

Every landscape in the world is full of these exact and beautiful adaptions, by which an animals fits into its environment like one cogwheel into another. The sleeping hedgehog waits for the spring to burst its metabolism into life. The humming-bird beats the air and dips its needle-fine beak into hanging blossoms. Butterflies mimic leaves and even noxious creatures to deceive their predator. The mole plods through the ground as if he had been designed as a mechanical shuttle.

So millions of years of evolution have shaped the grunion to fit and sit exactly with the tides. But nature—that is, biological evolution—has not fitted man to any specific environment. On the contrary, by comparison with the grunion he has a rather crude survival kit; and yet—this is the paradox of the human condition—one that fits him to all environments. Among the multitude of animals which scamper, fly, burrow and swim around us, man is the only one who is not locked into his environment. His imagination, his reason,

his emotional subtlety and toughness, make it possible for him not to accept the environment but to change it.

Jacob Bronowski

Clarification through Classification

Classification is one of the fundamental ways we have of making sense
of large numbers of anything. We break those numbers down into logical
groups. Linnaeus did us all a favor when he classified the bewildering variety
of animals on our planet. By dividing them up into logical groups, he made
sense out of chaos. (Of course, we ended up in a group that includes hamsters
and whales.)

Confronted by a topic that consists of a large group, writers will often
break it down into categories in order to clarify that topic for their readers.
They might, for instance, divide Shakespeare's plays into comedies, tragedies,
and histories. Or they might sort out Silicon Valley businessmen and find
that they fall into three categories: suits (IBM employees), sport coats (DEC
employees), and jeans (Apple employees). When you discover a passage that
classifies, all you do is introduce your summary with words that let your
reader know that fact. You might, for instance, introduce a summary of a
classification passage in the following ways:

The author classifies . . .
The author analyzes his topic by sorting it into . . .
The author breaks down _____ into three categories: . . .
The author describes four ways of . . .

You will discover the classification principle at work in the essay that we
have reprinted in Exercise 2-6.

Reminder: When you're summarizing an essay, look carefully at the
first paragraph. You're likely to find the author's own summary there. All
you have to do is put the author's summary into your own words; that will
serve as your topic sentence.

EXERCISE 2-6: *Writing a Summary*

In a single paragraph, summarize the essay that follows. As you construct your
introduction, be sure to let your reader know that the author is classifying a subject.
Remember, your first sentence should be an overview. Only then do you go on to
elaborate on that overview.

Main Street: The Agora of Rural America

During the Golden Age of Athens, the ancient Greeks regularly donned their hippest
togas and strolled through the agora: the marketplace. Today, a similar pastime thrives in
small towns throughout America. That pastime, of course, is known simply as cruising. In
Murray, Kentucky, the Dairy Queen not only sells cherry Blizzards and foot-long hot dogs,
but its parking lot serves as the turnaround point for cruisers. To a casual observer, all
cruisers look much the same, but a discriminating spectator can see that cruisers actually
fall into distinct categories.

The largest number of cruisers are the kids from the city. They cruise the streets in Z-cars and freshly polished Cutlass Broughams. They slouch behind the wheel, clad in pre-washed Guess jeans and oversized Generra shirts. Bruce Springsteen blasts through their open car windows from Sony Stereos equipped with graphic equalizers and power boosters. Cruising on a summer night is the *ne plus ultra* of their existence.

The rednecks have a different style. They drive GMC pickup trucks and wear Dingo boots and Levi 501s. Their right back pocket bulges, where a green and white tin of Skoal Bandits rests. The rednecks hang red bandannas from their rearview mirrors, and Hank Williams, Jr. sings about all his rowdy friends from giant rear speakers. Rednecks drink Mountain Dew and eat Moon Pies.

Later in the evening, the part-time cruisers, the college kids, wearing Reeboks and fraternity sweaters, join the parade. The college kids cruise for nostalgia's sake—they say——and spend most of the evening describing (1) how much better the cruising was in their day and (2) the immaturity of the present day high school cruisers.

When the caravan finally reaches its northernmost point, the DQ, some of the rednecks dismount from their 4 × 4's and line up at the counter for an ice cream. Meanwhile, a girl from a Stingray skitters across the parking lot. She is dressed like Cindy Lauper. A high school athlete struts over to a small group of sorority pledges. The college kids make fun of his leather pants and driving gloves. A college girl wearing a bandanna around her waist sits in her Ford Taurus, a gift from daddy. But the college kids don't stay long. Tomorrow's a school day and they have themes due at eight in the morning.

Murray's taxpayers who live along Main Street don't like the cruisers. They claim, rightly, that the cruisers are loud and boisterous. But the taxpayers are fighting a losing battle against tradition, the DQ, and The American Way. Besides, most members of Murray's city council who hear complaints by the Main Street residents were once Main Street cruisers themselves.

As I sit in front of the DQ, I notice a man in his mid-thirties standing at the other end of the table. He wears beige linen pants and a white Van Heussen dress shirt. Clinging to his neck is a five-year-old girl, his daughter no doubt, who is wearing most of her chocolate-dipped ice cream cone on her face. I overhear the man telling his friend that his wife is in San Francisco on business, so he and his daughter have come out for an ice cream cone. All of us look up as a Corvette lays down a strip of rubber on its way out of the DQ parking lot. The man with the child continues. He used to cruise Main Street, he says, in a blue 1964 Mustang convertible. But he has other things to worry about now, he says somewhat ruefully, than the sound of his radio, the color of his car.

Soon the man and his daughter are gone, and Main Street is left to the teenagers. All over America, all summer long, they come out at night, as regular as summer moths, and cruise and cruise, an endless parade of cars, trucks, and motorcycles. There's something elemental about it—like the dancing of bees or the mating strut of peacocks. At any rate, it's been going on since ancient Greece and shows no sign of slowing down. Indeed, it's a part of growing up in America's Heartland.

Kelli Burkeen

Summarizing an Essay That Argues

Just as the author can clarify an idea in a variety of ways, he or she can also argue an idea in a variety of ways. An arguer might compare IBM XTs to Apple Macintoshes in order to point out that one of them is superior to the other. An arguer may use, on a paragraph level, all of the various approaches that we have already discussed. He or she might, for instance, give examples or even describe a process. But the two most important tools are giving reasons and showing causes.

Your first job as a summarizer, then, is to be a good reader by stripping away everything but the bare bones of the argument, which will be either reasons or causes. You don't want to be summarizing minor points in an essay when you're supposed to be examining the basic argument.

To show how this works, let's consider a famous statement that was put forth in the Declaration of Independence. In the midst of all those words, there is a simple argument going on. The writers state their conclusion (or thesis):

> The history of the present King of Great Britain is a history of
> repeated injuries and usurpations, all having in direct object
> the establishment of an absolute tyranny over these states. To
> prove this, let facts be submitted to a candid world.

Then they discuss the reasons that led to the necessity to break away from Britain. Three of the numerous reasons are these:

1. King George has sent foreign mercenaries to plague us.
2. He has encouraged Indians to rebel against us.
3. He has not listened to our pleas for justice.

If you were giving a brief summary of the writers' argument, you would probably write something like this:

> Jefferson argues that Americans are breaking their ties with Britain
> because King George has been "tyrannical."

If you were writing a longer summary, you might write something like this:

> The signers of the Declaration of Independence argue that Ameri-
> cans are breaking their ties with Britain because King George, has,
> among other "tyrannical" acts, sent foreign mercenaries to plague
> the colonies, encouraged the Indians to raid the colonists' villages,
> and failed to listen to legitimate complaints.

And that's what you need to do when you summarize an essay: Break the argument down to its simplest parts, and then summarize those parts.

Like the writer who is clarifying something, the author who is arguing uses a variety of methods of presenting the material. But if you look deeper, you'll often see that underneath these "expository" methods, the author is arguing in one of two basic ways: either by giving *reasons* for a position, or by showing how one thing *caused* another.

It's helpful, though not crucial, for a summarizer to be able to communicate the author's method of argumentation. In fact, it's very difficult to tell in some essays if the author is giving reasons or showing a cause-and-effect relationship.

Arguments That Give Reasons

Probably the most common way of arguing is by listing reasons. In its simplest form, such an argument looks like this:

We should keep pet tigers out of school because

1. They aren't housebroken.
2. They roar while the teacher is trying to talk.
3. They bite.

Of course, there may be a lot of words before, between, and around those simple reasons. But that's your job when you're summarizing an argument: Separate the wheat from the chaff. Here's a hint: Look at the first sentence in each paragraph. The author will often state his or her reasons there. (More on this in the chapter on paraphrasing.) But remember, your first job is to summarize the author's basic argument. Then if you want to elaborate on that argument, list the author's reasons for adopting that position.

So a very brief summary of the tiger essay will look something like this:

The author argues that taking tigers to school is a bad idea.

Of course, you don't have to use the word "argue." Sometimes it is obvious that an argument is going on. Then your summary (a longer summary this time) will look something like this:

According to the author, taking tigers to school is a bad idea be-cause they mess on the floor, they are noisy, and they bite people.

Reminders: Authors usually insert a thesis statement, or main idea, in their introductions. If you discover the author's thesis statement, you've discovered, in effect, a summary of the essay. Your only job will be to put it in your words. Also, authors often use the first sentence of a paragraph as an overview, or summary, of the paragraph—in other words, a topic sentence. As a result, you'll usually find the main points of an essay in these topic sentences.

Now see if you can identify, and then summarize, Judy Syfers' argument in the essay below.

EXERCISE 2-7: *Writing a Summary*

In *Why I Want a Wife*, Judy Syfers argues by giving reasons. But because her style is ironic, a literal summary of her reasons would mislead the reader about Syfers' intentions. To drive this point home, we're going to ask you to write two summaries here. First, write a summary in which you take Syfers' ironic reasons as real ones. Then write a summary in which you recognize the sustained irony of the essay.

Why I Want a Wife

I belong to that classification of people known as wives. I am a wife. And, not alto-gether incidentally, I am a mother.

Not too long ago a male friend of mine appeared on the scene from the Midwest fresh from a recent divorce. He had one child, who is, of course, with his ex-wife. He is obviously looking for another wife. As I thought about him while I was ironing one evening, it suddenly occurred to me that I, too, would like to have a wife. Why do I want a wife?

I would like to go back to school so that I can become economically independent, support myself, and, if need be, support those dependent upon me. I want a wife who will work and send me to school. And while I am going to school I want a wife to take care of my children. I want a wife to keep track of the children's doctor and dentist appointments. And to keep track of mine, too. I want a wife to make sure my children eat properly and are kept clean. I want a wife who will wash the children's clothes and keep them mended. I want a wife who is a good nurturant attendant to my children, arranges for their schooling, makes sure that they have an adequate social life with their peers, takes them to the park, the zoo, etc. I want a wife who takes care of the children when they are sick, a wife who arranges to be around when the children need special care, because, of course, I cannot miss classes at school. My wife must arrange to lose time at work and not lose the job. It may mean a small cut in my wife's income from time to time, but I guess I can tolerate that. Needless to say, my wife will arrange and pay for the care of the children while my wife is working.

I want a wife who will take care of *my* physical needs. I want a wife who will keep my house clean. A wife who will pick up after my children, a wife who will pick up after me. I want a wife who will keep my clothes clean, ironed, mended, replaced when need be, and who will see to it that my personal things are kept in their proper place so that I can find what I need the minute I need it. I want a wife who cooks the meals, a wife who is a *good* cook. I want a wife who will plan the menus, do the necessary grocery shopping, prepare the meals, serve them pleasantly, and then do the cleaning up while I do my studying. I want a wife who will care for me when I am sick and sympathize with my pain and loss of time from school. I want a wife to go along when our family takes a vacation so that someone can continue to care for me and my children when I need a rest and a change of scene.

I want a wife who will not bother me with rambling complaints about a wife's duties. But I want a wife who will listen to me when I feel the need to explain a rather difficult point I have come across in my course of studies. And I want a wife who will type my papers for me when I have written them.

I want a wife who will take care of the details of my social life. When my wife and I are invited out by my friends, I want a wife who will take care of the babysitting arrangements. When I meet people at school that I like and want to entertain, I want a wife who will have the house clean, will prepare a special meal, serve it to me and my friends, and not interrupt when I talk about the things that interest me and my friends. I want a wife who will have arranged that the children are fed and ready for bed before my guests arrive so that the children do not bother us. I want a wife who takes care of the needs of my guests so that they feel comfortable, who makes sure that they have an ashtray, that they are passed the hors d'oeuvres, that they are offered a second helping of the food, that their wine glasses are replenished when necessary, that their coffee is served to them as they like it. And I want a wife who knows that sometimes I need a night out by myself.

I want a wife who is sensitive to my sexual needs, a wife who makes love passionately and eagerly when I feel like it, a wife who makes sure that I am satisfied. And, of course, I want a wife who will not demand sexual attention when I am not in the mood for it. I want a wife who assumes the complete responsibility for birth control, because I do not want more children. I want a wife who will remain sexually faithful to me so that I do not have to clutter up my intellectual life with jealousies. And I want a wife who understands that *my* sexual needs may entail more than strict adherence to monogamy. I must, after all, be able to relate to people as fully as possible.

If, by chance, I find another person more suitable as a wife than the wife I already have, I want the liberty to replace my present wife with another one. Naturally, I will expect a fresh, new life; my wife will take the children and be solely responsible for them so that I am left free.

When I am through with school and have acquired a job, I want my wife to quit working and remain at home so that my wife can more fully and completely take care of a wife's duties.

My God, who *wouldn't* want a wife?

Judy Syfers

Arguments That Show Cause and Effect

It isn't always easy to distinguish between essays that argue through reasons and essays that argue through cause and effect. Essays that discuss the cause of something—the kind we're going to treat in this section—show not only that one thing preceded another in time (a chronological development) but also *caused* it. In other words, the author traces a problem back to its source to try to show that something *in the past* caused the problem. (What's confusing is that some essays focus their attention on the cause, while others focus on the effects.)

If you have problems deciding whether an essay is using cause and effect or giving reasons, you might look at those three signposts in an essay: title, introduction, conclusion. Often the author will not only spell out the thesis, but also suggest what method will be used to carry out the argument.

To introduce your summary of a cause-and-effect argument, use words like these:

- **The author shows** that the loss of electricity in New York **caused** panic.
- **The author points out** that Nixon's poor appearance on television **caused** him to lose votes.
- **The author argues** that although the telephone was a wonderful invention, it also **caused** people to lose some of their privacy.

Of course, an author might not use the word "cause" or "effect" at all. He or she might use a synonym like "due to" or structure the sentence in such a way that the word "cause" or "effect" is not even present—as you see in the following two sentences.

- Society is falling apart **because** we were corrupted by ancient aliens. [That is, the aliens, sometime in the past caused the present dreadful state of society.]

- When the Normans overran England, the English language almost disappeared from official discourse; only the Saxon peasants kept it alive. [That is, the Norman invasion caused the near disappearance of English.]

But don't worry about it too much. If you can't decide if a writer is revealing a cause-and-effect relationship or giving reasons, just begin your summary with a generalized introduction that tells your reader that an argument is going on—something like this:

In *Commonweal*, Edmond Cruise contends that . . .

It's more important that your readers know that your source is arguing than they know what method he is using.

Reminder: Poor summarizers have tunnel vision; they focus in on a few individual sentences and lose sight of the passage's main idea. Back off and see the passage as a whole, like landscape photographers who step back so that they can capture a panoramic view of nature. Once you see the large picture, you can fill in the details.

Now see if you can identify the cause/effect relationship in the following assignment.

EXERCISE 2-8: *Writing a Summary*

Write a paragraph-length summary of the following essay that identifies the cause-and-effect relationship. Begin with an overview of the whole essay; then go on to fill out your paragraph.

New-Born Mother

"Talking babies" is bad form. Dinner party chat can wander around giving up smoking, the quality of the food, . . . the shortcomings of public transport and other yawns. But talking babies is beyond the pale. The rearing of children—and one can call it motherhood, since women continue to do it in far greater numbers than men—has low status and is therefore boring. Women apologize: "I'm just a mother," because they think it would be more interesting if they weren't. Working mothers submit to public values too and expect greater acknowledgement of the job, not the mothering.

Not that I am going over to the Mediterranean view which decrees child-bearing the destiny and only fulfillment of women; that too is a constricting prejudice. But to see the work of a mother in the crucial years of infancy when character is formed as a sequence of dirty nappies [diapers] is the equivalent of reviewing a love affair in terms of changing the bed sheets. The drudgery is present, of course: but having a baby is still the grandest rite of passage I have had to suffer.

The birth of a child hurls the mother—and the father—into a strange universe, moving powerfully according to its own laws, its inmost nature knowable only by participation, incommunicable to the uninitiate. Inside the womb, the baby has a certain degree of reality, as it beats and kicks, playing its own battery of drums, executing its big top feats under one's ribs. But this gives only a presentiment.

When the child, warm, wet, slippery, crying out, face crumpled from the sudden burst into the light, first wriggled in my arms on my belly I knew I had been taken over—it was unmistakable—by something that immediately made all the difference. I had crossed a boundary of existence, just like the baby. And for my husband, standing there beside the delivery couch, the attachment to the child was that moment made as fast. The passage of parenthood is instant, ferocious and irrefutable; it comes on you like being winded.

This is not to say that is love alone. The new world inspires rage and fear as well. The exhaustion of the first few weeks is hallucinatory. There are terrible tiny moments of grief, and the terror of loss, of harm, of failure. I have a friend who regularly sleepwalks, looking for her baby on the floor where she is certain she has fallen: I have woken crying out, ''No, not that, no!'' certain that one of us has rolled over and suffocated ours—when he lies safely asleep in his cot.

The pleasures of it have, at a more intense level, the quality of delight in finding a new aptitude: the exhilaration of first floating, realising one can swim, perhaps the wonder of a child standing free on his own legs for the first time. So much of mothering is involuntary, motivated at a level deep down, perhaps in the very DNA.

There is the phenomenon that took me entirely by surprise, that I had never heard of previously: the spontaneous spurting of milk. Sometimes, when my son cries, I feel the milk rise spontaneously in response. There is a scientific explanation for this: sympathy flowing between mother and infant releases oxytocin, a chemical which amongst other things is responsible for milk ''let-down.'' But like most scientific explanations, it leaves the mystery intact.

The symbiosis between infant and mother is fostered by intimacy in the first few hours and days, so several studies have reported; therefore one can say perhaps that maternal responses are learned rather than innate. But they *feel* instinctive. The baby's needs, rhythms, emotions hold sway not just over the practical side of life, but over the psychical as well. I swore for instance that I would never make goo goo eyes or squeal nonsense at any baby of mine. He or she would learn to listen to grown-ups behaving naturally. But immediately, I raised my voice, widened my eyes and gabbled. This instinct has its reasons, again the studies have found. Newborn babies focus more easily on staring eyes, and they hear more clearly sounds at a higher pitch. The child is master of the man.

It is only after I had been thrown into this new world of experience that I found friends talking about it too, telling me how they had felt with their first-born. Had I never listened before? I don't think it was only that. Motherhood is like a street gang in a ghetto: you learn the rules only after you've joined.

Its physiology alone is still misunderstood through prejudice and lack of inquiry. And it seems to me now not just an irony but a tragedy that, through the mistake of confusing sexual equality with sexual identity and the fear of betraying the feminist cause, the many other dimensions of this central female difference continue to be hidden from history and beggared of honour.

Marina Warner

EXERCISE 2-9: *Writing Assignment*

Obviously, writers don't summarize for its own sake. Summarizing is a means to an end. That's why we're going to ask you now to write an essay that *uses* the skill you've been working so hard on throughout this chapter. Respond to the ideas in the essay below by Nat Hentoff. Agree or disagree in part or in whole. Naturally, in your introduction you'll want to give an overview of your source's argument.

Then as you develop your argument, summarize ideas from your source so that your reader will know exactly what you're responding to.

When Nice People Burn Books

It happened one splendid Sunday morning in a church. Not Jerry Falwell's Baptist sanctuary in Lynchburg, Virginia, but rather the First Unitarian Church in Baltimore. On October 4, 1981, midway through the 11 A.M. service, pernicious ideas were burned at the altar.

As reported by Frank P. L. Somerville, religion editor of the *Baltimore Sun*, "Centuries of Jewish, Christian, Islamic, and Hindu writings were 'expurgated'—because of sections described as 'sexist.'

"Touched off by a candle and consumed in a pot on a table in front of the altar were slips of paper containing 'patriarchal' excerpts from Martin Luther, Thomas Aquinas, the Koran, St. Augustine, St. Ambrose, St. John Chrysostom, the Hindu Code of Manu V, an anonymous Chinese author, and the Old Testament." Also hurled into the purifying fire were works by Kierkegaard and Karl Barth.

The congregation was much exalted: "As the last flame died in the pot, and the organ pealed, there was applause," Somerville wrote.

I reported that news of the singed holy spirit to a group of American Civil Liberties Union members in California, and one woman was furious. At me.

"We did the same thing at our church two Sundays ago," she said. "And long past time, too. Don't you understand it's just *symbolic?*"

I told this ACLU member that when the school board in Drake, North Dakota, threw thirty-four copies of Kurt Vonnegut's *Slaughterhouse Five* into the furnace in 1973, it wasn't because the school was low on fuel. That burning was symbolic, too. Indeed, the two pyres—in North Dakota and in Baltimore—were witnessing to the same lack of faith in the free exchange of ideas.

What an inspiring homily for the children attending services at a liberated church: They now know that the way to handle ideas they don't like is to set them on fire.

The stirring ceremony in Baltimore is just one more illustration that the spirit of the First Amendment is not being savaged only by malign forces of the Right, whether private or governmental. Campaigns to purge school libraries, for example, have been conducted by feminists as well as by Phyllis Schlafly. Yet, most liberal watchdogs of our freedom remain fixed on the Right as *the* enemy of free expression.

For a salubrious change, therefore, let us look at what is happening to freedom of speech and press in certain enclaves—some colleges, for instance—where the New Right has no clout at all. Does the pulse of the First Amendment beat more vigorously in these places than where the Yahoos are?

Well, consider what happened when Eldridge Cleaver came to Madison, Wisconsin, last October to savor the exhilarating openness of dialogue at the University of Wisconsin. Cleaver's soul is no longer on ice; it's throbbing instead with a religious conviction that is currently connected financially, and presumably theologically, to the Reverend Sun Myung Moon's Unification Church. In Madison, Cleaver never got to talk about his pilgrim's progress from the Black Panthers to the wondrously ecumenical Moonies. In the Humanities Building—*Humanities*—several hundred students and others outraged by Cleaver's apostasy shouted, stamped their feet, chanted "Sieg Heil," and otherwise prevented him from being heard.

After ninety minutes of the din, Cleaver wrote on the blackboard, "I regret that the totalitarians have deprived us of our constitutional rights to free assembly and free speech. Down with communism. Long live democracy.''

And, raising a clenched fist, while blowing kisses with his free hand, Cleaver left. Cleaver says he'll try to speak again, but he doesn't know when.

The University of Wisconsin administration, through Dean of Students Paul Ginsberg, deplored the behavior of the campus totalitarians of the Left, and there was a fiercely denunciatory editorial in the Madison *Capital Times:* "These people lack even the most primitive appreciation of the Bill of Rights.''

It did occur to me, however, that if Eldridge Cleaver had not abandoned his secularist rage at the American Leviathan and had come to Madison as the still burning spear of black radicalism, the result might have been quite different if he had been shouted down that night by young apostles of the New Right. That would have made news around the country, and there would have been collectively signed letters to the *New York Review of Books* and *The Nation* warning of the prowling dangers to free speech in the land. But since Cleaver has long since taken up with bad companions, there is not much concern among those who used to raise bail for him as to whether he gets to speak freely or not.

A few years ago, William F. Buckley Jr., invited to be commencement speaker at Vassar, was told by student groups that he not only would be shouted down if he came but might also suffer some contusions. All too few liberal members of the Vassar faculty tried to educate their students about the purpose of a university, and indeed a good many faculty members joined in the protests against Buckley's coming. He finally decided not to appear because, he told me, he didn't want to spoil the day for the parents. I saw no letters on behalf of Buckley's free-speech rights in any of the usual liberal forums for such concerns. After all, he had not only taken up with bad companions; he was an original bad companion.

During the current academic year, there were dismaying developments concerning freedom for bad ideas in the college press. The managing editor of *The Daily Lobo*, the University of New Mexico's student newspaper, claimed in an editorial that Scholastic Aptitude Test scores show minority students to be academically inferior. Rather than rebut his facile misinterpretation of what those scores actually show—that class, not race, affects the results—black students and their sympathizers invaded the newspaper's office.

The managing editor prudently resigned, but the protesters were not satisfied. They wanted the head of the editor. The brave Student Publications Board temporarily suspended her, although the chairman of the journalism department had claimed the suspension was a violation of her First Amendment rights. She was finally given her job back, pending a formal hearing, but she decided to quit. The uproar had not abated, and who knew what would happen at her formal hearing before the Student Publications Board?

When it was all over, the chairman of the journalism department observed that the confrontation had actually reinforced respect for First Amendment rights on the University of New Mexico campus because infuriated students now knew they couldn't successfully insist on the firing of an editor because of what had been published.

What about the resignations? Oh, they were free-will offerings.

I subscribe to most of the journalism reviews around the country, but I saw no offer of support to those two beleaguered student editors in New Mexico from professional journalists who invoke the First Amendment at almost any public opportunity.

Then there was a free-speech war at Kent State University, as summarized in the November 12, 1982, issue of *National On-Campus Report*. Five student groups at Kent State are vigorously attempting to get the editor of the student newspaper fired. They are: "gay students, black students, the undergraduate and graduate student governments, and a progressive student alliance.''

Not a reactionary among them. Most are probably deeply concerned with the savaging of the free press in Chile, Uruguay, Guatemala, South Africa, and other such places.

What had this editor at Kent State done to win the enmity of so humanistic a grand alliance? He had written an editorial that said that a gay student group should not have access to student-fee money to sponsor a Hallowe'en dance. Ah, but how had he gone about making his point?

"In opening statements," says the *National On-Campus Report*, "he employed words like 'queer' and 'nigger' to show that prejudice against any group is undesirable." Just like Lenny Bruce. Lenny, walking on stage in a club, peering into the audience, and asking, "Any spics here tonight? Any kikes? Any niggers?"

Do you think Lenny Bruce could get many college bookings today? Or write a column for a college newspaper?

In any case, the rest of the editorial went on to claim that the proper use of student fees was for educational, not social, activities. The editor was singling out the Kent Gay/Lesbian Foundation. He was opposed to *any* student organization using those fees for dances.

Never mind. He had used impermissible words: Queer. Nigger. And those five influential cadres of students are after his head. The editor says that university officials have assured him, however, that he is protected at Kent State by the First Amendment. If that proves to be the case, those five student groups will surely move to terminate, if not defenestrate, those university officials.

It is difficult to be a disciple of James Madison on campus these days. Take the case of Phyllis Schlafly and Wabash College. The college is a small, well-regarded liberal arts institution in Crawfordsville, Indiana. In the spring of 1981, the college was riven with discord. Some fifty members of the ninety-odd faculty and staff wrote a stiff letter to the Wabash Lecture Series Committee, which had displayed the exceedingly poor taste to invite Schlafly to speak on campus the next year.

The faculty protesters complained that having the sweetheart of the Right near the Wabash River would be "unfortunate and inappropriate." The dread Schlafly is "an ERA opponent . . . a far-right attorney who travels the country, being highly paid to tell women to stay at home fulfilling traditional roles while sending their sons off to war."

Furthermore, the authors wrote, "The point of view she represents is that of an ever-decreasing minority of American women and men, and is based in sexist mythology which promulgates beliefs inconsistent with those held by liberally educated persons, and this does not merit a forum at Wabash College under the sponsorship of our Lecture Series."

This is an intriguing document by people steeped in the traditions of academic freedom. One of the ways of deciding who gets invited to a campus is the speaker's popularity. If the speaker appeals only to a "decreasing minority of American women and men," she's not worth the fee. So much for Dorothy Day, were she still with us.

And heaven [forbid] that anyone be invited whose beliefs are "inconsistent with those held by liberally educated persons." Mirror, mirror on the wall. . . .

But do not get the wrong idea about these protesting faculty members: "We subscribe," they emphasized, "to the principles of free speech and free association, of course."

All the same, "it does not enhance our image as an all-male college to endorse a well-known sexist by inviting her to speak on our campus." If Phyllis Schlafly is invited nonetheless, ''we intend not to participate in any of the activities surrounding Ms. Schlafly's visit and will urge others to do the same.''

The moral of the story: If you don't like certain ideas, boycott them.

The lecture committee responded to the fifty deeply offended faculty members in a most unkind way. The committee told the signers that ''William Buckley would endorse your petition. No institution of higher learning, he told us on a visit here, should allow to be heard on its campus any position that it regards as detrimental or 'untrue.'

''Apparently,'' the committee went on, ''error is to be refuted not by rational persuasion, but by censorship.''

Phyllis Schlafly did come to Wabash and she generated a great deal of discussion—most of it against her views—among members of the all-male student body. However, some of the wounded faculty took a long time to recover. One of them, a tenured professor, took aside at a social gathering the wife of a member of the lecture committee that had invited Schlafly. Both were in the same feminist group on campus.

The professor cleared her throat, and said to the other woman, ''You are going to leave him, aren't you?''

''My husband? Why should I leave him?''

''Really, how can you stay married to someone who invited Phyllis Schlafly to this campus?''

And really, should such a man even be allowed visitation rights with the children?

Then there is the Ku Klux Klan. As Klan members have learned in recent months, both in Boston and in Washington, their First Amendment right peaceably to assemble—let alone actually to speak their minds—can only be exercised if they are prepared to be punched in the mouth. Klan members get the same reception that Martin Luther King Jr. and his associates used to receive in Bull Conner's Birmingham.

As all right-thinking people knew, however, the First Amendment isn't just for anybody. That presumably is why the administration of the University of Cincinnati has refused this year to allow the KKK to appear on campus. Bill Wilkerson, the Imperial Wizard of the particular Klan faction that has been barred from the University of Cincinnati, says he's going to sue on First Amendment grounds.

Aside from the ACLU's, how many *amicus* briefs do you think the Imperial Wizard is likely to get from liberal organizations devoted to academic freedom?

The Klan also figures in a dismaying case from Vancouver, Washington. There, an all-white jury awarded $1,000 to a black high school student after he had charged the Battle Ground School District (including Prairie High School) with discrimination. One of the claims was that the school had discriminated against this young man by permitting white students to wear Ku Klux Klan costumes to a Hallowe'en assembly.

Symbolic speech, however, is like spoken or written speech. It is protected under the First Amendment. If the high school administration had originally forbidden the wearing of the Klan costumes to the Hallowe'en assembly, it would have spared itself that part of the black student's lawsuit, but it would have set a precedent for censoring symbolic speech which would have shrunken First Amendment protections at Prairie High School.

What should the criteria be for permissible costumes at a Hallowe'en assembly? None that injure the feelings of another student? So a Palestinian kid couldn't wear a PLO outfit. Or a Jewish kid couldn't come as Ariel Sharon, festooned with maps. And watch out for the wise guy who comes dressed as that all-around pain-in-the-ass, Tom Paine.

School administrators might say the best approach is to have no costumes at all. That way, there'll be no danger of disruption. But if there were real danger of physical confrontation in the school when a student wears a Klan costume, is the school so powerless that it can't prevent a fight? And indeed, what a compelling opportunity the costumes present to teach about the Klan, to ask those white kids who wore Klan costumes what they know of the history of the Klan. To get black and white kids *talking* about what the Klan represents, in history—and right now.

Such teaching is too late for Prairie High School. After that $1,000 award to the black student, the white kids who have been infected by Klan demonology will circulate their poison only among themselves, intensifying their sickness of spirit. There will be no more Klan costumes in that school, and so no more Klan costumes to stimulate class discussion.

By the way, in the trial, one offer of proof that the school district had been guilty of discrimination was a photograph of four white boys wearing Klan costumes to that Hallowe'en assembly. It's a rare picture. It was originally printed in the school yearbook but, with the lawsuit and all, the picture was cut out of each yearbook before it was distributed.

That's the thing about censorship, whether good liberals or bad companions engage in it. Censorship is like a greased pig. Hard to confine. You start trying to deal with offensive costumes and you wind up with a blank space in the yearbook. Isn't that just like the Klan? Causing decent people to do dumb things.

Nat Hentoff

— 3 —

Quoting

Using the *exact* words of other writers (rather than a summary or paraphrase) serves various purposes: You might want to quote a few pungent words to let your reader taste the flavor of your source; you might want to quote a passage to illustrate an idea that you've just summarized; and you might want to quote an authority to add weight to your ideas. However, quotations won't serve any purpose unless you know a few specific skills about handling them. Those skills are what this chapter is about.

IDENTIFYING YOUR QUOTATIONS

Failure to identify a quotation leaves behind a gap at the place where your prose ends and your quotation begins. Here's what one of those ugly gaps looks like:

> In the past, writers usually pointed to episodes in the Bible to support their belief in demons. "Did not the devil afflict Job with loathsome sores."

Obviously, there's something missing between the writer's words (sentence 1) and the quotation (sentence 2). Who said those words within the quotation marks? When were they said? Why were they said? What's the connection between the quotation and the statement that precedes it? When the writer doesn't leave behind clear, concise answers to those questions, determined readers will plough on, though they'll now be a little annoyed and even more confused. Your readers won't be confused if you construct identification bridges that look something like this:

> During the Renaissance, writers usually pointed to the Bible to support their belief in demons. For example, Francisco Guazzo, a seventeenth-century monk, asks a self-evident question to point out the

fact that a demon, the *supreme* demon in this case, shows up in the book of Job: "Did not the devil afflict Job with loathsome sores?"

What, then, are the requirements of an identification bridge? The minimum one is the name of the author, or source—as simple as this: "Joe Doakes says, . . . " In the block passage above, the writer tells us that the author of the quote is Francisco Guazzo. But you will usually want to say more. Most of the time, for instance, you will want to include a note about the relationship between your idea and the quotation. In the case above, that relationship, a simple one, is revealed by the phrase "for example." Include other matters if they seem relevant. In the above example, the writer thought it relevant to include Guazzo's vocation (monk) and the century in which he lived (seventeenth).

The point is to include whatever information you think is relevant. You might, for instance, want to tell your reader the title of the article in which the quote appeared—or even the name of the book or magazine. Of course, if the writer you're quoting is a writer for *Time* magazine, you won't be able to say much about the author. You would merely say something like this: "In an article in *Time* magazine, Robert Shirley writes that . . . " But if the writer you're quoting is a famous biochemist and your thesis has something to do with biochemistry, you would want to include the writer's expertise in your bridge. Use your common sense.

Even when you identify a quotation for your reader, you still may be baffled about how to incorporate that quotation into your prose smoothly and correctly. Happily, there are only a few basic sentence patterns to learn. In fact, if you will study the simple examples below, you will rarely meet a quotation situation that you can't handle.

At the Beginning

You might notice that you use a comma before a quotation when the verb in your introduction lacks a direct object (the first example below), whereas you use a colon when the verb contains a direct object (the second example).

La Rochefoucauld, a seventeenth-century aristocrat, remarked, "In the misfortunes of our best friends, we find something that is not displeasing."
La Rochefoucauld, a seventeenth-century aristocrat, made the following cynical observation: "In the misfortunes of our best friends, we find something that is not displeasing."
According to La Rochefoucauld, a seventeenth-century aristocrat, "In the misfortunes of our best friends, we find something that is not displeasing."

At the End

"In the misfortunes of our best friends, we find something that is not displeasing," La Rochefoucauld wrote.

"In the misfortunes of our best friends, we find something that is not displeasing." La Rochefoucauld's words are as painful now as they were in the seventeenth century when he wrote them.

In the Middle

Here is a simple example.

"In the misfortunes of our best friends," La Rochefoucauld wrote, "we find something that is not displeasing."

Notice that no punctuation is necessary when you slide into a quotation without a pause or precede a quotation with the word "that."

La Rochefoucauld, the seventeenth-century French aristocrat, once wrote that the suffering of our best friend produces a sensation that is not "displeasing."
La Rochefoucauld, the seventeenth-century French aristocrat, once said that "we find something that is not displeasing" when we see our best friend suffering.

EXERCISE 3-1: *Identifying and Presenting Quotations*

In short paragraphs of your own, summarize the following excerpts and incorporate quotations within those summaries. Quote a single word and a phrase or sentence from each of the paragraphs. The first piece is by Barbara Tuchman, the Pulitzer Prize-winning historian and author of the best-selling *The Guns of August*. The second piece is by Ernest Sackville Turner, the author of numerous social histories and for many years the editor of a British military magazine, *Soldier*.

A Distant Mirror: The Calamitous 14th Century

In the Rhineland . . . a new hysteria appeared in the form of a dancing mania. Whether it sprang from misery and homelessness caused by heavy spring floods of the Rhine that year, or whether it was the spontaneous symptom of a disturbed time, history does not know, but the participants were in no doubt. They were convinced that they were possessed by demons. Forming circles in streets and churches, they danced for hours with leaps and screams, calling on demons by name to cease tormenting them or crying that they saw visions of Christ or the Virgin or the heavens opening. When exhausted they fell to the ground rolling and groaning as if in the grip of agonies. As the mania spread to Holland and Flanders, the dancers appeared with garlands in their hair and moved in groups from place to place like the flagellants. They were chiefly the poor—peasants, artisans, servants, and beggars, with a large proportion of women, especially the unmarried. Sexual revels often followed the dancing, but the dominant preoccupation was exorcism of devils.

Barbara Tuchman

The Court of St. James's

Dressed and painted, [Queen Elizabeth] was a formidable sight. As she passed through the Presence Chamber on her way to chapel, preceded by her great officers, all fell on their knees as her eyes turned on them. By this time she was accustomed to see men and women lower their eyes on meeting hers, in deference to such glory. Fear of making a *gaffe* bore heavily on some. John Aubrey has a famous story of a young courtier who, when bowing low before the Queen, made an unfortunate noise. This humiliated him so much that he spent the next few years travelling in far places.

Edward Sackville Turner

WHEN TO QUOTE

There are no certain rules for knowing when to quote, so here are some uncertain ones: When you come across words that are strong or shocking or poetic or pithy, go ahead and quote them. When you come across words that are ironic or comic, go ahead and quote them. That is, communicate the flavor of your source when it *has* a strong flavor. Don't quote vanilla. Quote pistachio.

Let's say you are arguing that the United States is declining intellectually, and in your reading you run across these words, written by John Mason Brown.

Part of the American myth is that people who are handed the skin of a dead sheep at graduation time think that it will keep their minds alive forever.

That's pistachio. If you had merely tried to summarize Brown's idea, your reader would have missed the comic tone of the original. In fact, an ironic or comic passage is often impossible to summarize without distorting the original.

There will be times, however, when your source is such a widely recognized authority—someone like Einstein on physics, Mother Theresa on Catholic charity, or Donald Trump on himself—that you can lower your standards on quoting. (But even here, wait until your famous authority says something in a *somewhat* special way.) The writers of the following two sentences made the mistake of quoting words that are just too ordinary:

The senator said that he is "worried" that Congress is getting too unwieldy. Desmond Morris wrote, "A third form of verbalization is exploratory talking."

A common mistake in using quotations is using too many of them. "I hate quotations. Tell me what you know." That's what Ralph Waldo Emerson said back in the nineteenth century. That's what your readers will say if you quote too much. An essay with too many quotations looks old-fashioned and pretentious. It's easier to quote a passage than to put it in your own words, so lazy writers overquote. It's safer to quote a passage than to speak in your own voice, so timid writers overquote. So have a good reason for quoting and quote sparingly.

EXERCISE 3-2: *Choosing Appropriate Quotations*

Using the advice given thus far in this chapter, summarize each of the following
passages in a single sentence and quote *appropriate* words from each. Give each
summary an appropriate introduction, or bridge ("Spenser Klaw says . . . "), and
quote only a word or a short phrase from each. By the way, it might be helpful for
you to know that in the first passage below, the "Thomson" in the first line refers
to Samuel Thomson, a nineteenth-century American herbalist.

Belly My Grizzle

It was Thomson's passionate conviction that most physicians of the day were no better than
torturers and murderers. Their chief crime against suffering humanity, he argued, was their
insistence on dosing patients with "metallic" medicines, by which he mainly meant calomel, a widely used and horribly effective cathartic whose active ingredient was mercury. In
Thomson's view, the way to cope with illness was to administer certain herbal remedies—
he particularly favored lobelia, a powerful emetic—and to put the patient in a steam bath to
make him sweat. Thomson held that it was possible by using these methods to cure every
disease known to man, from dyspepsia and croup to cancer and tuberculosis.

Spenser Klaw

The March of Medicine

Once confirmed in its rights, *derivatio* [tradition] became a bloody tyrant whose rule was
unopposed for centuries. According to the authorities, in the event of any malady and without consideration for his state of general health the patient had to be bled at least three to
five times, with the loss of $1^3/4$ pints of blood on each occasion. Contemporary doctors were
under the illusion that the human body contained more than 24 lb. of blood. (Actually the
average figure is 12 lb.) They therefore believed that they could safely tap off 20 lb., and
they endeavoured to carry this out in practice unless the premature death of the patient
prevented them.

H. S. Glasscheib

MTV's Message

One potentially insidious aspect of music videos is that they can reach a very young audience. John Wright, director of the Center for Research on the Influence of Television on
Children at the University of Kansas, says videos are "well suited to the attention spans of
little bitty kids." At the Daybridge Learning Center in Overland Park, Kans., this year,
MTV stole Halloween; children came in wearing Madonna, Cyndi Lauper and Michael
Jackson costumes. Daybridge kindergarten teacher Susan Albers says she has seen pre-
schoolers cry when listening to "Thriller" because they had been frightened by the ghoulish video. And one second-grade boy has talked about undressing Madonna and marrying
her as soon as her husband dies.

Eric Gelman

HOW TO PUNCTUATE QUOTATIONS

Punctuation that is related to quotations follows most of the rules that govern
punctuation anywhere, so you shouldn't have much difficulty. But there are

a few curiosities—and one maddening eccentricity—that give fits to even the best of writers. We'll begin with the maddening eccentricity.

Punctuation with Quotation Marks

1. Suppress your common sense and *put periods and commas inside the final quotation marks.* The British are more reasonable than we are on this. They put periods and commas outside, where they belong. But because of a convention that started back when boys wore knickers, we're doomed, apparently forever, to put them inside, like this:

   - Wilson Mizner once said this about Hollywood: "It's a trip through a sewer on a glass-bottomed boat."

Place the period and comma inside no matter why you are quoting or how short your quotation is.

   - Jefferson was an admirer of John Locke's "Second Treatise."

Commas, too, go inside.

   - Marvin read Swift's "A Modest Proposal," but he didn't care much for it.

Now, having said all that, there is an exception. When you're using parentheses for in-text citations, as you will later in this book, put the periods outside the quotation marks. (This is also true, though it occurs more rarely, with commas, question marks, and exclamation marks.)

   - Robert Farquar, a noted entomologist, wrinkled his nose and squeaked, "Ooh, I just hate wiggly potato bugs" (56).
   - Robert Farquar, a noted entomologist, wrinkled his nose and squeaked, "Ooh, I just hate wiggly potato bugs, don't you" (56)?

2. Colons, semicolons, and dashes always go *outside* the final quotation marks.

   - Please include the following information in your review of "Young Goodman Brown": a description of the characters and a discussion of the theme.
   - The store owner sputtered, "Put down that comic book"; so I put down the comic book.
   - Winston Churchill once wrote, "A fanatic is one who can't change his mind and won't change the subject"—or something like that.

3. Placement of question marks and exclamation points varies. When you are quoting words that ask a question, put the question mark *inside* the quotation mark. When you are asking a question that ends with a quoted phrase, put the question mark *outside* the quotation mark. The same rule applies to the exclamation point.

- The guy in the mauve shirt asked me, "Hey bub, wanna good deal on a watch?"
- What did you think of "The Short Happy Life of Francis Macomber"?
- I love "The Short Happy Life of Francis Macomber"!

Correct Punctuation before a Quotation

1. When you introduce your quotation with a verb that lacks a direct object, set it off with a comma.

   - Brigid Brophy once said, "To my mind, the two most fascinating subjects in the universe are sex and the eighteenth century."
   - The thing explained, "Don't go into the room with the black door."
   - Josh Billings wrote to his sister, "As scarce as truth is, the supply has always been in excess of the demand."

2. When you introduce your quotation with a verb with a direct object, set it off with a colon.

   - Brigid Brophy once said this: "To my mind, the two most fascinating subjects in the universe are sex and the eighteenth century."
   - The thing explained the situation carefully: "Don't go into the room with the black door."
   - Josh Billings wrote these words: "As scarce as truth is, the supply has always been in excess of the demand."

3. When your introduction flows into the quotation without a grammatical break, don't use any punctuation at all.

   - Brigid Brophy once said that "the two most fascinating subjects in the universe are sex and the eighteenth century."
   - The thing told me not to enter the room with the "black" door.
   - Josh Billings wrote that truth is hard to come by, but even then "the supply has always been in excess of the demand."

Block Quotations

Set off long quotations, seven lines or more, by indenting five spaces from the left margin. This special indentation tells your reader that you are quoting, so *no* quotation marks are necessary. Even if your source is just beginning a paragraph, you don't need to indent any further than the five spaces you've already indented. Let's say that the first line in the example below is your introduction to a quotation, and it is, quite naturally, flush with the left margin. Then you indent five spaces and begin your block quotation.

In *Foolish Figleaves*? Richard H. Kuh writes,

> Until his death in 1966, aged forty, apparently from "acute morphine poisoning caused by an injection of an overdose,"

> Lenny Bruce was a nightclub entertainer billed as "the dirty-talking comic," and author of an autobiography, *How to Talk Dirty and Influence People.* His influence on the nation's police, however, had netted him half dozen or so arrests in less than three years—in Philadelphia, Chicago, San Francisco, Los Angeles, and New York—both on narcotics and on obscenity charges. In the courts and among a dedicated following his impact had been more propitious: most of these arrests had ended in dismissals or acquittals, and with each new one Bruce's claque, lauding both his and their own iconoclasm, had chanted swelling choruses of "persecution" at those with the temerity to have regarded their idol as subject to mortal laws.

You will rarely have the need to quote a complete paragraph—or even four lines. Quote sparingly. Remember how you feel when you are confronted by long, dense quotations in your textbooks.

By the way, block quotations (like research papers themselves) are usually double-spaced, though some writers like to set off a block quotation through single-spacing, even when the rest of their text is double-spaced.

Ellipses

Use ellipses (. . .) to indicate that you've left something out. For example, let's say you wanted to quote a portion of the following passage by Immanuel Kant.

> Cultivated to a high degree by art and science, we are civilized to the point where we are overburdened with all sorts of social propriety and decency.

You don't need to use an ellipsis to indicate the omission of words at the beginning of a quotation. Instead, merely break into the quotation, like this:

> Immanuel Kant once said that "we are civilized to the point where we are overburdened with all sorts of social propriety and decency."

Replace words left out of the middle of a quotation with an ellipsis. Don't destroy the grammatical structure of the source sentence when you omit these words, and don't destroy the sense of the sentence by leaving out something crucial.

> Immanuel Kant once said, "Cultivated . . . by art and science, we are civilized to the point where we are overburdened with all sorts of social propriety and decency."

When you leave out words at the end of a quotation, insert an ellipsis after the final punctuation.

> Immanuel Kant once said, "Cultivated to a high degree by art and

science, we are civilized to the point where we are overburdened with all sorts of social propriety. . . ."

Quotes within Quotes

Use single quotation marks for quotations within quotations.

- Ron Goodwin agreed that "Shakespeare was right when he said, 'How sharper than a serpent's tooth is an ungrateful child.' "
- According to Professor Snodgrass, " 'Heart of Darkness' is the greatest short story in our language."

It's easy to get mixed up when it comes time to put the above rule in practice, so we had better say a bit more on the subject. Let's suppose you want to quote some words by Benjamin Franklin that you have come across in a book by Harry Dundee. Don't be tempted to put the Franklin quotation in single marks (or in double *and* single marks) because Dundee is quoting it. The following quotation by Franklin, then, is correctly enclosed in double quotation marks.

- In Dundee's book, Benjamin Franklin says, "A used key is always bright."

Only if you are quoting Dundee and the Franklin quotation appears within the Dundee quotation do you use single marks.

- Dundee says, "Franklin's cleverest saying is 'A used key is always bright.' "

One more thing: If you need to quote within a block quotation, you may simply use the standard double quotation marks.

Brackets

1. Use brackets to insert notes to your reader. You will sometimes find it necessary to clarify an idea, a pronoun, or a problem in the tense of your quotation. Obviously, you cannot merely enclose your parenthetical insertion in parentheses because your reader would assume that the insertion is part of your quotation. It's conventional to use brackets for those insertions.

   - My father has always insisted, "Fame and fortune have never given me the joy which my childhood days in Possum Trot [Kentucky] gave me."

2. Use brackets to clarify the antecedent of a pronoun. In fact, you can make a direct substitution of your pronoun with your bracketed antecedent without an ellipsis. Let's say your source, the famous historian, Eileen Green, has written a sentence that looks like this:

- Later he would regret his sullen attitude and bitter words.

Here's how to handle that sentence if you were quoting it.

- Green says, "Later [Johnston] would regret his sullen attitude and bitter words."

You can also do it this way:

- Green says, "Later he [Johnston] would regret his sullen attitude and bitter words."

3. Use brackets and the Latin word "sic" to indicate that the error in spelling, grammar, or fact which you are faithfully quoting is your source's mistake, not yours.

- Randy Johnson claims that "Steinbeck's 'Chrysanthemummums' [sic] presents a laundry list of basic adult psychological needs."

4. Use brackets to change the verb tense of your quotation to make it coincide with the verb tense of your own text. Notice, once again, that you can substitute the appropriate tense for the original tense without using ellipses. If, for instance, the source you are quoting reads, "Your essay doesn't say anything," your quotation would look like this:

- I was stunned to discover my teacher's response to my term paper on the final page: He fumed that my "essay [didn't] say anything."

EXERCISE 3-3: *Punctuating Quotes and Using Ellipses*

Summarize the following paragraph in a single sentence. In a second sentence, introduce a quotation that consists of a complete sentence. In your bridge into that quotation, use a verb that doesn't contain a direct object. Also, omit extraneous material and indicate the omissions with an ellipsis.

Cruel Lib

It's an unattractive human truth, but every now and then someone should put it on record: most people—Christians used to acknowledge this fact without embarrassment—most people are not particularly talented or beautiful or charismatic. Set free to discover "the true self," they very often find nothing there at all. Men and women who determine "to do their own thing" commonly learn that they have little of note to do. Yet these people are harassed, shamed by the Zeitgeist and its glib armies into disparaging their conventional roles. The bubble gum tune goes like this: American civilization, through some spiteful, stupid conspiracy, means to thwart self-expression. We are all frustrated painters, explorers, starlets, senators. But there are times when it's more healthful to be frustrated than to have one's mediocrity confirmed in the light of common day.

D. Keith Mano

EXERCISE 3-4: *Punctuating Quotes and Using Brackets*

Summarize the following paragraph in a single sentence. In a second sentence, introduce a quotation that consists of a complete sentence. In your introduction to that quotation use a verb that contains a direct object. Also, use a bracket to identify the antecedent of a noun. (That means, of course, that you'll have to quote a sentence that contains a pronoun.)

"I Gave Him Barks and Saltpeter . . ."
The Lewis and Clark expedition passed the first winter in a hastily built but sturdy stockade, Fort Mandan, near the mouth of the Knife River, about fifty-five miles above the present Bismarck, North Dakota. Here, for six months, they lived, surrounded by some 4,000 aboriginals—Mandans and Minnetarees (Hidatsas). From the very beginning, these Indians exceeded the bounds of what white men considered conventional hospitality. To the explorers they proffered not only corn, beans, and squash but also wives, daughters, and sisters. To them, as to many other Indian tribes, this was no deviation from rectitude; it was an old, established, and entirely respectable custom. However, even for the Indians there were limits to hospitality, and as the long winter wore on, many of the "squars" began to sell their "favors" for a string of beads, a looking glass, or a piece of ribbon.

Paul Russel Cutright

EXERCISE 3-5: *Punctuating Quotes*

As you summarize the following paragraph, let your words flow into a quotation without a grammatical break.

For Her Own Good—the Tyranny of the Experts
During the 19th century the medical profession threw itself with gusto on the languid figure of the female invalid. Popular advice books written by physicians took on a somber tone as they entered into "The Female Functions" or "The Diseases of Women." The theories that guided medical practice from the late 19th century to the early 20th century held that women's *normal* state was to be sick. This was not advanced as an empirical observation but as physiological fact. Medicine had "discovered" that female functions were inherently pathological. Menstruation, that perennial source of alarm to the male imagination, provided both the evidence and the explanation. Menstruation was a serious threat throughout life—so was the lack of it.

Barbara Ehrenreich and Deirdre English

SOME FINAL NOTES ABOUT QUOTATIONS

Use and Abuse of Quotation Marks

Use quotation marks to identify the titles of essays, poems, songs, newspaper articles, and chapter titles. Underline (or italicize, if your word processor has the capability) titles of books, journals, plays, and films.

- William Blake's "Tyger" appears in an anthology called The Best of Blake.
- I read a chapter, "Inside the Darkroom," in a book called Photography.
- Did you read that essay, "Corn fields and Corncobs," in our freshman textbook?

Use quotation marks to identify expressions that you disagree with.

- The <u>National Inquirer</u> printed the "facts" about an alien living in the basement of the White House.

Use quotation marks to identify words that you are discussing merely as words.

- He was in love with the word "bitchen."

Don't use quotation marks for your own slang words or figurative language. If you're ashamed of using a word, don't use it. <u>*Don't*</u> do this:

- He was too "hip" to be believable.
- I don't consider myself a "pig."
- College life is the "pits."
- He has a "nose" for news.

There's just no reason for any of those quotation marks.

Documenting Quotations

If you're writing an essay or other informal paper, you needn't formally document a quotation with a footnote or an item on a works cited page. Merely identify the author in your introduction to the quotation, like this: "According to Judy Hillaire, a practicing neurosurgeon, . . ."

Of course, if you are writing something more formal, such as a research paper, you will have to give complete bibliographic information (such as the name of the magazine that Hillaire's essay was printed in, the month and year it was printed, and even the page numbers it occupied). We'll get to that in Chapter 6. For the time being, however, let's keep things simple.

It's now time to put your knowledge of how to handle quotations to good use.

EXERCISE 3-6: *Writing Assignment*

Write an essay in which you respond to Dalma Heyn's ideas in *Body Hate*. Agree or disagree in part or in whole with Heyn's main idea. In your introduction, you should let your reader know the gist of her essay. You might even use a quotation to serve as support for what you say the main idea is. Then as you argue, summarize and quote parts of Heyn's argument so that your reader will know exactly what you're responding to.

Body Hate

At the age of four, Katie knows what she hates: Fat, "Ewww . . . she's ugly," she says, pointing to a picture of a robust woman in the newspaper I'm reading. I scoop up this little pudge of a thing and say, What's the matter, you don't like curvy ladies? and she says no, she doesn't. I argue with her, carefully pointing out the miracle of female bodies; the reproductive significance of those curves and bulges, the sumptuous glory of it all. My speech is lyrical, but I am too late. I'm talking to a tiny little thing, someone who has Legos in her hand and cereal stuck to her hair, but someone whose mind is made up.

Millions of other three- and four-year-old girls equate fat with "badness" even before they can read. Katie will probably be on a self-imposed diet by the time she is nine (four out of five fourth-grade girls are) and, by the time she hits puberty, will react to her body filling out with a distress that gradually gives way to disgust. She may vomit or take laxatives to control her weight (as one out of eight first-year college women do). By 18, Katie's body image—that snapshot of herself she carries with her deep in her mind's eye—will be completely out of whack, a reflection not of her real contours, but of her worst imaginings. What she'll see in her mirror will be this same distortion of her real self—a fleshy, obese creature; a blob.

Bulimia, the body-racking binge-and-purge disorder that is now epidemic among successful corporate women as well as young girls in their teens and twenties, "is more than dieting gone haywire," says therapists Wayne and Susan Wooley, leading researchers in the field. "It comes from an obsession with thinness so intense it becomes the core of a woman's identity." The process of ingesting three pizzas and two quarts of ice cream, gagging to throw it up—then gorging again—doesn't make her feel nearly as powerless as the thought of watching her body becoming round and soft and vulnerable and feminine—like her mother's, her model of femininity; her legacy of powerlessness.

She wants to be lean and strong and tough, like a man. The traditional stuff of a woman's identity—love, sex, childbirth, caretaking—is precisely what the bulimic rejects most vehemently, for they sentence her to a powerlessness she fears more than anything.

Powerless? Who, us? With all our choices, with all our chances; with all the progress we've made?

Oh, please. Our society is more antifemale now than it has ever been. Pay scales remain a joke. The new divorce laws might be equitable if two men were parting, perhaps, but for women they're atrocious. Custody cases that would have been thrown out on their ears 10 years ago are now commonplace. The lack of care offered us seems to stem from some misguided notion of equality that assumes our needs not to be equally important as, but to be literally the same as, men's.

Normal women, current research shows, now suffer from the same body-image problems that bulimics do. Women who have no eating disorder, no weight problem—who have, objectively, fine, healthy bodies—look in the mirror and see "hideous" upper arms. When asked to assess the size of their body parts, they perceive them to be as much as twice as big as they are, and the more inaccurate they are, the worse they feel.

We call this body image a visual problem. "It's not distortion of body image," says therapist Steven Levenkron, a Manhattan eating disorders specialist, "it's an antifemale ethic about body image." We all know we look like women; we just wish—blindly, profoundly—that it weren't so.

Fashion magazines report that curves are back. While the all-bones look has indeed been chucked, it has been replaced with an even more elusive female ideal. Skinny, muscular legs, the taut abdomen of a 13-year-old, and arms with the muscle definition that comes from daily workouts—that's the body we want. Looking like an undeveloped adolescent girl is out. What's very much the rage is looking like a well-developed adolescent boy.

When was the last time you had a normal lunch in a restaurant—you know, where you eat bread with butter, dessert, maybe sugar and cream in your coffee? At restaurants all over the country, we are eating: a piece of broiled fish, no butter (or tuna, no mayo; or a chef's salad, dressing on the side); Perrier or club soda with lemon or lime, or perhaps a wine spritzer; coffee with artificial sweetener. "Public eating behavior is very discreet," notes Steven Levenkron. Privately we may hit the Haagen-Dazs and binge on David's Cookies, but did you ever see a corporate vice president down a hunk of chocolate at a business deal? "We've put this new demand on women that they be 'successful eaters,' " says Levenkron. "They must look like women who are eating to be thin."

The look of horror on my companion's face when he first saw Isabella Rossellini's body in the film Blue Velvet is accompanied by a gasp from the audience. That belly, that ample, white flesh; that departure from tan, from taut, from fit has the audience reeling—not with gratitude or pleasure or relief at finally seeing on the screen a woman's body when it isn't put through the daily rigors of exercise and diet. It is a gasp of disgust. And we're not talking real fleshiness here, don't forget. There's nothing fat going on. The woman is a model. A thin person.

Our phobia about fat, our revulsion at looking female, our trenchant self-loathing are a scandal. Yet we no longer wish to trace the source of our shame; we are too embarrassed and bored by even a phrase like "women's issues" to recognize a woman's issue when we see one. We prefer instead to battle our own intrinsic femaleness, to beat our bodies into the shape our psyches insist on, till both what we see and who we are don't jibe—just as what society says about the new female equality and how things are don't jibe. Like victims of some variation of the Stockholm syndrome, we so identify with men now that anyone thin enough and muscular enough to pass as one is okay by us. We have become our own worst enemies, perpetrators of antifemaleness without even knowing it. Oh, for a band of angry, strident, marching women, brassieres afire, eyes ablaze! Anything but this passivity!

But no, we say, nothing's wrong out there, it's us. The requirements for beauty, women hating? Hell, don't alter them, we'll just chop ourselves up instead. A surgical procedure called liposuction—which eliminates ugly lumps, Hoover style, for a mere $4,000 and two hours under the knife—is one of the fastest growing operations in the country. Tummy tucks are also very popular, cost about $5,000, and leave you as taut as a 10-year-old. Sure, that's it; liposuction on our thighs will take away our raging anxiety. A tummy tuck will render us less overwhelming. Science, triumphant once more over measly nature, will finally get rid of that powerless and unacceptable person in the mirror.

                                                                              Dalma Heyn

4

Synthesizing

When Herbie Hancock presses a certain key on his synthesizer, the note that emerges from the speaker is a synthesized sound; that is, it's a tone made up of sounds that have been "mixed," or combined, inside of Hancock's synthesizer. Writers who combine sources to create paragraphs or essays are also synthesizers. They're *idea* synthesizers. They take the ideas, the examples, and the descriptions of other writers and incorporate them into their own writing. Like Herbie Hancock, idea synthesizers make a new kind of music out of pieces of the old.

A MODEL SYNTHESIS

Let's look now at a simple example of a synthesis from a passage in an essay that appears in Chapter 12. The author, Kai Erikson, argues that the United States didn't have to drop the atomic bomb on Japanese civilians. Read the topic sentence carefully and then watch how Erikson weaves into his prose two sources that serve as examples of his topic sentence.

> The fourth option [to actually dropping the bomb on Hiroshima] involved a kind of *warning shot.* The thought here was to drop a bomb without notice over a relatively uninhabited stretch of enemy land so that the Japanese high command might see at first hand what was in store for them if they failed to surrender soon. Edward Teller thought that an explosion at night high over Tokyo Bay would serve as a brilliant visual argument, **and** Adm. Lewis Strauss . . . recommended a strike on a local forest, reasoning that the blast would "lay the trees out in windrows from the center of the explosion in all directions as though they were matchsticks," meanwhile igniting a fearsome firestorm at the epicenter.

Easy enough. The paragraph begins with an overview statement—in other words, a topic sentence—that encompasses the ideas from both sources. The paragraph includes an announcement of each source ("Edward Teller thought" and "Adm. Lewis Strauss recommended"). And it provides a transitional expression that shows the relationship between the ideas in the paragraph. In this case that relationship is so obvious (the second example is merely an addition to the first example) that the author merely provides the word "and" (which we have put in boldface) between the first and second source to show that they are coordinate ideas. That is a synthesized paragraph.

Now let's construct a synthesized paragraph of our own. We'll create it out of the raw material from two different sources in Chapter 10, the first by Geoffrey Cowley and the second by Robert White. Read these paragraphs first, and then go on to the analysis of the synthesis based on them.

> The killing is not without purpose; it has immense practical benefits. Animal models have advanced the study of such diseases as cancer, diabetes and alcoholism and yielded life-saving treatments for everything from heart disease to manic-depressive illness. Vaccines developed through animal research have virtually wiped out diseases like smallpox and polio. "Every surgical technique was tried first in animals," says Frankie Trull, executive director of the Foundation for Biomedical Research. "Every drug anybody takes was tried first in animals."
>
> Geoffrey Cowley

> Four years ago I was part of a surgical team trying to remove a malignant tumor from the brain of a nine-year-old girl. The operation failed because we could not stem the hemorrhaging in the brain tissue. We were unable to separate the little girl from the cancer that was slowly killing her. To buy time, we put her on a program of radiation.
>
> Concurrently we were experimenting in our brain-research laboratory with a new high-precision laser scalpel. Working with monkeys and dogs that had been humanely treated and properly anesthetized, we perfected our operating technique. Then, in July 1985, my associate, pediatric neurosurgeon Matt Likavec, and I used the laser to remove all of that little girl's tumor. Now 13, she is healthy, happy, and looking forward to a full life. The animal experiments had enabled us to cure a child we could not help 15 months earlier.
>
> Robert White

Now let's say we are writing a paper with this thesis: Animal research is necessary. One of the things we want to do is point out examples of animal research that have benefited humanity. A synthesis of the above two sources might look something like this:

Research on animals has alleviated human suffering. For instance, in a recent *Newsweek* article, Geoffrey Cowley points out that animal research has brought us closer to cures for cancer and diabetes and has enabled researchers to create vaccines for smallpox and polio. But animal research had helped in small, personal ways, too. Writing for *The Reader's Digest*, Dr. Robert White, a professor of neurosurgery, describes an operation he had performed on a 9-year-old girl. Because his initial attempts to remove a cancerous growth from the girl's brain failed when he encountered massive bleeding, he had to postpone any further surgery. He then put the girl on radiation treatments. In the following weeks Dr. White and his associate perfected the skills of a new laser scalpel on anesthetized monkeys and dogs. Only then were they able to go back and safely remove the girl's tumor. She is now a healthy 13-year-old.

THE ELEMENTS OF A SYNTHESIS

Now let's look more closely at certain important parts of the synthesis above.

Topic Sentence

This statement encompasses all of the ideas that you want to combine in your paragraph. In this case the statement is this: "Research on animals has alleviated human suffering."

Source Identifications within the Text

In this case, the first source is announced with "In a recent *Newsweek* article, Geoffrey Cowley points out . . . " The second source is introduced with "Writing for *The Reader's Digest*, Dr. Robert White, a professor of neurosurgery, describes . . . " These announcements help your reader keep *your* point of view separate from that of your sources. Without those little introductions, your reader would find it irksome, perhaps impossible, to keep track of whose point of view is being expressed at any particular time.

One more thing: If your source is a well-known expert in the field, your source introduction need consist only of his or her name and area of expertise. Let's say you come across a well-known authority who is quoted in a *Time* magazine essay. You don't have to mention the author, title, or even the name of the magazine in your introduction to that quote. All you need to say is this: "Dr. Robert White, a professor of neurosurgery, argues that . . . "

You'll want to vary these source identifications occasionally. Here are some of the possibilities.

Introductions for Sources with Authors' Names

According to Bruce Pickering, director of Rockdyne, . . .
Natalie Gittelson, in a *McCall's* essay, asserts that . . .

In a recent *Newsweek* essay, Carol Kimmel puts it this way:
This point is further supported by Robert Samuelson in a recent *American History* article. Samuelson points out that . . .

Introductions for Sources without Authors' Names

An essay in *U.S. News and World Report* observes . . .
According to an essay in *Science News* . . .

Subsequent Source Introductions

Once you have introduced a particular source in your paper, the following references need only mention the author's name. However, if you haven't mentioned a particular author for a while, use the author's first *and* last names in a subsequent identification. Indeed, if you haven't mentioned your source in a page or two, you might also repeat one of the identifying tags that you originally used.

The biochemist Fred Weathers also expresses great concern that . . .
According to the previously cited *Science News* article . . .
Bruce Pickering goes on to say:

The Relationship between Two Sources

In this case, the writer shows that relationship by announcing, "But animal research has helped in small, personal ways, too." That statement tells the reader two things about the examples from the second source: (1) that the examples coming up offer additional support for the topic sentence and (2) they differ in one small way. The word "but" signals that way.

Pay careful attention to the advice we have just given. You see, the heart of a synthesis lies not within the sources but within the writer's comments on those sources. The synthesizer's job is to introduce the sources, clarify their ideas, show the relationship between them, and discuss their implications. In fact, a synthesis is basically a dialogue between the writer and his or her sources. Without these running comments, a synthesis comes off looking mechanical and superficial—as if the writer had done little more than paste together the ideas of other writers.

Even the verbs you use when you introduce a source can act as implicit comments on your source's point of view. For instance, when you say, "Robert Felter continues to insist, . . . " you are telling your reader something about Felter's attitude toward his idea. If you are arguing with Felter, you might even say, "Robert Felter doggedly contends . . . " The point is, get involved with your sources. That involvement doesn't threaten your credibility; it greatly enhances it. Without that kind of running commentary, a writer comes off looking ill-informed about the topic.

ANNOUNCING YOUR SOURCES

There are two places when you ought to tell your reader that you are using a source: (1) when you use any source for the first time and (2) when you come back to a particular source after it has been interrupted by another source. Let's see how this works. Let's say you are going to use some information out of an essay by H. S. Glasscheib for the first time in your paper. Your prose might look something like this:

> In his essay "The Four Juices," H. S. Glasscheib reports that between 1827 and 1836 France's hospitals used between 5 and 6 million leeches a year.

You are now going to move to another source, so naturally you have to announce to your reader that you are changing your source—like this:

> But France wasn't alone in using bloodletting as a therapeutic tool. In England, for instance, doctors were spilling blood just as copiously as the French. Even kings were not spared. In describing the last days of Charles II, Ernest Sackville Turner, in *Call the Doctor*, says that the "merry monarch," who was already weak, had his flesh scarified, his veins tapped, and his skin "cupped" by the dozen or so doctors who were attending him.

Now, however, you want to go back to Glasscheib. You have to tell your reader that you are returning to the Glasscheib source.

> Perhaps it's not surprising that "therapeutic" bloodletting, according to H. S. Glasscheib, can be traced back to the practice of human sacrifice.

Let's put the whole thing together, with the "announcements" in boldface.

> **In his essay "The Four Juices," H. S. Glasscheib reports that** between 1827 and 1836 France's hospitals used between 5 and 6 million leeches a year to suck the blood of their patients. But France wasn't alone in using bloodletting as a therapeutic tool. In England, for instance, doctors were spilling blood just as copiously as the French. Even kings were not spared. **In describing the last days of Charles II, the social historian, Ernest Sackville Turner, says that** the "merry monarch," who was already weak, had his flesh scarified, his veins tapped, and his skin "cupped" by the dozen or so doctors who were attending him. Perhaps it's not surprising that "therapeutic" bloodletting, **according to H. S. Glasscheib,** can be traced back to the practice of human sacrifice.

Really there's nothing to it: Announce each source the first time you use it, and reannounce a source when you return to it after an absence. It may seem a nuisance to do so much announcing of your sources, but readers appreciate those announcements; they help them keep track of where you stop and your sources begin.

Remember, too, that even when you're using a single source throughout a paragraph, you still need to announce that source the first time you use it and then remind your reader, every so often within that paragraph, that you are using that same source.

Of course, a synthesis isn't always a combination of sources that agree with one another. You might want to combine sources that disagree. We'll use two more paragraphs from Chapter 10 to illustrate this point: the first by Steven Zak and the second by Robert White.

> Some researchers may insist that scientists should not be constrained in their quest for knowledge, but this is a romantic notion of scientific freedom that never was and should not be. Science is always constrained, by economic and social priorities and by ethics. Sometimes, paradoxically, it is also freed by these constraints, because a barrier in one direction forces it to cut another path, in an area that might have remained unexplored.
>
> Steven Zak

> My main objection is to regulations requiring animal-care-and-use committees to pass on all research proposals involving animals. While experiments begin with specific goals, a scientist never knows at the outset where the research will lead. Yet he may not deviate from the original plan—in order to pursue an unexpected opportunity—without first filling out costly, time-consuming paper work to obtain committee approval. New regulations governing the use of animals have already increased the financial burden on the nation's 127 medical schools by many millions of dollars annually. "But the real cost is that there will be less research," says Carol Scheman of the Association of American Universities, "and when research is slowed, people die."
>
> Robert White

Now let's say we are writing an objective description of the two sides of the controversy on animal rights. One of the issues of this controversy concerns the freedom of researchers to pursue whatever path that they deem necessary. Here, then, is what a synthesis of that issue might look like.

> One of the issues within the animal research controversy concerns the freedom of researchers to pursue whatever path they think best. A defender of the freedom of the researcher, Robert White, a professor of neurosurgery, argues that regulations that are too strict will hamper research and lead to more human suffering and death. A critic of research that uses animals, Steven Zak, calls research freedom a "romantic notion" because no one has perfect freedom any-

way. Zak then claims that constraints designed to alleviate animal suffering may actually aid research by forcing the researcher down a promising research path that he or she would not have otherwise traveled.

We don't mean to suggest that synthesis is only used within paragraphs. Writers who move from one source to another as they move from one paragraph to another are also synthesizing. In this case the transition from one source to another will usually be a topic sentence. But the same principles are valid: each new source needs a transition that moves the reader smoothly from one source to the next.

In one of the exercises below, you'll have a chance to write a short essay that incorporates the ideas of other writings.

EXERCISE 4-1: *Synthesizing*

Combine information from the following three excerpts to form a new, synthesized paragraph. Be sure to include all of the elements common to a synthesis: a topic sentence that encompasses all the ideas in the paragraph, announcements of sources, and a sentence that describes the relationship between the ideas. The three essays from which these paragraphs have been chosen deal with the problem of the "heroic" measures—respirating, blood transfusing, and so on—that are now taken to prolong life for terminally ill patients. Your topic sentence is this: The cost of all of these heroic medical measures is troubling.

On the Death of a Baby

The situation now exists in which it is very easy to turn on a respirator—no one's consent is even needed—and almost impossible to turn one off. Until our legal and moral codes become sophisticated enough to cope with our machinery, parents must have the right to decide whether or in what circumstances their tiny babies should be attached to respirators. Meanwhile, patients, families, hospitals, and society as a whole will continue to be plagued by new and agonizing problems created by the boom in life-support technology. . . .

At the end came a notice from the PHC business office, announcing in passionless figures that the hospital costs alone for Andrew Stinson's treatment came to $104,403.20 (of which all but $2100 has been paid). The bill is more than an accounting for charges for daily treatment. It is a reminder that through the six months of hospital experiments, failures, and arrogance, the meter was ticking—but someone else would pay. The IICU could continue to operate in splendid isolation, not only from our protests, but also from any sense of the financial impact of their solitary decisions.

Robert and Peggy Stinson

The Staggering Cost of Prolonging Life

William Greenberg is experiencing advanced forms of senility. Almost 30 years ago, in 1954, he developed diabetes. This was controlled with strict dieting and weight loss. At age 85 he had a severe heart attack and survived as a result of recent advances in drug therapy. He stopped working, changed his diet, began to take newly discovered drugs to lower the fatty substances in his blood, and by age 90 his coronary arteries were again functioning normally. But he began to lose his memory, fall frequently (a hip fracture was repaired after one such event), and lose his personal cleanliness so that he began to need constant care. Now at age 104 he is bedridden, recognizes no one, but has a healthy appetite and normally functioning heart, lungs, and kidneys. His care costs $80,000 annually. Who should pay the bills?

Thomas Chalmers and Alfred Stern

Test Case Is Shaped by Doctors' Ethics, One Man's Suffering

The hospital's chief attorney says the doctors' ethics outweigh a patient's right to privacy or to control his treatment and that [William] Bartling has not been steadfast in his request to die. For a while, Bartling's hands were tied down to prevent any suicide attempt.

The next step for Bartling—whose medical, hospital and legal bills since last spring have gone well over half a million dollars—is an appeal of a lower court's refusal to disconnect the respirator.

Andrew H. Malcolm

EXERCISE 4-2: *Synthesizing*

Let's say you are arguing this case: We should not use heroic medical measures to prolong the life of the terminally ill. Within that paper you include a paragraph that combines a description of the intense suffering of the terminally ill with at least one reason for our inability to confront the issue of allowing the dying patient to decide his or her own fate. Combine the following two sources to create that paragraph.

Nurse's Tale

Sandy was a five-year-old kid. I had been taking care of her for several months. She had a malignant brain tumor. They had operated several times, her head was shaved, and she had scars like zippers over her head. She got worse and worse and finally slipped into a coma. Her parents used to be at the hospital every day; they'd take turns minding Sandy's twin brothers, who were three years old. The mother couldn't stand it and finally took a bunch of sleeping pills. The doctors used to stand at the foot of the bed and shake their heads, saying, "Medicine can't do any more." The mother survived the pills and after that she used to talk to me. One night Sandy just stopped breathing and would you believe some nut jumped on her chest and her heart started beating again. They put her on a respirator. She got infected and then the doctors started giving her antibiotics, sticking her with needles all the time. The kid looked like a pincushion. She was getting all black-and-blue, and nothing seemed to touch the infection. She smelled awful. Sort of pungent and sickly sweet, like decaying tissue. I could even smell it when I was out of the room. It stuck in my nostrils, and if I breathed through my mouth I could taste it. My clothes and hair and skin smelled like it too.

She had been such a pretty little girl, and I really cared about her. I kept asking everyone how we could get her off that damn machine. Nobody could do it . . . although they all agreed it would be better if she died. They told me if her heart stopped again to walk slow before I called anyone. I knew what they meant. Her father came in one day and told me he couldn't stand it anymore. He was going to run as far away as he could get. I thought about the twins and about the mother. Sandy had died once.

Terry Daniels

We're the Prisoners of Medical Technology

We are becoming the prisoners of our medical abilities. Individual choice about death is being steamrolled by a medical profession afraid to act in the manner it believes best for patients, by legislators who refuse to touch such a political hot potato, and by a legal profession that seems to delight more in terrorizing physicians than in helping the terminally ill to exercise control over their final days.

Arthur Caplan

EXERCISE 4-3: *Synthesizing*

Let's say you are arguing the case for using heroic measures to prolong life. Within that paper you include a paragraph that combines sources that will support your side of the issue. Combine information from the following two sources.

When Doctors Play God

The hopelessly ill or dying patient creates the weightiest issue in bioethics, and no wholly satisfactory way has yet been found to deal with it. Doctors are sometimes accused of carrying heroic measures too far, a result, perhaps, of their natural instinct and training. "Saving a life is a very primitive reflex for a physician," says Dr. O. J. Sahler of the University of Rochester School of Medicine and Dentistry. Many doctors go further; they insist that the Hippocratic code is still literally valid. "The doctor's responsibility is to do everything he can to sustain lives," says Dr. Marshall L. Brumer of Ft. Lauderdale, Fla. Brumer would not withhold treatment from a victim of incurable cancer who is in pain and says he wishes to die. "Cures can come down the pipeline at any hour of the day," Brumer says. "To stand idly by and watch a person die is intolerable. Where does it stop? Where do you draw the line?"

Matt Clark

The Awful Privacy of Baby Doe

Among the infants thus doomed was a baby with Down's syndrome who had a routinely operable intestinal obstruction. . . . Drs. Duff and Campbell explained in the article that "his parents thought that surgery was wrong for their baby and themselves. He died seven days after birth." He died because he was retarded, although no one had any way of knowing how retarded he would be. (In 1984 the poster of the National Organization on Disability was a photograph of Matthew Starr, of Baltimore, reading the Torah during his bar mitzvah. Matthew has Down's syndrome, but that service was not simplified for him. He also wrote and read the traditional speech given by a boy entering the adult Jewish religious community.)

Nat Hentoff

EXERCISE 4-4: *Synthesizing*

Read the following three essays and write a small paper that objectively describes the two sides of the controversy over using "heroic" measures to prolong life. In this case you will not necessarily be combining sources within a single paragraph.

Don't Pull the Plug, Even on the Terminally Ill

The idea of the "good death" is taking firm root in our media culture. Death is part of life, its advocates say.

Indeed it is; so is tuberculosis when you willfully refuse the vaccine against it.

But there is an older idea in our collective psyche, one that Dylan Thomas expressed so well in his imperative, "Do not go gentle into that good night."

Humanity—and especially the medical profession—must fight to preserve life and enhance it.

William Bartling's experience at Glendale Adventist Medical Center pinpointed the dilemma of the "right to die." A 70-year-old man with multiple ailments, Bartling lived for seven months on a ventilator (commonly called a respirator) while his wife and attorney fought a legal battle to remove him precipitously from the ventilator and bring about his death.

It was clear to the five physicians treating him that Bartling did not want to die.

Yes, he nodded in a June 21 videotape deposition, he wanted to live. No, he didn't want to live on a ventilator. Yes, he knew that removing the ventilator could result in his death.

But on many occasions this same patient, who was being treated for depression in addition to his physical ailments, gestured frantically for nurses to return the ventilator to his throat when they removed it for cleaning.

And he continued to consent to and request ongoing therapeutic treatment. This was a man who consistently wanted to die?

This hospital and these doctors have no problem turning life-support machines off in comatose or brain-dead patients where the family and physicians are in agreement. In fact, they have done so.

But a cognizant, alert patient, who sits up in a chair and eats ice cream and who interacts with nurses on a regular basis, as Bartling often did, is another matter.

Are physicians and hospitals to be forced to aid and abet a suicide or homicide? Is a depressed patient to be "terminated" because he requests it on blue Monday—even if he changes his mind on Tuesday?

According to the 2nd District California Court of Appeal's Dec. 27 decision, yes.

The mission statement of Glendale Adventist speaks of treating the whole person, encompassing his physical, spiritual, and emotional needs. Its aim is to "nurture the patient's faith, allay his fears, and help the patient become more responsive to the healing process."

Bartling, who died Nov. 6 while still attached to the ventilator, was tragically typical of the patient who needs this kind of help.

Hippocrates had a simple rule in the training of physicians: "First, do no harm."

Acquiescing to an ambivalent patient's self-destructive moods would be doing just that kind of harm.

Jiggs Gallagher

It's a Costly Mistake That Just Denies Death

Like his predecessor Barny Clark, William Shroeder, the second man to permit doctors to put a polyurethane and chrome heart in his chest, is a brave man. No one would argue that. It takes guts to be a part of a new venture with high risk of pain, even agony.

And the doctors who designed and implanted the artificial heart are enterprising pioneers in their field. They have pushed their effort with care and conscience, with an eye towards saving lives later.

But with this second implant of an artificial heart, it's time to ask, Is it worth it? Should human life be extended at all cost? Should high tech medicine be brought to bear on every dying patient? Can society afford to divert limited resources into saving every life?

I think the answer to all these questions is no. The artificial heart experiment illustrates how far we have come in medicine, but it also raises some hard questions.

Medicine has already advanced to the point where many technically "dead" and dying people can be kept alive indefinitely. Machines can breathe for us, cleanse our waste, and circulate our blood.

As technical progress continues, the boundary between life and death is likely to become even cloudier. Are we prolonging life or extending death?

In many cases, it now must be said, we are extending death. In the case of the artificial heart, this is certainly so.

Doctors bristle at the idea of rationing medical care, and no one wants to or enjoys making the choice: Life or death?

But as we develop more new ways to save and restore life, doctors and society must develop better criteria to judge who to save and who to let die.

And we need to ask what that life will be like if it's saved. For Barny Clark, we now know the suffering was intense, relentless. Shroeder has already had a relapse. Some argue they pave the way for others. But it's doubtful the artificial heart will ever yield a good quality of life.

We pay a high price for costly high tech medical advances like the artificial heart. They save lives but they drive up the cost of care. Our tax dollars foot the bill (Medicare and Medicaid); the rest we pay for indirectly as companies charge more for their products to finance skyrocketing health insurance premiums.

Our medical priorities are backward. We spend billions on new treatments but very little on preventing disease.

Finally, the media is as guilty as the medical profession at focusing too much attention on high tech solutions. They glorify them, wallow in the wizardry of it all.

Making these brave patients and good doctors heroes is understandable, but it doesn't help us come to terms with the harsh choices we face as high tech medical solutions yield diminishing returns.

Steven Findlay

Best Medicine Is Love, Not Doses of Death

Words can be misleading. The semantic gymnasts of the death enhancement effort somersault across America, heralded by the media elite, creating the illusion that man not only has a "right to die," but that medicine has a "duty to help him out"!

Man, whether in possession of his rights or not, is going to die. From the first instant of his natural life at fertilization, he is destined for aging and ultimately death. But between the first spark of his life and the last spark of his life, he is always inviolably alive.

Man experiences, among other things, pain, anguish, joy, and laughter during his lifetime. Sometimes, toward the end of his natural life, he experiences more pain and anguish than usual. However, at no time during his natural life do others have the obligation, the duty, or the privilege of providing a means of death.

If a man does this for one of his fellow men, he, in fact, murders. And that is a crime.

What then is the basis for the "right to die" argument?

It is fatally flawed, misrepresented, and misunderstood by the public. When someone is in pain and suffers a great deal, his anguish may come forth, at times verbally, and he may perhaps express a wish that life would end.

The obligation we all face, in the situation, is to provide love and compassion. For by understanding and care, we express to the dying person our need to nurture him during his time of agony. We reinforce life.

Pain-relieving medication is a further response, which is never discussed by those who promote the "right to die." And, in this time of modern medicine, there's a great deal that can be done to manage the pain, make the patient at least moderately comfortable, while at the same time not giving in to his despair. We reinforce life.

The desire to hasten death must be countered in this age of machinery by the human emotions of love and concern.

"I want to go gently into the good night" must mean to us, "Help me now by sharing yourself that I might find peace in this agony of mine."

Approaching death or experiencing pain will never be easy, but it is within our capacity to provide either greater love during these tribulations, or, if we heed the harbingers of "death enhancement," to play God by ending life prematurely.

In a society as great as ours, let us hope that each of us finds, within ourselves, the capability of saying "I love you" by word and by action, so that as nature takes her course within the body of the one who is sick, we have provided the medicine of understanding rather than the doses of death, which, in time, will cause us a suffering unlike any we can imagine in this life.

Judie Brown

— 5 —

Writing a Critique

You and your friend Arnie emerge into the bright sun from Cineplex 30, where you just saw *Friday the 13th, Part Jillion: Jason Visits Disneyland.* Staring at a Jujube he's just picked from his teeth, Arnie turns to you and grunts, "Awesome flick." Arnie may not have known it, but he's just critiqued a movie. His critique is a primitive thing, to be sure—something like a burp of approval after a big meal—but it is a critique. But now you turn to Arnie and ask, "How come?" How come? How come "awesome"? Nobody's ever asked that of Arnie before. He's momentarily dumbfounded about how he's going to explain his gut response—his "critique."

That's what you'll be doing in this chapter, *explaining* your reactions to the ideas in essays. A critique, you see, analyzes a work of art—a painting, an opera, a movie, or an essay—to show how it works. We can begin by looking at the most vital part of the whole process, the reading of the essay.

ACTIVE READING

Most of our reading is done while our brains are idling. But reading in order to critique demands more of us. Our brains need to be active, alert, in gear. We need to think, question, disagree, agree. We need to react almost viscerally to the printed word.

Of course, before we can react, we have to understand. That's why it's a good idea to give the essay a cursory reading first. We need to see the shape and feel of the landscape before we dig into it. In this first reading, slow down at the title, introduction, topic sentences, and conclusion. (If you want to read more on these matters, see Chapter 1.)

After you have a feel for the essay, take a pencil in your hand. You'll want to leave a trail behind you—a trail of underlinings, checks, asterisks, and comments in the margin—so that you can go back and see where you've been.

But, you ask, what am I looking for? Good question. Unfortunately, we can't give a really good answer right now. (We'll be discussing that matter later in this chapter.) Each essay is different. Of course, very simply stated, what you're looking for are things to write about. In one essay you might like to write about the author's coarse diction. In another you might object to an author's carelessness with facts. In yet another you might like to argue with one of the author's assumptions. You just don't know *what* you'll find until you get there. It's kind of like opening a Christmas present—though sometimes it's more like opening a can of worms.

To give you a picture of what active reading looks like, we have actively read and marked up the Vance Packard essay from *The Waste Makers*, excerpted below. You'll get your chance to practice active reading later in this chapter; for the time being read the following essay and our responses to it.

The Waste Makers

extravagant?

Americans traditionally have liked to think of themselves as a frugal, hard-working, God-fearing people making sacrifices for the long haul. They have exalted such maxims of Ben Franklin as: "A man may, if he knows not how to save as he gets, keep his nose to the grindstone."

really?

What caused this "flamboyance"? Perhaps Americans only had more opportunity.

Puritanical traits were esteemed necessary to survival by the settlers struggling to convert forest and prairie into a national homeland. By the nineteenth century, however, a flamboyant streak was beginning to emerge clearly in the American character. Emerson observed that Americans, unlike Europeans, exhibited "an uncalculated, headlong expenditure." As more and more Americans found themselves living in metropolitan areas, hedonism as a guiding philosophy of life gained more and more disciples. People sought possessions more than formerly in emulation of, or competition with, their neighbors. Quite possibly, the environment of thickly settled areas brought a lessening of serenity and a feeling of

pop psychology!

Then again, maybe it didn't.

no kidding

What a leap: 19th cent. to atomic age.

chicken or the egg? Who created the demand?

stereotype

being swallowed up that impelled the people to strive for distinctive emblems and gratification through consumption. The growing availability of manufactured goods undoubtedly had a great deal to do with the rise in hedonism. The upheaval of wars and the uncertainty of life in an atomic era also contributed to the life-for-the-moment spirit.

During the fifties, however, another force came powerfully into play in the promotion of hedonism. Many marketers, as a calculated strategy, sought to promote a mood of self-indulgence in order to promote sales. The puritanical inhibitions of Americans were seen as blocking consumers from enjoying the wondrously rich, full new life that marketers were ready and eager to provide. . . .

The joys of self-indulgence were stressed, consciously or unwittingly, in many sales messages. A New York department store told women in a full-page advertisement: "Even If You Own a Dozen Coats, You Can't Afford to Miss. . . ." A San Francisco store featuring luxurious fixtures and accessories for bathrooms beckoned passers-by with the sign, "PAMPER YOURSELF! . . ."

Are customers really the helpless victims of such appeals?

An elderly supermarket operator in Indianapolis shook his head sadly as he pointed out to me all the "convenience" foods he was selling to bridge-playing wives. He muttered: "The husband works all day and then comes home to a dinky little pre-cooked pot pie." He said he would not permit them in his own home. Ready-to-serve meals are likely to cost up to 50 percent more than home-prepared meals.

Perhaps time is important: Evidently it is to those who buy the pies.

He told of jesting with one young redheaded wife who was inspecting his bakery-made cherry pies. He asked her why she didn't make one herself. She replied: "I wouldn't know how to begin." This elderly man began showing her by listing the ingredients. When he said "shortening," she asked "What's that?" He explained and began showing her how to roll out the crust. She wrinkled her pert nose and said, "It sounds terribly messy. I think I'll take this one here." Hundreds of wives, he told me with a shrug, buy his expensive jars of chicken a là king every week when they could make it themselves for less than a third the cost. . . .

condescending

"Pert" nose? I think Packard made up this whole episode.

Still another aspect of the promotion of hedonism, we should note, has been the drive to make Americans more impulsive in their shopping habits. Du Pont found that impulse buying in supermarkets had soared nearly a third in a decade. Supermarkets changed from being simple, stripped-down marts designed to pass on the economies of mass buying to the consumer. Originally they operated on a slim 12 percent markup. Now the supermarkets have become shimmering carnivals offering free automobiles as prizes, offering premiums, trading stamps, soft music, and hundreds of packages that have been shrewdly designed, at considerable expense, to present an imagery that will cry out to the passing shopper: "Grab me!" The result of all these changes in the supermarkets is that markups have risen on the average to nearly 20 percent.

So what's so bad about this?

My, we're so helpless.

I wonder what his source is for this figure?

Perhaps the most impressive report on the swing to hedonism was made by the research division of *The Chicago Tribune.* Its study, entitled *The New Consumer,* was based on a $100,000 study of homemakers from

three different social layers in the
suburbs of Chicago. At all three levels
a trend toward hedonism was evident. Mr. Martineau, director of research and marketing for the *Tribune*,
summed up the findings of the investigators as they related to this trend
in these words:

> There has been a shift from the   *What else?*
> philosophy of security and sav-
> ing to a philosophy of spending
> and immediate satisfaction . . .
> more self-indulgent spending, a
> tendency to equate standard of
> living with possession of materi-
> al goods. . . .

She's probably making   One wife said that the difference
more money than her   between herself and her parents was
parents did.   that she buys "new furniture and
lamps because we get tired of looking
at them any longer." Another woman
said; "Today, we're always looking to   *Why not?*
buy something that's a time saver so
that we can have more time to relax
and enjoy life." Still another woman
said that when she and her husband
buy draperies, rugs, and furniture
they hope the goods "don't last as
long as our parents' did."

Women in the . . . community of
Home Town, primarily a working-
class and lower-white-collar suburb,
revealed this same fascination with
accumulating material things. The report stated that in Home Town "the
gadget . . . becomes the symbol of
'finer living.' "

Vance Packard

AN EXERCISE IN ACTIVE READING

Now it's time for you to try your hand at active reading on the essay below,
Has Anyone Here Seen My Old Friend Jimi? Remember, as you read the essay

for the first time, focus your attention on the big picture. If you keep your mind on what the author is trying to do, the details of the essay will drop into place.

After you have a clear picture of the author's main concern, begin a second reading, this time with a pencil in your hand. Underline. Make little notes in the margin: Write a question mark when you doubt what the author claims. Write an exclamation mark when you agree strongly with something. Write "How true!" Or "What's the assumption here?" Or "Skimpy examples." Or "Bull!" Or "Needs another example here." Or "Ha!" Or "Is he right here? I remember differently." Or whatever. Make up your own marks. Read personally. We've increased the margins so that you'll have plenty of room for your comments. Later in this chapter you'll have a chance to sort out your comments and write a critique on the John Lee essay, but for now we need to describe what to critique and how to go about organizing one.

Has Anyone Here Seen My Old Friend Jimi?

Turning through the airwaves of frequency modulation, I hear so much music nonsense that I usually just turn the squawk box off. No longer, especially in the backward area I live in, can you find "free program" radio stations. By this I mean a station where the individual disc jockey may pick his own tunes to play. In this day and age *Billboard* dictates what everyone listens to. If Wham's synthesizer-laden sex single is in the Top 40, I can be assured that it will be played at least once every 2 hours. And if some punked-out metal band writes a song about strip bars, and then 500,000 mindless 14-year-old girls buy it, good ol' Top 40 FM saturates the atmosphere with their teeny-bopper psychosis. Give me the music of the fifties, sixties, and early seventies over this dreck any day.

To begin with, there's hardly anything played today that is actually music. Music, you might remember, is played on an instrument. So much of the "modern," state-of-the-art trash is nothing more than a talentless singer accompanied by a genius on a computer. No longer do we have the classic guitar work such as Eric Clapton masterfully playing the lead to "Layla," nor is there a Jimi Hendrix and his consummately skillful music. You may say, "Well, Jimi is dead." That's true. In fact, the few who are Jimi's heirs are a dying breed due to the Top 40 radio stations. Masters like Jimi played from the heart, not from the wallet. Of course there are exceptions, but if you'll look closely, the only exceptions are those diehard artists from the seventies who are still playing. The music of the Hollies, the Who, Jefferson Airplane, and especially the Beatles wasn't just comatose caterwauling. These singers and musicians often sang about current issues and human values. Maybe it is a good thing poor Jimi is dead. If he heard Z100, he'd surely roll over in his grave.

The visions I spoke of are another reason today's music is

garbage. Does the lyric "Bang your head" bring any concept to
mind? Well, besides axe-murdering your neighbors? Bon Jovi
tells us he is an outlaw wanted dead or alive. Radical concept
indeed! The only people who want him dead are the parents of
the sexually distraught teenagers.

What happened to groups such as Country Joe and The
Fish asking us, "What the hell are we fighting for?" or Neil
Young attempting to bring to light the plight of blacks in
"Southern Man"? These songs about moral issues, social dis-
turbances, and public awareness are, for the most part, history.
All I hear today is junk like Madonna telling me how she feels
like a virgin. Ha!

And that brings me to the subject of sex. Songs such as
"Like a Virgin," "Take You Down," "Love Touch," and George
Michael's "I Want Your Sex" are socially irresponsible. No
wonder today's youth is so sexually active and pregnancy rates
are so high. Although I don't believe in censorship, I do believe in decency, and I don't think local radio should force
such garbage on me. Long gone are the days of Buddy's girl
Peggy Sue or the Beatles wanting to hold some girl's hand. The
dream of the Everly Brothers have turned into a nightmare. The
innocence of the fifties has turned into perversion in the high-
tech eighties. Tunes such as Motley Crue's "Girls, Girls, Girls,"
with all of its T&A lyrics, have transformed rock music into an
aphrodisiac.

I have been asked many times why I still listen to the radio. Simple. I'm hoping someone new will come along and
turn modern music a full 180-degrees back to art, intellect, and
innocence. Like a fundamentalist Christian waiting for the Second Coming, I await the return of good music—and, thus far,
with the same futility as the eternally disappointed Christian.
Until the musical second coming arrives, I will stand by the ol-
dies like a Doberman Pinscher, undaunted by the onslaught of
modern "music." I own a radio, it is true, but I use it mainly to
amplify my records and tapes of past treasures of musical art.

                                                              John Lee

WRITING A CRITIQUE

What Can You Critique?

A critique can focus on a single idea from an essay, or it can deal with an
entire essay, focusing on its most conspicuous features. Just be sure to tell
your reader, in a thesis statement, what it is you're going to do.

Let's be a bit more specific now about just what you can talk about
during a critique. Here are some of the more common concerns of critiques.

1. An essay's ideas

- How logical is the author's thesis? To get at this, start by breaking down the essay. Is the main idea based on a cause-and-effect relationship or on reasons? (For more on this, see Chapter 2, pages 23–29.)
- Are there enough examples, and are they representative enough to be persuasive?
- How realistic is the idea? An idea may be logical but foolish.
- What kind of assumptions underlie the idea?
- Are the assumptions credible?

2. An essay's language

- Sentences too long and convoluted?
- Sentences clear?
- Diction too pompous? Too jargon-laden? Too coarse? Too vague?

3. An essay's tone

- Too pious? Too corny? Too sarcastic? Too condescending?

4. An essay's structure

- Clear thesis? Is it clear where the author is going?
- Introduction too long, too short?
- Topic sentences clearly related to thesis?
- Enough examples?
- Coherent? Do the ideas move smoothly and logically from one to another?

Sorting Out Your Responses

First, see if there is a focus to your comments. If there is, sharpen that focus by reading the essay again, pulling out other examples. If you find that you have an idea that seems to have potential, stop and briefly work it out on a piece of scratch paper. Here, then, are the kinds of theses that could be used for papers that have a single focus.

One assumption undermines the author's thesis.
Offensive language spoils the author's tone.
Exaggeration hurts the essay's effectiveness.
The essay is delightfully ironic and funny.
The author's nostalgia weakens her argument.

If there is no focus to your comments, you might want to write a critique that covers a variety of the ideas that you have about the paper. In that case, your thesis might look something like this.

The essay is clearly and cleverly written, but its thesis rests on a troublesome assumption.

However, don't try to cover everything you've noted in the margins. Omit or quickly run by minor points to get to the one or two points that you want to talk about.

"Looking at Billboards" has a few minor problems, but its strengths outweigh them by far. In particular, the essay is full of vivid examples and delicious irony.

An essay might be terribly logical but also mean-spirited. Speed by the essay's logicality to get to what struck you forcefully: its mean-spirited nature. An essay might be coarse but profound. Brush off the coarseness in a single sentence to get to the essay's profundity.

We can overlook the author's fondness for four-letter words because he has an important and profound message.

Organizing a Critique

1. Introduce the author, his or her title or special expertise (if any), the title of the piece you are going to critique, and a broad summary of the piece. In the case of "Has Anyone Seen My Old Friend Jimi?" there is no additional information about the author, so you won't be able to tell the reader anything about his expertise (That's often the case.) But he does have a clear thesis statement, and it is traditionally located.
2. Clarify, or elaborate on, your source's thesis and discuss any premises or assumptions that underlie that thesis. Remember, give the thesis a fair shake. This may take you a paragraph or so. You might even want to quote a few words to give the reader an idea of the tone of the piece.
3. Write your thesis. Now it's time to make your own statement. Perhaps you agree with Lee and you think he's done a marvelous job of showing the reader why he was led to his conclusion. Perhaps you *generally* agree with Lee but find that his whole attack on the problem is wrong. Perhaps you agree with Lee but find that he falls down in a couple of places. Perhaps you disagree with Lee's thesis. Whatever conclusion you arrive at, write it clearly.
4. Fill the body of your paper with an analysis of the piece. You planned your response to Lee's essay when you sorted out and elaborated on your marginal notes—and then put your plan down on paper in the form of a simple outline. Those sketchy points will become, of course, the topic sentences of your critique. You may want to divide the body into three sections: strengths, weaknesses, and overall assessment. Or into your reasons for why the piece is weak or strong or wrong-headed.
5. Come back, in some way or another, to your thesis. Writing conclusions are as easy as getting up and leaving friends you've been visiting. You can't, of course, get up and leave without an announcement of some kind. But you also don't want to draw out your leave-taking. Hosts don't enjoy standing at the door listening to forced small talk. If you have trouble getting out the door of your essay, we have a few suggestions.

- If you don't have anything that's worthy of your reader's time, merely rephrase your main idea. Like a sleepy host, your reader will be grateful for your brevity.
- Come back to your main idea with a fresh illustration or a quotation.
- Don't restate each point you've made.
- Make a separate paragraph out of your conclusion, even if it's a single sentence.

Another way of organizing a critique is to jump right in. In this method you don't begin by telling your reader what the essay is about. Instead, you begin by focusing on *your* thesis. Your first paragraph might look as simple as this:

> The essay "Has Anyone Seen My Old Friend Jimi?" is ruined by juvenile humor and coarse diction.

Of course, you might want to lead up to that statement. But if you don't have anything truly informative (or worth your reader's time), merely write a thesis for an introduction and get on with the body of your paper.

Before you critique an essay on your own, we need to illustrate what an actual full-blown critique looks like. We're now going to finish the job we started back on pages 61–65, where we actively read and wrote comments in the margin of the passage from *The Waste Makers*. We'll take you through this critique step by step. You might want to glance back at the Packard essay before you read this critique.

A CRITIQUE OF *THE WASTE MAKERS*

1. Introduce the author and the piece.

   > In *The Waste Makers*, Vance Packard, the author of numerous popular books on American consumer culture, attacks consumer "hedonism."

2. Clarify background and assumptions. Be objective here. You'll have plenty of time to jump on the author's ideas, if you so desire. For the time being, give a fair shake to the piece under question. This may take you a few paragraphs. You might even want to quote a few words to convey the tone of the piece in question.

   > Packard argues that Americans have come to view their purchases as ends in themselves. He decries the born-to-shop mentality that has come, he claims, to characterize American society since World War II. He is appalled by a housewife, with a "pert" nose, who buys a cherry pie at the supermarket rather than making it from scratch in her kitchen.

3. Write your thesis.

> Packard's essay is based on three somewhat dubious assumptions.

4. Develop your thesis in the body of your paper.

> The first of those assumptions is that Americans were once "frugal" and "God-fearing people making sacrifices for the long haul." And that the reason they didn't "waste" their money is that they had character—and that we, corrupt moderns that we are, don't.
>
> In fact, through the ages, people who have had money left over, after their basic needs have been taken care of, have always purchased those pleasing little things—red ribbons and other little geegaws—that they haven't absolutely needed. Our Puritan forefathers and foremothers would no doubt have spent more of their discretionary income on ribbons and geegaws if they had had more discretionary income. It's difficult to buy a new Sunday hat when you don't have the cash. Indeed, it's difficult to think of any affluent people in the past who haven't spent their discretionary income on baubles.
>
> Packard also assumes that in recent decades especially, cynical advertisers have broken down our "puritanical inhibitions"—and thus set free our hedonism to feast on the cornucopia of unnecessary products that American manufacturing produces. It is true, as Packard says, that advertisers try to persuade us to untie our purse strings. Anyone who has felt the pangs of new-car lust knows that advertising can be seductive.
>
> Advertising is seductive but we are not its helpless victims, as Packard would have it. Packard gives too much credit to the power of advertisers and too little credit to consumers. People are not unwilling pawns in the grip of advertisers. I like to think, even if Packard doesn't, that people have free will. We aren't pursuing the good life because advertisers have created a demand that wasn't there. We're pursuing the good life because, unlike our Puritan ancestors, we have the money to pursue it. It's as simple as that.
>
> What, after all, would Packard have us do with our discretionary income? Stow it away in savings banks for the long haul? The fact is, most of us do plan for our retirement. Beyond that, we are only passing it on to our children and burdening them with the temptations of consumer hedonism.
>
> Finally, Packard assumes, throughout his essay, that consumerism is somehow bad for the soul. Packard obviously agrees with the "elderly supermarket operator," who is ap-

palled that his women customers buy convenience foods. Like
the supermarket operator, Packard seems to assume that endless domestic drudgery is good for a woman's soul.

But there is nothing in the process of making a cherry pie
from scratch that is conducive to virtue. In fact, one might argue that the woman who buys a cherry pie at the supermarket
has more time to spend with her children, more time to read a
book, more time to pursue a vocation. After all, over 50 percent
of women are in the work force. Packard makes the rise of the
feminist movement a little easier to understand.

5. State your conclusions or come back to your thesis in some way.

Like Emerson, Thoreau, and other American Romantics,
Packard would have us return to life in a log cabin, reading the
Bible by the flickering light of a whale-oil lamp. Packard seems
to believe that our ancestors *chose* such a simple life. Actually,
most were constrained by economic necessity. But most of us
no longer live under that constraint.

In his hearty approval of the simple life, Packard is a
modern-day Puritan who has that old fundamentalist suspicion
that there's something wrong about personal pleasure.

That's all there is to it.

Now go back and write a critique of "Has Anyone Seen My Old Friend Jimi?"
Since you have already written notes in the margin, you are halfway home.
All that remains is to sort out your responses, write a simple outline, and
begin.

EXERCISE 5-1: *Critiquing an Essay*

There are a variety of essays in this book to critique, but the two essays printed
below are particularly amenable to analysis because they are feisty and opinionated.

Cruel Lib

Let's call him Fred. I met Fred during his junior year in college. All Fred wanted was love
and a rewarding sexual relationship—is that not an inalienable right by now? Fred was pur-
poselessly big, overweight. His arm flesh hung down, white as brandy Alexander, full of
stretch marks. His face, in contrast, was bluish: acne scars that might have been haphazard
tattooing. A nice guy, intelligent enough, but the coeds were put off. Fred wooed them at
mixers with his face half-averted, as if it were an illicit act.

Fred was without sexual prejudice: as they say, he could go both ways. There was a
militant gay-lib branch on campus. For months, struck out at mixers, he had considered
joining. It was a painful decision: if he came out of the closet, Fred knew, his mother and

father would probably go in—hidden there for shame. Yet mimeo sheets from gay lib offered a tacit, thrilling promise: new life, freedom. I remember the day Fred told me he had come out: he was relieved, optimistic. But being gay and free didn't cosmetize his face. When Fred let it all hang out, it just dangled there. After a while he noticed the good-looking gays dated the good-looking gays, as a first-string quarterback goes out with a homecoming queen. Fred had caused his family anguish for small compensation: he was now a wallflower in both sexes. Liberation. The tacit promise had been empty, and it had cracked his fragile spirit. Three months later Fred committed suicide.

Let's call her Gwen. The usual: $40,000 bilevel house, three kids, married to a good provider. Her unwed sister-in-law, however, ran the local women's-lib cell. Gwen's sister-in-law made fun of drudgery: dishes; that unending double-play combo, hamper to washer to dryer; the vacuum she used and the one she lived in. It seemed so *uncreative*. Creativity, you know, is another inalienable American right. Gwen was 34 and, good grief, only a housewife. There were wonderful, though unspecified, resources inside her. After some time marriage, in Gwen's mind, became a kind of moth closet.

Ms. Gwen is divorced now. Mr. Gwen still loves her; he has taken the children. Gwen enrolled in a community college, but she didn't do well. Term papers were drudgery. For some time she made lopsided ashtrays at a Wednesday-night ceramics class. She was free and bored to death with herself. Now Gwen drinks a lot; she has some talent in that direction. Her children, well . . . all three understand, of course, that they were exploiting Gwen for twelve and nine and seven years respectively.

It's an unattractive human truth, but every now and then someone should put it on record: most people—Christians used to acknowledge this fact without embarrassment—most people are not particularly talented or beautiful or charismatic. Set free to discover "the true self," very often they find nothing there at all. Men and women who determine "to do their own thing" commonly learn that they have little of note to do. Yet these people are harassed, shamed by the Zeitgeist and its glib armies into disparaging their conventional roles. The bubblegum tune goes like this: American civilization, through some spiteful, stupid conspiracy, means to thwart self-expression. We are all frustrated painters, explorers, starlets, senators. But there are times when it's more healthful to be frustrated than to have one's mediocrity confirmed in the light of common day.

Roles don't limit people; roles protect them. And, yes, most people need protection: deserve it. Not so long ago our society honored the wife, the mother and the father. These were titles that carried merit enough to justify a full human life. Remember the phrase, "It's like attacking motherhood." Times have changed. On the lecture circuit today, you can pull down a nice income plus expenses attacking motherhood.

Yet probably the cruelest of all libs is education lib. Ed lib hasn't been formally incorporated, but it's very well sustained by an immense bureaucracy of teachers, professors, administrators, foundations, Federal agencies. Strike a match and you learn inside the pad how John earned respect from his bowling team as a correspondence-school computer executive. And on the crosstown bus they tell you, *Don't prepare for tomorrow with yesterday's skills* (picture of a wheelbarrow). Or, *A mind is a terrible thing to waste.* Sure. But what about a pair of hands, damn it? Even at fifteen bucks per hour, we humiliate our labor force in a programmatic way. The elitism of it all is pernicious and disgusting.

Some few centuries ago another kind of lib prevailed. Christianity, they called it. Christian lib isn't a "now" item; it comes due in another life. Prerequisites are faith, works, humility: children are raised, things are made, to God's glory. Christians know personal gratification for what it is: a brummagem trinket. And this has been the shrewd beauty of Communism. Lenin cribbed his tactics from the New Testament. Liberation is promised through an arduous class struggle—but not in anyone's lifetime. This lib movement, moreover, functions within a powerfully structured, oppressive social system. Not only do totalitarian governments curtail personal liberty, but they are downright prissy when it comes to permissive sex. Yet people, in general, accept. Their roles are clear, and those roles are esteemed.

In this country . . . lib has become a growth industry. Many who are otherwise talentless have made it their profession. But what Ralph Nader will hold them accountable for the Freds and the Gwens, for those who have been dispirited by a society that no longer prizes sexual restraint or menial labor or the nuclear family? We have, I hold it self-evident, an inalienable right to be unliberated. This nation—another unattractive truth—doesn't need more personal freedom. The human spirit can be an unruly beast; a little restraint is wholesome. Let people be cherished for what they are, not for ambiguous thwarted gifts, or for the social responsibilities they default on. The men and women of Middle America have earned that small consideration. Really ''creative'' people will surface anyway. They usually do. And they will have their great rewards.

D. Keith Mano

Confessions of a Female Chauvinist Sow

I once married a man I thought was totally unlike my father and I imagined a whole new world of freedom emerging. Five years later it was clear even to me—floating face down in a wash of despair—that I had simply chosen a replica of my handsome daddy. True, the updated version spoke English like an angel but—good God!—underneath he was my father exactly: wonderful, but not the right man for me.

Most people I know have at one time or another been fouled up by their childhood experiences. Patterns tend to sink into the unconscious only to reappear, disguised, unseen, like marionette strings, pulling us this way or that. Whatever ails people—keeps them up at night, tossing and turning—also ails movements no matter how historically huge or politically important. The women's movement cannot remake consciousness, or reshape the future, without acknowledging and shedding all the unnecessary and ugly baggage of the past. It's easy enough now to see where men have kept us out of clubs, baseball games, graduate schools; it's easy enough to recognize the hidden directions that limit Sis to cake-baking and Junior to bridge-building; it's now possible for even Miss America herself to identify what *they* have done to us, and, of course, *they* have and *they* did and *they* are. . . . But along the way we also developed our own hidden prejudices, class assumptions and an anti-male humor and collection of expectations that gave us, like all oppressed groups, a secret sense of superiority (co-existing with a poor self-image—it's not news that people can believe two contradictory things at once).

Listen to any group that suffers materially and socially. They have a lexicon with which they tease the enemy: ofay, goy, honky, gringo. ''Poor pale devils,'' said Malcolm X loud enough for us to hear, although blacks had joked about that to each other for years. Behind some of the women's liberation thinking lurk the rumors, the prejudices, the defense systems of generations of oppressed women whispering in the kitchen together, presenting one face to their menfolk and another to their card clubs, their mothers and sisters. All this is natural enough but potentially dangerous in a revolutionary situation in which you hope to create a future that does not mirror the past. The hidden anti-male feelings, a result of the old system, will foul us up if they are allowed to persist.

During my teen years I never left the house on my Saturday night dates without my mother slipping me a few extra dollars—mad money, it was called. I'll explain what it was for the benefit of the new generation in which people just sleep with each other: the fellow was supposed to bring me home, lead me safely through the asphalt jungle, protect me from slithering snakes, rapists and the like. But my mother and I knew young men were apt to drink too much, to slosh down so many rye-and-gingers that some hero might well lead me in front of an oncoming bus, smash his daddy's car into Tiffany's window or, less gallantly, throw up on my new dress. Mad money was for getting home on your own, no matter what form of insanity your date happened to evidence. Mad money was also a wallflower's rope ladder; if the guy you came with suddenly fancied someone else, well, you didn't have to stay there and suffer, you could go home. Boys were fickle and likely to be unkind; my mother and I knew that, as surely as we knew they tried to make you do things in the dark they wouldn't respect you for afterwards and in fact would spread the word and spoil your rep. Boys liked to be flattered; if you made them feel important they would eat out of your hand. So talk to them about their interests, don't alarm them with displays of intelligence—we all knew that, we groups of girls talking into the wee hours of the night in a kind of easy companionship we thought impossible with boys. Boys were prone to have a good time, get you pregnant, and then pretend they didn't know your name when you came knocking on their door for finances or comfort. In short, we believed boys were less moral than we were. They appeared to be hypocritical, self-seeking, exploitative, untrustworthy and very likely to be showing off their precious masculinity. I never had a girl friend I thought would be unkind or embarrass me in public. I never expected a girl to lie to me about her marks or sports skill or how good she was in bed. Altogether—without anyone's directly coming out and saying so—I gathered that men were sexy, powerful, very interesting, but not very nice, not very moral, humane and tender, like us. Girls played fairly while men, unfortunately, reserved their honor for the battlefield.

Why are there laws insisting on alimony and child support? Well, everyone knows that men don't have an instinct to protect their young and, given half a chance, with the moon in the right phase, they will run off and disappear. Everyone assumes a mother will not let her child starve, yet it is necessary to legislate that a father must not do so. We are taught to accept the idea that men are less than decent; their charms may be manifold but their characters are riddled with faults. To this day I never blink if I hear that a man has gone to find his fortune in South America, having left his pregnant wife, his blind mother and taken the family car. I still gasp in horror when I hear of a woman leaving her asthmatic infant for a rock group in Taos because I can't seem to avoid the assumption that men are naturally heels and women the ordained carriers of what little is moral in our dubious civilization.

My mother never gave me mad money thinking I would ditch a fellow for some other guy or that I would pass out drunk on the floor. She knew I would be considerate of my companion because, after all, I was more mature than the boys that gathered about. Why was I more mature? Women are just people-oriented; they learn to be empathetic at an early age. Most English students (students interested in humanity, not artifacts) are women. Men and boys—so the myth goes—conceal their feelings and lose interest in anybody else's. Everyone knows that even little boys can tell the difference between one kind of a car and another—proof that their souls are mechanical, their attention directed to the non-human.

I remember shivering in the cold vestibule of a famous men's athletic club. Women and girls are not permitted inside the club's door. What are they doing in there, I asked? They're naked, said my mother, they're sweating, jumping up and down a lot, telling each other dirty jokes and bragging about their stock market exploits. Why can't we go in? I asked. Well, my mother told me, they're afraid we'd laugh at them.

The prejudices of childhood are hard to outgrow. I confess that every time my business takes me past the club, I shudder. Images of large bellies resting on massage tables and flaccid penises rising and falling with the Dow Jones average flash through my head. There it is, chauvinism waving its cancerous tentacles from the depths of my psyche.

Minorities automatically feel superior to the oppressor because after all, they are not hurting anybody. In fact, they feel they are morally better. The old canard that women need love, men need sex—believed for too long by both sexes—attributes moral and spiritual superiority to women and makes of men beasts whose urges send them prowling into the night. This false division of good and bad, placing deforming pressures on everyone, doesn't have to contaminate the future. We know that the assumptions we make about each other become a part of the cultural air we breathe and, in fact, become social truths. Women who want equality must be prepared to give it and to believe in it, and in order to do that it is not enough to state that you are as good as any man, but also it must be stated that he is as good as you and both will be humans together. If we want men to share in the care of the family in a new way, we must assume them as capable of consistent loving tenderness as we.

I rummage about and find in my thinking all kinds of anti-male prejudices. Some are just jokes and others I will have a hard time abandoning. First, I share an emotional conviction with many sisters that women given power would not create wars. Intellectually I know that's ridiculous; great queens have waged war before; the likes of Lurleen Wallace, Pat Nixon and Mrs. General Levelle can be depended upon in the future to guiltlessly condemn to death other people's children in the name of some ideal of their own. Little girls, of course, don't take toy guns out of their hip pockets and say ''Pow, pow'' to all their neighbors and friends like the average well-adjusted little boy. However, if we gave little girls the six-shooters, we would soon have to double the pretend body count.

Aggression is not, as I secretly think, a male-sex-linked characteristic: brutality is masculine only by virtue of opportunity. True, there are 1,000 Jack the Rippers for every Lizzie Borden, but that surely is the result of social forms. Women as a group are indeed more masochistic than men. The practical result of this division is that women seem nicer and kinder, but when the world changes, women will have a fuller opportunity to be just as rotten as men and there will be fewer claims of female moral superiority.

Now that I am entering early middle age, I hear many women complaining of husbands and ex-husbands who are attracted to younger females. This strikes the older woman as unfair, of course. But I remember a time when I thought all boys around my age and grade were creeps and bores. I wanted to go out with an older man: a senior or, miraculously, a college man. I had a certain contempt for my coevals, not realizing that the freshman in college I thought so desirable, was some older girl's creep. Some women never lose that contempt for men of their own age. That isn't fair either and may be one reason why some sensible men of middle years find solace in younger women.

I remember coming home from school one day to find my mother's card game dissolved in hysterical laughter. The cards were floating in black rivers of running mascara. What was so funny? A woman named Helen was lying on a couch pretending to be her husband with a cold. She was issuing demands for orange juice, aspirin, suggesting a call to a specialist, complaining of neglect, of fate's cruel finger, of heat, of cold, of sharp pains on the bridge of the nose that might indicate brain involvement. What was so funny? The ladies explained to me that all men behave just like that with colds, they are reduced to temper tantrums by simple nasal congestion, men cannot stand any little physical discomfort—on and on the laughter went.

The point of this vignette is the nature of the laughter—us laughing at them, us feeling superior to them, us ridiculing them behind their backs. If they were doing it to us we'd call it male chauvinist pigness; if we do it to them, it is inescapably female chauvinist sowness and, whatever its roots, it leads to the same isolation. Boys are messy, boys are mean, boys are rough, boys are stupid and have sloppy handwriting. A cacophony of childhood memories rushes through my head, balanced, of course, by all the well-documented feelings of inferiority and envy. But the important thing, the hard thing, is to wipe the slate clean, to start again without the meanness of the past. That's why it's so important that the women's movement not become anti-male and allow its most prejudiced spokesmen total leadership. The much-chewed-over abortion issue illustrates this. The women's-liberation position, insisting on a woman's right to determine her own body's destiny, leads in fanatical extreme to a kind of emotional immaculate conception in which the father is not judged even half-responsible—has no rights, and no consideration is to be given to his concern for either the woman or the fetus.

Woman, who once was abandoned and disgraced by an unwanted pregnancy, has recently arrived at a new pride of ownership or disposal. She has traveled in a straight line that still excludes her sexual partner from an equal share in the wanted or unwanted pregnancy. A better style of life may develop from an assumption that men are as human as we. Why not ask the child's father if he would like to bring up the child? Why not share decisions, when possible, with the male? If we cut them out, assuming an old-style indifference on their part, we perpetuate the ugly divisiveness that has characterized relations between the sexes so far.

Hard as it is for many of us to believe, women are not really superior to men in intelligence or humanity—they are only equal.

Anne Roiphe

6

Writing the Source Paper

The fact that you've come this far means, we hope, that you already know most of what there is to know about how to write a source paper. You've been summarizing, quoting, paraphrasing, synthesizing, and analyzing. You've even been informally documenting your sources. This chapter deals with the little of what's left—mainly, how to gather material in the library and put it in an acceptable form. But before we can begin, we have to know something about where you're starting from. Choose your scenario.

Scenario 1: You're choosing a source paper topic from one of the exercises at the end of Chapters 7 to 12, and you're not going beyond the essays in that chapter. In that case, begin with the next section, "Papers Based on Essays in This Book."

Scenario 2: You're writing a library source paper from scratch, using none of the topics in this book. In that case begin with "Papers Based on Library Research," page 79.

Scenario 3: You're choosing a source paper topic from one of the exercises at the end of Chapters 7 to 12, but you're going to supplement the essays in that chapter with essays you find in the library. In that case, you should read the next section and then go right to "The Initial Library Search," page 81.

PAPERS BASED ON ESSAYS IN THIS BOOK

There are eight or so essays on a limited topic in each of the last six chapters of this book. Indeed, the topics are so limited that you could write a small research paper without going beyond one of those chapters. If your instructor chooses that option for you, here is how to go about writing your paper.

Begin by reading the chapter introduction. If you want to deepen your understanding of the issues involved, read an essay or two from the chapter.

If the chapter contains essays on a controversial issue, you might browse through one essay on either side of the issue. The reading skills you learned in Chapter 2 should serve you well here.

Now choose one of the topics listed at the end of the chapter.

Prepare a preliminary outline. Even at this early stage, you should be able to break down your topic, or thesis, into three or four logical parts. For instance, if you had chosen to write a report on futile medical procedures from early medicine, you might divide your topic into these categories:

1. Bleeding
2. Purging
3. Exorcism

With this initial outline in hand, you will know what you are looking for when you read. Of course, you aren't locked into this preliminary outline. It merely serves as a starting point.

Go on to the next step: either "Taking Notes" on page 90 (scenario 1) or "Collecting Information in the Library" on page 85 (scenario 3).

PAPERS BASED ON LIBRARY RESEARCH

Finding Something to Write About

Remember, the thesis of a source paper, like the thesis of any other paper, is not just a topic, or subject. It's an idea or attitude *about* a topic. "Birds of the Amazon" is a topic; "The Plight of the Birds of the Amazon" is a topic *and* an idea about a topic—in other words, a thesis. So what you need to do now is move toward the kind of thesis on which you can write a paper. This section will help you.

Free Association

Let's say you're given the broad topic of "Flight" (or perhaps you're given complete freedom to choose your own broad topic). Begin by brainstorming, or free associating. On a sheet of paper, begin to copy down words related to flight that come immediately to mind. Here's a little list that we came up with:

Lindbergh
World War I
Wright brothers
Science fiction
Rockets
Icarus
Wind tunnels
Spads
Red Baron

World War II
Mars flight
Moon
Armstrong
One small step
SST
Spitfires

Each one of the items you've come up with is narrower than the broad topic you began with, so you're already closer to a thesis than you were. But you have to go further. You still need an idea or attitude *about* your narrower topic. So now take one of the most promising of your free-association words, perhaps the one that you're most curious about, and ask questions of it. Let's try the topic of Icarus, the Greek myth about the boy who plunged to his death when the wax that held his wings together melted from the sun's heat. Here are some questions you might ask.

- Was his flight based on a real event?
- I seem to remember a painting, a poem? What was that?
- Any real-life attempts to build a human-powered, wing-driven machine to fly in? What happened to them?
- What other theories of flight existed in ancient days? Before the twentieth century?

Now from this list of questions, choose one that seems the most promising. How about the last one? What other theories of flight existed before the twentieth century? If you refined your thesis just a bit further, it might turn out something like this: Before the flight of the Gossamer Condor, there were several other theories of how human-powered flight could be accomplished. Now you have an idea *about* flight. You don't know yet if you've come up with an acceptable thesis. You'll only know that after you've done a little preliminary work in the library, but at least you have something to begin with.

Narrowing the Topic
This method is a more formal version of free association. In this one you *think* your way through the narrowing process. Once again, begin with the broad topic, "Flight." Now begin to narrow the topic, like this.

Flight
Human-powered flight
Mythical human-powered flight
The Icarus myth
The Icarus myth in literature and art

That's not bad. How about a paper on the Icarus myth in literature and art? Of course, you might even be able to refine it further as you research it. You may find, for instance, that your thesis is still too broad. Or perhaps too narrow. Or you may even find that it's not workable because it's already been treated exhaustively in a single article or book. Or it may not be workable because there is not enough material in your library on the topic. (That last possibility is the *least* likely. You're far more likely to find too much on a topic than not enough.)

Reader's Guide to Periodical Literature

One of the easiest ways of moving toward a thesis is by browsing through a few pages of the *Reader's Guide to Periodical Literature*, which is located in the reference room of the library. (If you want to know more about this multivolume reference work right now, go to page 87.)

What you do is this: Look up your broad topic "Flight," and see what kinds of articles are there. The kinds of articles you find under "Flight" might pique your interest *and* suggest how you might restrict your topic. Figure 1 shows an actual page from the 1984–1985 issue of the *Reader's Guide*. Let's just browse around in it to see what's there.

Ah! Under the topic "Flight" you are given the direction *See also*, followed by a list of additional topics, one of which is "Manpowered aircraft—Flights." If you turn to the M pages in the *Reader's Guide*, you'll find articles on that topic. But let's go ahead and browse further on the page we're on. Ah! again. You discover two more intriguing topics under the topic "Flight": "Insects—Flight" and "Gliding and soaring" sound promising, don't they? How about "Flight simulators" and "Flightless birds"? Perhaps you can narrow one of these topics by looking it up and reading through the titles of articles that were written about it.

You see how this works, don't you? Browse until a topic piques your interest, and then look at the kinds of articles that are written about the topic.

The Initial Library Search

Don't go any further unless you have something that *resembles* a thesis. Without at least a fairly narrow topic you'll wander the library stacks forever, aimlessly picking up and casting aside useless books and magazines. A precisely defined topic will direct your steps around the library and bring you out before you turn dusty.

Even better: If you can prepare a preliminary outline at this point, go ahead and do so. That outline—which will consist merely of the main points in the body of your paper—will save you even more time in the library.

The Working Outline

Even at this early stage, common sense *might* enable you to prepare a simple outline of your paper. It doesn't have to be anything fancy. But you may be able to think of two or three of the main points that support your thesis. For instance, if you had this thesis, "What the atomic bomb looked like from the ground," you might be able to break it down into these logical parts:

Figure 1. *Reader's Guide, 1984–1985, p. 709.*

1. Descriptions of the initial blast
2. Descriptions of property damage
3. Descriptions of human injury

Think hard about your narrowed topic; you might be able to break it down into logical parts even before you begin. Of course, as you find out more about your topic, you'll be able to refine your working outline even further, but for now an outline, no matter how sketchy, is an awfully handy thing to have in your pocket as you enter the library for the first time.

Your First Session in the Library
Your first session will serve at least four purposes. It will

* Tell you more about your subject than you know now. That knowledge will enable you to refine your thesis, modify your thesis, or change your thesis entirely before you get too deep into it.
* Allow you to either prepare a working outline or refine your outline further.
* Reassure you that there is plenty of information available on your topic.
* Allow you to prepare a preliminary bibliography.

Before you jump cold into your library's card catalog, there is a place you can go to find out what kinds of headings the card catalog uses to sort its books. That place is *The Library of Congress List of Subject Headings*, which is usually located on a table near the card catalog itself. A quick browse through these two volumes can serve as a substitute for thumbing through hundreds of cards in various drawers of the card catalog itself.

When you search through the subject headings, start with fairly specific topics. That is, don't look under "Flight" right now. You'll probably find too much. Instead, look under "Greek myth," "Airplanes," "Icarus," "Human-powered flight," and any other narrower headings that you can think of. The list of subject headings will tell you which of these headings the card catalog uses. So if you don't find a heading under "Icarus," that means there's no sense in looking for that heading in the card catalog; it's not there.

After you have armed yourself with appropriate subject headings, you are now ready to tackle the card catalog itself. (For more specific information on what kind of information is listed on the actual cards, see page 85.) Jot down the call numbers of potentially useful books, and locate them in the stacks. Check out the promising ones.

Now you will want to see what is available in your library's magazine collection. Like the card catalog, your primary periodical index is the *Reader's Guide to Periodical Literature*. Monthly and quarterly issues of the *Reader's Guide* are collected in annual volumes. Begin with either the most recent volume or—if your topic deals with a specific event—the most appropriate volume. You will need to browse in your volume just as you did in *The Library of Congress List of Subject Headings* in order to find the subject heading the editors have used for your particular topic. Once you have determined your subject heading (or headings), write down the most promising entries under it. You will then probably want to go back 6 or 7 years in the annual volumes in order to determine what has appeared on your topic in the recent past. For more specific instructions on the *Reader's Guide*, including a sample page, see pages 82, 87.

Finally, with your list of magazine articles in hand, you will want to consult the front pages of one of the *Reader's Guide* volumes if you have any questions about the magazine title abbreviations, and you will want to consult the nearby circular file, an alphabetized list of the magazines that *your* library possesses. (The list is usually kept on a cylindrical metal file consisting of rotating panels.) Once you've determined which of the magazines your library has, you are ready to look up your articles, either in the library's periodical stacks or in its microfilm room.

At this point, after an hour or so of searching, you will probably have several books and magazine articles. So now sit down and browse through these sources piled around you to see how useful they are really going to be.

As you examine each book look for your topic in the table of contents and the index, and then skim over any relevant pages or chapters they direct you to. You might also want to scan any introductory or concluding chapters.

As you evaluate each of your magazine articles, read the introductory paragraphs and all bold-faced headings. Glance also at the lead sentences of the rest of the paragraphs, and take a close look at any illustrations—pictures, tables, and graphs.

The Preliminary Bibliography

Now that you have taken an initial survey of the magazine articles and books on your topic, it is time to make a list of the sources you intend to study further. Such a list will help you to locate your sources later on—should you need to—and it will provide the publication data that you will need to document the material from your notes.

You should make this collection of sources not on slips of paper but on 3 × 5 cards, listing one source per card. A simple book entry on a 3 × 5 card is shown in Figure 2. (For the formats for other kinds of entries, see pages 95–97.) This method will enable you to manipulate your list of sources at any time during your research. With cards, you can easily add or delete sources and alphabetize the entire list for your bibliography, which will be prepared according to a format recommended by the Modern Language Association. So, since you're going to have to get it all down correctly sooner or later, you might as well do it now. Then you'll be able to create your final bibliography in just a few minutes, and that may prove to be a godsend if you find yourself finishing your paper in the wee hours of the morning before it's due.

With a working outline and a preliminary bibliography in hand, you are now ready to read and take notes on your sources. The next section is basically a description of the more useful indexes you can use as you do your research. If you're interested right now only in the *process* of writing a source paper, skip the next section and go to "Taking Notes."

Call
number

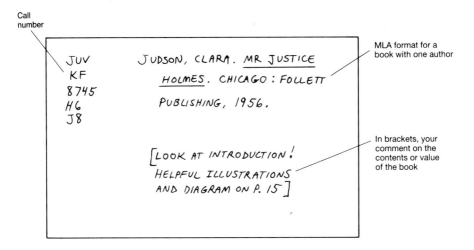

MLA format for a
book with one author

JUV
KF
8745
H6
J8

JUDSON, CLARA. MR JUSTICE

HOLMES. CHICAGO : FOLLETT

PUBLISHING, 1956.

[LOOK AT INTRODUCTION!
HELPFUL ILLUSTRATIONS
AND DIAGRAM ON P. 15]

In brackets, your
comment on the
contents or value
of the book

Figure 2. Bibliography card.

Collecting Information in the Library

There is a wealth of reference material in your library, including atlases, yearbooks, companions to literature, dictionaries of quotations, and so forth. Most reference rooms in college libraries have a card catalog that will tell you where these books are located. If your reference room doesn't have such a catalog, the main catalog will list reference works as well as books for the general reader.

The Card Catalog

You have probably been using the card catalog since your elementary school librarian introduced you to it in the third grade. So rather than spending time describing what you have known for years about the catalog, we'll just print a card here and then point out a few less familiar facts about the cards. Don't worry about the cryptic numbers at the bottom of the card. Most of that information is for librarians.

- You will find that the card catalog subject headings are surprisingly specific. If you want to know more about the Reims Cathedral in France, for example, look under that heading. Try a more general heading only if you cannot find your specific one.
- As you copy down information from a subject card for a potentially useful book, be sure to look at what the librarians call the "tracings" at the bottom of the card. The words you see there are cross-references. Subject cards for this book are also filed under these topics. If this book proves to be useful, other similarly useful volumes might be found under the headings which the tracings provide.
- Remember that all books *by* an author (the author cards) will appear before the books *about* an author. If you are looking for a critical biography of Charles Dickens, for example, flick quickly through the

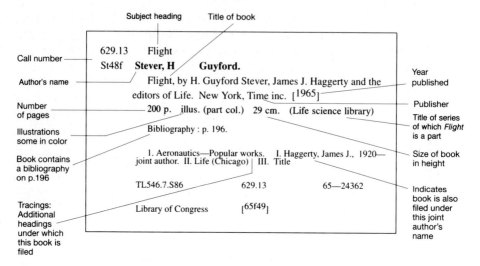

Figure 3. A card from the card catalog.

numerous cards containing the titles of his novels and essays and stop only when you see a subject heading appear at the top of the cards. It is only at this point the books written *about* Dickens begin.

- The familiar abbreviations "Dr." and "St." are alphabetized as if they were spelled out—as "doctor" and "saint."
- The Scottish prefix "Mc" is always alphabetized under "Mac." This is true of McGowan, McGregor, McCall, McDougal, or any other Mc name you can think of.
- Remember that in alphabetizing, just as "a" comes before "b," so also nothing comes before something. Alphabetizing is done word by word. For example, "New Zealand" will come before "Newark."
- If your topic is historical—for example, the Battle of Hastings—once you have looked up "Great Britain, History of," you will find that the cards are arranged chronologically, not alphabetically.
- You will discover that the card catalog doesn't end with the "Z" drawer. In a few drawers that follow, your library maintains a Shelf List, which catalogs all of its holdings according to their call numbers. This list provides you with an additional means of getting your hands on books which might be relevant to your topic. If you were a nursing major writing a paper on the endocrine system, for example, you could simply look up the Library of Congress classification heading for human anatomy (on a chart on your library's wall)—"QM"—and then look in the Shelf List drawers under "QM." There you would find all your library's human anatomy holdings—and most of these books will likely have something to say about the endocrine system.
- If, alas, the card catalog doesn't yield much on your topic and if your deadline isn't pressing, you can go to the *National Union Catalog* in your library's reference room. This huge, multivolumed work is the

card catalog of the Library of Congress in book form. If a book has been copyrighted and published in the United States, you are going to find it here. If looking under the same subject headings you used in the card catalog, you find potentially useful books in the *National Union Catalog*, you merely need to copy down the publication data. Armed with this information and with your instructor's help, you can borrow these books from other libraries in the country through your own library's interlibrary loan office. This service will usually make the books you need available to you (for a nominal fee) within 10 days. Hence, technically you can have access to the immense holdings of the Library of Congress without leaving your own library. You can also obtain xeroxed copies of articles from magazines that your library doesn't have by going through your library's interlibrary loan office.

Reader's Guide to Periodical Literature

The *Reader's Guide* is an index of over 200 general-interest magazines. It includes magazines like *Psychology Today*, which is designed for people who have an interest in psychology—but not a *specialist's* interest. If you were a practicing psychologist (or even a psychology major) writing an essay on your research specialty for your colleagues, you would need to go to more scholarly psychology periodicals. You won't find those listed in the *Reader's Guide*. (We have provided a list of specialized indexes in the very next section.) But if you were writing a paper for the so-called common reader, the *Reader's Guide* will usually be your first stop for periodical articles.

The monthly and quarterly issues of the *Reader's Guide* are collected in annual volumes. You will initially need to spend some time finding the subject heading which the editors have used for your topic. But once you have found the appropriate heading, your only remaining concern might be making sense of some of the abbreviated magazine titles. The abbreviation key is in the front of the volume.

Computer Index to Periodicals

Libraries around the country are supplementing conventional periodical indexes—as well as card catalogues—with computer systems. One of the best is a user-friendly system called InfoTrac. If your library has this system, you can use it to search for articles for a research paper. Believe us, it's a fast, slick way of doing research. Its only serious drawback is that its citations only go back 4 years. You'll have to use the *Reader's Guide* for articles printed before that time.

InfoTrac consists of a computer that accesses information compiled on laser disks and a small printer. The disks themselves contain citations from over 1100 periodicals. By contrast, the *Reader's Guide* indexes about 200. Other details about the system:

- InfoTrac was designed to be a general-information index. That is, it indexes just the kind of articles that you are apt to use in a research paper. Indeed, the database on the laser disks is called the General Periodicals Index.

- Many of the citations in *InfoTrac* are briefly described. None of those in the *Reader's Guide* are.
- InfoTrac is updated monthly. The *Reader's Guide* is updated quarterly.
- InfoTrac includes articles and news stories for the last 80 days of *The New York Times* and *The Wall Street Journal*, two newspapers that are troublesome to access otherwise.
- When you come across a citation that looks promising, all you do is hit the Print button and the printer attached to the main system prints out your citation.

InfoTrac, or a system like it, might ease your task of finding information. Check it out.

Specialized Indexes

Remember, the *Reader's Guide* covers only general-interest articles. There are other more specialized indexes that you might find helpful. Here are the more useful ones.

Applied Science and Technology Index, 1958–. (Before 1958 this was called the *Industrial Arts Index*, 1913–1957.)
Art Index, 1929–.
Biography Index, 1946–.
Biological and Agricultural Index, 1964–.
Book Review Index, 1905–.
Business Periodicals Index, 1958–.
Education Index, 1929–.
Engineering Index, 1884–.
Historical Abstracts, 1955–.
Humanities Index, 1974–. (Before 1974 this was called the *Social Sciences and Humanities Index*, 1965–1973, and, before that, the *International Index*, 1907–1965.)
Index to Legal Periodicals, 1908–.
Music Index, 1949–.
Social Sciences Index, 1974–.
United States Government Publications, 1895–.

Your college library probably has, on microfilm, a copy of every page *The New York Times* has ever printed, dating all the way back to 1913. And since it carries news articles, editorials, and feature articles, it can be an invaluable aid in your research. Many college libraries also have indexes to *The Wall Street Journal*, *The Christian Science Monitor*, and *The Washington Post*.

Special Dictionaries

The Oxford English Dictionary, also called *A New English Dictionary on Historical Principles*, is thirteen volumes. If you look up a word in this dictionary, it will not only tell you the spelling and meaning of a word, it will also tell you, through quotations, what that word has meant through the centuries, all the way back to the word's first appearance in print. Other specialized dictionaries include:

A Dictionary of Modern English Usage, by H. W. Fowler
Dictionary of Foreign Terms, by C. O. S. Mawson
A Dictionary of Slang and Unconventional English, by Eric Partridge
The Random House Dictionary of the English Language, 1967
Roget's Collegiate Thesaurus
Webster's Third New International Dictionary, 1981

Encyclopedias

You might be surprised to know the variety of encyclopedias that are available in a library. Did you know, for instance, that there is an *Encyclopedia of Pop, Rock and Soul*? Or that there is an *Encyclopedia of Mystery and Detection* and an *Official World Encyclopedia of Sports and Games*? We can't list them all, but for our purposes here are a few of the more promising encyclopedias:

General Encyclopedias

Chamber's Encyclopaedia
Collier's Encyclopedia
Encyclopedia Americana
Encyclopaedia Britannica
The New Columbia Encyclopedia

Special Encyclopedias

Dictionary of American History
Dictionary of the History of Ideas
Encyclopedia of the Biological Sciences
Encyclopedia of Painting
Encyclopedia of Philosophy
Encyclopedia of Psychology
Encyclopedia of World Art
An Encyclopedia of World History
International Encyclopedia of Higher Education
International Encyclopedia of the Social Sciences
McGraw-Hill Encyclopedia of Science and Technology
The New Grove Dictionary of Music and Musicians

Biographies

Current Biography
Contemporary Authors
Dictionary of American Biography
Dictionary of National Biography [British]

Dictionary of Scientific Biography
International Who's Who
Twentieth Century Authors
Who's Who in America?
Who's Who [British]
Webster's Biographical Dictionary

TAKING NOTES

This is where you're going to put to good use the skills you learned in Chapters 2 to 4.

There are a few hints we can offer about getting the information down onto note cards. For one thing, as you take notes you'll want to think ahead to the writing of your paper. You'll need to think, for instance, about what passages you'll be summarizing, what passages you'll be quoting, and what passages you'll be paraphrasing. Also, take more notes than you think you'll use and quote a little more than you think you'll quote. It's only a small waste of time to write something down in your notes that you don't use in your paper; it's a big waste of time to go back to the library because you need something that you failed to take down the first time you were there.

Most instructors will require that you take notes on 4 × 6 cards. There's a good reason for this. Though it's true that a research paper as short as the one you're doing could be accomplished almost as easily on sheets of paper, taking notes on 4 × 6 cards gives you a system that you can use for any writing project that comes your way, in or out of school. Besides, taking notes on cards allows you to manipulate the information a bit more easily.

Figure 4 shows a typical note card, along with an explanation of its parts.

WRITING THE PAPER

Once you have taken enough notes to thoroughly develop your paper, it's time to take out your working outline and write your paper from it. Perhaps now that you've thought about it some more, you can refine it further. You can begin to write the first draft from your note cards. In fact, before we go any further, we might stop here for a minute or so to offer some hints about outlining. (For an example of a properly structured outline—including the correct format to use when it comes time for you to type it up—see page 100.)

Writing the Final Outline

- If you can, keep all items that belong to a particular level parallel in their grammatical structure. That is, if the A item in a subhead begins with a noun, the B item should also begin with a noun.

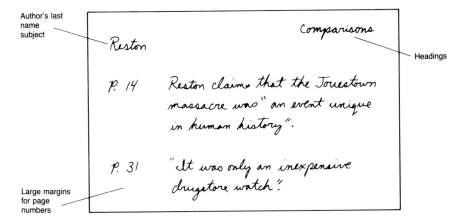

Author's last
name
subject

Reston

Comparisons

Headings

p. 14   Reston claims that the Jonestown
massacre was " an event unique
in human history".

p. 31   " It was only an inexpensive
drugstore watch".

Large margins
for page
numbers

Figure 4. Note card.

- Don't include your introduction or conclusion in the outline. An outline consists of only the points that appear in the *body* of the text.
- You needn't write complete sentences so long as your outline is clear without complete sentences.
- Your outline can be a mix of complete sentences, phrases, and clauses. But all items *on a particular level* of your outline should be consistent, either all complete sentences or all incomplete sentences. When you do have a mix, the main headings are usually complete sentences while the subheads are incomplete sentences.
- From your outline, a reader should be able to tell very easily how your paper is constructed. That is, your reader should be able to understand the relationship between your thesis and its main headings—and between your main headings and their subheadings. Believe us, outlines are *hard* to follow, so take some time with this.

Writing from Note Cards

With your outline in front of you, merely put the note cards in the order of your outline and then use them to write your paper. Naturally, you won't use all the material you've gathered. Worse, you may have to go back to the library to gather more material for a crucial part of your paper.

Your real problem here is to integrate the source material into your own writing. Your research paper should look like it's your thing, not just a patchwork of paraphrases and quotations joined together by *ands* and *according to*'s. But since you have already worked your way through Chapter 4, you should have no problem in handling your sources.

Announcing Your Sources

We have already discussed this matter of announcing your sources in Chapter 4, but it's important enough to bear repeating: Each time you use a particular source for the first time, tell your reader that you are using that source. And when you change a source, tell your reader, in an introduction to that source, that you are changing. Here, then, is a paragraph in which the writer does everything right in handling sources. We have put the source announcements in boldface. Look hard at them.

> Princes and kings had it no better than the common man when it came time to see the doctor. For instance, **in "Jeers and Chaos," Ernest Turner reports** that Charles II's last days were rendered hellish by a succession of doctors who scarified him, bled him, purged him, and "blew hellebore up his nostrils and set him sneezing." In fact, it's likely that members of the aristocracy suffered more than commoners *because* doctors attended on them. Poor people, usually to their good fortune, often had no doctor at all. **H. S. Glasscheib claims** that in the space of six short months, an ailing Louis XIII of France underwent 47 bleedings, 215 purgings, and 312 clysters. Indeed, doctors tried so many ungodly treatments on Charles II, **according to Ernest Turner,** that the only thing they didn't try was a "stomach brush."

As you see, the writer introduced the two sources, Ernest Turner and H. S. Glasscheib, the first time each was used and then reintroduced an earlier source ("according to Ernest Turner") when it was cited again after an interruption by the Glasscheib source.

DOCUMENTING SOURCES

In a sense you've been documenting your sources all along. Every time you introduced a summary or a quotation with words like these, "In Harold Klein's essay, 'Bring Back Opus,'" you were informally documenting your source. But, without going to enormous trouble, your readers would not be able to find the essay in their local library. For that, formal documentation is required. It goes a bit further. It tells readers *exactly* where they might find "Bring Back Opus." It tells them in what magazine the article appeared, in what month and in what year it appeared, and even on what pages it appeared. So complete documentation for Klein's essay would look something like this:

> Klein, Harold. "Bring Back Opus." American Culture May 1986: 44–56.

Now your readers can go to their library and find the same article that you used.

Why would they want to do that? Well, they might have become intrigued by your mention of the article and now they want to read the whole thing. Or they might want to check your facts. Or they might want to respond to your essay and they need the original article you used. Whatever their reason, you have given them enough bibliographic facts to make their search easy.

You might think of documentation as common courtesy. It gives credit to authors from whom you've borrowed, and it helps your readers locate the works you've used to write your paper. It also lends authority to your words.

We're going to simplify matters by describing the kind of documentation that the Modern Language Association (MLA) now recommends. There are other styles of documentation. The American Psychological Association (APA) has a somewhat different documentation style. The American Mathematical Society (AMS) uses yet another style. Newspapers, law reports, and government documents all use different documentation styles. When you write for these agencies, you'll be asked to use their styles. In the meantime, we'll use the MLA style of documentation. It's not *the* style for formal documentation. Rather, it's a serviceable, easy-to-use, generic format that will give you practice in following *a* style sheet.

Parenthetical Citations in the Text

When you borrow something from a source—a quotation or merely an idea—you need to tell your reader something about where you found that source. You do this by inserting information in parentheses immediately following your use of the source.

> Marvin Daughaday, the widely respected microbiologist, claims that amoebae are promiscuous (Daughaday 89).

That's all there is to it. The name in parentheses refers to the author of the work you got your information from, and the number refers to the page number.

If you mention, within your text, the name of your source when you introduce a summary or quotation, it's not necessary to mention the source's name again in your parenthetical citation. However, if you have any doubt about whether your reader might be confused, go ahead and include the name of your source as well as the page number.

The *parentheses itself* tells your readers to go to the end of your paper, where they will find a Works Cited page, which contains an alphabetized list of the sources you used to write your paper. If they go back there and trace their finger down to the Ds, they will find this item.

> Daughaday, Marvin. "Lust Under the Microscope." Bulletin of the American Microscope Association July 1948: 55–68.

Now your readers know how to find the article from which you are summarizing. (A sample Works Cited page appears on page 108.)

Once you know the basic principle of citing a source within a text, common sense alone will often tell you most of what you need to know when it comes to exceptions to the basic format. But just in case it doesn't, we will discuss them here.

Exceptions to the basic pattern of in-text citation.

- If you use more than one work by Daughaday in your paper, you'll have to add the name of the article you're referring to: (Daughaday, "Lust Under the Microscope" 89).
- When you refer to a play, put in the act and scene: (King Lear IV, i). No further bibliographic information is necessary on your Works Cited page.
- If you are referring to an anonymous work, merely put the title of the work in parenthesis: ("Microscopic Hijinks" 56). On the Works Cited page, list the work alphabetically by its title.
- If the title is long, you can use a shortened version, but be sure that the shortened version begins with the same word in the title that is alphabetized in your Works Cited page. A single word title, however, is probably *too* short.
- If your borrowing comes from a work that consists of more than one volume, you'll have to include the volume number and page number in parenthesis: (Bowles 5: 189).
- When you use the same information from two sources, include both sources within the parenthesis: (Howl 54; Bowles 175).

Note Page

As you write your paper, you may feel the need to make a comment that just doesn't seem to fit within your text. You may, for instance, want to provide an evaluative comment about a source. Or you may want to elaborate on an idea. Or you may just want to tell your reader something interesting related to your topic. A note page is where you can do these things. But don't feel obligated to provide a note page. Most papers don't have one. If yours does, here is how to handle these notes.

In your text, merely put a raised note number after the idea or source you want to comment on. Number these notes consecutively throughout your paper. That is, the first note will use a [1], the second a [2], the third a [3], and so on. Those numbers will direct your reader to a separate page, located just before the first page of your Works Cited page.

Works Cited Page

The Works Cited page is a separate page located at the end of your source paper. It contains an alphabetized list of all the works that you refer to in your paper.

Here's where your little stack of bibliography cards is going to come in handy. If you've kept up with these cards, all you have to do now is alphabetize them and type them, one item at a time, onto your Works Cited page. Here are the formats to use for those individual items on that Works Cited page.

Books and Articles within Books

One Author

> Johnson, Paul. <u>Intellectuals</u>. New York: Harper & Row, 1988.

Two Authors

> Adams, Betty, and Dominic West. <u>The Decline of Families</u>. Boston: Braumin and Sons, 1990.

Three Authors

> Clarey, Thomas E., Michael Donbey, and Cynthia Smith. <u>The Dilemma of Heroic Measures</u>. Toronto: Edmond Publishing, 1967.

More than Three Authors

> Berry, Frank, et al. <u>A History of the Movies</u>. Atlanta: Dombey and Sons, 1989.

Corporate Authorship

> Exxon Corporation. <u>The Story of Oil</u>. Chicago: The Exxon Press, 1979.

A Selection from an Anthology   *title A essay*

> Weinbaum, Stanley G. "A Martian Odyssey." <u>Science Fiction Hall of Fame</u>. Ed. Robert Silverberg. New York: Avon Books, 1970. 13–39.

Edition after the First

> McCrimmon, James M. <u>Writing with a Purpose</u>. 3rd ed. Boston: Houghton Mifflin, 1963.

An Edited Book Where Your Reference Is to the Author Who Is Edited

> Sterne, Laurence. <u>Tristram Shandy</u>. Ed. Ian Watt. Boston: Houghton Mifflin, 1965.

An Edited Book Where Your Reference Is to the Editor's Preface or Introductions

> Watt, Ian. Foreword. <u>Tristram Shandy</u>. By Laurence Sterne. Boston: Houghton Mifflin, 1965.

A Book That Has Been Republished

> Huxley, Aldous. <u>Brave New World</u>. 1932. New York: Bantam, 1953.

Translation

> Camus, Albert. <u>The Plague</u>. Trans. Stuart Gilbert. New York: Random House, 1948.

A Work in More than One Volume

> Durant, Will, and Ariel Durant. The Story of Civilization. 11 vols.
> New York: Simon Schuster, 1939–1967.

A Signed Item in an Encyclopedia

> Woolrych, Austin. "Cromwell, Oliver." Encyclopedia Americana.
> 1971 ed.

An Unsigned Item in an Encyclopedia

> "Cortland." Encyclopedia Americana. 1971 ed.

Magazines and Newspapers

Signed Article in a Monthly or Bimonthly Magazine

> Porter, Roy. "Before the Fringe: Quack Medicine in Georgian
> England." History Today Nov. 1986: 16–22.

A Signed Article in a Weekly Magazine

> Davis, Carole. "Reflexology." Health and Happiness 5 Aug. 1957:
> 45–46, 86.

Unsigned Article in a Magazine

> "Theme and Countertheme in A Clockwork Orange." British
> Literature Sept. 1967: 56–75.

Magazine with Continuous Pagination Throughout the Year

> Herman W. Roodenburg. "The Maternal Imagination: The Fears of
> Pregnant Women in Seventeenth-Century Holland." The Journal of
> Social History 21 (1988): 701–716.

Newspaper Editorial or News Story

> Lewis, Flora. "Creeping Freedom." The Courier-Journal 13 July
> 1989, sec. A: 4.

Book Review

> Cadge, Wilfred. "Confessions." Rev. of Fictions and Nonfictions, by
> Elaine Washer. Wildfire Fall 1987: 45–48.

Pamphlets and Bulletins

> The Safety Record of the Logging Industry. Pamphlet 23. Springfield,
> Oregon: Oregon Logging Association, 1978.

Nonprint Sources

Television or Radio Program

Japan: Electronic Tribe. PBS. 13 July 1989.

Recording   Video

Great Sea Battles of World War Two. Larson Wales. Simplex
   Communications. 1978.

Lecture

Herndon, Jerry. "Western Literature." Murray State University.
   Murray, Kentucky. 20 June 1990.

Interview

Brown, Barry. Personal Interview. Murray, Kentucky. 5 Aug. 1987.

A SAMPLE PAPER

This student paper can serve as an illustration of the points we have discussed throughout this book. We'll begin with a title page.

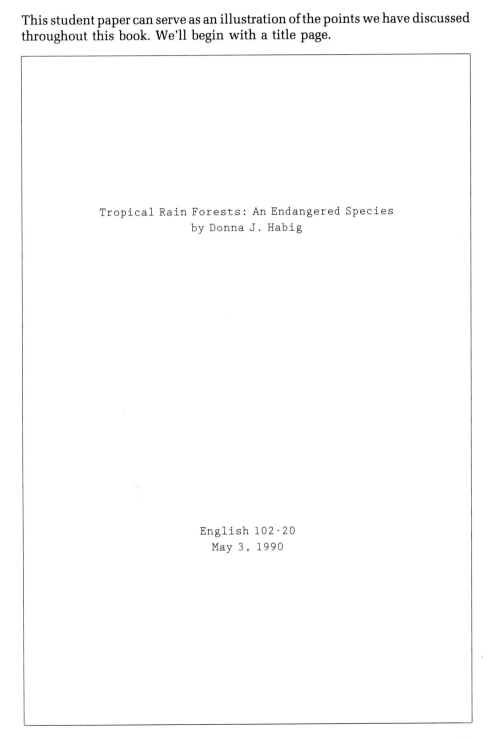

Tropical Rain Forests: An Endangered Species
by Donna J. Habig

English 102-20
May 3, 1990

Outline: Tropical Rain Forests: An Endangered Species

Thesis: Because the deforestation of tropical rain forests will seriously alter the world's environment, we must stop the destruction.

I. The causes of deforestation
   A. Population increases
      1. Housing space needed
      2. Farming space needed
      3. Energy sources needed
   B. Consumer demands
      1. Cattle ranching to meet beef demands
      2. Logging to meet timber demands
   C. Government policies
      1. Tax credits to ranchers
      2. International debt
II. The effect of deforestation
   A. Loss of a source of medicine and food
      1. Loss of current drug sources
      2. Loss of future medical cures and break-throughs
      3. Loss of food sources
   B. Environmental changes
      1. Decrease of rainfall
      2. Increase of temperature
      3. Destruction of flood control systems
III. The solutions to the problem of deforestation
   A. Limit agricultural production
   B. Eliminate international debt
   C. Form parks and reserves
   D. Implement education and public awareness programs

Tropical Rain Forests: An Endangered Species

Tropical rain forests, as defined by a recent <u>Mother Earth News</u> essay, are woodlands that get over 80 inches of rainfall per year and are close enough to the equator to be so unaffected by seasons that all the trees are evergreen (96). This definition, however, merely touches the surface of a rain forest's true identity. As Eugene Linden points out in a recent <u>Time</u> essay, rain forests are home to 50 to 80 percent of the earth's plant and animal species, though rain forests comprise only 7 percent of the earth's surface (32). A rain forest, hence, is a place teeming with diversity.

But this remarkable habitat is in grave danger of being completely destroyed within our lifetime. Eugene Linden warns that the current rate of destruction of these forests is 1000 times that which has transpired throughout history. Within the next 30 years, 100 species a day will become extinct (32). Unlike the disappearance of the dinosaurs, this extinction won't be caused by nature. It will be brought about by human societies whose modern priorities are in dramatic conflict with the preservation of conditions necessary for rain forest survival.

Numerous causes for tropical deforestation can be found. Some stem from population trends, some from consumer demands, and some from government policies.

The constant growth of human population has had a direct impact on deforestation. As Peter Raven observed in a recent address, the population is growing at an annual rate of 2.4 percent (473). Norman Myers summarizes the inevitable results of this growth in his book <u>The Primary Source</u>: Because more space is needed to house the growing population, more rain forests are cut down to supply building materials and to clear the areas for rural housing. Those who reside in this cleared space, moreover, clear still more rain forest because they must resort to farming for a livelihood (157). Obviously, as the population continues to grow, so will the number of people who must destroy the tropical rain forests to provide for their basic needs of food and shelter.

With the increased population come increased energy needs. According to Peter Raven, wood has become a major source of energy production. An estimated 1.5 billion people currently obtain energy from fuel wood. To meet this need, trees are being cut at rates much faster than new trees can be planted and grown. At the present rate, cutting timber for fuel could wipe out most tropical forests within three decades (474).

In recent years hydroelectric power has been used widely as an alternative to fuel wood, but, as David Schoonmaker observes, the results are the same for the rain forests: rather than being cut down, they are being flooded as engineers dam rivers to create reservoirs to provide water power at electricity generating plants. Like logging, flooding, too, kills the plant and animal species in the affected areas. Such hydroelectric projects are not prevalent in rain forests yet, but they could be as early as the year 2000. At that time, Schoonmaker says, Brazil alone hopes to have 100 new hydroelectric dams under construction (100).

We must not, however, indulge in pointing fingers of blame at other people in distant continents. David Schoonmaker insists that we as modern consumers play a significant role in the process of tropical deforestation. Logging, for example, accounts for a quarter of the deforestation in Brazil and is a major cause of deforestation in Southeast Asia (100). Half of the timber that is cut, according to Norman Myers, supplies energy, but the other half ends up in the advanced countries to meet consumer demands for wood products. Building materials, such as plywood, can be obtained from Southeast Asia at relatively cheap prices. For this reason, the United States is second only to Japan in hardwood imports. Hardwood furniture is also created by processing trees from the tropics. Though merely decorative rather than necessary, beautiful furniture, Myers insists, is widely viewed as a status symbol and purchased by affluent consumers with no regard for its ruinous effects upon rain forests (92, 101).

The leading cause of deforestation in Central and South America, Myers says, is cattle ranching (127). A Newsweek essay estimates that 260 acres of tropical rain forests are destroyed each day to provide grazing areas for cattle. The livestock industry is a dominant force in South America, too ("Hamburgers" 74). In 1980 alone, according to a Science News essay, cattle ranch development accounted for 72 percent of all of the rain forests which were destroyed in Brazil (Raloff 367).

The demand which drives this beef industry is fueled

primarily by one source--American consumers. The United
States is the biggest consumer, producer, and importer of
beef. Of the beef it imports, according to Norman Myers,
75 percent is from South America, while 17 percent is from
Central America. The United States imports so much beef
because beef imported from the tropics costs half that
which is raised within the country, and fast food chains,
in particular, rely on the cheaper imports to keep their
profits high. Also there is not enough grazing land in the
United States, Myers says, to raise all the cattle needed
to meet current U.S. consumer demands (129).

Yet Americans are not alone to blame when it comes to
the dramatic increase in cattle raising in recent decades.
As David Schoonmaker observes, Brazil's government offers
70 percent of its tax credits to cattle ranchers (100).
Janet Raloff, writing for Science News, agrees: Other economic advantages, such as accelerated depreciation, the
ability to write off operating losses against income
earned on other projects and highly subsidized credit
[mean that] ranch investors have earned up to 250 percent
on their investment. Ironically, ranchers would make
little profit at all if it were not for the government's
help (367).

Another politically linked cause of deforestation involves Third World government debts. Peter Raven suggests
that many Third World countries are so heavily in debt that
they must use practically any means they can to make debt
payments to the international banks. This desperation
leads to the exploitation of Third World natural resources
(474). Unfortunately, these countries don't seem to understand, or perhaps just don't care, that once all of
their natural resources are depleted, they will be much
worse off than they are now.

As difficult as these problems are to solve, the consequences of not solving them are so dire that we must make a
massive attempt at their solution. The destruction of the
tropical rain forests could quite simply alter the world
as we know it. The loss of biological diversity and a
dramatically altered environment will profoundly affect
people the world over.

Presently, the most serious danger resulting from
deforestation is the elimination of much of the earth's
biological diversity. Eugene Linden, writing for Time,
laments that many of the plant species that survived the

period when dinosaurs became extinct are disappearing now because of human carelessness (32). Most people, observes David Schoonmaker, don't realize what a vital role the vegetable world of the tropics play in their everyday lives. Twenty-five percent of all prescription drugs are derived from plants growing in tropical rain forests (98). The drug that is used to treat Hodgkin's disease, for instance, comes from a tropical plant (Raven 475).

Although tropical plants can now be grown in controlled environments, or their medical properties simulated from artificial substances, Adrian Forsyth and Kenneth Miyata argue in their book, Tropical Nature, that destroying the biological diversity found in the rain forests will eliminate future medical breakthroughs, and they point out that scientists at the National Cancer Institute have concluded that more than 70% of the plants known to produce compounds with anticancerous properties are tropical (211). Moreover, as Eugene Linden observes, three of the plants which provide the ingredients for drugs with the potential to treat AIDS grow exclusively in the tropical rain forests (33). Thus, if a species is driven to extinction before it can be scientifically studied, potential cures for cancer, AIDS, or other health problems will have been eradicated.

The staggering costs exacted by the loss of the world's tropical rain forests must be reckoned in terms of nutrition as well as in terms of disease prevention and treatment. As Peter Raven points out,

> Not all of a plant's benefits are medicine related: For example, three species of plants--rice, wheat, and corn--supply over half of all human energy requirements; only about 150 kinds of food plants are used extensively; and only 5000 kinds have ever been used. Many of these come to us from the tropics. It is estimated, however, that there may be tens of thousands of additional kinds of plants that could provide human food if their properties were fully explored and they were brought into cultivation (475).

Imagine the possibilities that new food sources could offer. They would give us new foods to try and new recipes to create. No longer would we have to rely on the same old foods to meet our nutritional needs. Yet, more importantly, new food sources could prove beneficial for feeding the hungry. Tropical species could be grown in Third World tropical cultures and used to feed the poverty-stricken. This would help alleviate the developing countries' dependence on outside help in providing for their people.

Another effect of deforestation is that it leaves the forest floor open to the sun's rays. Usually, according to David Schoonmaker, only 3 percent of the sunlight falling on a tropical rain forest reaches the ground (96). Cecie Starr and Ralph Taggart, authors of Biology: The Unity of Life, add that much of the sunlight that doesn't reach the ground is used by the trees and other plants for photosynthesis--the process of converting the sun's energy into chemical energy for use in manufacturing food from carbon dioxide and water (109). But without trees to provide protection, warn Adrian Forsyth and Kenneth Miyata, the ground absorbs and reflects the sunlight back into the atmosphere, producing an increase in temperature (213).

Such temperature increases, according to David Schoonmaker, are also produced merely by the fact that destroying trees on a wholesale scale wipes out a major source of carbon storage. Approximately 200 billion tons of carbon are bound up in rain forest plants. If not bound in plants, this carbon might be found as carbon dioxide in the atmosphere. A rise in carbon dioxide levels on this large scale would produce a greenhouse effect (98). The greenhouse effect, as Cecie Starr and Ralph Taggart define it, occurs when carbon dioxide levels in the upper atmosphere build up and reflect heat into the lower atmosphere, thus producing a global warming (758). Peter Raven estimates that global temperature could ultimately rise 3 to 5° C in the near future if deforestation is not controlled (475).

Deforestation also wipes out nature's own flood-control system. Adrian Forsyth and Kenneth Miyata put it this way: Instead of being filtered through the trees and absorbed through their roots, the rainwater just runs off the land, clogging rivers with silt and producing frequent, unpredictable flooding. The pounding rain makes hilly areas susceptible to mudslides, further clogging rivers (212).

All of the effects of deforestation discussed above combine to form still another effect: natural destruction. Peter Raven notes that decreased rainfall,

increased temperatures, and frequent flooding alter the
environment and climate enough to speed up the deteriora-
tion of the remaining tropical rain forests (475).

The inexorable nature of deforestation's causes and
the highly sobering implications of its effects, of
course, cry out for immediate solutions, but there are no
quick and easy solutions to this widespread destruction.
A combination of diverse actions, however, must be taken
to ensure the survival of the tropical rain forests.

The effort to solve the problem which would show the
quickest results would be to try to eliminate the greatest
cause of deforestation--tropical agricultural production. If beef and timber production could be controlled,
the rain forests would stand a chance of survival. Such
control could effectively be achieved through a variety of
methods.

Once they understand the immense problem, Americans
should, as the Time essay cited earlier suggests, refuse
to patronize fast-food chains, restaurants, and grocery
stores which sell or use meat purchased from countries
where tropical deforestation is a problem. This boycott,
if executed carefully, could decrease beef production in
Central America alone by as much as 90 percent ("Hamburgers" 94). David Schoonmaker adds that a boycott of timber
and wood products which originated in the tropics would
also result in a significant decrease in land destruction
(100). Successful boycotts would almost eliminate the
need to clear land for food, fuel, and building material
production.

Government intervention could also lead to a large
reduction in deforestation caused by cattle production.
Peter Raven asserts that if Brazil and other countries
which offer tax credits to cattle ranchers would do away
with such tax shelters, these ranchers would find clearing
new lands for expanded operations financially unfeasible.
After the financial fallout which would inevitably result,
moreover, vacant ranches could be turned back into agricultural farms to produce food for poverty-stricken people who would otherwise destroy forest regions to satisfy
their hunger. The areas could also be transformed into
timber plantations for fuelwood and plywood production.
These alternative uses of the cleared land would prevent
most future destruction, since, as Raven asserts,
"virtually all of the food, timber and fuelwood needs of

the tropics could be met by the intelligent use of [previously cleared] lands" (474, 477).

This solution, of course, would exact a high price for tropical countries' agricultural industries. Dramatic reductions in agricultural exports would harm already troubled economies. Peter Raven suggests that because such Third World land abuse is closely linked to Third World international debt, any solution must include a suspension of payments toward this debt--a suspension prompted by the realization that the world's environmental stability is at stake (477).

The formation of parks and reserves to aid in preserving biological diversity is a concept already in action. Although such preserves are beneficial in preventing commercial development of the land, this idea is not as promising as it seems. Eugene Linden points out that even if such an area is protected, it cannot be self-supporting unless it is relatively large. Smaller regions decline quickly because of biological factors such as an increased rate of inbreeding and a consequent loss of genetic variability (33). Hunting and poaching, moreover, according to Peter Raven, become more prevalent in such small animal-rich preserves (476). Therefore, such parks might merely delay the destruction of rain forests instead of stopping it altogether.

Perhaps the most obvious, and in my opinion the most valuable, tool in saving tropical rain forests is education. Public awareness and knowledge of the situation are what makes all other efforts in deforestation possible. If the people of all nations learn how devastating tropical deforestation really is, then they might be able to pressure those most responsible for the problem into stopping the destruction. Without public awareness, deforestation will likely continue unchallenged.

The collective efforts of people all over the world are the only solution to saving the tropical rain forests and preserving the environment of the earth for future generations. But until the governments and the general public make an effort to stop supporting deforestation, the destruction of one of the earth's most valuable natural resources will proceed until nothing can be done!

Works Cited

Forsyth, Adrian, and Kenneth Miyata. <u>Tropical Nature</u>. New
    York: Charles Scribner's Sons, 1984.

"Hamburgers Are Killing Trees." <u>Newsweek</u> 14 September
    1987:74.

Linden, Eugene. "The Death of Birth." <u>Time</u> 2 January
    1989: 32-35.

Myers, Norman. <u>The Primary Source</u>. New York: W. W.
    Norton and Company, 1984.

Raloff, Janet. "Unraveling the Economics of Deforesta-
    tion." <u>Science News</u> 4 June 1988: 366-367.

Raven, Peter H. "We're Killing Our World." <u>Vital
    Speeches of the Day</u> 15 May 1987: 472-478.

Schoonmaker, David. "Crisis in the Rain Forest." <u>Mother
    Earth News</u> July-August 1987: 94-100.

Starr, Cecie, and Ralph Taggart. <u>Biology: The Unity of
    Life</u>. Belmont: Wadsworth, Inc., 1989.

PART TWO

Following Through: Sources for Your Papers

—— 7 ——

Medicine Before Science:

The Treatment Was Successful but the Patient Died

INTRODUCTION

Before science revolutionized medicine, physicians were somewhat handicapped. They didn't know what the world was made of, they had only a hazy idea of what went on inside the human body, and they didn't have the foggiest notion of the existence of bacteria and viruses. It's difficult to think straight about human physiology when you believe that "life" consists of four elemental juices; it's hard to deal with diseases of the liver when you don't know the function of the liver; and you're unlikely to do much good for your patient when you slice open his body with a rusty knife and plunge your dirty hands into his body cavity. (The germ theory of disease wasn't generally known until the middle of the nineteenth century.)

Ignorance didn't inhibit the doctors in the slightest, and they went their merry way. They cut off legs, applied enemas, and drained their patients of blood. Instead of knowledge, they had theories, all kinds of theories—ancient theories, up-to-date theories, exotic theories, pious theories, and neat and tidy theories—none of which had the slightest basis in reality, though each was quite orthodox in its time and most were taught in the best universities.

One pious theory was that Satan, or creatures much like him, went to and fro on this earth, stopping every now and again to inflict the Black Death on humanity or a sharp pain in the belly of Goodwife Martha. There were, of course, philosophical problems that accompanied this theory: If God is good and all powerful, why does he allow Satan to cause so much suffering? But that was a problem for only a few airy theologians. The mass of people—along with most of the church authorities—believed that an evil force in the universe was causing all our pain. For the practitioner of the theory of demon-caused illness, there were two courses of action: exorcise the demons who dwelt in the sick person's body, or torture or kill the witch, Satan's subordinate, who had cast an evil eye on the sufferer. In this chapter we have included a seventeenth-century essay, "Of the Different Diseases Brought by Demons," written by a demonology enthusiast.

University-educated physicians usually embraced more secular theories. The most popular was the theory of the four humors, which had the imprimatur of ancient Greek authority and most contemporary universities to recommend it. According to this theory, the universe is made up of four elements: fire, water, earth, and air. Thus, if the universe is made up of four elements, there must be four humors, or juices, that make up life itself. This theory has a kind of symmetry to recommend it. At any rate, for thousands of years, physicians believed that life was made of red juice (evidenced in the blood), yellow juice (evidenced in secretions of bile), black juice (evidenced by secretions of the pancreas), and white juice (evidenced by secretions of the nose). As long as each of your humors was properly mixed and proportioned, you would remain healthy. But if one humor became predominant, you would fall into sickness. Treatment was simple: A physician who was well-versed in the theory of the humors would purge you of either your urine, feces, blood, or pus. In "The Four Juices," reprinted in this chapter, H. S. Glasscheib reports that some doctors drained off blood till their patients died. Now *that* is devotion to one's favorite theory.

In Book 4 of *Gulliver's Travels*, Jonathan Swift makes a bit of fun of the theory of humors. Gulliver, Swift's inveterate traveler, tells one of the talking horses that human doctors believe that

> all diseases arise from repletion; from whence they conclude that a great evacuation of the body is necessary, either through the natural passage, or upwards at the mouth. Their next business is, from herbs, minerals, gums, oils, shells, salts, juices, seaweed, excrements, barks of trees, serpents, toads, frogs, spiders, dead men's flesh and bones, birds, beasts, and fishes, to form a composition for smell and taste the most abominable, nauseous, and detestable that they can possibly contrive, which the stomach rejects with loathing and this they call a vomit. Or else from the same storehouse . . . they command us to take in at the orifice above or below (just as the physician then happens to be disposed) a medicine equally annoying and disgustful to the bowels, which relaxing the belly, drives down all before it; and this they call a purse, or a clyster. For nature . . . having intended the superior anterior posterior for ejection, these artists ingeniously considering that in all diseases nature is forced out of her seat; therefore to replace her in it, the body must be treated in a manner directly contrary, by interchanging the use of each orifice; forcing solids and liquids in at the anus, and making evacuations at the mouth.

Not all medical theories were as hard on patients. The theory of signatures, for instance, was usually benign in practice. Behind this theory, embraced by both doctors and folk practitioners alike, was the idea that man is a microcosm of the larger world, the macrocosm. Thus, ancient "researchers" needed only to discover which object of nature went with which human illness. "Researchers" usually discovered their medicines through colors and shapes. If the bark of a tree had a yellow tinge, they would try it out on their yellow-jaundiced patients. According to Benjamin Gordon's "Signature and Other Healing Concepts" (reprinted in this chapter), some physicians used pomegranate seeds to treat diseases that caused redness on the skin and the leaf of the liverwort (which sort of resembles the human liver) to treat liver diseases. The theory of signatures is not a very elegant theory, to be sure, but in the absence of any other theories, doctors were apparently determined to do *something* rather than nothing. A patient with a coin in her pocket must have been a strong inducement to do *something*.

It's all really quite amazing. For thousands of years doctors bled their patients until they were ashen-faced, they purged them until they were weak and dehydrated, and they carved off breasts with dirty knives, thus introducing infections into the wound. Yet sick people kept coming to them. Chronic pain will bring the strongest people to their knees, and suffering people will always do *something*. Even today some old men and women with inflamed joints wear copper bracelets to try to ease the pain of arthritis. Sometimes the only alternative to pain is to do nothing, and that is apparently too horrible to contemplate.

OF THE DIFFERENT DISEASES BROUGHT BY DEMONS

Francesco Maria Guazzo

Francesco Maria Guazzo was a seventeenth-century monk of the order of Saint Ambrose. In a century that witnessed the persecution of a variety of Christian heresies, Guazzo's enthusiasm for "discovering" and then rooting out "witches" was exceptional but not unique. This selection comes from a larger work called *Compendium Maleficarum*, where Guazzo blames most of humanity's ills—including almost all diseases—on the influence of Satan and the witches who were his subordinates. In ages of intense faith, at least before the scientific revolution, human suffering was often blamed on the Evil One. As Guazzo says, "Did not the devil afflict Job with loathsome sores . . . ?" But even with a sense of history, it's hard not to marvel at Guazzo's naiveté as he describes a 15-year-old girl who evacuates live eels and vomits 24 pounds of wine a day.

Avicenna and Galen and Hippocrates deny that it is possible for any diseases to **1.** be brought upon man by demons; and their view is followed by Pietro Pomponazzi and Levin Lemne, not because they did not believe that the demons, which they acknowledged to be evil, wished to cause disease, but because they held that every disease is due to natural causes. But that is no good argument: for is it not possible for sicknesses to spring from natural causes, and at the same time possible for demons

Source: Francesco Maria Guazzo, "Of the Different Diseases Brought by Demons," *Compendium Maleficarum.* 1608. Montague Summers (ed.), E. A. Ashwin (trans.). New York: Barnes and Noble, 1970. 105–106, 108–109.

to be the instigators of such sicknesses? The contrary opinion is held by Codronchi, Andrea Cesalpino, Jean Fernel, Franciscus Valesius the Spaniard, and other most learned physicians, together with S. Jerome (on Matt. iii), S. Chrysostom (*Homily* 54, on Matt. xvii), S. Thomas (I, 2, 115, art. 5), and other theologians. The jurists also, especially Burchard (*Decret.* XIX, *de re magica*), argue excellently on the same side. Grilland (2, 6, to number 13) has often been quoted to the same effect: but I prefer the firmer authority of the Holy Scriptures. Did not the devil afflict Job with loathsome sores from the soles of his feet to the crown of his head? Did not the devil put to an alien use the tongue and ears of him whom S. Matthew calls the Lunatic? Did not a devil afflict Saul with a black humour? The account is quite explicit, for it says that an evil spirit afflicted him, which went away when David played the harp.

Let us now see by what method the demon causes sickness. This has been clearly **2.** set forth by Franciscus Valesius, who says that the demon is the external cause of sickness when he comes from without to inhabit a body and bring diseases to it; and if the sickness has some material source he sets in motion its inner causes. Thus he induces the melancholy sickness by first disturbing the black bile in the body and so dispersing a black humour throughout the brain and the inner cells of the body: and this black bile he increases by superinducing other irritations and by preventing the purging of the humour. He brings epilepsy, paralysis and such maladies by a stoppage of the heavier physical fluids, obstructing and blocking the ventricle of the brain and the nerve-roots. He causes blindness or deafness, bringing a noxious secretion in the eyes or ears. Often again he suggests ideas to the imagination which induce love or hatred or other mental disturbances. For the purpose of causing bodily infirmities he distils a spirituous substance from the blood itself, purifies it of all base matter, and uses it as the aptest, most efficacious and swiftest weapon against human life: I say that from the most potent poisons he extracts a quintessence with which he infects the very spirit of life, and (as Cesalpino well observes, *De Daemonum Investigatione, c.* 16) so establishes his devil-made disease that human skill is hardly able to find a remedy, since the devil's poison is too subtle and tenuous, too swift and sure in killing, and reaches to the very marrow of the bones. But those more common maladies which are caused solely by some external injury or noxious breath, by means of certain instruments of witchcraft, unguents, signs, buried charms and such things, have no natural power for evil in themselves, but are merely symbols in response to which the demon fulfils his pact with a witch. This was pointed out by the same Andrea Cesalpino in Chapter 17 of the work above quoted.

A certain honest woman who had been legally married to one of the household **3.** of the Archduke formally deposed the following in the presence of a Notary. In the time of her maidenhood she had been in the service of one of the citizens, whose wife became afflicted with grievous pains in the head; and a woman came who said she could cure her, and so began certain incantations and rites. And I carefully watched (said this woman) what she did, and saw that, against the nature of water poured into a vase, she caused water to rise in its vessel, together with other ceremonies which there is no need to mention. And considering that the pains in my mistress's head were not assuaged by these means, I addressed the witch in some indignation with these words: "I do not know what you are doing, but whatever it is, it is witchcraft, and you are doing it for your own profit." Then the witch at once replied: "You will know in three days whether I am a witch or not.'' And so it proved; for on the third day when I sat down and took up a spindle, I suddenly felt a terrible pain in my body. First it was inside me, so that it seemed that there was no part of my body in which I did not feel horrible shooting pains; then it seemed to me just as if burning coals were being continually heaped upon my head; thirdly, from the crown of my head to the soles of my feet there was no place large enough for a pinprick that was not covered with a rash of white pustules; and so I remained in these pains, crying out and wishing only for death, until the fourth day. At last my mistress's husband told me to go to a certain tavern; and with great difficulty I went, whilst he walked before, until we were in front of the tavern. ''See!'' he said to me; ''there is a loaf of white bread over the tavern door.'' ''I see,'' said I. Then he said: ''Take it down, if you possibly can; for it may do you good.'' And I, holding on to the door with one hand as much as I could, got hold of the loaf with the other. ''Open it'' (said my master) ''and look carefully at what is inside.'' Then, when I had broken open the loaf, I found many things inside it, especially some white grains very like the pustules on my body; and I saw also some seeds and herbs such as I could not eat or even look at, with the bones of serpents and other animals. In my astonishment I asked my master what was to be done; and he told me to throw it all into the fire. I did so; and behold! suddenly, not in an hour or even a few minutes, but at the moment when that matter was thrown into the fire, I regained all my former health.

The same author tells in the same place the following story. An honest married **4.** woman deposed the following on oath. Behind my house (she said) I have a greenhouse, and my neighbour's garden borders on it. One day I noticed that a passage had been made from my neighbour's garden to my greenhouse, not without some damage being caused; and as I was standing in the door of my greenhouse reckoning to myself and bemoaning both the passage and the damage, my neighbour suddenly came up and asked if I suspected her. But I was frightened because of her bad reputation, and only answered, ''The footprints on the grass are a proof of the damage.'' Then she was indignant because I had not, as she hoped, accused her with actionable words, and went away murmuring; and though I could hear her words, I could not understand them. After a few days I became very ill with pains in the stomach, and the sharpest twinges shooting from my left side to my right, and conversely, as if two swords or knives were thrust through my breast; whence day and night I disturbed all the neighbours with my cries. And when they came from all sides to console me, it happened that a certain clay-worker, who was engaged in an adulterous intrigue with that witch, my neighbour, coming to visit me, took pity on my illness, and after a few words of comfort went away. But the next day he returned in a hurry, and, after consoling me, added: ''I am going to test whether your illness is due to witchcraft, and if I find that it is, I shall restore your health.'' So he took some molten lead and, while I was lying in bed, poured it into a bowl of water which he placed on my body. And when the lead solidified into a certain image and various shapes, he said: ''See! your illness has been caused by witchcraft; and one of the instruments of that witchcraft is hidden under the threshold of your house door. Let us go, then, and remove it, and you will feel better.'' So my husband and he went to remove the charm; and the clay-worker, taking up the threshold, told my husband to put his hand into the hole which then appeared, and take out whatever he found; and he did so. And first he brought out a waxen image about a palm long, perforated all over, and pierced through the sides with two needles, just in the same way that I felt the stabbing pains from side to side; and then little bags containing all sorts of things, such as grains and seeds and bones. And when all these things were burned, I became better, but not entirely well. For although the shootings and twinges stopped, and I quite regained my appetite for food, yet even now I am by no means fully restored to health. And when we asked her why it was that she had not been completely restored, she answered: There are some other instruments of witchcraft hidden away which I cannot find. And when I asked the man how he knew where the first instruments were hidden, he answered: "I knew this through the love which prompts a friend to tell things to a friend."

A tale surpassing all wonder is told in his *De Naturae divinis characterismis*, II, **5.** 4 by Cornelius Gemma, who relates that a fifteen-year-old girl of Louvain named Catarina Gualteri was sometime under his charge in the year 1571. She was given by a kinswoman of her own age something to taste, and when she had eaten it she at once showed extraordinary symptoms of sickness; for Gemma himself saw her every day void so many objects of such a size and nature that he would not have believed if it had been told him by anyone else. In the eighth month of her sickness with a great effort she voided from her back passage a live eel, perfectly formed, as thick as a thumb and six feet long, with scales and eyes and tail and everything belonging to an eel. He tells that, three days before it came out, not only the girl herself but also those near her heard the eel utter a sharp thin cry in her belly; and when it was coming out the girl said that she clearly felt that at the first attempt it drew back its head, and then came out with a rush. They killed and disembowelled the eel, and hung it high out of the reach of the animals; but it suddenly vanished. Meanwhile the girl began to vomit an immense quantity of fluid not unlike wine and of an unpleasant taste; and this continued for more than fourteen days, each day's vomiting weighing twenty-four pounds. Besides this she made water copiously two or three times a day. No tumour or external swelling could be seen in her stomach or anywhere in her body, and the girl ate and drank very sparingly, hardly taking a cup of wine or beer or other liquor; but her excretion of water was such that in two weeks she could easily fill two water-butts. After this flood of water she began to vomit a vast number of hairs of about a finger's length, some longer and some shorter, like those which fall from old dogs; and the quantity of the hairs grew each day so that she could easily have filled many full-sized balls. All this she vomited with much retching and difficulty. After a few days' interval there followed other vomitings of great balls of hair floating in a purulent sanies, and sometimes of the appearance of the dung of pigeons or geese; and in this pus were found bits of wood and tiny pieces of skin, some of the wood being various-sized pieces of living trees, as if they had been broken off from the trunks; these were of the thickness and breadth of a nail, spongy inside and black with old bark outside. Shortly afterwards her vomiting became as black as coal, so that you would have said that it was ink or the excretion of a cuttle fish, with minute pieces of coal in it; and each day she vomited two or three pounds, nearly always accompanied with more hairs than could be put into a walnut, all white and long and stiff. This continued for three days, and then in one single vomit she threw up two pounds of pure blood, as from an opened vein, unmixed with any other matter. After this blood, the black vomiting returned, as if the fluid had been dyed with pounded antimony, and each day there were five or six pounds of the fluid; and this prodigy continued for seven solid hours. The application of human and divine remedies brought some relief, during which the hairs were still ejected, but they were fewer and gradually became blacker and shorter every day, growing from auburn to dark and so to jet black, and it seemed that the vomiting broke them into minute particles, such was her virulent spitting; though at times it was more like mud. About the middle of September she vomited larger pieces of skin which seemed to be torn from her stomach, and they had the appearance of a thick fleshy membrane, tough and difficult to tear, like the choroid envelope of a foetus, and were marked with a network of veins, and were sometimes as much as half a palm in length. Immediately after these followed others much thinner but black right through, but still bearing the marks of veins, and in other respects not unlike the allantoid membrane. Last came membranes of a third kind, devoid of vasa, and thinner than any of the others, like the amnion yet differing from it in appearance and material; for though thin, they were remarkably tough, and in some marvellous manner larger. The fragments differed in size, but two especially were more than two palms wide and were deeply grooved: these split themselves from top to bottom and took the form of cancelled rhombs. I can compare them with nothing better than the slough of a viper, although I had never before seen anything comparable with them. But this was chiefly remarkable in them, that along the length of them there appeared a deeper groove marked sparsely with transverse marks, as appears in hoarseness of the lung. They had a hollow circular cavity within, a little narrower in the fastigium of one membrane, like the mark of a snake's head with a mastoid apophysis or a mamillary processus. In the end of the other there lurked something abdominal and asymmetrical, not unlike a bifurcated vertex. All these joined together clearly attained to the length and thickness of an eel, and I think that it was a papillary tubercle through which the eel breathed and, perhaps, drew into itself the needful solid and liquid nutriment.

After she cast up these membranes, there followed a vast quantity of stones, **6.** which she brought up always in the evening and at a fixed hour with much contortion and nausea. These stones were of the shape which is found in the ruins of old houses, and were solid, angular, and of various shapes and sizes, some as big as walnuts; and she vomited them not without danger of suffocation. Sometimes also they were coated with chalk and joined together, so that they could not be distinguished from stones pulled from a house wall.

Once in my presence she brought up an angular stone as big as a double chestnut, **7.** with very great difficulty, so that I manifestly saw her vomiting it and heard the sound of it falling into the basin, to the great horror both of my own mind and of those who were standing about. Immediately afterwards she brought up, but with less difficulty, a piece of wood as long and thick as a thumb. This was bound right round with a sort of thread. Meanwhile at intervals she still vomited hairs, but fewer and blacker. Then came that which would surpass all belief, for she brought up a hard triangular bone, hollow and spongy inside, such as was clearly a fragment of ox's leg, and the girl's father said he had seen such a one the day before in his broth. Without delay on the following day she vomited a number of bony objects, some sharp and some round, of various shapes and sizes, still mingled with hairs and stones: and last of all, pieces of glass and bronze. Gemma justly supposes that a demon was, with the permission of God, the originator of these prodigies, but that he nevertheless employed natural causes in their due order as far as he could.

WORKING WITH THE TEXT

Cultural and Historical References

In this section, the numbers at the margin refer to the numbered paragraphs in the selection itself.

1. Hippocrates, a fifth-century B.C. Greek physician, left behind a set of ethical rules that later became codified as the Hippocratic oath. Galen was a second-century Greek physician who, at that time, was *the* authority on human anatomy and physiology.

1. Avicenna was an eleventh-century Arabic philosopher and physician, Pietro Pomponazzi a sixteenth-century Italian philosopher, and Levin Lemne a sixteenth-century Dutch philosopher. Pomponazzi got into trouble with religious authorities for his opinion that disease was not caused by Satanic influence.

1. Codronchi, Cesalpino, Fernel, and Valesius had all written works that argued that disease *is* caused by supernatural agents.

1. St. Jerome was the fourth-century Latin scholar who wrote commentaries on the Bible and prepared an early version of the Bible, the Latin Vulgate. St. Thomas Aquinas was the famous thirteenth-century theologian who wrote copiously on all aspects of Christian theology. Buchard was the thirteenth-century bishop of Worms who had left behind a twenty-volume guide for the clergy.

2. Valesius was a sixteenth-century Spanish physician who was famous for his commentaries on ancient medical authorities.

4. Cornelius Gemma was a sixteenth-century Dutch physician, astrologer, and university professor.

Writing Assignments: The Paragraph

Be sure to provide an introduction for each paragraph writing assignment. That is, begin each paragraph with a phrase like this: "Thomas Brickle claims that. . . ." When it is relevant, you might also want to identify the expertise of the author ("Thomas Brickle, a New Testament scholar, claims that. . . ."), the name of the book or article, the century and country in which the work appeared, or any other circumstances that your readers might find significant.

1. Summarize Guazzo's work in a short paragraph. Be sure to write a topic sentence that identifies the author (and other pertinent information) and encompasses *all* that your summary paragraph will contain—including the fact that this selection by Guazzo serves two purposes. You'll probably want to quote a phrase to communicate the flavor of the original.

2. In a single paragraph, summarize, and quote from, paragraphs 4, 5, and 6. Pay special attention to your topic sentence.

3. Write a paragraph in which you offer an explanation for most of the maladies that Guazzo mentions in paragraph 2. Don't be too dogmatic.

4. Write a paragraph on the purpose of Guazzo's first paragraph. Summarize and quote to make your point.

Writing Assignments: The Short Essay

Use informal documentation for the short essays. That is, don't use footnotes or a Works Cited page to document your sources. Instead, cite only relevant information about your source, and keep that information *within* your text. Then follow the summary or quote with a page number in parenthesis. (Use the page numbers that you find in this book to represent the page numbers of the source.) Thus, your informal documentation will look something like this:

> In *The Romance of Medicine,* Benjamin Gordon, a professor of history, says that red wine was once believed to replenish a person's depleted blood supply (121).

1. After reading the introduction to this chapter, write a short paper that is sympathetic toward Guazzo and his interpretations of disease.

2. Write a paper on the sources of Guazzo's tales. How good is his evidence? How critically does he approach his evidence? Obviously the tales are not true, so what do you suppose lies behind these tales?

3. Write a paper on the first two paragraphs of Guazzo's work. Here are some matters you might analyze: his method of presentation, the purpose behind his first paragraph, and the leap of logic he makes in the first sentence in the second paragraph (not necessarily in that order).

SIGNATURE AND OTHER HEALING CONCEPTS

Benjamin Lee Gordon

It was an incurable optimist in *As You Like It* who said that there are "sermons in stones and good in everything." That sentiment might well be the slogan for the theory of signatures, which is as much a world view as it is a way of practicing medicine. Behind the theory lies the idea that each object of the natural world has written on it its purpose—if we could just read it. (God wouldn't have put an object there unless it were significant in some way to humanity, the climax of creation.) Thus, the mandrake root, which vaguely resembles the human form, must have a significant medical purpose. And in fact the mandrake root was used—and is still used in parts of the Far East—as an aphrodisiac and fertility drug. Lacking a knowledge of germs and infection, physicians found other explanations for diseases and their treatment.

At the time he wrote this book, Benjamin Lee Gordon was an ophthalmologist at the Shore Memorial Hospital, Somers Point, New Jersey. Hang on a little tight. This essay is filled with names of plants and medicines.

The doctrine *"signature"* is probably the earliest therapeutic system in the **1.** history of medicine. It was based on the belief that the Creator stamped all objects medically beneficial to mankind, and on the assumption that there is a connection of every part of the human body with a corresponding part in the world of Nature. This hypothesis originated in the ancient idea that man is a microcosm (little world) and each anatomical part of man has a counterpart in the macrocosm (larger world). Accordingly diseases readily respond to remedies bearing some real, symbolical, or fanciful resemblance to the diseased part either in appearance or structure. The doctrine of signature presupposes that there are specifics for all pathologic conditions, if man only could recognize them.

Color and shape were the two principal factors in selecting remedies. The **2.** signature of color played an important part in ancient Babylonia. According to R. Campbell Thompson, a mixture of a disemboweled yellow frog, gall, and curd was applied to the eye for the treatment of leukoma (an ocular disease characterized by a yellowish film upon the cornea of the eye). The yellow color of the frog was the signature of the yellow color of the leukomatous eye. Gall was also used by the ancient Egyptians and Hebrews for dislodging obscuring films of the eye of a leukomatous nature. The book of Tobit describes how the angel Raphael ordered the use of gall in the affected eye of Tobit, who had been blinded by leukoma.

Persons troubled with jaundice were treated with yellow drugs, tumeric, the roots **3.** of rhubarb, the flowers of saffron, or other yellow substances. A yellow coin or a yellow ribbon was part of the midwife's equipment. The system of signature still persists among certain classes of people. The writer recalls that during his early practice, when summoned to treat cases of icterus neonatorum (jaundice of the newborn) he occasionally noticed a yellow coin on the umbilicus or a yellow ribbon suspended from the neck of the newborn baby.

Scarlet fever, measles, or any other eruptive disease characterized by redness of **4.** the skin, was treated by covering the patient with scarlet blankets. In the treatment of smallpox, the patient was made to face red bed coverings, hangings, and other red substances and was made to drink liquids containing pomegranate seeds, mulberries, or other such drinks. It is recorded that Frederick I of Germany, when stricken with smallpox, ordered the regular draperies changed to red ones. The grandfather of Maria Theresa, who died of smallpox, was found wrapped, by order of the physician, in 20

Source: Benjamin Lee Gordon, "Signature and Other Healing Concepts," *The Romance of Medicine.* Philadelphia: F. A. Davis, 1949. 367–376.

yards of scarlet broadcloth. This treatment is still in vogue in Eastern Europe. In measles, for example, mothers darken the room and cover their children with red garments. John of Gaddesdin, physician to Edward II, while treating the son of the renowned king, took care that everything around the bed should be of a red color. He ascribed to this procedure the complete recovery of the prince, "without a vestige of a pustule remaining." According to Kaempfer, when any of the children of the Japanese Emperor are infected with smallpox, not only the wall chamber and the bed are covered with red hangings but also the people around the sick prince are clad in scarlet gowns.

In acute articular rheumatism, which is characterized by redness and swelling of **5.** the joints, a red flannel shirt that had been dyed nine times was applied to the parts. The idea of nine times was based on the sacredness of the number 9. According to Von Hahn, the Albanian peasants believe that if a blood-red stone is applied to the surface of a wound, it will stop the flow of blood. Skinned fresh red beans were put upon a bleeding skin surface after leeching because their reddish color was believed to insure hemostasis. Culpepper (1652), a well-known therapeutist of his day, wrote: "If a bean be parted in two, the skin being taken away, and laid upon the place where the Leeche hath been set that bleedeth too much, it stayeth the bleedings—The Huskes boiled in water to the consumption of a third part thereof stayeth a Lax and the Ashes of the Huskes made uppe wth Hogg's gress helpeth the old Pains, contusions and wounds of the sinews, the skiatica and the Gout. Beans eaten are extremely windy mete, but if after the Dutch fashion when they are half boiled you huske them and then seive them, they are wholesome food."

Red wine was employed by many people to replenish an exsanguinated person's **6.** blood. Red wine had a double function. It not only replaced lost blood but it also intoxicated the demon within the sick person's body, thus preventing him from sucking the blood of his victim.

The petals of the red rose, especially, bore the "signature" of the blood, and **7.** blood-roots or beets, on account of the red juice, were much prescribed for abnormal conditions of the blood. Red flowers were given for disorders of the vascular system. Red color has always been a factor in folk healing, particularly in China and New Zealand, where red was regarded as anathema to evil spirits. Red necklaces or beads, red ribbon, red coral rings, red bells on which the baby cut its teeth, and red pills had their superstitious associations. The familiar red sweater worn to prevent or counteract a cold and the red flannel muffler around the neck to treat sore throat and whooping cough, are employed not so much because of their wooly nature as because of their red color.

The color red was considered an acceptable substitute for blood. In Rome, for **8.** example, the face of the statue of Jove on the Capitol was dyed a deep red on all festive occasions. The Greeks, likewise, painted red the face and often the whole body of the wine-god Dionysus. Red is still used by primitive men everywhere in all types of magical rites.

Red is particularly employed medicinally. In China, for example, healers use red **9.** pills, write medical charms on red paper, and prescribe red silk braids for children's hair. Among the more ignorant and credulous of the Southern Negroes, the sovereign cure for syphilis is "red shanks tea."

Liverwort was employed in combating liver ailments because its leaf is shaped **10.**

like a liver. Lungwort, the leaves of which bear a fancied resemblance to the surface of the lungs, was considered good for pulmonary complaints. Heart-shaped leaves were placed over the sore breast of a nursing woman. Eye-bright, because its blossom resembles the pupil, was used in the treatment of disease of the eye; and the peony, when in bud, appearing like a man's head, was thought to be the most perfect signature available against the falling sickness.

Kidneywort was employed for renal disease because its leaves resemble a kidney.   **11.** Kidney beans were similarly prescribed on account of their shape. The use of beans in medicine had also an astrologic significance. The bean plant belonged astrologically to the planet Venus. It had to be gathered when Venus was in ascendance. Poppy-heads were claimed to be effective for head affections and lilies-of-the-valley were used for the cure of apoplexy. The rationale for this, according to Coles, was: ''as that disease is caused by the drooping of humors into the principal ventricles of the brain, so the flowers of the lily, hanging on the plants as if they are drops, are of wonderful use herein.'' Nettle tea is still a country remedy for nettle rash; prickly plants, like thistles and holly, were prescribed for pleuritic or other stitching pains, and the scales of the pine or of certain fish were used in toothache, because they resemble front teeth. Scorpion grass, sometimes known as forget-me-not, or mouse-ear, was used to treat the sting of a scorpion. Walnuts were prescribed for headache and meningitis because the kernels have some resemblance to the convolutions of the human brain. The shell was considered analogous to the human skull and husk analogous to the scalp.

The concept of signature was also applied to treating certain organs of the body   **12.** by administering similar organs of animals and humans. Liver, for example, was used in disease of the liver. A story is related of a Chinese woman who suffered from a severe hepatic disease and had been ordered by her physician to be transferred to a hospital which she disliked because of her fear of the ''white devils.'' Her devoted daughter-in-law took a kitchen knife, slashed her own abdomen, and sliced off a piece of what she thought was her liver and gave it to her mother-in-law. Cancer, which was believed to be caused by the growth of a toadlike body in the system, was treated by the application of a dried toad to the cancerous growth. A live worm was placed upon the stomach for intestinal worms. A remedy for asthma and shortness of breath was the administering of lung from a long-winded fox.

Certain roots of plants were used by ancient healers because of their resemblance   **13.** to the human body as a whole, or to one of its organs. Thus ginseng, named so, according to Grosler, because its root is forked and resembles the lower part of a human being, was ordered in paraplegia (paralysis of the lower part of the body). Ginseng root has been used in China as a remedy since ancient times; it was highly esteemed for its reputed lifegiving properties. When the root was brewed in a liquid, it was considered an *elixir vitae;* it was believed able to evolve into a living creature.

Thompson cites the following legend as told by a Chinese writer: ''The plant,   **14.** after growing for three centuries, is inspired through starlight by the spirits of the hills and rivers, then bursts into the shape and form of a man. In the course of time the new creature can leave the earth and dwell among the stars; but the most wonderful part about him is his white blood, which is a sovereign cure for all disease and a safeguard against mortality. It is very hard, however, to get this white blood; this divine *ichor.* To begin with, one must be extremely pious and must pray and fast for some while, before making the attempt. Then the plant spirit may be deluded into believing that a red paper lamp with seven purple stars is a *Great Bear,* as he is something of a star worshiper. A net is kept handy, the spirit caught, and his arms are cut with a knife of agate, and the drops of blood caught in a vessel of the purest jade. As a few drops will bring a dead man to life, they are naturally valuable.'' Ginseng, for a long while, formed the chief means by which the Koreans paid tribute to China. Its value varied in proportion to its resemblance to the male figure.

Another plant credited with similar properties and associated with legends like **15.** those connected with ginseng is Shang Luh. This plant has roots resembling the human form which are said to have the power of shrieking when gathered. Shang Luh is believed by the Chinese to grow upon the ground beneath which a dead man lies. The Chinese use this plant in magic after shaping the root into a mannikin. Internally, Shang Luh produced delirium and visual hallucinations enabling man to see demons. It was used in China as an ingredient in love philters, and has a reputation in the Far East for removing sterility. Shang Luh is often employed in China as a purgative, and applied externally for scrofula and swollen glands.

Atropa belladonna is one of the earliest plants believed to possess spiritual virtue. **16.** It was believed by the Greeks to have been produced by Atropos, one of the three Fates who were the ''arbiters of the life and death of mankind.'' The three goddesses, Clotho, Lachesis, and Atropos, were supposed to control all destinies. Atropos is pictured in mythology as clad in somber black robes, holding scissors in her hands, gathering up various sizes of thread, which, as chief of the Fates, she was privileged to cut according to the length of the person's life.

The use of Atropa belladonna in medicine among the ancients arose because of **17.** its fancied resemblance to the human form. This drug was condemned by Gerard in the following terms: ''It you follow my council deal not with it in any case and banish it from your gardens and the use of it also, it being a plant so furious and so deadly it bringeth upon such as have eaten thereof a dread sleep wherein many have died.''

The most mysterious and potent plant of all times is mandrake (mandragora). It **18.** was believed to possess a great spiritual and therapeutic virtue. Valuable as a hypnotic and aphrodisiac, its claim to therapeutic value was based on the real or imaginary resemblance of its root to the human form. Tales were at large that when the root was pulled from the earth, it groaned and shrieked so dismally that if the person who dug it up did not plug his ears with cotton or wax, he was in danger of death.

Saint Hildegard of Bingen (1136) exorcised the demon of love with mandragora. **19.** Johanna Rhode (1526) suggested the following prayer for a woman whose domestic happiness was interfered with by demons: ''Mandragora, I pray to thee to keep my cruel husband from doing any harm to me.''

Because of its real or fancied resemblance to a human being, mandrake from **20.** time immemorial was sought as a sexual stimulant in cases of impotence. Rachel, who desired to have children, purchased it from Leah at the price of Jacob's spending the night in Leah's tent. The fact that mandragora is a sedative rather than an aphrodisiac supports the less common view that Rachel was preparing for childbirth and she desired to secure mandrake to ease her pains. Mandrake is still used in the Near East for sterility, but also to assure an easy delivery. The close proximity of the ancient Hebrews to the Egyptians and Babylonians, who employed narcotics extensively, also suggested that the plant might have been employed purely for its actual physiological action and not for any of the mystical properties ascribed to it. Certainly Rachel, no longer young at the time of her first pregnancy, might well have expected a great deal of difficulty during labor.

Whether or not this interpretation be accepted, the words of such writers as 21. Dioscorides, Scrapion, and Isidorus, as well as the description by Theocritus of the birth of Ptolemy Philadelphus, leave no room for doubt that the usual employment of mandragora was as a general narcotic and that the use of narcosis in childbirth was not unknown to the ancients.

Painless births were reported on the island of Kos as early as 309 B.C. Queen 22. Berenice, mother of Ptolemy Philadelphus and wife of Ptolemy Logus, received some sedative, probably mandragora, during her delivery, as is testified by a contemporary writer: "For then the daughter of Antigone, weighed down with the throes, called out for Lucina, the friend of women in travail, and she with kind favor stood by her, and in sooth poured down her whole limbs an insensibility to pain, and so a lovely boy, like to his father, was born."

R. Campbell Thompson identifies mandrake with the Assyrian "*Namtar Gira*." 23. (Namtar was the god of plague and "*Namtar Gira*" (male) refers to the plant.) According to Ebers, the mandragora of Elephantine was used in Egypt in the manufacture of intoxicating and narcotic drinks and was employed in medicine and magic. Ancient Egyptians, while recognizing that a mysterious fluid circulated through their members which supplied them with health, vigor, and life, thought that its effect was transient; they frequently resorted to mandragora (called "*Sa* of life") to bolster it. Pythagoras referred to mandrake as anthropomorphic. The encyclopedist and agriculturist, Columella, alluded to it as being semi-human. Hildegard said it was fashioned out of the earth whereof God made Adam.

The medicinal properties of mandragora were recognized by Hippocrates, who 24. asserted that a small dose in wine, less than would occasion delirium, relieves depression and anxiety. Aristotle included mandragora, poppies (known in occult sciences as the "tears of the moon"), and darnel (rey grass) among the remedies that induce slumber. The Greeks ascribed to mandragora the power of exciting passionate love, and when mixed in wine or vinegar, the ability to promote conception.

Celsus recommended mandrake in headache, ulcerations, dyspnea, inflammation 25. of the womb, pains in the hip, liver, and spleen, hysterical fits, and loss of voice in females.

Mandrake played a prominent part in Roman medicine. Dioscorides (40–90 A.D.), 26. a surgeon of the army of Nero, used it, mixed in wine, as an anesthetic for surgical operations.

Pliny Secundus stated: "It is a well-ascertained fact that the root of mandragora 27. beaten up with oil and wine is a curative for defluxions and pains of the eyes, and, indeed, the juice of these plants forms an ingredient in many medicaments for the eyes. . . . When persons are about to gather this plant they take every precaution not to have the wind blowing in their faces; after tracing three circles around it with a sword they turn towards the west and dig it up. There are some marvelous effects related in connection with this plant. The root of it is said to bear a strong resemblance to the organs of either sex. . . . If a root resembling the male organ should happen to fall in the way of a man it will insure him of women's love. Hence it is that Phoan, the Lesbian, was so passionately beloved by Sappho.''

The traditions and legends about mandrake continued to accumulate rapidly in **28.** the early centuries of the present era, reaching a zenith in the Middle Ages, during which period it was considered a panacea for all evils, although its main therapeutic effects were still considered to be hypnotic and aphrodisiac.

In Germany, this manlike root was regarded as a talisman of great value. Women **29.** carried it as an amulet against sterility, as a charm to insure prosperity, and for other magical purposes. Many of the mandrake charms sold were spurious, having been made from different roots that were artificially shaped into a mannikin. In the Imperial Library of Vienna, several of these specimens have been reposing since 1680. They belonged to Emperor Rudolph II.

One of the most extraordinary specimens, presented by Charles Hatchett, may **30.** be observed in the museum of the Royal College of Surgeons in London. It consists of twin mannikins quaintly shaped to resemble heavily bearded human faces, having eyes, noses, foreheads, and hands accurately depicted.

In Palestine, Syria, and the rest of the Near East, there is still a flourishing **31.** business carried on with human-shaped roots. The artificial mandrake in Syria is often preferred to the genuine roots of the plant.

Mandrake has played an important part in classical English literature. Shakespeare **32.** makes many references to mandragora. In Othello, Iago remarks:

> "Not poppy nor mandragora,
>   Nor all the drowsy syrups of the world,
>   Shall ever medicine thee to that sweet sleep,
>   Which they owdst yesterday.''

Again, in Romeo and Juliet, Shakespeare refers to the terrible shrieks heard when **33.** uprooting the plant:

> "What with loathsome smells,
>   And shrieks like mandrakes torn out of earth,
>   That living mortals hearing them run mad.''

In Anthony and Cleopatra, the latter is made to exclaim: **34.**

> "Give me to drink mandragora
>   That I might sleep out this great gap of time
>   My Anthony is away.''

Besides mandragora the poppy plant has been recognized from early antiquity **35.** to possess medicinal properties. The famous botanist, Dioscorides, who lived about two thousand years ago, had this to say with reference to the poppy plant, "When in the morning the dew has vanished, the stigma disks and the lateral surfaces of the poppy heads are carefully incised with a knife. The issuing juice is stripped off with the finger, and put into an oblong bowl. After the juice has thickened, it is thoroughly kneaded and formed into cakes.'' Most ancient lethargics and soporifics probably contained poppy juice or opium, which is obtained from the unripe capsule of the poppy.

In the "Jew of Malta" Marlowe puts in the mouth of Barbas: **36.**

"I drank poppy and cold mandrake juice;
    And being asleep, belike they thought me dead
    And threw me over the walls."

WORKING WITH THE TEXT

Cultural and Historical References

In this section, the numbers at the margin refer to the numbered paragraphs
in the selection itself.

2. Tobit is one of the books of the Apocrypha in the Protestant Bible; it is
   one of the authorized, or canonical books, in the Catholic Bible.

5. A "leeche" is an old spelling for that sluglike creature that lives in
   ponds, where it attaches itself to anything that swims by and sucks its
   blood. In the old days, doctors used them to remove blood from their
   patients. They are still used occasionally to draw blood from capillaries.

5. At one time "mete" signified any food.

10. "Falling sickness" is an old term for epilepsy.

13. The root of the ginseng is still collected in Kentucky and other Southern
    states, where it is shipped to the Far East as an elixir to rouse flagging
    spirits, sexual and otherwise.

20. This episode with the mandrake occurs in Genesis 30:14–16.

27. The Greek poetess Sappho was thought to be a lesbian.

Writing Assignments: The Paragraph

Be sure to provide an introduction for each of the following paragraph writing
assignments. That is, begin each paragraph with a phrase like this: "Thomas
Brickle claims that. . . ." When it is relevant, you might also want to identify
the expertise of the author ("Thomas Brickle, a New Testament scholar,
claims that. . . ."), the name of the book or article, the century and country
in which the work appeared, or any other circumstances that your readers
might find significant. For more on this, see pp. 11–13 in Chapter 2.

1. In a paragraph, summarize this work by Gordon.

2. Explain the theory of signature, citing Gordon as your authority.

3. Describe the mandrake and its uses.

Writing Assignments: The Short Essay

Use informal documentation for these short essays. That is, don't use footnotes or a Works Cited page to document your sources. Instead, cite only

relevant information about your source, and keep that information *within* your text. Then follow the summary or quote with a page number in parenthesis. (Use the page numbers that you find in this book to represent the page numbers of the source.) Thus, your informal documentation will look something like this:

> In *The Romance of Medicine*, Benjamin Gordon, a professor of history, says that red wine was once believed to replenish a person's depleted blood supply (p. 121).

1. Write a paper that is sympathetic to the concept of signatures. The germ theory of disease, after all, wasn't discovered until the time of Louis Pasteur in the middle of the nineteenth century, so physicians were working in the dark. Besides, some of these treatments did alleviate symptoms.

2. Perhaps you know of a folk cure yourself. If you do, write an essay in which you combine your knowledge with material in this piece by Gordon. Devise your own thesis.

3. Look up the mandrake root episode in Genesis, in particular the "fertility contest" between Rachel and Leah, and write a paper on the unconscious humor in the story. Use something from the account in Gordon's essay within your essay.

AGAINST THE STOPWATCH

Ernest S. Turner

It's not easy to resist flinching as we contemplate a time when, without anesthetics, surgeons amputated legs, carved off women's breasts, and opened up body cavities. Reading this selection from Ernest Turner's essay might be enough to keep a person awake for a few nights contemplating the agony—and the fortitude—that accompanied humanity's accidents and diseases through most of our history.

The surgeons were passing through a frustrating phase. In spite of the limitless **1.** orgies of dissection in which they were supposed to have been indulging, many of them had inadequate knowledge of the human frame. John Bell in his *Principles of Surgery* (1826), has an alarming picture of the novice surgeon at work, 'faltering and disconcerted, hesitating at every step . . . agitated, miserable and trembling.' He continues:

'We see <u>untaught</u> men operating upon their fellow creatures in cases of life and **2.** death, in aneurism, lithotomy, hernia, trepan, without the slightest knowledge of the anatomy of the parts . . . feeling in the wound for things they do not understand, holding consultations amid the cries of the patient, or even retiring to consult about his case, while he lies bleeding in great pain and <u>awful</u> expectation; and thus, while

Source: Ernest S. Turner, "Against the Stopwatch," *Call the Doctor*. New York: St. Martin's Press, 1959. 175–178.

Note the language here

they are making ungenerous struggles to gain a false reputation, they are incurring reproachs which attend them through life.'

Bell deprecated the passion for operations which had characterised some of the surgeons of an earlier day—'as the cutting off of limbs, the searing of arteries, the sewing of bowels, the trepanning of skulls round and round, and all the excesses and horrors of surgery.' He deplored too, the vogue for 'mere whiffling agility' and the emphasis on speed 'merely to gratify the fools who estimate dexterity by no other criterion than the stopwatch.' A surgeon, he said, should cut swiftly when all is safe, slowly and cautiously when there is danger, 'yet we every day see surgeons cutting out harmless tumours with affected and cruel deliberation, and in the same hour plunging a gorget among the viscera with unrelenting rashness.'   **3.**

No doubt there was a certain amount of exhibitionism in the operating theatre. Yet a surgeon aware of the torture he was inflicting on an unanaesthetised patient could hardly be blamed for working with utmost speed and taking pride in saying to his audience, like Robert Liston, 'Now, gentlemen, time me.' Liston, who was said to have had a wrist strong enough to screw off a man's head, could amputate a leg at the thigh, single-handed, compressing the artery with his left hand, 'in as few seconds as a first-class sprinter takes to run a hundred yards.' Another surgeon was reputed to have taken off an arm at the shoulder while his colleague turned for a pinch of snuff.   **4.**

This rapidity of action makes it slightly, but only very slightly, easier to comprehend the stoicism of those whose limbs were removed while they were fully conscious. Very occasionally, an impressionable patient might be put into a trance, in the fashion popularised by Mesmer, before undergoing a minor operation, but for the majority there was no such release. Flesh might be numbed by tourniquets, or by chilling, but neither rum nor opiate sufficed wholly to still the imagination of the victim, especially if he listened to the surgeon telling his audience what he proposed to do. Soldiers and sailors, born to hardship, could face the ordeal of amputation more stolidly than the delicately nurtured, allowing their limbs to be lopped with little more than a grimace. At Corunna Sir David Baird was injured in his left arm near the shoulder, in such a way that the ordinary method of amputation was impossible and it was necessary to remove the arm from the socket. Baird sat at a table, on which he rested his right arm. Only when the left arm was finally severed from the body did he make a single exclamation of pain. Lord Raglan's cry to the surgeon at Waterloo has become a legend—'Here, don't take that arm away until I have taken the ring off the finger!' General Sir Harry Smith hobbled round with a ball embedded under the Achilles tendon of his foot. When the time for operating came he cocked his leg on the table and said to the surgeons, 'There it is, slash away.' The ball was jagged and the fibres had partly grown into it. Thus, the five-minute operation involved both extraction and dissection. A pair of forceps was broken in the process. There were examples of equal courage among the lower ranks, but there was rarely a chronicler standing by. To keep the whole business in perspective, it is worth remembering, as one chronicler has pointed out, that the pain from the initial incision from lithotomy was probably no greater than that sustained from one blow of the lash—and an errant soldier might be ordered to receive 500.   **5.**

So much for soldiers. But women, too, showed a daunting fortitude under the knife. A not infrequent operation was amputation, or partial amputation, of the breast,   **6.**

a task which was made no easier for the surgeon before Sir Astley Cooper's day because modesty allowed only the minimum area of the bosom to be exposed. There is a description of such an operation in that best-selling tale, *Rab And His Friends*, by Dr John Brown, of Biggar. The patient was an elderly Scotswoman identified only as Ailie. Young Brown, then a clerk at Minto House Hospital, Edinburgh, himself put up the notice, 'An Operation Today,' which served to pack the theatre with eager, noisy students. As Ailie walked in with her husband *and dog* one glance at her simple dignity was enough to reduce the audience to silence. The husband withdrew to a corner of the room and held the dog's head between his knees. Stretched on the table, Ailie took a quick look at her husband, closed her eyes and held young Brown's hand. During the operation the dog sensed that his mistress was suffering cruelly and gave an occasional angry yelp. His master had to hold him firmly under restraint. Ailie's face showed what she was suffering but she remained still and silent. When it was over and the wound was dressed she stepped down from the table, turned to the surgeon and students, then curtseyed, begging their pardon if she had behaved ill. The students wept like children. Ailie died shortly afterwards; she had waited too long for the surgeon to have a fair chance of saving her.

7. Another description of a breast operation, though the word breast is never mentioned, appears in Samuel Warren's *Diary of a Late Physician* (1832), one of the first popular works purporting to give glimpses from a doctor's private records. In Warren's account, the patient, a naval officer's wife, awaits the surgeon in her home, sitting in a chair in a white muslin dressing gown with an Indian shawl over her shoulders. She has sent the servants out of the house. The medical attendants pour her a glass of port, but she barely touches the glass with her lips. One of the attendants removes the shawl, and the patient then displaces as much of the dress as necessary. She looks fixedly over her shoulder at a letter from her husband, which is held there for the purpose. At the first incision she gives a convulsive shudder, and seems likely to faint, but after that she barely moves a limb or sighs. When it is over she proposes to walk to her bedroom, but is told she must be carried. Only when she is in bed does she swoon. Warren's style is melodramatic and often nauseous, and his book did not please the medical profession; but there is no doubt that the operation he describes was commonly carried out in very much that fashion. It was after watching the agony of a Highland woman undergoing a breast amputation that young James Simpson left the classroom in horror and went straight to Parliament House, Edinburgh, to seek work as a writer's clerk. Then he changed his mind and returned, saying, 'Can nothing be done to make operations less painful?'

WORKING WITH THE TEXT

Cultural and Historical References

In this and the next section, the numbers at the margin refer to the numbered paragraphs in the selection itself.

5. Franz Mesmer's last name has given rise to an English word. Can you guess what it is?

Writing Assignments: The Paragraph

Be sure to provide an introduction for each of the following paragraph writing assignments. That is, begin each paragraph with a phrase like this: "Thomas Brickle claims that. . . ." When it is relevant, you might also want to identify the expertise of the author ("Thomas Brickle, a New Testament scholar, claims that. . . ."), the name of the book or article, the century and country in which the work appeared, or any other circumstances that your readers might find significant. For more on this, see pp. 11–13 in Chapter 2.

1. Paraphrase paragraph 5. Quote Lord Raglan's cry somewhere within your paraphrase.

2. Paraphrase and quote from paragraph 6. Be sure to note that Turner got the details of the operation described here from a book called *Rab and His Friends*. A paraphraser lets the reader know that sort of thing. Can you tell if *Rab and His Friends* is fiction or nonfiction? (It's not easy.)

3. Write a paragraph in which you describe one particular person's fortitude as he or she underwent a surgical operation before the invention of effective anesthetics. Use a quote in your paragraph.

Writing Assignments: The Short Essay

Use informal documentation for these short essays. That is, don't use footnotes or a Works Cited page to document your sources. Instead, cite only relevant information about your source, and keep that information *within* your text. Then follow the summary or quote with a page number in parenthesis. (Use the page numbers that you find in this book to represent the page numbers of the source.) Thus, your informal documentation will look something like this:

> In *The Romance of Medicine*, Benjamin Gordon, a history professor, claims that it was once believed that red wine replenished a person's depleted blood supply (p. 121).

1. If you've ever undergone an operation, no matter how small, compare your operation with the operations performed on the patients in Turner's account.

2. Write a report in which you use two sources, this essay and a work you find in the library, to describe methods of deadening pain to prepare men and women for pre-nineteenth-century surgery.

3. Write a two-page summary, with quotes, of "Against the Stopwatch."

JEERS AND CHAOS

Ernest S. Turner

"For God's sake, let us sit upon the ground / And tell sad stories of the death of kings." Those words spoken by Shakespeare's Richard II might serve as a preface to this selection by Ernest Turner, who tells the sad story of the death of Charles II, England's "merry monarch" during the days of the Restoration. Before science began to offer treatments that actually worked, everyone—kings and peasants alike—suffered excruciating pain at the hands of physicians. Because physicians might be rewarded handsomely for curing a king, they were eager to try anything that might work. As a result, this essay offers brief descriptions of some of the most up-to-date orthodox medical treatments in the late seventeenth century.

1. The seventeenth century was a peculiarly difficult one for the English Court physicians, who were reduced to unseemly shifts to disguise the inadequacies of their knowledge. It was, of course, no easier for the Sun King's physicians, who had to conceal the fact of their young sovereign's syphilis not only from the public but from the patient himself, and who covered up an embarrassing attack of royal measles by issuing announcements of the expulsion of voracious, but fictitious, tapeworms from the royal body.

2. When James I's son Prince Henry lay dying the physicians could not agree on his treatment. Some, it appears, were reluctant to drain off too much royal blood. Others argued that 'in this case of extremity they must (if they meant to save his life) proceed in the cure as though he was some meane person.' Screwing up their courage, they bisected a cock and laid the reeking halves to the soles of the royal feet. Eventually James gave Sir Theodore Mayerne *carte blanche* to do what he liked; a risky step, since Mayerne was wont to prescribe nightmare items from gibbet and graveyard. For once, however, the physician declined to draw on his fund of novelties. He informed the King that he would never do anything unless on the advice of the other doctors, not wishing it to be said of him that he had slain the King's eldest son.

3. Among sad stories of the deaths of kings, the account of Charles II's last days is a horror-comic. When the monarch fell ill on a Sunday evening of a kidney disease, accompanied by convulsions, Dr Edmund King was faced with the decision of whether to bleed him without consent of the chief ministers of the Crown, well aware that the penalty for such an act was death. Nevertheless, he acted. For his presence of mind as much as for his strength of purpose the Privy Council voted him £1,000, which he never received, the award being commuted to a knighthood. Not long was Dr King alone with his patient; the number of physicians built up to a dozen and more, dwindling to six at night. For five days, under Sir Charles Scarborough, they used the King with vastly more vigour than they would have applied to a mean person. Macaulay's view was that they tortured him like an Indian at the stake. To drain off his blood they put cupping glasses to his shoulders, scarified his flesh and tapped his veins. Then they cut off his hair and laid blisters on the scalp, and on the soles of his feet they applied plasters of pitch and pigeon dung. To remove the humours from his brain they blew hellebore up his nostrils and set him sneezing. To make him sick they poured antimony and sulphate of zinc down his throat. To clear his bowels they gave him strong purgatives and a brisk succession of clisters. To allay his convulsions they gave him spirit of human skull. To lower his temperature they administered Peruvian bark. At various times they gave him juleps for his spasms, a gargle for his sore throat, soothing draughts to temper his thirst, tonics for his heart and ale and light broth for his

Source: Ernest S. Turner, "Jeers and Chaos," *Call the Doctor.* New York: St. Martin's Press, 1959. 43–45.

nourishment. Into the scarred and blistered hulk of a king they sent, now sedatives, now depth charges; cowslip, manna and mint, then Raleigh's antidote, with its animal, vegetable and mineral contents. Lest they be accused of neglect, they even administered bezoar. When the hulk slept, they woke it; when it spoke, they silenced it. In and out of the chamber passed physicians, priests, ministers, servants. On the Thursday night the King's mind was clear and undimmed. On the Friday morning they drew twelve more ounces of weak Stuart blood and then gave him heart tonics. He did not give in until noon, after apologising for being so long in dying. 'Three things only they denied him,' says Sir Arthur Bryant, 'light, rest and privacy; nothing else was left untried.' Sir Arthur is wrong; they did not try that stomach brush.

It is tempting to speculate how this gallant band would have risen to the challenge   **4.** which Louis XIV presented to his medical advisers in the following year. He was suffering severely from an anal fistula, the complaint which had carried off Richelieu. Among physicians and surgeons alike there was something like panic, for the operation to relieve this condition was but indifferently known. The only authority who could have tackled it confidently, John of Arderne, had been dead 300 years. As weeping crowds flocked to the churches, Charles François Felix experimented on hospital patients who were similarly afflicted and devised an instrument to make the operation less painful. Then, at seven o'clock one morning, Felix operated on the Sun King, who made no exclamation. At eight o'clock, though confined to bed, he held his morning reception as usual. Both monarch and surgeon could feel pride in the occasion. In Louis's eyes, surgery was now a liberal art, to be liberally rewarded. Felix, in whom the ordeal left a permanent tremble, received a sum of about £15,000, a country estate and a patent of nobility. He was now the only landed nobleman in France to treat for anal fistula.

William III seems to have suffered not only from the attentions of his physicians   **5.** but from their impertinence. In 1697 Dr John Radcliffe, whom the King paid 600 guineas a year, told him: 'Your juices are all vitiated, your whole mass of blood corrupted and the nutriment for the most part turned to water. But if your Majesty will forbear making long visits to the Earl of Bradford (a convivial peer) I will engage to make you live three or four years longer; but beyond that no physic can protect your Majesty's existence.' (The King died five years later.) In 1699 the King showed his swollen ankles to Radcliffe and asked, 'Doctor, what think you of these?' The reply was, 'Why, truly, I would not have your Majesty's legs for your three kingdoms.' The jest seems to have been ill received. . . .

WORKING WITH THE TEXT

Cultural and Historical References

In this section, the numbers at the margin refer to the numbered paragraphs in the selection itself.

1. The Sun King is Louis XIV, who ruled France from 1643 to 1715.
2. What do you suppose the "nightmare" items from the gibbet and graveyard consisted of? What does it mean to be given *carte blanche*

permission? Why is *carte blanche* in italics? How does one represent italics in writing?

3. "Cupping glasses" were glass cups which were evacuated of their air by heating. They were applied to the patient's skin in order to draw blood up to, and sometimes through, the surface. "Bezoar," an intestinal mass found mainly in ruminants like deer and cattle, was at this time used as an antidote for poison. See H. S. Glasscheib's essay, "The Four Juices," for a description of humours.

4. The author, Ernest Turner, is an Englishman, and they do things a bit differently in the British Isles than we do here. How do their typographical conventions concerning brackets and quotation marks differ from ours?

Writing Assignments: The Paragraph

Be sure to provide an introduction for each of the following paragraph writing assignments. That is, begin each paragraph with a phrase like this: "Thomas Brickle claims that. . . ." When it is relevant , you might also want to identify the expertise of the author ("Thomas Brickle, a New Testament scholar, claims that. . . ."), the name of the book or article, the century and country in which the work appeared, or any other circumstances that your readers might find significant. For more on this, see pp. 11–13 in Chapter 2.

1. Write a paragraph on the difference between England and the United States in the use of parentheses and quotation marks. (See paragraph 5.) If you need to, reread Chapter 3, pp. 39–43.

2. Write a paraphrase of paragraph 4. Look carefully at Turner's clever topic sentence, but write a straightforward one for your summary. Find a word or phrase to quote. (This won't be easy.) Why would you not want to quote "anal fistula"?

Writing Assignments: The Short Essay

Use informal documentation for these short essays. That is, don't use footnotes or a Works Cited page to document your sources. Instead, cite only relevant information about your source, and keep that information *within* your text. Then follow the summary or quote with a page number in parenthesis. (Use the page numbers that you find in this book to represent the page numbers of the source.) Thus, your informal documentation will look something like this:

> In *The Romance of Medicine*, Benjamin Gordon, a history professor, claims that it was once believed that red wine replenished a person's depleted blood supply (p. 121).

1. In Genesis 15:7–21 there is a story in which God, in the form of a fire pot, moves between the halves of a bisected animal. God's action seems

to be part of a solemn convenant with Abraham. Write an essay in which you offer an explanation for that episode. (Of course, you will need an annotated Bible, a Bible dictionary, or a Bible commentary for this assignment. In that way you can turn mere speculation into informed speculation.) Then describe the similar action in Turner's paragraph 2 and point out that there might be a connection between the two. You'll have to speculate, of course, about the purpose of bisecting an animal.

2. Write a short paper in which you describe and analyze Turner's use of thesis statement and topic sentences. (Turner's thesis statement doesn't encompass *all* paragraphs in this piece. Discuss that "problem" as well.)

3. Combining information in Turner's essay with information in "The Four Juices," write a short report that describes and exemplifies the use of bloodletting by physicians.

"I GAVE HIM BARKS AND SALTPETER. . . ."

Paul Russell Cutright

Paul Cutright's description of the medical problems and treatment on the Lewis and Clark expedition is, in effect, a description of the state of medicine in early nineteenth-century America. Considering the crude medicine of the day, it's surprising to learn that only one person died on the entire expedition. Cutright is a professor of biology at Beaver College in Pennsylvania and the author of two books: *The Great Naturalists Explore South America* and *Theodore Roosevelt the Naturalist.*

On February 23, 1803, Thomas Jefferson wrote the following letter to Dr. Benjamin **1.** Rush, professor of the Institute of Medicine at the University of Pennsylvania and the foremost American physician of his day:

Dear Sir: I wish to mention to you in confidence that I have obtained authority from Congress to undertake the long desired object of exploring the Missouri & whatever river, heading with that, leads into the Western ocean. About 10 chosen woodsmen headed by Capt. Lewis my secretary will set out on it immediately & probably accomplish it in two seasons. . . . It would be very useful to state for him those objects on which it is most desirable he should bring us information. For this purpose I ask the favor of you to prepare some notes of such particulars as may occur in his journey & which you think should draw his attention & enquiry. He will be in Philadelphia about 2 or 3 weeks hence & will wait on you.

As Jefferson stated to Rush, he had just obtained from Congress the necessary **2.** authorization to send a party to explore the unknown reaches of the Missouri River

Source: Paul Russell Cutright, " 'I gave him barks and saltpeter . . .' " *American Heritage.* December 1963: 58–60, 94–101.

and to find a route to the Pacific. To lead this party he had selected Captain Meriwether Lewis—who would, in turn, ask William Clark, the brother of George Rogers Clark, to share the demanding duties of command. Jefferson's letter to Dr. Rush also suggests that the President, who planned each step of the expedition with almost preternatural care, gave no serious thought at any time to engaging the services of a physician, being content to let Lewis and Clark handle whatever ills and miseries might befall the party.

This decision may have been made easier by his familiarity with Lewis' family **3.** background. Lewis' mother was a well-known Virginia herb doctor who had her own herb garden, grew and dispensed her own simples, and ministered regularly and faithfully to the sick of Albemarle County. Lewis shared his mother's interest in herbs and herb therapy and had acquired much of her knowledge. Clark also had medical training of sorts. Like Lewis, he carried in his head the usual frontiersman's storehouse of medical information: how to set a broken limb or remove an imbedded bullet, how to cope with croup, dysentery, and a wide range of other ailments. Being often closer to disease and disaster than to doctors, he found it imperative to know such things.

As Jefferson originally planned it, the expedition was too small to include a **4.** doctor; but his willingness to entrust medical matters to Lewis and Clark was no doubt also inspired by his own lack of sympathy with the physicians of his day. Living in the era of depleting remedies—purges, vomits, sweats, blisters—and of the bloodletting lancet, which was still by far the most-used medical instrument, Jefferson had good reason to distrust doctors. And yet, he did not hesitate to ask Dr. Rush to advise Lewis on medical matters relating to the expedition. Not long after the President had done so, Rush wrote back to say that he had furnished Lewis with "some inquiries relative to the natural history of the Indians," and "a few short directions for the preservation of his health." The latter present an interesting lesson in personal hygiene as it obtained early in the last century:

> When you feel the least indisposition, do not attempt to overcome it by labour or marching. Rest in a horizontal posture. Also fasting and diluting drinks for a day or two will generally prevent an attack of fever.
> To these preventatives of disease may be added a gentle sweat obtained by warm drinks, or gently opening the bowels by means of one, two, or more of the purging pills.
>
> Unusual costiveness [constipation] is often a sign of approaching disease. When you feel it take one or more of the purging pills. Want of appetite is likewise a sign of approaching indisposition. It should be obviated by the same remedy.
>
> In difficult and laborious enterprises and marches, eating sparingly will enable you to bear them with less fatigue & less danger to your health.
>
> Flannel should be worn constantly next to the skin, especially in wet weather.
>
> The less spirit you use the better. After being *wetted* or *much* fatigued, or *long* exposed to the night air, it should be taken in an *undiluted* state . . .
>
> Molasses or sugar & water with a few drops of the acid of vitriol

[sulphuric acid] will make a pleasant & wholsome drink with your
meals.

   After having had your feet much chilled, it will be useful to wash
them with a little spirit.

   Washing the feet every morning in *cold* water, will conduce very
much to fortify them against the action of cold.

   After long marches, or much fatigue from any cause, you will be
more refreshed by lying down in a horizontal posture for two hours,
than by resting a longer time in any other position of the body.

Rush would have been pained to learn how many of these rules Lewis and Clark **5.**
totally disregarded. They ignored his injunctions to rest for two whole hours in a
horizontal position with each indisposition and to wash their feet in cold water every
morning. The idea of fasting to make difficult marches less fatiguing held no appeal
for them whatever. Nor do we find in any of the journals mention of that "pleasant &
wholsome" drink compounded of sweetened water and sulphuric acid.

   Lewis and Clark's original budget was $2,500. Of this total, $90.69 went for **6.**
medicines. According to one calculation, their purchases included 1,300 doses of
physic, 1,100 of emetic, 3,500 of diaphoretic (sweat-inducer), and fifteen pounds of
febrifuge (fever-reducer), not to mention sizable amounts of drugs for blistering,
salivation, and increased kidney output. Thus equipped with everything from camphor
and calomel to tourniquets and clyster syringes, the medical team of Lewis and Clark
seemed ready for almost any contingency.

   Their historic journey to the Pacific began at the frontier town of St. Charles, **7.**
Missouri, on May 21, 1804. The expedition, consisting of some forty men, travelled
in three vessels, a fifty-five-foot keelboat and two smaller craft called pirogues. Lewis
and Clark would not see St. Charles again until September 21, 1806, two years and
four months later.

   They were a month and a half out of St. Charles before they encountered their **8.**
first potentially serious medical problem. On Wednesday, July 4, 1804, Clark wrote:
"ussered in the day by a discharge of one shot from our Bow piece . . . passed the
Mouth of a Bayeau . . . Came to on the L.S. [larboard side] to refresh ourselves & Jos.
Fields got bit by a Snake."

   This incident occurred north of present-day Atchison, Kansas, near the mouth of **9.**
a small stream which Lewis and Clark, in honor of the day, called Independence Creek,
the name it still bears. The snake that bit Joseph Fields was apparently innocuous. But
since the party was now on unfamiliar terrain where snakes might belie their appearance,
Lewis took no chances when he treated Fields, and applied a poultice of bark and
gunpowder.

   The frontiersman of that day employed many remedies for snake bite, their very **10.**
multiplicity affording the best evidence possible that none was entirely effective. Mark
Twain was conversant with one of the most common. Readers of *Huckleberry Finn*
will recall how Nigger Jim, after being struck by a rattler, grabbed the whiskey jug
and "begun to pour it down." This was one remedy the victims of snake bite found
inviting, and great faith was placed in its ability to neutralize snake venom. Doctors
as well as laymen regarded it as a sure-fire antidote. This belief was not only false but

dangerous: by speeding the flow of blood, alcohol only hastens distribution and absorption of the venom.

The great majority of the remedies employed for snake bite were in the form of **11.** poultices. Favorite materials included garlic, onions, radishes, freshly chewed tobacco, and a wide range of other plants. Poultices of bark and gunpowder, such as Lewis applied, also were used. A poultice today is something of an anachronism, like the powder horn and the potbellied stove. As a general rule it consisted of a warm mass of a glutinous or oleaginous material—bread, lard, corn meal, bran, macerated plant material—which, combined with substances of reputed therapeutic value, was spread on a small piece of cloth and applied to the afflicted part. Doctors of the day thought that poultices would not only draw out the poison or other cause of inflammation but also act as a painkiller, antiseptic, and counterirritant. In those days, panaceas were almost as common as infirmities.

Physicians, however, did not regularly use gunpowder as a therapeutic agent. **12.** Explorers, Indian fighters, and frontiersmen regarded it more highly, especially for snake bite. They were known on occasion to slash the bite, pour gunpowder on it, and then set fire to the powder. Many of them used gunpowder as a medicine because they had nothing else available. Some wounds thus treated undoubtedly healed, and, using *post hoc* reasoning, the victims unhesitatingly gave credit to the powder instead of to Mother Nature.

The bark employed by Lewis in treating Joseph Fields could have been that of **13.** the slippery elm (*Ulmus fulva*), the inner part of which is mucilaginous and was much used in poultices during the last century. But Lewis and Clark had with them fifteen pounds of pulverized Peruvian bark (cinchona), and when anyone used the word "bark" in those days, it almost always meant cinchona.

Cinchona, which contains quinine, was used for a wide assortment of diseases **14.** and afflictions, ranging from measles, dysentery, and dropsy to carbuncles and "ill-conditioned ulcers." One-third of Lewis and Clark's medical outlay had gone into pulverized Peruvian bark, an indication of their high regard for it.

The seventh of July, 1804, along that part of the wide Missouri just below the **15.** mouth of the Platte must have been a day of pitiless, penetrating heat. Clark wrote: "one man verry sick, Struck with the Sun, Capt. Lewis bled him & gave Niter which has revived him much."

The niter employed here in treating sunstroke was potassium nitrate, better known **16.** as saltpeter. Even today its usefulness as a diuretic and diaphoretic—for increasing urine discharge and inducing sweats—is recognized, though other drugs are more commonly employed for those purposes. Lewis and Clark had two pounds of saltpeter with them and used it in treating a variety of unrelated disorders.

Saltpeter may have been a relatively harmless remedy, but bloodletting was **17.** not—in fact, it may well have killed more patients than it cured. For centuries, beginning even before Hippocrates and continuing almost to the present, doctors believed that practically every malady known to man, from pleurisy and scarlatina to bilious fevers and bubonic plague, could be treated effectively by drawing off blood. The practitioners of this sanguinary art included not only the physician but also the apothecary, the bath keeper, even the barber—hence the blood-red stripes on his barber pole. Many used leeches, and were known as leech doctors, while others insisted on the sharp-edged lancet. Some had a device known as a scarificator, a box-shaped instrument that made several incisions instead of the lancet's one.

Regardless of what instrument he used, the bloodletter meant business. Disease **18.** was serious and demanded vigorous action. With a few, the stock apothegm was, "Bleed until syncope," which meant in essence, draw blood until the patient is unconscious. Those who survived did so, of course, in spite of bleeding; today doctors rarely resort to the treatment. It is sometimes indicated in *polycythemia vera*, a rare disease in which the number of red blood cells has increased abnormally, and in certain grave heart and lung disorders where reducing blood volume is beneficial. Too, bleeding occasionally does seem beneficial for sunstroke. According to Dr. William Osler, the famous teacher at Johns Hopkins, "In the cases in which the symptoms are those of intense asphyxia, and in which death may take place in a few minutes, free bleeding should be practiced . . ." But whether or not the treatment helped the sunstroke victim of the Lewis and Clark expedition, it is impossible to say.

Soon after, however, tragedy struck for the first and only time during the whole **19.** journey to the Pacific and back. On July 31, just above the mouth of the Platte, Sergeant Charles Floyd noted in his journal, "I am verry Sick and Has been for Sometime but have Recovered my helth again." But his recovery was only temporary. Three weeks later, on August 19, Clark wrote: "Serjeant Floyd is taken verry bad all at once with a Biliose Chorlick we attempt to relieve him without success as yet, he gets worst and we are much allarmed at his Situation . . ." Nothing, Clark said, would "Stay a moment on his Stomach or bowels."

The next day Sergeant Floyd died, probably of a ruptured, gangrenous appendix. **20.** The journals reveal nothing of measures attempted to save his life. The odds are that Lewis both bled Floyd and purged him with laxatives. If he did the latter, it may well have hastened Floyd's death, either by rupturing the appendix or by adding to the inflammatory material already in the peritoneal cavity. In any event, Lewis' efforts were to no avail; probably the best medical talent of that day could not have saved the sergeant, for surgery then was almost entirely limited to the surface of the body. It was not until 1887 that the first appendectomy was performed by Dr. John Morton in Philadelphia.

The Lewis and Clark expedition passed the first winter in a hastily built but **21.** sturdy stockade, Fort Mandan, near the mouth of the Knife River, about fifty-five miles above the present Bismarck, North Dakota. Here, for six months, they lived surrounded by some 4,000 aboriginals—Mandans and Minnetarees (Hidatsas). From the very beginning, these Indians exceeded the bounds of what white men considered convention- al hospitality. To the explorers they proffered not only corn, beans, and squash but also wives, daughters, and sisters. To them, as to many other Indian tribes, this was no deviation from rectitude; it was an old, established, and entirely respectable custom. However, even for the Indians there were limits to hospitality, and as the long winter wore on, many of the "squars" began to sell their "favors" for a string of beads, a looking glass, or a piece of ribbon.

Though the Indian men had no scruples about farming their wives out for the **22.** night, they were properly resentful if their offers were turned down without good reason. However, the evidence seems firm that Lewis and Clark themselves refused all such offers. It is most unlikely that they would have cheapened themselves in the eyes of their men in this manner and thus jeopardized the success of their mission.

Lewis and Clark had little to say in their journals about the sexual relations **23.**

between soldiers and squaws, or about the sordid sequelae. On January 14, 1805, at Fort Mandan, Clark noted: "Several men with the venereal cought from the Mandan women." And, a few days later: "one man verry bad with the pox [*i.e.* syphilis]." Again, on March 30, as the expedition prepared to resume the ascent of the Missouri: "Generally helthy except Venerial Complaints which is verry Common amongst the natives and the men Catch it from them."

The expedition leaders had anticipated venereal disease. Both men had served **24.** previous enlistments in the Army, and they knew something of the appetites and frailties of the average soldier. Thus, they carried ample supplies of mercury ointment, calomel (mercurous chloride), balsam copaiba, and *saccharum saturni* (sugar of lead), and they had armed themselves with four pewter urethral syringes. Lewis and Clark, however, make mention only of mercury in their treatment of venereal disease, which meant either mercury ointment or calomel or both. (Dr. Rush regarded mercury as the "Samson of the Materia Medica" in the treatment of syphilis.)

As is well known, syphilis manifests itself in three stages: a primary one extending **25.** from the appearance of the initial sore, a small red papule, or chancre, until the onset of constitutional symptoms; a secondary stage characterized by skin eruptions (the pox); and the tertiary, which shows up much later, often years after the original infection, in the form of general paresis, locomotor ataxia, or other equally grave disorders.

It is highly unlikely that Lewis cured any syphilitic cases using mercury. This **26.** drug may have been effective in clearing up evidences of the primary and secondary stages, but hardly the third. But it is obvious from his statements that Lewis believed that he had cured this disease in his men. For instance, on January 27, 1806, while camped at the mouth of the Columbia River, he said, "Goodrich has recovered from the Louis Veneri [*lues venerea*] which he contracted from an amorous contact with a Chinnook damsel. I cured him as I did Gibson last winter by the use of mercury." However, we note that six months later he admitted: "Goodrich and McNeal are both very unwell with the pox which they contracted last winter with the Chinook women."

If venereal disease was a constant nuisance, subzero weather was the expedition's **27.** most stubborn enemy during the long winter stay at Fort Mandan. On some nights the cold gripped the land so firmly that the sentinels relieved each other every half hour. Many of the men had to be treated for frostbite. Private Whitehouse, for instance, had his feet so badly frozen while scouring the snow-covered plains for game that he had to have a horse bring him in. Another man returned from a trip upriver with his face frostbitten. Indians reported one day that two of their men had frozen to death on the prairie while hunting buffalo.

Another tragic incident had its beginning late one afternoon when an Indian **28.** arived at the fort and was much distressed not to find his thirteen-year-old son there. That night, one of the coldest of the winter, the temperature dropped to forty below. In the morning, with the boy still missing, the Indians of the lower village turned out en masse to hunt for him. At about ten o'clock the boy limped into the fort and reported that he had spent the night in the snow protected only by a buffalo robe. Luckily he had survived, though his feet were badly frozen. A week later Lewis had to turn surgeon when it became necessary to amputate the toes of one of the boy's feet.

In this operation, if Lewis followed custom, he seared the cut surfaces with a hot **29.** iron. This was done to stop hemorrhage rather than to sterilize. With frozen members, however, there was ordinarily a minimum of bleeding if the surgeon cut through the dead tissue immediately beyond the living flesh. Lewis did not sew up the wounds as would be done today. If he had been cutting off a leg above the knee, for example, he might have taken two or three stitches, but not in minor surgery such as the removal of toes. Wounds were never sewed tight then, because they had to be left open to drain and to allow them to heal from inside out. All surgical steps—excision, cauterization, suturing—were taken, of course, without the aid of anaesthesia: back in the "good old days" surgery was a soul-scarring ordeal.

One of the most memorable events of that winter at Fort Mandan was the **30.** appearance of Sacagawea, the Bird Woman, whose name has become almost as familiar to present-day Americans as that of Pocahontas. Sister of a Shoshone chief, she was captured in 1800 by a war party of Minnetarees from the Knife River. In the attack, which took place at Three Forks, Montana, the Minnetarees killed several of the Shoshones and took Sacagawea and a number of other girls and boys prisoner. Some time later, a French trader, Toussaint Charbonneau, made her his wife. Since Charbonneau could speak the language of the Minnetarees, Lewis and Clark hired him as an interpreter. They also took along Sacagawea, thinking that she might be of value to them once they reached her people.

On February 11, 1805, Sacagawea gave birth to a son. Lewis, whose obstetrical **31.** role was a minor one, described the delivery:

> It is worthy of remark that this was the first child which this woman
> had boarn, and as is common in such cases her labour was tedious and
> the pain violent; Mr. Jessome [René Jessaume, a Frenchman the expe-
> dition hired as an interpreter in the Mandan country] informed me that
> he had frequently administered a small portion of the rattle of the rat-
> tlesnake, which he assured me had never failed to produce the desired
> effect, that of hastening the birth of the child; having the rattle of a
> snake by me I gave it to him and he administered two rings of it to the
> woman broken in small pieces with the fingers and added to a small
> quantity of water. Whether this medicine was truly the cause or not I
> shall not undertake to determine, but I was informed that she had not
> taken it more than ten minutes before she brought forth. Perhaps this
> remedy may be worthy of future experiments, but I must confess that I
> want faith as to its efficacy.

The child was christened Jean-Baptiste, though nicknamed Pomp (short for **32.** Pompey). Later Clark called a prominent rock formation on the Yellowstone, Pompey's Pillar. Pomp, with his mother and father, travelled with the party from Fort Mandan to the Pacific and back. He was seriously ill only once, when he was fifteen months old. On May 22, 1806, beside the Clearwater River, as the expedition waited for the melting of the snows in the Bitterroot Mountains, Lewis wrote:

> Charbono's Child is very ill this evening; he is cuting teeth, and for
> several days past has had a violent lax, which having suddonly stoped
> he was attacked with a high fever and his neck and throat are much
> swolen this evening. We gave him a doze of creem of tartar and flour
> of sulpher and applyed a poltice of boiled onions to his neck as warm
> as he could well bear it.

Most probably Pomp's trouble was tonsillitis complicated by an infected cervical **33.**
lymph gland. Lewis and Clark brought him around using not only cream of tartar,
flowers of sulphur, and onion poultices but also clysters (enemas) and a plaster of
basilicon which was, in Clark's words, "a plaster of sarve [salve] made of the rozen
of the long leafed pine, Beeswax and Bears oil mixed."

Cream of tartar (potassium bitartrate) is both diuretic and cathartic. It is best **34.**
known as an ingredient of baking powder. Combining it with flowers of sulphur, an
excellent fungicide and insecticide, would not have altered its effect. Lewis and Clark
probably would have used plain warm water, or water with soap, in the enemas they
gave Pomp.

Two months after the party left Fort Mandan, Sacagawea herself took sick and **35.**
nearly died. Her illness, which neither Lewis nor Clark could positively diagnose,
occurred on that stretch on the Missouri immediately above the mouth of the Marias
River, in present-day Montana. Since Lewis had gone ahead to look for the Great Falls
of the Missouri, Clark had charge of her case at first. He seems to have had no idea
what was wrong with her, but he was attentive and did all he could. On the first day
he bled her, and on the next, her condition having failed to improve, he bled her again.
The operation, he noted, "appeared to be of great service to her." On the fourth day
he gave her "a doste of salts," which seemed to be of no help at all, for the next
morning she was "excessively bad" and her case "somewhat dangerous." She
complained of abdominal pain and was "low spirited." Clark applied a bark poultice
to "her region."

When Lewis rejoined the main party, he found Sacagawea's pulse rapid, irregular, **36.**
and barely perceptible, and her condition "attended with strong nervous symptoms,
that of the twitching of the fingers and leaders of the arm." He immediately took
charge. He continued the "cataplasms [poultices] of bark and laudnum" instituted by
Clark and ordered a cask of mineral water brought from a spring on the opposite side
of the river. He had great faith in the efficacy of this water, since it was highly
impregnated with sulphur and "precisely similar to that of Bowyer's Sulphur Spring
in Virginia." He had Sacagawea drink freely of it and by evening was gratified to find
her pulse stronger and more regular, her nervous symptoms somwhat abated, and her
abdominal pain less severe. He believed that her trouble "originated principally from
an obstruction of the menis [menstrual fluid] in consequence of taking cold."

The next morning Sacagawea was so far improved that she asked for food and **37.**
ate as heartily as Lewis would permit of "broiled buffaloe well seasoned with pepper
and salt and rich soope of the same meat." To the medicine already prescribed, Lewis
now added fifteen drops of oil of vitriol, and considered her in "a fair way to recovery."
And she no doubt would have been if her husband, who had been given specific orders
to watch her, had prevented her from downing a meal of white apples and dried fish,
as a result of which her pains and fever returned. After employing army language to
tell Charbonneau what he thought of him, Lewis went to work on his patient again,
prescribing "broken dozes of diluted nitre [saltpeter] untill it produced perspiration
and at 10 P.M. 30 drops of laudnum." The latter was, of course, a tincture of opium,
widely used in those days to deaden pain and induce sleep. Lewis' customary dose of
thirty drops, about two cubic centimeters or one-half teaspoon, was not a big one; its
effect would probably be similar to that of a quarter-grain injection of morphine.

Although from here on the Indian woman's recovery was rapid and uncomplicat- **38.**
ed, her case seems to have been a prime example of the patient's recovering in spite
of the treatment. Certainly the purging and bleeding could have had no effect upon the
cure except to retard it. How much blood Clark withdrew is speculative. Some of the
doctors of the day removed only four to eight ounces; others were not satisfied until
they had siphoned off from a pint to a quart. Only a few casehardened dissidents were
dead set against withdrawing any at all. The removal of a quart is enough to cause
grogginess in an individual, and taking any more induces fainting spells. Phlebotomists
probably did not often measure the blood accurately; when they had taken what they
thought was enough they applied a tight bandage to stop the flow. Very serious infection
sometimes set in at such wounds, and it was by no means unheard of to have the patient
die as a result.

One harmful effect of excessive bleeding is to reduce the quantity in the blood **39.**
of calcium, magnesium, and potassium. The muscle twitching reported by Lewis in
Sacagawea may very well have been induced by a deficiency of such important
minerals. Also, bleeding in conjunction with purging and fever produces dehydration.
If the considerable amount of mineral water Lewis had his patient drink benefited her
at all, it was because it relieved dehydration and restored vital minerals.

The journals carry many references to dysentery and constipation, "cholick & **40.**
griping," "lax" and "relax," "heaviness of the stomach"—all debilitating conditions
referable to the gastrointestinal tract. Happily for Lewis and Clark, Missouri River
water was not then the devil's brew of topsoil, sewage, and industrial waste it is today.
They drank it neat for months on end. Only now and then did they suspect that it might
be the cause of any of their gastric or intestinal troubles.

For disorders of the digestive tract, Lewis and Clark dispensed pills and doses **41.**
of salts as they saw fit. On May 4, 1805, above the mouth of the Yellowstone, Lewis
wrote, "Joseph Fields was very sick today with the disentary had a high fever I gave
him a dose of Glauber salts, which operated very well, in the evening his fever abated
and I gave him 30 drops of laudnum." Glauber's salt (from J. R. Glauber, the German
chemist who originally prepared it) was sodium sulphate and was, like Epsom salts,
a well-known physic. Lewis and Clark had six pounds of it, which cost ten cents a
pound, and they did not hesitate to use it.

Early in June, 1805, Lewis, with four of his best men, left the mouth of the **42.**
Marias River and started on foot up the north bank of the Missouri. Clark and the rest
of the party followed by boat. Lewis had been "somewhat unwell with the disentary,"
but he set out nevertheless. As the day advanced, he developed a violent pain in the
intestines and a high fever. Since the medical supplies had been left with the main
party, Lewis "resolved to try an experiment with some simples," these being the
medicinal plants with which any good herb doctor would be familiar. His eyes soon
fell on the chockcherry, a small shrub (probably *Prunus virginiana*) that he had
encountered frequently along the Missouri. He had his men gather a number of the
twigs and, after stripping off the leaves, cut the twigs into pieces about two inches in
length. These were then boiled in water "untill a strong black decoction of an astringent
bitter tast was produced." At dusk Lewis drank a pint of this, and about an hour later
downed another. By ten o'clock he was perspiring gently, his pain had left him, and
his fever had abated. That night, all symptoms which had disturbed him having

disappeared, he slept soundly. The next morning at sunrise, fit and refreshed, he took another stiff swig of the drink and resumed his march.

In late July the party arrived at Three Forks, that geographically important site **43.** in southwestern Montana where the Jefferson, Madison, and Gallatin rivers (as Lewis and Clark named them) unite to form the Missouri. Clark was sick, "with high fever . . . & akeing." Upon learning that Clark had not had a bowel movement for several days, Lewis prevailed upon him to bathe his feet and legs in warm water and to take five Rush's pills, which he had "always found sovereign in such cases." The next morning, the medicine having "opperated," Clark felt better.

Rush's pills, a product of the "genius" of Dr. Benjamin Rush, were well-known **44.** in those days and referred to, often with some feeling, as Rush's "thunderbolts." Each consisted of ten grains of calomel and fifteen of jalap (a powdered drug prepared from the purgative tuberous root of a Mexican plant of the morning-glory family); they were a powerful physic. Lewis and Clark carried fifty dozen of these pills and, in treating gastrointestinal disturbances, it seems to have been a coin-tossing proposition whether they used the "thunderbolts" or Glauber's salts. . . .

Lewis and Clark could scarcely credit the high incidence of eye troubles among **45.** the Indians of the Columbia River basin. Wrote Clark:

> The loss of sight I have observed to be more common among all the
> nations inhabiting this river than among any people I ever observed.
> They have almost invariably sore eyes at all stages of life. The loss of
> an eye is very common among them; blindness in persons of middle
> age is by no means uncommon, and it is almost invariably a comcam-
> mitant of old age. I know not to what cause to attribute this prevalent
> deficientcy of the eye except it be their exposure to the reflection of
> the sun off the water to which they are constantly exposed in the occu-
> pation of fishing.

When the Indians came to Lewis and Clark to have their eyes treated, as they **46.** did increasingly in the succeeding months, Lewis had his own special eyewash: "a solution of white vitriol [zinc sulphate] and the sugar of lead [lead acetate] in the proportion of 2 grs. of the former and one of the latter to each ounce of water." Dropped into the eyes, it brought at least temporary relief.

The prevalence of sore eyes among the natives was not caused by anything as **47.** innocent as reflection of the sun from water. It was probably due to trachoma or venereal disease. Both appear to have been common in all stages of development among the Columbia Valley Indians, and in all age groups. Trachoma, a highly contagious form of conjunctivitis characterized by granulations on the conjunctival surfaces, may lead to partial or complete blindness. So may gonorrheal conjunctivitis (ophthalmia neonatorum), which babies can inherit from their mothers at birth. . . .

From beginning to end, the members of the expedition suffered from skin **48.** infections—boils, tumors, abscesses, and whitlows, these last being inflammations at the ends of the fingers and toes. Such infections could not be avoided. Cuts and skin abrasions which would allow the entrance of germs occurred daily, especially among the boatmen. Theirs was hardly child's play. In places they toiled waist-deep in water for hours on end, scrambling over sharp-edged rocks which cut moccasins to shreds.

At one time Lewis wrote: "Many of them have their feet so mangled and bruised with the stones . . . that they can scarcely walk or stand; at least it is with great pain that they do either."

Lewis and Clark, of course, knew nothing of the doctrine of sepsis. Pathogens, **49.** such as bacteria, protozoa, and viruses, had yet to be recognized for what they are: almost three-quarters of a century would elapse before the world would know of Louis Pasteur and the germ theory of disease. Physicians of this preantiseptic era treated skin infections with poultices and ointments, and Lewis and Clark followed standard practice. For instance, when Private John Potts' cut leg became inflamed and painful, Clark applied first a poultice of the root of the "Cowes" (*Cogswellia cous*), an herb of the Northwest, and later, another of "the pounded root & leaves of wild ginger [*Asarum caudatum*] from which he found great relief." Another time, when an Indian woman showed up with an abscess on the small of her back, Clark opened it and applied basilicon ointment. This was a salve for external application consisting ordinarily of such ingredients as resin, yellow wax, and lard.

Today, it is difficult to evaluate such treatments. If poultices were applied hot, **50.** as frequently happened, they may have been of some benefit. Or if they contained a blistering agent, such as Spanish fly (cantharides) or oil of mustard, they would have been effective as counterirritants. It is safe to say that poultices generally did no harm when applied to skin that was still intact.

Just six weeks before the end of the trip, near the mouth of the Little Missouri, **51.** Lewis was felled by a bullet which struck him, according to Sergeant John Ordway, "in his back side." As Lewis described it:

> . . . opposite to the birnt hills there happened to be a herd of Elk. . . . I
> determined to land and kill some of them accordingly we put too and I
> went out with [Private Peter] Cruzatte only. we fired on the Elk. I
> killed one and he wounded another, we reloaded our guns and took dif-
> ferent routs through the thick willows in pursuit of the Elk; I was in
> the act of firing on the Elk a second time when a ball struck my left
> thye about an inch below my hip joint, missing the bone it passed
> through the left thye and cut the thickness of the bullet across the hind-
> er part of the right thye; the stroke was very severe; I instantly sup-
> posed that Cruzatte had shot me in mistake for an Elk as I was dressed
> in brown leather and he cannot see very well; under this impression I
> called out to him damn you, you have shot me, and looked towards the
> place from whence the ball had come, seeing nothing I called Cruzatte
> several times as loud as I could.

Receiving no answer, Lewis rushed to the conclusion that he had been shot by **52.** Indians. Therefore, though in great pain, he quickly made his way back to the boat, where he ordered the men there to follow him and "give them battle and relieve Cruzatte." But Lewis' wound soon became so painful and his thigh so stiff that he could go no farther. The rest of the party went ahead and about twenty minutes later returned, bringing Cruzatte with them. They had encountered no Indians. Cruzatte was blind in one eye and near-sighted in the other; he had shot Lewis unintentionally and, because of embarrassment, had kept quiet when Lewis called to him.

Sergeant Gass helped Lewis introduce "tents of patent lint into the ball holes" **53.** and, later that evening, they applied a poultice of Peruvian bark. It was a nasty wound. When Clark first dressed it, Lewis fainted dead away.

In those days a tent consisted of a roll of lint, or linen, unsterilized of course. **54.** It was supposed to expedite drainage and, by keeping the surface of the wound open, to insure the formation of new tissue from the inside out. If a tent was not used, wounds tended to head at the surface, thus precluding drainage. In similar situations, surgeons today sometimes employ rubber tubes of various kinds, called drains, some of which are open, others filled with gauze.

On August 22, eleven days after Lewis had been shot, Clark reported, "I am **55.** happy to have it in my power to Say that my worthy friend Capt. Lewis is recovering fast, he walked a little to day for the first time. I have discontinued the tent in the hole the ball came out." Four days later he removed the tent from the other wound, and by September 9, his worthy friend could "walk and even run nearly as well as ever he could." And just in time. Two weeks later Lewis was in St. Louis enjoying a hero's welcome. For that, a man needed two good legs under him.

Lewis and Clark, though not medically trained, were men of obvious talent and **56.** vast common sense in whom the spirit of inquiry ran high. Of the two leaders, Lewis was better educated and more knowledgeable, with the logical and deductive mind of a good scientist. He was a man of many moods and sought solitude rather than companionship. Clark, on the other hand, was genial and gregarious, the friend of prince and pauper alike. It was to him the men turned with their problems. If, subsequently, either of the captains had studied medicine, it is reasonable to believe that he would have distinguished himself. Lewis, from what we know of him, would have come nearer being the astute, discerning diagnostician. Clark, certainly, would have had much the better bedside manner.

The one incontrovertible fact about the medical practice of Lewis and Clark is **57.** that in twenty-eight months of travelling some 8,000 miles in a land of thirsty sands, rampaging rivers, and unpredictable savages, they lost only one man, poor Sergeant Floyd, and the best medical men in the country—even, probably, Dr. Rush—could not have saved him. Thomas Jefferson, it would seem, made no mistake in entrusting the health and welfare, as well as the military command, of the party to these two resourceful, clear-headed frontiersmen. In fact, considering the primitive state of medicine in the world at that time, who can conscientiously insist that the expedition would have fared better in the hands of a qualified doctor than in those of Meriwether Lewis and William Clark?

WORKING WITH THE TEXT

Cultural and Historical References

In this section, the numbers at the margin refer to the numbered paragraphs in the selection itself.

  6. Can you tell, from the context, what "clyster syringes" were used for?

  16. In folklore, "saltpeter" is thought to be an antiaphrodisiac.

17. Note the gentle irony in Cutright's use of "sanguinary art."

41. "Laudnum" (correctly spelled "laudanum"), a mixture of opium and alcohol, was certain to make a person feel temporarily good, even if it did not heal.

49. In teenage folklore, what is "Spanish fly" supposed to do?

Writing Assignments: The Paragraph

Be sure to provide an introduction for each of the following paragraph writing assignments. That is, begin each paragraph with a phrase like this: "Thomas Brickle claims that. . . ." When it is relevant, you might also want to identify the expertise of the author ("Thomas Brickle, a New Testament scholar, claims that. . . ."), the name of the book or article, the century and country in which the work appeared, or any other circumstances that your readers might find significant. For more on this, see pp. 11–13 in Chapter 2.

1. Write a more orthodox introduction for "I gave him barks and saltpeter. . . ." In your introduction, give background and lead up to a clear thesis statement.

2. In a paragraph, summarize the Cutright essay. Use one quote.

Writing Assignments: The Short Essay

Use informal documentation for these short essays. That is, don't use footnotes or a Works Cited page to document your sources. Instead, cite only relevant information about your source, and keep that information *within* your text. Then follow the summary or quote with a page number in parenthesis. (Use the page numbers that you find in this book to represent the page numbers of the source.) Thus, your informal documentation will look something like this:

In *The Romance of Medicine*, Benjamin Gordon, a history professor, claims that it was once believed that red wine replenished a person's depleted blood supply (p. 121).

1. Write a paper in which you discuss the subtle verbal humor of Cutright's essay. For instance, in paragraph 5, Cutright says that Lewis and Clark ignored some of the advice given to them by Dr. Benjamin Rush. Then Cutright adds: "Nor do we find in any of the journals mention of that 'pleasant & wholsome drink' compounded of sweetened water and sulphuric acid." That is an example of irony because Cutright doesn't actually mean the drink was "pleasant & wholsome." Discuss that example and any other examples of ironic humor that you can find.

2. Compare your own experiences on an "expedition" (perhaps you've taken a long hike with the Boy Scouts or Girl Scouts) with those of Lewis and Clark. Devise your own thesis.

3. Write a satiric or critical paper on modern-day bureaucracy, using details from the first six paragraphs of the Cutright essay to contrast eighteenth-century governmental planning with that of the twentieth century.

4. *Post hoc* reasoning occurs when you come to the faulty conclusion that *because* a particular event preceded another event, the first event *caused* the second one. Cutright gives an example of *post hoc* reasoning in paragraph 12. Write a paper on other instances of *post hoc* reasoning in Cutright's descriptions of medical treatment on the Lewis and Clark expedition.

THE FOUR JUICES

H. S. Glasscheib

In the following essay, H. S. Glasscheib describes the theory of "humors," a description of the makeup of the world as well as a theory on which the treatment of disease was based. For thousands of years, the theory of humors was *the* orthodox theory among European physicians. Very briefly, the theory of humors claims that life consists of four "juices." As a result of their diagnosis of the particular mix of the four "humors," the doctor would bleed or purge the patient. Think of it. For thousands of years doctors applied treatments that routinely did more harm than good—and no one seemed to notice.

    This mucus and bile of which the philosopher speaks so contemptuously in his **1.** *Metaphysics* is physical man. According to the theory of the doctors of antiquity, life consisted of juices. The body was only the form and bed in which the life juices circulated. They recognised four of these, and described them as humours. This number originated from the natural philosophy of Empedocles who recognised the four elements—earth, water, air and fire—as the basic components of the world, and conceived all growth and decay as their mixture and decomposition.

    Every practical science needs a theory since otherwise the wealth of phenomena **2.** cannot be explained. Equally it needs a doctrine, otherwise it cannot be handed down to future generations. Both theory and doctrine were united for the healing art in the philosophy of Empedocles, the same rules of the elements applied in the macrocosm and in the microcosm and thereby reflected a higher general code of laws.

    Antiquity knew the red juice of the blood, the yellow juice of the bile which **3.** sometimes dyed the whole body yellow and the whitish juice of the secretions from the nose and lungs in the case of colds. Corresponding to the four elements there must naturally be four juices. And a fourth juice was discovered, black in colour and forming in the pancreas. Compared with these juices, the significance of the organs, which were recognised as preparers and manufacturers of the juices, took a back seat.

    In the light of the four juices theory, the patient's reactions were observed in **4.** order to recognise the course of diseases. In a common cold, for example, it was noticed

Source: H. S. Glasscheib, "The Four Juices," *The March of Medicine: The Emergence and Triumph of Modern Medicine.* Mervyn Savill (trans.). New York: Putnam's, 1964. 153–162, 164–166.

that the sick man secreted mucus from the nose and lungs. It was therefore considered that colds were caused by an excess of white gall and that "physis" (the power of nature) in the body sought to eliminate this nocive juice. The body's natural power therefore endeavoured to restore the disturbed harmony of the juices by expelling the excess.

But nature appeared to have other means at her disposal of putting an end to the   **5.**
unhealthy condition. The most impressive and best-known internal maladies in antiquity were malaria and pneumonia. In these two diseases the effects of physis could be observed and recognised most clearly. An attack of malaria manifested itself by cold with subsequent immoderate heat, whereupon the fever abated suddenly and was followed by heavy perspiration and urination. It was similar in the case of pneumonia. Hence the idea of the healing powers of fever.

The whole of medicine was founded on these observations. The disease originates   **6.**
from an excess formation of one of the four juices; the body, however, has the capacity for rendering the excess harmless, by "cooking" and expelling it from the body. The body is also in a position to get rid of the "guilty matter" by other means: it can evacuate it in diarrhoea through the bowels or after a long cooking process allow it to break through as pus.

It was also remarked, however, that in many cases physis could not on its own   **7.**
account bring about the expulsion of the guilty matter. Was it not then the duty of the doctor to give a hand?

In this event he only had to imitate the effects of nature. Herbs were discovered   **8.**
with sudorific and diuretic properties, and others which acted as powerful purgatives. By careful use of these in the case of a disease the doctor was to a certain extent a servant of nature, but he had to know and understand their power. Were he to fail in this respect and ignore the intentions of physis he did more harm than good. As a result the motto of the Hippocratic school was: *primum nil nocere* (above all do no harm).

The body had three doors through which it could evacuate nocive matter: through   **9.**
the skin in the form of sweat, through the kidneys as urine and through the bowels as faeces. But since there were four juices there must also be four exits. The doctors invented this fourth door in the shape of blood-letting.

The history of blood-letting is shrouded in the mists of time. We shall never   **10.**
know when and why the slitting of a vein, which often occurred in an injury, developed into a conscious measure for healing disease. Archaeological research has shown that as early as the Stone Age, sharp flints, mussel shells, fishbones and wood splinters were used to pierce a vein in order to tap off a certain amount of blood from the body. The same objects are still used today for blood-letting in some of the Polynesian Islands. All the ancient civilisations practised blood-letting, either as cupping, as in Babylonia, or by actual bleeding, as in Egypt. In the realm of the Aztecs bleeding was carried out with an obsidian knife, with which the ritual sacrifices were performed. In China alone blood-letting was not endemic: it was replaced by pin pricking and scalding which are still practised today—in other words, acupuncture.

The origin and significance of this practice is a matter of controversy. According   **11.**
to Pliny the Younger, man copied it from the instinctive behaviour of animals. The Egyptians must have observed how the hippopotamus, when it became nervous and restless, tore open its veins on the sharp reed stems, to obtain relief. A few thousand

years later the surgeon Dieffenbach observed the same behaviour on the part of his horse. In his opinion blood-letting did not "originate from an abstract idea but from a natural instinct which in certain circumstances drives men in an unhealthy state of excitement to wound themselves to be rid of an excess of blood. Calm and self-possession return after the bleeding. We find similar behaviour in animals. I once owned a horse which in the dog days bit the swollen veins in his flanks. This had a calming effect."

But these are all rational explanations which do not get to the root of the matter. **12.** Blood-letting was originally a rudimentary human sacrifice, an offering of human blood in place of the body, just as the pious Phoenician offered his semen instead of his manhood to the god Moloch, burning it in the sacrificial flame. The calm resulting from bleeding was of a religious nature; by the sacrifice of the blood it was believed that divine grace was ensured, and that a cure could be hoped for.

Hippocrates first gave blood-letting, within the framework of the juices theory, **13.** a scientific foundation; it was held to be the last means of driving the sick juices from the body and saving the patient, when sweating, purging and diuretics failed. The doctors of antiquity used this remedy sparingly and only in moments of great danger. History tells that in 1184 B.C. Polidarius, the son of Aesculapius successfully bled the mortally sick daughter of King Damaethos. She was not only restored to health but he won her hand and a kingdom. Since then bleeding was held in high esteem by the disciples of Aesculapius.

On account of the special circumstances surrounding it, blood-letting took on a **14.** magical significance. The pain of inflicting the small wound, and the blood flowing from the wound, exert a terrifying but fascinating effect, and it is known that maniacs grow calm as soon as they see the blood flowing from a wound.

Before practising this healing method, the arm was bound tightly with a broad **15.** bandage. If the vein were sufficiently swollen the doctor pressed it with the thumb of his left hand while with a knife he opened the vein with his right hand. The blood which flowed from the wound was caught in a bowl. It was allowed to cool in order to recognise the mixture of the juices. The veins in the elbow were usually chosen, but since it was desired to extract the blood as close as possible to the ailing part (it was believed that the evil juices collected there) any vein visible on the body was used for blood-letting.

The theory of juices demanded the evacuation of the harmful or excess juice in **16.** cases of sickness. It therefore became a "therapy of evacuation". If we add to this dieting and ordination of the way of life, we have the rough outlines of the whole therapeutic armoury of the doctors of antiquity. It was simple, and when used with intelligence and moderation it could prove successful in many cases, and in any case caused little harm.

This restricted, but harmonious and hermetic, healing art, was bequeathed to the **17.** European and the Arab worlds. But the West took the currants out of the cake like any child; it preferred the obvious practice of violent expulsions of the body juices by bleeding, purgatives, diuretics and sudorifics, while the prudence and moderation to be found in the old texts remained misunderstood and ineffectual.

With the misunderstood half-truths of classical medicine, the West assumed a **18.** weighty inheritance, which it had to chew and digest for a long time. The first exponents and teachers of the healing art in this case were the monks. As the only members of the community who could read and write, they alone were able to interpret the scholarly latin books. They dedicated themselves to the studying and copying of the texts with great devotion. Their special living conditions within the convent walls forced Western medicine on to particular paths. The monks lived as celibates under their vow of chastity, and the suppression of the sensual pleasures caused them great difficulties. The idea was current in classical medicine that *retentio semenis* (the withholding of the semen) led to blood poisoning. Avoidance of the accumulation of semen by sexual intercourse was therefore considered an important preventive measure, which had often been ordered by the classical and Arab doctors as a cure, even in the case of children.

According to the Christian view, however, extra-marital sexual intercourse was **19.** considered one of the most grievous sins a man could commit. There was one method, however, of countering the accumulation of semen and its consequences—bleeding. It was a regular, prescribed custom among the monks and the members of the orders. Every month, often under compunction, blood-letting took place in order to regulate the decay of the juices, and to aid the monks in their battle against the temptations of the flesh. From this, the theory developed that blood-letting in general was good for purifying the juices and the blood, on the principle that women were cleansed of their "evil juices" by nature with their menstruation. Thus the layman, too, submitted to blood-letting prophylactically. Thus blood-letting ceased to be an independent measure within the framework of the classical theory, and embarked on its sanguinary crusade in Western medicine.

Blood-letting became a preventive and a panacea. As a result both the sick and **20.** the healthy were bled. Neither sex nor age had any privilege: men and women, dotards and children had to submit to blood-letting. A man could consider himself lucky if he suffered from haemorrhoids. He alone was exempt; he was assured of a long life because the evil juices departed of their own accord through the bleeding "golden vein". Astrology, too, claimed its rights, and determined the days on which it would be favourable to perform the operation. So-called blood-letting calendars were published recording accurately when the vein was to be opened and bathing attendants were strictly forbidden to hang out their bowls when the stars were unfavourable.

Newly awakened medical scholasticism seized upon the problem of blood-letting, **21.** perverted it and propounded new questions which it was unable to solve. In the case of sickness, where should the blood-letting be performed, from which vein and in what quantity? Discussions on this theme were endless. The Arabs were of the opinion that a severe tapping of blood near the focus of the disease, as the doctors of antiquity had practised it, caused the healthy blood to flow there and mingle with the bad juices, thus leading to a worsening of the malady. They taught that in order to obtain the best results, a very small quantity of blood should be tapped, drop by drop, as far as possible from the actual seat of the disease, and on the opposite side of the body. For example, if the patient had a pain in his right ear, the vein in the left heel had to be opened. This practice was known as *revulsio*. At the outset this method prevailed on account of the great influence that Arabic medicine exercised in Europe. But after the fall of Constantinople (1453), when the Greek texts became better known in Europe, there was a return to the original Hippocratic method of drawing off the blood in great quantities as near as possible to the focus of the disease. This was known as *derivatio*. Endless discussions and polemics raged as to the expediency and justification of these methods. Since the arguments were equally strong for both methods, they finally led to mutual recriminations and a split in the camp of the doctors. After the fruitless and indecisive debates in the universities, the question was referred to the Emperor Charles V. Unfortunately he was greatly troubled at this time by the religious disputes of the Reformation, and it was certainly not the right moment to try to smooth out a medical conflict. But since a close relative of the emperor had just died, in spite of treatment according to Arabic methods, *revulsio* was rejected and *derivatio* won the day.

Once confirmed in its rights, *derivatio* became a bloody tyrant whose rule was **22.** unopposed for centuries. According to the authorities, in the event of any malady and without consideration for his state of general health the patient had to be bled at least three to five times, with the loss of 1^3_4 pints of blood on each occasion. Contemporary doctors were under the illusion that the human body contained more than 24 lb. of blood. (Actually the average figure is 12 lb.) They therefore believed that they could safely tap off 20 lb., and they endeavoured to carry this out in practice unless the premature death of the patient prevented them.

This heroic therapy continued to rule, becoming more sanguinary and exacting **23.** from century to century. Before collapsing from extravagance, it acquired an ally in the struggle against "harmful juices".

No stone was left unturned to expel the poison of the disease from the body even **24.** if it cost the life of the patient. To the sanguinary business of blood-letting was now added the unsavoury business of purging. If the nocive matter refused to be expelled through the vein, it must be driven out through the intestines. In addition to streams of blood, a mass of faeces was evacuated. But even this did not seem to satisfy the doctors. A new discovery, a worthy companion of bleeding, entered the scene to perfect this type of therapy—the clyster.

The clyster or enema was practised by the Egyptians in all its intimate refinements. **25.** They were reputed to have learnt it from the sacred ibis. When constipated this intelligent bird relieved itself with its curved beak aided by its very long neck. The Egyptians were quick to learn and imitated the ibis, using an instrument in the shape of the bird's beak. In the fifteenth century the clyster syringe was discovered by Professor Gatenaria of Pavia.

This syringe was hailed with undisguised joy, particularly in France. For three **26.** hundred years the enema was one of the favourite remedies in all cases of physical discomfort. During the first years of the reign of Louis XIV, it was the mode at the French court. Ladies and dandies alike had three to four enemas a day in order to acquire a fresh and healthy complexion and the rich bourgeoisie did not lag behind. Every morning a battalion of young fellows, the "*limonadiers des posterieurs*", emerged from the "*boutiques*", as the chemist shops were called in those days, armed with instruments of various calibre and dispersed through the streets in order "to converse with the other cheeks" as Molière expresses it.

There was a great choice of clyster mixtures, including extracts of orange **27.** blossom, angelica, bergamot and roses. The ladies of the Faubourg St. Germain, that classical home of boudoir erotics, concocted their own clysters from secret recipes whose ingredients they would not betray even to their best friends. No one was allowed to enter the boudoir during the preparation ceremony for fear that he might discover the secret formula.

In those gallant days of the Rococo Age, when the syringe stood at its peak of **28.** fame, artists vied with each other to combine aesthetic shapes with elegance and convenience in handling. Instruments, real works of art in their way, were made from tortoiseshell or mother-of-pearl inlaid with silver gilt. The expensive decoration delighted the eye and made people forget the unappetising purpose of the instrument.

To administer an enema "professionally" was considered a high art. Instructions **29.** were printed and the technique of the procedure described in every detail with solicitude and love and pretentiously erotic prose. We read, for example: "At the moment of the operation the patient must raise any obstructive veil. He should lie on his right side with knees drawn forward and do all that is demanded of him without shame or false modesty. The operator, for his part, as a skilled tactician must not take the place by storm but like a trained sharp-shooter prepare for action and fire as soon as he catches sight of the enemy. The operator must also behave with dexterity and consideration and refrain from any movement until he has the target in sight. Then he must kneel down with deference, bring up the instrument with the left hand without undue haste or eagerness, lower the pressure pump *amoroso*, and set it in motion *pianissimo*, with care and without jerking . . . ." (Bardanus.) And so on for pages and pages embellished with pictures and metaphors.

The apothecaries were the practitioners, although legally the bath attendants and **30.** surgeons were entitled to give enemas. Since the apothecaries looked after the preparation and mixture of the ingredients, they managed to gain control of the actual administration. But they misused their warrant so grossly by playing all manner of pranks and worse on their female patients that they were eventually forbidden to give enemas.

When used prophylactically the clyster was considered as a method of preserving **31.** health. Anyone who absorbed three enemas a day triumphed over the ravages of age and "blunted the ruthless tooth of time". In these circumstances it appeared only reasonable that these precious instruments should be carried on a journey. A day without the use of the clyster pump meant courting death. Even in gaol, prisoners of quality were not deprived of their daily enema.

Clysters purporting to possess the power of rejuvenating the body and increasing **32.** sexual potency were also on sale. They were much sought after by young people, and for a large fee the apothecaries were only too ready to mix the mysterious potion and administer it with the greatest discretion. These clysters were known as *restaurants*, implying renovation or reparation. Men who received the treatment believed in it implicitly, and behaved like youths, while old ladies became skittish.

The heyday of the clyster actually produced heroes of the erotic art, such great **33.** lovers as Casanova, the Duc de Richelieu (the great-nephew of the Cardinal) and Mazarin, who until their dotage (Richelieu was ninety-two) openly boasted of their potency. When the Duc de Richelieu married for the third time at the age of eighty-five he announced publicly that if the marriage with a young woman remained childless, it would be no fault of his.

The administering of clysters had become a mode. The age needed change and **34.** new combinations and forms. A very peculiar idea was now conceived—the tobacco clyster. Tobacco smoke was considered to have a purifying effect and to ease the severest stomach cramps. A suitable instrument was manufactured with the aid of which tobacco smoke could be blown into the bowel. The bath attendant or physician administered the clyster by puffing at his pipe. The effect was believed to be so superlative that the tobacco clyster was also used for fainting fits. For some time its use for reviving drowned people was obligatory.

Abundant use was made of the clyster for all manner of diseases. A fundamental **35.**

evacuation of the bowels was naturally the rule in any case of discomfort. Constipation was considered a serious danger, because it was feared that the "vapours" given off by the accumulating faeces poisoned the body and induced melancholy. Albrecht Dürer in his well-known engraving *Melancholy*, among the other symbols of science, has depicted the symbol of medicine in the lower corner, a clyster syringe of very small dimensions half-covered by the clothed female figure.

But how did people react to the unnatural procedure of being given an enema? **36.** Although everyone resorted to it, one never finds an objective verdict on the passive toleration of the act. Only from Luther do we get a professional opinion. When his doctor gave him enemas to cure his serious constipation, he noted in his diaries: "In that act reverence finds its culmination, for the doctors behave to their patients as the mother to her children."

The clyster hardly had to justify itself, but it had to battle for its name. In France **37.** when it was termed *lavement*, it aroused hostility from the Catholic clergy, because this term is reserved for certain ecclesiastical ceremonies. The court was highly indignant when the pious Madame de Maintenon, who dominated the Sun King, decreed that the word *lavement* was no longer to be used to define such an indecent treatment. It was decided to substitute the word *remede*. But despite the royal decree the term *lavement* remained in general use in France.

The clyster became the ally of blood-letting and purging—an unholy trinity **38.** which the doctors let loose upon the human race. Persons of quality and crowned heads in particular who were in the hands of the leading physicians felt the healing lash of this three-thonged knout. Within six months Louis XIII of France was subjected to 47 bleedings, 215 purgings and 312 clysters—two every day except holidays. His son, Louis XIV, would presumably have suffered worse had he not rebelled against the prescriptions of his doctors. During his reign he got away with a mere 38 blood-lettings. Nor were enemas particularly to his taste, and the doctors only managed to force a few hundred on him. On the other hand, he endured several thousand purgings, which his gluttony necessitated, in order to unburden the royal bowels. The record in cathartic therapy was undoubtedly held by King Charles II of England, who had to endure untold agonies before he was allowed to die, presumably of a brain haemorrhage. . . .

But cathartics reached their peak in Paris at the turn of the nineteenth century. **39.** There Broussais, the leading physician in France, had seized upon the Brownian theory of movement. This new theory of healing, which had originated in England, captivated the whole of European medicine. It maintained that the whole of life was merely a reaction to external and internal stimuli and that this proclivity to irritability was the very nature of life.

In his efforts to give the theory a scientific basis, Broussais traced it back to **40.** physiological events. Any superfluous irritation of a tissue led to an accumulation of blood in that tissue. A congestion accompanied by excessive heat, redness or swelling was called inflammation; excessive irritation led to local irritation and so on to the end result. Every disease could be traced to an inflammation, in other words to an excessive accumulation of blood at one part of the body. He now made a mistake, comprehensible in the light of contemporary methods of examination but which led him on a fatal path. While dissecting, Broussais noticed that in all corpses extravasation of blood was to be found in the mucus membranes of the gastro-intestinal canal. It was a normal post-mortem phenomenon, caused by the self-digestion of the dying cells, due to the release of the intestinal ferments. Since Broussais almost invariably saw this extravasation of blood in the alimentary canal, he mistook these insignificant post-mortem changes for excess of blood in the intestinal canal and traced all maladies to this primary cause, which he called "gastroenteritis".

In view of this concept, which seemed to have a sound pathological and **41.** anatomical basis, cathartics which were already restricted by medicinal therapy were triumphantly reinstated. It was expedient to try to control the excess of blood in the bowels by drawing if off and in dangerous cases, by the "saignée, coup sur coup", blood-letting repeated until the patient was bled white.

Once more patients were unscrupulously bled. Bleeding from countless incisions, **42.** they lay there like the victims of some blood-thirsty sacrifice so exhausted by the heavy loss of blood that they were hardly able to groan. The wounds often became infected and suppurated, so that the sick often died of dermatitis. It was heralded as a great step forward when Broussais conceived the idea in minor cases of blood-letting painlessly with the aid of leeches rather than by opening the veins.

The idea was not entirely new; the ancient medical books mention the leech and **43.** its use, and it had always been employed in popular medicine. Now it became the fashion, it was believed that the leech was capable of sucking all the deleterious matter from the body. The demand for these creatures was enormous. Soon every pond in France had been scoured of these valuable worms, and they had to be imported from Bohemia, Hungary and the Baltic countries. Between 1827 and 1836 the Paris hospitals alone used five to six million leeches annually at a cost of a million and a half francs.

France alone needed in the neighbourhood of thirty-three million leeches. In **44.** every ward, in the better-class hospitals, four to five hundred were used. They lay in readiness in rows of glass containers. The leeches were placed on the belly of the patient in order by their powers of suction to relieve the excess blood of gastro-enteritis. Applied in their hundreds they sucked the patient's belly until it looked like a black glittering coat of mail. Full of hope, doctors and patients alike watched the silent activity of their little helpers who, with their greedy suckers, were to draw out the sickness from the body.

The opponents of this method spoke sarcastically of "vampirism", and main- **45.** tained that more blood was being shed by Broussais' therapy than had been shed during the Revolution and the Napoleonic wars combined. In their irony they lagged far behind the truth. The hosts of leeches which Broussais had conjured from the slimy depths of ponds and engaged against the human race, for sixteen years in succession, annually sucked 1,680,000 litres of blood from the French people. If we add the loss of blood from ruthless blood-letting, we reach a figure which makes Broussais the bloodthirstiest man in world history, for at his instigation and on account of his error, twenty to thirty million litres of blood were shed in France alone.

The enthusiasm for this new therapy and the confidence it inspired was so **46.** boundless that to prove the correctness of Broussais' teaching, a certain student embarked upon a dangerous experiment. Before an assembled audience he allowed himself to be inoculated in the arm with fresh syphilitic pus, and immediately contracted the disease in its first stage. According to Broussais' doctrine this was to be regarded merely as a local irritation which would be held in check by a sympathetic enteritis. In accordance with the theory, when the enteritis was removed by copious blood-letting, the local disease would also be healed. With great courage and complete confidence the student submitted to the blood-letting, but the chancre refused to obey the theory and to heal, but grew ever larger. The glands in his armpits swelled and soon the unfortunate man's body was covered with sores. His belief in medicine and its infallible theories shattered, he committed suicide.

In the long run, however, the failure of this therapeutic "vampirism" could not **47.** be kept a secret. It was obvious that the patients died more quickly and in greater numbers from blood-letting cures than from less violent measures. A striking fact was its unfavourable comparison with the new homeopathy, which obtained better results with a few mild powders or drops. The ruthless and gruesome vampirism of the doctors drove the patients in their hosts to the homeopaths.

With one accord the doctors abandoned their blood-letting. Until the middle of **48.** the nineteenth century a panacea for every disease, it was now very seldom practised. The copper basins still used today by the barbers are a reminder of its former domination. Its bloodless allies, purgatives and clysters have survived the collapse, and have retained their place in the arsenal of medicine.

WORKING WITH THE TEXT

Cultural and Historical References

In this section, the numbers at the margin refer to the numbered paragraphs in the selection itself.

1. Sometimes authors assume too much of their readers. Glasscheib begins this essay by referring to a "philosopher," the author of *Metaphysics*. Did Glasscheib go too far? Do you know who this philosopher is?

1. Empedocles was a fifth century B.C. Greek philosopher.

2. If humankind is the microcosm, what is the macrocosm?

8. From the context, can you tell what "sudorific" properties are?

8. Hippocrates is the ancient Greek physician who left behind a set of ethical standards for physicians. It is impossible to say today just which rules Hippocrates left behind and which were added by his followers. At any rate, upon graduation from medical school many doctors today still take the Hippocratic oath.

10. "Cupping" is an old-fashioned way of removing blood by applying a heated glass cup, partially evacuated of its oxygen, to the flesh of the patient. This draws blood to the surface of the skin, and sometimes through the skin.

13. Aesculapius is the Roman god of medicine (the counterpart of the Greek god of medicine, Asclepius).

16. There are two signs in this paragraph that this is an English rather than an American book. What are they?

18. What does "the West" mean?

21. "Scholasticism" usually refers to the body of knowledge bequeathed to

the Middle Ages by classical scholars, in particular Aristotle, and the early Church fathers.

31. Using the context, can you tell what a "gaol" is?

33. Perhaps you know that Casanova was a real man. In real life, he was an eighteenth-century Italian sensualist whose full name was Casanova de Seingalt. What has the name come to mean?

35. Albrecht Dürer is the famous sixteenth-century German engraver and painter, believed by some to be the inventor of etching.

36. Martin Luther is the sixteenth-century German monk, whose ninety-five theses, nailed to the door of the Wittenburg cathedral started the Reformation.

47. Homeopathic medicine, still used occasionally today, treats illness through the administration of extremely minute doses of medicine.

Writing Assignments: The Paragraph

Be sure to provide an introduction for each of the following paragraph writing assignments. That is, begin each paragraph with a phrase like this: "Thomas Brickle claims that. . . ." When it is relevant, you might also want to identify the expertise of the author ("Thomas Brickle, a New Testament scholar, claims that. . . ."), the name of the book or article, the century and country in which the work appeared, or any other circumstances that your readers might find significant. For more on this, see pp. 11–13 in Chapter 2.

1. In a paragraph, write a description of the theory of the microcosm/ macrocosm. Glasscheib mentions the theory in his second paragraph. You'll probably have to look up more information.

2. Write a paragraph that describes the four means by which doctors drew out the bad "juices" from their patients.

3. Describe the use of leeches. See paragraphs 43 and 44.

Writing Assignments: The Short Essay

Use informal documentation for these short essays. That is, don't use footnotes or a Works Cited page to document your sources. Instead, cite only relevant information about your source, and keep that information *within* your text. Then follow the summary or quote with a page number in parenthesis. (Use the page numbers that you find in this book to represent the page numbers of the source.) Thus, your informal documentation will look something like this:

> In *The Romance of Medicine*, Benjamin Gordon, a history professor, claims that it was once believed that red wine replenished a person's depleted blood supply (p. 121).

1. Write a paper in which you explain the theory of the microcosm/

was finally settled, Vesalius set out immediately for Italy, the land of anatomy. He went to Padua and, on December 5, 1537, was ceremoniously promoted from the student body of the university to professor of surgery and anatomy.

He was barely twenty-three years old when he took office; but he already **9.** surpassed all the other members of his discipline, not so much by his knowledge as by his devotion to his profession. He began his lectures, as was customary in the university, by expounding the thousand-year-old views and teachings of Galen. At the time any other approach would have been unthinkable. Galen and Hippocrates were comparable to the Church Fathers; their theories had become accepted as dogma and to doubt them was heresy. But since Vesalius performed his own dissection, not confining himself as his predecessors had done to pointing to the organs from a distance, he began to see them as they really were, and they were often very different from what Galen had taught. The liver did not have five lobes but only two; Vesalius could find no vent from the pancreas to the stomach any more than he could find pores in the atrial septum of the heart. Had man undergone a change in the thousand years since Galen, or was Vesalius dealing with pathological organs? He was disturbed because he did not know the answer. He continued to expound the theories of Galen, but began to doubt their accuracy.

At the second and third public dissections he encountered the same discrepancies **10.** between text and reality, but this time they were more frequent. In the actual osteology, the contradictions were quite obvious. Vesalius knew every bone in the skeleton intimately because in his three years of enforced idleness he had held each of them a hundred times in his hand—but where then was the bi-partite lower jaw, the seven-pieced sternum and the leg bent outwards? Where had Galen obtained all his information; where had he seen it? It was maintained that the leg had gradually grown straight, thanks to the tubular-shaped hose, but what of the sternum, the lower jaw, the form of the pelvis, the behaviour of the knee? How could so many discrepancies and deviations be explained?

Vesalius's glance fell on the skeleton of a monkey, which he had recently **11.** dissected. Here were the bent thigh, the seven-pieced sternum, the knee bent outwards, here everything conformed to what Galen had written. Suddenly everything became clear to him: Galen had described the anatomy of an ape. Later he recognised that the pig and the dog had served as models for the inner organs, and that from these various components Galen had formulated the anatomy of a human being.

At the fourth public dissection, Vesalius put an end to his lip service, no longer **12.** using the Galen text but describing the organs as he saw them. Today we look upon this as a matter of course and accept it as the premise for a purely descriptive science such as anatomy. But it was apparently very difficult to establish this viewpoint.

We are faced here with a strange phenomenon common to the history of mind **13.** and to psychology: even the most simple visual event can become completely divorced from reality. Nothing was easier than to recognise that the human liver consisted of two lobes; but every anatomist after Galen continued to speak of the five-lobed liver, which the Greek had observed correctly in the pig, and had falsely taken to apply to a human being. But what are we to think of those anatomists who, more than two hundred years after Mondino's dissections, who held the human liver in their hand, examined it eagerly and then insisted that it had five lobes in accordance with Galen?

Herein lies the basis of the Middle Ages: its power of faith but also its intellectual **14.** obscurity, blindness and incapacity to see the simplest facts as they really were. With Vesalius came an awareness of reality, an awareness which was also manifesting itself in Italian painting. For the two had much in common and it was no accident that painting and anatomy developed simultaneously and in fact worked hand in hand. Fifty years earlier than Vesalius, Leonardo da Vinci had dissected thirty human corpses and drew accurate drawings of them. Vesalius realised that the anatomy of the human being now had to be rewritten, and for his work he solicited the aid of a painter, a compatriot from the Netherlands, Jan Kalkar, a member of the Titian school.

Kalkar was enamoured of the beauty he had learned in Titian's school, and was **15.** horrified by the idea of drawing parts of corpses. Vesalius persisted, and finally convinced his friend that this service to science would mean no dishonour to his art, and would perhaps bring him more fame than pictures painted "in the manner of Titian". Vesalius hung a skinned corpse by the head and armpits on a line in his study, and prepared it layer by layer. And, layer by layer, according to his explanations and directions, his friend had to draw the structures as they were laid bare. It was an exhausting task, and on account of Vesalius's pedantry, Kalkar was often on the point of flinging down his brush. But the effort was worth while; Vesalius's immoderate demands for accuracy and Kalkar's talent combined to produce a work of the greatest artistic expression, which still arouses our admiration today.

For lack of good embalming materials a corpse did not last very long, and since **16.** a whole system had to be described, some other part of the body inevitably had to be destroyed. Vesalius prepared muscles, arteries, nerves, intestines, sinews and cartilage. The corpse grew ever more denuded as work progressed; the bones stuck out more and more until finally only the naked skeleton remained. When Kalkar had completed the last plate of his skeleton, Vesalius wrote below it in verse:

> *Death strips the body of its finery;*
> *The rosy cheek turns pale, the form is broken.*

On August 1, 1542, after four years' work, Kalkar's 276 engravings and Vesalius's descriptive text were completed. The manuscript of the work: *De humani corporis fabrica, Libri VII*, was ready. It was a treatise of anatomy, *not* copied from the ancient authors, *not* drawn from dissected monkeys, pigs and dogs and attributing faulty constructions to the human body, but the first real treatise on human anatomy.

The seven books appeared in 1543, the same year that Copernicus published his **17.** six books on the heavenly bodies, *De revolutionibus Orbium Coelestium*. Vesalius's work aroused the most violent controversy, one might say horror, for Galen was still the revered, sacred authority, and it was considered almost blasphemous that a man should have the temerity to contradict his teachings. One of the first to cast a stone at Vesalius was his old teacher, Sylvius. In urgent letters he implored his pupil to recant in public anything contradictory to Galen. When Vesalius refused and claimed the right to portray anatomy as his own eyes revealed it, Sylvius composed a pamphlet full of the most poisonous invective, calling him a dilettante and a fool, maintaining that he had dissected pathological bodies and had thus fallen into error.

Vesalius was very distressed by the shower of abuse which his former teacher **18.** poured on his head. Other anatomists of repute, such as Eustachius in Rome and

Columbus in Padua, criticised Vesalius's work and maintained that they would prefer to err with Galen than to be proved right with Vesalius. Science in those days was so full of bigotry that traditional surmise triumphed over real proof.

WORKING WITH THE TEXT

Cultural and Historical References

In this section, the numbers at the margin refer to the numbered paragraphs in the selection itself.

2. The Flemish anatomist and physician Vesalius had the full name of Andreus Vesalius.

2. Galen was the second-century Greek anatomist and physician who left behind a number of studies of human anatomy. By the time of Vesalius, Galen had become *the* supreme authority on human anatomy, as you will see later in this selection.

9. Hippocrates is, of course, the ancient Greek physician who left behind a set of rules that were later codified into the Hippocratic oath.

10. If the root "oste" means bone, what do you suppose "osteology" means?

14. Titian is a famous Italian Renaissance painter.

15. You might go to the library and look up these paintings by Kalkar.

16. Interesting coincidence: two revolutionary works, one an accurate description of human anatomy by Vesalius and one an accurate description of the solar system by Copernicus, both appeared in the same year, 1543.

Writing Assignments: The Paragraph

Be sure to provide an introduction for each of the following paragraph writing assignments. That is, begin each paragraph with a phrase like this: "Thomas Brickle claims that. . . ." When it is relevant, you might also want to identify the expertise of the author ("Thomas Brickle, a New Testament scholar, claims that. . . ."), the name of the book or article, the century and country in which the work appeared, or any other circumstances that your readers might find significant. For more on this, see pp. 11–13 in Chapter 2.

1. Glasscheib begins this small biography on Vesalius in a traditional way—mainly, details about birthplace and family. Write a paragraph in which you defend or criticize this traditional opening. If you attack it, what is the alternative?

2. In a paragraph, discuss a topic sentence that Glasscheib might have constructed for paragraph 7.

3. Paraphrase, and quote from, paragraph 15. You'll have to back up a bit to explain the situation clearly.

Writing Assignments: The Short Essay

Use informal documentation for these short essays. That is, don't use foot-notes or a Works Cited page to document your sources. Instead, cite only relevant information about your source, and keep that information *within* your text. Then follow the summary or quote with a page number in parenthe-sis. (Use the page numbers that you find in this book to represent the page numbers of the source.) Thus, your informal documentation will look something like this:

> In *The Romance of Medicine*, Benjamin Gordon, a history professor, claims that it was once believed that red wine replenished a per-son's depleted blood supply (p. 121).

1. Write a paper on the interesting coincidence in paragraph 17, that two revoluionary works came out in the same year. Begin your essay by attributing your discovery of this fact to Glasscheib.

2. Write a paper on people's reluctance to change their opinions. Perhaps you've noticed a fact or self-evident idea that people choose to ignore. If so, combine your own observations with those of Glasscheib in paragraphs 13 to 18.

BELLY-MY-GRIZZLE

Spencer Klaw

''Belly-My-Grizzle'' is the story of Samuel Thomson, a nineteenth-century herb-and-root doctor who mounted an attack on orthodox physicians. With a rather far-fetched theory in hand, Thomson put his patients in a steam bath to sweat out the diseases and fed them lobelia, a powerful emetic, to purge them. Through these methods he claimed he could cure every disease known to humanity. Of course, orthodox treatments of the time—which consisted mainly of purging and bleeding, but no steam—weren't much better. In fact, one could make the case that Thomson did less harm than orthodox physicians. Spencer Klaw is a free-lance writer and frequent contributor to *American Heritage*.

In the late 1820's and 1830's American physicians found themselves with a **1.** major rebellion on their hands. The rebels were their own patients, or ex-patients, and the rebel leader was a onetime New Hampshire farmer and itinerant herb-and-root doctor named Samuel Thomson, who had published, in 1822, a book called *Thomson's New Guide to Health; or, Botanic Family Physician.*

On Thomson's recommendation, hundreds of thousands of Americans were no **2.** longer calling in conventionally trained and licensed physicians when they were sick. Instead, they were either doctoring themselves according to the instructions contained in the *New Guide to Health*, or were consulting disciples of Thomson who had set themselves up in business as botanic healers.

Source: Spencer Klaw, ''Belly-My-Grizzle,'' *American Heritage.* June 1977: 97–105.

It was Thomson's passionate conviction that most physicians of the day were no **3.** better than torturers and murderers. Their chief crime against suffering humanity, he argued, was their insistence on dosing patients with "metallic" medicines, by which he mainly meant calomel, a widely used and horribly effective cathartic whose active ingredient was mercury. In Thomson's view, the way to cope with illness was to administer certain herbal remedies—he particularly favored lobelia, a powerful emetic—and to put the patient in a steam bath to make him sweat. Thomson held that it was possible by using these methods to cure every disease known to man, from dyspepsia and croup to cancer and tuberculosis.

Thomson's rebellion was launched at a time when American physicians had been **4.** trying, with some success, to enhance their status (and incomes) by putting the practice of medicine on a more professional footing. Before the Revolution, and for some time afterward, in most parts of America anyone with a mind to do so had been at liberty to treat sick people and to call himself a doctor. But in the early 1800's the country's "regular" physicians, led by graduates of the medical schools of Columbia, Harvard, and the University of Pennsylvania, set out to change this. At their behest, state after state established licensing requirements for physicians and imposed penalties on persons practicing medicine without a license. At the same time, new medical schools were founded in the South and West, and young men were entering the profession in such numbers as to assure, before many more years, an adequate supply of licensed physicians for all but the most remote and sparsely settled regions of the country.

The nation's growing medical establishment began to react vigorously—and **5.** understandably—to the threat that Thomson posed to its members' self-esteem and to their pocketbooks. His notions about medicine were denounced as at once laughable and dangerous. In a book called *Humbugs of New-York* a New York physician named David Meredith Reese expressed the prevailing view in medical circles when he dismissed Thomsonian practitioners as uneducated quacks, noting by way of proof that their principal remedies were commonly known "by the classical and euphonious names of *screw augur! ram-cat!* and *hell-scraper!*" These names clearly point to the emetic action of lobelia, which was also known, for reasons that are not so clear, as "belly-my-grizzle."

Reese went on to charge that if anyone was killing innocent patients, it was **6.** the Thomsonians, whose medicine, he explained, had "systematic arrangements for clandestinely murdering its victims" in infirmaries where patients were "taken care of on the Thomsonian plan, until they either run away . . . or are quietly buried." (Thomson himself, early in his career, had been tried for the murder of one of his patients.) State and local medical societies called on the authorities to deal harshly with unlicensed practitioners, and some Thomsonians were actually thrown into jail.

But such tactics were unavailing. Between 1822 and 1839 the *New Guide to* **7.** *Health* went through thirteen editions and sold more than 100,000 copies. This was an astonishing total considering that the population of the United States in 1839 was less than seventeen million, and that a copy cost twenty dollars.

Thomsonians also founded, and supported with their subscriptions, some forty **8.** journals in which the theory and practice of Thomsonian medicine were expounded. Their pages were filled with stories of the miraculous healing powers of Thomsonian remedies. Typically these accounts told of patients who had been left for dead by their regular doctors—the latter were customarily referred to in terms like "these slick-tongued, high-minded, small-pillbag, metallic gentry"—and had been restored to robust health within twenty-four hours after swallowing their first dose of belly-my-grizzle. In one variation of the formula it was reported that an old lady in Crawford County, Missouri, had polished off most of a bottle of tincture of lobelia under the mistaken impression that it was whiskey. "I thought I would die," she was said to have told a local Thomsonian practitioner. "But sir, I did not die; for I commenced puking . . . and please God, sir, I have not had one hour's sickness since." . . .

Thomson's ideas fitted in beautifully with the spirit of Jacksonian democracy. **9.** Self-educated and self-made, Thomson argued that a free people could well dispense not just with doctors, but with lawyers and ministers and all other specially educated and, in his view, parasitic professional castes. It was all right with him if someone who had carefully studied his *New Guide to Health* should choose to apply its teachings to the cure of disease in others. But he thought it was much better for people to learn how to cure themselves, and toward the end of his life he was deeply troubled because some of his followers, including his own son John, wanted to establish Thomsonian medical schools. Such schools, he feared, would spawn a new elite, and "the benefit of my discoveries will be taken from the people generally, and, like all other crafts, monopolized by a few learned individuals."

But the egalitarian mood of the United States in the late 1820's and 1830's does **10.** not alone explain the remarkable popularity of Thomson's ideas. Quite apart from the way people had come to feel about bankers and lawyers, Americans had a specific—and justified—grudge against the medical profession. For this was the golden age of heroic medicine, when doctors were taught that it was their duty, at the first signs of illness, to attack it with harsh therapies—therapies that seldom did any good, and that were often far more unpleasant, and sometimes far more dangerous, than the illness itself.

One of the doctor's most trusted weapons in combating disease was the lancet, **11.** which was commonly used in treating even the most trivial disorders. "I remember that a horse kicked me once as Dr. Colby was passing the house," a survivor of the age of bloodletting wrote years later. "I was not injured much, yet mother called in the doctor, and he at once proceeded to bleed me—I presume on general principles."

Bleeding did tend to reduce a fever. But it often did so at the price of a throbbing **12.** headache and an overwhelming feeling of weakness, and it seems to have had no other beneficial effects. Bleeding was also dangerous. Many doctors believed in letting the blood flow until the patient lost consciousness, and some patients lost their lives as well. Reminiscing in 1878 about medical practice in Ohio in the first quarter of the nineteenth century, a contributor to the *Cincinnati Lancet and Clinic* recalled "a neighboring physician who proposed to cure and did cure common intermittent [*i.e.,* malaria] by blood-letting alone; he bled the patient till he was too weak to shake, and then the disease and the patient went off together." Physicians in Thomson's time also tormented patients by raising huge blisters on their bodies, breaking the blisters, and then irritating the resulting sores, a procedure that sometimes led to the development of ulcers and gangrene.

More widespread than either bleeding or blistering, and probably more dangerous **13.** as well, was the practice of stuffing sick people with calomel. Unpleasant even when taken in small quantities, in the huge doses favored by many doctors it often had terrible side effects on the patient's mouth and salivary glands. "It is but the other day," a Dr. G. C. Howard wrote in the *Boston Medical and Surgical Journal* in 1835, "that I saw a case of gastroenteritis, in which calomel was pushed till the countenance exhibited a most frightful appearance, owing to the excessive swelling of the cheeks, lips, tongue . . . and throat, while the saliva flowed in streams." Many doctors regarded these classic symptoms of mercury poisoning as hopeful signs that the drug was doing its work.

Howard, one of the few regular physicians who did not share the prevailing **14.** enthusiasm for calomel, went on to point out that patients who asked why they had to take the stuff did so at their peril. Their doctors, he wrote, "in the plenitude of their wisdom and power, are determined to inflict summary vengeance on them for their temerity and doubt, by a ten times more frequent and greater use of the article in question, than they otherwise would have done."

While most physicians were satisfied that bleeding, blistering, and purging were **15.** good for their patients, they did not agree on just why this should be so. Some believed, with the celebrated Dr. Benjamin Rush of Philadelphia, that virtually all disease was caused by an overstimulation of the blood vessels, and that this, in turn, was the result of too much blood in the system, a condition that the physician was in a position to correct with his lancet. (In cases of serious illness Rush advised tapping as much as four-fifths of the patient's blood supply—not all at once, to be sure, but in fairly short order.)

Other doctors had other theories, equally bizarre. Only a few were inclined to **16.** agree with Thomas Jefferson, who scoffed at all contemporary theory-spinners and put forward the radical notion that in many cases the physician's proper office was to stand aside and let nature do the healing.

Thomson, too, was a theory-spinner. Like Rush, he held that all disease stemmed **17.** from a single cause. In Thomson's view, that cause was a lack of bodily heat, brought about by the body's failure to digest food properly. Consequently the first step in a course of Thomsonian therapy was usually to steam the patient thoroughly.

"When the sweat rolls off as thick as your finger," a Maryland man noted in **18.** 1837, in a letter to his son, "the body is washed with cold water and the patient is straightway put to bed with hot bricks to bring back his heat. Then a powerful vomitive is administered, composed of *bay berry*, of cayenne (red pepper) and lobelia, which suffer naught impure to remain in the stomach, and all these herbs are mixed in 40 proof brandy, after which warm water is drunk until there has ensued the most extraordinary vomiting. Next, the patient rises and takes a second bath, like the first. He takes again to his bed, after having been laved with cold water and is surrounded with hot bricks and remains in bed for an hour. At the end of this time he takes two injections [*i.e.*, enemas] of penny royal, cayenne pepper and lobelia and the treatment is over for the day." Thomson also recommended various mild tonics, such as tincture of myrrh, "to give tone to the stomach and bowels, and prevent mortification."

All this was no more likely to cure a patient than bleeding or purging him. But **19.** Thomson's system had several advantages over conventional therapies. One was that a family owning a copy of the *New Guide to Health*, which even gave detailed instructions for building a home steam bath, did not need to call in a doctor when someone was sick. Another advantage was that Thomsonian remedies were relatively easy on the patient. There were practitioners, it is true, who tended to pour on the lobelia. Thomson sternly chided one such enthusiast who gave a patient nineteen treatments of Thomsonian medicine in a six-week period ''and then left her in a very weak and low condition (no wonder).'' But in the dosages recommended by Thomson, lobelia was not nearly as hard on the system as calomel.

20.   Thomson's do-it-yourself treatise was not the first book of its kind to come on the market. But it differed from earlier guides to botanic healing in that it included a lengthy autobiographical sketch, titled ''Narrative of the Life and Medical Discoveries of the Author.'' And the book's popularity no doubt stemmed in part from the pleasure many Americans got from Thomson's account of how a poor and uneducated farm boy, forced to rely on his native wit and powers of observation, nevertheless grew up to expose the greed and wrongheadedness of the medical profession.

21.   Thomson was born in Alstead, New Hampshire, in February, 1769. As he tells it in the ''Narrative,'' he attached himself in very early childhood to a local herb doctor, an old woman named Benton. When she went out to collect roots and herbs, Thomson writes, ''she would take me with her, and learn me their names, with what they were good for; and I used to be very curious in my inquiries, and in tasting everything that I found.''

22.   One plant that he soon tasted was lobelia. He was four years old at the time, he recalls, and had gone to look for his father's cows. While on this errand ''I discovered a plant which had a singular branch and pods . . . and I had the curiosity to pick some of the pods and chew them; the taste and operation produced, was so remarkable, that I never forgot it.'' Later, Thomson adds, he ''used to induce other boys to chew it, merely by way of sport, to see them vomit.''

23.   But it was not until some twenty years had passed that Thomson was persuaded that lobelia, a smallish plant with pale blue blossoms, could do more than just make people sick to their stomachs. There was, and is, disagreement as to whether Thomson was the first to use lobelia as a medicine. Lobelia is also called Indian tobacco, and it was well known to the Penobscot Indians before Thomson was born, although it is not clear whether they took it as a medicine or dried its leaves and smoked them.

24.   However that may be, Thomson's discovery of its curative powers was made on a summer day while he was cutting hay. As he recalls the incident in the ''Narrative,'' he cut a sprig of lobelia and offered it to one of his fellow mowers with the suggestion that he eat it. ''When we had got to the end of the piece, which was about six rods,'' Thomson writes, ''he said that he believed what I had given him would kill him, for he never felt so in his life. I looked at him and saw that he was in a most profuse perspiration . . . he trembled very much, and there was no more color in him than a corpse. I told him to go to the spring and drink some water; he attempted to go, and got as far as the wall, but was unable to get over it, and laid down on the ground and vomited several times.''

25.   Fortunately this medical experiment ended happily. Thomson helped his companion into the house, ''and in about two hours he ate a very hearty dinner, and in the afternoon was able to do a good half day's labor. He afterwards told me that he never had any thing do him so much good in his life; his appetite was remarkably good, and he felt better than he had for a long time.''

Soon afterward Thomson discovered the virtues of steam when he was able to **26.**
cure his two-year-old daughter of a disease he diagnosed as canker-rash by steaming
her every two hours for a week. As word of his prowess as a healer got around, more
and more people began coming to him for help, and in 1805 he gave up farming
altogether and became a full-time herb doctor, treating patients in Vermont, Massachusetts, and Maine, as well as in New Hampshire. Wherever he went he ran into fierce
opposition from regular physicians, one of whom, according to Thomson, tried to kill
him with a scythe as he was passing by the physician's door in Eastport, Maine. In
Salisbury, Massachusetts, on the complaint of a Dr. French, Thomson was arrested for
the murder of a young man named Ezra Lovett, whom he was alleged to have killed
with an overdose of lobelia. For more than a month in the cold fall of 1809 he was
confined to a filthy and verminous cell in the Newburyport, Massachusetts, jail, where
he had no chair, no table, no fire, no candle, no bed, and only a thin and dirty blanket.

Thomson was eventually acquitted after a character witness took from the hand **27.**
of the prosecutor a sample of the drug with which Thomson was said to have done the
deed and ate it in open court. When Thomson had recovered from the effects of his
confinement he resumed his work as a peripatetic healer, and the closing pages of the
"Narrative" are richly freighted with stories of his therapeutic triumphs. To give just
one example, Thomson tells of a young man who was being treated by Thomson's
enemy, Dr. French, following an accident in which three of his fingers had been cut
to the bone. After three weeks, upon being advised br Dr. French that he should have
the fingers amputated, the patient consulted Thomson; ten days later, with all fingers
intact, he was back on his job in a nail factory. Soon afterward, when Thomson asked
how his fingers were, "he said they were perfectly cured; he wished to know what my
bill was for attending him. I asked him what Dr. French had charged, and he said he
had sent his bill to his mother, amounting to seventeen dollars; I told him I thought
that was enough for us both, and that I should charge him nothing. His mother was a
poor widow depending on her labor and that of her son for a living."

Thomson's robust egalitarianism was coupled with a shrewd business sense. In **28.**
1813, nine years before the publication of his *New Guide to Health,* he had hit on an
ingenious scheme for propagating, and profiting from, his ideas. He patented his
therapeutic discoveries, and began selling certificates that conferred on the purchaser
"the right of preparing and using, for himself and family, the medicine and System
of Practice secured to Samuel Thomson by Letters Patent from the President of the
United States. . . ."

A certificate, or "right," cost twenty dollars, and with it the purchaser got written **29.**
instructions in the principles of Thomsonian medicine. At first these instructions were
contained in *The Medical Circular*, a pamphlet that Thomson had drafted while lying
on the floor of his Newburyport jail cell. Later, however, each purchaser of a right got
a copy of the *New Guide to Health.* To push the sale of his rights, Thomson appointed
regional agents—at one time there were forty-one in Ohio alone—who traveled about
in wagons loaded not only with copies of Thomson's book, but also with lobelia,
cayenne, bayberry, poplar bark, and other staples of Thomsonian medicine.

The country's regular doctors could not stop people from swallowing herbal teas, **30.**
or giving each other herbal enemas. But they did for a time make it hard for anyone
to earn his living as a Thomsonian practitioner. "Every medical society in [New York]

became virtually a police station, to which resorted spies and informers to communicate evidence for prosecutions,'' one historian has written. ''Many [botanic] practitioners were arrested and fined, many were fined and imprisoned for two months.''

The Thomsonians proved, however, to be formidable lobbyists. The New York **31.** legislature, for example, could scarcely ignore Samuel Thomson's son John when he arrived at the capitol in Albany with a pro-Thomsonian petition ninety-three feet long that he had personally trundled up State Street in a wheelbarrow. Moreover, the Thomsonians had a big edge over the regular doctors in that their arguments could so easily be elevated to a lofty patriotic plane. Thus Job Haskell, a leading champion of the Thomsonians in the New York legislature, charged that the law prohibiting botanic physicians from accepting fees was an insult to American democracy. ''Intrinsic merit, sir,'' he proclaimed, ''is the only qualification which ought to be required of any man to entitle him to practice physic or surgery; it is the only qualification necessary to carry a man from the humblest station under our republican government to the presidential chair.'' Warming to his work, Haskell spoke feelingly of ''the groans and shrieks of the millions who have been destroyed by the lancet and mineral medicines,'' and gave it as his opinion that ''if the awful sounds could burst upon this hall, that law [penalizing botanic practitioners] would be swept with indignation from your statute book. . . .'' In the end, such rhetoric was too much for the doctors to withstand, and in state after state, including New York in 1844, all laws regulating the practice of medicine were repealed. . . .

Within a few years after Thomson's death even practitioners who stuck closely **32.** to his system of therapeutics no longer cared to invoke his name. Curtis and his followers, perhaps believing that they could achieve true respectability only by disowning the unlettered farmer who had set them on the path of botanic medicine, soon dropped the name Independent Thomsonians, choosing instead to call themselves Botanico-Medicals or Physio-Medicals.

But it was to take the country's regular physicians more than fifty years to recover **33.** completely from the drubbing Thomson had given them. Millions of Americans went on dosing themselves with herbal remedies and consulting herbal practitioners. Some of these practitioners had picked up their trade on their own, but many were graduates of one of the twenty-odd schools of botanic medicine that were founded in the United States in the nineteenth century. In 1901 a medical historian named Alexander Wilder estimated that several thousand botanic, reformed, physiopathic and physio-medical doctors were still practicing in the United States. Most of them, according to Wilder, were treating patients pretty much along the lines laid down by Samuel Thomson nearly eighty years before.

Thomson's ideas also unquestionably influenced the founders of the eclectic **34.** school of medicine, which flourished in the middle and late years of the century. Most eclectics were graduates of orthodox medical schools, and while they did on occasion prescribe ''mineral'' medicines, they stuck mainly to vegetable remedies, and eschewed both calomel and the lancet. The first eclectics often went in for heroic botanic medicine, attempting to blast out disease with potent vegetable cathartics. Alexander Wilder, who was himself an eclectic physician, conceded that in the early years of the movement the medicines prescribed by eclectics were ''often distasteful and repulsive beyond the power of sensitive patients to endure.'' But as time went by the eclectics came to rely on inoffensive drugs, and to prescribe them in small quantities, on the sensible theory that often the best thing to do for a sick person was to help him to rest comfortably and, as a leading eclectic physician put it, to keep ''the bowels in such restful condition that they would not disturb the patient.''

After 1900, herbal medicines lost much of their appeal. Although able to hold **35.** their own in competition with calomel, they were completely outclassed by new and rational forms of therapy based on recent discoveries about human physiology and the nature of disease. As L. J. Henderson, a widely respected physiologist and medical sociologist, pointed out some forty years ago, doctors could at long last actually cure people, at least some of the time. ''I think it was about 1910 or 1912,'' Henderson observed, ''when it became possible to say of the United States that a random patient with a random disease consulting a doctor chosen at random stood better than a fifty-fifty chance of benefiting from the encounter.''

But while most botanic doctors were put out of business by the coming of **36.** scientific medicine, the voice of Thomson and his disciples can still be heard, at least faintly, in the land. The notion that simple herbal remedies are inherently superior to the dangerous chemicals prescribed by doctors continues to be given currency by books such as *Back to Eden*, a work described by its publisher as a ''million-copy best seller'' that came out in 1939 and is still selling briskly in health-food stores. Its subtitle is ''The Classic Guide to Herbal Medicine, Natural Foods, and Home Remedies,'' and its author, Jethro Kloss, devotes a good deal of space to lobelia. Describing Thomson's favorite remedy as ''a most efficient relaxant, influencing mucous, serous, nervous, and muscular structures,'' Kloss recommends its use for the treatment of ''coughs, bronchitis, asthma, whooping cough, pneumonia, hysteria, convulsions, suspended animation, tetanus, febrile troubles, etc.''

''Lobelia possesses most wonderful properties,'' Kloss goes on to say. ''It is a **37.** perfectly harmless relaxant. It loosens disease and opens the way for its elimination from the body. Its action is quick and more effective than radium.'' Nonpoisonous herbs like lobelia, Kloss concludes, will do everything that conventional doctors try to do with ''mercury, antitoxin, serums, vaccines, insulin, strychnine, digitalis, and all [their] poisonous drug preparations. . . .'' Samuel Thomson could not have put it better himself.

WORKING WITH THE TEXT

Cultural and Historical References

In this section, the numbers at the margin refer to the numbered paragraphs in the selection itself.

9. ''Jacksonian democracy'' is sometime described as popular democracy, in which independently minded common citizens take the reins of the government away from the big shots and grip them in their own hands. How is this like Thomson's plans for medical treatment?

10. What does the egalitarian mood of the country have to do with Thomson's popularity?

Writing Assignments: The Paragraph

Be sure to provide an introduction for each of the following paragraph writing assignments. That is, begin each paragraph with a phrase like this: "Thomas Brickle claims that. . . ." When it is relevant, you might also want to identify the expertise of the author ("Thomas Brickle, a New Testament scholar, claims that. . . ."), the name of the book or article, the century and country in which the work appeared, or any other circumstances that your readers might find significant. For more on this, see pp. 11–13 in Chapter 2.

1. In a paragraph, describe the comparison that Klaw makes between Jacksonian democracy and Thomsonian medicine.

2. In a paragraph, describe the theory that lay behind Thomson's treatments (paragraph 17) and the treatments that resulted from his theory.

3. Write a paragraph that follows this topic sentence: "Medical quackery of the past never quite goes away." Then summarize paragraphs 36 and 37.

Writing Assignments: The Short Essay

Use informal documentation for these short essays. That is, don't use footnotes or a Works Cited page to document your sources. Instead, cite only relevant information about your source, and keep that information *within* your text. Then follow the summary or quote with a page number in parenthesis. (Use the page numbers that you find in this book to represent the page numbers of the source.) Thus, your informal documentation will look something like this:

> In *The Romance of Medicine*, Benjamin Gordon, a history professor, claims that it was once believed that red wine replenished a person's depleted blood supply (p. 121).

1. Write a paper in which you try to explain why Thomson's medical treatments, though ineffective, were popular. (See in particular paragraphs 9 to 13.) If you can, combine your reasons with those of Klaw. If you can't come up with any beyond Klaw's, summarize his reasons and then elaborate on them, perhaps by adding to them historical examples that you can think of.

2. Write a paper in which you contrast the treatments for medical problems as recommended by Thomson and those recommended by orthodox physicians of the day.

3. Write a paper in which you criticize Thomson, perhaps by making fun of him a little. Paint Thomson as just another nineteenth-century quack. Emphasize his theory and the more extreme of his treatments.

4. Begin a paper with the quotation by L. J. Henderson in paragraph 35.

Fill the body of your paper with descriptions of Thomson's remedies for illness and orthodox remedies of the nineteenth-century. Paint both in the same critical light.

"FOR HER OWN GOOD"—THE TYRANNY OF THE EXPERTS

Barbara Ehrenreich and Deirdre English

Barbara Ehrenreich and Deirdre English are the authors of *Witches, Midwives, and Nurses* and *Complaints and Disorders: The Sexual Politics of Sickness.* In the work that we have reprinted, first published in *Ms.* magazine, Ehrenreich and English contend that nineteenth-century doctors based their treatment of women's medical problems on false stereotypes of female sexuality. This is the most controversial essay we have published in this chapter—and one of the most lively.

1. During the 19th century the medical profession threw itself with gusto on the languid figure of the female invalid. Popular advice books written by physicians took on a somber tone as they entered into "The Female Functions" or "The Diseases of Women." The theories that guided medical practice from the late 19th century to the early 20th century held that woman's *normal* state was to be sick. This was not advanced as an empirical observation, but as physiological fact. Medicine had "discovered" that female functions were inherently pathological. Menstruation, that perennial source of alarm to the male imagination, provided both the evidence and the explanation. Menstruation was a serious threat throughout life—so was the lack of it. According to Dr. Englemann, president of the American Gynecology Society in 1900:

> Many a young life is battered and forever crippled in the breakers of puberty; if it crosses these unharmed and is not dashed to pieces on the rock of childbirth, it may still ground on the ever-recurring shallows of menstruation, and lastly upon the final bar of the menopause where protection is found in the unruffled waters of the harbor beyond the reach of sexual storms.

2. The sickly, nervous woman of the upper or middle class with their unending, but fortunately nonfatal, ills became a natural "client caste" to the developing medical profession.

3. Meanwhile, the health of poor women received next to no attention from the medical profession. These women must have been at least as susceptible as wealthy women to the "sexual storms" doctors saw in menstruation, pregnancy, and so on, and they were definitely much more susceptible to the hazards of childbearing, tuberculosis, and of course, industrial diseases. Still, however sick or tired working-class women might have been, they certainly did not have the time or money to support a cult of invalidism. Dr. Dudley ruled poor women out as subjects for gynecological surgery on the simple ground that they lacked the leisure for successful treatment:

> The hardworking, daily-toiling woman is not as fit a subject for [gyne-

Source: Barbara Ehrenreich and Deirdre English. " 'For Her Own Good'—the Tyranny of the Experts," *Ms.* December 1978: 90, 92, 95–96, 98.

cological surgery] as the woman so situated in life as to be able to conserve her strength and, if necessary, to take a prolonged rest, in order to secure the best results.

So the logic was complete: better-off women were sickly because of their refined   **4.**
and civilized life-style. Fortunately, however, this same lifestyle made them amenable to lengthy medical treatment. Poor and working-class women were inherently stronger, and this was also fortunate, since their lifestyle disqualified them from lengthy medical treatment.

It was medicine's task to translate the evolutionary theory of women into the   **5.**
language of flesh and blood, tissues and organs. The result was a theory that put woman's mind, body, and soul in the thrall of her all-powerful reproductive organs. "The uterus, it must be remembered," Dr. F. Hollick wrote, "is the *controlling* organ in the female body, being the most excitable of all, and so intimately connected, by the ramifications of its numerous nerves, with every other part." Professor Hubbard addressing a medical society in 1870, observed that it seemed "as if the Almighty, in creating the female sex, *had taken the uterus and built up a woman around it.*"

To other medical theorists, it was the ovaries that occupied center stage. This   **6.**
passage written in 1870 by Dr. W. W. Bliss is, if somewhat overwrought, nonetheless typical:

> The gigantic power and influence of the ovaries over the whole animal
> economy of woman [*means*] that they are the most powerful agents in
> all the commotions of her system: that on them rest her intellectual
> standing in society; her physical perfection; and all that lends beauty to
> those fine and delicate contours . . . constant objects of admiration.

According to this "psychology of the ovary" woman's entire personality was   **7.**
directed by the ovaries, and any abnormalities, from irritability to insanity, could be traced to some ovarian disease.

It should be emphasized that woman's total submission to the "sex function"   **8.**
did not make her a *sexual* being. Women were urged by health books and doctors to indulge in deep preoccupation with themselves as "The Sex"; they were to devote themselves to developing their reproductive powers, and their maternal instincts. Yet doctors said that women had no predilection for the sex act itself. Hygiene manuals stated that the more cultured the woman, "the more is the sensual refined away from her nature," and warned against "any spasmodic convulsion" on a woman's part during intercourse lest it interfere with conception. Female sexuality was seen as unwomanly and possibly even detrimental to the supreme function of reproduction.

Since the reproductive organs were the source of disease, they were the obvious   **9.**
target in the treatment of disease. Any symptom—backaches, irritability, indigestion—could provoke a medical assault on the sexual organs. Historian Ann Douglas Wood describes the "local treatments" used in the mid-19th century for almost any female complaint:

> This [local] treatment had four stages, although not every case went
> through all four: a manual investigation, "leeching," "injections," and
> "cauterization." Dewees [an American medical professor] and Bennet,

a famous English gynecologist widely read in America, both advocated placing the leeches right on the vulva or the neck of the uterus, although Bennet cautioned the doctor to count them as they dropped off when satiated, lest he "lose" some. Bennet had known adventurous leeches to advance into the cervical cavity of the uterus itself, and he noted, "I think I have scarcely ever seen more acute pain than that experienced by several of my patients under these circumstances." Less distressing to a 20th-century mind, but perhaps even more senseless, were "injections" into the uterus. The uterus became a kind of catch-all, or what one exasperated doctor referred to as a "Chinese toy shop": water, milk and water, linseed tea, and "decoction of marshmellow . . . tepid or cold" found their way inside nervous women patients. The final step, performed at this time, one must remember, with no anesthetic but a little opium or alcohol, was cauterization, either through the application of nitrate of silver, or, in cases of more severe infection, through the use of much stronger hydrate of potassa, or even the "actual cautery," a "white-hot iron" instrument.

10. By the later part of the century, these fumbling experiments with the female interior gave way to the more decisive technique of surgery—aimed increasingly at the control of female personality disorders. There had been a brief fad of clitoridectomy (removal of the clitoris) in the 1860s, following the introduction of the operation by the English physician Isaac Baker Brown. Although most doctors frowned on the practice of removing the clitoris, they tended to agree that it might be necessary in cases of nymphomania, intractable masturbation, or "unnatural growth" of that organ.

11. The most common form of surgical intervention in the female personality was ovariotomy, removal of the ovaries—or "female castration." In 1906 a leading gynecological surgeon estimated that there were 150,000 women in the United States who had lost their ovaries under the knife. Some doctors boasted that they had each removed from 1,500 to 2,000 ovaries. Historian G. J. Barker-Benfield states:

> Among the indications were troublesomeness, eating like a ploughman, masturbation, attempted suicide, erotic tendencies, persecution mania, simple "cussedness," and dysmenorrhea [painful menstruation]. Most apparent in the enormous variety of symptoms doctors took to indicate castration was a strong current of sexual appetitiveness on the part of women.

12. The rationale for the operation flowed directly from theory of the "psychology of the ovary": since the ovaries controlled the personality, they must be responsible for any psychological disorders; conversely, psychological disorders were a sure sign of ovarian disease. Ergo, the organs must be removed.

13. One might think, given the all-powerful role of the ovaries, that an ovaryless woman would be like a rudderless ship—desexed and directionless. On the contrary, the proponents of ovariotomy argued, a woman who was relieved of a diseased ovary would be a *better* woman. One 1893 advocate of the operation claimed that "patients are improved, some of them cured . . . the moral sense of the patient is elevated . . .

she becomes tractable, orderly, industrious, and cleanly.'' Patients were often brought in by their husbands, who complained of their unruly behavior. Doctors also claimed that women—troublesome but still sane enough to recognize their problem—came to them "pleading to have their ovaries removed."

The reign of the uterus (and ovaries) was never entirely as tranquil and secure **14.** as the doctors might have wished. There was the constant threat of subversion by sexual feelings, arising from God knows what disorders of the brain or genitals. Nothing was more alarming than masturbation—known at the time as "self-abuse" or simply "the vice"—which could lead to menstrual dysfunction, uterine disease, lesions on the genitals, tuberculosis, dementia, and general decay. Parents were urged to watch their children for the first symptoms (pallor, languor, peevishness) and if necessary to strap their hands to their sides at night. Patients of both sexes were urged to "confess." In women even amorous thoughts inspired by reading, parties, flirtations, or "hot drinks" could upset the entire physiology. Doctors acknowledged a stern duty to oppose the reading of romantic novels as "one of the greatest causes of uterine disease in young women."

As the century wore on, the hegemony of the uterus appeared to grow ever **15.** shakier. More and more middle-class women were seeking college educations. To the doctors it seemed as if a new organ had entered the contest for power—the female brain. Nineteenth-century gynecology became absorbed in the combat between the brain and the uterus for dominion over the female persona.

The possibility of peaceful coexistence between the two organs was ruled out by **16.** the basic laws of physiology. Medical men saw the body as a miniature economic system, with the various parts—like classes or interest groups—competing for a limited supply of resources. Each body contained a set quantity of energy which could be directed variously from one function to another. Thus there was inevitably a tension between the different functions, or organs—one could be developed only at the expense of the others. Strangely enough, doctors saw no reason to worry about conflicts between the lungs and the spleen, or the liver and the kidneys, or other possible pairs of combatants. The central drama, in bodies male or female, was that great duel between the *brain* and the *reproductive organs*.

Needless to say, the desirable outcome of this struggle was different for the two **17.** sexes. Men were urged to back the brain, and to fight the debilitating effects of sexual indulgence.

In reverse but almost parallel terms, women were urged to throw their weight **18.** behind the uterus and resist the temptations of the brain. Because reproduction was woman's grand purpose in life, doctors agreed that women had to concentrate all their energy downward toward the womb. All other activity should be slowed down or stopped during the peak periods of uterine energy demand. At puberty, girls were advised to take a great deal of bed rest in order to help focus their strength on regulating their periods—though this might take years.

Pregnancy was also a period requiring intense mental vacuity. One theory had **19.** the brain and the pregnant uterus competing not only for energy, but for a material substance—phosphates. Every mental effort of the mother-to-be could deprive the unborn child of some of this vital nutrient, or would so overtax the woman's own system that she would be driven to insanity and require "prolonged administration of phosphates.'' Menopause brought no relief from the imperious demands of the uterus. Doctors described it as a ''Pandora's box of ills,'' requiring, once again, a period of bovine placidity.

But it was not enough to urge women in the privacy of the office or sickroom **20.** to side with the beleaguered uterus. The brain was a powerful opponent, as the advance of the Women's Movement and the growing number of educated women showed. So the doctors were led, beginning in the 1870s, into the ongoing public debate over female education.

Dr. Edward H. Clarke's book, *Sex in Education, or a Fair Chance for the Girls*, **21.** was the great uterine manifesto of the 19th century. It appeared at the height of the pressure for coeducation at Harvard, where Clarke was a professor, and went through 17 editions in the space of a few years. Clarke reviewed the medical theories of female nature—the innate frailty of women, the brain-uterus competition—and concluded, with startling but unassailable logic, that higher education would cause women's uteruses to atrophy!

Armed with Clarke's arguments, doctors agitated vociferously about the dangers **22.** of female education. R. R. Coleman, M.D., of Birmingham, Alabama, thundered this warning:

> Women beware. You are on the brink of destruction: you have hitherto
> been engaged in crushing your waists; now you are attempting to culti-
> vate your mind. You have been merely dancing all night in the foul air
> of the ballroom; now you are beginning to spend your mornings in
> study. . . . Science pronounces that the woman who studies is lost.

Dozens of medical researchers rushed in to plant the banner of science on the **23.** territory opened up by Clarke's book. Female students, their studies showed, were pale, in delicate health, and prey to monstrous deviations from menstrual regularity. A 1902 study showed that 42 percent of the women admitted to insane asylums were well educated compared to only 16 percent of the men—''proving,'' obviously, that higher education was driving women crazy. But the consummate evidence was the college woman's dismal contribution to the birthrate. An 1895 study found that 28 percent of female college graduates married, compared to 80 percent of women in general. The birthrate was falling among white middle-class people in general, and most precipitously among the college-educated.

The doctors and psychologists conceded that it was possible for a woman, if she **24.** were sufficiently determined, to dodge the destiny prepared for her by untold eons of evolutionary struggle, and throw in her lot with the *brain*. But the resulting ''mental woman'' could only hope to be a freak, morally and medically. ''She has taken up and utilized in her own life all that was meant for her descendants,'' G. Stanley Hall complained. ''This is the very apotheosis of selfishness from the standpoint of every biological ethic.'' Physically, the results were predictable: ''First, she loses mammary function,'' Hall wrote—since lactation seemed to represent woman's natural unselfish- ness. Some medical writings suggested that the loss of the mammary function would be accompanied by an actual loss of the breasts. ''In her evening gown she shows evidence of joints which had been adroitly hidden beneath tissues of soft flesh,'' wrote Arabella Kenealy, M.D., of the ''mental'' woman, ''and already her modesty has been put to the necessity of puffing and pleating, where Nature had planned the tenderest and most dainty of devices,'' *i.e.*, the breast.

The medical warnings against higher education did not go unheeded. Martha **25.** Carey Thomas, president of Bryn Mawr College, confessed that as a young woman she had been ''terror-struck'' after reading the chapters relating to women in Hall's mammoth work *Adolescence*, lest she ''and every other woman . . . were doomed to live as pathological invalids . . .'' as a result of their education. Martha Carey Thomas survived her education and pursued a full and demanding career, but there were also casualties. Dr. Margaret Cleaves of Des Moines ended by confessing the futility of her attempts at a career. In her own description she had been a ''mannish maiden'' from the start and had let her masculine ambition draw her into a medical education. But no sooner had she achieved her goal than she developed a galloping case of neurasthenia, or ''sprained brain'' as she called it.

The notion of the female body as the battleground of the uterus and the brain led **26.** to two possible therapeutic approaches: one was to intervene in the reproductive area—removing ''diseased'' organs or strengthening the uterus with bracing doses of silver nitrate, injections, cauterizations, bleeding, and so on. The other approach was to go straight for the brain and attempt to force its surrender directly. The doctors could hardly use the same kind of surgical techniques on the brain as they had on the ovaries and uterus, but they discovered more subtle methods. The most important of these was the ''rest cure''—the world-famous invention of Dr. S. Weir Mitchell.

The rest cure depended on the now-familiar techniques of 20th-century brainwash- **27.** ing—total isolation and sensory deprivation. For approximately six weeks the patient was to lie on her back in a dimly lit room. She was not permitted to read. If her case was particularly severe, she was not even permitted to rise to urinate.

The cure became immensely popular—largely because, unlike other gynecologi- **28.** cal treatments, this one was painless. As a result of the rest cure, Philadelphia (where Mitchell practiced) was soon ''the mecca for patients from all over the world.'' Jane Addams underwent the rest cure, but it was apparently unsuccessful since it had to be followed with six more *months* of rest during which Addams was ''literally bound to a bed'' in her sister's house.

The secret of the rest cure lay not in the soft foods, the massages, or even, **29.** ultimately, in the intellectual deprivation, but in the doctor himself. S. Weir Mitchell must be counted as one of the great pioneers; perhaps the greatest, in the development of the 20th-century doctor / patient relationship, or more generally, the expert / woman relationship. He was, by his own description, a ''despot'' in the sickroom. Patients were to ask no questions. His manner would be gentle and sympathetic one moment, abrupt and commanding the next. Now magnify Dr. Mitchell's authoritarianism by the conditions of the rest cure:

The patient has been lying in semi-darkness all day. She has not seen any other **30.** man, and no person but the nurse, for weeks. She is weak and languid from lying still for so long. Enter Dr. Mitchell. He is confident, commanding, scientific. He chides the patient for her lack of progress, or predicts exactly how she will feel tomorrow, in one week, in a month. The patient can only feel a deep gratitude for this particle of attention, this strange substitute for human companionship. She resolves that she *will* get better, as he has said she must, which means she will try to be a better woman, more completely centered on her reproductive functions.

It is as if Dr. Mitchell recognized that in the battle between the uterus and the **31.**

brain, a third organ would have to be called into play—the phallus. The "local treatments" of earlier decades had already proposed the need for direct male penetration to set errant females straight.

The physician, according to Mitchell, could heal by the force of his masculinity **32.** alone. This was, of course, the ultimate argument against female doctors: they could not "obtain the needed control over those of their own sex." Only a male could command the total submissiveness which constituted the "cure."

If the patient did not yield to Mitchell's erect figure at the bedside, he would **33.** threaten to bring out his own, literal phallus. For example, according to a popular anecdote, one patient failed to recover at the end of her rest.

> Dr. Mitchell had run the gamut of argument and persuasion and finally announced, "If you are not out of bed in five minutes—I'll get into it with you!" He thereupon started to remove his coat, the patient still obstinately prone—he removed his vest, but when he started to take off his trousers—she was out of bed in a fury!

WORKING WITH THE TEXT

Cultural and Historical References

In this section on vocabulary and cultural allusions, the numbers at the margin refer to the numbered paragraphs in the selection itself.

1. What do you suppose the authors mean when they say that menstruation is a "perennial source of alarm to the male imagination"?

15. "Hegemony" is a political word, meaning the domination of one state over another. How does that meaning fit here?

19. Where is the source for these quoted words: "prolonged administration of phosphates" and "Pandora's box of ills"?

21. The authors claim that Dr. Edward Clarke, in his book, *Sex in Education, or a Fair Chance for the Girls*, concludes that higher education would result in the atrophy of women's uteruses. Do you think that Ehrenreich and English need to support *their* claim by quoting something from Clarke's book?

28. Jane Addams (1860–1935) was a social worker who founded the famous Hull House in Chicago. She was also a leader in movements for women's suffrage and peace.

Writing Assignments: The Paragraph

Be sure to provide an introduction for each of the following paragraph writing assignments. That is, begin each paragraph with a phrase like this: "Thomas Brickle claims that. . . ." When it is relevant, you might also want to identify the expertise of the author ("Thomas Brickle, a New Testament scholar, claims that. . . ."), the name of the book or article, the century and country in which the work appeared, or any other circumstances that your readers might find significant. For more on this, see pp. 11–13 in Chapter 2.

1. Write a paragraph that discusses this question: Does what Ehrenreich and English say in the first sentence of paragraph 4 follow from what they've said thus far?

2. Summarize the episode concerning Dr. S. Weir Mitchell in paragraphs 29 to 34.

3. Write a paragraph or two—or a short paper if you like—in which you examine the author's generalizations, summaries, and quotations in paragraph 19.

Writing Assignments: The Essay

Use informal documentation for these short essays. That is, don't use footnotes or a Works Cited page to document your sources. Instead, cite only relevant information about your source, and keep that information *within* your text. Then follow the summary or quote with a page number in parenthesis. (Use the page numbers that you find in this book to represent the page numbers of the source.) Thus, your informal documentation will look something like this:

> In *The Romance of Medicine*, Benjamin Gordon, a history professor, claims that it was once believed that red wine replenished a person's depleted blood supply (p. 121).

1. Analyze the statistics in paragraph 23. Try to *explain* them. Why, for instance, might more educated women end up in insane asylums. And why might fewer women college graduates marry? Since your paper will be pure speculation, don't be too dogmatic about your conclusions.

2. Play devil's advocate. Take Ehrenreich and English to task for using male stereotypes, for overgeneralizing (using one doctor to represent the entire medical profession), and for exaggeration.

ESSAYS ON *MEDICINE BEFORE SCIENCE*

Short Essays

Use informal documentation for these short essays. That is, don't use foot-notes or a Works Cited page to document your sources. Instead, cite only relevant information about your source, and keep that information *within* your text. Then follow the summary or quote with a page number in parenthe-sis. (Use the page numbers that you find in this book to represent the page numbers of the source.) Thus, your informal documentation will look something like this:

> In *The Romance of Medicine*, Benjamin Gordon, a history professor, claims that it was once believed that red wine replenished a per-son's depleted blood supply (p. 121).

1. Write a report on the "sad tales of the death of kings" by combining information in "Jeers and Chaos" with paragraph 38 of "The Four Juices."

2. Write a report on the practice of bloodletting by combining material from "The Four Juices," "Belly-My-Grizzle," and "I gave him barks and saltpeter . . ."

3. Analyze the reasoning that lay behind the theory of signatures.

4. Use "I gave him barks and saltpeter . . ." to back the claims of Ehrenreich and English (in "For Her Own Good") that those who ministered to women's illnesses were preoccupied with women's sexual organs.

Long Essays

For rules governing formal documentation, see Chapter 6.

1. Write a paper on medical theories before the twentieth century.

2. Write a paper with this thesis: "Before the twentieth century, doctors allowed dogma to rule over simple observation."

3. Write a paper with this thesis: "Doctors before the twentieth century consistently violated the Hippocratic motto: 'First of all, do no harm.' "

4. Examine the reasoning and authority that lay behind the theory of signatures, the theory of demon-caused illness, and the theory of the four humors. Use the relevant essays in this chapter to support your points.

5. Describe and discuss the agonies of patients before the discovery of effective anesthesia.

8

The Jonestown Massacre:
How Could It Happen?

INTRODUCTION

In 1978 the members of a San Francisco cult, who had immigrated to a jungle in South America, lined up before a vat of strawberry punch which was laced with tranquilizers and cyanide. Their leader, a tall dark man by the name of Jim Jones, sat in a chair overlooking the vat. "Bring the babies first," he shouted. Obediently, many of the mothers brought up their babies and, with a syringe, squirted the poison down their babies' throats. After a short time nearly 900 of Jones's flock had committed suicide by drinking the poisoned punch.

After the news stories had died down, after the blame for the affair had landed first on one thing, then another, after newspaper editorialists had had their say—after all the immediate responses were over—one question, the really important question of the whole affair, remained in the air: How did those people get talked into destroying themselves?

Some of the writers who studied the Jonestown massacre looked to the past for an answer. There had been a few—but only a few—mass suicides before Jonestown. But they were remote and exotic affairs, generally heroic in nature, and they offered few instructive comparisons. The first-century Jews at Masada, for instance, had killed themselves in their stronghold rather than be taken by the invading Roman soldiers. But there is an essential difference between Masada and Jonestown: the Jewish defenders of Masada were doomed. The Roman army was at the gates, and there were likely to be few survivors among the defenders after the Romans swarmed through Masada. Only a few of the most gullible of the Jonestown "communards" believed that the U.S. government was going to massacre them.

In "The Lure of Our Many Cults," Henry Allen mentions the thousands of South American Indians who had committed suicide rather than continue to endure cruel and pitiless treatment by the Spanish conquistadors. But once again there is a difference between the two affairs: The members of Jim Jones's "church," unlike the Indians, were not the captives of a foreign army. Though some of the members were treated shabbily, their treatment can hardly be compared to the cruelties inflicted on the South American Indians by the Spaniards.

The list of these mass suicides is a short one. They seem so rare, in fact, that on the surface they resemble circus freak shows more than the stuff of normal human experience. But just as we know that the freak who sits on the platform staring back at us shares with us the deeper matters of the human heart, we also know that those who listened to Jones rant and then lifted the poison to their lips resemble us more than we would like to admit. In fact, we could probably find someone much like ourselves among the membership of the People's Temple. The membership of the church ranged from uneducated street blacks to privileged whites with postgraduate degrees.

There are other lessons. In an essay that we reprint in this chapter, Kenneth Wooden describes the radical lawyers who eased the way for Jim Jones by threatening those who stood in his way; the establishment politicians who needed precinct workers from Jones and gave him back respectability; the newspapers in San Francisco who wrote glowing stories about the People's Temple without checking too closely on the rumors that were coming out the People's Temple of Jim Jones.

But it's easy to find blame in cases like this: hindsight is always 20/20. So back to *the* question: How did Jim Jones talk those people into killing themselves? Why did the people drink the punch? Where was their will? How could they be such fools? Are people really that weak? We always come circling back to those questions because they are really personal questions. You see, underneath the question of why *they* did it is the unspoken question of whether we would have been that weak. And that question is *much* harder to answer. *Would I, under similar circumstances, have drunk the poison?*

A similar question arose in 1945 when Russian and American troops opened up the Jewish concentration camps. But the question then wasn't about the victims; it was about the oppressors. After the horror had been digested, the question that remained was the same: *Could I have been so evil?*

There were people who heard Jim Jones's spiel and didn't join the People's Temple. There were those who joined up, stayed for a while, and then quit. And there were a few in the jungle who ran away while the rest were drinking from the poisoned vat. Each of us hopes that we will be the ones who resist, that we will be the heroes when everyone around us is weakening. But most of us are not. In Jonestown, a handful; in Germany a few.

In his small way, Jones underwent a familiar metamorphosis. Like any number of idealists before him—Robespierre, Lenin, Mao Tse-tung, Mussolini—Jones grew to love power for its own sake. When the carnage was over, Jones's followers, in particular those who survived the Guyana experience, provided us with a close look at the process by which a person can evolve into a monster. That transformation illustrates, once again, the truth of Lord Acton's famous words: "Power tends to corrupt, and absolute power corrupts absolutely."

So a chapter like this can be instructive in a deep way. By the time you've read the essays in this chapter, you may not know more about *your* heart (though we hope you will), but you will see how power can seduce, and you will understand, in part at least, the reasons for the sheeplike behavior of Jim Jones's followers.

But it will take *essays*, because there's not a single essay that explains it all. You will see that the Jonestown massacre happened because a variety of forces converged at that jungle clearing. Jim Jones, megalomaniac and drug addict, was only the spider at the center.

The holocaust showed us that we could be oppressors; the Jonestown massacre showed us we could be victims.

THE LURE OF OUR MANY CULTS

Henry Allen

In this essay Henry Allen, a *Washington Post* staff writer, discusses the appeals of other cults of the 1960s and introduces a variety of psychological theories in his effort to account for Jones's megalomania and compelling power over his followers.

In an age in which everything was permitted, yet little seemed real, the Reverend **1.** Jim Jones promised a refuge.

At his Peoples Temples in California and in the jungles of Guyana, little enough **2.** was permitted—disciples surrendered property, privacy, logic, freedoms. And in a blaze of certainty lit by Jones's charisma, paranoia, deceits, and power lust, they found the final reality—death.

"They were smiling . . . they were genuinely happy," said Mark Lane, a lawyer **3.** for the cult who fled into the jungle just before the mass suicide began with the pouring of cyanide into babies' mouths.

Literate, adult Americans, supposedly immunized against such madness by 20th century education and science—these children of the Enlightenment—watched their own children, their spouses, and friends die in foaming convulsions, then waited—even happily—to fall dead in their turns. Only they could understand whatever message they tried to send with their deaths, so it died with them. But they were already long past appreciating this savage paradox.

Genuinely happy. If Lane is right, here lies the real terror for the rest of us. **4.**

All week, in the aftermath, historians groped for precedents, psychiatrists for **5.** motivations, community leaders for courses of action. How could this have happened? Could it happen again?

Source: Allen, Henry, "The Lure of Our Many Cults," *The Washington Post.* November 26, 1978, sec. c:1.

Except for the smugness of hindsights offered by foes of the mind-control cults **6.**
that have emerged in the last decade, there are no simple answers. Instead, a variety
of explanations rises out of fact and theory. None suffices in itself. But taken together,
they begin to show how the madness of one man could converge with the spirit of an
age in upheaval to weave a doomed nexus out of strands ranging from the most ancient
of human instincts and customs to the physiology of the mammalian brain.

The comfort, here, is cold indeed. For all that it was bizarre beyond thinking, we **7.**
don't need a Jim Jones to invoke the supernatural to explain the immolation in Guyana.
It was a human—frighteningly human—experience.

It has happened before. Scientists and historians rushed to sweep the carnage **8.**
into the corner of anomaly, but suicides—even mass suicides—for gods and principles,
right and wrong, have occurred in various contexts throughout history.

On April 15, A.D. 73, nearly 1,000 Jewish defenders of the fortress Masada killed **9.**
themselves rather than be taken prisoner by the besieging Romans. According to
Gibbon, the 4th and 5th centuries were marked by the willful martyrdoms of the
Donatists, who in seeking heaven "frequently stopped travelers on the public highways
and obliged them to inflict the stroke of martyrdom by promise of a reward, if they
consented_ and by the threat of instant death, if they refused to grant so very singular
a favor."

In the 13th century, the fervor of the Albigensians and Cathars (heretical sects **10.**
in southern France) to avoid the material and seek the spiritual led to numerous deaths
from self-willed starvation. A. Alvarez, author of *The Savage God*, writes that after
the conquest of the New World, "treatment at the hands of the Spanish was so cruel
that the Indians killed themselves by the thousands rather than endure it . . . In the
West Indies, according to the Spanish historian Girolamo Benzoni, four thousand men
and countless women and children died by jumping from cliffs or by killing each
other."

In the upheavals of the Industrial Revolution, the romantic rebellion turned **11.**
suicide into a fad. After the appearance of Goethe's novel, *The Sorrows of Young
Werther*, Europe was swept by Werther-like suicides. Before the end of World War II,
thousands of Japanese soldiers and civilians killed themselves en masse after island
battles rather than be dishonored by defeat or surrender. Vietnamese Buddhists
registered political protests by setting themselves afire in the 1960s. In 1970, about a
dozen French students killed themselves as a political gesture.

But these acts, however irrational, come within the pale of understanding. What **12.**
promise of heaven, or threat of disaster or dishonor, could have tempted the Peoples
Temple disciples?

There were no mercenaries, of course. There was little "situation" to become **13.**
hopeless. The Peoples Temple was hardly known outside California, much less under
attack, except for some West Coast media probes. Jones had sizable political clout—he
was head of the San Francisco Housing Authority—and a treasury that may have held
millions of dollars. He and his followers had everything, by conventional wisdom, to
live for.

But conventional American wisdom has never come to terms with the spiritual **14.**
upheavals and cult phenomena that started growing out of the disarray of American
society a decade ago. As a secular society, we've ignored the power of messianic

personalities and their persuasive techniques; and we've forgotten the terrible charm of absolutism—or paranoia—in an age of uncertainty.

"What you have to remember is that leaders like Jones always believe in **15.** what they're doing—it's a divine calling," says Syracuse University anthropologist Agehananda Bharati. "Once a person is embarked on this path, it will lead to a power quest. There's a point of no return, a snapping point. Suddenly you need more and more power to be sure of yourself—and the quest becomes linked to the divine calling.

"There are cults and cult leaders all over the world, and always have been. In **16.** the South Pacific we have the cargo cults [whose members believe in the imminent arrival of shiploads of goods and money, if they can only have complete faith that it will happen]. In India there are gurus such as Sai Baba, who has 10 million followers. But often, in other cults, something comes along to slow the momentum of the power quest. People object, for instance. Jones managed to escape that by taking his followers to Guyana where there was no media, no possibility of dissent or investigation."

The divine calling. Like most messiahs and prophets, Jones, a minister by **17.** profession, seems to have started with a vision. Around 1961 he saw a holocaust consuming Indianapolis, where he was living. (In *The Varieties of Religious Experience*, William James writes of "the psychopathic temperament in religious biography . . . The subjects here actually feel themselves played upon by powers beyond their will.") A few years later, in the archetypal pattern outlined by sociologist Max Weber, Jones had gathered a group of followers and led them to a new land in Ukiah, California. He established a multiracial community which quickly became a political force in Mendocino County. In 1971 he bought his Geary Street temple in San Francisco, then expanded to Los Angeles. He preached socialism and practiced faith healing, praised Huey Newton and Angela Davis, and expanded his apocalyptic vision by predicting a fascist takeover of America.

Being so sure of his ends, Jones had no doubt about means, a philosophy he **18.** passed along to disciples. According to cult defectors, Jones gained an estimated following of 20,000 by staging faith healings. As in all hermetic sects, there were levels of understanding. Those who suspected fraud justified it on the ground that it brought more recruits to the truth of Jim Jones. Jones claimed to be the inheritor of the spirit of Lenin, Jesus, Buddha and the brotherhood of man, to be God, some defectors recall. His means were beyond question.

Jones's paranoia, power and manipulation fed on themselves. His delusions, **19.** legitimized by his divine calling, had nothing to check them when he secluded his mission in the Guyana rain forest.

"This wouldn't have happened if they hadn't been so isolated," says Dr. J. **20.** Thomas Ungerleider of the UCLA Neuropsychiatric Institute. "With no feedback from the outside world you can do incredible things with peer pressure. Paranoia becomes a useful tool. It's a binding force. With it, you'll engage in peer-pressure activities even more."

And with paranoia, Jones' beliefs that vast conspiracies were arrayed against him **21.** only bolstered the certainty of the rightness of his cause, his delusions of importance, and his fears of losing it.

In fact, he may have been courting disaster all the time. "These people look **22.** desperately for martyrdom," says Bharati.

"He was irate at the light in which he had been portrayed in the media," Deborah **23.**
Layton Blakey testified last June. "He felt that as a consequence of having been
ridiculed and maligned, he would be denied a place in history. His obsession was with
his place in history. When pondering the loss of what he considered his rightful place
in history, he would grow despondent and say that all was lost."

He made his first mass suicide threat in September 1977, threatening the deaths **24.**
of all followers in a mere dispute over a custody case involving one child. The Guyana
courts backed off.

Just when it appeared that Representative Leo Ryan would end his investigative **25.**
mission to Jonestown with a relatively favorable impression, a knifing attempt and then
the airfield attack ensured doom. Finally, Jones had vindicated himself by fulfilling his
own holocaustic prophecies. He had no choice. His only way out was martyrdom, the
more spectacular the better. He had organized it well in advance, so that his followers
would die too, arms linked, fallen in embraces, testimony to his wisdom.

"It may be that as the cult phenomenon is receding, the cults get a sense of **26.**
desperation, a sense of need for still more desperate acts," says Yale psychiatrist
Robert Jay Lifton, author of *Thought Reform and the Psychology of Totalism.*

Like many of the cults and esoteric religions which began attracting Americans **27.**
in the late 1960s, Peoples Temple had lost a large part of its membership by 1978. As
the upheavals of a decade ago have eased in the somnolent '70s, religious refuges and
revelations have lost allure.

It's hard to remember, now, that the turn of the decade was called the third **28.**
"Great Awakening" by a number of scholars—the first two having been religious
revivals in the early 18th and 19th centuries.

Then, as in the late '60s, the nation was swept by proponents of ecstatic religion, **29.**
in which converts were invited to sense God first-hand, rather than through the
intermediaries of theology and sacraments.

The 1960s movement had two stages. In the first, the enemy was not Satan and **30.**
sin but establishment reason and technology, along with the reality they described.
Heroes included British psychiatrist R. D. Laing, who argued in *The Politics of
Experience* that schizophrenia was as valid a reality as establishment "sanity." And
there was humanist psychologist Abraham Maslow, who advocated the cultivation of
the sort of "peak experiences" which mark the lives of saints and prophets.

American spiritual life, often a drab business of church suppers and bingo games, **31.**
exploded with alternatives: Tibetan Buddhism, the mysterious wisdom of Carlos
Castaneda's Don Juan, meditation, glossolalia, primal screaming, biofeedback, and Zen
in the art of practically everything. LSD and other psychedelics became anodynes for
the situation once described in graffiti in a Boston men's room: "Reality is a crutch."

In short, everything became permitted, but reality—which religion ultimately **32.**
defines—became very unsure indeed. The problem was that this movement, rather than
attacking a well-entrenched establishment, was largely a symptom of its collapse in
the storm of Vietnam, racial strife, generational enmity, and rapidly shifting mores. It
publicly played itself out in Haight-Ashbury, where in 1967 a "summer of love"
turned into a nightmare of rape and drug addiction. Then the Charles Manson murders
in 1969 showed that LSD revelations could lead to lethal paranoia and messianic
delusion.

So when the second stage, the so-called mind-control cults, began to appear with **33.** many of the popular esoteric trappings but none of the chaos, the change was often greeted with relief.

In the mid-'60s, the Hare Krishna cult arrived in America. Far from "doing their **34.** own thing," cult members dressed in identical robes, men shaving their heads except for a top knot. With drums and finger cymbals they chanted for hours on street corners and harassed passersby for contributions. Like so many other cult members, they always looked tired, undernourished and ecstatic.

In 1968, David "Moses" Berg founded the fire-eyed Children of God to preach **35.** salvation in the face of the earthquake fever that swept the hip West Coast psyche that year. In 1971, a 13-year-old Indian named Guru Maharaj Ji arrived from India to found the Divine Light Mission. Meanwhile, Sun Myung Moon had come from Korea to build his Unification Church into the most controversial of all the cults, which seemed to exist in a constant barrage of charges ranging from financial malfeasance to brainwashing.

A host of smaller or less controversial movements accompanied the cults: **36.** Yogi Bhajan's 3HO group (one cell of which runs the Golden Temple Restaurant), Transcendental Meditation, and Rev. Jim Jones' Peoples Temple, among hundreds, perhaps thousands, of groups.

The quest was for certainty. Just as Christians in late antiquity had sought to flee **37.** the iron determinism of astrology, these cultists sought an escape from chaos. They tended to stress their identification with middle-class American values, often dressing conservatively.

"The cult promises to provide, and indeed does provide for the convinced **38.** convert, the assurance and absolutism the large society so conspicuously lacks," state S. P. Hersh of the National Institute of Mental Health and Ann Macleod of the University of Maryland, in a paper entitled "Cults and Youth Today." "Once the initial decision is taken—to join—the rest comes ready-made: what is right, what is wrong, who shall be saved and who not, how to eat, how to dress, how to live."

The cults represent what anthropologists have long identified in cultures around **39.** the world as a revitalization movement, following on what anthropologist Anthony F. C. Wallace calls "a period of cultural distortion," marked by such things as alcoholism, "extreme passivity and indolence, intragroup violence, disregard of kinship and sexual mores, irresponsibility in public officials . . ."

Examples of such movements include the Plains Indians' Ghost Dance movement **40.** in the late 19th century, the Boxer Rebellion in China, the South Seas cargo cults, and even the Bolshevik Revolution of 1917.

As Wallace explains it, a prophet has one or several hallucinatory visions, such **41.** as Jones's vision of a holocaust. He preaches his revelations to people "in an evangelistic or messianic spirit." Then "converts are made by the prophet. Some undergo hysterical seizures induced by suggestion in a crowd situation; some experience an ecstatic vision in private circumstances; some are convinced by more or less rational arguments . . ." The prophet changes his message to fit his needs. "In instances where organized hostility to the movement develops, a crystallization of counter-hostility against unbelievers frequently occurs, and emphasis shifts from cultivation of the ideal to combat against the unbeliever."

Such is the fate of a large number of American cults. That combat sometimes **42.** takes the form of ridiculously high-stakes gambles: the Children of God predicted the end of the world with the arrival of the comet Kohoutek; Guru Maharaj Ji's adherents rented the Houston Astrodome for a mammoth convention at which they predicted apocalyptic confirmation of their doctrine, even setting aside spaces in the parking lot for flying saucers.

More recently, the Transcendental Meditation movement tried to bolster declining **43.** membership with claims that they could teach adherents to levitate and fly.

The combat has taken harsher forms. In the past year, members of Synanon, a **44.** California group originally founded in the 1950s to treat drug addiction, have been accused of attempting to murder a prosecutor by putting a rattlesnake in his mailbox. Members of the Church of Scientology, another group dating from the '50s, were indicted for stealing files the government had maintained on the group. One prankster who hit Guru Maharaj Ji in the face with a pie later had his skull fractured with a hammer wielded, he charged, by a Divine Light Mission official. Last summer, a self-styled renegade Mormon prophet named Immanuel David, who had been visited like Jones by holocaustic visions, killed himself. The next morning his wife helped their seven children jump from their eleventh-floor hotel room, then followed them. And Jim Jones abandoned America, hurling back the threats of assassination and suicide that became fact last week.

"The unnatural passivism of [cult] members," is actually "a carefully muted **45.** aggressiveness," write Katherine V. Kemp and John R. Lion, professors of psychiatry at the University of Maryland School of Medicine.

The cults have flourished, too, because the American establishment, founded on **46.** rationalism and Lockean tabula rasa theories of the mind (in which mankind is seen to be infinitely educable, with no inborn predispositions) is extremely reluctant to admit that human beings may be innately susceptible to certain persuasive techniques. In *Battle for the Mind* and *The Mind Possessed*, British neurologist William Sargant has cited laboratory evidence gathered by Pavlov and his own observations of acute combat stress in World War II as part of a hypothesis that stress, if strong enough, "can produce a marked increase in hysterical suggestibility so that the individual becomes susceptible to influences in his environment to which he was formerly immune." Says anthropologist Bharati, "It can happen to anybody."

Former cult members recite a litany of stress they underwent: sleep deprivation, **47.** hunger, constant haranguing, and in the case of Peoples Temple, public beatings and threats of death.

Psychiatrist Lifton notes: "Mind control comes when you have total control of **48.** communication in an environment; when you have manipulation in an environment; when you have manipulation inside the group, such as constant self-criticism and confessing; and manipulation of individual guilt."

If Sargant is right, we are innately and physically susceptible. Ethologist Konrad **49.** Lorenz brings it into the realm of instinct in *On Aggression*. Once instilled with the sort of paranoia Jones purveyed, the follower is driven by "militant enthusiasm by which any group defends its own social norms and rites against another group not possessing them . . . One is ready to abandon all for the call of what, in the moment of this specific emotion, seems to be a sacred duty."

So lured by security and order, betrayed by physiology and instinct, cult members **50.** can be willing to follow their leaders even into death.

Some cult observers maintain that it is largely those who are mentally ill or close **51.** to it who join the cults. Dr. John Clark, a professor of psychiatry at the Harvard Medical School, has estimated from his studies that 58 percent of those who join cults are schizophrenic, either chronic or borderline. But he adds that 42 percent of those he examined were neither ill nor damaged.

In any case, we are left with the hideous vision of smiling disciples drinking **52.** cyanide. We can explain it away as a terrible accident, saying that the cult members were duped into thinking the exercise was just another rehearsal. We could claim that the cultists were forced to kill themselves. But that does not explain the smiles, the failure of more members to flee, the dying with arms linked with fellow disciples. In fact, a survivor recalls one woman objecting, only to be shouted down with cries of "traitor."

UCLA's Ungerleider speculates that "they may have killed themselves willingly **53.** out of what Anna Freud called 'identification with the aggressor.' It's a defense mechanism in hopeless situations, when the ego is overwhelmed. It explains why some Jews would actually help each other into the gas chambers in concentration camps." Even when the dying began, and panic twitched through the camp, Jones could keep the mad momentum going by insisting that they must "die with dignity."

We might do well to consider that they died knowingly, believing that death was **54.** beautiful, as Jones kept chanting into his microphone. Indeed, if they shared his paranoia, his vision of the holocaust, the fate that awaited the community after the murder of Representative Ryan was far worse than death.

In the terms of French sociologist Emile Durkheim, they had preached an **55.** "altruistic" suicide, for the glory of socialism. But when the time came, it was merely "anomic"—self-destruction in the face of the disintegration of all that was meaningful, a universe which existed only in their minds.

To his followers, Jones was a god whose power they could take into themselves **56.** merely by obeying him. It may have seemed, as they drank the cyanide, that for one moment they would share in ultimate power—the power of life and death. If, in the falling and convulsions, that moment ever came, no one will ever know.

WORKING WITH THE TEXT

Cultural and Historical References

In this section, the numbers at the margin refer to the numbered paragraphs in the selection itself.

3. "Enlightenment" refers to the intellectual movement in the eighteenth century which was devoted to reason and rationalism. It is also called the Age of Reason. With this in mind, what do you think Allen meant when he said that the members of the Jonestown cult were "children of the Enlightenment"?

6. Can you define "nexus" by its content?

8. What does Allen mean when he says that "historians rushed to sweep the carnage into the corner of anomaly"?

14. Versions of the word "messiah" are used in this paragraph and in paragraph 17. Why is the word particularly appropriate when used in the context of the Jonestown massacre?

16. Where is Guyana? Is there any place in the essay that tells us?

17. Huey Newton and Angela Davis were famous 1960s black radicals. Davis presently teaches in a California college.

31. *Zen and the Art of Motorcycle Maintenance* was the intriguing title of a best-selling book at the time when Allen wrote this essay for *The Washington Post.*

32. Charles Manson is presently in prison for his part as the charismatic leader of the Sharon Tate murders. Manson had "brainwashed" his followers into murdering the actress Sharon Tate and a number of her friends.

37. Why is astrology called "iron determinism"?

46. "Lockean tabula rasa" refers to John Locke's famous argument that the human brain is a blank slate at birth.

Writing Assignments: The Paragraph

Be sure to provide an introduction for each of the following paragraph writing assignments. That is, begin each paragraph with a phrase like this: "Thomas Brickle claims that. . . ." When it is relevant, you might also want to identify the expertise of the author ("Thomas Brickle, a New Testament scholar, claims that. . . ."), the name of the book or article, the century and country in which the work appeared, or any other circumstances that your readers might find significant. For more on this, see pp. 11–13 in Chapter 2.

1. Write a paragraph in which you explain the purpose of paragraphs 9 to 11 in the light of paragraph 12.

2. Paragraph 51 seems to contradict paragraphs 46 to 50. Explain.

3. In a paragraph, summarize and quote from this essay.

Writing Assignments: The Short Essay

Use informal documentation for these short essays. That is, don't use footnotes or a Works Cited page to document your sources. Instead, cite only relevant information about your source, and keep that information *within* your text. Then follow the summary or quote with a page number in parenthesis. (Use the page numbers that you find in this book to represent the page numbers of the source.) Thus, your informal documentation will look something like this:

In *The Romance of Medicine*, Benjamin Gordon, a history professor, claims that it was once believed that red wine replenished a person's depleted blood supply (p. 121).

1. Look up information on the Masada mass suicides or the Donatists and contrast those suicides with those of the Jim Jones cult.

2. Look at paragraph 8, in which Allen says that "historians rushed to sweep the carnage into the corner of anomaly." Begin a paper with that idea, and then show why it is either right or wrong.

3. Look up the Cargo Cult (alluded to in paragraph 16), and show how it differs in one significant essential from the Jim Jones cult.

4. Allen's essay offers up a variety of theories to account for the Jonestown massacre. Choose one and develop it into an essay. Begin your essay by mentioning that there are other theories, but that you want to discuss what you think is the most significant.

THE CULT OF DEATH

Tom Mathews

Tom Mathews, a senior writer for *Newsweek*, gives an early blow-by-blow account of Congressman Ryan's trip to Guyana to investigate the conditions at Jonestown and of the tragic events which this investigation triggered: the assassination of members of Ryan's entourage and the mass suicide and massacre of over 900 People's Temple members.

"Alert! Alert! Alert! Everyone to the pavilion!" The Rev. Jim Jones was on the **1.** loudspeaker, summoning the members of his Peoples Temple to their last communion. Dutifully, they gathered round; some of them, without a doubt, knew what was in store. "Everyone has to die," said Jones. "If you love me as much as I love you, we must all die or be destroyed from the outside." Mothers grasped their children to their breasts. "What have they done?" one screamed. Jones ordered his medical team to bring out "the potion," a battered tub of strawberry Flavour-aide, laced with tranquilizers and cyanide. "Bring the babies first," he commanded.

At the fringes of the huge crowd, armed guards fingered guns and bows and **2.** arrows. Some families edged forward voluntarily. Others held their ground. The guards moved in, grabbing babies from recalcitrant mothers and holding them up to let "nurses" spray the poison down their throats with hypodermics. A man shoved a gun into the ribs of Rauletter Paul, who was clutching her year-old son, Robert Jr. "You dumb bitch," he shouted. "You better do it or we're going to shoot your ass off." Tears streaming down her face, she shot the poison into the baby's mouth, and he immediately began to scream and go into convulsions.

Many walked willingly up to the poison vat and took away their cups of Flavour- **3.** aide. "We'll all fall tonight," said one, "but he'll raise us tomorrow." One old man

Source: Tom Mathews, "The Cult of Death," *Newsweek.* December 4, 1978: 38–44, 49–53.

resisted violently; he was thrown to the ground, his jaws were pulled upon, and a cupful of poison was poured down his throat. "It is time to die with dignity," said Jones on the loudspeaker.

'Mother! Mother!'

After they had drunk their potions, members of the Peoples Temple were led away by **4.** the armed guards and told to lie in rows, face down. Family groups often held hands or embraced. Within minutes, they began to gasp and retch. Blood flowed from their mouths and noses. On his raised chair on the pavilion stage, Jones kept saying, "I tried. I tried. I tried." Then he cried "Mother! Mother!" Finally, there was a shot. Jones toppled over backward, a bullet hole in his head. And a terrible silence began to settle over the camp deep in the South American jungles of Guyana.

The apocalyptic end of Reverend Jones and his Peoples Temple last week was **5.** a tragedy that strained all comprehension. The carnage in Jonestown conjured up comparisons with the Zealots of Masada, who killed each other rather than surrender to Rome in A.D. 73, and the 1,000 Japanese civilians who hurled themselves from a cliff in Saipan as American troops took control of the island during World War II. But in this case it was not the passions of war that had prompted the self-slaughter, but rather the paranoid fantasies of a single leader. Somehow, in Jones's twisted reason, a fact-finding mission by U.S. Congressman Leo Ryan became a mortal collision that left more than 900 people—Jones's followers, newsmen, Ryan and Jones himself—dead.

Explanations for the disaster could be drawn only from the murky pathology of **6.** madness and mass indoctrination. Jim Jones, 47, was a self-appointed messiah with a vision of a socialist paradise on earth and a lust for dominion over his fellow man. He attracted hundreds of fanatic followers, whose fierce loyalty and slavish work on his behalf smacked of the psychological disintegration that accompanies brainwashing. His success, and its awful consequences, posed disturbing questions about the flourishing of cults that has given the U.S. everything from saffron-robed devotees of Lord Krishna to the weird regimen and ugly threats of Synanon. It was as if all the zany strains of do-it-yourself religion and personality-cult salvation that have built up in America had suddenly erupted with ghastly force. And to add a touch of the macabre to the tragic, the scene was a faraway jungle outpost where corpses bloated under the tropical sun and the pile of bodies was so thick that the original count turned out to be too low by half.

The heart-of-darkness tragedy at Jonestown actually began in San Francisco **7.** eighteen months ago when Ryan received some bad news from an old friend named Sam Houston, an AP photographer. Houston's son Bob, 31, had been found dead, his body mangled, in the railroad yard where he worked. The day before, Houston told Ryan, Bob said he planned to quit the Peoples Temple. The police didn't know whether they were dealing with an accident or a murder. Shaken, Ryan vowed to keep an eye on the Peoples Temple and he hired a special staff investigator. Over the next several months, parents and friends of Jonestown commune members told him that Jones was keeping his followers prisoners in Guyana. A former Jones bodyguard said Jones practiced physical and psychological torture regularly. Tim and Grace Stoen, two dissident communards, claimed Jones was holding their 6-year-old son hostage in

Jonestown. And last spring, Debbie Blakey, the colony's financial secretary, fled Guyana with the most chilling report of all: Jones was collecting $65,000 a month in social-security checks due elderly communards—and running regular mass-suicide drills.

Staff Warnings

Other sources, however, said Jonestown was a counter-culture paradise. Jones's **8.** attorney, Charles Garry, a San Francisco radical who had numbered Huey Newton and Angela Davis among his clients, called the colony "a jewel that the whole world should see." Last summer, Ryan resolved to see it for himself, despite warnings from his staff. "He knew it was relatively dangerous," Ryan's daughter, Pat, 25, said last week.

On Nov. 1, Ryan sent Jones a telegram. "I am most interested in a visit to **9.** Jonestown and would appreciate whatever courtesies you can extend," he wired. On Nov. 6, a reply arrived from lawyer Mark Lane, best known for challenging the Warren Commission's report on the John F. Kennedy assassination. Jones had hired Lane to collect evidence proving that intelligence agents were infiltrating and harassing Jonestown. Lane wrote Ryan that if the congressman staged a "witch hunt" in Guyana, Jones might embarrass the U.S. by fleeing to "two anonymous countries" (apparently the Soviet Union and Cuba) that were willing to offer him refuge.

Ryan decided to go ahead with his trip, and he welcomed reporters who asked **10.** to go along. "He felt the press was his best protection," said Joe Holsinger, a Ryan aide. The Washington Post assigned its South America correspondent Charles Krause, The San Francisco Examiner sent reporter Tim Reiterman and photographer Greg Robinson and The San Francisco Chronicle sent reporter Ron Javers. NBC News assigned reporter Don Harris and cameraman Bob Brown—both news veterans of Vietnam. "We all assumed they would be pretty safe—since no one would kill a congressman," said West Coast producer Steve Friedman of NBC's "Today" show.

Not all the members of Ryan's party shared the same comfortable assumption. **11.** In Washington, Ryan's legislative aide Jackie Speier, who was also making the trip, wrote out a will addressed to her parents. Speier, 28, also made sure that Ryan's own will was in order. The day before the trip, she tucked the two wills into envelopes and left them in her desk. Then she packed her bags. In Los Angeles, Bob Brown told his wife, Connie, and adopted Vietnamese daughter, Kim, that he was having frightening premonitions. The day he set off, he had breakfast with a friend. "Goodbye," he said. "I won't see you again."

On Nov. 14, the entire group flew to Georgetown (population: 164,000), the **12.** sleepy, tin-roofed capital of Guyana. For a time, it looked as if Ryan might get no further. On Wednesday, he began to dicker for permission to enter Jonestown, a 90-acre enclave carved out of thick jungles 150 miles northwest of Georgetown. His contact was Sharon Amos, one of the commune's public-relations people who presented her unwelcome guest with long scrolls bearing the signatures of hundreds of Jonestown-ers. They read coldly, "Many of us have been visited by friends and relatives. However, we have not invited, nor do we care to see, Congressman Ryan." Word came that Jones was ill and wouldn't talk. But Ryan decided he would go to Jonestown whether Jones gave permission or not.

Then, Lane and Garry flew in to break up the impasse. The two lawyers, who **13.** openly spoke of the commune's commitment to integration and egalitarian values, radioed Jones. "You have two alternatives," Garry told Jones. "You can tell the Congress of the United States, the press and the relatives to go ---- themselves. If you do that, it's the end of the ball game. The other alternative is to let them in—and prove to the world that these people criticizing you are crazy."

When Garry and Lane promised to escort the party and make sure that things **14.** ran smoothly, Jones finally gave in. The two lawyers made a dash for the airport and caught up with Ryan. His party had ballooned to nineteen members including nine newsmen and four relatives of commune members. At 3 p.m., their Twin Otter took off for Port Kaituma, a small fishing village with a landing strip nestled in thick jungles 6 miles north of Jonestown. When they landed one hour later, they were greeted by an angry group of Jonestowners, including one man with a gun. After some more bargaining, Ryan's group finally boarded a dump truck for the hour drive to Jonestown on a twisting dirt road bordered with dense jungle brush.

The scene at Jonestown was surprisingly pleasant. They found children on swings **15.** in a small playground and cheery communards baking bread and doing laundry. Commune members trotted alongside the guests, smiling and asking polite questions. Jones's wife, Marceline, led the welcoming delegation. "You must be hungry," she said. "The food is waiting at the pavilion." She led the party to a building with a corrugated-tin roof and open walls, where Jones, perspiring and looking ill, was waiting. He sat down with Ryan and the others to a dinner of smoked pork, eddoes (a root vegetable), coffee and tarts. The commune's small band broke into the Guyanese national anthem—and a chorus of "America the Beautiful."

Jones then threw a two-hour soul review for his guests. There was an eight-man **16.** band—made up of electric guitars, drums and saxophones. Old women sang old-fashioned blues. Younger communards wailed modern soul and rock songs. Ryan interviewed 40 commune members as the show went on. Finally, Ryan stood up, took a mike and said, "I can tell you right now that by the few conversations I've had with some of the folks here already this evening that . . . there are some people who believe this is the best thing that ever happened in their whole lives." The crowd cheered for nearly twenty minutes.

Bad Vibes

If the good vibes were thunderous, they soon began to appear a bit suspect to Ryan **17.** and the newsmen. At one point, the congressman noticed that all of the commune's elderly white members were mechanically clapping and swaying to the beat of the throbbing soul music. "Look at that man's face, just look at his face," Ryan said to the Post's Krause, pointing out Tom Kice Sr., a middle-aged white in a gray crew cut who was bobbing about with glazed eyes. But when reporters edged out into the crowd to ask a few questions, most of the communards gingerly moved away.

Krause had been sitting next to Jones. He recalled that Grace Stoen had told him **18.**
that Jones was vain and power hungry despite all his protestations of humility—and
that he filled out his sideburns with eye liner. Krause looked closely. ''It was true,''
he reported to the Post later. Jones suddenly exploded in rage at one of the newsmen's
questions: ''Threat of extinction! I wish I wasn't born at times. I understand love and
hate. They are very close.'' And when newsmen pressed him on the reports of physical
punishments in the camp, he shouted, ''I do not believe in violence . . . I hate power.
I hate money . . . All I want is peace. I'm not worried about my image. If we could
just stop it, stop this fighting. But if we don't, I don't know what's going to happen
to 1,200 lives here.''

Overnighting at the Bar

At 10 p.m., the entertainment ended. One of Jones's lieutenants told Jones that the **19.**
reporters had secured lodgings in Port Kaituma and would be driven there for the night.
The reporters had made no such arrangement; some argued that they wanted to stay
overnight to get a better fix on living conditions in the commune. ''Get them out of
here. I will not have them staying here overnight,'' Jones whispered to his wife. The
newsmen and the relatives were driven to the Weekend Bar, a tiny nightspot in Port
Kaituma. They persuaded the owner to let them sleep on the living-room floor of his
house nearby. A local cop told the newsmen that the Jonestowners had at least one
gun, an automatic rifle, registered with the Guyanese authorities.

Ryan, Speier, Lane, Garry and two others were allowed to spend the night in **20.**
Jonestown. Lane went to bed early. Garry stayed up into the night, discussing the day's
events with Jones, who was in good spirits. His 103-degree fever had vanished and he
seemed in control. A red-letter day, Garry told him. Ryan had been impressed—things
were going well.

Jones also seemed cheerful the next morning. Ryan and the other overnight guests **21.**
were given a hearty breakfast of pancakes and bacon. The dump truck went into Port
Kaituma to bring back the newsmen. Then the atmosphere began to sour. Krause
discovered four barnlike buildings that turned out to be dormitories. When he attempted
to get into one of them—Jane Pittman Place—he was turned away. The newsmen
protested. After Garry and Lane prevailed on the commune's leaders to let the reporters
in, they discovered about five dozen elderly communards jammed into a small room
with long lines of bunk beds. ''It was like a slave ship,'' said Lane. Things took a turn
for the worse when Jones agreed to sit for an interview with Harris. For 45 minutes,
he sat stonily under the eye of Bob Brown's mini-camera while Harris peppered him
with hard questions about weapons, drugs and corporal punishment. Finally Harris
asked about the gun the newsmen had heard about the night before. ''A boldfaced lie,''
said Jones. Then Harris showed him a crumpled note from a communard who had
asked Harris for help in leaving Jonestown. Jones's eyes narrowed slightly and his
voice tightened. ''People play games, friend,'' he said icily. ''They lie. What can I do
with liars? Are you people going to leave us? I just beg you, please leave us . . .
Anybody that wants to can get out of here . . . They come and go all the time.''

The possibility of real defections seemed to have rattled Jones badly. After the **22.**
interview, Ryan told him, ''Jim, there's a family of six here that wants to leave.'' Jones

grew furious. "I feel betrayed," he shouted. "It never stops." "He just freaked out," said Garry. "It was as if all hell broke loose." When Jones began to rant about liars and traitors, Garry stepped in quickly to calm him. "Let them go," he told Jones. "Who gives a shit if six leave or 60? It won't change what you've done here." Jones mumbled that he had been stabbed in the back. Garry grew more and more worried. "I just wanted to get out of there," he recalled.

At 3 p.m. Saturday, Ryan was summoned to the pavilion. An American Indian **23.** named Al Simon wanted to leave with his three children; Simon's wife refused to let the children go. Garry and Lane persuaded the parents to let a court decide the matter. Ryan then assured Jones that he would not call a Congressional investigation when he returned home. He had just thanked Lane and Garry for making the trip possible. With no warning, a Jones lieutenant named Don Sly grabbed him around the throat and put a 6-inch fishing knife to his chest. "Congressman Ryan, you are a mother----er," Sly yelled. Garry and Lane grappled with Sly; Ryan fell free; Sly's hand was cut; blood splattered on Ryan's shirt. Jones stood watching. "Does this change everything?" he asked. "It doesn't change everything," said Ryan. "But it changes things."

'This Is Hell'

With Ryan finally aboard, the commune dump truck set off for Port Kaituma at 3:15. **24.** Near the airstrip, the entire family of Gerry Parks caught up with the truck and begged to be taken along. Parks, his wife, Patty, his brother, Dale, their mother and two children had arrived in Jonestown last spring. Parks had buttonholed the congressman earlier and whispered, "We gotta get outta here, this is hell." But his wife had refused to leave—until she saw the commune's security forces hauling out a stash of automatic weapons. "They started getting out the big stuff and she finally knew it was coming down on us," said Parks.

Another, more sinister latecomer also joined Ryan's party: Larry Layton, 32, a **25.** thin, blond, white man who had been one of Jones's close followers. "He's not really going," objected Dale Parks. "This is a plot—something is going to happen." The plea was dismissed, but it was prophetic. After the dump truck left the commune, Jones summoned Lane. He told him that other communards were also bound for the airstrip. "This is terrible, terrible, terrible," he said. "There are things you don't know. Those men who left a little while ago to go into the city are not going there. They love me and they may do something that will reflect badly on me. They've going to shoot at the people and their plane. The way Larry hugged me, a cold hug, told me."

At about 4:30 p.m., the Ryan entourage arrived at the Port Kaituma dirt airstrip. **26.** At about the same time, a white Cessna six-seater touched down and ten minutes later, a nineteen-seat, twin-engine Otter landed. The planes did not have enough seats for all the members of Ryan's party. He had promised to take all the defectors out first and they crowded nervously forward. "The congressman said I could go on the first plane," grumped Layton as the Otter began to load. He discreetly made for the Cessna when Ryan personally started frisking the passengers boarding the Otter.

The two planes began to warm up their engines. Aboard the Cessna, Layton **27.** suddenly whipped out a pistol and fired three shots, wounding two of the other commune defectors aboard the plane. Then his gun jammed. Dale Parks and Vernon Gosney wrestled the gun from his hands. Layton jumped from the plane and fled.

At the same moment, Harold Cordell, another of the commune defectors, looked **28.** out of the window of the Otter and saw a Jonestown tractor pulling a trailer onto the runway. Men armed with automatic pistols, semi-automatic rifles and shotguns suddenly stood up in the trailer. Gerry Parks also saw the trailer. "Now we're going to get it," Parks thought. His wife, Patty, stood in the Otter's doorway. Shots snapped out, her head shattered and blood and brain tissue splashed into Cordell's lap. Tom and Tina Bogue, children of dissident Jonestowners, sprinted to the Otter's door. Both were wounded in a new hail of gunfire but they managed to slam the door shut. "If those children hadn't shut that door," said their mother, Edith, "those gunmen might have gotten on the plane—and we'd all be dead now."

Ryan and the newsmen on the ground outside the Otter were not so fortunate. **29.** Waving aside Guyanese civilians on the airstrip, the assassins in the tractor-trailer bore down on the two planes, firing as they came. Reiterman took a slug in his left arm; another fractured his wrist and blew off his watch. Javers was wounded in the shoulder. Krause was wounded slightly in the hip. All three sprinted for cover and survived. But the gunmen cut down cameraman Brown at the tail of the Otter. Photographer Greg Robinson fell near the port engine, his body riddled by bullets. Harris and Ryan dived behind the plane's starboard wheel. The tractor-trailer pulled around the right side of the plane—and the gunmen killed both men.

Steven Sung, 44, an NBC soundman connected to Brown by a cable, fell 2 feet **30.** from the cameraman. He put his arm over his head and feigned death. "The next thing I heard, they were walking toward us," he said. "Someone shot Bob Brown in the leg . . . He screamed 'ouch' or 'shit' . . . and next thing I know, the guy came close and blow his brain off . . . the next thing I know I have tremendous pressure, explosion right next to my head and my arm feel like falling apart." The gunmen walked up to Ryan, Harris and Robinson and fired point-blank at their heads.

As the shooting erupted, a squad of Guyanese soldiers armed with rifles stood **31.** guarding a crippled Guyanese plane at the end of the airstrip. "We need guns," shouted NBC field producer Bob Flick, who rushed up seeking help. The guards turned away. Oddly enough, the gunmen also withdrew, leaving behind eight wounded. The terrified survivors dragged themselves from the planes. Some fled into the jungle at the edge of the airstrip. Embassy official Richard Dwyer, wounded in the thigh, took charge of the others. Night fell. The survivors huddled miserably, still fearing that the assassins would return to finish the job. A Guyanese nurse refused to come to the field to treat the victims and the local medical dispensary declined to send bandages and medication. Some residents even demanded tips when the survivors asked them to bring water to the airfield. Finally, the most seriously wounded were placed in an army tent at the end of the airstrip, and the others holed up in a nearby saloon called the Rum House.

Back at the commune, Reverend Jones had a very different plan in mind. At **32.** about 5 p.m., the camp loudspeaker summoned everyone in Jonestown to the pavilion. Garry and Lane walked over, stopping to talk to Jones. He seemed calm and controlled. "Some of those people who left had no intention of leaving," he said. "They went to kill somebody . . . and they've taken every gun in the place."

'We All Die'

Jones told the two stunned lawyers to wait at a guest cottage. "Feeling is running very **33.**
high against you two," he said. "I can't say what might happen at the meeting." At
the guest house, two young communards named Pancho and Jim Johnson stood by the
door, rifles at the ready. "We all going to die," Pancho said. "It's a great moment—we
all die." The two guards explained that Jones was ordering a revolutionary suicide to
protest racism and Fascism. "Isn't there any alternative?" asked Lane. When the two
said there was none, Lane popped up hopefully: "And Charles and I will write about
what you do?" The notion seemed to please the guards. They turned to leave. "How
do we get out of here?" asked Lane. Pancho waved some directions, and Garry and
Lane ran into the jungle.

In retrospect, Jones's plan seemed clear: Layton was to kill the pilot of the Otter **34.**
as it was flying over the jungle, causing a crash that would wipe out Ryan, the newsmen
and the defectors. Anyone left behind at the airstrip would be finished off by the
gunmen in the tractor-trailer.

Afraid that the plan might fail, Jones prepared his followers for death. First he **35.**
sounded the alarm for a White Night, the sect's suicide plan. With a shock, Stanley
Clayton, 25, a cook, realized that this was no drill. Ordinarily, Jones allowed the cooks
to skip White Nights because they had to prepare food for the commune when a drill
was over. This time, a grim bodyguard came to the camp kitchen and ordered the cooks
to the pavilion.

Standing at his throne, a wooden chair on a raised dais inside the pavilion, Jones **36.**
told the crowded assemblage that Ryan's plane would fall from the sky. Time passed.
Nothing happened. Finally the camp's dump truck returned from the airstrip. Two of
Jones's lieutenants rushed up and whispered to him. He grabbed a microphone. "The
congressman is dead . . . and the journalists," he said. "The GDF [Guyanese Defense
Forces] will be here in 45 minutes . . . We must die with dignity."

A Jug of Cyanide

In a tent next to the pavilion, Larry Schact, a medical-school graduate who acted as **37.**
camp doctor, prepared a vat of strawberry Flavour-aide. He dumped a quantity of
painkillers and tranquilizers into the pinkish-purple brew. Finally, Jones ordered Schact
and Joyce Touchette, one of the leaders of the commune, to bring forth "the potion."
Half-gallon jugs of cyanide was then poured into it. The tub was placed at the edge
of the pavilion. Jones ordered the mothers of Jonestown to bring their children forward,
and the killing began.

For a while, Jones sat calmly on his "throne" and watched the carnage unfold. **38.**
More and more members began to balk. The resistance angered Jones. He finally
stepped down from the throne. With guards at his side, he waded among his followers,
whipping them on to finish the ghastly rite. "Hurry, hurry, hurry," he shouted. "The
man was crazy," said Clayton. "He was out of his mind."

In the swirling confusion, a few of Jones's followers managed to escape. Clayton, **39.**
a street-wise kid from San Francisco, told guards he had been assigned to count the
living; he made his way to the camp's library tent, hid, then fled into the jungle when

a guard at the tent door turned aside. Odell Rhodes, 36, leaned against a fence, waiting for his turn at the poison tub and thinking ''about a chance to get out of there.'' When a nurse asked him to go to the camp's nursing station for a stethoscope, he eagerly volunteered; he hid under the building until the enforced suicide ceremony was nearly over. Then he managed to sneak off into the jungle. He made it to Port Kaituma—and sounded the first alarm on the Jonestown apocalypse.

Before Guyanese authorities could reach the camp, Jones and his inner circle **40.** completed the suicide pact. A death squad poisoned the commune's water supply in an attempt to kill cattle, chickens and pigs. Mr. Muggs, the camp's mascot monkey, was shot. Two brightly colored parrots, a tankful of fish in the commune's school aquarium and one yellow dog survived, not much more. Jones's mistress, Maria Katsaris, and eleven disciples put their poison cups in a bread pan and small pail and carried them down to Jones's house. Five died in one bedroom, seven in another. Katsaris was shot. When the death trip was nearly complete, Jones finished it: he put a gun to his head and pulled the trigger.

Lane, 51, and Garry, 69, heard the shots as they plunged into the jungle beyond **41.** Jonestown. They struck out for the road to Port Kaituma. Emerging on a trail lined with cassava plants, and catching sight of two strange men hauling boxes on their shoulders, they ducked back into the bush and stayed there for 26 hours. Lane ripped strips from some extra sets of underwear to mark a trail, and the two lawyers eventually reached Port Kaituma, considerably on the outs with one another. ''It was utter madness to go in there,'' Garry said in anguish last week. ''Mark Lane knew about everything; the guns, the drugs, the suicide pact—and he never told anyone.''

It took Guyanese authorities more than twelve hours to reach the stranded **42.** survivors of the Ryan party, in part because the Port Kaituma airstrip had no lights for night landings. At about 6 a.m., the first Guyanese Army units arrived. The survivors were flown to Georgetown that afternoon. As the evacuation planes lifted off, the dazed survivors could still see the bodies of Ryan, Harris, Robinson, Brown and Parks lying where they fell. The U.S. Air Force dispatched a C-141 medical plane to Georgetown, and the badly wounded were ferried back to Andrews Air Force Base near Washington, where they were recovering last week.

The sight that met the Guyanese troops when they entered Jonestown was as **43.** horrifying as anything out of a Hitlerian death camp. Bodies lay everywhere. The troops also found a trunk crammed with 803 U.S. passports and scores of social-security checks that the older members had turned over to Jones. More than $1 million in cash also turned up.

Anxious Relatives

For a time, how many people had died in Jonestown was very much a mystery. After **44.** making a preliminary count of the victims, Guyanese officials set the figure first at 373, then at 409. The discrepancy between that number and the total cache of passports sparked rumors that hundreds of communards had fled Jonestown for the jungle. Anxious relatives in Georgetown and the United States cautiously hoped that Jones might not have taken all his flock with him.

Their hopes were dashed. The U.S. Government dispatched a team of graves- **45.**

registration and body-identification experts to Jonestown to help the Guyanese measure the toll and to return the bodies of the Jonestown victims. In a terse news conference, Air Force Capt. John Moscatelli, spokesman for the body-removal task force, said the initial count of the Guyanese had been "seriously in error." He set a revised figure of 780 "with more to come." The problem, he explained, was that the bodies had fallen in stacks. Adults lay on top of children, big people on small people, making it easy to miss many of the victims. As the body detail worked its way inward from the perimeter of the dying ground to the center, the stacks grew deeper—and the count rose to more than 900.

Air Force pilots made a last sweep over the jungle beyond the commune looking **46.** for survivors. Choppers flew low, announcing over loudspeakers that it was safe to come out of hiding. "There were absolutely no sightings," said one U.S. official. "They must be dead, they must be dead," wept Claire Janaro, who sat sobbing in the Georgetown Hotel as the search went on. She had hoped that her two children, Maury and Daren, had somehow escaped death.

Not all of the communards died in Jones's holocaust. In Washington, the State **47.** Department and FBI warned police in San Francisco and Los Angeles to look out for more suicides in the Temple's surviving enclaves. None occurred last week. In Port Kaituma, police arrested Layton and charged him with Ryan's murder. They also took into custody—and later released—three of Jones's lieutenants, Mike Prokes, Tim Carter and Mike Carter, who turned up in Port Kaituma after the deaths. And they arrested Charles Beikman, charging him with the murder of Sharon Amos and her three children.

'An Insane Element'

In Georgetown, the cult's office was sealed off, and 46 followers, including the **48.** basketball team, were put under house arrest. Steven Jones, 19, leader of the Georgetown Temple followers, disavowed his father. "There was an insane element in the leadership," he said. Despite the disclaimer, some Jonestown survivors said they feared the younger Jones as much as his father.

A C-141 military air transport brought the bodies of Ryan and the newsmen back **49.** to the United States. The congressman's body was in a metal casket. The newsmen were in plain, wooden coffins. Harris was buried in Vidalia, Ga., where he had started out as a local radio broadcaster and where local people still knew him by his original name: Darwin Humphrey. Ryan was buried on a gloomy, rain-washed afternoon in South San Francisco. Dozens of congressmen, and California's Gov. Jerry Brown attended the ceremonies in Golden Gate National Cemetery. In the will that aide Jackie Speier had attended to before the trip, Ryan had asked to be buried in that place so his "ghost will be looking out over the bay he loved so much."

Had Ryan and the newsmen really understood what they were getting into when **50.** they set off for Jonestown? Some of Ryan's aides charged angrily last week that the State Department should have been more alert to the dangers of the Peoples Temple. State Department officials said that they had warned Ryan of flying in a small plane over uncharted jungle into a dirt airstrip that was remote, far from local police protection and beyond easy reach of the two-man United States mission in Georgetown. They also maintained that they had warned Ryan that the Peoples Temple had become "increasingly hostile" to outsiders. "But at no time did any of us think that there was any physical danger to his person," said one unhappy department officer.

'Jones Became a Devil'

The future of the Peoples Temple was another intriguing question. Less than three **51.** dozen of Jones's followers were left in the Temple's buff, brick church in San Francisco last week. Eleven adherents turned up there alongside lawyers Lane and Garry for a post-mortem press conference. "Jones became a devil," said Lane. "If you cannot be God, you don't just fall back to the rank and file . . . If you win, you're Moses, if you lose, you're Charles Manson." The remaining communards denied reports that Jones had organized a team of trained assassins. They said they would try to keep up the Temple's anti-racist, humanitarian good works. But from the beginning the Peoples Temple was very much a one-man show and without leader Jones, it seemed unlikely that it could survive.

As for Jones, there was some worry for a time that he wasn't really dead. In the **52.** Bay Area last week, worried defectors from the Peoples Temple kept bodyguards posted against the possibility that he still had hit men in place to carry out vengeance against those who had left him. But a metal coffin with the name "Rev. Jimmie Jones" scrawled upon it arrived at Dover Air Force Base in Dover, Del., when the Air Force began ferrying the Jonestown victims back home last week. When they opened the coffin, the body inside was unrecognizable. A technician had to peel the skin from one hand to make a set of fingerprints. It was Jones.

WORKING WITH THE TEXT

Cultural and Historical References

In this section, the numbers at the margin refer to the numbered paragraphs in the selection itself.

5. The New Testament book of Revelations is also called the Apocalypse—a revelation of impending catastrophe. Why does this word fit the Jonestown massacre so well?

6. Perhaps you've seen devotees of Krishna, an Indian god, begging on city streets.

6. "Synanon" began as a California-based drug treatment group but evolved into a cultish, quasi-religious organization.

7. Throughout this essay, Mathews uses "communards" to refer to the members of the Jonestown cult. Look up the word to see why it is particularly appropriate.

21. Do you know who Jane Pittman is?

51. Charles Manson was the leader who directed his followers to murder Sharon Tate and others. Manson is presently in a California prison.

8. Huey Newton and Angela Davis were black radicals, favorites of the counterculture mentioned above. Davis is currently a Marxist philosophy professor in a California university.

Writing Assignments: The Paragraph

Be sure to provide an introduction for each of the following paragraph writing assignments. That is, began each paragraph with a phrase like this: "Thomas Brickle claims that. . . ." When it is relevant, you might also want to identify the expertise of the author ("Thomas Brickle, a New Testament scholar, claims that. . . ."), the name of the book or article, the century and country in which the work appeared, or any other circumstances that your readers might find significant. For more on this, see pp. 11–13 in Chapter 2.

1. Summarize the article.
2. Explain the contrast that Mathews makes between Masada and Saipan —and Jonestown.

Writing Assignments: The Short Essay

Use informal documentation for these short essays. That is, don't use footnotes or a Works Cited page to document your sources. Instead, cite only relevant information about your source, and keep that information *within* your text. Then follow the summary or quote with a page number in parenthesis. (Use the page numbers that you find in this book to represent the page numbers of the source.) Thus, your informal documentation will look something like this:

> In *The Romance of Medicine*, Benjamin Gordon, a history professor, claims that it was once believed that red wine replenished a person's depleted blood supply (p. 121).

1. Describe how the opinions of the two radical lawyers, Charles Garry and Mark Lane, change as the story of Jonestown unfolds.
2. Write a paper on the mixed reactions to Jones's call for suicide.
3. Mathews suggests a number of reasons for the willingness of the people to commit suicide. Write a report on those reasons.
4. Look up the mass suicide at Masada and contrast it with the Jonestown massacre.

TWO PERSPECTIVES ON JONESTOWN

Deborah Layton Blakey and Jim Jones

Deborah Blakey joined the People's Temple in 1971 at the age of 18. By 1977 she had become the Temple's financial secretary and a confidant of Jones. She moved to Jonestown, Guyana, in 1977 and finally defected in June of 1978. The first description, or "perspective," of Jonestown is a signed affidavit written by Blakey and her attorney, Jeff Haas, shortly after her arrival back in the United States from Guyana in June 1978. At that point it was the most damning single account of life under Jim Jones in the Guyana colony. The second perspective consists of excerpts from letters which Jones wrote to U.S. reporters extolling his grand social experiment in Guyana, which was founded on the principles of socialism and Marxism. Blakey's perspective, unfortunately, proved to be the accurate one.

Affidavit of Deborah Layton Blakey
Re the Threat and Possibility
of Mass Suicide
By Members of the People's Temple

I, Deborah Layton Blakey, declare the following under penalty of perjury:

1. The purpose of this affidavit is to call to the attention of the United States government the existence of a situation which threatens the lives of United States citizens living in Jonestown, Guyana.

2. From August, 1971 until May 13, 1978, I was a member of the People's Temple. For a substantial period of time prior to my departure for Guyana in December, 1977, I held the position of Financial Secretary of the People's Temple.

3. I was 18 years old when I joined the People's Temple. I had grown up in affluent circumstances in the permissive atmosphere of Berkeley, California. By joining the People's Temple, I hoped to help others and in the process to bring structure and self-discipline to my own life.

4. During the years I was a member of the People's Temple, I watched the organization depart with increasing frequency from its professed dedication to social change and participatory democracy. The Rev. Jim Jones gradually assumed a tyrannical hold over the lives of Temple members.

5. Any disagreement with his dictates came to be regarded as "treason". The Rev. Jones labelled any person who left the organization a "traitor" and "fair game". He steadfastly and convincingly maintained that the punishment for defection was death. The fact that severe corporal punishment was frequently administered to Temple members gave the threats a frightening air of reality.

6. The Rev. Jones saw himself as the center of a conspiracy. The identity of the conspirators changed from day to day along with his erratic world vision. He induced the fear in others that, through their contact with him, they had become targets of the conspiracy. He convinced black Temple members that if they did not follow him to Guyana, they would be put into concentration camps and killed. White members were instilled with the belief that their names appeared on a secret list of enemies of the state that was kept by the C.I.A. and that they would be tracked down, tortured, imprisoned, and subsequently killed if they did not flee to Guyana.

7. Frequently, at Temple meetings, Rev. Jones would talk non-stop for hours. At various times, he claimed that he was the reincarnation of either Lenin, Jesus Christ,

Source: Deborah Layton Blakey and Jim Jones, "Affidavits," *Guyana Massacre: The Eyewitness Account.* New York: Berkley, 1978. 187–194, 205–210.

or one of a variety of other religious or political figures. He claimed that he had divine powers and could heal the sick. He stated that he had extrasensory perception and could tell what everyone was thinking. He said that he had powerful connections the world over, including the Mafia, Idi Amin, and the Soviet government.

8. When I first joined the Temple, Rev. Jones seemed to make clear distinctions between fantasy and reality. I believed that most of the time when he said irrational things, he was aware that they were irrational, but that they served as a tool of his leadership. His theory was that the end justified the means. At other times, he appeared to be deluded by a paranoid vision of the world. He would not sleep for days at a time and talk compulsively about the conspiracies against him. However, as time went on, he appeared to become genuinely irrational.

9. Rev. Jones insisted that Temple members work long hours and completely give up all semblance of a personal life. Proof of loyalty to Jones was confirmed by actions showing that a member had given up everything, even basic necessities. The most loyal were in the worst physical condition. Dark circles under one's eyes or extreme loss of weight were considered signs of loyalty.

10. The primary emotions I came to experience were exhaustion and fear. I knew that Rev. Jones was in some sense "sick", but that did not make me any less afraid of him.

11. Rev. Jones fled the United States in June, 1977 amidst growing public criticism of the practices of the Temple. He informed members of the Temple that he would be imprisoned for life if he did not leave immediately.

12. Between June, 1977 and December, 1977, when I was ordered to depart from Guyana, I had access to coded radio broadcasts from Rev. Jones in Guyana to the People's Temple headquarters in San Francisco.

13. In September, 1977, an event which Rev. Jones viewed as a major crisis occurred. Through listening to coded radio broadcasts and conversations with other members of the Temple staff, I learned that an attorney for former Temple member Grace Stoen had arrived in Guyana, seeking the return of her son, John Victor Stoen.

14. Rev. Jones has expressed particular bitterness toward Grace Stoen. She had been Chief Counselor, a position of great responsibility within the Temple. Her personal qualities of generosity and compassion made her very popular with the membership. Her departure posed a threat to Rev. Jones' absolute control. Rev. Jones delivered a number of public tirades against her. He said that her kindness was faked and that she was a C.I.A. agent. He swore that he would never return her son to her.

15. I am informed that Rev. Jones believed that he would be able to stop Timothy Stoen, husband of Grace Stoen and father of John Victor Stoen, from speaking against the Temple as long as the child was being held in Guyana. Timothy Stoen, a former Assistant District Attorney in Mendocino and San Francisco counties, had been one of Rev. Jones' most trusted advisors. It was rumored that Stoen was critical of the use of physical force and other forms of intimidation against Temple members. I am further informed that Rev. Jones believed that a public statement by Timothy Stoen would increase the tarnish on his public image.

16. When the Temple lost track of Timothy Stoen, I was assigned to track him down and offer him a large sum of money in return for his silence. Initially, I was to offer him $5,000. I was authorized to pay him up to $10,000. I was not able to locate

him and did not see him again until on or about October 6, 1977. On that date, the Temple received information that he would be joining Grace in a San Francisco Superior Court action to determine the custody of John. I was one of a group of Temple members assigned to meet him outside the court and attempt to intimidate him to prevent him from going inside.

17. The September, 1977 crisis concerning John Stoen reached major proportions. The radio messages from Guyana were frenzied and hysterical. One morning, Terry J. Buford, public relations advisor to Rev. Jones, and myself were instructed to place a telephone call to a high-ranking Guyanese official who was visiting the United States and deliver the following threat: unless the government of Guyana took immediate steps to stall the Guyanese court action regarding John Stoen's custody, the entire population of Jonestown would extinguish itself in a mass suicide by 5:30 P.M. that day. I was later informed that Temple members in Guyana placed similar calls to other Guyanese officials.

18. We later received radio communication to the effect that the court case had been stalled and that the suicide threat was called off.

19. I arrived in Guyana in December, 1977. I spent a week in Georgetown and then, pursuant to orders, traveled to Jonestown.

20. Conditions at Jonestown were even worse that I had feared they would be. The settlement was swarming with armed guards. No one was permitted to leave unless on a special assignment and these assignments were given only to the most trusted. We were allowed to associate with Guyanese people only while on a "mission".

21. The vast majority of the Temple members were required to work in the fields from 7 A.M. to 6 P.M. six days per week and on Sunday from 7 A.M. to 2 P.M. We were allowed one hour for lunch. Most of this hour was spent walking back to lunch and standing in line for our food. Taking any other breaks during the workday was severely frowned upon.

22. The food was woefully inadequate. There was rice for breakfast, rice water soup for lunch, and rice and beans for dinner. On Sunday, we each received an egg and a cookie. Two or three times a week we had vegetables. Some very weak and elderly members received one egg per day. However, the food did improve markedly on the few occasions when there were outside visitors.

23. In contrast, Rev. Jones, claiming problems with his blood sugar, dined separately and ate meat regularly. He had his own refrigerator which was stocked with food. The two women with whom he resided, Maria Katsaris and Carolyn Layton, and the two small boys who lived with him, Kimo Prokes and John Stoen, dined with the membership. However, they were in much better physical shape than everyone else since they were also allowed to eat the food in Rev. Jones' refrigerator.

24. In February, 1978, conditions had become so bad that half of Jonestown was ill with severe diarrhea and high fevers. I was seriously ill for two weeks. Like most of the other sick people, I was not given any nourishing foods to help recover. I was given water and a tea drink until I was well enough to return to the basic rice and beans diet.

25. As the former financial secretary, I was aware that the Temple received over $65,000 in Social Security checks per month. It made me angry to see that only a fraction of the income of the senior citizens in the care of the Temple was being used for their benefit. Some of the money was being used to build a settlement that would earn Rev. Jones the place in history with which he was so obsessed. The balance was

being held in "reserve". Although I felt terrible about what was happening, I was afraid to say anything because I knew that anyone with a differing opinion gained the wrath of Jones and other members.

26. Rev. Jones' thoughts were made known to the population of Jonestown by means of broadcasts over the loudspeaker system. He broadcast an average of six hours per day. When the Reverend was particularly agitated, he would broadcast for hours on end. He would talk on and on while we worked in the fields or tried to sleep. In addition to the daily broadcasts, there were marathon meetings six nights per week.

27. The tenor of the broadcasts revealed that Rev. Jones' paranoia had reached an all-time high. He was irate at the light in which he had been portrayed by the media. He felt that as a consequence of having been ridiculed and maligned, he would be denied a place in history. His obsession with his place in history was maniacal. When pondering the loss of what he considered his rightful place in history, he would grow despondent and say that all was lost.

28. Visitors were infrequently permitted access to Jonestown. The entire community was required to put on a performance when a visitor arrived. Before the visitor arrived, Rev. Jones would instruct us on the image we were to project. The workday would be shortened. The food would be better. Sometimes there would be music and dancing. Aside from these performances, there was little joy or hope in any of our lives. An air of despondency prevailed.

29. There was constant talk of death. In the early days of the People's Temple, general rhetoric about dying for principles was sometimes heard. In Jonestown, the concept of mass suicide for socialism arose. Because our lives were so wretched anyway and because we were so afraid to contradict Rev. Jones, the concept was not challenged.

30. An event which transpired shortly after I reached Jonestown convinced me that Rev. Jones had sufficient control over the minds of the residents that it would be possible for him to effect a mass suicide.

31. At least once a week, Rev. Jones would declare a "white night", or state of emergency. The entire population of Jonestown would be awakened by blaring sirens. Designated persons, approximately fifty in number, would arm themselves with rifles, move from cabin to cabin, and make certain that all members were responding. A mass meeting would ensue. Frequently during these crises, we would be told that the jungle was swarming with mercenaries and that death could be expected at any minute.

32. During one "white night", we were informed that our situation had become hopeless and that the only course of action open to us was a mass suicide for the glory of socialism. We were told that we would be tortured by mercenaries if we were taken alive. Everyone, including the children, was told to line up. As we passed through the line, we were given a small glass of red liquid to drink. We were told that the liquid contained poison and that we would die within 45 minutes. We all did as we were told. When the time came when we should have dropped dead, Rev. Jones explained that the poison was not real and that we had just been through a loyalty test. He warned us that the time was not far off when it would become necessary for us to die by our own hands.

33. Life at Jonestown was so miserable and the physical pain of exhaustion was so great that this event was not traumatic for me. I had become indifferent as to whether I lived or died.

34. During another "white night", I watched Carolyn Layton, my former sister-in-law, give sleeping pills to two young children in her care, John Victor Stoen and Kimo Prokes, her own son. Carolyn said to me that Rev. Jones had told her that everyone was going to have to die that night. She said that she would probably have to shoot John and Kimo and that it would be easier for them if she did it while they were asleep.

35. In April, 1978, I was reassigned to Georgetown. I became determined to escape or die trying. I surreptitiously contacted my sister, who wired me a plane ticket. After I received the ticket, I sought the assistance of the United States Embassy in arranging to leave Guyana. Rev. Jones had instructed us that he had a spy working in the United States Embassy and that he would know if anyone went to the embassy for help. For this reason, I was very fearful.

36. I am most grateful to the United States government and Richard McCoy and Daniel Weber; in particular, for the assistance they gave me. However, the efforts made to investigate conditions in Jonestown are inadequate for the following reasons. The infrequent visits are always announced and arranged. Acting in fear for their lives, Temple members respond as they are told. The members appear to speak freely to American representatives, but in fact they are drilled thoroughly prior to each visit on what questions to expect and how to respond. Members are afraid of retaliation if they speak their true feelings in public.

37. On behalf of the population of Jonestown, I urge that the United States Government take adequate steps to safeguard their rights. I believe that their lives are in danger.

I declare under penalty of perjury that the foregoing is true and correct, except as to those matters stated on information and belief and as to those I believe them to be true.

Executed this 15 day of June, 1978 at San Francisco, California.

Jim Jones Writes:

The warm, gentle tradewinds have come up and the glow of the evening is subsiding **1.** quickly into the clear, star-filled night. There is such peace here. There can't be anything so fulfilling anywhere as living this communal life. We watered the garden today. We grouped into bucket brigades to haul water to a two-and-a-half acre plot where we are experimenting with a North American crop. We sang and laughed and joked the whole time, and in the spirit of joy in our accomplishment, urged each other on to a faster pace. We had the whole job done in two hours. I love to work. I was at the beginning of the line, bringing spring water up out of the well that brims full no matter how much we take from it. One who leads is also one who works. And working together this way, we are making the land produce faster than we can clear it.

I work in the fields whenever I can—whenever I am not helping coordinate the **2.** defense against the attacks on us in the United States. It strikes me as immensely sad that the vast majority of people submit to the regimentation and extreme tension of a highly technological society. They pay such a high price in strokes, hypertension, physical diseases and mental stress. And yet those who dare to live for high ideals rather than the mediocrity, apathy and indifference that are the order of the day, become the objects of vindictive harassment.

Cooperative living provides such security. It provides the structure to see that **3.** everyone's needs are met. It maximizes everyone's own individual creativity and allows time for pursuit of individual interests. We have classes in rugmaking, weaving, tanning hide, canning, and myriad academic subjects. Seniors and youth alike are learning every type of craft, carpentry, welding, electrical work and even medicine. We have the best nutrition and a very high level of preventive medicine. Each resident has a blood pressure and TPR test (temperature, pulse and respiration) every week.

We enjoy every type of organized sport and recreational games. Musical talents **4.** and arts are flourishing. We share every joy and every need. Our lives are secure and rich with variety and growth and expanding knowledge.

What kind of security can money buy to compare to this? I cannot help thinking **5.** about someone like Howard Hughes—one of the richest men in the world who died of neglect and lack of proper medical attention. Or John Paul Getty, a billionaire who refused to pay a ransom for his own grandson and kept payphones in his mansions. When we had a nursing home years ago in the Midwest, a well-to-do gentleman was on his deathbed; his relatives started fighting over his handkerchief and bedside belongings the minute he lost consciousness. I was sure the failing man was hearing them bicker. A nursing assistant who was present at the time, Mary Tschetter, had to ask them to leave the room. Carrie Langston, a member of our church, worked for years taking care of very wealthy elderly people, and said that sometimes even before they passed, their families came in and stripped their homes of all their possessions.

Here, even though we are under the financial burden of developing this agricultural **6.** project, we paid for cosmetic surgery for one of our members whose appearance was marred from birth. We could hardly afford to do this, but her psychological development was being hampered, and to us, human values are more important than material things. Surely living for oneself, amassing individual wealth or fighting to stay on top of the pack is no way to live. Your personality and your worth become defined by what you own rather than by what you are or can do for others. When you are without ideals, you live alone and die rejected.

We have got to find a way to share the wealth of the world more equitably. It **7.** seems unless America learns this, she will meet as tormented an end as the multi-millionaires she has spawned. In a very real sense, we came here to avoid contributing to the destruction which the country of our birth continues to inflict on less prosperous nations. How can one live free of guilt when one's resources go to sponsor the kind of atrocity I recently read about that took place in Rhodesia? A child was forced to beat his own father, a Black African leader, on the privates until they were severed from his body. The father died from the beating. Several of the persons directing the atrocity were members of the U.S. military, one of them a major. How can individual Americans consider themselves blameless when their money, through agencies like the International Monetary Fund, is used to destabilize popularly elected governments such as in Portugal? Just America's past sins alone should cause one to feel guilt. Here we have the clean feeling that we are not contributing to this kind of abuse of power. Perhaps people of conscience in America can challenge such policies privately, but how can you avoid the feeling that you're compromising what you stand for?

I will be back one day. But just as others who have been courageous enough to **8.** stand up and speak their minds in America have paid the final price—whether revolutionary as the first Americans who believed in liberty or death, or whether non-violent, like Martin Luther King—I also expect to die for my beliefs. And in these days you don't have to be as great a man as Martin Luther King to die for taking a stand.

For all those who would be concerned about our eventual fate, you should know **9.** we have found fulfillment. We have gotten ourselves together. We share every moment. When I see the seniors happy and productive, when I see the children gather to perform a play, I know we have lived. Life without principle is devoid of meaning. We have tasted life based on principle and now have no desire to ever live otherwise again. You do not know what happiness is until you have lived up to your highest. You should come. Often I wish I could be there with you, but I had no choice. They were going to harm youngsters and seniors, and I am a leader who could not leave one soul who looks to me for guidance to that fate. I feel it is my duty to protect them from senseless destruction. We were being set up by provocateurs. I am not about to let us be used as an excuse to bring hardship down on the people of the United States.

Now there is peace. For the seniors there is freedom from loneliness and the **10.** agony of racism. For the children, as simple a relief as no more bedwetting or bad dreams. We have found security and fulfillment in collectivism, and we can help build a peaceful agricultural nation.

I know some of you there will suffer for the ideas you now guard carefully behind **11.** closed doors. One civil rights leader has called to tell us the same writers who were after us have come around to check on him. But when you have stood up for your rights, when you have done all you can for oppressed people, there is no longer any fear. I know well that I am not as articulate as Martin Luther King, Jr., Malcolm X or Eugene V. Debs, but my head is on straight and I am well-trained for battle. No one could be more fearless or principled. Neither my colleagues nor I are any longer caught up in the opiate of religion nor the narcissistic indulgences of trying to keep ourselves young. And yet, in the balmy tropical sun and gentle breezes, we have shed the physical afflictions of the dog-eat-dog world. Arthritis, diabetes, kidney ailments, hypertension—they have been reduced to almost nothing here.

We have found a healthy and meaningful existence. There are high relationships **12.** here, ones that do not come just out of sex, but by sharing and living the highest ideals. We have passed beyond alienation and have found a way of living that nurtures trust—one that could speak to a society grown cynical and cold.

It is obvious someone or some group wants to denigrate what is going on here. **13.** A long time ago a high-ranking official had told us we would be having difficulty in the future. We did not pay much attention at the time, but now it all fits together like pieces to a puzzle. A powerful agency he had mentioned was, as crazy as it sounds, threatened because we were too effective at organizing people of all races to work together. In the eventuality of economic crisis, it was thought we would have too much organizing potential among the economically deprived of all races. Organization for survival of the poor was not on their agenda.

He told us also that there were individuals planted in our ranks who would try **14.**

to promote terrorist activities. When this in fact happened, we were reluctant to credit their motives to deceit, and we regarded them as ignorant and youthful fanatics. But now, when we see these same ones who tried to steer us on a violent course being picked up and dignified by some of the media—with no thought given to challenging their word with as much as a lie detector test—it is obvious that the official's warning was correct. We have provocateurs in our midst.

There have been so many obstructions thrown in our way throughout the years. **15.** We had thought several years ago to do a documentary film about our work in alternatives to drug addiction, anti-social behavior, and violence. The next morning, after having discussed our ideas over the telephone, we received a phone call from an "agent" for some "movie producer" offering a face-to-face meeting for a promising contract. When we checked through the police to locate the source of the call, we found an office building with no such company where someone could have easily been waylaid in a corridor. It is difficult to convey this kind of intrigue that has followed us in a few short lines—there have been very sophisticated attempts to set me up like this. There have been more death threats and attempted frame-ups than I can begin to count, not only on me and my family, but also on many of the church leaders.

Even if the powerful were to succeed in smearing and destroying this one voice **16.** for racial and economic justice, it is ridiculous that they underestimate the intelligence of the general public, the little man I have represented who had no voice. Someone will *always* rise up to speak again. People are beginning to see through the overkill that has been perpetrated against civil rights leaders, and I believe the people will prevail.

WORKING WITH THE TEXT

Cultural and Historical References

In this section, the numbers at the margin refer to the numbered paragraphs in the selection itself.

Affidavit of Deborah Layton Blakey
3. Berkeley, California, is the site of the University of California at Berkeley and was a center for countercultural activities at the time this was written.

7. Lenin was one of the leaders of the Russian Revolution and its first premier.

7. Idi Amin was the power-mad, bloodthirsty Ugandan dictator during the 1970s.

Jim Jones Writes
9. What do you suppose a "provocateur" is? Guess at the meaning and then look it up in the dictionary.

11. Malcolm X was a leader of the Nation of Islam and a black radical. He was assassinated by members of an opposing faction.

11. Eugene Debs was an early twentieth-century American labor leader and socialist candidate for president a number of times.

Writing Assignments: The Paragraph

Be sure to provide an introduction for each of the following paragraph writing assignments. That is, begin each paragraph with a phrase like this: "Thomas Brickle claims that. . . ." When it is relevant, you might also want to identify the expertise of the author ("Thomas Brickle, a New Testament scholar, claims that. . . ."), the name of the book or article, the century and country in which the work appeared, or any other circumstances that your readers might find significant. For more on this, see pp. 11–13 in Chapter 2.

1. Write a paragraph summary of Blakey's affidavit.
2. Write a paragraph summary of Jones's essay.
3. In a paragraph, contrast Jones's ideas about sharing the wealth in paragraph 7 with Blakey's description in paragraph 23.

Writing Assignments: The Short Essay

Use informal documentation for these short essays. That is, don't use footnotes or a Works Cited page to document your sources. Instead, cite only relevant information about your source, and keep that information *within* your text. Then follow the summary or quote with a page number in parenthesis. (Use the page numbers that you find in this book to represent the page numbers of the source.) Thus, your informal documentation will look something like this:

> In *The Romance of Medicine*, Benjamin Gordon, a history professor, claims that it was once believed that red wine replenished a person's depleted blood supply (p. 121).

1. Contrast the Blakey affidavit with Jones's account. Pick just a couple of points to contrast. For instance, you might want to contrast Jones's ideas about sharing the wealth in paragraph 7 with Blakey's description of his personal style in paragraph 23.
2. Write a paper explaining why Jones admired Eugene Debs and Malcolm X.
3. Using details from Blakey's affidavit and Jones's essay, write a paper in which you illustrate Jones's paranoia.

WHY 900 DIED IN GUYANA

Carey Winfrey

Carey Winfrey, a member of *The New York Times* news team which covered the events in Guyana, discusses the events leading up to the Jonestown carnage. In order to explain how Jones was able to exert such powerful control over the members of the People's Temple, Winfrey went to the surviving Temple members for their perspectives on Jim Jones and his appeal.

Why did they die? Perhaps no explanation will ever satisfy completely. But to **1.** review the massacre months later through the eyes of those most deeply involved is to discover a dozen different clues in the deadly dynamics of Guyana, from faith to fear to murder.

We know now through firsthand witnesses that once Jim Jones learned of the **2.** Port Kaituma killings of a Congressman, three journalists and a "defector," events moved quickly. Jones called his followers to the main pavilion.

According to reports of a tape recording of the commune's last hour, he began **3.** by telling them: "I tried to give you a good life. In spite of all I tried to do, a handful of our people who are alive"—presumably meaning other defectors—"have made our lives impossible." Then, referring to the earlier airstrip killings, he continued: "There's no way to detach ourselves from what's happened today. We are sitting on a powder keg. If we can't live in peace, let's die in peace."

For some—their identities irrevocably intertwined with Jones—his suggestion **4.** sufficed. As Odell Rhodes, a survivor who escaped while the killings took place, put it, "Some of these people were with Jim Jones for 10 or 20 years. They wouldn't know what to do with themselves without him." Another voice on the tape: "Dad has brought us this far; my vote is to go with Dad."

Christine Miller, an elderly woman, asked why they couldn't flee instead to **5.** Russia. Jones answered calmly that the Russians wouldn't want them now because they had been disgraced by the killings at Port Kaituma. "I want my babies first," he then commanded. "Take my babies and children first."

Stanley Clayton, another eyewitness escapee, testified at the Guyana inquest that **6.** many in the commune seemed at first to think it was just another drill. In calling for "babies first," Jones surely knew that mothers duped into killing their children would want to take their own lives.

Clayton testified that, in some cases, "nurses took babies right out of their **7.** mothers' arms. The mothers were frozen with shock, scared out of their wits." The nurses then squirted the deadly liquid down the children's throats, sending them into convulsions.

"After you watched your child die," Paula Adams—a Jones follower who survived because she was in Georgetown that Saturday—speculated later, "you'd think, 'What's there to live for. I may as well die.'"

When most of the babies were dead or dying, Clayton testified, "people began **8.** realizing this was really taking place."

The crowd grew restive. Jones took another tack. "He kept telling them, 'I love you. I love you. It is nothing but a deep sleep,'" Clayton recalled. "'It won't hurt you. It's just like closing your eyes and drifting into a deep sleep.'"

Then, Clayton said, Jones stepped into the crowd and began guiding people **9.**

Source: Carey Winfrey, "Why 900 Died in Guyana," *The New York Times Magazine.* February 25, 1979: 39–40, 42, 44–46, 50.

toward the vat of fruit drink and cyanide. Jones's wife, Marceline, also walked among the followers, embracing them and saying, "I'll see you in the next life."

Jones himself did not believe in reincarnation, but he knew that many of his **10.** followers did. "We'll all fall tonight," one communard said, stepping forward for his cup of poison, "but he'll raise us tomorrow."

According to Rhodes, Jones told the group that if they didn't drink the potion, **11.** they would be tortured and the men castrated by the Guyanese Army. "Troops will come in here," Rhodes quoted Jones as saying. "They will torture our babies. They will kill everybody. It's better that we die with dignity." The many who shared his paranoia about a C.I.A.-Treasury Department-Guyana Defense Forces conspiracy to destroy the Temple undoubtedly believed him.

Jones "made them feel that in a couple of hours the army was going to be there **12.** and take them and put them in concentration camps," Stephan Jones said later. Stephan, the cult leader's natural son, escaped the carnage. As a member of the Jonestown basketball team, he had gone to Georgetown for a game.

To those who felt death inevitable, Jones's repeated entreaties to "die with **13.** dignity" would have proved powerfully persuasive, former followers agreed. "If I was down there," said Grace Stoen, "I would say I'd rather go down bravely than be shot in the back. That's the choice they had."

Others may have felt that they had run out of alternatives. Virtual prisoners in **14.** a jungle outpost 150 miles from a major airport, lacking money, resources or passports, many must have believed they had come too far, repudiated too much, to turn back.

"In San Francisco, they'd have run," said Willard Gaylin, a psychiatrist who is **15.** president of the Institute of Society, Ethics and the Life Sciences. "And once a few ran, it would have changed the whole dynamic and power of the group. But where the hell were they going to run to in Guyana?"

For some, a return to the United States was psychologically out of the question, **16.** as Dr. Hardat Sukhdeo, a Guyanese-born cult specialist now working in New Jersey, observed. "They were people in Jonestown," he said of the survivors he interviewed in Georgetown. "For the first time in their lives they were persons." Michael Carter, one of three who escaped with a suitcase containing more than half a million dollars, offered another version of the same thought. "A lot of the people," he said, "had nothing else but the People's Temple and Jonestown."

One more factor in their acquiescence was Jones's call for "revolutionary **17.** suicide"; the belief, as Michael Carter reconstructed it, that "we're going to show how a force of so many people can do so much to shape the world." Two who apparently shared this belief were the guards sent to warn (or possibly to kill) the two visiting Temple attorneys, Charles Garry and Mark Lane.

"It's a great moment—we all die," Mr. Garry later reported one of the guards **18.** saying. "They had this smile on their faces. They said they were going to die, that it was a pleasure to die for revolutionary suicide, that this is the way it's got to be done as an expression against racism and fascism."

The group need was also critical. For many, the anxiety of being separated from **19.** the group—which even at the last moment represented love and security—perhaps outweighed fear of death. Odell Rhodes related that, as he was escaping, he came upon a dormitory full of elderly members. They all said they wanted to join in the suicides.

Some asked him to escort them to the pavilion. Others, who could walk, picked themselves up and made their own way.

When 74-year-old Hyacinth Thrash awoke the next morning, after sleeping **20.** through the holocaust, she panicked. "I thought everybody had run off," she explained after she was rescued. "I started crying and wailing, 'Why did they leave me? Why did they leave me?' "

"It may be a less sick thing," Dr. Gaylin said of suicide, "when it's done as **21.** part of the group than when it's done individually, because of the immensity of group pressure on insecure people."

The haste inherent in the event, giving the communards little time to think things **22.** over, also helps account for the compliance. "If I was one of the first," Michael Carter admitted, "I think I would have done it willingly. I think as things went on, I would have tried to rebel. I can't imagine no one tried to rebel, [at least] 30 or 40. I know a majority followed him willingly." But, given time, Carter said, "there was definitely a minority in Jonestown of at least 30 people who would have rebelled, with a hundred more in the closet."

Some did rebel. In addition to Rhodes and Clayton, 79-year-old Grover Davis **23.** simply walked away from the pavilion and hid in a ditch. "I didn't want to die," he said later.

There is evidence that others also didn't want to die. Mr. Clayton testified that **24.** Jones, backed by security guards, pulled some people from their seats and propelled them forcibly toward the vats of poison.

A report by Dr. Leslie Mootoo, the Guyana Government's chief medical examiner, **25.** noted that several of the 39 bodies he examined showed punctures "consistent" with injections. He and police estimated that at least 70 persons might have received injections. Mr. Rhodes said he saw some people injected when the poison they took orally failed to kill them.

By one reckoning—counting the 70 "rebels" as murdered, as well as 260 **26.** children and five elderly women who may have mistaken the poison for routine medication—perhaps a third of those who died at Jonestown were not suicides at all. But by almost any other reckoning, murder and suicide became so hopelessly intermingled that it was impossible to tell which was which.

The signs were there for some time. **27.**

Grace Stoen, one of Jim Jones's closest aides, remembers that, in September **28.** 1972, Lester Kinsolving wrote a series of skeptical newspaper articles detailing Jones's claims as faith healer and prophet. "That bad press just freaked Jones out and he got even more paranoid."

A year later, by her recollection, Jones expounded the idea of mass suicide. **29.** "We've got to go down in history," she recalls him saying in September 1973. " 'We've got to be in the history books.' And he said, 'Everyone will die, except me of course. I've got to stay back and explain why we did it: for our belief in integration.' "

Two days later, the defection of eight Temple teen-agers ushered in a new era **30.** at the Temple. "We hated those eight with such a passion because we knew any day they were going to try bombing us," Neva Sly, a former member recalled recently. "I mean Jim Jones had us totally convinced of this."

The defections, following so rapidly the first mention of "revolutionary suicide," **31.**
may also have persuaded Jones to set the notion aside—at least temporarily. For it was
not until about three years later, according to Mrs. Stoen, that the idea came up again.
On New Year's Day, 1976, Jones told about 30 inner-circle followers that he loved
them so much he would lift his abstinency rule and allow them each a glass of wine.
When all had drunk, he informed them that they would be dead within an hour. Mrs.
Stoen says that while she didn't believe him, others did. She recalls Walter Jones, who
was attending his first meeting as a member of the Planning Commission, standing up
and saying that he just wanted to know "why we're dying. All I've been doing is
working on bus engines ever since I got here and I want to know that I'm dying for
something more than being a mechanic working on all these buses."

Mrs. Sly, whose husband, Don, threatened Representative Leo J. Ryan with a **32.**
knife at Jonestown, also believed Jones that evening. She remembers Jones telling the
assemblage that the F.B.I. or the C.I.A. was closing in and would kill everyone. "I
had so much going through my mind that the 30 minutes was like 20 hours." After
a while, Mrs. Sly reported, "Jones smiled and said, 'Well, it was a good lesson. I see
you're not dead.' He made it sound like we needed the 30 minutes to do very strong,
introspective kind of thinking. We all felt strongly dedicated, proud of ourselves."

Today Mrs. Sly, whose son died at Jonestown, says she had not been afraid of **33.**
death that evening. After all, she says, Jones "taught that it would be a privilege to
die for what you believed in, which is exactly what I would have been doing."

Deborah Layton Blakey has an equally chilling memory of the same evening. **34.**
She said that Jones took her and a handful of other trusted aides into a room and asked
their advice about how to kill off the entire Planning Commission. He suggested
sending the group on an airplane trip, she said. Once aloft, "one of us would shoot
[the pilot] and the whole plane would go down. And that way he'd have the whole
P.C. dead. Then he thought of taking all the buses and running them off the Golden
Gate Bridge.

"His big concern," Mrs. Blakey continued, "was that people were starting to **35.**
leave his church, P.C. people. He got scared and thought the best thing to do was just
kill them off."

Those gathered on the Golden Gate Bridge for a Memorial Day service for those **36.**
who jumped from the landmark, might also have heard intimations of things to come.
Jones, an invited speaker, departed from his prepared text to extemporize about the
depressing effect a New West magazine article, by San Francisco reporters Marshall
Kilduff and Philip Tracy, was having on him and his congregation.

"These past few days," Jones said, "we as a congregation of several thousand **37.**
have undergone a considerable amount of pressure. It seems that there are elements in
society, very wrongfully, who want to use us as an embarrassment to this administration.
So I can empathize [with suicide victims].

"This week my son said to me," he continued, " 'For the first time Dad, I felt **38.**
like committing suicide . . . Maybe it might cause people to care if I jumped off the
bridge while you were speaking.' We worked our way through that, but I think that
perhaps we all should identify closely with that kind of personal experience. Because
at one time or another we have all felt the alienation and the despair. I think the despair

got to me yesterday. If it hadn't been for an Academy Award-winning actress joining our church . . . I think I would have been in a suicidal mood myself today for perhaps the first time in my life.'' (Jones was mistaken; Jane Fonda, the ''Academy Award-winning actress,'' visited but did not join the People's Temple.)

Less than a year later, in March 1978, Jones would write a letter to United States **39.** Senators and Representatives. ''We at People's Temple,'' he said, ''have been the subject of harassment by several agencies of the U.S. Government and are rapidly reaching the point at which our patience is exhausted. . . . I can say without hesitation that we are devoted to a decision that it is better even to die than to be constantly harassed from one continent to the next.''

There are further clues to the tragedy in the life histories of the people themselves. **40.**

Long before threats of suicide had appeared in letters to Congressmen, the **41.** People's Temple had helped drug addicts break their addictions, offered food and shelter to the destitute, run schools and senior-citizen centers, reformed prostitutes and found jobs for the uneducated. It helped an illiterate black woman become a nurse and a heavy drug-user become a doctor. Although the reality never matched the Temple's stated egalitarian aims, and although some racial friction always existed, blacks and whites worked together in considerable harmony.

Neva Sly remembers that, at her first visit to the Temple in 1967, ''a force of **42.** love just slapped you in the face.'' Within a month, she and her husband had moved to Ukiah, Calif., to work full time ''for the cause. It was the greatest feeling to me, that I was really giving my all to something.''

''When we first joined, it was beautiful, interracial humanitarianism,'' Jeannie **43.** Mills, another defector, recalls. ''When you walked into the church, everybody greeted you with hugs. I had never experienced this kind of love before.''

''I went into this group to serve mankind by building a tightly knit utopian **44.** society which would be a model,'' said Grace Stoen's husband, Tim, a lawyer who was Jones's most trusted adviser until he defected in April 1977 and became his most hated traitor. ''I wanted utopia so damn bad I could die. In fact, I fully expected to die. I really took to heart that verse in Ecclesiastes: 'Whatsoever thy hand findeth to do, do it with thy might.' '' Mr. Stoen, then an assistant district attorney, gave the Temple his house, turned over his salary, sold his Porsche sports car, and began buying his suits at the Salvation Army.

At the center of the tragic scene, holding it all together, was Jim Jones—darkly **45.** handsome, spellbindingly loquacious and, by the evidence available to most members, committed to the ideals he espoused.

''Jim Jones was warm, friendly, outgoing,'' recalls Harold Cordell, who joined **46.** the ''church'' at the age of 18 in 1956 and stayed for 20 years. ''There were outings for young people. He made young people feel they were part of something. He was meeting the needs of senior citizens. There were programs for the poor. It looked like a good thing. I saw a place I could relate to and feel like I was a part of something, I wanted to feel I was contributing to society. I wanted to do good works.''

''Jones was a master mythmaker,'' adds Stoen. ''I've never seen anybody who **47.** could weave the tapestry of a utopian dream so beautifully.''

But the tapestry never appealed to a broad constituency. In his first four months as a new member, Stoen brought some 35 lawyer friends to hear Jones speak, fully expecting each to be quickly converted, as he had been. To his surprise, not one returned a second time.

Stoen estimates that, in 10 years, somewhere between 50,000 and 100,000 people **48.** came to hear Jones speak. But, he says, despite Jones's boasts of 20,000 members, the actual membership never exceeded 3,000.

In the main, the Temple attracted two kinds of people: white, upper-middle-class **49.** idealists and uneducated, disenfranchised blacks. The latter outnumbered the former by about 4 to 1; but whites, notably white women, held most of the leadership positions. Jones once referred to his rank-and-file members as ''the refuse of America.''

''I remember some black mothers would tell you they had seven sons and five **50.** were in prison,'' says Tim Stoen. ''Nobody else had ever taken them and looked them in the eye and said, 'I love you,' which Jim would do. When I saw Jim kiss old black ladies on the cheek and their eyes would light up, I would cry, I was so touched.''

In the ''self-analysis'' letters that Jones asked his Jonestown followers to write **51.** to him last July, feelings of guilt and worthlessness ran rampant.

''Historically, I have been very insecure,'' wrote Tom Grubbs, the Jonestown **52.** high-school principal. ''Had a very strong inferiority complex all my life, felt frightfully inadequate. . . . I want to work every damn minute I'm not asleep, largely so I don't have to face my feelings of unworthiness, inadequacy, insecurity.''

Agreeing to do whatever the leader asks in exchange for relief from feelings of **53.** worthlessness and guilt is a familiar pattern, says Dr. Stanley Cath, a psychiatrist and student of cults at Tufts University. ''Anyone in a group like this says, 'My God, if I'm thrown back on myself, and have to put up with what I put up with before . . .' Then he says of the leader: 'You converted me, you snapped something, you gave me the light and I didn't feel that way anymore. You stopped the pain.' ''

The self analysis letters, rich in avowals of redemption and gratitude, support **54.** Dr. Cath's thesis.

''After meeting you I found out that I didn't no anything about love,'' wrote **55.** Odel Blackwell to Jones, ''because you are all love. . . . I love you & Mother, and what you say do I will do it, because I no what ever you tell me to do, I can do it if I try.''

''Jim Jones was the best friend I ever had,'' said Bea Orsot Grubbs, a survivor. **56.** ''When I couldn't pay the rent once, he paid the rent. Nobody else ever did that, including my rich relatives.''

Returning to the United States on an airplane two weeks after the massacre, Mrs. **57.** Grubbs, 52 years old, tried to explain why the year she spent in Jonestown was ''the happiest of my life.'' ''I never had the feeling of being treated different because I was a black woman,'' she said. ''I was respected for my mind and what I could offer people as a whole. We lived in a cooperative community. We shared with each other, caring for people other than yourself. That was very fulfilling.''

Last July, Mrs. Grubbs had written to Jones that ''I would never betray you, no **58.** matter what. . . . I shall not beg for mercy either in that last moment. I shall proudly die for a proud reason.'' But Mrs. Grubbs was not called upon to put her loyalty to the ultimate test. She was 150 miles away, in Georgetown to keep a dental appointment, during the mass suicides.

As Jim Jones's message of love turned gradually to one of hate and fear, Grace **59.** and Tim Stoen, Alfred Cordell, Deborah Layton Blakey, Neva Sly and others grew disillusioned. But because they were committed followers who had entrusted their identities, as well as their financial resources, to his care—who had sacrificed homes, possessions, husbands and wives to their belief in a higher calling—breaking away was a complicated, painful process.

"Once people have made the commitment," Dr. Gaylin observes, "they're **60.** invested in the truth of that decision. They become frightened to go back on it. It's terrifying to go back."

"We always blamed ourselves for things that didn't seem right," Neva Sly **61.** remembered. "I think we suffered from a lack of confidence."

Jones seemed to have an answer for everything. His end-justifies-the-means **62.** philosophy accommodated most doubts. "He had a vision in his mind of a perfect world," Tim Stoen said, that "will come about only when people destroy their own egos from within and replace them with a collective ego. And in order to get people to do that you sometimes have to play tricks. . . . He may have to set you up and embarrass you: Have your spouse attack you in front of everybody so that you can think less of yourself. And after a while, because you think less of yourself, the instinct for self-preservation is more and more destroyed."

Jones dismissed protests against family separations on the grounds that personal **63.** alliances diminish concern for the oppressed. He explained his requests for self-incriminating documents as simple tests of loyalty; tests most were willing to take. "Oh, heavens, yes, I'd totally incriminate myself on anything," Mrs. Sly remembered. "I was loyal. I was dedicated. I believed. I totally believed in this cause. Why wouldn't I go through a loyalty test?"

Mr. Stoen said he agreed to sign a paper certifying that Jones had fathered his **64.** child because "I loved the man and I thought, O.K., his reason for asking me to do so was that if I ever defect from the organization, it would cause me embarrassment."

"You didn't know how to get away," said Grace Stoen. "You didn't know **65.** where to go. You didn't know who could help you. You always thought you would be found. And there were always these threats that you would be killed."

"Even though everyone is making good reports and making good fronts," a **66.** prophetic communard wrote last July, "we could be sliding downhill to sink." The slide would be rapid.

In the beginning, Jones had little trouble persuading his people to go to Jonestown: **67.** As Neva Sly recalls, "To me, my God, it was the greatest privilege in the world to get to go to Guyana. Gee whiz, to be able to work to build paradise! Whooo!"

Tim Stoen also remembers Jonestown with something like fondness. "Everything **68.** would run pretty happily when Jim was not around," he says of the three months he spent there in 1977. Deborah Layton Blakey also recalls working in the fields in the summer of 1977 and thinking, "Jonestown would be nice if Jim Jones weren't here."

But Jones was there. He had arrived that June, shortly after delivering his Golden **69.** Gate Bridge suicide speech and only days before the New West magazine article he so feared was published. He fled San Francisco telling Temple members there that he would be imprisoned for life if he did not do so.

"I came here with no feeling of a future," he later told a Guyanese interviewer. **70.**

"Our movement was dead. If I didn't come here, our movement was finished. We would be destroyed in the U.S.A."

In Jonestown, Jones gained close to total control. He confiscated all passports, **71.** and forbade the communards to leave the compound without permission. Beatings, sexual humiliations, solitary confinement—all became commonplace. By last September, according to testimony of former residents, all mail into and out of Jonestown was censored by a four-member committee. Five armed guards patrolled the commune each night to prevent defections.

But it was as the only source of news in the isolated jungle compound that Jones **72.** derived his final power over men's minds. At last he was able to paint a world entirely in hues of his own choosing. For hours on end, and sometimes all night, Jones used the camp loudspeakers to amplify his nightmare vision of a "fascist, racist, imperialist" United States determined to put black people in concentration camps and to destroy Jonestown. Money his followers had spent in the United States, he told them, had financed C.I.A. killings of black babies and of socialists all over the world. He expressed admiration for Charles Manson and the kidnappers of former Italian Prime Minister Aldo Moro.

Disoriented by the isolation, by low-protein diets and little sleep, the people of **73.** Jonestown did not doubt their leader. By September 1977, the communards were starting their days by looking for mercenaries at the jungle's edge and finishing them with self-recriminations. "I feel so guilty," Carrie Langston wrote, "about the money I spent and the food and drinks. I sure didn't know I was helping to murder people."

To commit suicide as an individual, Jones would say, was terrible: You would **74.** be reborn into the world of 5,000 years ago and have to live 500 lifetimes just to get back to the 20th century. But a "revolutionary death" put one on a higher plane.

"If I could die," wrote Clifford Geig, expressing a common refrain, "I would **75.** like it to be a revolutionary death where I would take some enemies down with me. That would be the final goal of my life."

"I'll be glad to die for Communism," said Maryann Casanova. "I want to help **76.** make a world where no one has to be born in a capitalist system."

Eleven-year-old Mark Fields wrote to Jones last July that "if the capitalists came **77.** over the hill I'd just drink the potion as fast as I could do it. I wouldn't let the capitalists get me but if they did I'd indour it. I would not say a word. I'd take the pain and when I couldn't stand it anymore I'd pass out."

The attempt by Grace and Tim Stoen to regain custody of their 6-year-old son, **78.** known as John-John, hastened the denouement. Jones's rational and irrational fears came into sharp focus. By holding John-John hostage, Jones felt he could keep the Stoens quiet and punish them as well. (Mrs. Stoen says she did not take her son with her when she left the People's Temple in 1976 because she feared for his life. By the time her husband left the Temple, Jones had sent John-John to Guyana.)

In August 1977, the Stoens obtained a ruling from a California judge granting **79.** them custody and ordering Jones's appearance in court. By then, both Jones and the boy were in Guyana where—with the help of the affidavit Stoen had signed years before as an act of loyalty—Jones claimed to be the boy's natural father.

In September, Jeffrey Haas, an attorney representing the Stoens, arrived in **80.** Guyana. He succeeded in obtaining a bench warrant ordering the child removed from

Jonestown. According to Deborah Blakey and Charles Garry, Jones's attorney, the issuance of the bench order led Jones to issue his first threat to destroy the Jonestown commune.

Mrs. Blakey, who was manning the People's Temple radio in San Francisco at **81.** the time, remembers that she was told by Jones "to get in touch with [Deputy Prime Minister Ptolemy] Reid, who was in the United States; to call him and tell him that unless something was done in Guyana, they'd have 1,100 people dead in Jonestown. "They were all in a big circle. Jones said: 'O.K., listen, my people are with me.' You could hear them all saying 'Yeah!' in the background. You could hear them all the way to San Francisco.' "

"He freaked out," recalls Charles Garry, who spoke to Jones by telephone at **82.** the time. "He said, 'This child cannot go because he'll be ruined.' He said, 'We are all so solid that if something happens to any one of us, it's happening to all of us.' "

The Guyanese did not enforce the order for the child's removal, and Jones called **83.** off his suicide threat. Later he assured Garry that it had simply been a ploy.

But according to Mrs. Blakey, who came to Jonestown three months afterward, **84.** Jones issued similar threats on two other occasions when he felt threatened and under attack: once when Guyanese officials asked that the People's Temple doctor, Laurence E. Schacht, take his internship in a Georgetown hospital and again when the Guyanese asked to place a Guyanese teacher in the Jonestown school.

"If things didn't sound exactly the way he wanted them to be," Mrs. Blakey **85.** said, "he'd call for a 'black night' "—a term Jones converted to "white night" because he considered whites, not blacks, the enemy.

"One time, it was 3 or 4 in the morning," she said, "people had to jump out **86.** of their bunks, grab their kids and run up to the main pavilion. They took a head count. You'd give your name to this woman and the guards would go search the cabins. You stayed there 12 hours, maybe 20. He'd discuss how the mercenaries were coming. He'd throw out maybe five variables and ask what you'd rather do: Go to Africa and help the people there fight imperialism? Go to Russia? Go to Cuba? Somebody would say 'No, no, let's stay here and fight it out to the death.' You never knew if you were going to live through it or not."

On one such night, according to Mrs. Blakey, after telling the group that the **87.** situation was hopeless, Jones told everyone to line up. They were all given small glasses containing a red liquid and told it was poison; they would be dead in 45 minutes. After the time had passed, Jones informed them that they had been through a loyalty test. Now he knew that the communards would do as they were told.

Mrs. Blakey says she had drunk the liquid that night because "the whole pavilion **88.** was surrounded by guards. You also knew that if it was not the real thing and you said, 'No,' and lived through it, you'd have your butt kicked severely. After a while after you continually had these 'white nights,' after you'd seen your best friends beaten up and you were estranged from your family, after a while you just wanted to be dead."

Stephan Jones, the surviving son, says he spoke out against a mass suicide during **89.** a "white night" last May. "They're going to say we're fanatics," he told the group. "It's not going to be understood. But I got shut up. I got booed down by everybody."

He reports that his mother, Marceline Jones, also argued with Jones against a **90.** mass suicide, but only in private. "Mother would say, 'You can't kill 914 people.

There are going to be people [left] alive, brain-damaged. It's going to be a horrible scene.' '' But his father always countered that the only alternative was torture.

By all indications, Jones was deteriorating physically as well as mentally. Three **91.** months before the mass suicides, he asked Carlton B. Goodlett, a San Francisco physician to come to Jonestown to examine him. Jones was a diabetic who had run a 103-degree fever for a month before the examination, Dr. Goodlett said, adding that he suspected a rare, often fatal, but treatable fungal disease (progressive coccidioidomycosis). Jones promised the physician that he would enter the hospital after Representative Ryan's visit. Others, including Odell Rhodes, who knew the signs, said Jones was an amphetamine addict.

"I told myself I was looking at a man in decay," a reporter traveling with Ryan **92.** later recounted. At one point, he said, Jones babbled almost incoherently. "Threat of extinction! I wish I wasn't born at times. I understand love and hate. They are very close. . . . I do not believe in violence. I hate power. I hate money. All I want is peace. I'm not worried about my image. If we could just stop it, stop this fighting. But if we don't, I don't know what's going to happen to 1,200 lives here."

In a matter of hours, the world found out.   **93.**

WORKING WITH THE TEXT

Cultural and Historical References

In this section, the numbers at the margin refer to the numbered paragraphs in the selection itself.

10. The Communards were members of the Paris Commune of 1871; by extension it means the member of a religious group.

72. Charles Manson was the leader of a California counterculture group. His members were, some say, "brainwashed" into murdering the actress Sharon Tate and six of her friends. Manson and some of his followers are now in a California prison. Manson comes up for parole every now and then. So far he's been denied.

72. Aldo Moro was kidnapped and killed by Italian radicals a few years before this essay was written.

Writing Assignments: The Paragraph

Be sure to provide an introduction for each of the following paragraph writing assignments. That is, begin each paragraph with a phrase like this: "Thomas Brickle claims that. . . ." When it is relevant, you might also want to identify the expertise of the author ("Thomas Brickle, a New Testament scholar, claims that. . . ."), the name of the book or article, the century and country in which the work appeared, or any other circumstances that your readers might find significant. For more on this, see pp. 11–13 in Chapter 2.

1. Write a paragraph that begins with "Not all of those who died committed suicide." Use a quote somewhere in your paragraph.
2. Summarize one of the reasons why members of the People's Temple committed suicide. Use a quote somewhere in your paragraph.
3. Write one or two paragraphs on Jones's paranoia. Use a quote somewhere in your paragraph.

Writing Assignments: The Short Essay

Use informal documentation for these short essays. That is, don't use footnotes or a Works Cited page to document your sources. Instead, cite only relevant information about your source, and keep that information *within* your text. Then follow the summary or quote with a page number in parenthesis. (Use the page numbers that you find in this book to represent the page numbers of the source.) Thus, your informal documentation will look something like this:

> In *The Romance of Medicine*, Benjamin Gordon, a history professor, claims that it was once believed that red wine replenished a person's depleted blood supply (p. 121).

1. Write a paper that analyzes the People's Temple members' uncritical views of communists and capitalists.
2. Why do you suppose the great bulk of Jones's members consisted of highly educated, upper-class whites and poorly educated lower-class blacks?
3. Write an essay on what you think are the two or three most compelling reasons for Jones's appeal.

TWO WHITE NIGHTS

James Reston, Jr.

When James Reston wrote *Our Father Who Art in Hell*, the book from which the following excerpts were taken, he was a lecturer at the University of North Carolina and the author of three novels. In the following excerpts Reston discusses the tape transcripts of two "white night" sessions which Jones presided over during 1978. The first one, which took place on the night of May 13, clearly reveals Jones's madness. On the second one, the night of November 18, the mass suicide occurred.

May 13, 1978

It was midafternoon on May 13, his forty-seventh birthday, the day, he would tell his **1.** host later, that he died. May 13 was the day he gave up thinking he could communicate

Source: James Reston Jr., *Our Father Who Art in Hell.* New York: New York Times Books, 1981. 259–268, 323–329.

his Goodness to them. Somewhere high above Trinidad, as their plane sped toward New York, Deborah Blakey was beginning her story to Richard McCoy. In Jonestown, as Jones began the white night early, he seethed with the thought that she had picked his birthday to defect as a special twist in his suffering soul. But he was not ready to announce to them the real reason that they might die later in the evening.

It began in the alabaster heat of the afternoon, with the electric sound of the   **2.** insects, the murmurings and small movements of things underfoot, the shimmering waves of the swelter rising from the banana fields, the kiskadees, with their necrotically yellow throats, hopping gregariously on the ground, and the carrion crows soaring overhead, all mixing with the voices and the static of their radio, talking breathlessly to San Francisco in "tongues," as he called their codes, lending an air of prodigious crisis. There had to be a good reason for their "stand" that day, and the Bishop conjured a trilateral attack. In Georgetown, the Minister of Health Affairs was demanding that Dr. Larry Schacht come to town for a three-month residence, so he could qualify for licensing. But Jones felt that he could not lose his young Albert Schweitzer even for three days. Over that issue alone, even this uncritical congregation might have balked at the inevitable lineup. But in San Francisco, the Concerned Relatives were peddling their accusatory petition again. A press conference was only hours away, where the Temple from Jonestown via radio would answer the charges yet again, to the profound boredom of the press. But a licensing dispute and yet another momentous press conference still needed bolstering, and so, at that very moment, Jones informed them, the Attorney General of the United States had entered the case. He was deciding whether to come after John Victor Stoen.

To repulse this pincer movement, they were presenting their war demands. In   **3.** Georgetown, the situation was uneasy, unsettled, dangerous, for their friend, the Prime Minister, was in Russia, and whenever the Prime Minister was gone, Guyana was a "land of emergency." One only had to consult history to know how many coups take place when the leaders are gone. They should recall that on that other terrible white night in September 1977, "when we came so close, my darlings," Burnham had also been abroad. They had been promised there would be no interference in their affairs, and wasn't it curious that the pressure on the doctor came just now? From "our" black and Indian origins, "we" are tired of broken promises, he told them, wrapping the cloak of epic struggle once again around their imagined problem. The doctor would not go to Gerogetown, not for three weeks or three days. For anyone who even considered coming to Jonestown to get him, the implication would be very strong. They would come in at their own risk. And simultaneously, the "vast news conference" three hours hence over the radio would make the difference in what happened not simply with the measly Attorney General of the United States . . . but with the U.S. Congress! (His skill for making the smallest claim grandiose was boundless.) They should rejoice in the power of their revolution, for when the whole U.S. government came down on you like this, you knew you were doing something right.

With the radio crackling beside him, he drew the issue. He had made his decision.   **4.** He would not allow the Attorney General to take away John Victor, for they had solid intelligence that the evil official was ready to shoot the child full of deprogramming chemicals, as if deprogramming were a chemical matter. He was beyond the point of crying now. It was time for decision, for action. There were options. He could slip through the jungle into Brazil or Venezuela and make his way back to Babylon to take care of the class enemies. Perhaps he would elicit the help of his Central American connections, some dictator or another. Then in America, depraved like the ''fleshpots of Egypt,'' he could take care of the enemies and then die gallantly for ''all the children of the world, for this Communist collective, and for Principle.'' Jonestown could be left in Mother Marceline's charge, and they would obey her . . . at the point of a gun.

His apparent successor stood by his side through this exposition, constantly **5.** taking his blood pressure, no longer the sugary sentimental conciliator. In the reedy, sharp voice of the dictator's handmaiden, she chimed in: ''I'll tell you one thing: if you're counting on me letting you out, forget it. I would kill you before I'd let you harm one of these children [as if anyone had suggested that] . . . I'm telling you right now, it'd be a great honor to die for this cause tonight. I'd fight to the very last breath in my body against these devils.'' She shook with passion, in a voice aged overnight by thirty years it seemed, but who exactly the devils were stayed obscure. He patted her with a trainer's pride.

''We've been at this thirty years, and she's still ready to fight. That's a long time **6.** to be with a fighter. And some [of] you aren't ready to fight now!''

In the rear of the Pavilion, the coaching of the various members who would **7.** answer questions from the San Francisco press (if any showed up) about their health and happiness began. Among the coaches were Richard Tropp, who wrote their initial statements, and Jann Gurvich. There was only a space of three hours to ''press time.'' But it soon became clear that the coaching was not going well. Harriet Tropp, a lawyer and Richard Tropp's sister, called to him from the rear of the Pavilion.

''It's not going well, Dad,'' she announced.   **8.**

''They're not trying hard enough,'' Jones roared.   **9.**

''They're trying, but it doesn't come out natural.''   **10.**

A flunky jumped for the microphone.   **11.**

''Don't you *dare* dispute Dad in a white night, woman,'' he hissed. ''Don't you **12.** ever do that.''

She recoiled with her sin. ''I apologize, Dad. I'm truly sorry. I forgot myself,'' **13.** she said. It had been ordained that these graduates of law school, members of the California bar, and other professionals must remember that principle of silence in white nights more than the rest.

Jones tolerated her mistake this time. ''They're not trying hard enough,'' he **14.** repeated. ''If they really hated their relatives, it would come across. If you can't come across, you're a fucking traitor. You people say you can't do, you can't do. I stuttered and stammered as a child, couldn't get a sentence out. So you better talk back there, because our lives are resting on you. No mealy mouthing, either. It better come through strong. You better be getting with it, because if you don't, your ass is going to be kicked all the way to the learning crew, or, farther than that, to the psychological department.''

He had tried many things to sustain at a peak the level of their hate toward their **15.** relatives. A month before during a ''catharsis'' over mercenaries, the entire community had filed before the microphone to describe what slow torture and death they would recommend for their kin in Babylon, and it had become a creative competition to see which of them could make the Bishop laugh the highest and longest with their ghoulish

fantasies, most of which began with the sex organs. In the end, two suggestions tied
for the prize. One ninety-year-old black woman had proposed to build a big white
church, put all her relatives in it, and then burn it to the ground. And an eight-year-
old boy had suggested killing his mother, cutting her up and poisoning the pieces,
then feeding the bits to his remaining relatives. To that, the Bishop's laugh trilled
uncontrollably from bass to contralto prestissimo for an endless set of measures. There
was no joy in the percussive offensive sound, only triumph and bloodlust, as he
contemplated the poisonous feast. The laugh hung high in the air, like contagious ether.

But now, at a serious moment, when it was no longer his form of entertainment, **16.**
somehow the fire had left them. The first act of *this* passion play centered on a tawdry
little interrogation of Stanley Clayton, the cook who would survive on cunning in six
months. Clayton bore a special burden, which was the flip side of Jann Gurvich's. He
was the nephew of Huey Newton, the high priest of revolutionary suicide, and a valid
rebel. Elitists and elite revolutionaries alike had to be denigrated. Clayton's interrogation
displayed not so much the banality as the seediness of evil, for he was "on the floor"
for a high Jonestown transgression: only hours after his black companion named Janice
had departed for Georgetown, he had lain with a white woman. It was a sin that put
one more scar in the psyche of the white members, making them want to take
blowtorches and sear their skin darker, as Jones put it. The moral of the interrogation
was that they all had no more loyalty than chickens, certainly not as much as dogs.

Jones often thought of chickens, dogs, and domesticated animals when he wanted **17.**
to teach his missionaries something important about themselves. In another moment,
he lectured a child he saw remove the wing from an insect. "The world is so full of
pain, son," he said gently. "Don't torture things. Because if you don't learn sensitivity
for life young, you sure won't learn it later. I don't want to see any more of you kids
stepping on bugs or teasing dogs, or we're going to tease *you* in the public service
union." It launched him into his favorite theme. "I've got a strong sentimentality
about animals. Take that anteater of ours some of you want to put back out in the
jungle. You complain about its smell, but I'll tell you this. I'd rather smell some of
these animals than some of you humans." His voice rose to receive their applause and
then receded. "If you put that anteater out, it will die. A tiger will get it in nothing
flat. When it climbs up on you, it doesn't want to hurt you; it just has such big claws.
So you can't put it out. It doesn't know how to fend for itself anymore.

"That's the problem when you domesticize something. It can't function anymore **18.**
in its natural habitat. When something comes to me, animal or human, I feel a
responsibility for it, so can't we build a cage for that anteater?"

His metaphor escaped them, so he moved to chickens, always surer ground. No **19.**
one seemed to mind his transitions anymore. "I can't even eat chickens. I've watched
too many of them die. They die calmly if you love them, but you can tell instinctively
that they know what's coming. They get excited. . . ." With disgust, he noticed
someone sleeping before him. "OK, sleep on. I know it don't make any difference to
you about chickens. But you know, there may be a step up some day. Someone might
decide to chop your head off."

But that was in a calmer moment, as one judged calm in Jonestown, and now, **20.**
in his "rage of love," it was Stanley Clayton's chicken-like infidelity that tormented
him—so different, say, than a dog's loyalty toward his master. "Ever since as a child

I saw a dog die, I wanted to commit suicide. It was the first time I felt guilt. But I still had some little dogs and cats alive, and I had to keep care of them, so I stayed alive for some thirty-nine-odd years more. Just little animals I stayed alive for, because I didn't know who was going to feed them, and I was *too young to know how to kill them.* . . . Then a little later, my mom needed me, and then some poor soul down the road, poor and minority. Then always blacks wanted me for their champion. It's always been that way. So you can do what you want to, while I do all the thinking, but I'm bored and disgusted and sick with you who do so little for socialism when you have such a good example to follow.''

It was as if he needed Stanley Clayton to bridge the stations of his martyrdom **21.** in this last passion. So from the origin of his guilt, he moved back to Stanley. Why, he wanted to know, had contract killers once come after Stanley?

"I can't think why, Dad," Stanley mumbled.   **22.**

"The gangland doesn't come after you just because you're Huey Newton's **23.** nephew. Who was after you?"

"I ran the streets a little, Dad."   **24.**

"What'd you market? Did you sell dope on the streets?"   **25.**

"Did a little of that, Dad."   **26.**

"Shit, I'm just as black as you [at least his hair was] . . . and I'd starve to death **27.** before I pushed that stuff on any of my black or Indian brothers. I consider you a class enemy now, Stanley," and he turned away as members leapt from the audience and started beating on Clayton, tearing his shirt. But the tearing affronted Jones's chintziness. "Would you quit tearing Stanley's clothes!" he barked. "I usually win these god-damned white nights, and if we're unlucky enough to get through this one, he'll need something to wear. . . . But there'll be one come we don't get through. I'd like for a white night to come and not pass."

Clayton's cheated companion, Janice, was brought forward, as well as Dr. Larry **28.** Schacht. For after Clayton's sin had been discovered, it had been decided that Janice should "relate" to the doctor, so overworked and uncomforted as he was. The first act now had its triangle. Soon it came out that Stanley had tried one last time to make Janice stay with him, rather than flee to the doctor. Jones made him describe his move.

"In that last talk with Janice in the loft, Stanley, what were you trying to get **29.** accomplished? Don't tell me. I know. All that babified talk, you wanted her to feel sorry for you, so she wouldn't go with that doctor, weren't you, Stanley?"

"That's true, Dad."   **30.**

"So you could get more nooky, right?"   **31.**

"Yes, Dad."   **32.**

"That line is so old, Stanley, it's boring. I can't image what the choice is between **33.** you and the doctor anyway. I've lain with women that made my skin crawl, men and women, but if I lay down next to someone, I would like to imagine that they were thinking slightly above the capacity of an ape. . . . The Office said *no* to one more chance, and you tried to con her into it. Did you make love that last time, Stanley?"

"No, Dad."   **34.**

"Well, that's one breakthrough for women's emancipation."   **35.**

"It's clear Stanley is a homosexual," Dr. Schacht offered, a curious rebuke for **36.** one who had had his own episodes.

"It takes two years for a man to be honest about his homosexuality," the Bishop **37.** proclaimed. "I've had to do it for this movement, with great big football players, twice your size, Stanley, big bucks of men, and they oohed and ahed. I don't have to tell no street man like you about this, though, now do I, Stanley?"

"No, Dad, I've done that."   **38.**

"Good, Stanley. See, you're growing," and then as if all the host had not heard, **39.** he repeated Stanley's admission of homosexuality. "That's good you can be honest about that. I've got a hell of a sex drive, and it's all oriented toward women. But if women had the proper pride, they ought to become a legion of Amazons, become lesbians, and never take a look at one of us. Because only then would they be capable of fighting a revolution. But you women get moony-eyed around men, you go crazy, and you can't do a thing for the cause. And you men are no different. All your intelligence goes to your balls. All you who are in love are in trouble."

They had arrived at the next station: his fantastic and selfless sexual prowess, **40.** their moony-eyed impotence.

"How long can he fuck, Janice?" he asked.   **41.**

"About two minutes."   **42.**

"Two minutes? Two minutes! Oh, you women sell out for such a pittance. OK, **43.** so you had a two-minute fuck, what else did you have in common? Did you ever go to college, Stanley?"

"I took a three-week college course once," Stanley mumbled.   **44.**

"So here we sit in the middle of a white night, not knowing whether we're going **45.** to die tonight, being bored by a two-minute fuck and a three-week college course."

His gale of laughter swept over them, and when it dissipated he launched yet **46.** again into the apocryphal legend of his eight-hour heroics with Karen Layton. And then with Grace Stoen. And then with others, but "I won't tell [on] the black ones." Then an aide brought him the draft press statement, and Stanley got a moment's respite. Jones looked at the clock which he had set up beside him. Only two hours to doomsday, he said offhandedly. He mouthed the words of the draft written by Richard Tropp, and translated into oratory for them.

"We will be like the valiant heroes of the Warsaw ghettos, before we are through. **47.** If you can't understand that willingness to die, if necessary rather than compromise, then you will never understand the integrity, honesty, and bravery of the People's Temple. . . .''

He approved it and turned back to Stanley.   **48.**

"Now, where were we, Stanley?"   **49.**

"I was telling you about sex, Dad."   **50.**

"*You* were telling *me* about sex, me, the maestro of revolutionary sex! Oh, **51.** c'mon, Stanley. What were we saying?"

"You were talking about your eight-hour. . . ."   **52.**

"Why'd you remember eight hours, Stanley?"   **53.**

"Well, me being only a two-minute driver, eight hours be more than I could **54.** strive for."

"More than you could strive for? You'd have to be a maniac to strive for eight **55.** hours, unless you were helping a revolution."

"That's true, Dad."   **56.**

''I remember every painful minute of it. You people who believe in love, you're **57.** fools. You can't fuck for no seven hours. You women can't take no seven-hour fuck, and all you have to do is lay there. Only saw one woman who could take it, and she had to be a masochist. But she grew out of it, and she's a good revolutionary now. Hell, I can fuck fifteen times a day, and I've got to worry about all of you at the same time. But the only fuck I want now is *the orgasm of the grave*.''

He called for his wife to take his blood pressure, because he felt it rising. One **58.** hour and fifty minutes to go. He dared not take any more medicine, because he feared he might be too tranquillized when they arrived at the moment of history. So he called for a portion of brandy instead. Meanwhile, Dr. Schacht stepped in as fabulist.

''The other night, as Dad was pouring out his soul to try and save the likes of **59.** you, he had a small stroke. He couldn't see a thing, and later in the night he had three convulsions, three seizures. But he didn't bother you with that. Dad's been saying it for a long time: life is shit. Any life outside of this collective is shit. Every relationship is shit. You people who think you're loved. You're not loved, you're needed. All I want is to die a revolutionary death. And I don't want to get involved in a relationship that might sidetrack me.''

Something in Schacht's narration touched Jones's sentimentality. He recalled the **60.** senior who had told him the nicest thing the other day, and how rarely nowadays he heard nice things from them. She had said if there were no enemies, she would still pick this place to end her life, because it was so beautiful. How sweet. How lovely of her to say that. Usually, their comments were different, and he slid into his flapjack mammy's voice again. '' 'I didn't get my food today.' 'I didn't get the right medicine.' 'They made me wait five minutes in line.' That's all I ever hear.''

An old woman in the back waved her hand to get her food. **61.**

''Don't worry, honey. They'll get the food to you. You'll eat before you die.'' **62.** That touched his funny bone, and he laughed, but his amusement shifted to melancholy quietly. ''Never saw anything like it. They'd eat as they were lowered into the grave. Sometimes, I don't know where you people's heads are. . . . OK, Stanley, give us some news.''

''How's that, Dad?'' **63.**

''Give us some news, I said. Here I throw my voice away four or five hours a **64.** day, giving the news. . . .''

The fabulist jumped back in. ''You ought to be grateful that Dad pours all this **65.** news out to you, so you know what's going on in the world. It's fantastic.''

''Well, I've been back in the kitchen today, and I didn't hear too good,'' Stanley **66.** tried stupidly, knowing it would get him nowhere.

''That's OK, Stanley, it doesn't have to be today's news,' Jones said leniently. **67.** ''We'll give you *any* day.''

''I try to keep up with it, Dad, but, you know, back in the kitchen. . . .'' **68.**

''*Any* news, Stanley!'' **69.**

''Zimbabwe?'' **70.**

''Good, Zimbabwe. Where's Zimbabwe? Southeast Asia?'' **71.**

''Naw, Africa.'' **72.**

''That's good. What part of Africa?'' **73.**

''South Africa.'' **74.**

"OK, that's close enough. What about Zimbabwe?"   **75.**

"They won their struggle over there."   **76.**

"Four hundred fifty of their children were tortured yesterday. I told that on the   **77.** news this morning. . . . *I can't live with this.* Marceline, take this blood pressure again. I think it's getting to the danger level. C'mon, Stanley. C'mon, man. I can't take this. What are we having this white night for?"

"We're having a white night, Dad, because . . . our enemies are walking around   **78.** our building in San Francisco with some type of paper, protesting something. That's just a sketch of it, but I have this problem of hearing, and. . . ."

Jones's breath was becoming progressively heavier on the microphone.   **79.**

"Protesting what, Stanley?" he smoldered, low, ominous.   **80.**

"Demanding that they get John Victor, but I didn't hear exactly. . . ."   **81.**

"Who's coming after John Victor?"   **82.**

"Tim and Grace."   **83.**

"Not on your life. Tim and Grace come in here, they'd get their brains blown   **84.** out. It'd take more than Tim and Grace."

"Well, the noise back in the kitchen. . . ."   **85.**

"Hey, Stanley. Hey, Stanley," someone whispered from behind the podium, and   **86.** Stanley fell for it.

"You fuckers are too stupid to deal with me," Jones said, close now, ever so   **87.** close, to the brink. "He whispered your name and you turned around and you say you can't hear. . . . You people just tear me apart. You tear me apart. YOU'RE KILLING YOUR LEADER. The CIA hasn't been able to do it. I know what causes my blood pressure to rise. It's risen 20–30 points on both ends. . . ."

He snapped, bursting into cascading sobs.   **88.**

". . . Oh, how I cried for the people in *Roots*," he sobbed. "When the Fiddler   **89.** says 'free at last' as he lay dying, how I cried. I've been a slave all my life. Nothing I saw in that movie was as horrible as I've had to endure. To feel for a thousand people, to worry about them night and day! My heart breaks so many times every day, because I see so much that pains me, so much.

"This is a perfect society compared to the United States, but it was not what I   **90.** wanted. I never thought we'd be faced with multimillion-dollar lawsuits. I've been in this *litte prison* for nearing a year now. Made no name. Made no prestige outside, because the best way I could serve you was to stay out of the news and not be forging ahead in the limelight. But this is not my cup of tea. I'm a speaker. I'm a revolutionary, a tactical leader, a strategist. But that was not what was needed, because that would endanger our babies and our seniors. But it's dead. You're the only thing that's alive in me, and that's dying.

"Some people have an unlimited capacity for evil, my darlings. I tried America,   **91.** from one coast to the other. I took you around and saw that every city was the same. If I could have found one better than San Francisco, I would have taken you to it. I'd have liked to fight there. But we didn't have a chance to win a revolution there. All we had was a chance to see old people and children tortured. Here we can die on our own terms."

From his depravity to his cruelty to his sobs, he moved now onto the plane of   **92.** the hypnotic, his clerical, teaching tone establishing itself, his soothing sounds rising and pausing with great effect.

"That's what Jesus said: No man, no man will take my life. . . . I will lay it   **93.**

down . . . lay it down when I get ready. Some Christians don't understand us because we're more Christian than they will ever be. . . . And Paul said that it's all right to give your body to be buried . . . but be sure you've got charity in your heart. Charity means Principle. What is pure love? Communism . . . In other words, Paul was saying, give your body to be burned. Set it afire, if necessary to convey a revolutionary message, but be sure you've got Communism in your heart.''

His substitutions were often brilliant, but wherever the spirit of Jim Jones may **94.** now reside, St. Paul would probably like to have a little chat with him about the use Jones made of his doctrine. In Jones's mind, a secular image had invaded his rhetoric, an image of the 1960s had merged with St. Paul: the bonze in his orange robes dousing himself with gasoline before the American Embassy and setting himself afire. . . .

November 18, 1978

Jones assumed his pedestal, adjusting the scepter microphone. For the last time, this Prince of Omega, the Caesar Godhead, left his secular station and invested himself in the Office.

"I've tried to give you a good life," the Master began. "In spite of all that I've **95.** tried, a handful of our people, with their lies, have made our life impossible. There's no way to detach ourselves from what's happened today.''

Those who left had committed the "betrayal of the century." Those who remained **96.** sat on a powder keg. They could not simply wait for the catastrophe to overwhelm them. That was not what they had in mind for their babies. He invoked Jesus, restoring Christianity for a fleeting moment.

"It was said by the greatest of prophets from time immemorial: No man takes **97.** my life from me. I lay down my life. . . . If we can't live in peace, then let's die in peace.''

As they applauded, he warmed to the theme of betrayal. The synthesizer music **98.** began. The soft tones of a spiritual singer washed over them. He repeated the words of an idolater: if this experiment had worked for but one day, it had been worthwhile. It was time to touch them all. All his languages, all his tricks, all his voices must go on display. This was his sermon in the swamp. He was calling in all his debts, and the tape of history was rolling.

"What's going to happen here in a matter of mintues is that one of our people **99.** on that plane is going to shoot the pilot—I know that. I didn't plan it," he lied, "but I know it's going to happen. They're gonna shoot that pilot and down comes that plane in the jungle. And we had better not have any of our children left when it's over, because they'll parachute in here on us," parachute in as if they were the avenging angels of a wrathful Sky God. The suggestion brought the first scream of hysteria.

"So my opinion is that you be kind to children, and be kind to seniors and take **100.** the potion like they used to take it in ancient Greece, and step over quietly, because we are not committing suicide. It's a revolutionary act. We can't go back, and they won't leave us alone. They're now going back to tell more lies, which means more congressmen. And there's no way, no way, we can survive.''

His opinion, his decree thus announced, he called for discussion. Was there **101.** dissent? Never, never dispute the Father in a white night; it was a law burned into their minds. If there was dissent, it would be planned. His foil searched for her courage. As she did, he talked on, building his case. If the children were left, they would be butchered. If they went on a hunger strike, they would be striking against their Guyanese friends. It was too late for them to get their enemies—that would have to be left to the angels. Finally, the foil asked about Russia. The debate raged, Jones's deception on the Soviet covenant made clear, but it was too late for Russia, and he grew bored with the subject.

"I look at all the babies and I think they deserve to live," the foil, Christine 102.
Miller, said.

"I agree, but much more, they deserve peace."   103.

"We all came here for peace," she said.   104.

"Have they had it?" he retorted, besting her. They, not her.   105.

"No."   106.

"I tried to give it to you. I've laid my life down practically. I practically died 107.
every day to give you peace." His self-piety, his sacrifice again. Could they rise, or descend, to his level? "And you still don't have peace. You look better than I've seen you in a long while, but still it's not the kind of peace that I wanted to give you. A person's a fool to continue to say that you're winning when you're losing."

To light candles, to curse the darkness: before, this was how they posed their 108.
dilemma. Now the twain were joined. Before, he had scoffed at the Epistles of Paul: "Servants, obey all things in your masters, according to the flesh, not with eye service as men pleasers, but in singleness of heart, fearing God. . . . Masters, give unto your servants that which is just and equal, knowing that ye also have a master in heaven." Now in his vainglory, he evoked Paul.

"Paul said there is a man born out of this season. I've been born out of this 109.
season just like all you are, and the best testimony we can make is to leave this goddamn world."

The servants cheered, the raptures of slaves. The master ordered the potion. The 110.
crystals from 500-gram plastic bottles sprinkled into the purple solution of flavored drink. The syringes were scattered on the wooden picnic tables by the fistfuls, needles attached to some, making them weapons. Dr. Schacht marshaled his nursing corps. Ruletta Paul, twenty-four years of age, wife of Robert Paul, leader of the fugitive band that had slipped into the jungle that morning, stepped forward with her child in her arms. For her special guilt, atonement was to serve as first example. The child opened its mouth. The doctor squirted the liquid far back toward the uvula. "Children," Paul had told the Colossians, "obey your parents in all things, for this is well pleasing unto the Lord."

For Dr. Schacht, the problem was purely scientific: how to concoct a mixture 111.
that would kill quickly, painlessly, almost pleasantly. As the Bishop told them more than a year before, this had been worked out carefully by a Father who was deeply loving, a people who were truly caring. Dr. Schacht had poured in the appropriate measure of liquid Valium. Had he measured wrong?

"Oh, God, we're dying. It's starting to hurt," someone cried.   112.

"Great God, who said that?" Jones asked in irritation, then relented. "Come on 113.
up and speak, honey." He harked back to their enemies. They were responsible for this.

"We win. We win when we go down. Tim Stoen don't have nobody else to hate. 114.
He'll destroy himself." So that was their victory. They must all die, so that Timothy

Stoen would be deprived of an object for his hatred. For this inane absurdity, it took the Prophet's clairvoyance. Christine Miller was going too far. The foil was becoming sincere. She punctured his ridiculousness, and the centurions began to heckle her. "You're afraid to die." "You're no fucking good, God dammit." "You're only standing here because of him." She absorbed the abuse, as she watched the babies and small children being carried out into the field. Jones made a show of protesting her dissent, as he directed the communion.

"Hold it. Everybody hold it. Not much longer. Lay down your burdens. I'm **115.** going to lay my burden down by the riverside. . . . When they start parachuting out of the air, they will shoot some of the innocent babies. Can you let them take your babies?"

The congregation responded as it had been taught. Did no one pinch himself? **116.** Did someone not, at least, exchange a quizzical glance with his neighbor? Jann Gurvich? Christine Miller reached for her last argument, her final challenge.

"You mean you want to see John die?"   **117.**

For a year and a half he had entwined their blood with his: *they* must face death **118.** to prevent *his* child from being snatched away. How important was his blood tie now? What was the shape of his selfishness?

"What?" he said, startled, buying a second to think.   **119.**

"You mean you want to see John, the little one, die?"   **120.**

"John? John? Do you think I'd put John's life above others? He's no different **121.** to me than any of these children here. He's just one of my chldren. I don't put one above another. I can't separate myself from your actions or his actions. If you'd done something wrong, I'd stand for you. If they wanted to come and get you, they'd have to take me."

Christine receded into the mass. He complimented her. She was honest, and she **122.** had stayed with him, not running away with the betrayers. Her life was precious to him, as precious as John Victor Stoen's. Now, he could get on with it. Now, he saw that this was the will of the sovereign being. The Sky God was reinstalled. Had they noticed that only white people had betrayed them? Even he was deceived at the end. As the children came for their potion, he blessed them. Peace. Peace. Peace. Peace. Peace. The peace of God which passeth all understanding.

"I've tried so very, very hard from the time we were here," he groaned. **123.** "Together it's just easy. It's easy. Yes, my love."

"At one time I felt just like Christine," a woman said, "but after today I don't **124.** feel anything, because the people that left here were white, and I know that it really hurt my heart."

"It broke your heart, didn't it?" he said, selectively sentimental.   **125.**

His adopted son came to him, whispering the news from the airstrip. He announced **126.** it frantically: "It's all over, all over. What a legacy! What a legacy!" Ryan was dead. Many of the traitors were dead. The red brigade had showed them justice. Theirs had been an act of provocation. His voice rose with urgency. The process was too slow. Children's screams filled the arena.

"No, no, please, no," a boy's scream pierced the pandemonium.   **127.**

He issued orders. "Please get some medication. There's no convulsions with it **128.** . . . ."

There *were* convulsions. There was vomiting. The potion took four minutes to **129.** work. He wanted it to work faster. The Guyanese soldiers were coming. Quicker. Keep moving. Faster. It was an administrative problem. A nurse tried to help.

"The people that are standing there in the aisles will have to move," her flat **130.** usher's voice announced. "Everybody get behind the table and back this way, okay? There's nothing to worry about. Everybody keep calm and try to keep your children calm. They're not crying from pain. It's just a little bitter tasting. We have lots of little children here and we will serve them."

He called for Annie McGowan, so the business of transferring the Temple fortune **131.** to the Russians could be conducted amid the growing carnage. As he did, the head of security stepped forward to testify on his past experience of therapy to the dying, of how he had experienced the reincarnation of others, of how pleasurable getting a new body was, new and free of the nagging deficiencies of this one. He might have been describing an orgasm; perhaps this was Jones's orgasm of the grave, reaching its climax in the process of reincarnation.

"You'll never feel so good, family. I tell you, you'll never feel so good as how **132.** that feels."

It was the cue for other last testimonies to Father. **133.**

"Folks, this is nothing to cry about," a celebrant rejoiced. "We should be happy **134.** about this. We should cry when we come into this world. But when we leave it, we leave it peacefully. I was just thinking about Jim Jones. He has suffered and suffered and suffered. I'm looking at so many people crying. I wish you could not cry . . . but just thank Father."

There were still communicants who clapped. More gratitudes were delivered, but **135.** the Bishop was getting short-tempered.

"Please, for God's sake, let's get on with it. We have lived as other people have **136.** lived and loved. We have had as much of this world as you're gonna get. Let's just be done with it. Let's be done with the agony of it."

But the agony of it persisted, the organ strains and the Valium doing little to **137.** dampen the pain. These things take time. It would take three hours to finish the job. By "serving" the little children first, Jones's managerial talent surfaced again: having murdered their children, how strong could the parents' will to live be? He fortified their guilt for this crime against nature with a metaphysical argument: They could not separate themselves from the crimes of their archangels.

"You can't separate yourself from your brother and sister. No way I'm going to **138.** do it. I refuse. I don't know who killed the Congressman, but as far as I'm concerned, *I* killed him. You understand what I'm saying. *I* killed him." They understood: they had killed him too.

The Bishop preached on, repeating his exhortations, shifting blame to his enemies, **139.** harping on the worthlessness of this life, and embracing death as a friend, while Mother Marceline circulated among the crowd, hugging them, telling them she would see them in the next life. They should lay down their lives by the riverside. It was the River Styx now. Several times, the devil implied he might survive his hell.

"Do you think you can endure long enough in a safe place to write about the **140.** goodness that has been done?" someone shouted over the din. Think of the literature Albert Speer produced from Spandau.

"I don't know how in the world I will ever write about us," he replied mournfully. **141.**
"It's just too late."

Later, he wailed, "They can take me and do anything they want, whatever they **142.**
want to do with me. But I want to see you go. I don't want to see you go through this
hell anymore. No more, no more, no more. . . . "

The reverberation of his voice was overwhelmed by the screams of children. **143.**

Pandemonium was hell's capital, and no amount of his brilliant, loathsome **144.**
oratory or his organ player's dirge or his monster-doctor's Valium could keep the place
from consorting with chaos. On the perimeter, the centurions trained their rifles and
crossbows. Some waded into the herd to help inject the obstreperous. At his children's
antics, Father grew angry.

"Stop these hysterics," he scolded. "This is not the way for socialistic Commu- **145.**
nists to die." He was right about that, at least. "We must die with some dignity. We
had no choice. Now we have some choice."

He meant the choice of the group, not the choice of the individual, but the two **146.**
were dangerously moving into opposition.

"You think they are going to allow this to be done, allow us to get by with **147.**
this?" . . . This crime against humanity he seemed to mean. "You must be insane."
The growing weakness of his noble arguments occurred to him. His accent shifted to
their crime, their responsibility, his naked power.

"Mother, mother, mother, please mother, please mother, please, please, please, **148.**
please. Don't do this, don't do this. Lay down your life with your child, but don't do
this." Be mannerly in your slaughter.

"We are doing this for *you*?" a woman shouted at him. Was it a final, bleating **149.**
rebuke?

He ignored it. "Free at last. Peace. Keep your emotions down. Keep your **150.**
emotions down, children. It will not hurt if you will be quiet," as if hurting, like the
slight bitter taste of the potion, was the point.

As youthful screams melded with music, he tried history. **151.**

"It's never been done before, you say? It's been done by every tribe in history, **152.**
every tribe facing annihilation. All the Indians of the Amazon are doing it right now.
They refuse to bring any babies into the world. They kill every child. They don't want
to live in this kind of world. . . . The Eskimos? They take death in their stride." His
final identification was with the aborigines of the world.

But they would not be dignified, not his notion of it, anyway. **153.**

"Quit telling them they are dying!" he demanded, as if lying to the children was **154.**
more dignified. "If you adults would stop some of this nonsense! ADULTS! ADULTS!
ADULTS! I call on you to stop this nonsense. I call on you to quit exciting your
children when all they are doing is going to quiet rest. I call on you to stop this now,
if you have any respect at all. Are we black, proud, and socialists?"

"YES," came the diminished response. **155.**

". . . or what are we? Now stop this nonsense now." **156.**

"All over, and it's good." This cadence suggested the Bible again. And God **157.**
saw everything he had made, and behold, it was very good. "No sorrow that it's all
over," he sighed. "Hurry. Hurry, my children. Hurry. Let's not fall into the hands of
our enemy. Hurry, my children. Hurry."

The children were gone. The old and the infirm were next. From somewhere **158.**
came still more to try to please him with flatteries. For once, he needed no further
gratification.

"Where's the vat, the vat, the vat? Where's the vat? The vat with the green **159.**
potion." He brushed them aside, matter-of-factly mistaking the color of the stuff.
"Bring it here so the adults can begin. If you fail to follow my advice, you will be
sorry. *You will be sorry.*"

In the radio room Maria Katsaris directed the final details. Three aides, all white, **160.**
were called and given their mission to carry the letters and the cash to Feodor
Timofeyev. Later, all security bearing arms, some twenty-five people, were summoned.
There was to be no mayhem among the guards at the end. Meanwhile, Katsaris
messaged to Georgetown in code what was happening. Angels were to be dispatched
to Georgetown hotels to murder the remaining enemies there, particularly Timothy
Stoen. Then they were to kill themselves. How was it to be done? the question returned.
They had no firearms in Georgetown, no potion. Slowly, in Morse code, the letters
came back: K-N-I-F-E.

Then Katsaris gave her last order to the radio operator.   **161.**

"Now tell Georgetown that we're having a power failure," she ordered. This **162.**
transmitted, she held out her hand. The operator yanked a critical part from the
transmitter and handed it to her. She walked off to her private ceremony in the West
House, dying in Jim Jones's bed.

WORKING WITH THE TEXT

Cultural and Historical References

In this section, the numbers at the margin refer to the numbered paragraphs
in the selection itself.

1. The "he" in this first paragraph is Jim Jones. Deborah Blakey was an
   administrator in the People's Temple who became disenchanted and
   left the group.
4. Babylon was the city in Mesopotamia that represented corruption to
   Old and New Testament prophets.
4. The phrase "fleshpots of Egypt" is used in Exodus. Some of the Jews
   treking across the desert began to wish they had never left their cozy
   life in Egypt. They missed the "fleshpots of Egypt," that is, the pots in
   which they cooked their food. The phrase has come to mean any kind
   of high living.
16. A "passion play" is the story of the last hours of Jesus.
16. Huey Newton was the leader of the Black Panthers, a revolutionary
    group that was active during the 1960s.
20. "Socialism" is an economic system in which the means of production
    are controlled by the state. A communist government is a socialist
    government.

46. In common parlance, "apocryphal" means an imaginary event. It is named after the books of the Apocrypha between the Old and New Testaments in Protestant Bibles.

47. The Warsaw ghetto was a Jewish ghetto before World War II. When Nazis began to deport Jews to the concentration camps, the Jews turned the ghetto into a stronghold and offered armed resistance. After months of struggle and deprivation, the Jews were finally defeated when the Nazis brought in tanks and destroyed the ghetto.

89. *Roots* is one of the highest-rated television miniseries of all time. It tells the story of African slaves who were brought to the United States.

94. "Omega" is the last letter in the Greek alphabet. In time it came to mean death or last things. Knowing that, what does "Prince of Omega" mean when the phrase refers to Jim Jones?

99. One of Jesus' last sermons is called the Sermon on the Mount. Do you see why Reston calls Jones's sermon a "Sermon in the Swamp"?

125. The "red brigades" were composed of Western European radicals in the early 1970s.

140. The River Styx is the river in classical mythology that divides the world of the living from the world of the dead.

141. Albert Speer, a Nazi, wrote his memoirs while imprisoned in Spandau for war crimes.

145. In *Paradise Lost*, Pandemonium is the capital of Hell.

Writing Assignments: The Paragraph

Be sure to provide an introduction for each of the following paragraph writing assignments. That is, begin each paragraph with a phrase like this: "Thomas Brickle claims that. . . ." When it is relevant, you might also want to identify the expertise of the author ("Thomas Brickle, a New Testament scholar, claims that. . . ."), the name of the book or article, the century and country in which the work appeared, or any other circumstances that your readers might find significant. For more on this, see pp. 11–13 in Chapter 2.

1. Explain the point Jones is trying to make in his discussion of wild and tame animals in paragraphs 17 to 18.

2. Explicate in some detail the "fleshpots of Egypt" metaphor in paragraph 4.

3. A "foil" is a person who enhances the distinctive characteristics of another. Explain why Reston calls Christine Miller a "foil." Look at paragraphs 102 to 103, 115, 117 to 123.

4. What are the "substitutions" that Miller alludes to in paragraph 94? Look up the original passage in St. Paul that Jones alludes to in paragraph 93. Write a paragraph that shows how Jones uses the Biblical passage.

Writing Assignments: The Short Essay

Use informal documentation for these short essays. That is, don't use foot-notes or a Works Cited page to document your sources. Instead, cite only relevant information about your source, and keep that information *within* your text. Then follow the summary or quote with a page number in parenthe-sis. (Use the page numbers that you find in this book to represent the page numbers of the source.) Thus, your informal documentation will look something like this:

> In *The Romance of Medicine*, Benjamin Gordon, a history professor, claims that it was once believed that red wine replenished a per-son's depleted blood supply (p. 121).

1. Explain how two biblical metaphors—Babylon and the fleshpots of Egypt—work. What is Reston suggesting? What is Jones suggesting?
2. Explain why Reston calls this night a "passion play." What is Reston saying about Jones's perception of his role in history, his megalomania? How does the image serve as an ironic contrast?
3. Write a paper on peer pressure and the last act at Jonestown.

POLITICS + PUBLIC RELATIONS = POWER

Kenneth Wooden

At the time he wrote *The Children of Jonestown,* the book from which the following excerpt is taken, Kenneth Wooden was a special correspondent of *The Chicago Sun-Times*. He has written extensively on the exploitation of children in *Weeping in the Playtime of Others* and elsewhere. In the following selection, Wooden discusses how Jones avoided political and media scrutiny by courting establishment figures and reporters with a line of liberal and progressive rhetoric. As a result, as Wooden points out, Jones was the recipient of much highly positive publicity until just before the Jonestown carnage.

Saturday evening, November 18, 1978, Dr. Carlton Goodlett, a physician, the **1.** publisher of the Oakland *Sun Reporter,* and a powerful voice in the black community of northern California, was dining with friends at a private home with a beautiful view of San Francisco Bay. The phone rang twice that evening, and Dr. Goodlett's world fell apart.

The caller was San Francisco Mayor George Moscone. Frantically, he informed **2.** his friend that People's Temple in San Francisco had just told him it had received unconfirmed reports, via shortwave from Guyana, that Congressman Leo Ryan and his investigating party had been ambushed and killed. Reverend Jim Jones and his followers also were killing themselves at that very moment.

Goodlett, personal physician, close friend, and strong supporter of Jim Jones, **3.**

Source: Kenneth Wooden, "Politics + Public Relations = Power," *The Children of Jonestown.* New York: McGraw-Hill, 1981. 91–101, 103–115.

was visibly shaken and refused to believe what he had heard. He asked Mayor Moscone to do some further checking on what had to be a preposterous rumor. In the second call, the mayor confirmed the unbelievable, and they both "broke down and cried like babies."

It was symbolic that these two men—one a powerful city politician and the other 4. a prominent newspaper publisher—heard the news and shared the grief together. Dr. Goodlett and Mayor Moscone were key members of the coalition Jones had built to enhance his own political power base—a base initiated in Mendocino County and perfected in San Francisco, from which he rose to impressive heights. Using slick public relations and cleverly duping the press, Jones gained the reputation of a humanitarian whose religious works were dedicated to helping the poor and uplifting society's failures. In fact, he was a power broker, with an army of political workers who, at his command, would march for his choice of potential politicians or elected office holders.

Without question, Jones hoodwinked the politicians. In keeping with the ritual 5. of American politics, the power moguls, including Governor Jerry Brown and Mrs. Jimmy Carter, heaped praise on this man of whom they knew literally only one thing—that he could provide a host of dedicated, tireless campaign workers. As the children labored in the "grass roots," far removed from the eyes of the public and the candidates, Jones built a reputable powerhouse. From its center he weathered major assaults from defectors who, knowing the truth, battered its ramparts in vain to save their loved ones.

Jones' influence peddling began in the summer of 1965, when a black Cadillac 6. pulled into Ukiah, which was to be his first California base. In the car was Jones, his wife, Marceline, and their interracial family of four children. Armed with information his Ukiah scout had gleaned for him while he himself was in Brazil, Jones arrived with a plan to completely dominate the area that he claimed would "provide safety from nuclear fallout." The townspeople never knew what hit them.

With efficient speed, the minister found employment for the busload of 100 loyal 7. followers from Indianapolis who had uprooted their lives and livelihoods to remain close to their god. Soon, every key office in the local and county governments had a People's Temple member employed and reporting back to Jim Jones. With objectives similar to those of a military operation, they penetrated and controlled or neutralized basic community departments and communications.

The *Ukiah Daily Journal* was an important but easy target. Jones provided its 8. editor with a free houseworker and nurse for his ailing wife. When the editor's daughter-in-law had her first baby, Reverend Jones paid the hospital bill and later supplied the man with a young, attractive receptionist—Maria Katsaris. The publisher of the *Journal* was most appreciative for the many ads Jones brought to the paper: The two established a congenial relationship from which flowed a series of complimentary stories on Jones, the dedicated altruist. Since the *Journal* was the only newspaper in the area, Jones had effectively counterchecked future critics.

People's Temple began building a massive promotional campaign. Pictures of 9. adorable children graced the brochures, handouts, and press releases. Smiling innocents, with the right touch of "religious connotation"—"Whatever measure you use to give, large or small, will be used to measure what is given back to you": Luke 6:30—lent heart-robbing appeal to financial solicitations that filled mailbags, which in turn filled mail trucks and eventually filled Jones' bank accounts.

It was during this time, too, that hundreds of children and senior citizens were **10.** packed into buses, and the "Caravan of Hope" began its 10,000-mile, three-week trip across the country, attracting glowing editorial comments on their behavior and performance. In addition to their own literature, church members handed out a booklet entitled *Family Council on Crime Resistance,* excellent for families coping with crime, but hypocritical in its objective: Jones was criminally destroying the family fibers of his own following.

With the public relations campaign in full swing, Jones simultaneously developed **11.** a political machine worthy of the envy of any politician. Again, the children and senior citizens formed the vital nucleus. Ukiah-Redwood Valley, in Mendocino County, provided their basic training. One of the people to benefit was Mrs. Wayne Boynton, then chairman of the Mendocino County Republican Party, of which Jones was a member. Mrs. Boynton talked with the *Los Angeles Times* after the massacre:

> They [Temple membership] were a dream come true. They would do
> precinct work. They would get information from the courthouse. They
> would do the grubbies—addressing envelopes, making phone calls.
> They'd do anything you'd ask, and so quickly you couldn't believe it.

According to children and parents interviewed by this writer, Mrs. Boynton's **12.** work was completed in record time because Jones forced the children and adults to stay up all night to do it.

Fifteen-year-old Linda Myrtle described the mandatory work done by young **13.** "volunteers" for one candidate Jones was supporting: "We would leave school and go to the Wirth headquarters and man the phones and ask people were they going to vote for Congressman Wirth. And if they said no, or whatever, we'd write it down."

A father whose four children were drafted into the workings of the Temple's **14.** political machine stated: "He [Jones] exploited the children unmercifully in his political activities. Using the telephone directory, the kids would spend endless hours copying down names and writing letters for candidates."

Other political chores included passing out leaflets the day before election and **15.** going door-to-door for Jones' chosen candidates.

Year-round, for young and old, Wednesday was letter-writing night, and everyone **16.** had to work a minimum of six hours. Jim Cobb described the technique as he remembered it during his teens in People's Temple: "We would look at telephone books and get a first name here and a last name there and make up false names." Richard D. Tropp, who won a Woodrow Wilson Fellowship and had dreams of becoming a writer, headed up the letter-writing committee. Each person was given a copy of a letter Tropp had composed and an instruction sheet for variations of the draft letter. The following instruction sheet applied to a letter addressed to then Vice President Nelson Rockefeller.

Special Letter to Go Out—Everyone Must Write

Write a short letter thanking Vice-President Rockefeller for giving such
a superb speech. Our Pastor, Jim Jones, thinks so very much of you

(respects you, etc.) and appreciated all that you said at the Religion in American Life dinner the other night. Some—say that Pastor Jones told you about his great speech.

You can also say things like:

—I think you are a great Vice-President.

—I wish you the best of success.

—All of our members at People's Temple Christian Church think the world of you.

—We need leaders like you in these times.

—Pastor Jones has always taught us to appreciate and respect governmental leaders, and has praised you often for your concern for people, etc.

—It is important to see leaders in government taking an interest in (and honoring) our nation's religious leaders.

—We've looked to you often for wisdom and guidance and have found you to be a tremendous inspiration.

—I want you to know that whoever Pastor Jim Jones respects, I respect. And he thinks the world of you. You have done so much for the country, and for the office of the Vice-President.

—You have shown courage and wisdom in so many issues, etc.

Do not seal your letter. Please have it done by tomorrow night's meeting. It can be short. Put it in a stamped envelope, and address it to:

> Vice-President Nelson Rockefeller
> Washington, D.C.

Put your return address on the letter. Use a previous address if you wish. Some can use a variation on this address—say Vice-President Rockefeller, *or* Nelson A. Rockefeller. Some can put on his address Office of the Vice-President, or Vice-President of the United States.

Other projects of People's Temple were constant, consistent reminders to the **17.** political machine that Jones was essential to its success:

1. The Temple bakery turned out cakes for the bereaved survivors listed in the daily obituary columns.
2. Telephone banks were set up before elections. Temple members called registered voters and solicited their votes for Jones' hand-picked candidates.
3. Children and adults canvassed door-to-door before the election, using the personal approach to get out the vote for the Temple's selected candidate.
4. Little children, particularly, worked long, hard hours passing out campaign literature. Called adorable by the voters, they were most effective.
5. People's Temple contributed sizable sums so that the candidates would not forget.
6. Jones supported both slates or candidates without either side's knowledge. That way, he was always the winner.
7. Finally, People's Temple Church served as a large and enthusiastic forum to feed the egos of candidates.

With political wars come the spoils, and Jones knew exactly what he wanted. **18.**
Important jobs in sensitive governmental departments (Mendocino County Welfare
Department, the office of the district attorney, the sheriff's office, the Police Dispatch
Unit) became increasingly available to People's Temple members. Strategically placed,
these people monitored their offices and departments and reported anything that hinted
of potential trouble for Jones. It is small wonder that when teacher Ruby Bogner, who
had filed a threat and harassment charge against People's Temple, inquired years later
about the outcome of the charge, she was told that no record of such a complaint
existed.

The patronage system so effectively isolated Jones from governmental scrutiny **19.**
that he was awarded high public profile appointments—foremanship of the Mendocino
County Grand Jury and a seat on the County Juvenile Justice and Delinquency
Prevention Board. These posts gave him a public platform from which he generated
additional publicity. The publicity, in turn, provided him with more recruits for his
church, and the increasing membership gained him more workers, more control, and
more power.

With virtually total conquest of the communities of Ukiah and Redwood Valley, **20.**
Jones began to recruit talent to serve his designs for expanded political action, massive
public relations, and legal protection. San Francisco was his talent-draft choice. The
minister knew that the volatile 1960s, with the Civil Rights upsurge, three assassinations,
the Vietnam war, and the drug culture, had burned out many young people. He also
realized that the San Francisco Bay Area was a magnet for disenchanted idealists.
Combining charm and revolutionary rhetoric, he captivated some young, very bright
minds and enlisted them to help him lead People's Temple into the 1970s.

The purchase of a fleet of buses gave his public relations "army" rapid mobility **21.**
as he enlarged his weekend services to both Los Angeles and San Francisco. During
the early forays, he and his lieutenants visited local church services and rated the
ministers' performances. He also met with San Francisco politicians, evaluated their
strengths and weaknesses, and made index cards on them for future use. These early
days of scouting and reporting formed the basis for his overall strategy and actions in
that city.

After six years of solid growth and political muscle-testing in Mendocino County, **22.**
Jones was ready for the move to San Francisco. In the spring of 1971, a long line of
buses and cars left Redwood Valley and transferred the People's Temple central
operation to a new location on Geary Street in the Fillmore district—the heart of the
black community—of San Francisco.

Almost overnight, the Temple's propaganda program was in full operation. In **23.**
the tradition of Father Divine, Pastor Jim offered free meals, good health care, and
convincing oratory on social justice. Realizing that his "good works" would attract
members of black churches in the Fillmore district, Jones and his aides devised a plan
to overcome the expected bitter opposition from black clergymen. The strategy was to
win the confidence of one man: Carlton B. Goodlett, Ph.D., M.D., president of the
National Newspaper Publishers Association and a leading figure in the black community, who had once run for governor against former Governor Edmund G. "Pat"
Brown, and whose political views were "pro-Marxist socialism."

Dr. Goodlett already had been profiled and categorized by People's Temple staff, **24.**

and Jones knew Dr. Goodlett long before the black leader had ever heard of Jim Jones. Starting with his quarry's name on a small 3 by 5 index card, Jones charmed his way into the man's heart and confidence. Goodlett would become his personal physician, his friend, and his defender in death.

As Jones predicted, the Fillmore clergymen were threatened by the inroads he **25.** was making into their memberships. During this crucial period, they formed a delegation to talk to Dr. Goodlett about the "white intruder." After listening to their complaints, Goodlett offered this advice:

> Listen, this man (Jones) looks to me like he's pretty successful in inter-preting the functional gospel. I don't know what brand of whiskey he drinks, but if he drinks a special brand of whiskey, you better drink it yourselves.

So impressed was Goodlett with Jones that any time public criticism was leveled at People's Temple or its pastor, the publisher would place his respected newspaper at Jones' disposal to defend himself.

Goodlett was not the only member of the press seduced by Jones and his apparent **26.** good works. *San Francisco Chronicle* columnist Herb Caen wrote glowing accolades on People's Temple, and Steve Gavin, city editor of the *San Francisco Examiner,* attended Temple services and a testimonial dinner for the minister. Even after the Jonestown massacre, Gavin told Jeannie Kasindorf of *New West Magazine:*

> [Jones] was a very exciting, very impressive person who said all the right things . . . possibly the most fascinating person I've ever met. He invited me to the service and it was a real high, this joyous kind of feeling of love and caring for each other.

Jones' overtures to the press were effective for the first six years in San Francisco. **27.** His public image grew with each new article on his amazingly innovative drug abuse program, lunches for senior citizens, and crime prevention programs for youths. The newspapers reported everything the minister wanted in print, including his $500 donation to the family of California Highway Patrol Officer Al Turner, who was shot on the job, and a People's Temple contribution of $4,400 "in defense of the press."

In January 1973, the *San Francisco Chronicle* accepted $500 from Jones' "Free **28.** Press Fund" in good faith. In an article expressing his thanks, the publisher, Charles deYoung Thieriot, described People's Temple for his readers:

> Called less formally PT, the church is best known and highly regarded for its social works, which include housing and feeding senior citizens and medical convalescents, maintaining a home for retarded boys, reha-bilitating youthful drug users and assisting non-members as well as members of the faith through college and legal difficulties.

So within eighteen months of opening the new church on Geary Street, Jones could comfortably count on the support of and promotion from local media. He also knew the exact needs of the politicians. He and his workers, dubbed "the troops," soon became an awesome commodity in political circles. Said one high Democratic State Committee staff person, "They were made to order. You should have seen it—old ladies on crutches, whole families, little kids . . .'' Jones was noted for his ability to turn out a crowd of 2,000 with only a six-hour notice.

The minister's public relations plan also called for the infiltration of other **29.** influential organizations with media and political connections. While going through the San Francisco Temple Church with *NBC News,* this writer found a NAACP membership card for Larry Layton (who has been tried in Guyana for his role in the shooting of Congressman Ryan and others). Layton was one of 300 members of People's Temple for whom Jones paid the ten-dollar membership dues in the NAACP. They literally took over the local branch, and shortly thereafter, Jones was elected to the board of directors. A similar move was made to take over the Black Leadership Forum in San Francisco, but an astute change in the bylaws by its membership saved that organization.

At the same time, an internal master plan was devised for use in discrediting any **30.** critics of People's Temple, whether defectors or investigators from the media or government. The plan was called ''Diversions Department'' and operated as described in Jim Cobb's lawsuit against Jones:

A. *Defectors & Critics Division:* To divert individual persons, particularly ex-members of People's Temple and outspoken critics thereof,
   from publicizing and from organizing in opposition to the practices
   of defendants JONES and PEOPLE'S TEMPLE, by threatening
   such persons with death and injury to their persons and properties,
   including threats that their homes will be burned;
B. *Government & Media Division:* To divert agencies of government
   and of the media from investigating the practices of defendants
   JONES and PEOPLE'S TEMPLE by:
   (1). ''Bombarding'' them with continual mass volumes of letters
   written in longhand by People's Temple members conscripted as
   part of ''letter-writing committees'' which allege various types of
   unjustified harassment; and
   (2). Making anonymous telephone calls to agencies of government
   and the media, which accuse totally innocent persons selected at
   random of heinous crimes and immoral acts (particularly crimes and
   acts related to those for which defendant JONES feared he was
   about to be accused); and
C. *General Public Division:* To divert the public from focusing upon
   the questionable practices of defendants JONES and PEOPLE'S
   TEMPLE by publishing press releases and other communications
   which falsely accuse the critics of such practices as being sexual
   deviates, terrorists, drug traffickers or child molesters.

The operation was used liberally in general, but most extensively against Tim **31.** Stoen after he defected and joined forces with the Concerned Relatives. A People's Temple letter to the U.S. Agency for International Development charged: ''The Stoens instigated his [Jones] relationship with Grace, over Tim's pleas to protect his reputation from embarrassment of threatened exposure of his transvestite patterns.''

The coalition Jones built between political leaders and the media gave him an **32.** unassailable position in the power structure of San Francisco up to the mid-1970s. His army of political ''volunteers'' were used to support whomever he wished to put in office. To the powerful weapons at his command was added another—fear. As word spread that Jones wouldn't hesitate to discredit or destroy anyone who got in his way or crossed him or his cause, more and more politicians felt uneasy about him.

The years 1975 and 1976 were his political zenith. In 1975, George Moscone **33.** ran for mayor and Joe Freitas for district attorney. Jones threw his workers—children, teen-agers, and elderly—behind the two men, and they both won very tight races—Moscone by a mere 4,000 votes and Freitas by about 9,000. The closeness of these elections gave Jones significant new leverage, prompting State Assemblyman Willie Brown's assessment: ''In a tight race like the ones that George and Joe had, forget it without Jones.'' Jones was rewarded with the appointment to chairmanship of the city's Housing Authority, and Tim Stoen, then his trusted lawyer, joined the staff of District Attorney Freitas.

With this high public profile, more awards began to come, some of them **34.** engineered by Jones and his staff. In April 1975, he was named ''one of the 100 most oustanding clergymen in the nation'' by Religion in American Life, Inc., an interfaith organization. Dr. Goodlett's newspaper, the *Sun Reporter*, presented him with a ''Citizen's Merit Award'' for his dedication to social justice. And in January 1976, a most coveted award, ''Humanitarian of the Year,'' was bestowed on Pastor Jones by the *Los Angeles Herald*. This award gave People's Temple a platform from which to boast of its generous financial support to worthy causes and organizations: the Fresno Bee Newsmen, the Telegraph-Hill Medical Clinic, American Cancer Society, Mendocino County Heart Association, Sickle-Cell Anemia Testing Program, Educational Broadcasting Stations, Big Brothers of America; and to antihunger groups: Bread for the World, North of Market Senior Escort Program, and even the Police Fishing Program.

While all this was merely token support to further build Jones' credibility in the **35.** Bay Area, it paid off when state Democratic Officials solicited his help with a scheduled visit from Rosalyn Carter, who was campaigning for her husband's successful bid for the Presidency. Jones had already figured prominently in campaign functions for Lieutenant Governor Mervyn Dymally, Governor Jerry Brown, Tom Hayden (husband of actress Jane Fonda), and others.

In retrospect, Mrs. Carter's visit to San Francisco on September 14, 1976, was **36.** not one of the Secret Service's finest hours. The rally for the future First Lady was held at a Market Street storefront serving as the Democratic campaign headquarters for Jimmy Carter. People's Temple buses parked behind the store after depositing the children and elderly, who strategically filled the front rows of chairs. Jones arrived with a score of armed bodyguards, some of whom were convicted felons with records of aggravated assault.

The United States Secret Service worked hand in hand with Jones's security **37.**

force, searching the area for bombs and "suspicious characters who may be armed."
At one point, a bodyguard of Jones' pointed to a man he suspected of carrying a
weapon. The Secret Service agent duly approached and searched the man. At the same
time, a Democratic official spotted a gun on one of Jones' bodyguards and voiced his
concern to the Secret Service, but was told it was "OK."

Since the audience was packed with People's Temple members, Jones received **38.**
more applause than anyone, including Mrs. Carter. She and her advance team were
most impressed and pleased with Jones and the enthusiastic turnout. She readily agreed
to his request for a private audience later in the day.

That evening, Jones pulled into the prestigious Stanford Court Hotel's courtyard **39.**
in a chauffeured limousine, followed by two other cars. To the amazement of the Carter
people and the Secret Service, Jones entered the hotel with at least a dozen armed
bodyguards in dress suits. It took some intense reassuring and quiet but firm maneuvering
by the Carter advance team to separate the guards from Jones.

No one knows precisely what was discussed, but close aides to the minister **40.**
reported that the Guyana project and Carter's campaign in California were priority
subjects. Apparently, a mutually satisfactory agreement was reached, for shortly
afterward, 200 to 250 "volunteers" from People's Temple turned up to work for the
Central Committee's "Get-Out-The-Vote" drive for Carter. According to party officials, the Temple youths and senior citizens made up more than 10 percent of the entire
state's campaign volunteer effort.

On September 25, 1976, eleven days after Mrs. Carter's entourage left San **41.**
Francisco, the Establishment turned out en masse to honor Reverend Jim Jones at his
church. The guest list was a political spectrum, from the chairman of the Republican
Party in Mendocino County to leading Democrats in San Francisco. There was Angela
Davis on the far left, and a leading member of the John Birch Society on the far right.
In between were all the important politicians, media, and civic personalities of the city:
Lieutenant Governor Mervyn Dymally, State Senator Milton Marks, Mayor George
Moscone, District Attorney Joseph Freitas, Supervisor Robert Mendelsohn, Police
Chief Charles Gain, Dr. Goodlett of the *Sun Reporter*, Steve Gavin of the *San Francisco
Chronicle*, and members of the Gay Movement.

As the children of People's Temple unobtrusively provided entertainment and **42.**
served food, State Assemblyman Willie Brown, the master of ceremonies, added
another jewel of praise to the cult leader's promotional crown:

> Jim Jones is a rare, rare, rare specimen. Jim Jones is a symbol of what
> we all ought to be about . . . Jim Jones is, in my opinion, a true human
> being. Let me present to you what you should see every day when you
> look into the mirror in the early morning hours. Let me present to you
> a combination of Martin Luther King, Angela Davis, Albert Einstein,
> Chairman Mao . . .

The crowd roared its approval with a standing ovation.

With an eye on expanding horizons, Jim Jones also sought public approval by **43.**
national leaders. The Temple's files show endorsements from, among others, the late
Hubert H. Humphrey, Jane Fonda, and Roy Wilkins. (This respectability later proved

very costly to the parents who, fighting to free their children from the cult, were rebuffed and neutralized in their efforts.)

> The work of Reverend Jones and his congregation is testimony to the positive and truly Christian approach to dealing with the myriad problems confronting our society today.
>
> Hubert H. Humphrey

> During this period when there are such serious problems with which our minorities are faced, it is encouraging to learn that there is such an effective effort which is being made by the People's Temple.
>
> Roy Wilkins

> Much of what America needs to resolve its overwhelming social problems has become embodied into the life of Jim Jones and the works of People's Temple.
>
> Jane Fonda

> Reverend Jim Jones has been a friend to hundreds of youth in the city, and his church has rehabilitated many from drug use, helped young people out of legal difficulty and antisocial patterns . . . His church has taken . . . children abandoned by parents and unwanted by agencies.
>
> Joseph E. Hall
> NAACP, San Francisco branch

> Ninety-nine percent of all the work done by People's Temple is in service to the elderly, poor families, and troubled youth . . . It is most unfortunate that some people . . . feel threatened by this simple organization and philosophy of service.
>
> Art Agnos, majority whip
> California State Assembly

> I am grateful . . . for . . . the work of the People's Temple Christian Church in defending the First Amendment guarantees of freedom of the press . . . and in running the ranch for handicapped children.
>
> Walter F. Mondale

> I say without qualification that this church has been second to none in preventing crime . . . They have donated thousands of dollars to city-sponsored fund drives for the purpose of creating summer jobs for youth and programs for cultural enrichment. They have sent some of their wayward youth to their large agricultural mission in South America entirely at their own cost.
>
> Joe Johnson, former deputy mayor
> City of San Francisco

At different times when Vice President Mondale and Attorney General Griffin **44.** Bell visited San Francisco, Jim Jones was invited to meet with Mondale on Air Force One and with Bell at a private dinner at the home of the influential lawyer Robert Wallach. Now the reverend's political clout spanned the nation—from a black ghetto on the West Coast to the White House and the halls of the Justice Department in Washington.

Amidst the adulation for Jim Jones from the uninformed and the compromised, **45.** a handful of inquisitive reporters had their doubts. As far back as 1972, Lester Kinsolving, religious editor for the *San Francisco Examiner*, prepared a series of articles on the minister. Two installments—''The Prophet Who Raises the Dead'' and ''Healing Prophet Hailed as God''—were published before management buckled under a barrage of letters and phone calls and nonstop picketing by People's Temple children and adults. The picketing got extensive TV and newspaper coverage. However, not one reporter questioned why the children, who marched all day without a rest or lunch, were not in school. No mention was made, either, of the children's dinner of dry peanut butter sandwiches (partially frozen) and a small drink of Kool-Aid while they continued to march.

In 1977, Gordon Lindsay, of the *National Enquirer*, also wrote an exposé on **46.** Jones, but threats of libel action made the national weekly decide not to run it. Marshall Kilduff, of the *San Francisco Examiner*, was more tenacious when he asked his editor, Steve Gavin, if he could look into People's Temple. Gavin, by his own admission, was impressed with Jones and did not give his reporter permission to investigate either the church or its leader, who by now was constantly surrounded by armed guards and refused to be interviewed.

Kilduff took his story concept to *New West Magazine*, where senior editor Kevin **47.** Starr liked the idea for an investigative piece and gave the young reporter the green light. It was not an easy assignment. Jim Jones knew almost immediately that someone was investigating him; he also knew that neither he nor his power base—the People's Temple—could withstand a critical examination. On Valentine's Day in 1977, Starr was visited by a group of People's Temple lawyers and other personnel. The next day, Starr wrote to Marshall Kilduff:

> A large delegation from the PT called upon me yesterday and con-
> vinced me that further publicity at this time would have a bad effect
> upon the church's ministry. *New West Magazine* has no wish to inter-
> fere with the most important work of the PT at this time. *New West
> Magazine* is very interested in maintaining good community relations. I
> am therefore asking you not to do the PT story.

A copy of the letter was sent to Jim Jones.

Kilduff then took the story to the *San Francisco Magazine*, but it too turned **48.** down the idea after a visit from the same People's Temple delegation. The investigation appeared to be dead until a new ownership took over *New West*. Kevin Starr was out, and Rosalie Muller Wright, the new editor, liked the story and assigned Phil Tracy to work with Marshall Kilduff on the piece.

Jones now attempted to kill the story in two ways. First, he applied pressure on **49.** *New West*. Rupert Murdoch, the new owner, was inundated in New York with letters and phone calls, as were the advertisers, who were urged to pull their ads out of the publication. This time most of the letters were not fictitious. They were from the powerful whom Jones had helped. Even the San Francisco branch of the American Civil Liberties Union intervened to try to kill the exposé.

Second, the Temple's propaganda mill went into overtime operation. Reams of **50.** heartwarming stories flooded the public and the mailboxes of Temple supporters. Photos of children were used extensively in a series of new brochures about the People's Temple in Guyana. One photograph showed more than fifteen little children holding toys, sucking their thumbs, but all waving "a fond goodbye to Pastor Jones as he leaves to come back to California." In a special Thanksgiving message, Jones wrote:

> Each day the children grow more self-assured, blossoming in all their
> beauty and creativity, free to express themselves and so healthy and
> happy . . . The seniors seem to have grown younger . . . the little chil-
> dren look forward eagerly to their visit to the seniors' homes. The
> medical clinic has been compared to Dr. Schweitzer's hospital in
> Africa . . .

For the first time, Jones played down the appeal for money as he closed his **51.** informative letter with: "I urge you to take advantage of this opportunity to express your gratitude and strengthen your point of contact with the spirit of Love."

When it became apparent that publication of the *New West* article was imminent, **52.** Jones panicked, and in what appeared to be a spontaneous decision, hustled the children out of the country to Guyana. The People's Temple Agricultural Project Progress Report for the summer of 1977 was hastily prepared and widely distributed. The brochure depicted a jungle paradise with beautiful children in school situations, playing in the playground, always smiling and waving to the photographer—thus documenting the image that Jones needed to counter the bad publicity expected from the *New West* article.

The Temple's own newspaper, *People's Forum*, cranked out articles about how **53.** effectively Jones was helping children, as well as other child-related articles: "Our Children Are Our Wealth," "Black Child Development," "Youth Crime," "Hunger in the U.S.: Children Without Food," and, ironically, "Children Brutalized." Newspaper rehashes of favorable articles bordered on the ridiculous—for example, the column by Guy Wright in the *San Francisco Examiner*, June 9, 1977. Entitled "Fresh Start in a Jungle for the City Misfits," the piece relied entirely on Jones for information in telling how youngsters were going straight in the jungle under the wise and kind tutelage of Father Jones. Wright ended the article with this alleged statement by a troubled teen-ager of his first day in Jonestown, as Jones described it:

> He [Jones] told about a new arrival who woke up to the tropical dawn,
> the song of exotic birds, the soft kiss of the trade winds. The young
> man threw his arms out and shouted, "Man, the Fillmore has seen the
> last of me!"

To the credit of *New West Magazine*, Jones, with all his power and diverse **54.** contacts, failed to control the media in San Francisco totally. Two weeks before publication of its exposé, Jim Jones fled the country, never to return again alive. With him went the remainder of the children and senior citizens. His political workers were transplanted in a foreign country where, without their knowledge, Jones offered their services to the Prime Minister for future elections.

From the jungle, Jones and his faithful planned a counteroffensive. The strategy **55.**

was threefold: 1) Use the politicians and media to neutralize the *New West* charges of abuse in People's Temple, 2) discredit the informers and obtain glowing comments from "impartial observers," and 3) totally cloud the issue by bringing on Mark Lane, the notorious exposer of government "conspiracies," to act as legal counselor.

Sympathetic politicians and press fell quickly into line. The mayor's office issued **56.** the following statement concerning the magazine exposé:

> I have read the recent well-publicized article concerning the Reverend
> Jim Jones and the PT and find it to be a series of allegations with ab-
> solutely no hard evidence that the Rev. Jim Jones has violated any
> laws, either local, state or federal. The Mayor's Office does not and
> will not conduct any investigations on the Rev. Jones or the PT.

District Attorney Joe Freitas announced, however, that his office, under the **57.** jurisdiction of his special prosecutor, Robert Graham, would conduct an investigation into the affairs of People's Temple, but nothing ever came of it.

Columnist Herb Caen wrote that Jones was most anxious to return to the States **58.** to defend himself but couldn't act against the advice of his attorney. He then quoted Jones' public relations man, Mike Prokes: "This campaign against Jim is orchestrated at the highest level, perhaps FBI or CIA." Dr. Goodlett leveled his criticism at the people who had given the two reporters their information for the *New West* story, calling them "malcontents, psychoneurotics, and, in some instances, provocateurs—probably Establishment agents."

A notable religious leader, Reverend John V. Moore, former superintendent of **59.** the United Methodist Church of northern California, and his wife visited "impressive and amazing" Jonestown during the summer of 1978 to see their two daughters and grandson. On his return, Moore had this to say:

> I had a feeling of freedom. Neither in Georgetown, with twenty-five or
> thirty people coming and going all the time with total freedom, nor at
> the project itself did I have any feeling that anybody was being re-
> strained or coerced or intimidated in any way.

The most powerful weapon employed by People's Temple in its counterattack, **60.** however, was attorney Mark Lane, who, after a quick trip to Jonestown, thundered to the press that he would soon file a multimillion-dollar suit against various government agencies for their conspiracy to destroy Jonestown. "The long silence has ended, and the offensive is about to begin," he vowed.

Lane then told the press a story, overlooked in the aftermath of the tragedy, to **61.** prove his conspiratorial claim. According to him, twenty employees of Interpol (the International Criminal Police Commission) were sent on a "trans-jungle trek . . . armed with rocket launchers and small arms" to free the children of Jonestown from its reported evil influence. The group, Lane continued,

> was [instructed] to fire on the colony's generator building, darkening
> the compound, cut their way through barbed wire, and trek over mine
> fields to rescue the children. . . . Not finding these conditions, they con-
> tented themselves with sniping at the compound for six days, and after

being invited in and treated well, they felt used by the people who sent them.

Lane also claimed at that time to have a "full statement by the leader" of the alleged battalion, but he never released it.

Goodlett's paper, the *Sun Reporter*, published Lane's findings. Under a picture **62.** of happy, smiling Temple children holding a large poster that said, "FREE," the caption read:

> The People's Temple settlement in Jonestown, Guyana, has been described as an armed camp, where people are held against their will and harshly disciplined. Attorney Mark Lane says he has investigated the charges and found them to be false and part of a government-inspired plot to destroy this unique experiment in socialist living. The youngsters at Jonestown, pictured above, appear to agree with Lane's assessment . . .

In a confidential, attorney/client communication, titled "Projected Offensive Program for the People's Temple," Mark Lane gave Jim Jones the perfect scapegoat(s) he needed to divert attention away from how terrifying life had become in the Temple, especially at Jonestown:

> Even a cursory examination reveals that there has been a coordinated campaign to destroy the People's Temple and to impugn the reputation of its leader, Bishop Jim Jones. This campaign has involved various agencies of the U.S. Government, agencies of various states and the action of numerous individuals who at the present time cannot be proven to have a working relationship with the state or federal authorities. Among the suspect organizations are the Central Intelligence Agency, the Federal Bureau of Investigation, the Internal Revenue Service, the U.S. Post Office, the Federal Communication Commission and their agents and employees.

In the same memo, under the heading "Public Relations Counter-Offensive," **63.** Lane suggested that Marceline Jones, Terri Buford, and he "embark upon a campaign following the San Francisco press conference in which we appear on numerous radio and TV talk programs." The aim was to "create an appropriate and trustful image of the People's Temple among organizations on the Left in the U.S. and among Black organizations in the U.S."

At the very end, still another public relations extravaganza was planned—a **64.** benefit dinner honoring Jones to show continuing community support for him. Fliers were printed announcing the $25-per-person, tax-deductible dinner program, entitled "A Struggle Against Oppression," at the Hyatt Regency Hotel on December 2, 1978.

Listed as master of ceremonies was the powerful California state assemblyman, **65.** Willie L. Brown, Jr. Among the speakers were to be attorneys Mark Lane and Charles Garry, with Dick Gregory the special guest speaker. On the back of the flier, under the endorsements of seventy-six prominent leaders in the Bay Area, was a picture of three beautiful children. Next to the photograph was a quote from Jim Jones:

When I see the seniors happy and productive—when I see the children of every race gathered together to perform a play—I know we are living to the fullest. Life without principles is devoid of meaning. We have tasted life based on total equality, and now we have no desire to live otherwise.

After the massacre, those invited to speak at the benefit had their excuses. Willie **66.** Brown complained that Jones "hustled us politicians," and Dick Gregory blamed the CIA. Mark Lane wrote a book in which he said the "strongest poison" was not that "placed in the mouths of the children in Jonestown," but rather the poison of conspiracy directed at him, Lane, by the government and the press.

WORKING WITH THE TEXT

Cultural and Historical References

In this section, the numbers at the margin refer to the numbered paragraphs in the selection itself.

24. Father Divine was the charismatic black religious leader who lived in luxury among his poor parishioners.
42. Angela Davis, a Black radical who was involved in radical politics in the late 1960s and 1970s, is now a professor in a California university.
43. Chairman Mao is Mao Tse-tung, a leading theorist and premier of the Chinese Communist Party until he died in 1976.

Writing Assignments: The Paragraph

Be sure to provide an introduction for each of the following paragraph writing assignments. That is, begin each paragraph with a phrase like this: "Thomas Brickle claims that. . . ." When it is relevant, you might also want to identify the expertise of the author ("Thomas Brickle, a New Testament scholar, claims that. . . ."), the name of the book or article, the century and country in which the work appeared, or any other circumstances that your readers might find significant. For more on this, see pp. 11–13 in Chapter 2.

1. Analyze Wooden's introduction in paragraphs 1 to 4. Contrast it to a conventional introduction.
2. Describe the reactions of Willie Brown, Dick Gregory, and Mark Lane after the massacre.

Writing Assignments: The Short Essay

Use informal documentation for these short essays. That is, don't use footnotes or a Works Cited page to document your sources. Instead, cite only relevant information about your source, and keep that information *within* your text. Then follow the summary or quote with a page number in parenthesis. (Use the page numbers that you find in this book to represent the page numbers of the source.) Thus, your informal documentation will look something like this:

> In *The Romance of Medicine,* Benjamin Gordon, a history professor, claims that it was once believed that red wine replenished a person's depleted blood supply (p. 121).

1. Describe and analyze what establishment politicians got from Jones.
2. Explain the *San Francisco Chronicle's* part in the rise of Jones and the People's Temple.
3. Describe Mark Lane's complicity in the rise and defense of Jim Jones and the People's Temple.

GLIMPSES OF THE PEOPLES TEMPLE

Tim Reiterman and John Jacobs

When Tim Reiterman and John Jacobs wrote *Raven: The Untold Story of the Rev. Jim Jones and His People,* the book from which the following excerpts were taken, they were staff reporters for *The San Francisco Examiner.* Reiterman was a member of Leo Ryan's entourage, which made the fateful visit to Jonestown in November 1978. The following excerpts from *Raven: The Untold Story,* the most comprehensive book to date, describe incidents in the darkening world of the Peoples Temple, during 1971, 1977, and 1978.

Ukiah, California, 1971

It was Sunday morning in 1971, shortly before eleven o'clock. Clouds of dust billowed **1.** over the Temple parking lot as car after car pulled off Road E. Soon the metal folding chairs were filled. The microphones were in place, the long cords in order. The musicians fussed with their instruments, then an impatient hush exploded into applause as Jim Jones took the stage wearing satiny red robes over a white turtleneck sweater. A swath of hair angled across his forehead. Sunglasses with fashionable dark wire-rims masked his eyes. He took a position behind the pulpit where a high barstool-like padded seat made him appear to be standing.

Upon receiving the proper cue, Loretta Cordell, plain-looking and pinched-faced, **2.** dipped her head in an imaginary downbeat and started to pound on the organ. Others played guitars and wind instruments. Bob Houston, with his trombone, stood tall among them.

With his arms keeping time, Jones led the singing, his baritone voice rising and **3.** falling to the tune "Amen."

"We live and die for free-eee-dom. **4.**
We live and die for free-eee-dom!" **5.**

Source: Tim Reiterman and John Jacobs, *Raven: The Untold Story of the Rev. Jim Jones and His People.* New York: E. P. Dutton, 1981. 145–150, 345–349, 432–434, 445–447.

Then a sweet chorus, dominated by women and children: **6.**
"Free-eee-dom. *Free-eee-dom. Free-dom.*"   **7.**

Peoples Temple was becoming a nation unto itself. It could claim its own **8.**
president for life, its own unique mix of people, its own institutions, its creeds and
liturgy, its dietary and sexual practices, its justice and educational systems. Jim Jones
had fashioned his Temple with input from many: Jesus Christ, Karl Marx, Father
Divine, Joseph Stalin, Adolf Hitler, Mahatma Gandhi, Martin Luther King, Jr., and
Fidel Castro; also Lynetta Jones, Myrtle Kennedy, Marceline Baldwin, and a Pentecostal
lady from Lynn, Indiana. For Peoples Temple was in essence a reflection of what he
thought best.

The church and many of its people had been bonded permanently to an extraordi- **9.**
nary man who was a victim of his own experience. He swallowed whole his environment
and personal history, and spit out bits of it every time he spoke. His single greatest
ache was the loneliness and lack of acceptance he felt as a child. It was no great
mystery why communism and communalism appealed to Jim Jones. People were his
labor of love, his hedge against loneliness, and ultimately against history.

From the pulpit, Jones bombarded his people with almost impressionistic messag- **10.**
es. Because the catch words of love, brotherhood, unity and equality defied challenge,
his contradictory messages defied analysis. Sexual and family identities were dashed.
"Break down the barriers," Jones cried. "Lose your ego. Become selfless. Don't
establish superficial relationships on the outside." As he kept track of the personal
lives of hundreds of members, he not only showed them he cared for each of his
"children," he also located the wedge that would alienate them from family and
society. They confessed to each other, and criticized each other openly, purging old
values. They lived together, worked together in love, and when it was in the interest
of the Temple, informed on each other.

The exhilaration of having a family and a cause that could save the world kept **11.**
them going around the clock, giving until they were spent. But it was Jones's personal
magic—above all the black magic, webs of ideas and disguised threats—that weaned
people from their pasts and tied them to the Temple's future.

Total commitment was demanded piece by piece. As he declared in a 1970 **12.**
newsletter: "One must not worship things. Treat heat and cold alike. Pain and blessing
are just alike. . . . Have firm convictions. Don't vacillate!" Only thoughts existed and
mattered, he said. "If your mind is negative in attitude . . . it will produce disease and
likewise if positive, there is a great deal of information to indicate that one can almost
obtain eternal youth, the cessation of cellular death. . . ."

Jones promised essentially eternal life and protection. And he buttressed his **13.**
promise with the concept of reincarnation. It helped explain the deification of Jones,
the presence of a God-force in his body. It also allowed him to borrow from the auras
of great historical and religious figures—pharaohs, Christ, Buddha, Lenin among
them—and claim to be their reincarnation. But most significantly, he used the concept
to comfort those members who might have to suffer and give their bodies for the cause.
Death was not final, he told them. And in so convincing them, he grasped control of
individual lives that went qualitatively beyond that of any world leader in history.

"We live and die for free-eee-dom," they sang.
"Free-eee-dom. Free-eee-dom. Free-dom."

"No more poverty!" Jones shouted, then led the chorus again. He talked over **14.**
the singing, through the singing, directing them, bringing them down the home stretch
so he could speak:

"I'm here to show you as a sample and example that you can bring yourself up **15.**
with your own bootstraps," he began to approving shouts.

"And you can become your own God!" he promised. "Not in condescension **16.**
but in resurrection and upliftment from whatever economic condition, injustice or
racism or servitude which you have had to endure. Within *you* rest the keys of
deliverance.

"We ask for no condescending saviors," he went on, criticizing Father Divine, **17.**
"that has been pawned off on every breast. And I, God that came from earth of earth,
this dust of this toils and fields, hardships of labor, from the lowest of economic
positions, from the misery of poverty near the railroad tracks, I came to show you that
the only God you need is within you."

"Yeah," they cried, the male voices overpowering. "Right!!"   **18.**

"None other!" Jones repeated. "That's my purpose in being here. When that **19.**
transition comes, there shall be no need for Gods, any other kind of ideology. Religion,
the opiate of the people, shall be removed from the consciousness of mankind. There
shall no longer be any need for anything religious when freedom comes."

"Yeah." They nodded heads and waved hands, revived. They were with him **20.**
every step of the way.

"I came in the power of God in religion. . . . All the power you said God had, **21.**
I have. [I've] come to make one final dissolution, one final elimination of all religious
feeling. Until I have eradicated it from the face of the earth, I will do all the miracles
you said your God would do and never did." His voice quickened. "I shall heal you
of all the diseases, [provide the cures] that you prayed for that never happened. . . ."

Pausing, he reminded them all how he warned a woman and saved her from fire, **22.**
how he had had a crippled woman dancing around the room. As he addressed his
people, he scanned the faces before him, hundreds of them, his son Stephan in his shirt
and tie nearby with the microphones, the rest of his family, his faithful friends Jack
Beam and Archie Ijames, Grace Stoen with her arms folded over her bulging abdomen,
Bob Houston peering through his black-rimmed glasses, and many more. Even through
his glasses, Jones's gaze could be felt, through the force of his presence and the voice,
that tool that kept them in their hard metal seats when their backs ached, their legs
went numb and their bladders and bowels threatened to burst.

"I see some," he said raising his voice, "are not aware what God is. The only **23.**
thing that brings perfect freedom, justice and equality, perfect love in all its beauty
and holiness is socialism. *Socialism!*"

A roar of assent echoed through the church and out the louvered windows opened **24.**
to pick up a cross-draft. Their hands and voices pushed him onward:

"I have taken myself a body, the same one that walked on the [ancient] plains **25.**

. . . of whom Solomon said his hair was as black as a raven, and he would shave as Isaiah said, 7:20, with a razor. I *come* shaved with a razor! I *come* with the black hair of a raven! I come as God socialist!''

The shouts—''All right. *All right.* Yeah''—drowned him out.   **26.**

Proceeding more deliberately now, as if clarifying a point, he said, ''I shall show **27.** you, from time to time, proofs of that, so that you will have no further need of religion because the highest authority tells you. I come to you doing all the things you have ever imagined God to do and you have never seen done. . . .

''It's beautiful to know God is a socialist worker. He is one of the people. He **28.** is all that you have desired, all the freedom, justice, all the sensitivity in minds.

''And I must say it's a great effort to be God.''   **29.**

There was not a single snicker from the audience.   **30.**

For his first miracle of the day, Jones called out a man named John to convince **31.** people that nothing, no matter how seemingly insignificant, is lost in the consciousness of a socialist worker God. ''My brother John came to me last week,'' he said gesturing to the black man. ''You were concerned that something was lost. He lost it miles and miles away. Well, my spirit retrieved it for you today.''

Then, to hoots and howls, Jones held out an object. John came for his miraculously **32.** recovered credit card. ''God damn!'' another man shouted in amazement.

With organ music and people keeping time with their hands, Jones shouted over **33.** them like some Bible thumper, urging people not to hate because it boomerangs, decrying loopholes that let the rich escape taxes, calling for freedom from the bondage of the aristocratic rich. Then, in frantic and seemingly incoherent fashion, Jones railed about the theft of the Bill of Rights, the spread of social disease, drug abuse by eight- and nine-year-olds and drug pushing to fourth graders even here, in rural Redwood Valley. No heavenly God could cope with those things, could he? He reminded them of his own miracles and parapsychology—and social goals—all in one breathless rush.

''If you don't need a God, fine. But if you need a God, I'm going to nose out **34.** that God. He's a false god. I'll put the right concept in your life.

''You understand the mystery? If you don't have a God and you're already **35.** believing that you have to build a society to eliminate poverty, racism and injustice and war, I will not bother you.

''But,'' he exclaimed, ''if you're holding onto that sky God, I'll nose him out, **36.** ten lengths every time!!!

''Will you tell me you believe in God out there?'' he shrieked in anger at **37.** imaginary doubters. ''So what? What's your sky God ever done? Two out of three nations in the world are hungry. Misery in every one of your homes. . . .'' His voice rose to a crescendo: ''The only happiness you've found is when you've come to this earth God!''

Waiting for their cries to die down, he went on. ''When you came to your socialist **38.** worker father, some of you never knew the fulfillment of happiness, you never knew that anyone cared. Your children were in difficulties. No one came to the jails. You prayed to your sky God and he never heard your prayers. You asked and begged and pleaded in your suffering, and he never gave you any food. He never gave you a bed, and He never provided a *home*. But *I, Your socialist worker God*, have given you *all* these things.''

Then, in display of power, as though to demonstrate that no harm would befall **39.** blasphemers, he slammed a black Bible to the floor. There were cheers. "No fears of doing that," he said, almost out of breath. "Say what you feel. Tap all the resources of energy within you!

"No, it's not sacred. You won't die if. . . ." He flung the book down again. "If **40.** you drop it. You won't die if you stand on it." He put both feet on the book, the toes of his shoes hanging over the edge, and tottered a little.

His audience delighted in the performance, reveled in his rebelliousness; they **41.** too were above the Bible that had guided the lives of so many of them. "You won't die if you jump up and down on it."

Jones calmed himself purposefully. "I talk pretty loud. Hope I didn't strain your **42.** ears."

They laughed and spoke in unison, "All right." **43.**

He told them, "I want you to realize that *you* must be the scripture, that any **44.** other scripture other than you and the word that I am now imparting is idolatry."

"Yeah!" They were with him again. He urged and they urged back. They were **45.** one.

"I know where I am going. I know what I believe. And I know what I'm doing," **46.** Jones hollered, straining for a peak. "And I've got a principle that will carry me on if the world passes away.

"When your world has failed you, I'll be standing," he murmured, braking **47.** himself, savoring each word as if it were being handed down from the Almighty. "Because I am freedom. I am peace. I am justice. . . . I AM GOD!!!!"

They went wild, cheering, cheering, cheering. **48.**

"See socialism as God in me," he told them. "Look upon me harmoniously. **49.** Every service I've said that socialism has a higher dimension than the three dimensions. You don't have to worry about that God up there," he told those who still believed in a heavenly Being. "*I* can heal your back when your spine's wasting away and your doctor says you can't be helped, and I cure it. *You're free! You're free of God! I want you to penalize that old God up there!"* He was ranting now, shouting at the heavens, challenging.

"If you're all-powerful, *send* one of your magic wands," he mocked. "*Send* **50.** your electric lightning. *Send* your thunder. Let it rain!" He stopped to give God a chance to perform. Nothing happened. The people chortled.

That contest won, Jones took it one step further. "When I was laying on springs **51.** with no covers, and the rain was pouring through the roof of my old ramshackle house, and they told me to pray to God . . . there was no God that came. The rain kept pouring. I had a beam of consciousness. I said there shouldn't be any poor; there shouldn't be any private property."

The pain of poverty and disadvantage flowed from his voice; a matter-of-fact **52.** righteousness, vengeance, swelled his chest. "Every time I take a drive in the country, and I see 'Private Property—No Trespassing,' I take those signs down." Approving laughter all around. "When I want to trespass, I just trespass. Because they *robbed* the people to get it! They took it from my people, the Indians! They came and shot down our babies! Raped our mothers!" His words boomed like cannon fire. "They took our babies and stripped off the scalps!"

He jumped from Indians to the preciousness of children of mixed races, to sex. **53.**
"It's come up that there have been bisexual and homosexual patterns [among church members]," he said. "And we got somebody coming in that won't tell the facts. And they say . . . I am a great lover. Now I know what you told me." He pauses, and there is silence. One by one, he points them out with his index finger, one cluck of his tongue for each. He was making their admissions for them, those homosexuals, latent and otherwise.

Raising his volume preacherly and righteously, he said, "There can be nothing **54.** going on in the bedroom, until mankind is liberated! There's no freedom in that bedroom! I've come to one of you! I've come to all of you! As I said, you'd all be happier to admit it."

"Right," a woman called out.   **55.**

"Right," a man called out. "Right" came a whole chorus of voices.   **56.**

Jonestown, Guyana, 1977

Despite the litany of allegations back home, no outsider visiting Jonestown for the first **57.** time could fail to be impressed by the physical site itself. The people, through sheer hard work and perseverance, had converted three hundred acres of dense jungle into a neatly laid out, administered and maintained town of nearly a thousand people. One needed only to walk the boardwalks to see the pride that had gone into constructing the colony—the row upon row of weeded crops on either side of the long road into Jonestown and around the cottages and dormitories, the vegetable beds and citrus groves planted in and around the settlement.

Visitors coming from Port Kaituma passed under a large sign hanging over the **58.** road: GREETINGS, PEOPLES TEMPLE AGRICULTURAL PROJECT. Behind the sign was a guarded gate—nothing more than a chain across the road—and a small security shack equipped with radio and tall antenna; routinely the guards advised Jonestown of approaching visitors. Along the roadsides, plantain groves and acres of cassava flourished. A final turn into the compound revealed the banana shed, kitchen and eating area on the right. Surrounding buildings included showers and toilets, sheds to dry and store food, an outdoor laundry area and even an herb center. On the other side of the road rose the dominant structure—the Jonestown pavilion—an open-air structure with a peaked aluminum roof. Here Jim Jones held his meetings and here the band played. Immediately adjacent to the pavilion stood two long school rooms with green canvas roofing. Beyond the pavilion, five large sexually segregated dormitories had been built for single women, problem children and the elderly. Beyond those lay a cluster of small wooden cottages. Other buildings were interspersed throughout the compound: the nursery, preschool center, the radio room and an outdoor play area. On opposite ends of Jonestown stood East House—accommodations for overnight visitors—and West House, home to Jim Jones; these cabins were named after early communes in Redwood Valley.

With the logistical problems of the initial influx behind them, the Jonestown **59.** administrators could practically watch the place run itself. The organizational plan, with modifications owing to the poor soil, was essentially working. Joyce Touchette ran the kitchen, central supply and laundry. Charlie Touchette oversaw construction, mechanics, the wood and machine shops, transportation and power generation. Marceline Jones, who commuted between Jonestown and San Francisco, ran the medical department when she was around. Tom Grubbs ran the school. Johnny Brown Jones, Carolyn Layton and Harriet Tropp served as Jim Jones's chief administrative officers: "the triumvirate." Stephan Jones sat on the steering committee, which planned for the farm's future, basing its decisions on reports from heads of various departments—banking, sewage, sanitation and engineering, roads, public relations, movies, video and guests, livestock and agriculture.

Jonestown's workforce was comprised of about 950 Peoples Temple members, **60.** two-thirds female. Nearly 70 percent were black, 25 percent were white, and the rest a smattering of mulatto, Hispanic, American Indian and Asian. Nearly three hundred were under eighteen years old.

An extensive report to the Guyanese government in the summer of 1977 detailed **61.** the progress of these pioneers. A preliminary draft was sent to the San Francisco temple with a note from Harriet Tropp: "[It] does show that the project is indeed something other than a 'penal colony.' "

The section on cassava production illustrated the care taken to use every bit of **62.** the precious resources available: the cassava mill could grate one hundred pounds of cassava root in three minutes. The gratings then were pressed; when the starch settled in the resulting liquid, the remainder was boiled, strained, then cooked down to a heavy syrup called cassareep. This was used to flavor foods and to make fudge. The starch was used for cooking and in the laundry center. The leftover cassava pressings were made into flour that was mixed in pig feed or turned into bread.

Eddoes, a root similar to sweet potatoes, were planted in 900-foot beds. The **63.** orchard, upward of a thousand immature trees, yielded only small fruit. But the agriculture section expected a crop of 1,000 pineapples and harvested 2,000 pounds of bananas a month. As the settlers invented a mechanical planter and their farming methods improved, they experimented with a wide variety of crops: onions, mung and cutlass beans, even coffee.

The pig population had grown from one young boar and five small pigs in 1975 **64.** to 130 animals. Pork, though served only when outsiders visited, was plentiful—and regularly sold downriver to earn income for the farm. The chicken population of several hundred soon multiplied to a thousand.

The Jonestown kitchen, though spartan by American standards, nevertheless was **65.** efficient and came equipped with large commercial refrigerators and icemakers, two gas and kerosene stoves and large aluminum sinks. It stayed open around the clock, as teams of workers took turns preparing the meals. At first the diet was varied: fresh fruit and vegetables, rice, chicken, cheeses and bread, among other things. A hand-dug well provided excellent water for cooking, drinking, cleaning, laundry and bathing.

The medical unit was well staffed and supplied. A large room served as an **66.** infirmary and drug dispensary. Detailed medical records, even a gynecological history of each woman, were kept.

Don Fields, who held a doctorate in pharmacology, manned the dispensary. The **67.** medical personnel included Dr. Larry Schact, who had interrupted his internship to come to Jonestown, plus a pediatrics practitioner and a respiratory therapist. A registered nurse was on duty twenty-four hours a day.

The hard-working staff soon learned to cope with health hazards of a jungle life. **68.**

They had workers kill off mosquito larvae to prevent outbreaks of malaria. The herb staff experimented with various teas to treat serious cases of constipation, a common consequence of the increasingly starchy diet. The seriously ill were taken to Matthews Ridge or, if necessary, to Georgetown.

The preschool nursery was a wood frame cottage with a corrugated metal roof. **69.** A rising sun had been painted on its wall, in back of the sandbox. Toys, crayons, children's books and dolls were arranged on ledges. A clipboard held "preschool stool reports." The day's lesson plan was chalked on a blackboard: "1) Perceptual motor skills; 2) water colors; 3) play dough; 4) paper cutting; and 4) sandbox, manipulative toys."

Elementary school classes were organized according to ability. The learning pace **70.** was individualized. In addition to the three R's, the students were taught physical and earth sciences, social science "with emphasis on Guyanese history and culture," socialism, arts, crafts and music. The high school provided vocational and technical education, stressing agricultural skills.

For many of the several hundred senior citizens, Jonestown might well have **71.** seemed better than life in America, especially for southern blacks who came via the ghettos. Nearly two hundred seniors turned over monthly social security checks to the church, but in return they enjoyed a measure of security. All their needs were met, and they no longer had to fear urban crime. By and large, seniors could relax. Those not desiring to work on communal projects could tend small gardens. All could visit the library for books or watch videotapes. Sometimes they took short nature hikes on carefully marked trails. It was difficult for some, but they adjusted out of necessity to crowding, strange food and weather, and other negative conditions. Still, they shared a sense of community in Jonestown—and some believed that Jones was God. None was in a position to pack up and leave.

Not all was work, hardship and structured activities. Occasionally, Stephan Jones **72.** would face his stereo speakers toward the cottages and turn up the volume. People would gather spontaneously to sing and dance. Visitors provided relief from the routines, too. When outsiders came to Jonestown, Jim Jones would pull out the stops; the settlers could count on pork or chicken for dinner, with several kinds of vegetables and sometimes a piece of pie. The Jonestown Express and the Soul Steppers would provide the musical entertainment while comedians did their slapstick routine. When the band got cooking—soul, gospel, rhythm and blues, disco—everyone would join in.

Above all, the pioneer spirit kept Jonestown alive. Despite the hardship, this **73.** group of city people had carved a new life in the rain forests of South America. Most new arrivals felt a special sense of adventure. They also felt their experiment was significant: that they were building a model for socialism.

Nevertheless, factionalism developed with the sudden arrival of so many people. **74.** Stephan Jones and some other early settlers resented the well educated new arrivals, who second-guessed their work. When one so-called expert suggested "a better method" for milling lumber, they invited him to try. Then they gloated after he managed less than 10 percent of the regular crew's production and gave up.

It did not take long for one woman to realize that Jonestown was not for her. **75.** During her May 1977 visit to the Promised Land, "Mrs. B." became convinced that people were losing weight rapidly on a high-carbohydrate diet. As a city person, she was put off by jungle sanitation; she did not like using a cold water shower and an outhouse, or wiping with a newspaper. The flies pestered her so much that she had to eat with one hand and shoo them off with the other. It rained nearly every day, leaving the ground constantly muddy. Mildew crawled everywhere.

Mrs. B. got the impression that Temple leaders did not want her to speak with **76.** her friends from San Francisco—James and Irene Edwards and Emmett Griffith, Sr., and his wife Mary—who had arrived earlier. Yet the two couples privately told Mrs. B. that they were not getting enough to eat. Edwards, a powerful man well over six feet, looked as though he had lost fifty pounds. Both couples wanted to go home. (Earlier, of course, I had heard what another friend, Le Flora Townes, believed about Edwards's weight loss—that he was not emaciated but fit, and happy, in Jonestown.)

Such revelations had made Mrs. B. afraid to speak to anyone else about leaving; **77.** she feared being reported. She believed others were unhappy, too, but were stranded without money or passports. Someone advised her to pin any cash she had to her underwear, so it would not be taken away or stolen.

Though she was squired around hospitably, some hardship and brutality could **78.** not be hidden from her. People worked from sunup to sundown, performing the most grueling physical work in the broiling sun. The children were pushed to the point of unquestioning obedience. In one case, a child who defecated in his pants was forced to wear the soiled garments on his head and to go without food while watching others eat. An eleven-year-old boy who said he was tired of hearing about Father's sacrifices was knocked down by one man, and Charlie Touchette had to throw his body over the boy to prevent him from being hurt further. As punishment, some were made to eat hot peppers. Edwards told her of one offender who had a pepper jammed up his rectum. Other guilty parties had their heads shaved. Mrs. B. also heard Marceline Jones and Maria Katsaris lecture a women's meeting, saying sex was banned, because there was time only for labor.

To complain was to be punished. So Mrs. B. used ruse to return to the United **79.** States. The others—the unhappy and the true believers alike—were doomed to stay behind.

On a daily basis, Jones had to deal with the dashed expectations of the many **80.** settlers who recognized that Jonestown, their tropical paradise, really resembled a primitive jungle workcamp. Jones had to crush any thought of leaving or escape, but that was no more difficult than disabusing them of their fantasies. At last, he had people where he wanted them—on another continent, in a jungle with no law except his own. Their isolation was complete. Events in the world—and reality itself—would be filtered exclusively through him. His lust for control could be almost sated.

Jonestown, Guyana, Spring and Summer, 1978

The agonizingly long meetings and catharsis sessions continued, as did the Russian **81.** language drills. News reports were broken by Jones's petty announcements from his house, such as "Attention, attention, attention. My fever is down, slightly, to 104." The food worsened. On many nights, the rank and file saw little other than rice and gravy. Whereas bananas had once been plentiful and freely available, people now were disciplined for swiping them from the banana shed.

In August, anticipating a series of visitors from the United States, Jones added **82.**
a new routine to the meetings. Playing interrogator or reporter, he would fire hostile
questions at his people, then give critiques of their taped replies. He wanted to make
sure that no one, wittingly or unwittingly, would ever confirm any of the accusations
against Jonestown.

One night he ordered Carl Hall, a seventy-four-year-old black man from Los **83.**
Angeles, to approach the microphone:

"Tell me, sir, what do you like about Jonestown?" inquired Jones, adopting a **84.**
broadcaster's tone.

"We're all treated the same, on an equal basis," stammered Hall. "And the **85.**
great work you're doing."

"Don't talk to *me*," Jones corrected. "Talk to me like you're talking to a **86.**
reporter. . . . How's the food here?"

"The food is excellent," Hall said quickly.   **87.**

"What kind of food do you eat?" Jones pressed.   **88.**

"We eat three meals a day and they're all good."   **89.**

"What kind of food," Jones insisted. "Tell me about your diet!"   **90.**

"Well, in the morning, I have one to two eggs and toast." At that, people broke **91.**
up with laughter. Eggs for breakfast were as rare as a U.S. Embassy visit.

"You're sharp, brother," Jones said, approvingly.   **92.**

"And at lunch we have bread and soup, and the soup is very delicious," Hall **93.**
added, warming to the exercise.

"Bread and soup, hmmm," said Jones, thinking out loud. "Mention fruit and **94.**
salad. What's that soup the Russians eat, and they're the healthiest people in the world?
Borscht. But you know Americans. They gotta have a bunch of shit that gives them
cancer. . . . How many people live with you?"

"Fourteen." At that, everyone groaned and laughed.   **95.**

"That's what I was afraid of," Jones said sharply. "Don't ever say that. Say **96.**
four or five. Say 'two couples. My wife and I are retired.' Don't talk about fourteen
'cause the average American wouldn't understand it."

This exchange, like those in other nightly sessions with other participants, **97.**
continued for more than an hour. Jones patiently coached Hall on how to answer such
questions as why he decided to come to Jonestown and why he did not want to return
to the United States. When Jones ran out of questions, he asked for help from the
audience. A little kid named Jim came up with some winners, such as "Do you have
any weapons here?"

"No, we don't," Hall said.   **98.**

That was not good enough for Jones. " 'We are peaceful people,' " he coached, **99.**
" 'nonviolent.' I'd look shocked. 'Weapons? What are you talking about?' That's a
very good question. 'Do you beat people here?' "

"No, they don't," said Hall.   **100.**

" 'Do you sock people, hit people, any kind of brutality?' " pressed Jones. " 'No, **101.**
of course not,' " he said, answering his own question. "Look shocked. Even though
some people in the past have grown up because of strong measures. But reporters don't
give a good goddamn. They just want copy."

The little boy asked Hall, "Do you put people in boxes?"   **102.**

"Yeah," echoed Jones. "Do we ever put people in boxes?" **103.**

"No, they don't," was all Hall could manage to reply. **104.**

"I'd say, 'That's ridiculous. That's a stupid question, sir. I don't mean to be **105.** offensive, but that's ridiculous. We don't use any form of brutality. We reason things out.' "

The little boy piped up again. "What's the tower back there?" **106.**

"That was a bright question," Jones said. "Give him a treat. Call it the pagoda. **107.** 'You mean the pagoda?' Act like it's a pagoda. 'They're making slides for children to play from there, and if we have dry spells, they can spot fires.' That makes sense, you hear? Don't initiate anything with people if they're trying to harm you."

Jones's "pagoda" was indeed the security tower, manned twenty-four hours a **108.** day by guards, scanning the camp for malingerers and potential deserters.

Jonestown, Guyana, Fall, 1978

If there were any lingering doubts that Jim Jones had lost touch with reality, his **109.** September 25, 1978, letter to President Jimmy Carter should have silenced them. The minister, who had chatted on the phone with the First Lady two years earlier, now felt compelled to tell the President of the United States his rationale for siring John Stoen. The five-page, single-spaced letter was marked URGENT URGENT URGENT, with copies to Secretary of State Cyrus Vance and the State Department's Guyana Desk.

The tone was frantic: Jim Jones and the Peoples Temple were being destroyed **110.** by enemies, including rumormongers at the U.S. Embassy, and by defectors who stole thousands of dollars and "planned to blow up bridges . . ." and "poison the water supply of Washington, D.C." For one not intimate with Temple developments, the letter must have read like the incoherent ramblings of a lunatic. What Jones wrote about the Stoen child was particularly telling:

"The schemes against us include some of the most devious stratagems imaginable. **111.** One of the principles told me several years ago, in tears: 'I have to quit my job . . . I have to leave the church. My wife is going to leave me. But she is attracted to you. Will you please have sex with her?' . . . Well, I checked with my wife and the church board, and they thought it would be alright if I went ahead to satisfy this desperate man's plea—they reasoned that this woman was distraught or confused enough to tell all kinds of lies about the church. . . . I went into the relationship, and although I used preventatives, she got pregnant.

"And now, six years later, a big issue is being made over the child. . . . these **112.** people are attempting to use a child as a pawn to discredit and ruin my work."

Jones had begun to see himself as a ruler of a sovereign city-state: writing letters **113.** to the President of the United States, receiving visiting foreign dignitaries. His letter to Jimmy Carter was tame compared to his daily broadcasting over Jonestown loudspeakers.

Life there was growing more surreal by the week. The drugs—injectable Valium, **114.** Quaaludes, uppers, barbiturates, whatever he wanted—had taken hold of him. His voice, once so riveting, now sounded pathetic, raspy, as if he were very drunk or his tongue coated with peanut butter. Words collided with each other in slow motion. He would read from typed notes, but often not finish sentences. Sometimes, as he sat in

West House, barely gripping the army field phone that connected him to the radio room, he could not read at all. In that case, Larry Schacht or Mike Prokes might prompt him by reading the sentence first and urging him to repeat it or, if Jones was really in bad shape, they would read it themselves after making excuses. Once, Schacht announced that Jones was in the next room combing his hair in anticipation of a visit from King Hussein of Jordan.

Somehow Jones got himself in shape on October 2 for the long-awaited visit **115.** from Soviet Consul Feodor Timofeyev. Timofeyev's colleague from Tass had visited in April and sent a glowing report back to the Soviet Union. But Timofeyev was the man who really mattered, the man on whom the Temple pegged its naïve notion that nine hundred expatriate Americans would be welcome in Russia. They spent countless hours practicing phrases in Russian to impress the Russian diplomat.

The program for Timofeyev got under way with Temple singer Deanne Wilkinson **116.** delivering a political protest song in a rich and hauntingly beautiful voice, with organ accompaniment. Then Jim Jones stepped to the microphone.

"For many years," Jones said, "we have made our sympathies publicly known. **117.** The United States is not our mother. The USSR is our spiritual motherland." A tremendous ovation greeted his words. "Ambassador Timofeyev, we are not mistaken in allying our purpose and our destiny with the destiny of the Soviet Union."

The Russian consul stepped forward, greeting the eager crowd in Russian. "On **118.** behalf of the USSR," he said, switching to a halting English, "our deepest and most sincere greetings to the people of the first socialistic and communistic community from the United States of America in Guyana and in the world."

He continued with lavish praise, pausing to explain at length the history of the **119.** Soviet Union since 1917 and to defend its policies. Wishing the collective continued great success, he concluded: "It is a great pleasure to see how happy you are being in a free society."

After the speech, Jones led everyone in a hand-clapping, gospel-style rendition **120.** of various socialist songs, including one that was repeated again and again:

"We are communists today and we're communists all the way.
Oh, we're communists today and we're glad."

Whatever personal strength and discipline Jones had marshaled for the Timofeyev **121.** visit was exhausted the next day. When he returned to the loudspeaker for news, announcements and lectures on fascism, he sounded drugged again. But he poured out his words faster than he could enunciate them, as if he were on stimulants. At one point, he threatened Public Service for anyone who said Christ's birth was more important than the Russian Revolution. . . .

Notes

The Hair of the Raven
This chapter is based on a Peoples Temple videotape of the service in Ukiah. The quotes are taken verbatim from the tapes, with editing for length; the description comes from observing the tape and from numerous interviews with Temple members. The analysis is our own.

Heaven on Earth?

Interviews
Stephan Jones; Mike Touchette; Charlotte and Walter Baldwin; Mike Carter; Dale Parks; Mrs. B., who requested anonymity.

Materials
Marceline's letters home to her parents, provided by the Baldwins; Peoples Temple tape recording of Jones and Jerry obtained under FOIA from FBI, dated Oct. 21, 1976, labeled Q735; Jonestown progress report to the government, summer 1977; Temple death list compiled Nov. 1978.

The Downward Spiral

Interviews
Tim Carter; Mike Carter; Mike Touchette; Stephan Jones; Sandy Bradshaw; Dale Parks.

Materials
Nearly 300 "Dear Dad" letters recovered from Jonestown by various news correspondents, including Jacobs; Temple tape recording obtained under FOIA, dated April 17, 1978, labeled Q736.

In the Hands of a Madman

Interviews
Stephan Jones, Mike Touchette; Lee Ingram; Dale Parks; Mike Carter; Tim Carter.

Materials
Temple tape recordings recovered by FBI from Jonestown and obtained under FOIA—Oct. 1, 1978, Q352, Oct. 2, Q401, undated labeled Q271; records of punishments recovered from typed "Instructions" of Oct. 16, 17 and 20, 1978, found by *San Jose Mercury* reporter Peter Carey; inventory of Jonestown drugs from *San Francisco Examiner* article of Dec. 28, 1978, by reporters James A. Finefrock, Peter H. King and Nancy Dooley; undated Temple recording after Timofeyev visit of Oct. 1, labeled Q393 by the FBI.

WORKING WITH THE TEXT

Cultural and Historical References

In this section, the numbers at the margin refer to the numbered paragraphs in the selection itself.

8. Father Divine was the black spiritual leader who spouted socialist rhetoric while living in luxury among his poor parishioners.

23. "Socialism" is the economic system in which the government controls

the means of production. Socialism is opposed to capitalism, or private enterprise, in which individuals control most of the means of production.

Writing Assignments: The Paragraph

Be sure to provide an introduction for each of the following paragraph writing assignments. That is, begin each paragraph with a phrase like this: "Thomas Brickle claims that. . . ." When it is relevant, you might also want to identify the expertise of the author ("Thomas Brickle, a New Testament scholar, claims that. . . ."), the name of the book or article, the century and country in which the work appeared, or any other circumstances that your readers might find significant. For more on this, see pp. 11–13 in Chapter 2.

1. In a paragraph summarize and quote from Jones's sermon in paragraphs 1 to 56.
2. Summarize and quote from paragraph 71, Jonestown's appeal to poor people.

Writing Assignments: The Essay

Use informal documentation for the short essays. That is, don't use footnotes or a Works Cited page to document your sources. Instead, cite only relevant information about your source, and keep that information *within* your text. Then follow the summary or quote with a page number in parenthesis. (Use the page numbers that you find in this book to represent the page numbers of the source.) Thus, your informal documentation will look something like this:

> In *The Romance of Medicine*, Benjamin Gordon, a historian, says that it was once believed that red wine replenished a person's depleted blood supply (p. 121).

1. Analyze Jones's sermon in paragraphs 1 to 56.
2. Describe some of the bits and pieces of ideas that Jones picked up from Jesus, Marx, Stalin, and Hitler. See paragraph 8.
3. Describe the appeal of Jonestown. Begin by reading paragraph 73.
4. Contrast Jones's appeal to poor blacks with his appeal to educated whites.

ESSAYS ON *THE JONESTOWN MASSACRE*

Short Essays

Use informal documentation for these short essays. That is, don't use foot-notes or a Works Cited page to document your sources. Instead, cite only relevant information about your source, and keep that information *within* your text. Then follow the summary or quote with a page number in parenthesis. (Use the page numbers that you find in this book to represent the page numbers of the source.) Thus, your informal documentation will look something like this:

> In *The Romance of Medicine*, Benjamin Gordon, a historian, says that it was once believed that red wine replenished a person's de-pleted blood supply (p. 121).

1. Collect material from two or three essays on the reasons that Jones gave for the necessity for suicide.

2. Using the material from two or three essays, write a short report on the scene at the punchbowl.

3. Write a short report on physical conditions at Jonestown. Use two or three essays to support your description.

4. Using two or three essays, trace the idea of suicide within the People's Temple.

5. Show how Jones broke down family relationships in order to increase Temple members' dependence on him. Use material from two or three essays.

Long Essays

For rules governing formal documentation, see Chapter 6.

1. Using three or four sources, show how Jim Jones kept his members in line.

2. Using three or four sources, show that underneath the egalitarian trappings of the People's Temple, its leader, Jim Jones, was actually a racist.

3. Write a documented paper on Jones's relations with the press.

4. Write on socialism and Jim Jones. Was he a socialist? Was he a commu-nist? If he wasn't either of these, what was he?

5. Show that the success of the Temple was the result of social and political conditions during the early 1970s.

6. Write a paper on how strongly seductive the People's Temple was. What exactly did it offer people? Use three or four essays in your analysis.

7. Show how Jones was able to rise through his manipulation of people's liberal or radical politics.

8. Discuss Jim Jones's obsessive preoccupation with power, his fear of losing it, and his efforts to maintain it.

—— 9 ——

Good Country People:
What Is the Author Up To?

INTRODUCTION

A sense of unease. That's the best way to describe one's initial encounter with a Flannery O'Connor story. Where *is* she going with this story? And later, after you have put down the book, Where *have* I been?

It's not the words on the page. They make perfect sense. In fact, they're comfortingly familiar. They look like so much modern prose: full of irony, laced with wit, all carefully crafted—a *New Yorker* kind of prose. But behind those modern words, you sense the presence of an author who is urgently whispering. The voice is muffled, you're on the other side of the door, and even with your ear to the door you can't quite make it out.

There is an urgency in her voice. And it's not hard to see why, once you know a little about the woman behind the words. O'Connor was *different.* She was a Roman Catholic in the Protestant Deep South, she was an orthodox Christian when very few "serious" fiction writers were, and she wrote some of her best stories while in the grip of a terminal disease. The urgency of her message seems in some way a response to her life. She once wrote that she had to take "violent means" to communicate her message to a "hostile" audience. A "hostile" audience. That's us.

"I see from the standpoint of Christian orthodoxy," O'Connor says in "The Fiction Writer and His Country." That's where Flannery O'Connor begins, and knowledge of that fact is where readers have to begin if they want to understand the words on the other side of the door.

Notice that O'Connor doesn't merely describe herself as a Christian, but as an *orthodox* Christian, and that is a big difference. Whatever else that word means today, in 1955 in the Catholic church it almost always meant a literal understanding of heaven and hell. Not a hell of the mind, not a hell

on earth, not hell as metaphor. Salvation, then, is the most important thing
a person can earn in this world. Not goodness—salvation, being saved.

O'Connor took her Christianity seriously, and that throws everyone off.
Listen to the tone of her voice as she describes the position of a Christian in
modern society:

> The novelist with Christian concerns will find in modern life
> distortions which are repugnant to him, and his problem will
> be to make these appear as distortions to an audience which is
> used to seeing them as natural.

Once again, O'Connor sees us, her audience, as cooperating with a society
that she finds "repugnant," and she is somehow going to have to shock us
into understanding why we see distortions as natural.

At first glance, O'Connor sounds like many another modern American
writer who finds modern life "repugnant." Sinclair Lewis, Kurt Vonnegut,
Norman Mailer, and many many more—these writers all seem to find modern
life repugnant. But Flannery O'Connor must have found it repugnant in a
special way. To an orthodox Christian, society isn't repugnant merely because
it is not caring enough, or didn't pass the ERA amendment, or whatever.
Modern society is repugnant because it has turned away from Christ, is losing
its soul, is evil. Those are not the themes of modern writers, but they are the
themes of Flannery O'Connor.

That's why O'Connor is initially baffling. Modern readers just do not
expect a writer like O'Connor. We *expect* the dark world of Hemingway; we
expect the satire on the middle classes in Sinclair Lewis; we *expect* William
Faulkner, James Joyce, Jean Paul Sartre. In short, we *expect* modernity. What
we don't expect is an orthodox Christian.

And O'Connor doesn't help us any. Her stories look, on their surface at
least, like midcentury American fiction. But underneath that modern gloss
is old-fashioned, orthodox Christianity.

It's like coming across a country church on a Greenwich Village street.

GOOD COUNTRY PEOPLE

Flannery O'Connor

Here is the text of your topic for this chapter: a most intriguing story by one of
the most gifted of all American writers who have appeared on the scene since
World War II.

Besides the neutral expression that she wore when she was alone, Mrs. Freeman **1.**
had two others, forward and reverse, that she used for all her human dealings. Her
forward expression was steady and driving like the advance of a heavy truck. Her eyes
never swerved to left or right but turned as the story turned as if they followed a yellow
line down the center of it. She seldom used the other expression because it was not
often necessary for her to retract a statement, but when she did, her face came to a

Source: Flannery O'Connor, ''Good Country People,'' *The Complete Stories.* New York: Farrar, Straus &
Giroux, 1972. 271–291.

complete stop, there was an almost imperceptible movement of her black eyes, during which they seemed to be receding, and then the observer would see that Mrs. Freeman, though she might stand there as real as several grain sacks thrown on top of each other, was no longer there in spirit. As for getting anything across to her when this was the case, Mrs. Hopewell had given it up. She might talk her head off. Mrs. Freeman could never be brought to admit herself wrong on any point. She would stand there and if she could be brought to say anything, it was something like, "Well, I wouldn't of said it was and I wouldn't of said it wasn't," or letting her gaze range over the top kitchen shelf where there was an assortment of dusty bottles, she might remark, "I see you ain't ate many of them figs you put up last summer."

They carried on their most important business in the kitchen at breakfast. Every **2.** morning Mrs. Hopewell got up at seven o'clock and lit her gas heater and Joy's. Joy was her daughter, a large blonde girl who had an artificial leg. Mrs. Hopewell thought of her as a child though she was thirty-two years old and highly educated. Joy would get up while her mother was eating and lumber into the bathroom and slam the door, and before long, Mrs. Freeman would arrive at the back door. Joy would hear her mother call, "Come on in," and then they would talk for a while in low voices that were indistinguishable in the bathroom. By the time Joy came in, they had usually finished the weather report and were on one or the other of Mrs. Freeman's daughters, Glynese or Carramae, Joy called them Glycerin and Caramel. Glynese, a redhead, was eighteen and had many admirers; Carramae, a blonde, was only fifteen but already married and pregnant. She could not keep anything on her stomach. Every morning Mrs. Freeman told Mrs. Hopewell how many times she had vomited since the last report.

Mrs. Hopewell liked to tell people that Glynese and Carramae were two of the **3.** finest girls she knew and that Mrs. Freeman was a *lady* and that she was never ashamed to take her anywhere or introduce her to anybody they might meet. Then she would tell how she had happened to hire the Freemans in the first place and how they were a godsend to her and how she had had them four years. The reason for her keeping them so long was that they were not trash. They were good country people. She had telephoned the man whose name they had given as a reference and he had told her that Mr. Freeman was a good farmer but that his wife was the nosiest woman ever to walk the earth. "She's got to be into everything," the man said. "If she don't get there before the dust settles, you can bet she's dead, that's all. She'll want to know all your business. I can stand him real good," he had said, "but me nor my wife neither could have stood that woman one more minute on this place." That had put Mrs. Hopewell off for a few days.

She had hired them in the end because there were no other applicants but she **4.** had made up her mind beforehand exactly how she would handle the woman. Since she was the type who had to be into everything, then, Mrs. Hopewell had decided, she would not only let her be into everything, she would *see to it* that she was into everything—she would give her the responsibility of everything, she would put her in charge. Mrs. Hopewell had no bad qualities of her own but she was able to use other people's in such a constructive way that she never felt the lack. She had hired the Freemans and she had kept them four years.

Nothing is perfect. This was one of Mrs. Hopewell's favorite sayings. Another **5.** was: that is life! And still another, the most important, was: well, other people have their opinions too. She would make these statements, usually at the table, in a tone of gentle insistence as if no one held them but her, and the large hulking Joy, whose constant outrage had obliterated every expression from her face, would stare just a little to the side of her, her eyes icy blue, with the look of someone who has achieved blindness by an act of will and means to keep it.

When Mrs. Hopewell said to Mrs. Freeman that life was like that, Mrs. Freeman **6.** would say, "I always said so myself." Nothing had been arrived at by anyone that had not first been arrived at by her. She was quicker than Mr. Freeman. When Mrs. Hopewell said to her after they had been on the place a while, "You know, you're the wheel behind the wheel," and winked, Mrs. Freeman had said, "I know it. I've always been quick. It's some that are quicker than others."

"Everybody is different," Mrs. Hopewell said.   **7.**
"Yes, most people is," Mrs. Freeman said.   **8.**
"It takes all kinds to make the world."   **9.**
"I always said it did myself."   **10.**

The girl was used to this kind of dialogue for breakfast and more of it for dinner; **11.** sometimes they had it for supper too. When they had no guest they ate in the kitchen because that was easier. Mrs. Freeman always managed to arrive at some point during the meal and to watch them finish it. She would stand in the doorway if it were summer but in the winter she would stand with one elbow on top of the refrigerator and look down on them, or she would stand by the gas heater, lifting the back of her skirt slightly. Occasionally she would stand against the wall and roll her head from side to side. At no time was she in any hurry to leave. All this was very trying on Mrs. Hopewell but she was a woman of great patience. She realized that nothing is perfect and that in the Freemans she had good country people and that if, in this day and age, you get good country people, you had better hang onto them.

She had had plenty of experience with trash. Before the Freemans she had **12.** averaged one tenant family a year. The wives of these farmers were not the kind you would want to be around you for very long. Mrs. Hopewell, who had divorced her husband long ago, needed someone to walk over the fields with her; and when Joy had to be impressed for these services, her remarks were usually so ugly and her face so glum that Mrs. Hopewell would say, "If you can't come pleasantly, I don't want you at all," to which the girl, standing square and rigid-shouldered with her neck thrust slightly forward, would reply, "If you want me, here I am—LIKE I AM."

Mrs. Hopewell excused this attitude because of the leg (which had been shot off **13.** in a hunting accident when Joy was ten). It was hard for Mrs. Hopewell to realize that her child was thirty-two now and that for more than twenty years she had had only one leg. She thought of her still as a child because it tore her heart to think instead of the poor stout girl in her thirties who had never danced a step or had any *normal* good times. Her name was really Joy but as soon as she was twenty-one and away from home, she had had it legally changed. Mrs. Hopewell was certain that she had thought and thought until she had hit upon the ugliest name in any language. Then she had gone and had the beautiful name, Joy, changed without telling her mother until after she had done it. Her legal name was Hulga.

When Mrs. Hopewell thought the name, Hulga, she thought of the broad blank **14.** hull of a battleship. She would not use it. She continued to call her Joy to which the girl responded but in a purely mechanical way.

Hulga had learned to tolerate Mrs. Freeman who saved her from taking walks **15.**
with her mother. Even Glynese and Carramae were useful when they occupied attention
that might otherwise have been directed at her. At first she had thought she could not
stand Mrs. Freeman for she had found that it was not possible to be rude to her. Mrs.
Freeman would take on strange resentments and for days together she would be sullen
but the source of her displeasure was always obscure; a direct attack, a positive leer,
blatant ugliness to her face—these never touched her. And without warning one day,
she began calling her Hulga.

She did not call her that in front of Mrs. Hopewell who would have been incensed **16.**
but when she and the girl happened to be out of the house together, she would say
something and add the name Hulga to the end of it, and the big spectacled Joy-Hulga
would scowl and redden as if her privacy had been intruded upon. She considered the
name her personal affair. She had arrived at it first purely on the basis of its ugly sound
and then the full genius of its fitness had struck her. She had a vision of the name
working like the ugly sweating Vulcan who stayed in the furnace and to whom,
presumably, the goddess had to come when called. She saw it as the name of her
highest creative act. One of her major triumphs was that her mother had not been able
to turn her dust into Joy, but the greater one was that she had been able to turn it herself
into Hulga. However, Mrs. Freeman's relish for using the name only irritated her. It
was as if Mrs. Freeman's beady steel-pointed eyes had penetrated far enough behind
her face to reach some secret fact. Something about her seemed to fascinate Mrs.
Freeman and then one day Hulga realized that it was the artificial leg. Mrs. Freeman
had a special fondness for the details of secret infections, hidden deformities, assaults
upon children. Of diseases, she preferred the lingering or incurable. Hulga had heard
Mrs. Hopewell give her the details of the hunting accident, how the leg had been
literally blasted off, how she had never lost consciousness. Mrs. Freeman could listen
to it any time as if it had happened an hour ago.

When Hulga stumped into the kitchen in the morning (she could walk without **17.**
making the awful noise but she made it—Mrs. Hopewell was certain—because it was
ugly-sounding), she glanced at them and did not speak. Mrs. Hopewell would be in
her red kimono with her hair tied around her head in rags. She would be sitting at the
table, finishing her breakfast and Mrs. Freeman would be hanging by her elbow outward
from the refrigerator, looking down at the table. Hulga always put her eggs on the
stove to boil and then stood over them with her arms folded, and Mrs. Hopewell would
look at her—a kind of indirect gaze divided between her and Mrs. Freeman—and
would think that if she would only keep herself up a little, she wouldn't be so bad
looking. There was nothing wrong with her face that a pleasant expression wouldn't
help. Mrs. Hopewell said that people who looked on the bright side of things would
be beautiful even if they were not.

Whenever she looked at Joy this way, she could not help but feel that it would **18.**
have been better if the child had not taken the Ph.D. It had certainly not brought her
out any and now that she had it, there was no more excuse for her to go to school
again. Mrs. Hopewell thought it was nice for girls to go to school to have a good time
but Joy had "gone through." Anyhow, she would not have been strong enough to go
again. The doctors had told Mrs. Hopewell that with the best of care, Joy might see
forty-five. She had a weak heart. Joy had made it plain that if it had not been for this

condition, she would be far from these red hills and good country people. She would be in a university lecturing to people who knew what she was talking about. And Mrs. Hopewell could very well picture her there, looking like a scarecrow and lecturing to more of the same. Here she went about all day in a six-year-old skirt and a yellow sweat shirt with a faded cowboy on a horse embossed on it. She thought this was funny; Mrs. Hopewell thought it was idiotic and showed simply that she was still a child. She was brilliant but she didn't have a grain of sense. It seemed to Mrs. Hopewell that every year she grew less like other people and more like herself—bloated, rude, and squint-eyed. And she said such strange things! To her own mother she had said—without warning, without excuse, standing up in the middle of a meal with her face purple and her mouth half full—"Woman! do you ever look inside? Do you ever look inside and see what you are *not*? God!" she had cried sinking down again and staring at her plate, "Malebranche was right: we are not our own light. We are not our own light!" Mrs. Hopewell had no idea to this day what brought that on. She had only made the remark, hoping Joy would take it in, that a smile never hurt anyone.

The girl had taken the Ph.D. in philosophy and this left Mrs. Hopewell at a **19.** complete loss. You could say, "My daughter is a nurse," or "My daughter is a schoolteacher," or even, "My daughter is a chemical engineer." You could not say, "My daughter is a philosopher." That was something that had ended with the Greeks and Romans. All day Joy sat on her neck in a deep chair, reading. Sometimes she went for walks but she didn't like dogs or cats or birds or flowers or nature or nice young men. She looked at nice young men as if she could smell their stupidity.

One day Mrs. Hopewell had picked up one of the books the girl had just put **20.** down and opening it at random, she read, "Science, on the other hand, has to assert its soberness and seriousness afresh and declare that it is concerned solely with what-is. Nothing—how can it be for science anything but a horror and a phantasm? If science is right, then one thing stands firm: science wishes to know nothing of nothing. Such is after all the strictly scientific approach to Nothing. We know it by wishing to know nothing of Nothing." These words had been underlined with a blue pencil and they worked on Mrs. Hopewell like some evil incantation in gibberish. She shut the book quickly and went out of the room as if she were having a chill.

This morning when the girl came in, Mrs. Freeman was on Carramae. "She **21.** thrown up four times after supper," she said, "and was up twict in the night after three o'clock. Yesterday she didn't do nothing but ramble in the bureau drawer. All she did. Stand up there and see what she could run up on."

"She's got to eat," Mrs. Hopewell muttered, sipping her coffee, while she **22.** watched Joy's back at the stove. She was wondering what the child had said to the Bible salesman. She could not imagine what kind of a conversation she could possibly have had with him.

He was a tall gaunt hatless youth who had called yesterday to sell them a Bible. **23.** He had appeared at the door, carrying a large black suitcase that weighted him so heavily on one side that he had to brace himself against the door facing. He seemed on the point of collapse but he said in a cheerful voice, "Good morning, Mrs. Cedars!" and set the suitcase down on the mat. He was not a bad-looking young man though he had on a bright blue suit and yellow socks that were not pulled up far enough. He had prominent face bones and a streak of sticky-looking brown hair falling across his forehead.

"I'm Mrs. Hopewell," she said. **24.**

"Oh!" he said, pretending to look puzzled but with his eyes sparkling, "I saw **25.**
it said 'The Cedars' on the mailbox so I thought you was Mrs. Cedars!" and he burst
our in a pleasant laugh. He picked up the satchel and under cover of a pant, he fell
forward into her hall. It was rather as if the suitcase had moved first, jerking him after
it. "Mrs. Hopewell!" he said and grabbed her hand. "I hope you are well!" and he
laughed again and then all at once his face sobered completely. He paused and gave
her a straight earnest look and said, "Lady, I've come to speak of serious things."

"Well, come in," she muttered, none too pleased because her dinner was almost **26.**
ready. He came into the parlor and sat down on the edge of a straight chair and put
the suitcase between his feet and glanced around the room as if he were sizing her up
by it. Her silver gleamed on the two sideboards; she decided he had never been in a
room as elegant as this.

"Mrs. Hopewell," he began, using her name in a way that sounded almost **27.**
intimate, "I know you believe in Chrustian service."

"Well yes," she murmured.   **28.**

"I know," he said and paused, looking very wise with his head cocked on one **29.**
side, "that you're a good woman. Friends have told me."

Mrs. Hopewell never liked to be taken for a fool. "What are you selling?" she **30.**
asked.

"Bibles," the young man said and his eye raced around the room before he **31.**
added, "I see you have no family Bible in your parlor, I see that is the one lack you
got!"

Mrs. Hopewell could not say, "My daughter is an atheist and won't let me keep **32.**
the Bible in the parlor." She said, stiffening slightly, "I keep my Bible by my bedside."
This was not the truth. It was in the attic somewhere.

"Lady," he said, "the word of God ought to be in the parlor."   **33.**

"Well, I think that's a matter of taste," she began. "I think . . ."   **34.**

"Lady," he said, "for a Chrustian, the word of God ought to be in every room **35.**
in the house besides in his heart. I know you're a Chrustian because I can see it in
every line of your face."

She stood up and said, "Well, young man, I don't want to buy a Bible and I **36.**
smell my dinner burning."

He didn't get up. He began to twist his hands and looking down at them, he said **37.**
softly, "Well lady, I'll tell you the truth—not many people want to buy one nowadays
and besides, I know I'm real simple. I don't know how to say a thing but to say it. I'm
just a country boy." He glanced up into her unfriendly face. "People like you don't
like to fool with country people like me!"

"Why!" she cried, "good country people are the salt of the earth! Besides, we **38.**
all have different ways of doing, it takes all kinds to make the world go 'round. That's
life!"

"You said a mouthful," he said.   **39.**

"Why, I think there aren't enough good country people in the world!" she said, **40.**
stirred. "I think that's what's wrong with it!"

His face had brightened. "I didn't inraduce myself," he said. "I'm Manley **41.**
Pointer from out in the country around Willohobie, not even from a place, just near
a place."

"You wait a minute," she said. "I have to see about my dinner." She went out **42.**
to the kitchen and found Joy standing near the door where she had been listening.

"Get rid of the salt of the earth," she said, "and let's eat." **43.**

Mrs. Hopewell gave her a pained look and turned the heat down under the **44.** vegetables. "*I* can't be rude to anybody," she murmured and went back into the parlor.

He had opened the suitcase and was sitting with a Bible on each knee. **45.**

"You might as well put those up," she told him. "I don't want one." **46.**

"I appreciate your honesty," he said. "You don't see any more real honest **47.** people unless you go way out in the country."

"I know," she said, "real genuine folks!" Through the crack in the door she **48.** heard a groan.

"I guess a lot of boys come telling you they're working their way through **49.** college," he said, "but I'm not going to tell you that. Somehow," he said, "I don't want to go to college. I want to devote my life to Chrustian service. See," he said, lowering his voice, "I got this heart condition. I may not live long. When you know it's something wrong with you and you may not live long, well then, lady . . ." He paused, with his mouth open, and stared at her.

He and Joy had the same condition! She knew that her eyes were filling with **50.** tears but she collected herself quickly and murmured, "Won't you stay for dinner? We'd love to have you!" and was sorry the instant she heard herself say it.

"Yes mam," he said in an abashed voice, "I would sher love to do that!" **51.**

Joy had given him one look on being introduced to him and then throughout the **52.** meal had not glanced at him again. He had addressed several remarks to her, which she had pretended not to hear. Mrs. Hopewell could not understand deliberate rudeness, although she lived with it, and she felt she had always to overflow with hospitality to make up for Joy's lack of courtesy. She urged him to talk about himself and he did. He said he was the seventh child of twelve and that his father had been crushed under a tree when he himself was eight year old. He had been crushed very badly, in fact, almost cut in two and was practically not recognizable. His mother had got along the best she could by hard working and she had always seen that her children went to Sunday School and that they read the Bible every evening. He was now nineteen year old and he had been selling Bibles for four months. In that time he had sold seventy-seven Bibles and had the promise of two more sales. He wanted to become a missionary because he thought that was the way you could do most for people. "He who losest his life shall find it," he said simply and he was so sincere, so genuine and earnest that Mrs. Hopewell would not for the world have smiled. He prevented his peas from sliding onto the table by blocking them with a piece of bread which he later cleaned his plate with. She could see Joy observing sidewise how he handled his knife and fork and she saw too that every few minutes, the boy would dart a keen appraising glance at the girl as if he were trying to attract her attention.

After dinner Joy cleared the dishes off the table and disappeared and Mrs. **53.** Hopewell was left to talk with him. He told her again about his childhood and his father's accident and about various things that had happened to him. Every five minutes or so she would stifle a yawn. He sat for two hours until finally she told him she must go because she had an appointment in town. He packed his Bibles and thanked her and prepared to leave, but in the doorway he stopped and wrung her hand and said that not on any of his trips had he met a lady as nice as her and he asked if he could come again. She had said she would always be happy to see him.

Joy had been standing in the road, apparently looking at something in the distance, **54.** when he came down the steps toward her, bent to the side with his heavy valise. He stopped where she was standing and confronted her directly. Mrs. Hopewell could not hear what she said but she trembled to think what Joy would say to him. She could see that after a minute Joy said something and that then the boy began to speak again, making an excited gesture with his free hand. After a minute Joy said something else at which the boy began to speak once more. Then to her amazement, Mrs. Hopewell saw the two of them walk off together, toward the gate. Joy had walked all the way to the gate with him and Mrs. Hopewell could not imagine what they had said to each other, and she had not yet dared to ask.

Mrs. Freeman was insisting upon her attention. She had moved from the **55.** refrigerator to the heater so that Mrs. Hopewell had to turn and face her in order to seem to be listening. "Glynese gone out with Harvey Hill again last night," she said. "She had this sty."

"Hill," Mrs. Hopewell said absently, "is that the one who works in the garage?" **56.**

"Nome, he's the one that goes to chiropracter school," Mrs. Freeman said. "She **57.** had this sty. Been had it two days. So she says when he brought her in the other night he says, 'Lemme get rid of that sty for you,' and she says, 'How?' and he says, 'You just lay yourself down acrost the seat of that car and I'll show you.' So she done it and he popped her neck. Kept on a-popping it several times until she made him quit. This morning," Mrs. Freeman said, "she ain't got no sty. She ain't got no traces of a sty."

"I never heard of that before," Mrs. Hopewell said. **58.**

"He ast her to marry him before the Ordinary," Mrs. Freeman went on, "and **59.** she told him she wasn't going to be married in no *office.*"

"Well, Glynese is a fine girl," Mrs. Hopewell said. "Glynese and Carramae are **60.** both fine girls."

"Carramae said when her and Lyman was married Lyman said it sure felt sacred **61.** to him. She said he said he wouldn't take five hundred dollars for being married by a preacher."

"How much would he take?" the girl asked from the stove. **62.**

"He said he wouldn't take five hundred dollars," Mrs. Freeman repeated. **63.**

"Well we all have work to do," Mrs. Hopewell said. **64.**

"Lyman said it just felt more sacred to him," Mrs. Freeman said. "The doctor **65.** wants Carramae to eat prunes. Says instead of medicine. Says them cramps is coming from pressure. You know where I think it is?"

"She'll be better in a few weeks," Mrs. Hopewell said. **66.**

"In the tube," Mrs. Freeman said. "Else she wouldn't be as sick as she is." **67.**

Hulga had cracked her two eggs into a saucer and was bringing them to the table **68.** along with a cup of coffee that she had filled too full. She sat down carefully and began to eat, meaning to keep Mrs. Freeman there by questions if for any reason she showed an inclination to leave. She could perceive her mother's eye on her. The first round-about question would be about the Bible salesman and she did not wish to bring it on. "How did he pop her neck?" she asked.

Mrs. Freeman went into a description of how he had popped her neck. She said **69.** he owned a '55 Mercury but that Glynese said she would rather marry a man with only a '36 Plymouth who would be married by a preacher. The girl asked what if he had a '32 Plymouth and Mrs. Freeman said what Glynese had said was a '36 Plymouth.

Mrs. Hopewell said there were not many girls with Glynese's common sense. **70.** She said what she admired in those girls was their common sense. She said that reminded her that they had had a nice visitor yesterday, a young man selling Bibles. "Lord," she said, "he bored me to death but he was so sincere and genuine I couldn't be rude to him. He was just good country people, you know," she said, "—just the salt of the earth."

"I seen him walk up," Mrs. Freeman said, "and then later—I seen him walk **71.** off," and Hulga could feel the slight shift in her voice, the slight insinuation, that he had not walked off alone, had he? Her face remained expressionless but the color rose into her neck and she seemed to swallow it down with the next spoonful of egg. Mrs. Freeman was looking at her as if they had a secret together.

"Well, it takes all kinds of people to make the world go 'round," Mrs. Hopewell **72.** said. "It's very good we aren't all alike."

"Some people are more alike than others," Mrs. Freeman said.   **73.**

Hulga got up and stumped, with about twice the noise that was necessary, into **74.** her room and locked the door. She was to meet the Bible salesman at ten o'clock at the gate. She had thought about it half the night. She had started thinking of it as a great joke and then she had begun to see profound implications in it. She had lain in bed imagining dialogues for them that were insane on the surface but that reached below to depths that no Bible salesman would be aware of. Their conversation yesterday had been of this kind.

He had stopped in front of her and had simply stood there. His face was bony **75.** and sweaty and bright, with a little pointed nose in the center of it, and his look was different from what it had been at the dinner table. He was gazing at her with open curiosity, with fascination, like a child watching a new fantastic animal at the zoo, and he was breathing as if he had run a great distance to reach her. His gaze seemed somehow familiar but she could not think where she had been regarded with it before. For almost a minute he didn't say anything. Then on what seemed an insuck of breath, he whispered, "You ever ate a chicken that was two days old?"

The girl looked at him stonily. He might have just put this question up for **76.** consideration at the meeting of a philosophical association. "Yes," she presently replied as if she had considered it from all angles.

"It must have been mighty small!" he said triumphantly and shook all over with **77.** little nervous giggles, getting very red in the face, and subsiding finally into his gaze of complete admiration, while the girl's expression remained exactly the same.

"How old are you?" he asked softly.   **78.**

She waited some time before she answered. Then in a flat voice she said, **79.** "Seventeen."

His smiles came in succession like waves breaking on the surface of a little lake. **80.** "I see you got a wooden leg," he said. "I think you're brave. I think you're real sweet."

The girl stood blank and solid and silent.   **81.**

"Walk to the gate with me," he said. "You're a brave sweet little thing and I **82.** liked you the minute I seen you walk in the door."

Hulga began to move forward.   **83.**

"What's your name?" he asked, smiling down on the top of her head.   **84.**

"Hulga," she said.   **85.**

"Hulga," he murmured, "Hulga. Hulga. I never heard of anybody name Hulga **86.** before. You're shy, aren't you, Hulga?" he asked.

She nodded, watching his large red hand on the handle of the giant valise.   **87.**

"I like girls that wear glasses," he said. "I think a lot. I'm not like these people **88.** that a serious thought don't ever enter their heads. It's because I may die."

"I may die too," she said suddenly and looked up at him. His eyes were very **89.** small and brown, glittering feverishly.

"Listen," he said, "don't you think some people was meant to meet on account **90.** of what all they got in common and all? Like they both think serious thoughts and all?" He shifted the valise to his other hand so that the hand nearest her was free. He caught hold of her elbow and shook it a little. "I don't work on Saturday," he said. "I like to walk in the woods and see what Mother Nature is wearing. O'er the hills and far away. Pic-nics and things. Couldn't we go on a pic-nic tomorrow? Say yes, Hulga," he said and gave her a dying look as if he felt his insides about to drop out of him. He had even seemed to sway slightly toward her.

During the night she had imagined that she seduced him. She imagined that the **91.** two of them walked on the place until they came to the storage barn beyond the two back fields and there, she imagined, that things came to such a pass that she very easily seduced him and that then, of course, she had to reckon with his remorse. True genius can get an idea across even to an inferior mind. She imagined that she took his remorse in hand and changed it into a deeper understanding of life. She took all his shame away and turned it into something useful.

She set off for the gate at exactly ten o'clock, escaping without drawing Mrs. **92.** Hopewell's attention. She didn't take anything to eat, forgetting that food is usually taken on a picnic. She wore a pair of slacks and a dirty white shirt, and as an afterthought, she had put some Vapex on the collar of it since she did not own any perfume. When she reached the gate no one was there.

She looked up and down the empty highway and had the furious feeling that she **93.** had been tricked, that he had only meant to make her walk to the gate after the idea of him. Then suddenly he stood up, very tall, from behind a bush on the opposite embankment. Smiling, he lifted his hat which was new and wide-brimmed. He had not worn it yesterday and she wondered if he had bought it for the occasion. It was toast-colored with a red and white band around it and was slightly too large for him. He stepped from behind the bush still carrying the black valise. He had on the same suit and the same yellow socks sucked down in his shoes from walking. He crossed the highway and said, "I knew you'd come!"

The girl wondered acidly how he had known this. She pointed to the valise and **94.** asked, "Why did you bring your Bibles?"

He took her elbow, smiling down on her as if he could not stop. "You can never **95.**

tell when you'll need the word of God, Hulga," he said. She had a moment in which she doubted that this was actually happening and then they began to climb the embankment. They went down into the pasture toward the woods. The boy walked lightly by her side, bouncing on his toes. The valise did not seem to be heavy today; he even swung it. They crossed half the pasture without saying anything and then, putting his hand easily on the small of her back, he asked softly, "Where does your wooden leg join on?"

She turned an ugly red and glared at him and for an instant the boy looked **96.** abashed. "I didn't mean you no harm," he said. "I only meant you're so brave and all. I guess God takes care of you."

"No," she said, looking forward and walking fast, "I don't even believe in **97.** God."

At this he stopped and whistled. "No!" he exclaimed as if he were too astonished **98.** to say anything else.

She walked on and in a second he was bouncing at her side, fanning with his **99.** hat. "That's very unusual for a girl," he remarked, watching her out of the corner of his eye. When they reached the edge of the wood, he put his hand on her back again and drew her against him without a word and kissed her heavily.

This kiss, which had more pressure than feeling behind it, produced that extra **100.** surge of adrenalin in the girl that enables one to carry a packed trunk out of a burning house, but in her, the power went at once to the brain. Even before he released her, her mind, clear and detached and ironic anyway, was regarding him from a great distance, with amusement but with pity. She had never been kissed before and she was pleased to discover that it was an unexceptional experience and all a matter of the mind's control. Some people might enjoy drain water if they were told it was vodka. When the boy, looking expectant but uncertain, pushed her gently away, she turned and walked on, saying nothing as if such business, for her, were common enough.

He came along panting at her side, trying to help her when he saw a root that **101.** she might trip over. He caught and held back the long swaying blades of thorn vine until she had passed beyond them. She led the way and he came breathing heavily behind her. Then they came out on a sunlit hillside, sloping softly into another one a little smaller. Beyond, they could see the rusted top of the old barn where the extra hay was stored.

The hill was sprinkled with small pink weeds. "Then you ain't saved?" he asked **102.** suddenly, stopping.

The girl smiled. It was the first time she had smiled at him at all. **103.**

"In my economy," she said, "I'm saved and you are damned but I told you I **104.** didn't believe in God."

Nothing seemed to destroy the boy's look of admiration. He gazed at her now **105.** as if the fantastic animal at the zoo had put its paw through the bars and given him a loving poke. She thought he looked as if he wanted to kiss her again and she walked on before he had the chance.

"Ain't there somewheres we can sit down sometime?" he murmured, his voice **106.** softening toward the end of the sentence.

"In that barn," she said.   **107.**

They made for it rapidly as if it might slide away like a train. It was a large two- **108.**
story barn, cool and dark inside. The boy pointed up the ladder that led into the loft
and said, "It's too bad we can't go up there."

"Why can't we?" she asked.   **109.**

"Yer leg," he said reverently.   **110.**

The girl gave him a contemptuous look and putting both hands on the ladder, **111.**
she climbed it while he stood below, apparently awestruck. She pulled herself expertly
through the opening and then looked down at him and said, "Well, come on if you're
coming," and he began to climb the ladder, awkwardly bringing the suitcase with him.

"We won't need the Bible," she observed.   **112.**

"You never can tell," he said, panting. After he had got into the loft, he was **113.**
a few seconds catching his breath. She had sat down in a pile of straw. A wide sheath
of sunlight, filled with dust particles, slanted over her. She lay back against a bale, her
face turned away, looking out the front opening of the barn where hay was thrown
from a wagon into the loft. The two pink-speckled hillsides lay back against a dark
ridge of woods. The sky was cloudless and cold blue. The boy dropped down by her
side and put one arm under her and the other over her and began methodically kissing
her face, making little noises like a fish. He did not remove his hat but it was pushed
far enough back not to interfere. When her glasses got in his way, he took them off
of her and slipped them into his pocket.

The girl at first did not return any of the kisses but presently she began to and **114.**
after she had put several on his cheek, she reached his lips and remained there, kissing
him again and again as if she were trying to draw all the breath out of him. His breath
was clear and sweet like a child's and the kisses were sticky like a child's. He mumbled
about loving her and about knowing when he first seen her that he loved her, but the
mumbling was like the sleepy fretting of a child being put to sleep by his mother. Her
mind, throughout this, never stopped or lost itself for a second to her feelings. "You
ain't said you loved me none," he whispered finally, pulling back from her. "You got
to say that."

She looked away from him off into the hollow sky and then down at a black **115.**
ridge and then down farther into what appeared to be two green swelling lakes. She
didn't realize he had taken her glasses but this landscape could not seem exceptional
to her for she seldom paid any close attention to her surroundings.

"You got to say it," he repeated. "You got to say you love me."   **116.**

She was always careful how she committed herself. "In a sense," she began, **117.**
"if you use the word loosely, you might say that. But it's not a word I use. I don't
have illusions. I'm one of those people who see *through* to nothing."

The boy was frowning. "You got to say it. I said it and you got to say it," he **118.**
said.

The girl looked at him almost tenderly. "You poor baby," she murmured. "It's **119.**
just as well you don't understand," and she pulled him by the neck, face-down, against
her. "We are all damned," she said, "but some of us have taken off our blindfolds
and see that there's nothing to see. It's a kind of salvation."

The boy's astonished eyes looked blankly through the ends of her hair. "Okay," **120.**
he almost whined, "but do you love me or don'tcher?"

"Yes," she said and added, "in a sense. But I must tell you something. There **121.**
mustn't be anything dishonest between us." She lifted his head and looked him in the
eye. "I am thirty years old," she said. "I have a number of degrees."

The boy's look was irritated but dogged. "I don't care," he said. "I don't care **122.**
a thing about what all you done. I just want to know if you love me or don'tcher?"
and he caught her to him and wildly planted her face with kisses until she said, "Yes,
yes."

"Okay then," he said, letting her go. "Prove it."   **123.**

She smiled, looking dreamily out on the shifty landscape. She had seduced him **124.**
without even making up her mind to try. "How?" she asked, feeling that he should
be delayed a little.

He leaned over and put his lips to her ear. "Show me where your wooden leg **125.**
joins on," he whispered.

The girl uttered a sharp little cry and her face instantly drained of color. The **126.**
obscenity of the suggestion was not what shocked her. As a child she had sometimes
been subject to feelings of shame but education had removed the last traces of that as
a good surgeon scrapes for cancer; she would no more have felt it over what he was
asking than she would have believed in his Bible. But she was as sensitive about the
artificial leg as a peacock about his tail. No one ever touched it but her. She took care
of it as someone else would his soul, in private and almost with her own eyes turned
away. "No," she said.

"I known it," he muttered, sitting up. "You're just playing me for a sucker." **127.**

"Oh no no!" she cried. "It joins on at the knee. Only at the knee. Why do you **128.**
want to see it?"

The boy gave her a long penetrating look. "Because," he said, "it's what makes **129.**
you different. You ain't like anybody else."

She sat staring at him. There was nothing about her face or her round freezing- **130.**
blue eyes to indicate that this had moved her; but she felt as if her heart had stopped
and left her mind to pump her blood. She decided that for the first time in her life she
was face to face with real innocence. This boy, with an instinct that came from beyond
wisdom, had touched the truth about her. When after a minute, she said in a hoarse
high voice, "All right," it was like surrendering to him completely. It was like losing
her own life and finding it again, miraculously, in his.

Very gently he began to roll the slack leg up. The artificial limb, in a white **131.**
sock and brown flat shoe, was bound in a heavy material like canvas and ended
in an ugly jointure where it was attached to the stump. The boy's face and his
voice were entirely reverent as he uncovered it and said, "Now show me how to
take it off and on."

She took it off for him and put it back on again and then he took it off himself, **132.**
handling it as tenderly as if it were a real one. "See!" he said with a delighted child's
face. "Now I can do it myself!"

"Put it back on," she said. She was thinking that she would run away with him **133.**
and that every night he would take the leg off and every morning put it back on again.
"Put it back on," she said.

"Not yet," he murmured, setting it on its foot out of her reach. "Leave it off **134.** for a while. You got me instead."

She gave a little cry of alarm but he pushed her down and began to kiss her **135.** again. Without the leg she felt entirely dependent on him. Her brain seemed to have stopped thinking altogether and to be about some other function that it was not very good at. Different expressions raced back and forth over her face. Every now and then the boy, his eyes like two steel spikes, would glance behind him where the leg stood. Finally she pushed him off and said, "Put it back on me now."

"Wait," he said. He leaned the other way and pulled the valise toward him and **136.** opened it. It had a pale blue spotted lining and there were only two Bibles in it. He took one of these out and opened the cover of it. It was hollow and contained a pocket flask of whiskey, a pack of cards, and a small blue box with printing on it. He laid these out in front of her one at a time in an evenly-spaced row, like one presenting offerings at the shrine of a goddess. He put the blue box in her hand. THIS PRODUCT TO BE USED ONLY FOR THE PREVENTION OF DISEASE, she read, and dropped it. The boy was unscrewing the top of the flask. He stopped and pointed, with a smile, to the deck of cards. It was not an ordinary deck but one with an obscene picture on the back of each card. "Take a swig," he said, offering her the bottle first. He held it in front of her, but like one mesmerized, she did not move.

Her voice when she spoke had an almost pleading sound. "Aren't you," she **137.** murmured, "aren't you just good country people?"

The boy cocked his head. He looked as if he were just beginning to understand **138.** that she might be trying to insult him. "Yeah," he said, curling his lip slightly, "but it ain't held me back none. I'm as good as you any day in the week."

"Give me my leg," she said. **139.**

He pushed it farther away with his foot. "Come on now, let's begin to have us **140.** a good time," he said coaxingly. "We ain't got to know one another good yet."

"Give me my leg!" she screamed and tried to lunge for it but he pushed her **141.** down easily.

"What's the matter with you all of a sudden?" he asked, frowning as he screwed **142.** the top on the flask and put it quickly back inside the Bible. "You just a while ago said you didn't believe in nothing. I thought you was some girl!"

Her face was almost purple. "You're a Christian!" she hissed. "You're a fine **143.** Christian! You're just like them all—say one thing and do another. You're a perfect Christian, you're . . ."

The boy's mouth was set angrily. "I hope you don't think," he said in a lofty **144.** indignant tone, "that I believe in that crap! I may sell Bibles but I know which end is up and I wasn't born yesterday and I know where I'm going!"

"Give me my leg!" she screeched. He jumped up so quickly that she barely saw **145.** him sweep the cards and the blue box into the Bible and throw the Bible into the valise. She saw him grab the leg and then she saw it for an instant slanted forlornly across the inside of the suitcase with a Bible at either side of its opposite ends. He slammed the lid shut and snatched up the valise and swung it down the hole and then stepped through himself.

When all of him had passed but his head, he turned and regarded her with a look **146.** that no longer had any admiration in it. "I've gotten a lot of interesting things," he said. "One time I got a woman's glass eye this way. And you needn't to think you'll catch me because Pointer ain't really my name. I use a different name at every house I call at and don't stay nowhere long. And I'll tell you another thing, Hulga," he said, using the name as if he didn't think much of it, "you ain't so smart. I been believing in nothing ever since I was born!" and then the toast-colored hat disappeared down the hole and the girl was left, sitting on the straw in the dusty sunlight. When she turned her churning face toward the opening, she saw his blue figure struggling successfully over the green speckled lake.

Mrs. Hopewell and Mrs. Freeman, who were in the back pasture, digging up **147.** onions, saw him emerge a little later from the woods and head across the meadow toward the highway. "Why, that looks like that nice dull young man that tried to sell me a Bible yesterday," Mrs. Hopewell said, squinting. "He must have been selling them to the Negroes back in there. He was so simple," she said, "but I guess the world would be better off if we were all that simple."

Mrs. Freeman's gaze drove forward and just touched him before he disappeared **148.** under the hill. Then she returned her attention to the evil-smelling onion shoot she was lifting from the ground. "Some can't be that simple," she said. "I know I never could."

WORKING WITH THE TEXT

Cultural and Historical References

In this section, the numbers at the margin refer to the numbered paragraphs in the selection itself.

16. Vulcan is the god of fire and craftsmanship. His importance here is that despite his ugliness, the most beautiful woman in creation, Venus, is hopelessly in love with him. Knowing that, what is Hulga saying about her name change?

18. Nicolas de Malebranche, a seventeenth-century French philosopher, is one of the philosophers that Hulga studied at the university.

20. This passage is a description of scientific materialism, the idea that science is only concerned with empirical knowledge—that which can be counted and measured.

52. "He who losest his life shall find it." This is Pointer's down-home quotation of Jesus' famous words. You might come back to this at the end of the story and think about it some more, in particular in connection with Joy/Hulga.

Writing Assignments: The Paragraph

Be sure to provide an introduction for each of the following paragraph writing assignments. That is, begin each paragraph with a phrase like this: "Thomas Brickle claims that. . . ." When it is relevant, you might also want to identify the expertise of the author ("Thomas Brickle, a New Testament scholar, claims that. . . ."), the name of the book or article, the century and country in which the work appeared, or any other circumstances that your readers might find significant. For more on this, see pp. 11–13 in Chapter 2.

1. O'Connor is sometimes said to be very good at writing dialogue. Explain how dialogue reveals character in paragraphs 6 through 11.

2. Why is that onion an "evil-smelling" onion in paragraph 148? How does it reinforce Mrs. Freeman's character?

3. In a paragraph, draw a parallel between Mrs. Hopewell's attitude toward the Freeman family and her attitude toward Manley Pointer.

4. Explain O'Connor's description near the end of the story (paragraph 146) in which Joy/Hulga, looking out of the barnloft opening, sees Manley Pointer's "figure struggling successfully over the green speckled lake." What does that sentence mean? Is he literally walking on water? Is O'Connor making an allusion to Jesus walking on water? If so, why would O'Connor do that?

Writing Assignments: The Short Essay

Use informal documentation for these short essays. That is, don't use footnotes or a Works Cited page to document your sources. Instead, cite only relevant information about your source, and keep that information *within* your text. Then follow the summary or quote with a page number in parentheses. (Use the page numbers that you find in this book to represent the page numbers of the source.) Thus, your informal documentation will look something like this:

> In "An Explication of Good Country People," Virgil Scott, professor emeritus at Michigan State University, says that Joy is a "spiritual as well as a physical cripple" (p. 293).

Before reading any essays about "Good Country People," write an essay on what you think this story means. If you're baffled, don't feel alone. It's not easy to say, after one reading, what the story is about. You might want to reread the introduction to this chapter. And you might want to reread the story a few times. Don't fret. If you think hard about the story and offer up a thoughtful interpretation, you'll be fulfilling the assignment.

THE FICTION WRITER AND HIS COUNTRY

Flannery O'Connor

This is the essay in which O'Connor most clearly sets forth her purpose for writing fiction. If you have been skeptical of critics' claims that O'Connor's themes center around her Catholic faith, in this piece the author herself should clear up your doubts.

Source: Flannery O'Connor, "The Fiction Writer and His Country," *Mystery and Manners.* Sally and Robert Fitzgerald (eds.). New York: Farrar, Straus & Giroux, 1969. 25–35.

Among the many complaints made about the modern American novelist, the **1.** loudest, if not the most intelligent, has been the charge that he is not speaking for his country. A few seasons back an editorial in *Life* magazine asked grandly, "Who speaks for America today?" and was not able to conclude that our novelists, or at least our most gifted ones, did.

The gist of the editorial was that in the last ten years this country had enjoyed **2.** an unparalleled prosperity, that it had come nearer to producing a classless society than any other nation, and that it was the most powerful country in the world, but that our novelists were writing as if they lived in packing boxes on the edge of the dump while they awaited admission to the poorhouse. Instead of this, the editorial requested that they give us something that really represented this country, and it ended with a very smooth and slick shift into a higher key and demanded further that the novelist show us the redeeming quality of spiritual purpose, for it said that "what is most missing from our hothouse literature" is "the joy of life itself."

This was irritating enough to provoke answers from many critics, but I do not **3.** know that any of those who answered considered the question specifically from the standpoint of the novelist with Christian concerns, who, presumably, would have an interest at least equal to that of the editors of *Life* in "the redeeming quality of spiritual purpose."*

What is such a writer going to take his "country" to be? The word usually used **4.** by literary folk in this connection would be "world," but the word "country" will do; in fact, being homely, it will do better, for it suggests more. It suggests everything from the actual countryside that the novelist describes, on to and through the peculiar characteristics of his region and his nation, and on, through, and under all of these to his true country, which the writer with Christian convictions will consider to be what is eternal and absolute. This covers considerable territory, and if one were talking of any other kind of writing than the writing of fiction, one would perhaps have to say "countries," but it is the peculiar burden of the fiction writer that he has to make one country do for all and that he has to evoke that one country through the concrete particulars of a life that he can make believable.

This is first of all a matter of vocation, and a vocation is a limiting factor which **5.** extends even to the kind of material that the writer is able to apprehend imaginatively. The writer can choose what he writes about but he cannot choose what he is able to make live, and so far as he is concerned, a living deformed character is acceptable and a dead whole one is not. The Christian writer particularly will feel that whatever his initial gift is, it comes from God; and no matter how minor a gift it is, he will not be willing to destroy it by trying to use it outside its proper limits.

The country that the writer is concerned with in the most objective way is, of **6.** course, the region that most immediately surrounds him, or simply the country, with its body of manners, that he knows well enough to employ. It's generally suggested that the Southern writer has some advantage here. Most readers these days must be

* In talks here and there Flannery O'Connor often alluded to this challenge on the part of the *Life* editorial. Once she said: "What these editorial writers fail to realize is that the writer who emphasizes spiritual values is very likely to take the darkest view of all of what he sees in this country today. For him, the fact that we are the most powerful and the wealthiest nation in the world doesn't mean a thing in any positive sense. The sharper the light of faith, the more glaring are apt to be the distortions the writer sees in the life around him."

sufficiently sick of hearing about Southern writers and Southern writing and what so many reviewers insist upon calling the "Southern school." No one has ever made plain just what the Southern school is or which writers belong to it. Sometimes, when it is most respectable, it seems to mean the little group of Agrarians that flourished at Vanderbilt in the twenties; but more often the term conjures up an image of Gothic monstrosities and the idea of a preoccupation with everything deformed and grotesque. Most of us are considered, I believe, to be unhappy combinations of Poe and Erskine Caldwell.

7. At least, however, we are all known to be anguished. The writers of the editorial in question suggest that our anguish is a result of our isolation from the rest of the country. I feel that this would be news to most Southern writers. The anguish that most of us have observed for some time now has been caused not by the fact that the South is alienated from the rest of the country, but by the fact that it is not alienated enough, that every day we are getting more and more like the rest of the country, that we are being forced out not only of our many sins, but of our few virtues. This may be unholy anguish but it is anguish nevertheless.

8. Manners are of such great consequence to the novelist that any kind will do. Bad manners are better than no manners at all, and because we are losing our customary manners, we are probably overly conscious of them; this seems to be a condition that produces writers. In the South there are more amateur authors than there are rivers and streams. It's not an activity that waits upon talent. In almost every hamlet you'll find at least one lady writing epics in Negro dialect and probably two or three old gentlemen who have impossible historical novels on the way. The woods are full of regional writers, and it is the great horror of every serious Southern writer that he will become one of them.

9. The writer himself will probably feel that the only way for him to keep from becoming one of them is to examine his conscience and to observe our fierce but fading manners in the light of an ultimate concern; others would say that the way to escape being a regional writer is to widen the region. Don't be a Southern writer; be an American writer. Express this great country—which is "enjoying an unparalleled prosperity," which is "the strongest nation in the world," and which has "almost produced a classless society." How, with all this prosperity and strength and classlessness staring you in the face, can you honestly produce a literature which doesn't make plain the joy of life?

10. The writer whose position is Christian, and probably also the writer whose position is not, will begin to wonder at this point if there could not be some ugly correlation between our unparalleled prosperity and the stridency of these demands for a literature that shows us the joy of life. He may at least be permitted to ask if these screams for joy would be quite so piercing if joy were really more abundant in our prosperous society.

11. The Christian writer will feel that in the greatest depth of vision, moral judgment will be implicit, and that when we are invited to represent the country according to survey, what we are asked to do is to separate mystery from manners and judgment from vision, in order to produce something a little more palatable to the modern temper. We are asked to form our consciences in the light of statistics, which is to establish the relative as absolute. For many this may be a convenience, since we don't live in

an age of settled belief; but it cannot be a convenience, it cannot even be possible, for the writer who is a Catholic. He will feel that any long-continued service to it will produce a soggy, formless, and sentimental literature, one that will provide a sense of spiritual purpose for those who connect the spirit with romanticism and a sense of joy for those who confuse that virtue with satisfaction. The storyteller is concerned with what is; but if what is is what can be determined by survey, then the disciples of Dr. Kinsey and Dr. Gallup are sufficient for the day thereof.

In the greatest fiction, the writer's moral sense coincides with his dramatic sense, **12.** and I see no way for it to do this unless his moral judgment is part of the very act of seeing, and he is free to use it. I have heard it said that belief in Christian dogma is a hindrance to the writer, but I myself have found nothing further from the truth. Actually, it frees the storyteller to observe. It is not a set of rules which fixes what he sees in the world. It affects his writing primarily by guaranteeing his respect for mystery.

In the introduction to a collection of his stories called *Rotting Hill*, Wyndham **13.** Lewis has written, "If I write about a hill that is rotting, it is because I despise rot." The general accusation passed against writers now is that they write about rot because they love it. Some do, and their works may betray them, but it is impossible not to believe that some write about rot because they see it and recognize it for what it is.

It may well be asked, however, why so much of our literature is apparently **14.** lacking in a sense of spiritual purpose and in the joy of life, and if stories lacking such are actually credible. The only conscience I have to examine in this matter is my own, and when I look at stories I have written I find that they are, for the most part, about people who are poor, who are afflicted in both mind and body, who have little—or at best a distorted—sense of spiritual purpose, and whose actions do not apparently give the reader a great assurance of the joy of life.

Yet how is this? For I am no disbeliever in spiritual purpose and no vague **15.** believer. I see from the standpoint of Christian orthodoxy. This means that for me the meaning of life is centered in our Redemption by Christ and what I see in the world I see in its relation to that. I don't think that this is a position that can be taken halfway or one that is particularly easy in these times to make transparent in fiction.

Some may blame preoccupation with the grotesque on the fact that here we have **16.** a Southern writer and that this is just the type of imagination that Southern life fosters. I have written several stories which did not seem to me to have any grotesque characters in them at all, but which have immediately been labeled grotesque by non-Southern readers. I find it hard to believe that what is observable behavior in one section can be entirely without parallel in another. At least, of late, Southern writers have had the opportunity of pointing out that none of us invented Elvis Presley and that that youth is himself probably less an occasion for concern than his popularity, which is not restricted to the Southern part of the country. The problem may well become one of finding something that is *not* grotesque and of deciding what standards we would use in looking.

My own feeling is that writers who see by the light of their Christian faith will **17.** have, in these times, the sharpest eyes for the grotesque, for the perverse, and for the unacceptable. In some cases, these writers may be unconsciously infected with the Manichean spirit of the times and suffer the much-discussed disjunction between sensibility and belief, but I think that more often the reason for this attention to the perverse is the difference between their beliefs and the beliefs of their audience. Redemption is meaningless unless there is cause for it in the actual life we live, and for the last few centuries there has been operating in our culture the secular belief that there is no such cause.

18. The novelist with Christian concerns will find in modern life distortions which are repugnant to him, and his problem will be to make these appear as distortions to an audience which is used to seeing them as natural; and he may well be forced to take ever more violent means to get his vision across to this hostile audience. When you can assume that your audience holds the same beliefs you do, you can relax a little and use more normal means of talking to it; when you have to assume that it does not, then you have to make your vision apparent by shock—to the hard of hearing you shout, and for the almost-blind you draw large and startling figures.

19. Unless we are willing to accept our artists as they are, the answer to the question, "Who speaks for America today?" will have to be: the advertising agencies. They are entirely capable of showing us our unparalleled prosperity and our almost classless society, and no one has ever accused them of not being affirmative. Where the artist is still trusted, he will not be looked to for assurance. Those who believe that art proceeds from a healthy, and not from a diseased, faculty of the mind will take what he shows them as a revelation, not of what we ought to be but of what we are at a given time and under given circumstances; that is, as a limited revelation but revelation nevertheless.

20. When we talk about the writer's country we are liable to forget that no matter what particular country it is, it is inside as well as outside him. Art requires a delicate adjustment of the outer and inner worlds in such a way that, without changing their nature, they can be seen through each other. To know oneself is to know one's region. It is also to know the world, and it is also, paradoxically, a form of exile from that world. The writer's value is lost, both to himself and to his country, as soon as he ceases to see that country as a part of himself, and to know oneself is, above all, to know what one lacks. It is to measure oneself against Truth, and not the other way around. The first product of self-knowledge is humility, and this is not a virtue conspicuous in any national character.

21. St. Cyril of Jerusalem, in instructing catechumens, wrote: "The dragon sits by the side of the road, watching those who pass. Beware lest he devour you. We go to the Father of Souls, but it is necessary to pass by the dragon." No matter what form the dragon may take, it is of this mysterious passage past him, or into his jaws, that stories of any depth will always be concerned to tell, and this being the case, it requires considerable courage at any time, in any country, not to turn away from the storyteller.

WORKING WITH THE TEXT

Cultural and Historical References

In this section, the numbers at the margin refer to the numbered paragraphs in the selection itself.

6. Edgar Allen Poe is, of course, the author of horror tales like *The Telltale Heart* and *The Masque of the Red Death.* Caldwell is the author of *God's Little Acre,* a lusty novel of crude, uneducated Southerners.

11. Alfred Kinsey authored books on sexual behavior. Gallup is the famous pollster.

15. "Redemption by Christ" means the saving of one's soul through the intercession of Christ. According to the Christian faith, humanity lost its way in Eden through the disobedience of Adam and Eve, and it therefore has to be "redeemed" by a second Adam, Jesus Christ.

17. The Manichees believe that the universe is a stage for a battle between equally powerful forces of good and evil. O'Connor may be only using the word "Manichee" to mean "heretic."

17. "Disjunction between sensibility and belief" means that one's religious beliefs have been removed, or cut off from, one's intellectual life.

19. A "revelation" is a message from heaven, or, by extension, a sudden enlightenment that can't quite be explained.

21. "Catechumens" is a Catholic term meaning those who are in the process of being taught the principles of the Christian faith.

Writing Assignments: The Paragraph

Be sure to provide an introduction for each of the following paragraph writing assignments. That is, begin each paragraph with a phrase like this: "Thomas Brickle claims that. . . ." When it is relevant, you might also want to identify the expertise of the author ("Thomas Brickle, a New Testament scholar, claims that. . . ."), the name of the book or article, the century and country in which the work appeared, or any other circumstances that your readers might find significant. For more on this, see pp. 11–13 in Chapter 2.

1. Explicate paragraph 21, O'Connor's conclusion. How does the paragraph serve to emphasize what she has been saying? Begin your paragraph with words like these: "In 'The Fiction Writer and His Country,' Flannery O'Connor argues. . . . " Then show how her conclusion supports what you have said.

2. Explain the point that O'Connor is making about Elvis Presley in paragraph 16. How does the remark on Elvis support O'Connor's topic sentence?

3. Summarize paragraph 13.

Writing Assignments: The Short Essay

Use informal documentation for these short essays. That is, don't use footnotes or a Works Cited page to document your sources. Instead, cite only relevant information about your source, and keep that information *within* your text. Then follow the summary or quote with a page number in parenthesis. (Use the page numbers that you find in this book to represent the page numbers of the source.) Thus, your informal documentation will look something like this:

> In "An Explication of Good Country People," Virgil Scott, professor emeritus at Michigan State University, says that Joy is a "spiritual as well as a physical cripple" (p. 293).

1. O'Connor plays on various meanings of the word "country" in paragraph 4. Explicate her meanings.
2. What is O'Connor trying to say in this essay? Get to the heart of it in your first paragraph, and then elaborate on that heart in the rest of your essay.
3. Paragraph 18 is the most quoted paragraph of this essay. Take that paragraph and apply it to "Good Country People."
4. Discuss O'Connor's remark about her Catholicism (or Christianity) and how it affects her writing.

THE HABIT OF BEING

Flannery O'Connor

The Habit of Being is an edited collection of letters which Flannery O'Connor wrote to various correspondents during her lifetime. In the following letters O'Connor makes some interesting comments on "Good Country People."

To Robert Giroux

26 February 55

I have just written a story called "Good Country People" that Allen and Caroline both **1.** say is the best thing I have written and should be in this collection. I told them I thought it was too late, but anyhow I am writing now to ask if it is. It is really a story that would set the whole collection on its feet. It is 27 pages and if you can eliminate the one called "A Stroke of Good Fortune," and the other called "An Afternoon in the Woods," this one would fit the available space nicely. Also I remember you said it would be good to have one that had never been published before. I could send it to you at once *on being wired.* Please let me know.

Giroux wired Flannery that every effort would be made to include the story. **2.**
After he had read it, he wrote suggesting that an appearance by the mother and Mrs. Freeman at the end might improve it. Flannery recognized the value of the suggestion and added the sentences that are now a part of the story.

7 March 55

I like the suggestion about the ending of "Good Country People" and enclose **3.**

Source: Flannery O'Connor, *The Habit of Being*, Sally Fitzgerald (ed.). New York: Farrar, Straus & Giroux, 1979. 75, 78, 170–171.

a dozen or so lines that can be added on to *the present end*. I enclose them in case you can get them put on before I get the proofs. I am mighty wary of making changes on proofs . . .

To Ben Griffith

4 May 1955

I am writing Harcourt, Brace to send you an advance copy of *A Good Man Is Hard* **4.** *to Find*, which is my collection of short stories (ten) due to be published June 6. There is one very long story in it, 60 pages, that I would like you to see, and another called "Good Country People" that pleases me no end. You will observe that I admire my own work as much if not more than anybody else does. I have read "The Artificial Nigger" several times since it was printed, enjoying it each time as if I had had nothing to do with it. I feel that this is not quite delicate of me but it may be balanced by the fact that I write a great deal that is not fit to read which I properly destroy. . . .

24 August 56

. . . About GCP ["Good Country People"] let me say that you are not reading **5.** the story itself. Where do you get the idea that Hulga's need to worship "comes to flower" in GCP? Or that she had never had any faith at any time? or never loved anybody before? None of these things are said in the story. She is full of contempt for the Bible salesman until she finds he is full of contempt for her. Nothing "comes to flower" here except her realization in the end that she ain't so smart. It's not said that she has never had any faith but it is implied that her fine education has got rid of it for her, that purity has been overridden by pride of intellect through her fine education. Further it's not said that she's never loved anybody, only that she's never been kissed by anybody—a very different thing. And of course I have thrown you off myself by informing you that Hulga is like me. So is Nelson, so is Haze, so is Enoch, but you cannot read a story from what you get out of a letter. Nor I repeat, can you, in spite of anything Sister Sewell may say, read the author by the story. You may but you shouldn't—See T. S. Eliot.

That my stories scream to you that I have never consented to be in love with **6.** anybody is merely to prove that they are screaming an historical inaccuracy. I have God help me consented to this frequently. Now that Hulga is repugnant to you only makes her more believable. I had a letter from a man who said Allen Tate was wrong about the story that Hulga was not a "maimed soul," she was just like us all. He ended the letter by saying he was in love with Hulga and he hoped some day she would learn to love him. Quaint. But I stick neither with you nor with that gent here but with Mr. Allen Tate. A maimed soul is a maimed soul.

I have also led you astray by talking of technique as if it were something that **7.** could be separated from the rest of the story. Technique can't operate at all, of course, except on believable material. But there was less conscious technical control in GCP than in any story I've ever written. Technique works best when it is unconscious, and it was unconscious there.

What Fr. Simons was talking about saying "Lutheran sensibility" he explained **8.** this way: Luther said a man was like a horse, ridden either by Christ or the devil. My characters are ridden either, said he, by Christ or the devil and therefore lack any self-determination, hence Lutheran sensibility. ?????????

What you say about your experience last August and since all rings true to me **9.** though I have never experienced anything like that myself. When you are born in it I suppose that is gift enough without asking for anything else. In any case you now have the Church and don't need anything else. And that about Edith Stein rings true too. I have been reading about eternity in a book of Jean Guitton's called *The Virgin Mary*—one that [a friend] left here—and have had considerable light thrown on the subject for me. He says that eternity begins in time and that we must stop thinking of it as something that follows time. It's all very instructive and I recommend it.

Sunday I am to entertain a man who wants to make a movie out of The River. **10.** He has never made a movie before but is convinced The River is the dish for him— a kind of documentary, he said over the telephone. It is sort of disconcerting to think of somebody getting hold of your story and doing something else to it and I doubt if I will be able to see my way through him. But we shall see. How to document the sacrament of Baptism???????

WORKING WITH THE TEXT

Cultural and Historical References

In this section, the numbers at the margin refer to the numbered paragraphs in the selection itself.

1. Robert Giroux was O'Connor's friend and publisher. Allen Tate, an influential Southern literary critic, and Caroline Gordon, a writer of fiction, were married to one another.

4. "The Artificial Nigger" is a story by Flannery O'Connor.

5. Nelson, Haze, and Enoch are characters in stories by O'Connor. T. S. Eliot, the author of *The Waste Land* and other poems, was a modernist in technique and a conservative in politics and religion (much like O'Connor herself).

8. Martin Luther began the Protestant Reformation when he posted 95 theses on the door of the Wittenberg Cathedral.

Writing Assignments: The Paragraph

Be sure to provide an introduction for each of the following paragraph writing assignments. That is, begin each paragraph with a phrase like this: "Thomas Brickle claims that . . . ." When it is relevant, you might also want to identify the expertise of the author ("Thomas Brickle, a New Testament scholar, claims that. . . ."), the name of the book or article, the century and country in which the work appeared, or any other circumstances that your readers might find significant. For more on this, see pp. 11–13 in Chapter 2.

1. Summarize *The Habit of Being.*
2. Summarize O'Connor's letter to Giroux.

Writing Assignments: The Short Essay

Use informal documentation for those short essays. That is, don't use foot-notes or a Works Cited page to document your sources. Instead, cite only relevant information about your source, and keep that information *within* your text. Then follow the summary or quote with a page number in parenthe-ses. (Use the page numbers that you find in this book to represent the page numbers of the source.) Thus, your informal documentation will look something like this:

> In "An Explication of Good Country People," Virgil Scott, professor emeritus at Michigan State University, says that Joy is a "spiritual as well as a physical cripple" (p. 293).

1. Discuss Alan Tate's comment in paragraph 6 about the man who said he was in love with Hulga. Is there anything lovable about Hulga? Or is Tate right in saying that Hulga is repugnant?
2. Giroux evidently suggested to O'Connor that she come back to Hopewell and Freeman at the end of her story. Should O'Connor have done it? Look carefully at those paragraphs that O'Connor added. Do they weaken the ending? How are they related to the theme of the story?
3. Argue with one of O'Connor's statements in paragraph 5.

FLANNERY O'CONNOR: "GOOD COUNTRY PEOPLE"
Virgil Scott

Virgil Scott, professor emeritus at Michigan State University, is co-editor of *Studies in the Short Story* (1968) and author of various articles on contemporary literature. In this essay Scott presents a straightforward, unpretentious, and convincing discussion of "Good Country People."

The late Flannery O'Connor was Roman Catholic, and many of her stories depict **1.** "sick souls" in a sick spiritual environment—a world of secularism and materialism (in the broad scientific sense), a world in which intangible values and concepts (not just God, but sin, virtue, love, salvation) are now meaningless myths. It is [a] world in which "intelligent" people desire "to know nothing of nothing." The quotation which is the philosophical core of this story can, of course, be interpreted in more than one way, and to the writer it is "some evil incantation in gibberish." To her, such intellectual and philosophical soil and climate provide good growing weather for "maimed souls."

Source: Virgil Scott, "Flannery O'Connor: 'Good Country People,' " *The Instructor's Manual for Studies in the Short Story* (3rd ed.). New York: Holt, Rinehart & Winston, 1968. 29–32.

"Good Country People" invites discussion on other than thematic and symbolic **2.** grounds. It is tremendously effective just for its characterization; no writer that I know of has the ear that Miss O'Connor had for the cliché or the art to make the cliché bring a human being to life for us. At the same time, "Good Country People" is, thematically, one of Miss O'Connor's bitterest stories. The central story of Joy-Hulga and Manley Pointer makes its point clearly enough. The atheist Hulga, with her wooden leg, myopic vision, and weak heart, is clearly a spiritual as well as a physical cripple. Originally named Joy, she has, with the maturity acquired through education, put away childish things and taken the ugliest name she can think of. She has, in fact, made ugliness a way of life. Her perpetual facial expression is one of outrage and her manners are deliberately rude. She "does not like dogs, cats, birds, flowers, nature, or young men" and love "is not a word I use. I don't like illusions." As for what in a superstitious and ignorant age were called sins or virtues we find that, "as a child she had sometimes been subject to feelings of shame but education had removed the last traces of that as a good surgeon scrapes for cancer." "Unless ye become as a little child ye shall not see the kingdom of heaven," but Hulga's only tie with childhood now is a yellow sweatshirt with a faded cowboy on it, an affectation which she considers funny. Spiritually speaking, Hulga has "achieved blindness by an act of will and means to keep it"; she has "seen through to nothing"; she has put her faith in one thing, her wooden leg, "which she takes care of as someone else would her soul." To put this in Hulga's terms, "she is saved, the boy damned."

Manley Pointer, for whom Bibles are heavy, who comes "not from a place, just **3.** from near a place," who like Hulga claims a weak heart, who is fascinated by accidents (the crushing of his father) and with the artificial parts of partial human beings (glass eyes, wooden legs) would make an appropriate lover for Hulga. His "serious thoughts" are fatuous, but no more gibberish than the passages Hulga underlines in books; and his "I hope you don't think that I believe in that crap!" is her philosophy robbed of its learned jargon. Like Hulga—who is shocked by his hypocrisy—Manley has a few vestiges of old faith, belief, and superstition left to him; "you got to say you love me," he says to the girl. But fundamentally he has "been believing in nothing ever since [he] was born."

The seduction scene is as obscene as anything in contemporary literature. That **4.** obscenity stems not from any biological detail but from the ironic context in which the scene is developed; not only love but lust is absent. Hulga's motive is to seduce the young man intellectually, to change his beliefs "into a deeper understanding of life," to turn them into "something useful." His motive is to reduce her to helplessness by robbing her of the symbol of her spiritual infirmity (which is at the same time her one crutch). What makes the scene obscene is not the hypocrisy on both sides, not the depiction of loveless love, not the translation of normal heterosexuality into a fascination with taking an artificial leg on and off, and not even Hulga's sick fantasy in which Manley takes her leg off every night and puts it back on every morning. The obscenity (I can think of no more apt a term than this) comes from the religious context in which the seduction is carried out, one which reminds us of what love was in another spiritual context. Thus Manley's earlier misquotation ("He who losest his life shall find it") becomes for Hulga "like surrendering to him completely. It was like losing her own life and finding it again, miraculously, in his"—and the "his" is not only not capitalized, it is followed by Manley's "You got me instead." This juxtaposition of Christ and Manley is matched by Manley placing before her a box of condoms, a flask of whiskey, a pack of cards with obscene pictures on the back, "like one presenting offerings at the shrine of a goddess"; not only is Manley the New Christ, Hulga is now the New Virgin. The spiritual sickness is finally captured in Hulga's fleeting vision of the leg "slanted forlornly across the inside of the suitcase with a Bible at either side of its opposite ends."

Fully half the story is devoted to Mrs. Hopewell and Mrs. Freeman and her **5.** family; moreover, the first half is from Mrs. Hopewell's point of view. Why? Are these two any more than an ironic Greek chorus? Do they serve a more important function than holding to an "evil-smelling" onion shoot while they add one more ironic note to the story? If so, what function do they serve?

For one thing, the opening scenes extend the story's meaning beyond a single **6.** sick and pathetic girl. Mrs. Hopewell's clichés, for example, are as empty of meaning as Hulga's philosophy. In some instances, scenes here are balanced against the seduction scene; in Carramae's wedding, for example, religion is nearly as debased as it is in the seduction scene. But Mrs. Hopewell and Mrs. Freeman also serve the story in other ways. Miss O'Connor frequently uses Jonsonian names for her characters, and in "Good Country People" all the names (Hopewell, Freeman, "Caramel," "Glycerine," Joy, Manley Pointer, probably even Lyman) have either spiritual or theological connotations. With Mrs. Hopewell and Mrs. Freeman, these connotations are essentially "protestant," if we define this term as a break with established tradition, an individual interpretation of scripture or religious conscience. Through its Jonsonian names the story can be interpreted as a kind of theological allegory, operating thematically in somewhat the same way as *Pilgrim's Progress*. Mrs. Freeman—described by Mrs. Hopewell as "good country people," "the salt of the earth"—is fascinated (as is Manley) by "secret infections, hidden deformities, assaults upon children. Of diseases, she preferred the lingering or incurable." Mrs. Freeman (ironically, a servant) is also the mother of one daughter married and pregnant at fifteen and of another who has curious dates. Similarly, Mrs. Hopewell—whose total intellectual equipment consists of meaningless and fatuous clichés, who is divorced, whose Bible is "somewhere in the attic," who reacts to compliments with "What are you selling?"—Mrs. Hopewell is the mother of Joy-Hulga. We cannot, perhaps, press the theological and allegorical implications of "Good Country People" too far. But it does remind me that historically the modern world began with the Reformation.

WORKING WITH THE TEXT

Cultural and Historical References

In this section, the numbers at the margin refer to the numbered paragraphs in the selection itself.

2. "Myopic" means shortsighted. What does this mean when it's used to describe a person?

2. The "Greek chorus" mentioned here was a fixture of ancient Greek

tragedies. The chorus served to comment on the action taking place. Knowing that, what is an "ironic Greek chorus"?

Writing Assignments: The Paragraph

Be sure to provide an introduction for each of the following paragraph writing assignments. That is, begin each paragraph with a phrase like this: "Thomas Brickle claims that. . . ." When it is relevant, you might also want to identify the expertise of the author ("Thomas Brickle, a New Testament scholar, claims that. . . ."), the name of the book or article, the century and country in which the work appeared, or any other circumstances that your readers might find significant. For more on this, see pp. 11–13 in Chapter 2.

1. Comment on Manley Pointer's name.
2. Discuss the implications of Joy changing her name to Hulga.

Writing Assignments: The Short Essay

Use informal documentation for these short essays. That is, don't use footnotes or a Works Cited page to document your sources. Instead, cite only relevant information about your source, and keep that information *within* your text. Then follow the summary or quote with a page number in parenthesis. (Use the page numbers that you find in this book to represent the page numbers of the source.) Thus, your informal documentation will look something like this:

> In "An Explication of Good Country People," Virgil Scott, professor emeritus at Michigan State University, says that Joy is a "spiritual as well as a physical cripple" (p. 293).

1. "Good Country People" might be seen as a pointed criticism, from a Catholic point of view, of fundamentalist Protestantism. Respond to this idea. See paragraph 16 for a comment on the Catholic-Protestant theme.
2. How is religion debased in Carramae's wedding?
3. How is the phrase "to know nothing of nothing" relevant to the story?

GOOD COUNTRY PEOPLE

David Eggenschwiler

David Eggenschwiler, an associate professor of English at the University of Southern California, has authored numerous essays on British and American literature. This excerpt focuses almost exclusively on the character and motives of Joy-Hulga Hopewell.

Source: David Eggenschwiler, *The Christian Humanism of Flannery O'Connor.* Detroit: Wayne State University Press, 1972. 52–57.

Joy-Hulga Hopewell of "Good Country People" is the most complex of Miss **1.**
O'Connor's demonic intellectuals. A stout, thirty-two-year-old woman with a Ph.D.
and a wooden leg, Hulga is in many ways a case study in repression and neurotic
compensation, although she is not just that, as man is never just a psychological case
to the Christian humanist. When she was ten years old, her leg was shot off in a hunting
accident. At thirty-two she has never danced, never been kissed, and, in her mother's
terms, has never had "any *normal* good times." Instead, she reads philosophy.
Ironically, because of a bad heart (and perhaps because of her more psychological
infirmities), Hulga lives at home on her mother's farm, surrounded by the unsophisticat-
ed and earthy people she scorns. Miss O'Connor emphasizes the sensuous and emotional
sterility of the character by contrasting her with the daughters of the hired help:
"Glynese, a redhead, was eighteen and had many admirers; Carramae a blonde, was
only fifteen but already married and pregnant."

Mrs. Freeman, the girls' mother, further intensifies the contrast by gossiping **2.**
continuously and minutely about her daughters' bodily functions: she keeps the
Hopewells informed daily about Carramae's morning sickness, with full accounts of
her eating and vomiting, and she recounts how Glynese got rid of a sty by letting her
chiropractic boyfriend pop her neck while she lay across the seat of his car. Thus, in
the background of Hulga's life there is an intensely physical mixture of sexuality,
courtship, and common bodily ailments: a continuous reminder that man is partly an
animal.

Hulga, however, is intent on denying that such matters are important. Most **3.**
obviously, she cultivates her ugliness, avoiding any social contests with the Glyneses
of the world and opposing her mother's cheerful belief that "people who looked on
the bright side of things would be beautiful even if they were not." She lumbers around
the house in a sweatshirt with a faded cowboy on it, exaggerating her deformity and
feeling continuous outrage. She is particularly proud of having changed her name from
"Joy" to "Hulga": "One of her major triumphs was that her mother had not been
able to turn her dust into Joy, but the greater one was that she had been able to turn
it herself into Hulga."

Obviously, Hulga has not succeeded in becoming indifferent to her deformity; **4.**
she is preoccupied with it, intent upon proving an indifference, which is disproved by
the intent. Because she cannot really admit to herself that she is infirm, that she is dust,
she tries to remake herself into something more apparently ludicrous than dust, into
Hulga; thereby, she will seem to be in control of her condition, to have willed herself
to be deformed as a jesting reply to the "normal" people around her. . . . She even
treasures her deformity and suffering for making her different, and she is quite sensitive
about her wooden leg and her adopted name, for they are very personal matters and
are important to her as psychological symbols. In fact, she fancifully, yet really quite
seriously, attributes special powers to her new name and the self-willed ugliness it
represents: "She had a vision of the name working like the ugly sweating Vulcan who
stayed in the furnace and to whom, presumably, the goddess had to come when
called." Through this brief fantasy, with its clear sexual implications, the ugly outcast
triumphs, as in the common mythical pattern of the dwarfs, humpbacks, and ugly
magicians of the world who enchant the beautiful princesses. But what magic could
come from dust, from an ordinary crippled girl who looked on the bright side of things?

Better to be a sweating Vulcan, especially if one could feel responsible for the transformation and if one still knew that beneath the disguise was another self, laughing at the masquerade.

To supplement her mortification of the flesh, Hulga also maintains a feeling of **5.** intellectual superiority by confounding wit with wisdom. Because she realizes that the people around her are often foolishly conventional in their ideas and values, she thinks that she lives without illusions, which is ridiculous, because her illusions are only more sophisticated than theirs. In a parody of popularized existentialism, she claims that she is "one of those people who see *through* to nothing" and that she has "a kind of salvation" because she sees that there is nothing to see. In both of these claims she is proudly asserting her role as the mocker and negater, but in neither does she understand that "nothing" can be the object of experience. Her claim that there is "nothing to see" means merely that she does not find anything to see, not that "nothing" can be the object of metaphorical sight. Her "nothing" is hypothetical, abstract, a philosophical cliché; it has little in common with the "nothing" that Kierkegaard and other existentialists make the object of dread. This is made clear by the passage which Mrs. Hopewell finds in one of the books Hulga has been reading:

> "Science, on the other hand, has to assert its soberness and seriousness afresh and declare that it is concerned solely with what-is. Noth-ing—how can it be for science anything but a horror and a phantasm? If science is right, then one thing stands firm: science wishes to know nothing of nothing. Such is after all the strictly scientific approach to Nothing. We know it by wishing to know nothing of Nothing." These words had been underlined with a blue pencil and they worked on Mrs. Hopewell like some evil incantation in gibberish. She shut the book quickly and went out of the room as if she were having a chill.

Although Mrs. Hopewell's superstitious response to the unknown is comic, it is intuitively right. For Hulga such a passage *is* an incantation to ward off the experience of nothing, and Hulga remains emotionally safe because she, too, wishes to know nothing of nothing. Thus, whatever is disturbing she eliminates through a trite nihilism, which she in turn renders harmless to herself through a scientific positivism (which, if the argument were extended, would be negated by the nihilism). Her philosophical position is nonsensical, for it has developed out of neurotic needs, her need to escape her socially and physically incomplete self, her dread of nothing, her realization that she is dust like all of mankind. So she becomes a ridiculous case of the satirist satirized and the rationalist revealed as irrational.

She is as fully absurd when she sets out to enlighten an apparently naive and **6.** religious Bible salesman, an action which she thinks to be altruistic and objectively experimental. Her motives are actually selfish and psychologically complex. She clearly wants to disillusion the young man to demonstrate her superiority, to recreate him as she thinks she has recreated herself, and she wants to continue her defensive attack on the good country people whom she scorns. Yet her plan for his philosophical education reveals less obvious, perhaps even more repressed, motives. She intends to seduce him and then lead him into the realization that there is nothing to see: "She imagined that she took his remorse in hand and changed it into a deeper understanding of life. She took all his shame away and turned it into something useful." Miss O'Connor's choice of seduction as Hulga's method is good comic psychology. Hulga's assumption that sexual remorse and shame would lead to her pseudo-nihilistic view of life reveals much about her own unconscious and the sexually neurotic bases of her philosophy. Also, one might well suspect the disinterestedness of a plan that would involve her own sexual initiation, especially since it would be executed on an apparent bumpkin who would offer little psychological threat to the inexperienced woman and tutor.

The murkiness of Hulga's motives and her lack of self-knowledge make her quite **7.** vulnerable to the bogus rube; in fact, she even considers running away with him. In the first place, she is moved that the boy sees "the truth about her," since he claims that her wooden leg makes her different from everyone else. She does not realize that he is even more of a morbid fetishist than she is. She imagines that, after they have run away, "every night he would take the leg off and every morning put it back on again," a fantasy that suggests her neurotically sublimated sexuality, her desire to relax her defenses, and her need to admit dependence. In the second place, she sentimentally has imagined the boy as a natural man: good, innocent, childlike, and intuitive, the antithesis of what she thinks herself to be. This image, which he helps to encourage, is an obverse reflex of her cynicism; it is almost proverbial that the same person may well be a worldly cynic and a naive sentimentalist, since he who is not whole may see alternately from different extremes.

The climax of the story is a violent attack on Hulga's illusions. As the Bible **8.** salesman drops his disguise as good country people, he reveals that he is more cynical than she, that his sexual attitudes toward her are brutal and obscene, and, most importantly, that his belief in nothing is far more radical than hers. Faced with what seemed to be an adoring, childlike boy, Hulga felt safe enough to experience emotions that she had previously protected herself against; when her defenses have been lessened, she is confronted with an image of what she has pretended to be, with a real, diabolical nihilist who exposes her name-changing and philosophizing as mere adolescent posturing. Having been emotionally and psychologically seduced, Hulga is the one who is educated; for the first time she is forced to *"see through* to nothing," an experience far less comfortable than she had imagined. As she is left behind in a state of near shock, without her glasses, her wooden leg, or her feigned self-sufficiency, her old self has been burned away, and she might be forced into a free choice that may be a new beginning. Perhaps it might even lead to her accepting her own body with its deformity and sexual desire, to accepting the ironies inherent in man's spiritual-corporeal nature.

WORKING WITH THE TEXT

Cultural and Historical References

In this section, the numbers at the margin refer to the numbered paragraphs in the selection itself.

4. Vulcan is the ugly god of fire and craftsmanship. Venus, the most beautiful woman in creation, was hopelessly in love with him. What does this mean to Hulga?

5. Existentialism begins, says Jean Paul Sartre, with atheism.

7. A "fetishist" is one who is sexually aroused by otherwise nonsexual objects such as shoes and feet.

Writing Assignments: The Paragraph

Be sure to provide an introduction for each of the following paragraph writing assignments. That is, begin each paragraph with a phrase like this: "Thomas Brickle claims that. . . ." When it is relevant, you might also want to identify the expertise of the author ("Thomas Brickle, a New Testament scholar, claims that. . . ."), the name of the book or article, the century and country in which the work appeared, or any other circumstances that your readers might find significant. For more on this see pp. 11–13 in Chapter 2.

1. What is Joy's "neurotic compensation"?

2. Do the names Glynese and Carramae suggest anything anything to you? How do they contrast with Hulga's name? See Hulga's comment on the two sisters' names.

Writing Assignments: The Short Essay

Use informal documentation for these short essays. That is, don't use footnotes or a Works Cited page to document your sources. Instead, cite only relevant information about your source, and keep that information *within* your text. Then follow the summary or quote with a page number in parentheses. (Use the page numbers that you find in this book to represent the page numbers of the source.) Thus, your informal documentation will look something like this:

> In "An Explication of Good Country People," Virgil Scott, professor emeritus at Michigan State University, says that Joy is a "spiritual as well as a physical cripple" (p. 293).

1. Write on Eggenschwiler's comment that Hulga "cultivates ugliness."

2. How is Hulga's leg a symbol? Symbol of what? What does it mean to Hulga? Discuss in an essay.

3. In paragraph 8, Eggenschwiler says that Hulga is "educated at the end." In what way is she educated? Write an essay.

4. How can this story be interpreted as a Christian story? Write an essay on that question.

5. In a short paper, disagree with Eggenschwiler's idea about the Vulcan image in paragraph 4.

GOOD COUNTRY PEOPLE

Preston M. Browning

In this selection from Browning's book, *Flannery O'Connor*, the author analyzes
in particular the childlike qualities of Joy-Hulga Hopewell. Browning is a professor
of English at the University of Illinois at Chicago Circle.

In "Good Country People" there appears a lively specimen of the criminal- **1.**
compulsive, as well as a family relationship in which a positivist and a positive
thinker prominently figure. Joy and her mother, Mrs. Hopewell, make up the prime
configuration: the disaffected young rebel, more often than not cynical but most
certainly imbued with pretensions to intellectualism, and typically alienated from the
smug, uncritical parent; the parent, self-satisfied, optimistic, endowed with what seems
an inexhaustible repertoire of platitudes of a moral or religious cast but actually
dedicated to philistine values and the profit motive. Mrs. Hopewell, as her name
implies, is a regular subscriber to the "life can be beautiful" philosophy. In contrast
to her daughter Joy, whose distinguishing features are a nasty disposition and an
artificial leg, Mrs. Hopewell staunchly maintains that "people who looked on the bright
side of things would be beautiful even if they were not." Joy is brilliant but cynical,
and derives a perverse pleasure from affronting her mother's flaccid optimism with a
look expressing her characteristic emotion of outrage. Joy's perversity prompts her to
adopt the name Hulga, the most unpleasant sound she can think of; and she complements
the ugliness of her new name with a sullen rudeness of behavior to her mother and the
latter's "companion," Mrs. Freeman. A self-styled atheist, with a Ph.D. in philosophy,
Hulga is rendered almost physically ill by the intensity of her contempt for what she
considers the utterly fatuous and banal world of her mother, who appears incapable of
thought more profound than the sentiment that "good country people"—of whom, in
her opinion, Mrs. Freeman is a notable example—are "the salt of the earth."

Into this world there suddenly intrudes another representative of "good country **2.**
people" (or so Mrs. Hopewell assumes), an itinerant Bible salesman named Manley
Pointer. Appearing to be the very essence of innocence and naïveté, Pointer has little
difficulty ingratiating himself with Mrs. Hopewell and matches her clichés with unctious
pieties about "Chrustian service" and "real honest people," nowadays only to be
found "way out in the country."

As attracted to his apparent innocence as she is repelled by his platitudinous **3.**
religious attitudes, and finding a common identity with Manley (they both have a not
unsymbolic "heart condition"), Joy agrees to accompany the boy on a picnic. Lying
in bed that evening Hulga anticipates the role she will play in the Bible saleman's
"education."

> She imagined that the two of them walked on the place until they came
> to the storage barn beyond the two back fields and there, she imagined,
> that things came to such a pass that she very easily seduced him and
> that then, of course, she had to reckon with his remorse. True genius

Source: Preston M. Browning, Jr., *Flannery O'Connor*. Carbondale, Ill: Southern Illinois University Press,
1974. 42–51.

can get an idea across even to an inferior mind. She imagined that she took his remorse in hand and changed it into a deeper understanding of life. She took all his shame away and turned it into something useful.

As the condescending Eve, Hulga will lead Manley into knowledge—not, however, knowledge of good and evil, but a more austere perception that both good and evil are illusions. "I'm one of those people who see *through* to nothing," she tells him. "We are all damned . . . but some of us have taken off our blindfolds and see that there's nothing to see. It's a kind of salvation."

The denouement of the story is at once pathetic and ironically comic. Hulga and **4.** the salesman do indeed enter the storage barn and climb to the loft, but here, Hulga's coldly calculating intelligence forsakes her completely. Earlier, while walking in the woods, she had allowed Pointer to kiss her, and at that time her mind was described as "clear and detached and ironic . . . regarding him from a great distance, with amusement but with pity." In the barn she kisses him with seeming passion, although "her mind" all the while "never stopped or lost itself for a second to her feelings." Pointer declares his love for Hulga and demands that she permit him to remove her artificial leg as proof of her love for him. This she refuses to do until he announces that it is her artificial leg which fascinates him. "It's what makes you different. You ain't like anybody else." And this, of course, is Hulga's undoing, literally and figuratively. Allowing her secret pride in her "difference" and her submerged self-pity to becloud her "clear and detached and ironic" vision, Hulga gives Pointer her leg and immediately loses that mastery over him on which her entire scheme depends. Feeling himself now in command, Pointer takes from his valise a hollowed-out Bible containing a small whiskey flask, a pack of pornographic cards, and a box of contraceptives. Hulga the cynic, the believer in nothing, is at first too startled to speak; when at last she does respond, it is in a voice described as "almost pleading": " 'Aren't you,' she murmured, 'aren't you just good country people?' " Pointer answers with a surly "Yeah . . . but it ain't held me back none"; and when Hulga complains furiously that he's "a perfect Christian," i.e., a thoroughly hypocritical one, this young man whom she has assumed to be the epitome of "real innocence" disabuses her once and for all of *her* illusions: " 'I hope you don't think,' he said in a lofty indignant tone, 'that I believe in that crap! I may sell Bibles but I know which end is up and I wasn't born yesterday.' " As he disappears out of the loft, with Hulga's leg safely ensconced in his valise, along with souvenirs of other similar escapades, Pointer delivers his *coup de grâce*: "And I'll tell you another thing, Hulga . . . you ain't so smart. I been believing in nothing ever since I was born!" While Hulga remains in the barn, her face "churning" with anger, Mrs. Hopewell and Mrs. Freeman watch Pointer crossing over the meadow to the highway. Mrs. Hopewell, with splendid unconscious irony, refers to the Bible salesman as "so simple" and adds, typically, "but I guess the world would be better off if we were all that simple." Mrs. Freeman's reply reveals her essential character: "Some can't be that simple . . . I know I never could."

One critic has maintained that the story continues past its natural conclusion at **5.** the moment of "symbolic defloration," but Flannery O'Connor had, I think, good reasons for giving the last word to Mrs. Freeman. For the wife of the hired hand plays a significant role in the story's thematic development. The long first paragraph is devoted to her; and her interest in physical deformities and monstrosities, developed in some detail in the narrative, is either integral to the story's purpose or the tale contains not one superfluous paragraph but two—the last *and* the first. Both paragraphs, however, are necessary, for the story largely concerns deformations of the body which reflect corruptions of the spirit; and this theme is advanced just as surely, though more subtly, through the relation of Hulga and Mrs. Freeman as it is through that of Hulga and Pointer. Mrs. Freeman is *free* of the illusions which blind both mother and daughter, seeing more deeply into Hulga's soul than does Mrs. Hopewell, who is too preoccupied with efforts to improve "the child's" disposition to attempt to understand her.

After the ritual name changing, Mrs. Hopewell continues to call her "child" **6.**
Joy, but in time Mrs. Freeman begins to use the adopted name, thereby causing Hulga extreme annoyance, since in so doing she invades the private domain bounded by the name, the self-created self it is meant to designate, and the artificial leg which is symbolic of the entire psychic structure. When Mrs. Freeman treads profanely upon this sacred soil, Hulga is inclined to "scowl and redden as if her privacy had been intruded upon."

> She considered the name her personal affair. . . . One of her major tri-
> umphs was that her mother had not been able to turn her dust into Joy,
> but the greatest one was that she had been able to turn it herself into
> Hulga. However, Mrs. Freeman's relish for using the name only irri-
> tated her. It was as if Mrs. Freeman's *beady steel-pointed eyes had
> penetrated far enough behind her face to reach some secret fact* [em-
> phasis added].

Mrs. Freeman, whose attraction to "the details of secret infections, hidden deformities, assaults upon children" is boundless, has in truth discovered a "secret fact" and the fact has much to do with the significance for Hulga of the artificial leg. Mrs. Freeman is fascinated by the leg, but it is a "secret infection," spiritual and psychological in nature, of which the leg provides intimations, toward which her eyes inevitably gravitate.

It is, of course, not only Mrs. Freeman who is fascinated by the leg but also **7.**
Pointer, as is made clear through numerous "signals,"one being the first question he asks Hulga on the day of the picnic: "Where does your wooden leg join on?" Earlier, when he had engaged Hulga in conversation preparatory to asking her for the date, Pointer had gazed at her "with open curiosity, like a child watching a new fantastic animal at the zoo. . . . His gaze seemed somehow familiar but she could not think where she had been regarded with it before." The gaze *is* familiar since it is merely a masculine version of Mrs. Freeman's concentrated and penetrating stare, the similarity made unmistakable when Pointer's eyes, after he has successfully separated Hulga from her leg and is casting compulsive glances at it, are described as "like two steel spikes." As Pointer, near the story's end, is to expose Hulga's pretenses, so Mrs. Freeman has already done earlier. Her "beady steel-pointed eyes" have discerned that Hulga is not what she would like to be taken for—a tough-minded, unsentimental, sophisticated materialist. Her comment, after spying Pointer and Hulga talking together following the salesman's initial appearance at the Hopewell farm, that "[s]ome people are more alike than others," infuriates Hulga, for it indicates that Mrs. Freeman has

taken the true measure of Hulga's supposed cynical detachment from all normal human relations.

On the level of conscious awareness Hulga believes that she allows Pointer a   **8.** limited degree of intimacy because his innocence will afford her a rare opportunity to be the "professor" of atheism and nothingness which her physical disabilities generally preclude. Actually Hulga longs for the warmth of human contact, longs in fact for a relationship in which she can play the dual roles of protected child and adoring mother. Though hardly aware of her hunger, Hulga covets an innocence identical to that which she imagines to be fundamental to Pointer's character. The true "secret fact" is that Hulga desires a return to Eden, to the life of play which constitutes the world of childhood, a prelapsarian existence of unity and uninterrupted mutuality. Consciously wishing to be Eve of the temptation, unconsciously she seeks the condition of Eve before the fall. This is one of the story's great ironies; another is that Mrs. Hopewell, for all her obtuseness, is correct: Joy-Hulga *is* a child.

That this is the case becomes evident in the barn loft when Hulga surrenders to   **9.** Pointer's blandishments. The following description of Hulga's highly emotive reaction to Pointer's comment that "You ain't like anybody else" is crucial for a just appraisal of her self-deceptive pose as the aloof, self-contained, rationalistic intellectual.

> She sat staring at him. There was nothing about her face or her round freezing-blue eyes to indicate that this had moved her; but she felt as if her heart had stopped and left her mind to pump her blood. She decided that for the first time in her life she was face to face with real inno-cence. This boy, with an instinct that came from beyond wisdom, had touched the truth about her. When after a minute, she said in a hoarse high voice, "All right," it was like surrendering to him completely. It was like losing her own life and finding it again, miraculously, in his.

The final lines are remarkable not only for the suggestion of parody of the Gospel parable, which, in fact, Pointer had recited the previous day in the Hopewell sitting room (the devil quoting scripture!), but also for the hints they give concerning Hulga's "secret." On several previous occasions Hulga has mentioned "salvation," the intended meaning of the word always being her enlightened view of the reality of Nothing. Here a more powerful and more authentic impulse toward salvation is manifest; a salvation whose terms—surrender, losing one's life, finding it again miraculously in the life of another and thereby experiencing spiritual resurrection—par-allel exactly the scheme of Christian redemption. Yet it is not Christian redemption for which Hulga yearns but rather a state of being which makes such redemption unnecessary. To be reborn into innocence, to shed the weight of consciousness and pain which life in the world entails—it is salvation of this sort which is Hulga's deepest desire.

Numerous details might be cited to support this conclusion. When, for instance, **10.** Hulga kisses Pointer she does so "as if she were trying to draw all the breath out of him." But his breath is described as "clear and sweet like a child's" and his kisses are "sticky like a child's"; since breath is a traditional symbol of spirit, it would appear that Hulga compulsively attempts to draw into herself Pointer's supposedly "clear and sweet" spirit. When Pointer mumbles incoherently of his love, Hulga's role as the mother redeemed by the purity of her child is intimated by the boy's murmurings, which are "like the sleepy fretting of a child being put to sleep by his mother." That the relationship as she comes to imagine it is one of childhood playfulness becomes more evident when Manley practices taking off the leg and replacing it, finally exclaiming, with an expression resembling that of a delighted child: " 'See!' . . . 'Now I can do it myself!' " Hulga's total immersion in this image of life-as-endless-play is expressed most vividly in her fantasy of "run[ing] away" with Pointer to an Edenic world where each day would end with Pointer's loving removal of the leg and each new day begin with his putting it "back on again." In such a world, Hulga is both mother and child, protectress and protected, lover and beloved. The roles unite because in this world, created out of Hulga's profoundest longing, all of the antinomies, the vexing contradictions, the soul-taxing dichotomies of real existence have been overcome. Hulga's dream is, finally, a dream of human wholeness and for a few moments the reader is inclined to share her vision. Yet quickly it is shown to be the very essence of Hulga's sin because of her desire to circumvent, without the suffering which redemption always entails, what the author considers the primary datum of the human situation—the fallen nature of man.

This fantasy, the culmination of Hulga's progressive revelation of her hidden **11.** self, is followed immediately by Pointer's disclosure of his true character. The explosive fury provoked in Hulga is thus to be accounted for not only as her predictable indignation at having been tricked by the "perfect Christian" who turns out to be a lewd, voyeuristic fraud, but more fundamentally as pure outrage occasioned by the betrayal of one whom she has come to consider a destined soulmate. The depth of Hulga's need for something in which she can believe and trust is illustrated by her pained cry that Pointer is "just like them all [i.e., the fraudulent "perfect Christians" she has known]—say one thing and do another." Though superficially she resembles the rationalist Sheppard, Hulga's more profound kinship is with a character such as Hazel Motes, in that both seek innocence and truth in a world which knows little of either.

Hulga's dream of running away to a world more capable of fulfilling the **12.** elemental human desire for unity and *joy* (it is, of course, her Joy-identity which is primary and which seeks realization in her dream) indicates how badly scarred she has been by life itself, not merely by the loss of the leg. The lost leg is an objective correlative of the lost unity of childhood, just as the wooden leg is an objective correlative of the pretended cynicism which is Hulga's self-protective response to adult reality. (It can hardly be a matter of chance that the key event in her fantasy of joyful existence is the removal of her leg by the childlike Pointer.) Self-exiled from the "grown-up" world whose fraudulence and cant she detests and cut off from the childhood world of playful bliss of which she has only unconscious or preconscious memories, Joy-Hulga dangles in limbo.

"Good Country People" gives us an admirable example of that depth of character **13.** which eludes easy classification. A typology of the sort I have suggested is frequently useful for character analysis and thematic interpretation. For example, Pointer's status as a "criminal-compulsive" is clear. But it is unwise to read this body of fiction exclusively in terms of categories of character type, whether those I have proposed or some others. This is a conclusion which will become clearer in the discussion of *The*

Violent Bear It Away; but "Good Country People" demonstrates the point with sufficient force to establish its validity.

Yet it *is* possible at the most obvious level of interpretation to say that Flannery **14.** O'Connor's intention in the dramatic encounter of Hulga and Pointer appears to be the exposure of a facile, superficial, and finally sentimental nihilism as it meets head-on a nihilism which, while entirely nonintellectual, is nonetheless real and implacable. Seen from this vantage point, Hulga's mean-spirited perversity proves merely a façade; and when she is compelled to acknowledge the existence of perversity profounder than her own—more a part of the true scheme of things, because partaking more fully of evil as a metaphysical reality—she responds with incredulity, shock, and impotent outrage. Thus is portrayed Hulga the positivist, experiencing the shock of evil which initiates her into what Hawthorne called "the sinful brotherhood of mankind." In this respect Hulga is like many another O'Connor character who experiences a sense of utter helplessness as he is made to confront a dimension of reality whose very existence his positivism or his positive thinking has prompted him to deny or ignore.

WORKING WITH THE TEXT

Cultural and Historical References

In this section, the numbers at the margin refer to the numbered paragraphs in the selection itself.

1. A "positivist" is a person who believes that the only way to real knowledge is through sense impressions.

1. A "philistine" was originally one of the idolaters with whom the Israelites came into conflict. Later the word came to mean a smug and ignorant person indifferent to aesthetic and cultural values.

8. "Prelapsarian" is the state of humankind before the Fall in Eden.

11. Sheppard is the main character in O'Connor's story "The Lame Shall Enter First." Motes is the main character in O'Connor's short novel, *Wise Blood*.

Writing Assignments: The Paragraph

Be sure to provide an introduction for each of the following paragraph writing assignments. That is, begin each paragraph with a phrase like this: "Thomas Brickle claims that. . . ." When it is relevant, you might also want to identify the expertise of the author ("Thomas Brickle, a New Testament scholar, claims that. . . ."), the name of the book or article, the century and country in which the work appeared, or any other circumstances that your readers might find significant. For more on this, see pp. 11–13 in Chapter 2.

1. For what purpose does Hulga wear her sweatshirt?

2. Why does Hulga call Mrs. Freeman's two daughters Glycerin and Caramel?

3. Comment on Browning's statement, in paragraph 1, that one member of the family is a positivist, the other a positive thinker. Which is which? Why?

4. What do you suppose Browning means when he says that in "Good Country People" there "appears a lively specimen of the criminal-compulsive"? Who is a criminal-compulsive? Why? Where does he get the idea that a character in the story is a criminal-compulsive?

Writing Assignments: The Short Essay

Use informal documentation for these short essays. That is, don't use footnotes or a Works Cited page to document your sources. Instead, cite only relevant information about your source, and keep that information *within* your text. Then follow the summary or quote with a page number in parentheses. (Use the page numbers that you find in this book to represent the page numbers of the source.) Thus, your informal documentation will look something like this:

> In "An Explication of Good Country People," Virgil Scott, professor emeritus at Michigan State University, says that Joy is a "spiritual as well as a physical cripple" (p. 293).

1. Browning says that "Good Country People" focuses on the "deformation of the body which reflects corruptions of the spirit." Discuss that statement.

2. What does Browning mean when he says, in paragraph 9, that Pointer is the devil who quotes scripture?

3. Write an essay on the idea that Hulga does believe in something. Focus your attention on the seduction scene.

GOOD COUNTRY PEOPLE

Frederick Asals

Frederick Asals has some interesting things to say about the relationship between the two older women in the story, Mrs. Hopewell and Mrs. Freeman, and how their relationship mirrors another, more "sinister," relationship in the story. Asals, an associate professor of English at York University in Toronto, has authored articles on Emily Dickinson, Nathaniel Hawthorne, Ralph Waldo Emerson, and, of course, Flannery O'Connor.

"Good Country People" presents a generational relationship within a family, in **1.** this case mother and daughter, but essential as that pairing is, it is not at the dramatic center of the story. The pivotal action is of course Joy-Hulga's encounter with the Bible

Source: Frederick Asals, *Flannery O'Connor: The Imagination of Extremity.* Athens, Ga.: University of Georgia Press, 1982. 102–108.

salesman, a confrontation that focuses and ironically reflects the other relationships in the story, that between the two older women, Mrs. Hopewell and Mrs. Freeman, and those of the girl with each of them. For Mrs. Hopewell, life is apparently summed up in her stock of clichés, and the dialogues with Mrs. Freeman that begin the story are exercises in hackneyed oneupmanship:

> "Everybody is different," Mrs.Hopewell said.
> "Yes, most people is," Mrs. Freeman said.
> "It takes all kinds to make the world."
> "I always said it did myself."

Mrs. Hopewell's supply of platitudes runs to the genteel and the uplifting. On her outraged daughter she urges the virtues of a "pleasant expression," a "pleasant" manner, and such cheery advice as "a smile never hurt anyone," but to her bewildered dismay, the girl responds to none of this. "It seemed to Mrs. Hopewell that every year she grew less like other people and more like herself—bloated, rude and squint-eyed."

This evolution is of course precisely what her daughter intends. As in "A View 2. of the Woods," naming again defines the shift: Joy's changing her name to Hulga is a deliberate defiance of her mother, a self-definition that sets her against everything Mrs. Hopewell stands for. "She saw it," O'Connor writes, "as the name of her highest creative act. One of her major triumphs was that her mother had not been able to turn her dust into Joy, but the greater one was that she had been able to turn it herself into Hulga." In this self-created rebirth, the girl believes, the ugly name acts as a mask for a private inner sense of identity: "She had a vision of the name working like the ugly sweating Vulcan who stayed in the furnace and to whom, presumably, the goddess [Venus] had to come when called." Cut off from the possibility of physical beauty by her "hulking" body and her wooden leg, Hulga emphasizes her outer ugliness in dress, manner, and action, but she secretly cherishes the vision of an inner self that is beautifully unique.

Forced by her physical disabilities to live at home, the girl's existence has become 3. one continuous gesture of outraged rejection of the life around her. If her mother refuses to deal with anything but the genteel surfaces of life, Hulga scorns those surfaces and plunges into the "depths," acquiring a Ph.D. in philosophy and disdaining "any close attention to her surroundings." If Mrs. Hopewell approaches life with a naïve optimism, her daughter embraces atheistic nihilism, "see[ing] *through*" the surfaces of things "to nothing." Point by point, the girl has, she thinks, defined a self that is the antithesis of her mother's.

The mysterious appearance of the Bible salesman at the Hopewell home provides 4. the first real test of that self called Hulga. As he presents himself, he seems a living embodiment of Mrs. Hopewell's most cherished clichés. "Honest," "sincere," "genuine," "simple," "earnest," "the salt of the earth," with his Bible-quoting and his missionary aspirations, he convinces the girl that at last she is "face to face with real innocence." Towards that innocence her feelings are deeply ambivalent. What she tells herself is that he is clay to be molded by her own "deeper understanding of life," an "inferior mind" to be instructed by "true genius," and she vaguely projects the aftermath of a seduction in which she transforms his inevitable remorse into "something useful.'' But what these fantasies of superiority reckon without is her unadmitted desire that someone pay homage to the goddess within.

The Bible salesman says that their meeting must have been fated ''on account **5.** of what all [we] got in common,'' but all that they seem to have in common is a potentially fatal heart condition. Their apparent roles are a typical set of O'Connor antitheses—the academic and the country bumpkin, the sophisticate and the innocent, the cynical atheist and the naïve Christian—antitheses that reach their comic high point in the barn where, as the boy whines for a declaration of love, the girl gives him a crash course in nihilist epistemology. But in the sudden role reversal that takes place in that barn, we discover what a genuine *Doppelgänger* this Bible salesman is.

The boy says of the wooden leg (which she treats ''as someone else would his **6.** soul, in private and almost with her own eyes turned away''), ''It's what makes you different. You ain't like anybody else.'' It is then that her outer cynicism drops and the girl reveals her underlying belief in real innocence: ''This boy, with an instinct that came from beyond wisdom, had touched the truth about her.'' The shrine of the goddess has been approached at last and with an attitude apparently ''entirely reverent.'' Her surrender to him is thus of more than her body, it is of her entire sense of self; and when she allows him to remove the leg, she becomes dependent on him for more than physical wholeness. Now he reveals to her who the true innocent is.

For the girl has not, as she thinks, escaped her mother and her mother's values: **7.** the entire identity of Hulga is built on them. Her academic nihilism is riddled with such clichés as ''We are all damned . . . but some of us have taken off our blindfolds and see that there's nothing to see. It's a kind of salvation.'' If the language is more sophisticated than any at Mrs. Hopewell's command, it is no less trite, and the smug self-deception underlying it (''I don't have illusions'') is, if anything, greater. Willfully blind to the world around her and complacent in her notion of self-created uniqueness, she has gained her sense of disdainful superiority precisely from her contemptuous acceptance of her mother's view of things. In kissing the boy, as we have seen, she falls into a parody of the maternal role, and when his childlike innocence becomes no longer credible, she asks, ''Aren't you . . . aren't you just good country people?'' The question is the ironic equivalent of Mrs. Hopewell's conviction that he is exactly that—a conviction her daughter has clearly shared.

As the mask of Hulga drops and reveals beneath it none other than Mrs. **8.** Hopewell's little girl Joy, it does so in response to the disappearance of the mask of the Bible salesman, of Manley Pointer, as he has called himself. And the face that looks forth from beneath *that* mask is the face of the nihilist the girl has claimed to be. She has pretended to be reborn into nothingness, but *he* has ''been believing in nothing ever since I was born.'' Although we get only a glimpse of what lives beneath that mask—apparently, like The Misfit, the Bible salesman thrives on ''meanness,'' in this case with a flair for the fetishistic—we see enough to grasp how uncannily mask and reality correspond to the Joy and Hulga identities of the girl. As the roles reverse themselves and his assumed innocence disappears into cynicism, so her superficial worldliness gives way to sentimental naïveté. If Manley Pointer turns out to be as hollow as the Bible he reveals in the barn, so Hulga is as empty as the wooden leg it was based on. "Like one presenting offerings at the shrine of a goddess," he takes from that Bible and places before her the contraceptives, whiskey, and pornographic cards that are a cruelly fitting devotion to the deified self. That self had been a sham; it is the girl, not the Bible salesman, who has the innocence of the child. Although he piously cites the text "He who losest his life shall find it," she is the one who truly believes in such a possibility, secularized though it is. For when she surrenders to him the privacy of the leg, "it was like losing her own life and finding it again, miraculously in his." The text, of course, works here ironically: it is the precise formula for their exchange of apparent identities.

The climax of his role as mocking double comes in a vicious parody of the **9.** intellectual clichés the girl has earlier mouthed at him. Accused of hypocrisy, he replies indignantly, "I hope you don't think . . . that I believe in that crap! I may sell Bibles, but I know which end is up and I wasn't born yesterday and I know where I'm going!"

But if the values here are the nihilistic ones the girl has professed, the idiom is **10.** the folk cliché so dear to Mrs. Hopewell, and the wedding of the two exposes with resonant finality how closely identified mother and daughter in truth are. Indeed, on this level "Good Country People" inverts the action of "A View of the Woods," for when Hulga is revealed as Joy, this apparent antithesis of her mother emerges as virtually a replica. The intricate set of reflections does not, however, end here, for the Bible salesman is not the only representative of those "good country people" in the story.

Mrs. Hopewell is of the opinion that Mrs. Freeman is also one of these "real **11.** genuine folks" and all the evidence ironically supports her. As Mrs. Freeman herself remarks, "Some people are more alike than others." Like the Bible salesman, she thrives on the exploitation of others' suffering—"Mrs. Freeman had a special fondness for the details of secret infections, hidden deformities, assaults upon children. Of diseases, she preferred the lingering or incurable"—and her persistent fascination with the girl's artificial leg is reflected and fulfilled in his successful theft of it. Even her "beady steel-pointed eyes" reappear at a higher pitch of intensity in his "like two steel spikes" as they leer at the filched trophy. If Joy at last turns out to be truly her mother's daughter, so Mrs. Freeman emerges as a symbolic mother to the Bible salesman. And as he is given the last triumphant word in his duel with the girl, so Mrs. Freeman, characteristically pulling an "evil-smelling onion shoot" from the ground, has the final ironic word in the story: " 'Some can't be that simple [as the Bible salesman appeared to be],' she said. 'I know I never could.' "

The relationship between the two women which frames the central action thus **12.** turns out to be a less sinister version of the encounter between their real and symbolic children. Like her daughter, Mrs. Hopewell persuades herself that she is in control of the situation, and like her she is self-deceived, for it is Mrs. Freeman with her mechanical, "driving" gaze, her imperviousness, and her ability always to get the last word who dominates their relationship. If "Good Country People" does not quite present parallel plots—the central encounter becomes a dramatic reversal, the framing action remains static and ongoing—it does set before us four characters in interlocking reflective relationship, like facing mirrors slightly askew. The Bible salesman has the role of the classic double figure, but he is only the center of the set of images and identities that cast back mocking versions of one another. "Everybody is different," all agree, whether as folk banality or as the secret nourishing of the hidden self; but what the story dramatizes is how appallingly small and superficial those differences are. Some people are indeed more alike than others.

WORKING WITH THE TEXT

Cultural and Historical References

In this section the numbers at the margin refer to the numbered paragraphs in the selection itself.

2. Vulcan is the ugly god of fire and craftsmanship. The beautiful goddess, Venus, was hopelessly in love with him.

8. The Misfit is a nihilistic murderer in another of O'Connor's stories, "A Good Man Is Hard to Find."

10. "A View of the Woods" is a story in the O'Connor collection *Everything That Rises Must Converge.*

Writing Assignments: The Paragraph

Be sure to provide an introduction for each of the following paragraph writing assignments. That is, begin each paragraph with a phrase like this: "Thomas Brickle claims that. . . ." When it is relevant, you might also want to identify the expertise of the author ("Thomas Brickle, a New Testament scholar, claims that. . . ."), the name of the book or article, the century and country in which the work appeared, or any other circumstances that your readers might find significant. For more on this, see pp. 11–13 in Chapter 2.

1. In a paragraph, explain how Hulga is a doppelganger of Manley Pointer. Begin by looking up the word "doppelganger" in a good dictionary.

2. In paragraph 2 Asals only suggests what the Vulcan image means to Hulga. Write a paragraph on what it means.

Writing Assignments: The Short Essay

Use informal documentation for these short essays. That is, don't use footnotes or a Works Cited page to document your sources. Instead, cite only relevant information about your source, and keep that information *within* your text. Then follow the summary or quote with a page number in parenthesis. (Use the page numbers that you find in this book to represent the page numbers of the source.) Thus, your informal documentation will look something like this:

In "An Explication of Good Country People," Virgil Scott, professor emeritus at Michigan State University, says that Joy is a "spiritual as well as a physical cripple" (p. 293).

1. Asals says that the Pointer-Hulga relationship is "ironically reflected in the Hopewell-Freeman relationship." How does it differ?

2. What are Hulga's illusions? Refer to comments by Asals as you develop your paper.

3. Write a paper on the Vulcan image in paragraph 2. What does it mean to Hulga? How does it fit Hulga? How does it reveal her secret life? What does that secret life consist of?

ROUGH BEASTS AND MYSTERIES: IRONY AND VISION IN FLANNERY O'CONNOR'S 'GOOD COUNTRY PEOPLE'

Patricia A. Deduck

In this essay, Patricia Deduck focuses her attention on Flannery O'Connor's almost unique vision among twentieth-century American writers—a vision of Christian mystery and revelation in a scientific age. According to Deduck, Joy-Hulga represents those who have rejected a spiritual view of life (or, in O'Connor's more specific terms, a Christian view of life) and have embraced, to their misfortune, an existentialist view of the universe. An interesting sidelight in this essay is Deduck's argument, early on, that O'Connor shared significant physical and psychological traits with her creation, Joy-Hulga.

Flannery O'Connor is a writer who, as one critic puts it, "reacquaints a scientific **1.** age with the eternal mystery of life."[1] Indeed, as evidenced by her fiction, and in her writings about the craft of fiction, the apperception of mystery is seen by O'Connor as the essential *raison d'être* of the writer. "The writer," she claims, "puts us in the middle of some human action and shows it as it is illuminated and outlined by mystery."[2] And again, she writes: "What he [the writer] sees on the surface will be of interest to him only as he can go through it into an experience of mystery itself. His kind of fiction will always be pushing its own limits outward toward the limits of mystery."[3] In her story, "Good Country People," Flannery O'Connor takes the reader with her through the surface of an encounter between a thirty-two year old Ph.D. with an artificial leg and a traveling Bible salesman and into an experience of the mysteries of life—the interdependence of goodness and evil, the often gratuitous gift of grace, the redemptive power of sudden revelation. Because the story deepens the sense of mystery and because it contains recurrent characters and themes, it serves as a good introduction to Flannery O'Connor's work and thought.

Written in 1955 and included in the collection, *A Good Man is Hard to Find*, **2.** "Good Country People" is an unusual O'Connor story in that it was written in four

Source: Patricia A. Deduck, "Rough Beasts and Mysteries: Irony and Vision in Flannery O'Connor's 'Good Country People,'" *Proceedings of the Conference of College Teachers of English of Texas,* Vol. XLIX. Sept. 1984.

days. In general, O'Connor spent months writing her stories, followed by months of revising and modifying them. But, as she noted in a letter to a friend, the four-day composition of "Good Country People" was "the shortest I have ever written anything in, just sat down and wrote it."[4] In other letters, O'Connor referred to "Good Country People" as "a very hot story" written "at the last minute," a story "that pleases me no end."[5]

As some critics propose, O'Connor's pleasure may have to do with the creation of **3.** the character Joy-Hulga, whom one critic calls "the author's cruelest self-caricature."[6] While it is possible to make some comparisons between Joy-Hulga and O'Connor on the basis of their physical conditions—Joy-Hulga has an artificial leg, as a result of a hunting accident in her childhood, and a weak heart; O'Connor was stricken with disseminated lupis, and as a result of medication which weakened her bones, eventually had to use a cane and then aluminum crutches with arm supports to walk—these similarities are not, I believe, particularly important. A greater significance may be found in the fact that both the author and her protagonist share the condition of alienation. O'Connor, as almost all her critics point out, was alienated from the dominant assumptions of her culture; she was an outsider not only as a woman and a Southerner, but also as a Roman Catholic living in the deep South. Joy-Hulga is an outsider not only by virtue of her education and intellectual interests, but also by virtue of her being an atheist-existentialist in a fundamentalist family. Out of her awareness of her own multiple alienation, O'Connor may indeed have conceived Joy-Hulga as her fictional counterpart.

However, we would be doing the story and its author a disservice to place too **4.** much emphasis on its biographical dimensions. While the impetus for O'Connor's writing of "Good Country People" may lie in the personal realm, the story itself presents in both its narrative situation and its themes, a more universal vision, which is, ultimately, the hallmark of O'Connor's fiction. And the author herself often warned the reader against purely biographical analysis.

> Fiction doesn't lie, but it can't tell the whole truth. What would you
> make out about me just from reading "Good Country People"? Plenty,
> but not the whole story. Anyway, you have to look at a novel or a sto-
> ry as a novel or a story; as saying something about life colored by a
> writer, not about the writer colored by life. She distorts herself to make
> a better story so you can't judge her by the story.[7]

What can be judged by the story is the depth of O'Connor's spiritual vision of the mystery of life. Like many of her stories, "Good Country People" focuses on a spiritually crippled human being and recounts the sudden revelation that forces the character to understand herself in new terms, with new objectivity, while confronting the usually painful consequences of her past blindness.

The story, very simply, presents us with the encounter of its protagonist, Joy- **5.** Hulga Hopewell—Ph.D. in philosophy, thirty-two years old, an amputee, living with her rather simplistic and superficial mother—with a traveling Bible Salesman, nineteen years old, named Manley Pointer. Joy-Hulga sets out to seduce the salesman, but ends up betrayed and helpless in a hayloft after he steals her artificial leg. The story engages us with several favorite O'Connor themes: change of identity and transformation, the limits of subjective perception, and the achievement of wisdom through folly. Structurally, the story follows a typical O'Connor format. We are presented with the protagonist in her typical, daily environment, and come to understand her orientation to life and to others through her history and her interaction with those surrounding her. Then the story builds to a climax as the result of an encounter with an outsider who in some way challenges the perceptions, illusions, and comfortable assumptions of the protagonist. Joy-Hulga is first presented against the empty, trite conversation of her mother and the wife of their tenant farmer, Mrs. Freeman. Mrs. Hopewell is a rather simple, well-meaning woman, who sees the world in dualistic terms: people, for example, can be divided into two groups—"trash" and "good country people." Both Mrs. Hopewell and Mrs. Freeman continually spout shallow aphorisms and are disgustingly optimistic. The grossness and insensitivity of these two provide a strong contrast to the hypersensitivity of Joy-Hulga and partially account for her alienation and frustration. Joy-Hulga's loss of her leg when she was only ten years of age, (it was, we are told, "literally blasted off" and yet she "had never lost consciousness") must have been a traumatic experience and led her to her sense of despair and her renunciation of God. This renunciation is symbolized by her changing her name from Joy to Hulga, a name which, we are told, she had arrived at first purely on the basis of its ugly sound, but then the full genius of its fitness had struck her. "She saw it as the name of her highest creative act. One of her major triumphs was that her mother had not been able to turn her dust into Joy, but the greater one was that she had been able to turn it herself into Hulga."

Her physical deformity is also meant to reflect her spiritual incompleteness or **6.** lameness. She has rejected Christianity not on personal grounds, but on the basis of philosophical considerations. In its place, Joy-Hulga embraces the secular doctrine of existentialism, which has led her to believe only in nothingness. Indeed, we see this from the books that Joy-Hulga reads, one of which contains a passage on "Nothing" (which she has underlined). The words, we are told, work on Joy's mother, when she reads them, "like some evil incantation in gibberish." The passage gives us some insight into Joy's position.

> If science is right, then one thing stands firm: science wishes to know
> nothing of nothing. Such is after all the strictly scientific approach to
> Nothing. We know it by wishing to know nothing of Nothing.

These words take on even greater significance during the seduction scene, when Joy-Hulga tells the Bible salesman: "I don't have illusions. I'm one of those people who see through to nothing." And later, "We are all damned, but some of us have taken off our blindfolds and see that there's nothing to see. It's a kind of salvation." Thus, the character of Joy-Hulga reveals the existentialist dilemma—the violent struggle to believe in nothing, to renounce the religious orientation passed on by her mother and society. That such renunciation is a struggle is indicated by Joy-Hulga's eyes, for she is described as having "the look of someone who has achieved blindness by an act of will and means to keep it." Joy-Hulga wishes to know nothing of nothing, but her encounter with Manley Pointer forces her to confront certain realities, while it tests the firmness of her secular faith.

To understand the epiphany Joy-Hulga experiences as a result of her liaison with **7.**

Pointer, we must examine her attitude toward her artificial leg, an important symbol in the story. We are told that "she was as sensitive about the artificial leg as a peacock about his tail. No one ever touched it but her. She took care of it as someone else would his soul, in private and almost with her own eyes turned away." Just as the leg is a symbol of deprivation (it is meant to replace the "nothingness" of her missing limb), it is also a symbol of her difference. Indeed, it is this difference that the salesman points to—"You ain't like anybody else," he says—a statement which, the narrator notes, "touched the truth about her." Joy-Hulga's leg has thus become for her an object rather than part of her body; yet it is an intimate part of her, as the soul is. Still, she "stumps" and "bangs loudly," "hulks around" on it when she walks, indicating that she is perhaps as contemptuous of it as she is of the notions of God and the soul. By virtue of both symbolic dimensions—deprivation and difference—the leg suggests that the philosophy of negation with which Joy-Hulga has propped up her life is also artificial—"strapped on" rather than integral to her being, "ending in an ugly jointure," that is, it does not complete her in a harmonious way as a human being.

In the seduction scene, it is the leg which Manley Pointer seems most interested **8.** in and, indeed, he asks Joy-Hulga to prove her love by showing him where it joins on. When she agrees to, we are told that "it was like losing her own life and finding it again, miraculously, in his." Pointer handles the leg with "reverence" and "tenderness." Joy-Hulga imagines "she would run away with him and that every night he would take the leg off and every morning put it back on again." Her fantasies of the night before had been just as simplistic and naive. She had imagined that "she very easily seduced him and that then, of course, had to reckon with his remorse. She imagined that she took his remorse in hand and changed it into a deeper understanding of life. She took all his shame away and turned it into something useful." The irony, of course, is that reality does not conform to Joy's expectations. Pointer turns out to be not the naive, inexperienced child Joy-Hulga has imagined him to be. He has come prepared with some pornographic playing cards, whiskey, and a package of contraceptives, which he takes from a hollowed-out Bible. Then he refuses to give Joy back her leg after he has removed it, and throws himself on her. She is shocked and in her horror she resorts to questions like, "Aren't you just good country people?" and then screams, "You're a Christian, you're a fine Christian!" Here she uses, to no avail, the very platitudes for which she had scorned her mother. Joy-Hulga is revealed to be much like her mother—she is incapable of belief in nothingness, yet also incapable of professing a belief in its opposite, in this case, love and trust of another human being. Pointer's response is to tell her, "I'm as good as you any day in the week. I may sell Bibles, but I know which end is up and I wasn't born yesterday and I know where I'm going."

Joy-Hulga, of course, has not known where she was going. Her intellectual pride, **9.** her condescension towards others, her deliberate rudeness, and her flirtation with nihilism have blinded her to the realities of her situation. Like her leg, her philosophy has been easily removed, and in its absence, she is helpless and dependent. It is the salesman, himself a fake Christian, who exposes Joy-Hulga as a fake atheist, who causes her to see that her pride and assumed superiority are merely ignorance and gullibility. "You just a while ago said you didn't believe in nothing," Pointer says scornfully, and then, packing up her leg in his suitcase, informs her: "You ain't so smart. I been believing in nothing ever since I was born!"

Thus, Joy-Hulga is left, literally and philosophically, without a leg to stand on. **10.** Pointer has also taken her glasses, so she is left, too, to deal with her blindness. She had failed to recognize the significance of her encounter with the salesman. Confronted with a true nihilist, she is made to acknowledge the reality of evil (her own and Pointer's), the "nothingness" of her philosophical beliefs, and to realize her vulnerability. Her philosophy of negation has been "blasted away" as suddenly and irrevocably as her leg had been. When she learns the true physical value of her leg, she also realizes the uselessness of an artificially-engendered philosophy. Perhaps the greatest irony is that Manley Pointer, the nineteen-year old uneducated embodiment of evil and nihilism, who turns out to be as phoney as Joy-Hulga, is instrumental in bringing her to wisdom, by his humiliation of her and her beliefs. It is this that Flannery O'Connor would point to as "mystery."

The power of O'Connor's fiction, as "Good Country People" illustrates, lies in **11.** the irony that emerges from an extremely objective view of reality. Neither Joy-Hulga nor Manley Pointer is a "good" character, nor is either completely evil. Rather, from O'Connor's brutally honest depiction, both are lacking, both are grotesque or misfits in some way. And yet, O'Connor elicits a certain compassion for both. Even though most critics have shown little sympathy for Manley Pointer, I believe we cannot exclude him from ours. His stealing of the leg may seem to be a heinously evil act, but his initial attraction to and subsequent admiration for Joy-Hulga appear sincere and genuine and are fed by her pretended interest in him. He too has been cheated by being scorned and rejected, and he carries away with him only an artificial limb, not the love or fellowship we may assume he had hoped for. I believe such a view would be appropriate to the spirit of O'Connor's vision. As she has said, in response to reviews that called the collection, *A Good Man is Hard to Find*, brutal and sarcastic: "The stories are hard because there is nothing harder or less sentimental than Christian realism. I believe that there are many rough beasts now slouching toward Bethlehem to be born and that I have reported the progress of a few of them." As "Good Country People" reveals in its portraits of several of these "rough beasts," to Flannery O'Connor, life, in all its homeliness, its paradox, even its brutality, is not only worthy of the attentions of art, but more, responsive to the human desire to find meaning, order, and spiritual perfection through the redeeming apperception of mystery.

Notes

[1] Alfred L. Castle, "Karl Jaspers and Flannery O'Connor: The Hermeneutic of Being in 'A Good Man is Hard to Find,' " *Southwest Philosophical Studies*, 6 (April 1981), p. 134.

[2] Flannery O'Connor, "Replies to Two Questions," in Melvin J. Friedman and Lewis A. Lawson (Eds.), *The Added Dimension: The Art and Mind of Flannery O'Connor* (New York: Fordham University Press, 1966), p. 254.

[3] Flannery O'Connor, *Mystery and Manners* (New York: Farrar, Straus and Giroux, 1961), p. 42.

[4] Letter to "A." (1 June 1956), in Sally Fitzgerald (Ed.), *The Habit of Being* (New York: Vintage, 1980), p. 160.

[5] Letters to Sally and Robert Fitzgerald (1 April 1955) and to Ben Griffith (4 May 1955), *op. cit.*, pp. 76 & 78.

[6] Stanley Edgar Hyman, *Flannery O'Connor*, 54, "University of Minnesota Pamphlets on American Writers" (Minneapolis: University of Minnesota Press, 1966), p. 16.

[7] Letter to "A." (19 May 1956), *op. cit.*, p. 158.

[8] Letter to "A." (20 July 1955), *op. cit.*, p. 90.

WORKING WITH THE TEXT

Cultural and Historical References

In this section, the numbers at the margin refer to the numbered paragraphs in the selection itself.

1. "Mystery" is a technical Christian term that means a religious truth that is revealed through Christ. Late in this paragraph Deduck elaborates on that definition.

1. "Grace" is also a technical Christian word for the divine love—or other gifts—that is freely given to individuals or humanity.

6. "Existentialism" is a philosophy, usually associated with Jean Paul Sartre, which is atheistic, materialistic, and pessimistic.

11. The "rough beasts" in this paragraph refers to the rough beast in W. B. Yeats's. "The Second Coming," a poem in which the beast represents the cold and cruel nature of the cycle of civilization that will follow the present Christian cycle.

Writing Assignments: The Paragraph

Be sure to provide an introduction for each of the following paragraph writing assignments. That is, begin each paragraph with a phrase like this: "Thomas Brickle claims that. . . ." When it is relevant, you might also want to identify the expertise of the author ("Thomas Brickle, a New Testament scholar, claims that. . . ."), the name of the book or article, the century and country in which the work appeared, or any other circumstances that your readers might find significant. For more on this, see pp. 11–13 in Chapter 2.

1. Explain Deduck's description of what the artificial leg means to Hulga. See paragraph 7.

2. Summarize paragraphs 3 and 4. Quote at least one passage from those paragraphs.

3. Describe the purpose of paragraph 2. Can it be justified? Or is it off-track? What does it add to the essay? How does it detract?

4. Deduck spends paragraphs 2 and 3 on biography and then begins paragraph 4 with an interesting comment on the use of biography. Describe Deduck's movement from paragraph 2 to paragraph 4, including, if you wish, a critical comment or two on the sequence.

Writing Assignments: The Short Essay

Use informal documentation for these short essays. That is, don't use footnotes or a Works Cited page to document your sources. Instead, cite only relevant information about your source, and keep that information *within* your text. Then follow the summary or quote with a page number in parenthe-

ses. (Use the page numbers that you find in this book to represent the page numbers of the source.) Thus, your informal documentation will look something like this:

> In "An Explication of Good Country People," Virgil Scott, professor emeritus at Michigan State University, says that Joy is a "spiritual as well as a physical cripple" (p. 293).

1. Read W. B. Yeats's "The Second Coming" and point out similarities between Yeats's vision in that poem (you may need help with it) and O'Connor's vision as explained by Deduck. See Deduck's last paragraph in particular.

2. Draw specific contrasts between Hulga and her mother. What exactly has Hulga rejected from her mother's world? How is that rejection portrayed? Quote from Deduck's essay at least once in your paper.

3. Deduck says in paragraph 10 that Hulga has been brought to "wisdom." Write a paper in which you show where and how O'Connor indicates that Hulga has been changed for the better by her encounter with Manley Pointer.

4. O'Connor says, in paragraph 11, that there are some "rough beasts" in her story. Write a paper in which you show who those rough beasts are.

ESSAYS ON *GOOD COUNTRY PEOPLE*

Short Essays

Use informal documentation for these short essays. That is, don't use footnotes or a Works Cited page to document your sources. Instead, cite only
relevant information about your source, and keep that information *within*
your text. Then follow the summary or quote with a page number in parenthesis. (Use the page numbers that you find in this book to represent the
page numbers of the source.) Thus, your informal documentation will look
something like this:

> In *The Romance of Medicine*, Benjamin Gordon, a history professor,
> claims that it was once believed that red wine replenished a per-
> son's depleted blood supply (p. 121).

1. Disagree with anything in one of the critical essays.

2. Gather up the various comments about Mrs. Freeman and write a paper
   on her part in the story.

3. Gather up comments about the names of the characters and write a
   paper about O'Connor's use of names to suggest ideas.

4. Analyze the various connections between Hulga and Manley Pointer
   and point out the similarities between the two. Begin by showing how
   much they *seem* to differ. Use at least three essays.

Long Essays

For rules governing formal documentation, see Chapter 6.

1. Begin an essay with this statement by Virgil Scott: "The late Flannery
   O'Connor was a Roman Catholic, and many of her stories depict 'sick
   souls' in a sick environment." Along the way support your analysis
   with paraphrases and quotations from two writers in addition to Scott.

2. After having read the critical essays in this chapter, explicate "Good
   Country People." Quote and paraphrase from at least three essays.

3. Using three or four critical essays, write an essay in which you show
   that the heart conditions of Hulga and Pointer are spiritual as well as
   physical.

— 10 —

Animal Rights:

Where Do We Draw the Line?

INTRODUCTION

Since the publication of Peter Singer's *Animal Liberation* in 1975, more and more Americans and Europeans have begun to question a basic cultural assumption with which we have lived comfortably for centuries: that because we, as humans, worship a higher being, have created a complicated means of communication, and were even, some believe, created in God's image, we have every right to exploit the rest of the living world for our purposes—and that the pain suffered by animals to enhance our welfare is of little account. Indeed, even in recent history, the laws that prohibited cock fighting and bear baiting were enacted not necessarily to prevent cruelty to animals but to prevent the moral degradation of those who might get pleasure from watching cocks tear one another apart and dogs mangle chained bears.

In the past decade or so, however, such assumptions have been vigorously attacked. Animal rights advocates insist that the cultural assumption that the welfare of nonhuman species is always subordinate to human interests is the equivalent of racism. They call it "speciesism." Failing to recognize inherent rights shared by all living creatures, the animal rights advocates say, is analogous to our culture's past failure to recognize the humanity of black slaves. What animals may not share with us—intellect and language—is not relevant. It is what animals *do indeed* share with us that counts: the capacity to experience physical and psychological pain. Cruelty to animals, hence, is wrong because animals suffer, not merely because such activity diminishes human moral character. Those who defend animals insist that if we are not willing to sacrifice or exploit "marginal" human beings—infants, the very old, or the severely retarded—to advance our welfare, then we have no right to impose suffering and death upon nonhumans for such purposes.

The goals of the numerous animal rights organizations which have emerged over the past two decades vary. The more extreme among them would have us gradually rid ourselves of all domestic pets and become vegetarians. For the time being, however, most of these groups have focused upon an issue less threatening to the general public—the use of laboratory animals in medical and psychological research. According to federal estimates, laboratories "use up" some 17 million to 22 million animals annually, including some 50,000 cats, 61,000 primates, 180,000 dogs, 554,000 rabbits, and millions of mice and rats.

Animal rights activists make their case against the animal research industry by simply describing, usually in graphic detail, specific examples of research reported on in professional journals—examples which sometimes involve the torture and death of thousands of animals, all sacrificed for studies whose conclusions were self-evident, trivial, or redundant. The particulars of such studies do tend to leave the general public outraged; indeed, the exposure of one such study conducted on dogs by the Pentagon several years ago triggered an avalanche of angry mail, much more mail than that prompted by the bombing of civilian populations in North Vietnam in the early 1970s. Some of the more militant groups, moreover, have punctuated their rhetoric with raids on animal research centers, sit-ins, and boycotts of cosmetic products which have been developed with animal experimentation. These tactics have had an inhibiting influence on the research community.

Animal researchers have reacted with dismay to the heat their studies have engendered. While conceding that in a few cases some researchers have been neglectful and irresponsible with their research animals, they adamantly insist that they have been vigilant in their efforts to minimize needless animal suffering, and numerous research institutions have reacted to recent criticism by adopting more stringent standards for animal care and study. The federal government, too, has expressed its concern by amending the 1970 Animal Welfare Act in 1985 to provide more rigorous requirements for the care of laboratory animals.

What the research community fears, however, is that animal rights activists will gain enough public support to virtually cripple the medical research that has been the very basis for *all* of the medical advances over the past 100 years. They insist that *every* wonder drug, *every* life-saving surgical procedure, *every* effective psychological therapy was first tried on animals, and they predict that the rush of medical technology will slow to a trickle without the preliminary experimental research that must be conducted on animals. The issue, for them, doesn't finally boil down to moral principles. What is at stake for us all, they argue, is nothing less than a practical strategy for human survival.

Animal rights activists aren't convinced by such talk. They insist that most such research could be radically reduced with no real human loss and that necessary experimental research could be performed on computer models. Researchers retort that such assumptions are hopelessly naive.

The controversy over animal rights may be a new arrival on the scene, but it is certainly no flash in the pan. Indeed, as long as we share this planet with nonhuman creatures, we're surely going to worry—as well we should—about our proper relationship with them.

ANIMAL LIBERATION

Peter Singer

Peter Singer, the author of *Democracy and Civil Disobedience, Practical Ethics, The Expanding Circle,* and several other books, is a former Radcliffe lecturer at University College, Oxford and is now Director of the Centre for Human Bioethics at Monash University in Melbourne, Australia. The following selection is an excerpt from the book credited with sparking the animal rights movement in the United States. Just prior to this excerpt, Singer has presented nearly thirty-five pages of examples of laboratory experiments, all described in professional journals, which involve agony, torture, and death for myriad mammals. Singer contends that the studies involving these animals were self-evident, trivial, or redundant. In the following paragraphs he attacks the research industry's callousness, laziness, and negligence in connection with the use of animals in research, and he goes on to prescribe solutions for the problem.

How can these things happen? How can a man who is not a sadist spend his **1.** working day heating an unanesthetized dog to death, or driving a monkey into a lifelong depression, and then remove his white coat, wash his hands, and go home to dinner with his wife and children? How can taxpayers allow their money to be used to support experiments of this kind? And how can students go through a turbulent era of protest against injustice, discrimination, and oppression of all kinds, no matter how far from home, while ignoring the cruelties that are being carried out on their own campuses?

The answers to these questions stem from the unquestioned acceptance of **2.** speciesism. We tolerate cruelties inflicted on members of other species that would outrage us if performed on members of our own species. Speciesism allows researchers to regard the animals they experiment on as items of equipment, laboratory tools rather than living, suffering creatures. Sometimes they even refer to the animals in this way. Robert White of the Cleveland Metropolitan General Hospital, who has performed numerous experiments involving the transplanting of heads of monkeys, and the keeping alive of monkey brains in fluid, outside the body, has said in an interview that:

> Our main purpose here is to offer a living laboratory tool: a monkey "model" in which and by which we can design new operative techniques for the brain.

And the reporter who conducted the interview and observed White's experiments found his experience

> a rare and chilling glimpse into the cold, clinical world of the scientist, where the life of an animal has no meaning beyond the immediate purpose of experimentation.[1]

Source: Peter Singer, *Animal Liberation.* New York: Avon Books, 1977. 62–67, 69–70, 74–86, 89–91.

This "scientific" attitude to animals was exhibited to a large audience in **3.**
December 1974 when the American public television network brought together Harvard
philosopher Robert Nozick and three scientists whose work involves animals. The
program was a follow-up to Fred Wiseman's controversial film *Primate*, which had
taken viewers inside the Yerkes Primate Center, a research center in Atlanta, Georgia.
Nozick asked the scientists whether the fact that an experiment will kill hundreds of
animals is ever regarded, by scientists, as a reason for not performing it. One of the
scientists answered: "Not that I know of." Nozick pressed his question: "Don't the
animals count at all?" Dr. A. Perachio, of the Yerkes Center, replied: "Why should
they?" while Dr. D. Baltimore, of the Massachusetts Institute of Technology, added
that he did not think that experimenting on animals raised a moral issue at all.[2]

As well as the general attitude of speciesism which researchers share with other **4.**
citizens there are some special factors operating to make possible the experiments I
have described. Foremost among these is the immense respect that we still have for
scientists. Although the advent of nuclear weapons and environmental pollution have
made us realize that science and technology need to be controlled to some extent, we
still tend to be in awe of anyone who wears a white coat and has a PhD. In a
well-known series of experiments Stanley Milgram, a Harvard psychologist, has
demonstrated that ordinary people will obey the direction of a white-coated research
worker to administer what appears to be (but in fact is not) electric shock to a human
subject as "punishment" for failing to answer questions correctly; and they will
continue to do this even when the human subject cries out and pretends to be in great
pain.[3] If this can happen when the participant believes he is inflicting pain on a human,
how much easier is it for a student to push aside his initial qualms when his professor
instructs him to perform experiments on animals? What Alice Heim has rightly called
the "indoctrination" of the student is a gradual process, beginning with the dissection
of frogs in school biology classes. When the budding medical student, or psychology
student, or veterinarian, reaches the university and finds that to complete the course of
studies on which he has set his heart he must experiment on living animals, it is difficult
for him to refuse to do so, especially since he knows that what he is being asked to
do is standard practice in the field.

Individual students will often admit feeling uneasy about what they are asked to **5.**
do, but public protests are very rare. An organized protest did occur in Britain
recently, however, when students at the Welsh National School of Medicine in Cardiff
complained publicly that a dog was unnecessarily injected with drugs more than 30
times to demonstrate a point during a lecture. The dog was then killed. One student
said: "We learned nothing new. It could all have been looked up in textbooks. A film
could be made so that only one dog dies and all this unnecessary suffering is stopped."[4]
The student's comment was true; but such things happen routinely in every medical
school. Why are protests so rare?

The pressure to conform does not let up when the student receives his degree. **6.**
If he goes on to a graduate degree in fields in which experiments on animals are usual,
he will be encouraged to devise his own experiments and write them up for his PhD
dissertation. We have already seen examples of work by PhD students—one student
was a member of the team that irradiated beagles at the University of Rochester, [a
study involving] the electric shocking of ducklings was work toward a PhD; and so

was [an] experiment involving thirst and electric shock. . . . Naturally, if this is how students are educated they will tend to continue in the same manner when they become professors, and they will, in turn, train their own students in the same manner.

It is not always easy for people outside the universities to understand the rationale   **7.** for the research carried out under university auspices. Originally, perhaps, scholars and researchers just set out to solve the most important problems and did not allow themselves to be influenced by other considerations. Perhaps some are still motivated by these concerns. Too often, though, academic research gets bogged down in petty and insignificant details because the big questions have been studied already, and have either been solved or proven too difficult. So the researcher turns away from the well-ploughed fertile fields in search of virgin territory where whatever he learns will be new, although the connection with a major problem may be more remote. So we find articles in the scientific journals with introductions like the following:

> Although swelling from trauma and inflammatory agents has been the subject of investigation for years, meager information exists on the quantitative changes that occur over a period of time. . . . In the present study a simple method was developed for measuring the volume of the rodent tail, and the changes which occur after standardized trauma have been reported.[5]

The "simple method" involves severely injuring the tails of seventy-three unanesthetized mice; and it is difficult to see how measuring the swelling of the tail of mouse can tell us much about anything—except the amount a mouse's tail swells. Here is another example: While "the effects of controlled hemorrhage resulting in reversible and irreversible shock have been studied in detail" there are "relatively few articles concerned with the controlled study of exsanguinating hemorrhage"—that is, hemorrhage that drains the body of all its blood, or at least until death occurs. Noting that patterns of dying from suffocation, drowning, and other causes have been studied in detail but that studies of the general pattern of death from exsanguinating hemorrhage have been "based on experiments performed on very few animals," experimenters gave sixty-five dogs an anesthetic that permitted "quick recovery . . . and study of the dying process without the influence of deep anesthesia." They then opened the aortic cannula in each dog and watched them go through a period they termed "the agonal state" which took up to ten minutes and was terminated by death. The experimenters describe their report as "merely a description of observations" and not an attempt to elucidate the mechanisms of the changes observed.[6]

When we read reports of experiments that cause pain and are apparently not even   **8.** intended to produce results of real significance we are at first inclined to think that there must be more to what is being done than we can understand—that the scientist must have some better reason for doing what he is doing than his report indicates. Yet as we go more deeply into the subject we find that what appears trivial on the surface very often really *is* trivial. Experimenters themselves often unofficially admit this. H. F. Harlow, whose experiments on monkeys I described earlier, was for twelve years editor of the *Journal of Comparative and Physiological Psychology*, a journal which publishes more reports of painful experiments on animals than almost any other. At the end of this period, in which Harlow estimates he reviewed about 2,500 manuscripts submitted for publication, he wrote, in a semihumourous farewell note, that "most experiments are not worth doing and the data attained are not worth publishing."

On reflection, perhaps this is not so surprising. Researchers, even those in **9.** psychology, medicine, and the biological sciences, are human beings and are susceptible to the same influences as any other human beings. They like to get on in their careers, to be promoted, and to have their work read and discussed by their colleagues. Publishing papers in the appropriate journals is an important element in the rise up the ladder of promotion and increased prestige. This happens in every field, in philosophy or history as much as in psychology or medicine, and it is entirely understandable and in itself hardly worth criticizing. The philosopher or historian who publishes to improve his career prospect does little harm beyond wasting paper and boring his colleagues; the psychologist or medical researcher, or anyone else whose work involves experimenting on animals, however, can cause severe pain or prolonged suffering. His work should therefore be subject to much stricter standards of necessity.

Once a pattern of animal experimentation becomes the accepted mode of research **10.** in a particular field, the process is self-reinforcing and difficult to break out of. Not only publications and promotions but also the awards and grants that finance research become geared to animal experiments. A proposal for a new experiment with animals is something that the administrators of research funds will be ready to support, if they have in the past supported other experiments on animals. New nonanimal-using methods will seem less familiar and will be less likely to receive support.

Those government agencies in the United States, Britain, and elsewhere that **11.** promote research in the biological sciences have become the major backers of experiments on animals. Indeed, public funds, derived from taxation, have paid for the vast majority of the experiments described in this chapter. Many of these agencies are paying for experiments that have only the remotest connection with the purposes for which the agencies were set up. . . .

Since these experiments are paid for by government bodies, it is hardly necessary **12.** to add that there is no law that prevents the scientist from carrying them out. There are laws that prevent ordinary people from beating their dogs to death, but a scientist can do the same thing with impunity, and with no one to check whether his doing so is likely to lead to benefits that would not occur from an ordinary beating. The reason for this is that the strength and prestige of the scientific establishment, supported by the various interest groups—including those who breed animals for sale to laboratories —have been sufficient to stop all attempts at effective legal control.

In the United States the only federal law on the matter is the Animal Welfare **13.** Act of 1970, which amended a 1966 act. The law set standards for the transportation, housing, and handling of animals sold as pets, exhibited, or intended for use in research. So far as actual experimentation is concerned, however, it effectively allows the researcher to do exactly as he pleases. One section of the law requires that those facilities which register under the act (and neither government agencies doing research nor many small facilities have to register) must lodge a report stating that when painful experiments were performed without the use of pain-relieving drugs this was necessary to achieve the objectives of the research project. No attempt is made to assess whether these "objectives" are sufficiently important to justify the infliction of pain. Under these circumstances the requirement does no more than make additional paperwork.

You can't, of course, electric shock a dog into a state of helplessness if you anesthetize him at the same time; nor can you produce depression in a monkey while keeping him happy with drugs. So you can truthfully state that the objectives of the experiment cannot be achieved if pain-relieving drugs are used, and then go on with the experiment as you would have done before the act came into existence. . . .

14.   When are experiments on animals justifiable? Upon learning of the nature of many contemporary experiments, many people react by saying that all experiments on animals should be prohibited immediately. But if we make our demands as absolute as this, the experimenters have a ready reply: Would we be prepared to let thousands of humans die if they could be saved by a single experiment on a single animal?

15.   This question is, of course, purely hypothetical. There never has been and there never could be a single experiment that saves thousands of lives. The way to reply to this hypothetical question is to pose another: Would the experimenter be prepared to carry out his experiment on a human orphan under six months old if that were the only way to save thousands of lives?

16.   If the experimenter would not be prepared to use a human infant then his readiness to use nonhuman animals reveals an unjustifiable form of discrimination on the basis of species, since adult apes, monkeys, dogs, cats, rats, and other mammals are more aware of what is happening to them, more self-directing, and, so far as we can tell, at least as sensitive to pain as a human infant. (I specified that the human infant be an orphan to avoid the complications of the feelings of parents, although in so doing I am being overfair to the experimenter, since the nonhuman animals used in experiments are not orphans and in many species the separation of mother and young clearly causes distress for both.)

17.   There is no characteristic that human infants possess to a higher degree than adult nonhuman animals, unless we are to count the infant's potential as a characteristic that makes it wrong to experiment on him. Whether this characteristic should count is controversial—if we count it, we shall have to condemn abortion along with experiments on infants, since the potential of the infant and the fetus is the same. To avoid the complexities of this issue, however, we can alter our original question a little and assume that the infant is one with severe and irreversible brain damage that makes it impossible for him ever to develop beyond the level of a six-month-old infant. There are, unfortunately, many such human beings, locked away in special wards throughout the country, many of them long since abandoned by their parents. Despite their mental deficiencies, their anatomy and physiology is in nearly all respects identical with that of normal humans. If, therefore, we were to force-feed them with large quantities of floor polish, or drip concentrated solutions of cosmetics into their eyes, we would have a much more reliable indication of the safety of these products for other humans than we now get by attemptng to extrapolate the results of tests on a variety of other species. The radiation experiments, the heatstroke experiments, and many other experiments described earlier in this chapter could also have told us more about human reactions to the experimental situation if they had been carried out on retarded humans instead of dogs and rabbits.

18.   So whenever an experimenter claims that his experiment is important enough to justify the use of an animal, we should ask him whether he would be prepared to use a retarded human at a similar mental level to the animal he is planning to use. If his

reply is negative, we can assume that he is willing to use a nonhuman animal only because he gives less consideration to the interests of members of other species than he gives to members of his own—and this bias is no more defensible than racism or any other form of arbitrary discrimination.

Of course, no one would seriously propose carrying out the experiments described **19.** in this chapter on retarded humans. Occasionally it has become known that some medical experiments have been performed on humans without their consent, and sometimes on retarded humans; but the consequences of these experiments for the human subjects are almost always trivial by comparison with what is standard practice for nonhuman animals. Still, these experiments on humans usually lead to an outcry against the experimenters, and rightly so. They are, very often, a further example of the arrogance of the research worker who justifies everything on the grounds of increasing knowledge. If experimenting on retarded, orphaned humans would be wrong, why isn't experimenting on nonhuman animals wrong? What difference is there between the two, except for the mere fact that, biologically, one is a member of our species and the other is not: But *that*, surely, is not a morally relevant difference, any more than the fact that a being is not a member of our race is a morally relevant difference.

Actually the analogy between speciesism and racism applies in practice as well **20.** as in theory in the area of experimentation. Blatant speciesism leads to painful experiments on other species, defended on the grounds of its contribution to knowledge and possible usefulness for our species. Blatant racism has led to painful experiments on other races, defended on the grounds of its contribution to knowledge and possible usefulness for the experimenting race. Under the Nazi regime in Germany, nearly 200 doctors, some of them eminent in the world of medicine, took part in experiments on Jews and Russian and Polish prisoners. Thousands of other physicians knew of these experiments, some of which were the subject of lectures at medical academies. Yet the records show that the doctors sat through medical reports of the infliction of horrible injuries on these ''lesser races'' and then proceeded to discuss the medical lessons to be learned from them without anyone making even a mild protest about the nature of the experiments. The parallels between this attitude and that of experimenters today toward animals are striking. Then, as now, the subjects were frozen, heated, and put in decompression chambers. Then, as now, these events were written up in a dispassionate scientific jargon. The following paragraph is taken from a report by a Nazi scientist of an experiment on a human being, placed in a decompression chamber; it could equally have been taken from accounts of recent experiments in this country on animals:

> After five minutes spasms appeared; between the sixth and tenth minute respiration increased in frequency, the TP [test person] losing con-sciousness. From the eleventh to the thirtieth minute respiration slowed down to three inhalations per minute, only to cease entirely at the end of that period . . . about half an hour after breathing had ceased, an autopsy was begun.[7]

Then, as now, the ethic of pursuing knowledge was considered sufficient justification for inflicting agony on those who are placed beyond the limits of genuine moral concern. Our sphere of moral concern is far wider than that of the Nazis; but so long as there are sentient beings outside it, it is not wide enough.

To return to the question of when an experiment might be justifiable. It will not **21.** do to say: "Never!" In extreme circumstances, absolutist answers always break down. Torturing a human being is almost always wrong, but it is not absolutely wrong. If torture were the only way in which we could discover the location of a nuclear time bomb hidden in a New York City basement, then torture would be justifiable. Similarly, if a single experiment could cure a major disease, that experiment would be justifiable. But in actual life the benefits are always much, much more remote, and more often than not they are nonexistent. So how do we decide when an experiment is justifiable?

We have seen that the experimenter reveals a bias in favor of his own species **22.** whenever he carries out an experiment on a nonhuman for a purpose that he would not think justified him in using a human being, even a retarded human being. This principle gives us a guide toward an answer to our question. Since a speciesist bias, like a racist bias, is unjustifiable, an experiment cannot be justifiable unless the experiment is so important that the use of a retarded human being would also be justifiable.

This is not an absolutist principle. I do not believe that it could *never* be justifiable **23.** to experiment on a retarded human. If it really were possible to save many lives by an experiment that would take just one life, and there were *no other way* those lives could be saved, it might be right to do the experiment. But this would be an extremely rare case. Not one tenth of one percent of the experiments now being performed on animals would fall into this category. Certainly none of the experiments described in this chapter could pass this test.

It should not be thought that medical research would grind to a halt if the test **24.** I have proposed were applied, or that a flood of untested products would come onto the market. So far as new products are concerned it is true that, as I have already said, we would have to make do with fewer of them, using ingredients already known to be safe. That does not seem to be any great loss. But for testing really essential products, as well as for other areas of research, alternative methods not requiring animals can be and would be found. Some alternatives exist already and others would develop more rapidly if the energy and resources now applied to experimenting on animals were redirected into the search for alternatives.

At present scientists do not look for alternatives *simply because they do not care* **25.** *enough about the animals they are using.* I make this assertion on the best possible authority, since it has been more or less admitted by Britain's Research Defence Society, a group which exists to defend researchers from criticism by animal welfare organizations. A recent article in the *Bulletin* of the National Society for Medical Research (the American equivalent of the Research Defence Society) described how the British group successfully fought off a proposed amendment to the British law regulating experiments that would have prohibited any experiment using live animals if the purpose of that experiment could be achieved by alternative means not involving animals. The main objections lodged by the Research Defence Society to this very mild attempt at reform were, first, that in some cases it may be cheaper to use animals than other methods, and secondly, that:

> in some cases alternatives may exist but they may be unknown to an investigator. With the vast amount of scientific literature coming out of even a very narrow field of study it is possible that an investigator may not know all that is now known about techniques or results in a particular area. . . .

(This ignorance would make the experimenter liable to prosecution under the proposed amendment.)

What do these objections amount to? The first can mean only one thing: that **26.** economic considerations are more important than the suffering of animals; as for the second, it is a strong argument for a total moratorium on animal experiments until every experimenter has had time to read up on the existing reports of alternatives available in his field and results already obtained. Is it not shocking that experimenters may be inflicting agony on animals only because they have not kept up with the literature in their field—literature that may contain reports of methods of achieving the same results without using animals? Or even reports of similar experiments that have been done already and are being endlessly repeated?

The objections of the Research Defence Society to the British amendment can **27.** be summed up in one sentence: the prevention of animal suffering is not worth the expenditure of extra money or of the time the experimenter would need to read the literature in his field. And of this "defense," incidentally, the National Society for Medical Research has said:

> The Research Defence Society of Great Britain deserves the plaudits of
> the world's scientific community for the manner in which it expressed
> its opposition to this sticky measure.[8]

It would not be appropriate here to go into the alternatives to animal experiments **28.** that are already available. The subject is a highly technical one, more suited for researchers than for the general reader. But we already have the means to reduce greatly the number of animals experimented upon, in techniques like tissue culture (the culture of cells or groups of cells in an artificial environment); mathematical or computer models of biological systems; gas chromatography and mass spectrometry; and the use of films and models in educational instruction. Considering how little effort has been put into this field, the early results promise much greater progress if the effort is stepped up.[9]

In some important areas improvements can easily be made without using animals. **29.** Although thousands of animals have been forced to inhale tobacco smoke for months and even years, the proof of the connection between tobacco usage and lung cancer was based on data from clinical observations of humans.[10]

The US government is pouring billions of dollars into research on cancer. Much **30.** of it goes toward animal experiments, many of them only remotely connected with fighting cancer—experimenters have been known to relabel their work "cancer research" when they found they could get more money for it that way than under some other label. Of all cancers, lung cancer is the biggest killer. We know that smoking causes 80–85 percent of all lung cancer—in fact this is a "conservative" estimate, according to the director of the National Cancer Institute.[11] In a case like this we must ask ourselves: can we justify inflicting lung cancer on thousands of animals when we know that we could virtually wipe out the disease by eliminating the use of tobacco? And if people are not prepared to give up tobacco, can it be right to make animals suffer the cost of their decision to continue smoking?

Of course, it must be admitted that there are some fields of scientific research **31.** that will be hampered by any genuine consideration of the interests of animals used in experimentation. No doubt there have been genuine advances in knowledge which would not have been attained as easily or as rapidly without the infliction of pain on animals. The ethical principle of equal consideration of interests does rule out some means of obtaining knowledge, and other means may be slower or more expensive. But we already accept such restrictions on scientific enterprise. We do not believe that our scientists have a general right to perform painful or lethal experiments on human beings without their consent, although there are cases in which such experiments would advance knowledge far more rapidly than any alternative method. My proposal does no more than broaden the scope of this existing restriction on scientific research.

32. Finally, it is important to realize that the major health problems of the world largely continue to exist, not because we do not know how to prevent disease and keep people healthy, but because no one is putting the manpower and money into doing what we already know how to do. The diseases that ravage Asia, Africa, Latin America, and the pockets of poverty in the industrialized West are diseases that, by and large, we know how to cure. They have been eliminated in communities which have adequate nutrition, sanitation, and health care. Those who are genuinely concerned about improving health and have medical qualifications would probably make a more effective contribution to human health if they left the laboratories and saw to it that our existing stock of medical knowledge reaches those who need it most.

33. When all this has been said, there still remains the practical question: what can be done to change the widespread practice of experimenting on animals? Undoubtedly some action at the government level is needed, but what action precisely? And how can we succeed now when previous efforts failed? What can the ordinary citizen do to help bring about a change?

34. Unlike many other much needed reforms, this one does not lack popular support. We have already seen that in the United States a larger number of people wrote to the Defense Department about the beagle experiments than about the bombing of North Vietnam. In Britain, too, members of Parliament have reported receiving more mail from constituents concerned about the use of animals in laboratories than about the nation's entry into the European Common Market.[12] A British opinion poll conducted in 1973 found that 73 percent of the electors disapproved of the use of animals in the testing of weapons, toiletries, and cosmetics. Barely one in ten actually approved of these practices; however, only about one in four knew that animals actually were being used to test weapons and cosmetics.[13]

35. So the problem is not so much one of altering the views of the public. There is a huge amount of ignorance to be dispelled, but once the public knows what goes on there is little doubt that the public will disapprove, and disapprove strongly. The problem is one of channeling the attitudes of the public through the machinery of politics into effective action. On this topic the *Bulletin* of the National Society for Medical Research has again had some revealing things to say, this time about how the democratic process was frustrated by the British Parliament when the mild amendment I referred to earlier was brought up:

> Parliament spent so much time discussing the proposed amendment that it eventually died without a vote being taken. The utmost delicacy was used in avoiding any stand on the bill . . . The bill died, yet no-one

can be accused of voting against it. Therefore each member of Parliament is able to face the animal lobby in his home district.[14]

Why do legislators try so hard to fool their constituents, instead of working to **36.** remedy the situation against which their constituents' anger is rightly directed? In part, no doubt, it is because they are overly influenced by scientific, medical, and veterinary groups. In the United States, these groups maintain registered political lobbies in Washington, and they lobby hard against proposals to restrict experimentation. In any case, since legislators do not have the time to acquire expertise in these fields, they rely on what the "experts" tell them. But this is a moral question, not a scientific one, and the "experts" usually have an interest in the continuation of experimentation, or else are so imbued with the ethic of furthering knowledge that they cannot detach themselves from this stance and make a critical examination of what their colleagues do. Legislators must learn that when discussing animal experimentation they have to treat the medical, veterinary, psychological, and biological associations as they would treat General Motors and Ford when discussing air pollution. These groups should be given an opportunity to state their case, but they cannot be regarded as impartial authorities, and above all they cannot be entrusted with setting or enforcing standards of animal care.

Nor is the task of reform made any easier by the fact that there are now large **37.** companies involved in the profitable business of breeding or trapping animals and selling them to research laboratories. As a research veterinarian has said in testimony before the US House of Representatives House Appropriations Committee: "An entire new industry has been developed . . . with several of the larger companies having obtained international status with stock traded regularly on the major exchanges of the world."[15] The veterinarian was testifying in favor of more federal dollars to pay for more housing, equipment, technicians, and so on; but for those interested in curtailing animal experimentation, the existence of this industry is another obstacle, both because large companies are prepared to spend money to oppose legislation which will deprive them of their profitable-markets, and because they use all the sophisticated selling techniques of other companies to increase the use of their products and expand their markets.

In journals like *Lab Animal,* a publication of United Business Publications, Inc., **38.** the breeding and trapping companies promote their wares as if they were new cars or another brand of cigarettes. "Demand our '74 model, the CD2F1 hybrid mouse," Charles River Breeding Laboratories, Inc., of Wilmington, Massachusetts, tells its potential customers in full-page advertisements; and in another issue it announces that, having taken over Primate Imports Corporation of Port Washington, New York, it can now supply, "Direct from trapping," "almost any species of monkey you desire. Squirrels, Baboons, Rhesus, Capuchins, Stumptails, Pigtails, African Greens, Chimpanzees and others." Meanwhile salesmen from companies of this sort, and those that sell cages and other equipment used with laboratory animals, visit educational institutions around the world, encouraging the use of animals in experimentation.

Whatever reforms are proposed, therefore, the most pressing need is that they **39.** include in a central, decision-making role a group of people totally free of any personal stake in the use of animals for research. Only in this way could effective control become a reality. United Action for Animals has proposed a ''Public Science Council,'' consisting of nonanimal-using scientists, which would have authority to regulate the sums of public money that go into research in fields in which animals are used. By insisting on the replacement of animal-using methods by alternative methods not involving animals it would be possible for such a council to foster the growth of a new and more humane approach to scientific inquiry. This approach might not even require legislation, so far as the United States is concerned. All that would be necessary is that the research grants, public contracts, training grants, fellowships, and other awards now given to animal-using scientists be redirected toward other methods. A council of this sort might also contain representatives of the general public. The public provides the money for most scientific research; and the public has the right to direct the way in which its funds are used.

Until some major change in national policy has been effected, citizens can work **40.** on a more local level to make known what is happening all around the country, and quite possibly at universities and commercial laboratories in their own community. Students should refuse to carry out experiments required for their courses. Students and the animal welfare organizations should study the academic journals to find out where painful experiments are being carried out. They should then demonstrate against those university departments that abuse animals. Pressure should be put on universities to cut off funds to departments that have a bad record in this respect, and if the universities do not do so this should be publicized. Since universities are dependent on public good will for financial support, this method of protest should be effective. No doubt the cry will be raised that such demands are a restriction of ''scientific freedom,'' but as there is no freedom to inflict agony on humans in the name of science, why should there be any freedom to inflict agony on other animals? Especially where public funds are involved, no one has a right to the freedom to use these funds to inflict pain.

The vital role played by public funds in the use of animals for experimentation **41.** suggests another political tactic. During the American involvement in Vietnam, opponents of that war withheld a portion of their taxes, roughly the proportion of the national revenues that went toward the war, as a way of emphasizing their opposition to the war. Such tactics should only be used in extreme cases; but perhaps this case is sufficiently extreme. Obviously experimenting on animals only uses a tiny fraction of the funds that went toward the war in Vietnam, although no figures are available to show how much is spent on animal experiments. A token tax withholding, say 1 percent of the tax payable, would cover the amount actually spent, and serve as a symbolic form of protest that would enable every taxpayer to express his opposition to the use made of his taxes.

By publicly exposing what is happening behind closed laboratory doors, protesting **42.** against these things, writing letters to those legislators who provide the funds for them, withholding taxes, and publicizing the records of candidates for public office before elections, it may be possible to bring about a reform. But the problem is part of the larger problem of speciesism and it is unlikely to be eliminated altogether until speciesism itself is eliminated. Surely one day, though, our children's children, reading about what was done in laboratories in the twentieth century, will feel the same sense of horror and incredulity at what otherwise civilized people can do that we now feel when we read about the atrocities of the Roman gladiatorial arenas or the eighteenth-century slave trade.

Notes

[1] *Scope* (Durban, South Africa), 30 March 1973.
[2] "The Price of Knowledge," broadcast in New York, 12 December 1974, WNET/13; transcript supplied courtesy WNET/13 and Henry Spira.
[3] S. Milgram, *Obedience to Authority* (New York: Harper & Row, 1974). Incidentally, these experiments were widely criticized on ethical grounds because they involved human beings without their consent. It is indeed questionable whether Milgram should have deceived participants in his experiments as he did; but when we compare what was done to them with what is commonly done to nonhuman animals, we can appreciate the double standard with which critics of the experiment operate.
[4] *South Wales Echo,* 21 January 1974.
[5] S. Rosenthal, "Production and Measurement of Traumatic Swelling," *American Journal of Physiology,* 216 (3) p. 630 (March 1969).
[6] R. Kirimli, S. Kampschulte, P. Safar, "Patterns of dying from exsanguinating hemorrhage in dogs," *Journal of Trauma,* 10 (5) p. 393 (May 1970).
[7] From the transcript of the "Doctors Trial," Case I, *United States v Brandt et al.* Quoted by W. L. Shirer, *The Rise and Fall of the Third Reich* (New York: Simon & Schuster, 1960), p. 985. A brief account of the Nazi experiments can be found in this book, pp. 979–991; for a fuller account, see A. Mitscherlich and F. Mielke, *Doctors of Infamy* (New York, 1949).
[8] *Bulletin of the National Society for Medical Research,* 24 (10) October 1973.
[9] For further details see Terrence Hegarty, "Alternatives," in *Animals, Men and Morals;* Mr. Hegarty is an adviser to the Fund for the Replacement of Animals in Medical Experiments (for address, see Appendix 3). United Action for Animals, New York, has also published a series of reports on alternative methods, under titles like: "How Isolated Organs Can Be Used in Research, Testing and Teaching"; "Alternatives in Car Crash Research"; "Mathematical Modelling in Biomedical Research"; and "Abstracts Regarding Testing of Environmental Chemicals."
[10] E. Wynder and D. Hoffman, in *Advances in Cancer Research,* 8, 1964; see also the Royal College of Physicians of London report, *Smoking and Health* (1962) and studies by the US Health Department. I owe these references to Richard Ryder, "Experiments on Animals," in *Animals, Men and Morals,* p. 78.
[11] Hearings before the Committee on Appropriations, Subcommittee on Departments of Labor and Health, Education and Welfare Appropriations, House of Representatives, 1974, Pt. 4, National Institutes of Health, pp. 83, 87.
[12] *Bulletin of the National Society for Medical Research,* 24 (10) October 1973.
[13] From an address by Richard Ryder, reported in *RSPCA Today,* Summer 1974. The poll was conducted by N.O.P. Market Research Ltd.
[14] *Bulletin of the National Society for Medical Research,* 24 (10) October 1973.
[15] *Journal of the American Veterinary Medical Association,* 160, p. 1568 (1972).

WORKING WITH THE TEXT

Cultural and Historical References

In this section, the numbers at the margin refer to the numbered paragraphs in the selection itself.

2. Can you define "speciesism" from the context in which it appears? Check your definition with the definition that Singer gives later in paragraphs 14 to 20.

4. Perhaps you've probably already heard about the Stanley Milgram study

in other courses. The 1965 study is frequently cited by teachers who are trying to show how susceptible people are to social conditioning by authority figures.

21. Can you define "absolutist answers" from the context in paragraphs 21 and 23?

Writing Assignments: The Paragraph

Be sure to provide an introduction for each of the following paragraph writing assignments. That is, begin each paragraph with a phrase like this: "Thomas Brickle claims that. . . ." When it is relevant, you might also want to identify the expertise of the author ("Thomas Brickle, a New Testament scholar, claims that. . . ."), the name of the book or article, the century and country in which the work appeared, or any other circumstances that your readers might find significant. For more on this, see pp. 11–13 in Chapter 2.

1. Write a paragraph in which you define "speciesism," and illustrate your definition with examples from Singer's essay.

2. Write a paragraph in which you cite details from paragraphs 4 and 5 on how from childhood we are conditioned by authority figures to do what we innately deem to be morally or physically repulsive.

3. Write a paragraph in which you paraphrase Singer's reservations about "absolutist answers" in paragraphs 19 to 23. You may want to dispute Singer's opinion here. Can you think of situations in which an absolutist answer is appropriate? Cite some examples from your own experience.

Writing Assignments: The Short Essay

Use informal documentation for these short essays. That is, don't use footnotes or a Works Cited page to document your sources. Instead, cite only relevant information about your source, and keep that information *within* your text. Then follow the summary or quote with a page number in parentheses. (Use the page numbers that you find in this book to represent the page numbers of the source.) Thus, your informal documentation will look something like this:

In *Animal Liberation,* Peter Singer asks an intriguing question, ". . . if people are not prepared to give up tobacco, can it be right to make animals suffer the cost of their decision to continue smoking" (p. 328)?

1. Write an essay in which you summarize, in some detail, Singer's answers to the question he asks in his first paragraph: "How can these things happen?" In other words, what causes the callous lack of concern among members of the scientific community for the suffering of laboratory animals? Pay particular attention to paragraphs 1 to 13.

2. Write an essay in which you use Singer's analogy which introduces the

term "speciesism" and compares it closely to racism (paragraphs 14 to 20). Analyze the analogy and show how it is useful (or misleading).

3. Write an essay in which you paraphrase Singer's proposals for severely curtailing the number and types of medical and psychological experimentation which inflict severe pain on laboratory animals (paragraphs 21 to 41).

4. Write an essay in which you demonstrate with specific examples the idea that those in medical or psychological research have frequently damned their own position or substantiated Singer's position with things they have said or done. Convincing examples are scattered throughout Singer's essay.

NEW DEBATE OVER EXPERIMENTING WITH ANIMALS

Patricia Curtis

In the following selection, Patricia Curtis, a freelance writer and author of a book on animal rights, analyzes the complex issues involved in research involving animals. She cites numerous grisly examples of laboratory abuse.

1. The professor was late leaving the medical school because he'd had to review papers by his third-year students in experimental surgery. It was well after 11 when he wearily drove his car into the garage. The house was dark except for a hall light left on for him. His wife and youngsters were already asleep, he realized, and the professor suddenly felt lonely as he fit his key in the lock. But even as he pushed open the door, Sabrina was there to welcome him. She was always waiting for him, lying on the rug just inside the door.

2. The little dog leaped up ecstatically, wagging her tail and licking the professor's hand. The professor stroked her affectionately. She flopped on her back and grinned at him as he tickled her chest and belly; then she jumped to her feet and danced around his legs as he walked into the kitchen to get something to eat. Sabrina's exuberant joy at his return never failed to cheer him.

3. Early next morning, the professor drove back to the medical school and entered the laboratory. He noticed that a dog on which one of his students had operated the previous afternoon still had an endotracheal tube in its throat and obviously had not received pain medication. He must be more strict in his orders, he thought to himself. Another dog had bled through its bandages and lay silently in a pool of blood. Sloppy work, the professor thought—must speak to that student. None of the dogs made any sounds, because new arrivals at the laboratory were always subjected to an operation called a ventriculocordectomy that destroyed their vocal cords so that no barks or howls disturbed people in the medical school and surrounding buildings.

4. The professor looked over the animals that would be used that day by his surgery students. He came across a new female dog that had just been delivered by the dealer.

Source: Patricia Curtis, "New Debate over Experimenting with Animals," *The New York Times Magazine.* December 31, 1978: 18, 20–21, 23.

Badly frightened, she whined and wagged her tail ingratiatingly as he paused in front of her cage. The professor felt a stab. The small dog bore an amazing resemblance to Sabrina. Quickly he walked away. Nevertheless, he made a note to remind himself to give orders for her vocal cords to be destroyed and for her to be conditioned for experimental surgery.

American researchers sacrifice approximately 64 million animals annually. Some **5.** 400,000 dogs, 200,000 cats, 33,000 apes and monkeys, thousands of horses, ponies, calves, sheep, goats and pigs, and millions of rabbits, hamsters, guinea pigs, birds, rats and mice are used every year in experiments that often involve intense suffering. The research establishment has generally insisted that live animals provide the only reliable tests for drugs, chemicals and cosmetics that will be used by people. Researchers also believe that animal experiments are necessary in the search for cures for human illnesses and defects. There is no question that many important medical discoveries, from polio vaccine to the physiology of the stress response, have indeed been made through the use of animals. Thus universities, medical and scientific institutions, pharmaceutical companies, cosmetics manufacturers and the military have always taken for granted their right to use animals in almost any way they see fit.

But increasing numbers of scientists are beginning to ask themselves some hard **6.** ethical questions and to re-evaluate their routine use of painful testing tools such as electric shock, stomach tubes, hot plates, restraining boxes and radiation devices. A new debate has arisen over whether all such experiments are worth the suffering they entail.

Strongly opposing curtailment of animal experimentation are groups such as the **7.** National Society for Medical Research, which insists that any such reduction would jeopardize public safety and scientific progress. The N.S.M.R. was formed to resist what it considers the threat of Government regulation of animal research and to refute the charges of humane societies. Many scientists, however, although they firmly believe that some animal research is necessary, no longer endorse such an absolutist approach to the issue.

''Some knowledge can be obtained at too high a price,'' writes British physiologist **8.** Dr. D. H. Smyth in his recent book ''Alternatives to Animal Experiments.''

''The lives and suffering of animals must surely count for something,'' says **9.** Jeremy J. Stone, director of the Washington-based Federation of American Scientists, which has devoted an entire newsletter to a discussion of the rights of animals.

According to physiologist Dr. F. Barbara Orlans of the National Institutes of **10.** Health, ''Within the scientific community there's a growing concern for animals that has not yet had a forum.'' Dr. Orlans is president of the newly formed Scientists' Center for Animal Welfare, which hopes to raise the level of awareness on the part of fellow scientists and the public about avoidable suffering inflicted on lab animals, wildlife and animals raised for meat. ''We will try to be a voice of reason. We can perhaps be a link between scientists and the humane organizations,'' Dr. Orlans explains. ''We hope also to provide solid factual data on which animal-protection decisions can be based.''

Another link between researchers and humane organizations is a new committee **11.** comprising more than 400 doctors and scientists that has been formed by Friends of Animals, a national animal-welfare group. Headed by eight M.D.'s, the committee is

making a survey of Federally funded animal-research projects. Friends of Animals
hopes that the study will expose not only needless atrocities performed on animals, but
also boondoggles involving taxpayers' money.

One reason scientists are no longer so indifferent to the suffering they inflict on **12.**
animals is the discoveries that science itself has made. We now know that many animals
feel, think, reason, communicate, have sophisticated social systems and even, on
occasion, behave altruistically toward each other. Communication by sign language
with higher primates, demonstrations of the intelligence of dolphins and whales,
observations of the complex societies of wolves and other animals, and many other
investigations have narrowed the gap between ourselves and the rest of the animal
kingdom, making it more difficult to rationalize inhumane experiments. Dr. Dallas
Pratt, author of "Painful Experiments on Animals," points out that "among the rats
and mice, the computers and oscilloscopes, there is Koko"—referring to the young
gorilla whom a California primatologist has taught a working vocabulary of 375 words
and concepts in sign language and who has even learned to take snapshots with a
Polaroid camera. It's hard not to feel squeamish about subjecting animals to inhumane
experiments when they possess almost human intelligence.

The thinking of researchers is also beginning to be affected by the growing **13.**
movement for animal rights. The rising concern for the welfare of animals is seen by
some people as a natural extension of contemporary movements promoting civil rights,
women's rights, homosexual rights, human rights and children's rights. Public interest
in preserving endangered species is based first on an increasing awareness of the
complexity and fragility of ecosystems, and second on the notion, still much debated,
that any species of plant or animal, from the lowly snail darter to the blue whale, has
the right to continue to exist. From here it is only a short logical step to the belief that
animals have the right to exist without suffering unnecessarily.

Near the top of the list of animal-welfare activists' causes is putting an end to **14.**
inhumane experiments on laboratory animals. In Great Britain, where a vigorous
antivivisection movement has existed for more than a century, a clandestine group
called the Animal Liberation Front conducts commando-style raids on laboratories,
liberating animals and sabotaging research equipment. A.L.F. members have also been
known to slash tires and pour sugar in the gas tanks of trucks used by animal dealers
who supply labs. To be sure, this group of zealots hasn't made much of a dent in
England's vast research community, but it does appeal to a gut reaction on the part of
many Britons against animal research.

Animal-rights activists are not merely sentimental do-gooders and pet-lovers. **15.**
They have mounted a philosophical attack on the traditional Western attitude toward
animals, branding it as "speciesist" (like racist or sexist), a term derived from the
word "speciesism," coined by psychologist and author Dr. Richard Ryder. The
Australian philosopher Peter Singer, in his influential 1975 book "Animal Liberation,"
argued that the "speciesist" rationalization, "Human beings come first," is usually
used by people who do nothing for either human or nonhuman animals. And he pointed
out the parallels between the oppression of blacks, women and animals: Such oppression
is usually rationalized on the grounds that the oppressed group is inferior.

In 1977, when outraged antivivisectionists heard about some highly unpleasant **16.**
electric-shock and burn experiments conducted on young pigs in Denmark, they wasted

no time in pointing out the irony that the tests were being conducted by Amnesty International, the human-rights organization. Amnesty International was attempting to prove that human prisoners could be tortured without leaving any marks, and pigs were used because of the similarity of their skin to ours. (The tests were subsequently discontinued.)

Paradoxically, the public tends to be "speciesist" in its reaction to animal **17.** experimentation: For many people, a test is permissible when it inflicts pain on a "lower" animal like a hamster, but not when the victim is a dog. When it was discovered in the summer of 1976 that the American Museum of Natural History was damaging the brains of cats and running painful sex experiments on them, hundreds of people picketed in protest. The museum's Animal Behavior Department defended itself on the grounds that the research was intended to gain a better understanding of human sexual responses. Animal-rights groups, scientists among them, were not convinced of the necessity of the tests, which came to an end only when the chief researcher retired. But the protesters made no stir about the pigeons, doves and rats that suffered in the same laboratory.

If United States Army researchers had used guinea pigs instead of beagles when **18.** they tried out a poison gas, they probably would not have provoked the public outcry that resulted in the curtailment of their funding in 1974. When a few Avon saleswomen quit their jobs last spring after reading about painful eye-makeup tests the company conducts on rabbits, they did not complain about the thousands of guinea pigs and rats Avon routinely puts to death in acute-toxicity tests.

It is not known whether any single vertebrate species is more or less immune to **19.** pain than another. A neat line cannot be drawn across the evolutionary scale dividing the sensitive from the insensitive. Yet the suffering of laboratory rats and mice is regarded as trivial by scientists and the public alike. These rodents have the dubious honor of being our No. 1 experimental animals, composing possibly 75 percent of America's total lab-animal population. As Russell Baker once wrote, "This is no time to be a mouse."

Rats and mice are specifically excluded from a Federal law designed to give **20.** some protection to laboratory animals. The Animal Welfare Act, passed in 1966 and amended in 1970, is administered by the Department of Agriculture and covers only about 4 percent of laboratory animals. Animal advocates worked hard for the bill, which sets some standards for the housing of animals in laboratories and at the dealers' facilities from which many of them are obtained. But the law places no restrictions on the kinds of experiments to which animals may be subjected. It does indicate that pain-relieving drugs should be used on the few types of animals it covers—but it includes a loophole so as not to inhibit researchers unduly. If a scientist claims that pain is a necessary part of an experiment, anesthetics or analgesics may be withheld.

One standard test conducted on rats by drug companies is called the "writhing **21.** test" because of the agonized way the animals react to irritants injected into their abdomens. Paradoxically, this test assesses the efficacy of pain-killers, which are administered only after the rats show signs of acute suffering.

Equally common are psychological experiments in "learned helplessness" that **22.** have been conducted on rats, dogs and other kinds of animals. In some of these tests, caged animals are given painful electric shocks until they learn certain maneuvers to obtain their food. As they become adept at avoiding the shocks, the researchers keep changing the rules so that the animals have to keep learning more and more ways to avoid shocks. Ultimately no way remains to escape, and the animals simply give up and lie on the floors of their cages, passively receiving shock after shock. Researchers have attempted to draw parallels between "learned helplessness" and depression in human beings, but some critics have difficulty perceiving their necessity. "What more are we going to learn about human depression by continuing to produce immobility in animals?" asks former animal experimenter Dr. Roger Ulrich, now a research professor of psychology at Western Michigan University.

Electric shock is widely used on many different kinds of animals in various types **23.** of research. In one experiment typical of a series that has been under way since 1966 at the Armed Forces Radiobiology Research Institute in Bethesda, Md., 10 rhesus monkeys were starved for 18 hours and then "encouraged" with electric prods to run rapidly on treadmills. This went on for several weeks before the monkeys were subjected to 4,000 rads of gamma-neutron radiation. Then they were retested on the treadmills for six hours, and subsequently for two hours each day until they died. Mean survival time for the vomiting, incapacitated monkeys was recorded in A.F.F.R.I.'s report as 37 hours. Dogs have been used in similar experiments, whose purpose is to get an idea of the effects of radiation on human endurance.

Now A.F.F.R.I. and other American research facilities are having to look for new **24.** sources of monkeys. In March 1978, the Government of India banned further export of rhesus monkeys to the United States. The native population was dwindling and Prime Minister Morarji R. Desai cited violations of a previous agreement that restricted the use of rhesus monkeys to medical research under humane conditions. "There is no difference between cruelty to animals and cruelty to human beings," the ascetic Prime Minister stated. The International Primate Protection League, a four-year-old watchdog group whose members include many scientists and especially primatologists (Jane Goodall, for one), had spread word in the Indian press that American scientists were using rhesus monkeys in grisly trauma experiments. According to the Primate Protection League, these tests included dipping monkeys in boiling water at the University of Kansas, shooting them in the face with high-powered rifles at the University of Chicago, and slamming them in the stomach with a cannon-impactor traveling at a speed of 70 miles per hour at the University of Michigan.

"I feel justified in stating that fully 80 percent of the experiments involving **25.** rhesus monkeys are either unnecessary, represent useless duplication of previous work, or could utilize nonanimal alternatives," wrote Illinois Wesleyan University biologist Dr. John E. McArdle, a specialist in primate functional anatomy, in a letter to Prime Minister Desai, who so far has held firm despite pressure from the American scientific community to rescind the ban. In the meantime, researchers are making do with non-Indian rhesus monkeys and a close relative, the crab-eating macaque.

One of the arguments in favor of animal tests is that under the controlled **26.** circumstances of the experimental laboratory they are likely to be objective and consistent. But the results of the same tests conducted on the same kinds of animals often differ from one laboratory to the next. When 25 cooperating companies, including Avon, Revlon and American Cyanamid, conducted a comprehensive study of eye- and skin-irritation tests using rabbits, the results varied widely. The study concluded that these tests "should not be recommended as standard procedures in any new regulations" because they yielded "unreliable results."

One of these tests, the Draize Ophthalmic Irritancy Test, is used to evaluate the **27.** effect upon the eyes of household and aerosol products, shampoos and eye makeup. Rabbits are used because their eyes do not have effective tear glands and thus cannot easily flush away or dissolve irritants. The animals are pinioned in stocks and their eyes are exposed to a substance until inflammation, ulceration or gross damage occurs.

Many investigators concede that the data provided by such experiments are often **28.** inconsistent and that the stresses caused by crowded cages, callous treatment, pain and fear can affect animals' metabolisms and thus confuse test results. "Since there is hardly a single organ or biochemical system in the body that is not affected by stress," says Dr. Harold Hillman, a British physiologist, "it is almost certainly the main reason for the wide variation reported among animals on whom painful experiments have been done."

Very often, different species respond differently to substances or situations. The **29.** rationale for many animal tests is that they predict human reactions, but thalidomide, for example, did not produce deformities in the fetuses of dogs, cats, monkeys and hamsters. On the other hand, insulin has been proved harmful to rabbits and mice although it saves human lives.

Researchers are becoming increasingly dubious about the efficacy of the LD/50, **30.** a test for acute toxicity that consists of force-feeding a group of animals a specific substance until half of them die, ostensibly providing a quantitative measure of how poisonous the substance is. In "Painful Experiments on Animals," Dr. Pratt asks what we learn from forcing hair dye or face powder into a dog or rat through a stomach tube until its internal organs rupture.

One small victory for animal-welfare activists that was hailed by many American **31.** scientists was the 1975 Canadian ban on the use of vertebrate animals by students participating in science fairs. Children had been awarded prizes for attempting heart-transplant surgery on unanesthetized rabbits, amputating the feet of lizards, performing Caesarean operations on pregnant mice, bleeding dogs into a state of shock and blinding pigeons. Remarking that such "experiments" were a distortion of the spirit of research, science-fair officials ruled out all such projects except observations of the normal-living patterns of wild or domestic animals.

In this country, the search for adequate substitutes for laboratory animals was **32.** officially launched last summer when the year-old American Fund for Alternatives to Animal Research made its first grant—$12,500 to a biology professor at Whitman College in Walla Walla, Wash. The award to Dr. Earl William Fleck will help finance his development of a test substituting one-celled organisms called tetrahymena for animals in screening substances for teratogens, agents that can cause birth defects. It is expected that the test, if and when perfected, will be cheaper, quicker, more accurate and certainly more humane than putting thousands of pregnant animals to death.

According to veterinarian Thurman Grafton, executive director of the National **33.** Society for Medical Research, people who talk about alternatives to animals are creating false hopes. "These new technologies can only be adjuncts to the use of animals," he claims. "While they serve a purpose in furnishing clues as to what direction a type of research might take, you will always ultimately need an intact animal with all its living complications and interchanging biochemical functions to properly assay a drug."

"Not so," says Ethel Thurston, administrator of the American Fund for Alterna- **34.** tives. "Enough progress has already been made to indicate that certain techniques can completely replace animals."

Several of these techniques have been developed over the last five years in Great **35.**
Britain, where the Lord Dowding Fund for Humane Research has given grants totaling
more than $400,000 to dozens of scientists engaged in research aimed at finding
experimental substitutes for animals. Dowding is currently financing several develop-
mental studies of the Ames Test, a promising technique invented by a Berkeley
biochemistry professor, Dr. Bruce Ames, that uses salmonella bacteria rather than
animals to determine the carcinogenic properties of chemicals. (It was the Ames Test
that recently revealed the possible carcinogenic dangers of certain hair dyes.) Another
Dowding Fund recipient, research physician Dr. John C. Petricciani, now with the Food
and Drug Administration, has devised a method of assessing how tumors grow by
inoculating the tumor cells into skin from 9-day-old chicken embryos instead of into
living animals.

Animal tests are frequently replaced by other methods discovered and developed **36.**
by scientists like Dr. Ames who are not trying to avoid the use of animals per se but
are simply searching for simpler and more cost-efficient ways to achieve their goals.
Dr. Hans Stich, a Canadian cancer researcher, for example, has devised a new test for
detecting carcinogenicity in chemicals; it uses human cells, takes one week and costs
only about $260. The traditional method, using rats and mice, takes three years and
costs approximately $150,000.

In addition to egg embryos, bacteria and simple organisms, possible substitutes **37.**
for animals include tissue cultures, human and other mammal cells grown in test tubes,
and organ banks. Preserved human corneas, for instance, might be used to spare rabbits
the agony of the Draize test. Computers could also play a role if researchers used them
fully to analyze experimental data, predict the properties of new drugs, and test
theoretical data. Computers can even be programmed to simulate living processes.
Mechanical models and audio-visual aids can and do substitute for animals as teaching
instruments. Simulated human models could provide valid information in car-crash
tests.

Last winter, Representative Robert F. Drinan, Democrat of Massachusetts, **38.**
introduced a bill authorizing the Department of Health, Education and Welfare to fund
projects aimed at discovering research methods that would reduce both the numbers
of animals used in laboratories and the suffering to which they are subjected.

Meanwhile, medical and military research and an unending stream of new **39.**
pharmaceutical, cosmetic and household products are resulting in an ever-increasing
use of animals in the laboratory.

The most recent and thorough exploration of alternatives is Dr. D.H. Smyth's **40.**
book "Alternatives to Animal Experiments," which examines every option and weighs
its pros and cons. He concludes that there is certainly reason to hope that the numbers
of laboratory animals can be drastically reduced, but also warns that it is unlikely a
complete phasing out of animal experimentation will happen soon. "By the time we
can produce complete alternatives to living tissue," Dr. Smyth writes, "we will not
need those alternatives because we will already understand how living tissues work."

Still, Dr. Smyth asks, "Does this mean we can perpetrate any cruelty on animals **41.**
to satisfy scientific curiosity in the hope that it will one day be useful? To me it
certainly does not. . . . Everyone has a right to decide that certain procedures are
unacceptable."

Richard Ryder calls animal experimenters to task for trying to have it both ways: **42.**
Researchers defend their work scientifically on the basis of the *similarities* between
human beings and animals, but defend it morally on the basis of the *differences*.

And there's the rub: The differences aren't as reassuringly clear-cut as they once **43.**
were. We now know that some animals have a more highly developed intelligence
than some human beings—infants, for example, or the retarded and the senile. Dr.
Ryder asks, "If we were to be discovered by some more intelligent creatures in the
universe, would they be justified in experimenting on us?"

WORKING WITH THE TEXT

Cultural and Historical References

In this section, the numbers at the margin refer to the numbered paragraphs
in the selection itself.

4. Using context alone, a reader can often make an intelligent guess about
   the meaning of a word. Make an intelligent guess about the meaning of
   "ingratiatingly" and then check your definition in a dictionary.

11. "Boondoggles": as you see, professional writers descend to the colloqui-
    al occasionally.

14. If "vivisection" means cutting into live animals, what does "antivivisec-
    tion" mean?

19. Russell Baker writes a syndicated humor column for *The New York
    Times*. Can you imagine a better job?

24. Why do you suppose Curtis calls the Indian prime minister an "ascetic"?
    Does that tag have any bearing on the prime minister's position?

24. Jane Goodall is a famous primatologist who studied African apes.

Writing Assignments: The Paragraph

Be sure to provide an introduction for each of the following paragraph writing
assignments. That is, begin each paragraph with a phrase like this: "Thomas
Brickle claims that . . . ." When it is relevant, you might also want to identify
the expertise of the author ("Thomas Brickle, a New Testament scholar,
claims that . . . ."), the name of the book or article, the century and country
in which the work appeared, or any other circumstances that your readers
might find significant. For more on this, see pp. 11–13 in Chapter 2.

1. Summarize paragraphs 1 to 4. Be sure to let your reader know the
   distinctive quality of these paragraphs.

2. Write a paragraph that begins this way: "Patricia Curtis describes a
   number of cruel experiments that use living animals."

Writing Assignments: The Short Essay

Use informal documentation for these short essays. That is, don't use foot-notes or a Works Cited page to document your sources. Instead, cite only relevant information about your source, and keep that information *within* your text. Then follow the summary or quote with a page number in parentheses. (Use the page numbers that you find in this book to represent the page numbers of the source.) Thus, your informal documentation will look something like this:

> In *Animal Liberation*, Peter Singer asks an intriguing question, ". . . if people are not prepared to give up tobacco, can it be right to make ani-mals suffer the cost of their decision to continue smoking" (p. 328)?

1. Although the Curtis essay seems to be a report (rather than an argument), what side do you think the author is on? Cite evidence to support your argument. Look at paragraphs 32 to 35 and the conclusion in particular.

2. Analyze the makeup of Curtis's introduction in paragraphs 1 to 4.

3. Using Curtis's examples, argue either that we should draw a line between higher and lower animals or that we should not. Somewhere in your essay, tackle the problem of exactly *where* the line should be drawn.

4. Argue either for or against "speciesism." In other words, is speciesism a valid position for a human to take, or is it more akin to racism and sexism? See paragraphs 15 to 17 in particular.

THINKING ANIMAL THOUGHTS

Lance Morrow

This essay by Lance Morrow, a senior writer for *Time*, is a thoughtful and balanced discussion of the interests and rights which clash in the contemporary controversy over animal rights.

The dogs would die anyway. They would be strays, caged in shelters, ready to **1.** be "put to sleep." The idea was that the Defense Department's new Wound Laboratory would pay about $80 for each dog. When the time came for research to proceed, the dogs would be anesthetized with pentobarbital, suspended in nylon mesh slings and shot with a 9-mm Mauser from a distance of twelve or 15 feet. The dogs would then be carried into a lab, and people studying to be military surgeons would examine the damage and learn something about gunshot wounds, which might some day save human lives on a battlefield.

It is a harsh moral configuration. The Wound Laboratory is perfectly designed to **2.** bring on a confrontation between the zealot and the omelet maker (the omelet maker being the one who always insists that you can't make an omelet without breaking a few

Source: Lance Morrow, "Thinking Animal Thoughts," *Time*. October 3, 1983: 35–36.

eggs). The issue is framed exactly: animal life is forfeit to the potential gain of human life. An ironist would point out that the Wound Laboratory would put animals to death in order to perfect the human talent to make war—and that war is humanity's most dramatic bestiality. Inevitably, the idea of the Wound Laboratory received publicity, and it stirred up the fury of what is becoming one of the more aggressive American constituencies. The Defense Department decided that it would not start shooting dogs there until it had studied the question further.

The notion of an Animal Rights Movement can be faintly satirical, especially if **3.** it is seen as the *reductio ad absurdum* of other rights movements. It smacks of a slightly cross-eyed fanaticism that might have amused Dickens, of battle-axes who file class-action suits in behalf of canaries. The movement has its truncheon rhetoric. Its ungainly equivalent of racism and sexism is "speciesism." Just as there is the male chauvinist pig, there presumably must be (so to speak) the human chauvinist pig.

But the animal rights issue has developed a peculiar power. Although a candidate **4.** running on an animal liberation ticket in 1984 might provoke witticisms about dark horses and fat cats, he or she would receive a respectably serious share of popular sympathy, if not of the popular vote. It is not some revolution that has suddenly come to critical mass, but it is there, a presence.

The situation of animals stirs people in a profound way that is sometimes difficult **5.** to explain. Thoreau wrote, "It often happens that a man is more humanely related to a cat or a dog than to any human being." Sometimes the love of animals bespeaks an incapacity for the more complicated business of loving people; mental patients who react to other humans with fear and loathing can develop calm, tender relationships with puppies. Animals are usually perfectly themselves, not the elaborately perverse psychological mysteries that people seem to become. Animals, if not rabid, have a certain emotional reliability. But being on the side of the animals does not always make one a good guy. It is wise, when beginning a discussion of the subject, to remember that Hitler was a vegetarian.

And yet the matter of animals and their claims in the world is morally fascinating. **6.** What are animals for? What is the point of animals? To ask such questions is mere speciesism, of course. The human race walks around enveloped in an aura of narcissism that would be laughable to any other animal bright enough to appreciate it. Privileged to possess presumably the highest, undoubtedly the dominant intelligence on the planet, humans assume that the rest of creation was provided for their convenience. But people are not merely predators with a taste for meat. The relationship between humans and animals is deep and primitive and ambiguous, both violent and sometimes deeply loving. People admire some animals, and shoot them precisely because they admire them. They wish to kill the tiger to take on his powers, to kill the deer to feel some deep, strange beauty in the deed, a fatal oneness. People fear some animals and devour others. Human teeth are not designed the way they are in order to eat tofu and alfalfa sprouts, but to tear and grind meat.

One medical theorist, Dr. Paul D. MacLean, has suggested that when a man lies **7.** down on a psychiatrist's couch, a horse and a crocodile lie down beside him. People, according to MacLean's theory, have not one but three brains: neomammalian (the human), paleomammalian (the horse) and reptilian (the crocodile). Certain primitive tribesmen make no distinction between human and animal life but assume that all life is roughly the same. It simply takes up residence in different forms, different bodies. Higher cultures do not make that organic assumption; they are haunted by the animal in man, by the idea of animals as their lower nature, the fallen part, the mortal. The clear blue intelligence of civilization, they think, is imprisoned in the same cell, the body, with its Caliban, the brute undermind.

That assumption is a bit of a slander upon the animal kingdom, of course. It **8.** arises from an egocentric and spiritually complicated habit of mankind. People use animals not only for food and clothing and scientific experiment and decoration and companionship, but also, most profoundly, for furnishing the human mind with its myths. Victor Hugo wrote, "Animals are nothing but the forms of our virtues and vices, wandering before our eyes, the visible phantoms of our souls." We become those elaborately varied creatures, we take their forms. Odysseus' companions were transformed into swine, but in the metamorphosis, their intelligence remained human, unaffected. In reality, when men are transformed into beasts, for whatever reason (anger, greed, lust, drugs), their intelligence is usually very much affected, for the worse. Unlike Odysseus' men, they keep their human forms but assume the character of beasts.

Animals, being so specifically themselves, so characteristic, have always been a **9.** powerful source of metaphor with which to describe human behavior. The lion is courage. The bull is strength. Christian allegory codified creatures and thus abstracted them: the hyena was impurity, the deer was the Christian longing for immortality, the pelican was redemption. Animals inhabit every corner of human fantasy and literature. They come bounding up out of the subconscious like tigers in a child's nightmare. They come in the form of snakes in Eden and albatrosses and white whales and in other forms purely fanciful, like dragons and unicorns.

Human beings sometimes have difficulty seeing animals dispassionately and **10.** according them the dignity of an objective existence. Animals tend to be either embodiments of ideas and phantasms or else cellophaned food units. As there is a can of soup, so there is a leg of lamb. The mind does not linger on what the leg of lamb used to be attached to or the messy process by which it was detached and turned into groceries. The technique, both physically and psychologically, is one of dissociation.

The lamb that owned that leg had life once. The issue of animal rights poses the **11.** complicated question of why one life—the lamb's, for example, or that of the dog destined for the Wound Laboratory—should be sacrificed for the nourishment or medical interest of another life, that of a human being. Every year research of one kind or another kills more than 60 million animals, including 161,000 dogs and 47,000 monkeys. Many of them die in the cause of presumably worthy medical study. Animal rights people become more militant when they ask questions about some other experiments: Why should rabbits be killed, for example, by having a new mascara tested on their eyes?

If human beings assume that they were created in the image of God, it is not **12.** difficult for them to see the vast and qualitative distance between themselves and the lesser orders of creation. The Bible teaches that man has dominion over the fish of the sea, the fowl of the air, the cattle and every creeping thing. Perhaps the rise of the animal rights movement is a symptom of a more secular and self-doubting spirit (although that could not be said of another animal lover, St. Francis of Assisi).

The human difference is known, to some, as the immortal soul, an absolute **13.** distinction belonging to man and woman alone, not to the animal. The soul is the human pedigree—and presumably the dispensation to slay and eat any inferior life that crosses the path. But in a secular sense, how is human life different from animal life? Intelligence? Some pygmy chimps and even lesser creatures are as intelligent as, say, a severely retarded child; if it is not permissible to kill a retarded child, why kill the animals? Self-awareness? Some creatures, such as chimpanzees, notice themselves in the mirror; others, such as dogs, do not. Laughter? (Max Eastman said that dogs laugh, but they laugh with their tails.) Conscience? The gift of abstract thought? An institutional memory that permits them to record experience and develop upon it, generation upon generation?

14. Descartes said that animals are mere "machines." If that is true, dropping a lobster into a pot of boiling water is about the same as dropping in an automobile transmission. The question of how to treat animals, how to think about them, usually revolves around the mystery of what animal consciousness is like. Is it all mere surface, pure eyeball and animal reflex, season and hunger and adrenal spurts of terror or breeding lust, a dumb, brute, oblivious ritual of the genes? Researchers occasionally find disconcerting evidence that animals are capable of unexpected intellectual feats, like the chimps at the Yerkes Regional Primate Research Center at Emory University who are learning a form of language. In any case, it may be risky for human beings to insist too much on the criterion of self-awareness; people are fairly oblivious themselves. Socrates said that the unexamined life is not worth living. If that is true, half the world's population should be suicidal.

15. But even if the lobster feels no pain in the pot, or the steer is just a dumb brute lumbering into the abattoir, they do have life. The offense against them—if there is one—is not essentially the pain we inflict upon them, but the fact that we deprive them of life. Albert Schweitzer constructed many saintly paragraphs about "reverence for life." He would lift an earthworm from a parched pavement and place it tenderly on the grass; he would work in the stuffy atmosphere of a shuttered room rather than risk the danger that a moth might immolate itself in his lamp.

16. The rest of the race is not so fastidious. The world has its hierarchy of tooth and claw, that savage orderliness one watched as a child in Disney nature films, all those gulping, disgusting ingestions by which the animal kingdom proceeds on its daily rounds. It is a slaughterous ripping, the hunt and kill, that is also somehow dreamy and abstract. The big fish eat the little fish and the folks eat the chickens. Various living things are destined to perish in the jaws of others, and the best that our civilization has been able to do is to draw the line at cannibalism. "Nature is no sentimentalist," Emerson wrote. "Providence has a wild, rough, incalculable road to its end, and it is of no use to whitewash its huge, mixed instrumentalities, or to dress up that terrific benefactor in a clean shirt and white neckcloth of a student in divinity."

WORKING WITH THE TEXT

Cultural and Historical References

In this section, the numbers at the margin refer to the numbered paragraphs in the selection itself.

  2. Knowing what "moral" means, what do you suppose "moral configuration" means?

2. Have you heard this omelet metaphor before? If you haven't, can you figure out what it means from the context?

3. Knowing that a truncheon is a club, what is Morrow suggesting by the term "truncheon rhetoric"?

7. Caliban is the brutish, half-animal, half-human creature in Shakespeare's *The Tempest*.

12. St. Francis of Assisi was the ascetic medieval priest who cared for the poor and the sick—but who also had a special fondness for animals. It is said that while living alone in the forest, St. Francis preached his sermons to the animals, and they enjoyed listening to them.

14. René Descartes was the French philosopher who separated religious thinking from scientific thinking and thus helped to pave the way for the scientific revolution.

15. An "abattoir" is a French word for slaughterhouse.

15. Albert Schweitzer was the physician, Christian scholar, and humanitarian who spent years in Africa ministering to the people. He was also a composer and organist.

Writing Assignments: The Paragraph

Be sure to provide an introduction for each of the following paragraph writing assignments. That is, begin each paragraph with a phrase like this: "Thomas Brickle claims that. . . ." When it is relevant, you might also want to identify the expertise of the author ("Thomas Brickle, a New Testament scholar, claims that. . . ."), the name of the book or article, the century and country in which the work appeared, or any other circumstances that your readers might find significant. For more on this, see pp. 11–13 in Chapter 2.

1. Morrow ends paragraph 5 with this statement: "Hitler was a vegetarian." Show that fair-minded writers sometimes bring up contrary evidence, and use Morrow's statement about Hitler as an example.

2. In a paragraph, summarize Morrow's discussion of the consequences to animals of the belief in a human soul. See paragraphs 12 to 13.

Writing Assignments: The Short Essay

Use informal documentation for these short essays. That is, don't use footnotes or a Works Cited page to document your sources. Instead, cite only relevant information about your source, and keep that information *within* your text. Then follow the summary or quote with a page number in parenthesis. (Use the page numbers that you find in this book to represent the page numbers of the source.) Thus, your informal documentation will look something like this:

In *Animal Liberation*, Peter Singer asks an intriguing question, ". . . if people are not prepared to give up tobacco, can it be right to make animals suffer the cost of their decision to continue smoking" (p. 328)?

1. Morrow's essay might be called a meditation rather than an argument. Using Morrow's essay as your starting point, discuss what a meditation is.

2. Analyze Morrow's essay and try to decide if he is on one side or the other. Be fair. Don't disregard evidence that supports what your opponents might say.

3. Argue with Morrow's statement that "Human teeth are not designed the way they are in order to eat tofu and alfalfa sprouts, but to tear and grind meat." You may have to do a little research on human teeth before you write.

4. Describe Morrow's use of animal metaphors. Expand his analysis by adding your own animal metaphors.

5. In paragraph 14, Morrow seems to conclude there is no essential difference between humans and animals. Can you come up with an essential difference?

ANIMALS IN RESEARCH: THE CASE FOR EXPERIMENTATION

Frederick A. King

Frederick King is director of the Yerkes Regional Primate Research Center of Emory University and the chairman of the American Psychological Association's Committee on Animal Research and Experimentation. As the title of his essay indicates, King is a strong defender of the use of animals in experimental research. His primary focus here is upon psychological research—an area that has come under heavy fire from animal rights advocates.

1. The Mobilization for Animals Coalition (MFA) is an international network of more than 400 animal-protectionist organizations that address themselves to a variety of issues, including hunting, trapping, livestock protection, vegetarianism and pets. Their primary concern, however, is an adamant opposition to animal research. Some groups with the movement want to severely curtail research with animals, but the most visible and outspoken faction wants to eliminate it.

2. The astonishing growth of this activist movement during the past three years has culminated this year in an intense attack on the use of animals in psychological research. This past spring, John McArdle of the Humane Society of the United States charged that torture is the founding principle and fundamental characteristic of experimental psychology, and that psychological experimentation on animals among all the scientific disciplines is "the ideal candidate for elimination. No major scientific endeavor would suffer by such an act." A recent pamphlet published by the MFA stated, "Of all these

Source: Frederick A. King, "Animals in Research: The Case for Experimentation," *Psychology Today.* September 1984: 56–58.

experiments, those conducted in psychology are the most painful, pointless and repulsive.''

The following specific allegations have been made by the MFA: Animals are **3.** given intense, repeated electric shocks until they lose the ability even to scream in pain; animals are deprived of food and water and allowed to suffer and die from hunger and thirst; animals are put in isolation until they are driven insane or die from despair and terror; animals are subjected to crushing forces that smash their bones and rupture their internal organs; the limbs of animals are mutilated or amputated to produce behavioral changes; animals are the victims of extreme pain and stress, inflicted out of idle curiosity, in nightmarish experiments designed to make healthy animals psychotic.

Such irresponsible accusations of research cruelty have consistently characterized **4.** the publications of the MFA. However, a recent study by psychologists D. Caroline Coile and Neal E. Miller of Rockefeller University counters these charges. Coile and Miller looked at every article (a total of 608) appearing in the past five years in journals of the American Psychological Association that report animal research. They concluded that none of the extreme allegations made by the MFA could be supported.

Coile and Miller admit that charges of cruelty may have gone unreported or been **5.** reported elsewhere but, they say, if such studies did occur, ''they certainly were infrequent, and it is extremely misleading to imply that they are typical of experimental psychology.''

Furthermore, there are standards and mechanisms to ensure that research animals **6.** are treated in a humane and scientifically sensible way. These mechanisms include the Federal Animal Welfare Act of 1966 (amended in Congress in 1970, 1976 and 1979); periodic inspection of all animal-research facilities by the Department of Agriculture; visits by federal agencies that fund animal research and are increasingly attentive to the conditions of animal care and experimental procedures that could cause pain or distress; and a comprehensive document, ''Guide for the Care and Use of Laboratory Animals,'' prepared by the National Academy of Sciences. In addition, virtually every major scientific society whose members conduct animal research distributes guidelines for such research. Above and beyond all of this, most universities and research institutes have animal-care committees that monitor animal research and care. This will include detailed information about how each institution complies with the new regulations as well as a requirement that animal-research committees include not only the supervising laboratory veterinarian and scientists but also a nonscientist and a person not affiliated with the institution. These committees will review programs for animal care, inspect all animal facilities and review and monitor all research proposals before they are submitted to agencies of the United States Public Health Service. The committees will also have the power to disapprove or terminate any research proposal.

This is not to say that research scientists are perfect. There will be occasional **7.** errors, cases of neglect and instances of abuse—as is the case with any human endeavor, whether it be the rearing of children, the practicing of a trade or profession or the governing of a nation. But a high standard of humane treatment is maintained.

The choice of psychological research for special attack almost certainly stems **8.** from the fact that such research is viewed as more vulnerable than are studies of anatomy, physiology or microbiology. In the minds of many, psychology is a less well-developed science than the biological sciences and the benefits that have accrued from psychological research with animals are less well known. Hence, it is more difficult to grasp the necessity for animal research in behavioral studies than it is in biomedical studies.

Anyone who has looked into the matter can scarcely deny that major advances **9.** in medicine have been achieved through basic research with animals. Among these are the development of virtually all modern vaccines against infectious diseases, the invention of surgical approaches to eye disorders, bone and joint injuries and heart disease, the discovery of insulin and other hormones and the testing of all new drugs and antibiotics.

The benefits to humans of psychological research with animals may be less well **10.** known than those of medical research but are just as real. Historically, the application of psychological research to human problems has lagged considerably behind the applied use of medical research. Mental events and overt behavior, although controlled by the nervous system and biology of an organism, are much more difficult to describe and study than are the actions of tissues or organ systems. To describe the complex interplay of perceptions, memories, cognitive and emotional processes with a physical and social environment that changes from moment to moment, elaborate research designs had to be developed. Since even a single type of behavior, such as vocalization, has so many different forms, a wide variety of ways of measuring the differences had to be developed. Finally, because much psychological research makes inferences from behavioral observations about internal states of an organism, methods were needed to insure that the interpretations were valid. Such complexities do not make the study of animal or human behavior less scientific or important than other kinds of research, but they do make it more difficult and slow its readiness for clinical applications. Examples include the use of biofeedback, which had its origin in studies of behavioral conditioning of neuromuscular activities in rats and other animals. Today, biofeedback can be used to control blood pressure and hypertension and help prevent heart attacks. In the case of paralyzed patients, it can be used to elevate blood pressure, enabling those who would otherwise have to spend their lives lying down to sit upright. Biofeedback techniques also are used in the reduction and control of severe pain and as a method of neuromuscular control to help reverse the process of scoliosis, a disabling and disfiguring curvature of the spine. Biofeedback can also be a cost-effective alternative to certain medical treatments and can help avoid many of the complications associated with long-term drug use.

Language studies with apes have led to practical methods of teaching language **11.** skills to severely retarded children who, prior to this work, had little or no language ability. Patients who have undergone radiation therapy for cancer can now take an interest in nutritious foods and avoid foods that have little nutritional value, thanks to studies of conditioned taste aversion done with animals. Neural and behavioral studies of early development of vision in cats and primates—studies that could not have been carried out with children—have led to advances in pediatric ophthalmology that can prevent irreversible brain damage and loss of vision in children who have cataracts and various other serious eye problems.

Behavioral modification and behavioral therapy, widely accepted techniques for **12.** treating alcohol, drug and tobacco addiction, have a long history of animal studies investigating learning theory and reward systems. Programmed instruction, the application of learning principles to educational tasks, is based on an array of learning studies in animals. These are but a few examples of the effectiveness and usefulness for humans of psychological research with animals.

Those opposed to animal research have proposed that alternatives to animal **13.** research, such as mathematical and computer models and tissue cultures, be used. In some cases, these alternatives are both feasible and valuable. Tissue cultures, for example, have been very effective in certain toxicological studies that formerly required live animals. For psychological studies, however, it is often necessary to study the whole animal and its relationship to the environment. Visual problems, abnormal sexual behavior, depression and aggression, for example, are not seen in tissue cultures and do not lend themselves to computer models. When human subjects cannot be used for such studies, animals are necessary if the research is to be done at all. It follows from this that even if humans might benefit from animal research, the cost to animals is too high. It is ironic that despite this moral position, the same organizations condone—and indeed sponsor—activities that appear to violate the basic rights of animals to live and reproduce. Each year 10,000,000 dogs are destroyed by public pounds, animal shelters and humane societies. Many of these programs are supported and even operated by animal-protectionist groups. Surely there is a strong contradiction when those who profess to believe in animal rights deny animals their right to life. A similar situation exists with regard to programs of pet sterilization, programs that deny animals the right to breed and to bear offspring and are sponsored in many cases by antivivisectionists and animal-rights groups. Evidently, animal-rights advocates sometimes recognize and subscribe to the position that animals do not have the same rights as humans. However, their public posture leaves little room for examining these subtleties or applying similar standards to animal research.

Within the animal-protectionist movement there are moderates who have confi- **14.** dence in scientists as compassionate human beings and in the value of research. Their primary aims are to insure that animals are treated humanely and that discomfort in animal experimentation is kept to a minimum. It is to this group that scientists and scientific organizations have the responsibility to explain what they do, why and how they do it and what benefits occur.

I believe that the values guiding contemporary animal research represent prevail- **15.** ing sentiment within the scientific community and, indeed, within society at large. And I believe that these values are congruent with those of the moderates within the animal-protectionist movement. As articulated by ethicist Arthur Caplan, rights, in the most realistic sense, are granted by one group to another based on perceived similarities between the groups. Plainly, animals lack those characteristics that would allow them to share in the rights we grant to humans. We do not grant domestic animals the right to go where they wish or do what they want because they are obviously unable to comprehend the responsibilities and demands of human society. In fact, we do not as a society even grant all domestic animals and pets the right to live.

This does not mean, however, that we do not have a moral responsibility to **16.** animals. I believe, along with Caplan and the scientific research community at large, that we hold a moral stewardship for animals and that we are obliged to treat them with humane compassion and concern for their sentience. Many animal forms can and do feel pain and are highly aware of their environment. This awareness makes them worthy of our respect and serious concern. Caplan is certainly correct when he says that this moral obligation ought to be part of what it means to be a scientist today. Scientific inquiry into the nature of our living world has freed us from ignorance and superstition. Scientific understanding is an expression of our highest capacities—those of objective observation, interpretive reasoning, imagination and creativity. Founded on the results of basic research, often conducted with no goal other than that of increased understanding, the eventual practical use of this knowledge has led to a vastly improved well-being for humankind.

Extremists in the animal-rights movement probably will never accept such **17.** justifications for research or assurances of humane treatment. They may reject any actions, no matter how conscientious, that scientists take in realistically and morally reconciling the advance of human welfare with the use of animals. But, fortunately, there are many who, while deeply and appropriately concerned for the compassionate treatment of animals, recognize that human welfare is and should be our primary concern.

WORKING WITH THE TEXT

Cultural and Historical References

In this section, the numbers at the margin refer to the numbered paragraphs in the selection itself.

16. "Sentience" means "consciousness, awareness of self, feeling." One of the significant disagreements between the two sides of the animal rights controversy concerns just how much sentience an animal has.

Writing Assignments: The Paragraph

Be sure to provide an introduction for each of the following paragraph writing assignments. That is, begin each paragraph with a phrase like this: "Thomas Brickle claims that. . . ." When it is relevant, you might also want to identify the expertise of the author ("Thomas Brickle, a New Testament scholar, claims that. . . ."), the name of the book or article, the century and country in which the work appeared, or any other circumstances that your readers might find significant. For more on this, see pp. 11–13 in Chapter 2.

1. Show how King uses a scientific study to undermine the arguments of his opponents. See paragraphs 1 to 4.

2. Show how King's fair-minded paragraph 7 actually strengthens his case. Begin your paragraph with a topic sentence that looks something like this: "Taking account of one's weaknesses can actually make one's argument stronger because it shows the writer to be fair-minded."

Writing Assignments: The Short Essay

Use informal documentation for these short essays. That is, don't use footnotes or a Works Cited page to document your sources. Instead, cite only relevant information about your source, and keep that information *within* your text. Then follow the summary or quote with a page number in parentheses. (Use the page numbers that you find in this book to represent the page numbers of the source.) Thus, your informal documentation will look something like this:

> In *Animal Liberation,* Peter Singer asks an intriguing question, ". . . if people are not prepared to give up tobacco, can it be right to make animals suffer the cost of their decision to continue smoking" (p. 328)?

1. Describe and comment on the idea in paragraph 15 that animal research is justified, in part anyway, because it is consistent with the idea that "animals lack those characteristics that would allow them to share in the rights we grant to humans."

2. One of King's purposes in his essay is to separate the extremists in the animal rights movement from the moderates. Show where and how he does this.

3. Describe and argue with King's attack on the animal rights groups' support of humane society and animal shelter activities.

4. Argue with King's basic position.

5. Show how King adds to the persuasiveness of his argument when he shows signs of compassion toward animals.

THE FACTS ABOUT ANIMAL RESEARCH

Robert J. White

Robert White is director of neurological surgery at Cleveland Metropolitan General Hospital and professor of neurosurgery at Case Western Reserve University Medical School. The "facts" which White reveals involve the vital role that animal research plays in the advancements in brain surgery and other life-saving medical procedures.

1. Four years ago I was part of a surgical team trying to remove a malignant tumor from the brain of a nine-year-old girl. The operation failed because we could not stem the hemorrhaging in the brain tissue. We were unable to separate the little girl from the cancer that was slowly killing her. To buy time, we put her on a program of radiation.

2. Concurrently we were experimenting in our brain-research laboratory with a new high-precision laser scalpel. Working with monkeys and dogs that had been humanely treated and properly anesthetized, we perfected our operating technique. Then, in July 1985, my associate, pediatric neurosurgeon Matt Likavec, and I used the laser to

Source: Robert J. White, "The Facts about Animal Research," *Reader's Digest.* March 1988: 127–132.

remove all of that little girl's tumor. Now 13, she is healthy, happy, and looking forward to a full life. The animal experiments had enabled us to cure a child we could not help 15 months earlier.

There is virtually no major treatment or surgical procedure in modern medicine **3.** that could have been developed without animal research. Work with dogs and other animals led to the discovery of insulin and the control of diabetes, to open-heart surgery, the cardiac pacemaker and the whole area of organ transplantation. Polio, which once killed some 30,000 people annually and crippled thousands of children, has been almost totally eradicated in the United States by preventive vaccines perfected on monkeys. By working with animals, researchers have raised the cure rate for children afflicted with acute lymphocytic leukemia from four percent in 1965 to 70 percent today.

Animal research has vanquished smallpox and enabled us to immunize our **4.** children against mumps, measles, rubella and diphtheria, and to defend them against infections by means of an arsenal of medical "magic bullets" called antibiotics.

Animals, too, have profited from this research. Many a family pet has had **5.** cataracts removed, has undergone open-heart surgery or wears a pacemaker, and many animals have benefited from vaccines for rabies, distemper, anthrax, tetanus and feline leukemia.

Regulatory Straitjacket. The dramatic medical strides of the past 50 years far **6.** exceed the progress in all of previous history. Unhappily, the next 50 years may not see comparable accomplishments. We owe this cloudy outlook to a radical element within the animal-rights movement, spearheaded by People for the Ethical Treatment of Animals (PETA) and other anti-vivisectionist groups, whose leaders insist that *all* research involving animals must cease. These extremists are applying pressure at every level of government, trying to fashion a regulatory straitjacket that is sure to slow medical progress.

Rep. Robert Mrazek (D., N.Y.) and Sen. Wendell Ford (D., Ky.) have introduced **7.** companion bills in Congress that would effectively prohibit the sale of pound animals for any medical research funded by the National Institutes of Health (NIH). Twelve states already have banned such sales, and five more have similar legislation under active consideration.

In addition, Rep. Charles Rose (D., N.C.) has introduced a bill that would, in **8.** effect, give animals "standing" in court. Should the bill pass, anyone who decides that an animal has been misused in an animal-research facility could file suit in the animal's behalf against the government. Thus, misguided radicals could choke our courts with nuisance suits.

Economic Realities. It is not hard to understand why opponents of research **9.** with animals have received such a sympathetic response. The idea conjures up images of experiments on beloved family pets. But the fact is that over 90 percent of the more than 20 million animals used annually in medical research are mice, rats and other rodents. A small percentage are farm animals and monkeys, and less than one percent are dogs and cats.

About 200,000 dogs and cats are abandoned *each week* in the United States. **10.** These are animals that people have left to roam the streets, forage in garbage dumps and run wild. After a waiting period in the pound, during which time any pet picked up accidentally may be claimed by its owner or adopted, the animals are put to death. It is only after this waiting period has expired that medical researchers purchase a few already doomed animals—in 1986, for example, less than two percent of them. That same year, about one-tenth of our dog and cat populations—some ten million animals—were destroyed.

Researchers obtain animals from pounds because the cost for each is usually $15   **11.** or less, while animals bred by commercial suppliers for research purposes cost several hundred dollars. If medical centers are prohibited from purchasing pound animals, many researchers will not be able to afford to continue their work.

This is nowhere more evident than in Massachusetts, one of the world's most   **12.** productive medical-research centers and the first state to ban totally the sale of pound animals for medical-research purposes. The high cost of commercially supplied dogs has forced noted Harvard Medical School physiologist Dr. A. Clifford Barger to cut back on work aimed at finding cures for hypertension and coronary-artery disease. "The dog is essential to the study of such diseases," says Dr. Barger. "In the end, it's the public that is going to suffer."

In the November 1986 issue of *The Washingtonian* magazine, Katie McCabe   **13.** recounted another aspect of the Massachusetts pound law: at Massachusetts General Hospital "cost factors have forced Dr. Willard Daggett to limit his cardiovascular studies to the rat heart, which severely limits the research questions that can be explored and applied to human cardiac patients."

Additionally, regulations governing the way we care for research animals have   **14.** already increased costs substantially, and animal-rights activists continue to make new proposals to drive costs higher. "It has even been proposed that dogs used in research have individual, isolated runs so they can defecate in privacy," says Dr. Mark Ravitch, surgeon-in-chief-emeritus at the University of Pittsburgh's Montefiore Hospital. "All of this has little to do with dog welfare, and everything to do with raising the price of medical research."

Shackled Experiments.   The public should have confidence that the animals   **15.** used in our medical-research laboratories are well treated. Every federally funded facility has an "institutional animal-care-and-use committee," one of whose functions is to ascertain that animals are being cared for properly. The committee must include a medical-research scientist, a non-scientist, someone not affiliated with the institution, and a veterinarian. Additional monitoring is provided by federal agents.

I certainly have no objection to these safeguards. Government-funded projects   **16.** involve many thousands of scientists in some 800 institutions, and the probability that there won't be some carelessness is zero. But all good researchers insist that animals be treated humanely—not only out of compassion but also because valid work depends on clean, healthy research subjects that are not victims of physical or emotional stress.

Charles McCarthy, Director of NIH's Office for Protection from Research Risks,   **17.** says: "We have had a half-dozen abuse cases since 1981. Either animals have not been properly cared for—usually over a long weekend—or an attendant has not conscientiously provided an animal with adequate anesthetics. But we have *never* run into a sadist who got his kicks inflicting pain on animals."

My main objection is to regulations requiring animal-care-and-use committees   **18.** to pass on all research proposals involving animals. While experiments begin with specific goals, a scientist never knows at the outset where the research will lead. Yet he may not deviate from the original plan—in order to pursue an unexpected opportunity—without first filling out costly, time-consuming paper work to obtain committee approval. New regulations governing the use of animals have already increased the financial burden on the nation's 127 medical schools by many millions of dollars annually. "But the real cost is that there will be less research," says Carol Scheman of the Association of American Universities, "and when research is slowed, people die."

Damaging Setbacks.   Public-opinion polls have shown that nearly 80 percent **19.** of us approve of the use of animals in medical experimentation. I am convinced that most Americans are unaware of the devastating effect animal-rights extremists are having on such research. Frankie L. Trull, president of the Foundation for Biomedical Research, says, "People don't realize that they are being steamrollered. They may not recognize what is happening until a lot of damage has been done."

The damage is already considerable. For example, Stanford University's proposal **20.** to build a state-of-the-art animal laboratory and a new biology building met with opposition from the Palo Alto Humane Society. First objecting to the lab, partly out of concern for the well-being of Stanford's animals, the Society later joined in an appeal to delay construction of the biology building on the basis of possible environmental damage. These delays will cost Stanford some $2 million.

What are the human stakes? Stanford University scientists have already developed **21.** a permanent cure for diabetes in mice. It isn't known yet whether this will lead to a permanent cure for human diabetes, but there is a strong basis for optimism. If this dream is to be realized, research must proceed with more mice, then with larger animals.

Animal-rights activists like to claim that work accomplished with animals can **22.** be done by other means, that we can unlock medical mysteries with computers and with cell cultures grown in test tubes. But, as yet, there is no computer that can even come close to matching the nervous system that tells a mouse how to move a leg or a monkey a finger.

How can researchers using cell cultures, which do not have bones, develop a **23.** treatment for arthritis or other bone diseases? How can cell cultures help us to perfect the surgical techniques used in organ transplantation? For the foreseeable future the answers to such questions can be found only by scientists working with living species.

Intimidation Tactics.   Not content to impose their views through lawful means, **24.** fringe elements of the animal-rights movement have resorted to terrorist activity. Last April, intruders who left behind graffiti and vandalized university vehicles set afire an unfinished veterinary diagnostic laboratory at the University of California's Davis campus, causing damage estimated at $3.5 million. A few months later a group calling itself "The Band of Mercy" took 28 cats from a Department of Agriculture research center in Beltsville, Md. Eleven of these cats had been infected with a parasite, Toxoplasm gondii, which infects pregnant women and causes some 2000 birth defects annually in the United States. The incident severely hampered the work of researchers who were investigating the effects of the parasite in animals as a potential source for infection in not only pregnant women but also victims of AIDS and other diseases that weaken the immune system.

The international Animal Liberation Front (ALF) was identified by California's **25.**
attorney general, John Van De Kamp, as among the state's three most active terrorist
organizations during 1985. In a foray into the City of Hope National Medical Center
in Duarte, the ALF did sufficient damage to set back a cancer research project by two
years. At a University of California at Riverside research facility, the ALF destroyed
$683,500 worth of equipment and records, painted walls with slogans and turned loose
467 animals, including a monkey involved in a program to improve the lives of
blind children. By last September, animal-rights groups throughout the country had
perpetrated 26 such serious crimes at medical-research facilities over a two-year period.

We are a people who love animals, but we must be realistic. Through the ages **26.**
we have harvested animals for food, clothing, shelter, and in this century alone medical
scientists working with animals have played a major role in increasing our average
life-span from 50 to 75 years. What a tragic disservice to ourselves and future
generations if we allow the animal-rights extremists to quell this marvelous momentum!

What to do? First, an important don't: Don't be misled by emotional and false **27.**
propaganda. The animals in our reputable research laboratories are *not* being wantonly
tortured by sadistic scientists. Such reports should not be taken seriously. . . .

Do we want to wipe out leukemia? Alzheimer's? AIDS? Diabetes? Do we want **28.**
better vaccines, more effective treatments and cures for high blood pressure, coronary-
artery disease, stroke and myriad other ills? All of these things and more are possible
within the next 25 years, some of them sooner, because of the work medical scientists
are now doing with animals. But they can't be accomplished if we surrender to the
mindless emotionalism and intimidation of the animal-rights fanatics. The choice is
ours.

WORKING WITH THE TEXT

Cultural and Historical References

In this section, the numbers at the margin refer to the numbered paragraphs
in the selection itself.

1. In the nineteenth century, antivivisectionists were those who opposed
   cutting into live animals. The word seems to have broadened through
   the years. Now antivivisectionists usually include groups opposed to
   animal research of all kinds.

27. "Wanton" means both "cruel" and "unchaste." Which does White
    mean?

Writing Assignments: The Paragraph

Be sure to provide an introduction for each of the following paragraph writing
assignments. That is, begin each paragraph with a phrase like this: "Thomas
Brickle claims that . . . ." When it is relevant, you might also want to identify
the expertise of the author ("Thomas Brickle, a New Testament scholar,

claims that . . . ."), the name of the book or article, the century and country in which the work appeared, or any other circumstances that your readers might find significant. For more on this, see pp. 11–13 in Chapter 2.

1. In paragraph 3, White *seems* to say that animal research is solely responsible for improvements in the survival rates of children with acute lymphocytic leukemia. Does he *actually* say that? Does he imply it? Is he discounting the years of research that hospitals like St. Judes in Memphis have been doing on children with acute lymphocytic leukemia? Write a paragraph about this matter.

2. Summarize paragraphs 1 to 2.

3. Extremists within the animal rights movement have hurt their case. Develop a paragraph based on that topic sentence. Use White's examples.

Writing Assignments: The Short Essay

Use informal documentation for these short essays. That is, don't use footnotes or a Works Cited page to document your sources. Instead, cite only relevant information about your source, and keep that information *within* your text. Then follow the summary or quote with a page number in parentheses. (Use the page numbers that you find in this book to represent the page numbers of the source.) Thus, your informal documentation will look something like this:

> In *Animal Liberation*, Peter Singer asks an intriguing question, ". . . if people are not prepared to give up tobacco, can it be right to make animals suffer the cost of their decision to continue smoking" (p. 328)?

1. Write a paper on the ways in which paragraph 18 strengthens or weakens White's argument.

2. Write an essay in which you analyze White's personalized introduction. Does it take away from the objectivity of his essay? Does it add to its effectiveness?

3. Discuss the pros and cons of the legislation put forward by Representative Mrazek and Senator Ford prohibiting the sale of pound animals for animal research funded by the National Institutes of Health.

OF PAIN AND PROGRESS

Geoffrey Cowley

Geoffrey Cowley, a senior writer for *Newsweek*, analyzes the issues involved in the controversy over animal rights, cites numerous examples of questionable uses of laboratory animals, and surveys the tactics of militant animal rights groups. You

Source: Geoffrey Cowley, "Of Pain and Progress," *Newsweek*. December 26, 1988: 50–55, 57, 59.

might want to treat this essay as an update of the Curtis article, and determine how the issues have evolved since 1978.

For 14 years, Michiko Okamoto heard nothing but praise for the medical **1.** experiments she performed on animals. By force-feeding barbiturates to groups of cats for periods of several weeks, then cutting off their supplies, the Cornell University pharmacologist learned a lot about the dynamics of addiction and withdrawal. She showed that the moderate drug doses prescribed by physicians can, over time, be as physically addictive as the fixes sold on the street. And she explained why addicts die from overdoses even after their bodies have grown tolerant of particular drugs. Okamoto's work won numerous grants from the National Institute on Drug Abuse (NIDA) and her findings are cited in standard medical texts. According to Keith Killam, a professor of pharmacology at the University of California, Davis, the cat experiments are "a shining crystal example of how to do science."

Steve Siegel of Trans-Species Unlimited, a Pennsylvania-based animal-rights **2.** group, calls them "the worst of the worst." Last year Siegel's group mounted a massive campaign against Okamoto. It printed brochures describing, in her own words, how her cats would stand "trembling [and] salivating" after she suddenly stopped pumping drugs into their stomachs—how they would hiss at imagined tormentors or collapse and die "during or soon after periods of continuous convulsive activity." For four months Trans-Species' supporters picketed Okamoto's laboratory and barraged her with phone calls. Cornell and NIDA officials received more than 10,000 letters condemning the experiments.

This fall, after making a statement that was widely, if mistakenly, viewed as a **3.** promise to stop the cat studies, Cornell and Okamoto surrendered. In an unprecedented gesture, they wrote NIDA to say they would forfeit a new $530,000 three-year research grant.

It was, depending on your perspective, a moral victory for abused and innocent **4.** creatures or a defeat for science and medicine. Either way, the case of the Cornell cats was just the latest example of America's growing preoccupation with the moral status of animals. Scholars say more has been written on the subject in the past 12 years than in the previous 3,000. And grassroots organizations are proliferating wildly. Just 15 years ago, talk of animal welfare was pretty well confined to the humane societies. Today there are some 7,000 animal-protection groups in the United States, with combined memberships of 10 million and total budgets of some $50 million. Says Carol Burnett, spokeswoman for the Washington-based group People for the Ethical Treatment of Animals: "We're really gaining steam."

That's not to say everybody's riding the same train. The activists' demands range **5.** from securing better lab conditions to setting all animals free, and their tactics range from letter writing to burglary. Yet they've become a potent collective presence. Animal advocates have sponsored numerous local ballot initiatives to regulate the treatment of farm animals, or ban the use of animals in product-safety tests, or exempt school kids from mandatory dissection lessons. They've declared war on the fur industry, agitated against particular scientists, as in the Cornell case, and organized to block construction of new animal-research facilities. At Stanford University, plans for a new $18 million animal lab were held up for more than a year when the Palo

Alto Humane Society opposed the project before the county board of supervisors. Construction is now under way, but the delay cost the university more than $2 million.

There has been civil disobedience, too—even violence. Just last month a woman **6.** affiliated with the animal-rights cause was arrested outside the United States Surgical Corp. in Norwalk, Conn., and charged with planting a radio-controlled pipe bomb near the company chairman's parking place. Fires and break-ins, many of them linked to the militant Animal Liberation Front, have caused millions of dollars' worth of damage at labs around the country. The fear of such incidents is fast turning research centers into bunkers. After two bomb threats and at least five attempted break-ins, officials at Emory University's Yerkes Regional Primate Research Center recently spent hundreds of thousands of dollars on new alarms and electronic locks. Other institutions, including Harvard Medical School, have taken similar steps.

In short, the debate over animal rights is forcing basic changes in the way **7.** universities, corporations and government agencies do business. More than that, it's prompting a reconsideration of mankind's place in the web of life. As the political scientist Walter Truett Anderson observes in his recent book "To Govern Evolution," the cause of animal rights is not just a passing fancy. It is a "principled attempt to redefine some of our most basic concepts about the nature of political rights and obligations."

Immense Benefits

The number of creatures used in research, education and product testing each year is **8.** indeed staggering. Though estimates run as high as 100 million, federal agencies place the total at 17 million to 22 million—a figure that includes some 50,000 cats, 61,000 primates, 180,000 dogs, 554,000 rabbits and millions of mice and rats (which fill 80 to 90 percent of the demand).

The killing is not without purpose; it has immense practical benefits. Animal **9.** models have advanced the study of such diseases as cancer, diabetes and alcoholism and yielded lifesaving treatments for everything from heart disease to manic-depressive illness. Vaccines developed through animal research have virtually wiped out diseases like smallpox and polio. "Every surgical technique was tried first in animals," says Frankie Trull, executive director of the Foundation for Biomedical Research. "Every drug anybody takes was tried first in animals."

By the same token, today's animal research may lead to better medicine in the **10.** future. Right now, researchers at the University of California School of Medicine, Davis, are infecting Asian rhesus monkeys with the simian AIDS virus, to see whether early treatment with the drug AZT will keep them from developing symptoms. Because the monkeys normally get sick within 10 months of infection—not the three to five years common in humans—the study will determine quickly whether the same treatment might save human lives.

At Houston's Baylor College of Medicine, Glen Martin and Brenda Lonsbury- **11.** Martin are using rabbits to study the hearing loss caused by environmental noise. By attaching small speakers to a rabbit's ears, the researchers can give the animal a large daily dose of noise resembling that of a blow-dryer or a factory or a construction site, and plot its effect. Knowing exactly how particular kinds of noise affect hearing would, of course, help us avoid the most dangerous ones. It might also suggest strategies for cleaning up the auditory environment.

At Emory University's Yerkes center, other researchers are performing cataract **12.** surgery on healthy baby rhesus monkeys, hoping to devise better postsurgical therapies for the human children who undergo the operation. After performing the surgery, neurobiologist Ronald Boothe and his colleagues give different monkeys slightly different rehabilitative treatments, all of which involve placing an opaque contact lens over the good eye and a corrective lens in the wounded eye. After a year of therapy, the researchers kill the animal and dissect their brains to see which treatment has promoted the most development within the visual cortex. "We have kids being born who are going to go blind without this research," Boothe says. "By me doing this research, we can prevent them from going blind. Most people, given that choice, will think it's justified."

Moral Costs

If the issue were that simple, animal experimentation might never have become so **13.** controversial. But as the philosopher Peter Singer demonstrated in 1975, it's not. In a book called "Animal Liberation," Singer questioned the assumption that securing practical benefits for mankind automatically justifies experimentation on other animals. Indeed, he condemned that notion as "a form of prejudice no less objectionable than prejudice about a person's race or sex," and he urged that we "consider our attitudes from the point of view of those who suffer by them."

To provide that perspective Singer had only to recount what scientists themselves **14.** had written in mainstream professional journals. In a chapter titled "Tools for Research," he sampled the recent literature from such diverse fields as toxicology and psychology, and it wasn't easy reading. He described standard government tests in which beagles were fed pesticides or bombarded with radiation until they lay bleeding from the mouth and anus. And he recounted numerous experiments in which psychologists subjected intelligent animals to fear or hopelessness or "psychological death" in crude attempts to analyze these emotional states.

In a 1972 paper in the Journal of Comparative and Physiological Psychology, for example, researchers at the Primate Research Center in Madison, Wis., described placing baby monkeys alone in a stainless-steel tank for periods of up to 45 days. They wanted to see whether confinement in this "well of despair" would cause lasting psychological damage. It did. The animals exhibited what the researchers termed "severe and persistent psychopathological behavior of a depressive nature." But the paper stressed the preliminary nature of this finding, saying further studies were needed to determine whether the symptoms could be "traced specifically to variables such as chamber shape, chamber size, duration of confinement [or] age at time of confinement." (No such experiments have been conducted at the Madison center since 1974.)

In other papers, the same scientists described efforts to gauge the effects of child **15.** abuse on young monkeys. In one experiment they designed mechanical surrogate mothers who would eject sharp brass spikes as the youngsters hugged them. The experience seemed to have no serious effect; the infants "simply waited until the spikes receded and then returned and clung to the mother." So, in a refinement of the experiment, the researchers forcibly impregnated females who had been driven mad through social isolation, and turned them loose on their own offspring. "One of [the mothers'] favorite tricks," they wrote, "was to crush the infant's skull with their teeth."

These programs were not mere atrocities, Singer argued. They were examples of **16.** scientists "doing what they were trained to do, and what thousands of their colleagues do." The peer-reviewed journals were brimming with similar stories. Researchers studying how punishment affects learning suspended dogs in hammocks and administered shocks through electrodes taped to their paws. Other investigators, curious to know how various drugs would affect a subject's responsiveness to punishment, implanted electrodes near pigeons' genitals, gave them drugs, then shocked them every time they pecked keys they'd learned to associate with food.

If Singer's work gave birth to a new social movement, a young activist named **17.** Alex Pacheco helped it grow. Pacheco, who was moved by Singer's book to help organize the group People for the Ethical Treatment of Animals (PETA), took a job in 1981 as a lab assistant at the Institute for Behavior Research in Silver Spring, Md. Once he had his own keys, he was able to spend several months sneaking in at night to document the mistreatment of 17 monkeys being used in a study of spinal-cord injury. Researchers had severed nerves to the monkeys' arms and were testing their ability to use the crippled limbs by shocking the animals when they failed. Pacheco's widely publicized photographs showed monkeys covered with open, infected wonds. Some had chewed the ends off their fingers. All were confined to filth-encrusted cages just a foot and a half wide.

Steady Progress

Since then, similarly troubling conditions have come to light at a number of respected **18.** research centers. Yet all parties seem to agree that the general situation has improved markedly since 1980. The number of animals destroyed in experiments, however staggering, has declined steadily as researchers have come up with cheaper and more humane alternatives, such as cell cultures and computer models. And scientists using live animals have, as a general rule, become more conscientious and more accountable. "A lot of people are learning, a lot are trying," says Ingrid Newkirk, the British-born activist who founded PETA with Alex Pacheco eight years ago.

One of the first tangible changes came about in 1985, when Congress passed a **19.** series of amendments to the federal Animal Welfare Act, the law governing animal care in laboratories and other nonfarm facilities. The amendments have yet to be implemented by the Department of Agriculture, which enforces the act (they remain stalled in the federal budget office). But they mark a new congressional commitment to the "three R's" preached by moderate groups like the Animal Welfare Institute and the Humane Society of the United States: *reduction* in the number of animals sacrificed, *refinement* of techniques that cause suffering and *replacement* of live animals with simulations or cell cultures.

Specifically, the amendments call for the creation of a national data bank that **20.** will list the results of all animal experiments and thus prevent needless repetition. All laboratories using live animals are required, under the amendments, to set up animal-care committees and submit to annual inspections. Facilities housing dogs must let them exercise, and those housing primates must provide for their "psychological well-being."

Rather than wait for the new rules to go into effect, many institutions have **21.** adopted reforms on their own. Most research facilities—including all that receive funds from the National Institutes of Health—now have committees that review proposed animal experiments. And some primate facilities, such as Yerkes and New York University's LEMSIP (Laboratory for Experimental Medicine and Surgery in Primates), are going out of their way to keep the animals mentally and emotionally stimulated. To encourage social contact among the 250 chimpanzees that LEMSIP uses in AIDS and hepatitis research, veterinarian James Mahoney has constructed wire-mesh tunnels between their cages. If an experiment requires keeping the animals separated, he makes sure they can see each other through sheets of Plexiglass. And to ward off the boredom that can turn lab chimps into blank-eyed psychotics, he gives them games.

Small Pleasures

He may place tubs of frozen Kool-Aid outside the chimps' cages, then give them pieces **22.** of plastic tubing that can be used as long-distance drinking straws. Noodling tube into tub for an occasional sip can provide hours of entertainment. In a variation on the theme, Mahoney passes out plastic tubes stuffed with raisins and marshmallows and lets the chimps use willow branches to extract the treats, just as they would termites from a hollow log in the wild. The animals' latest craze is cleaning their own teeth with toothbrushes and admiring the results in hand-held mirrors.

The reforms haven't been confined to research laboratories. For 50 years, **23.** consumer-protection laws have effectively required that cosmetics and household products be tested on animals before being sold to humans. But major firms have recently started seeking, and finding, less noxious methods of quality control. The LD-50 test, which consists of gauging the dose of a given substance needed to exterminate half of the animals in a test group, is already falling by the wayside; a survey by the Food and Drug Administration shows that its use has declined by 96 percent since the late 1970s. The Draize test for irritancy, which involves squirting high concentrations of possible irritants into the eyes of rabbits, is still the industry standard. But Procter & Gamble now exposes rabbits to concentrations somewhat closer to those a consumer might encounter. And it has joined other firms in pledging to halt all animal tests as soon as alternatives are available.

Still, the changes of the past decade hardly signal a new consensus on the proper **24.** use of animals. Some scientists consider the reforms excessive. University of Mississippi physiologist Arthur Guyton, for example, warns that the trend toward stricter regulation threatens the very future of science. Even the 1985 amendments to the Animal Welfare Act could prove ruinously expensive, he says. The "very arbitrary" rules governing cage size might force labs all over the country to remove their facilities. "While medical research using animals has not been killed outright," Guyton concludes, "it is slowly bleeding to death."

Activists, for their part, complain that the reforms have been too modest. A lot **25.** of needless suffering is still being perpetrated in the name of science and medicine, they say. Consider the situation at Sema Inc., a government contract laboratory in Rockville, Md., where AIDS and hepatitis experiments are conducted on chimpanzees. Visitors aren't normally welcome, but the renowned primatologist Jane Goodall got a tour of the facility last year, and later wrote an article for The New York Times, describing what she saw.

Unlike LEMSIP's chimps, Sema's spend years of their lives in total isolation, **26.** confined to tiny boxes that resemble nothing so much as microwave ovens. After watching a chimp stare blankly into space as her caretaker approached, Goodall wrote, "I shall be haunted forever by her eyes and by the eyes of the other infant chimpanzees I saw that day. Have you ever looked into the eyes of a person who, stressed beyond endurance, has given up, succumbed utterly to the crippling helplessness of despair?" Katherine Bick, deputy director of the National Institutes of Health, denies that the situation is really so grim. She adds, as she did last spring, that larger, better cages are on the way. Meanwhile, says PETA's Pacheco, conditions sanctioned by the federal government are "needlessly driving intelligent animals insane."

Empty Cages

Even more divisive is the question of where science should be headed. Many activists **27.** dream of a day when all the cages are empty. "Our bottom line," says Newkirk, "is a day when there are no animals in labs." Researchers find that idea ludicrous. They tend to dismiss it as a product of ignorance ("People with no science education don't recognize that the pyramid of knowledge, built upon basic research, depends on animals," says one federal official), or of sentimentality ("a bizarre elevation of a touchy-feely, do-gooder's view of the world," in the words of Yerkes administrator Frederick King).

The moral dilemma behind all this bitterness was nicely crystallized in a recent **28.** report by the National Research Council. "Research with animals has saved human lives, lessened human suffering and advanced scientific understanding," the authors observe, "yet that same research can cause pain and distress for the animals involved and usually results in their death."

It would be nice, of course, if there were alternatives to vivisection that could **29.** deliver the same benefits without the death and suffering. But there is a limit to what can be accomplished with cell cultures and computer models. "You can't mathematically model this disease," says Murray Gardner, head of the U.C. Davis team studying early drug treatment in AIDS-infected monkeys. "You've got to experiment in a living system, where all the things we don't know about are going on."

The question is whether the practical benefits of vivisection constitute a moral **30.** justification for it. If mankind's interest in finding a better treatment for AIDS *doesn't* justify conducting lethal experiments on individual humans, an ethicist might ask, why does it justify performing them on monkeys? Why doesn't a monkey deserve moral consideration? What is the relevant difference between a human subject and an animal subject?

To reply that the human is *human* and the animal isn't only begs the question. **31.** Peter Singer likens it to sanctioning racial discrimination on the ground that white people are white and black people aren't. Another possible answer is that we humans enjoy certain *God-given* prerogatives. We are, after all, the only creatures the Bible says were made in God's image. "Most Judeo-Christian religions make distinctions about the special nature of man," says Frederick Goodwin, director of the Alcohol, Drug Abuse and Mental Health Administration. "To me, that is a distinct, qualitative difference between our primate relatives and man."

The Evidence?

It may be a difference, but it's not an empirical, observable one. It has to be taken on **32.** faith. Are there certain things *about* humans that make us inherently more valuable than other animals? Language and rational thought are the two traits usually cited as setting *Homo sapiens* apart. Yet there are plenty of humans who *lack* language and reason—babies, the senile, the insane—and the thought of performing medical experiments on them is abhorrent. Why, if a severely retarded child is too precious to sacrifice, is a chimp of superior intelligence fair game?

Maybe there is no reasoned moral justification. Maybe animal experimentation **33.** is best understood in purely practical terms, not as a prerogative or an obligation but as a strategy for survival. Whatever the answer, scientists can no longer afford to pretend that their critics' moral concerns are frivolous. Profound questions are being raised, and ignoring them won't make them go away.

WORKING WITH THE TEXT

Cultural and Historical References

In this section, the numbers at the margin refer to the numbered paragraphs in the selection itself.

13. The first essay in this chapter is a selection from Peter Singer's *Animal Liberation.*

25. Jane Goodall is the noted primatologist who spent years in Africa studying apes.

Writing Assignments: The Paragraph

Be sure to provide an introduction for each of the following paragraph writing assignments. That is, begin each paragraph with a phrase like this: "Thomas Brickle claims that. . . ." When it is relevant, you might also want to identify the expertise of the author ("Thomas Brickle, a New Testament scholar, claims that. . . ."), the name of the book or article, the century and country in which the work appeared, or any other circumstances that your readers might find significant. For more on this, see pp. 11–13 in Chapter 2.

1. Write a paragraph in which you summarize what animal rights groups

have done to curtail the use of laboratory animals in psychological research (paragraphs 1 to 6).

2. Write a paragraph in which you summarize the roles that Peter Singer and Alex Pacheco have played in the emerging animal rights movement (paragraphs 13 to 17).

3. Write a paragraph in which you discuss the complex issue of sacrificing animals for human welfare (paragraphs 30 to 32).

Writing Assignments: The Short Essay

Use informal documentation for these short essays. That is, don't use footnotes or a Works Cited page to document your sources. Instead, cite only relevant information about your source, and keep that information *within* your text. Then follow the summary or quote with a page number in parentheses. (Use the page numbers that you find in this book to represent the page numbers of the source.) Thus, your informal documentation will look something like this:

> In *Animal Liberation*, Peter Singer asks an intriguing question, ". . . if people are not prepared to give up tobacco, can it be right to make animals suffer the cost of their decision to continue smoking" (p. 328)?

1. Write an essay in which you summarize and comment on the evidence that Cowley presents demonstrating the "immense benefits" of using laboratory animals in medical and psychological research (paragraphs 1, 8 to 12).

2. Summarize the efforts the federal government and the research community have made in response to intense pressure from animal rights advocates (paragraphs 18 to 23).

3. Develop and illustrate Cowley's concluding observation that "maybe animal experimentation is best understood in purely practical terms, not as a prerogative or an obligation but as a strategy for survival." Consult paragraphs 18 to 23 and 30 to 32.

IS A LAB RAT'S FATE MORE POIGNANT THAN A CHILD'S?

Jane McCabe

Jane McCabe and her husband live in northern California. They have a daughter who was born with cystic fibrosis and whose treatment and therapy depend heavily upon research involving laboratory animals. McCabe makes an impassioned, highly personal defense of such research.

I see the debate about using animals in medical research in stark terms. If you **1.**

Source: Jane McCabe, "Is a Lab Rat's Fate More Poignant Than a Child's?" *Newsweek.* December 26, 1988: 55.

had to choose between saving a very cute dog or my equally cute, blond, brown-eyed daughter, whose life would you choose? It's not a difficult choice, is it? My daughter has cystic fibrosis. Her only hope for a normal life is that researchers, some of them using animals, will find a cure. Don't misunderstand. It's not that I don't love animals, it's just that I love Claire more.

Nine years ago I had no idea that I would be joining the fraternity of those who **2.** have a vital interest in seeing that medical research continues. I was a very pregnant woman in labor; with my husband beside me I gave birth to a 7-pound 1-ounce daughter. It all seemed so easy. But for the next four months she could not gain weight. She was a textbook case of failure to thrive. Finally a hospital test of the salt content in her sweat led to the diagnosis of cystic fibrosis.

The doctor gave us a little reason for hope. "Your daughter will not have a long **3.** life, but for most of the time, it will be a good life. Her life expectancy is about 13 years, though it could be longer or shorter. As research continues, we're keeping them alive longer."

"As research continues." It's not a lot to rely on but what's our alternative? We **4.** haven't waited passively. We learned how to take care of our little girl; her medical problems affect her digestion and lungs. We protected her from colds, learned about supplemental vitamins and antibiotics. We moved to California where the winters aren't so harsh and the cold and flu season isn't so severe. Our new doctor told us that the children at his center were surviving, on the average, to age 21. So far, our daughter is doing well. She is a fast runner and plays a mean first base. She loves her friends and is, in general, a happy little girl. All things considered, I feel very lucky.

How has research using animals helped those with CF? Three times a day my **5.** daughter uses enzymes from the pancreas of pigs to digest her food. She takes antibiotics tested on rats before they are tried on humans. As an adult, she will probably develop diabetes and need insulin—a drug developed by research on dogs and rabbits. If she ever needs a heart-lung transplant, one might be possible because of the cows that surgeons practiced on. There is no animal model to help CF research, but once the CF gene is located, new gene-splicing techniques may create a family of mice afflicted with the disease. Researchers would first learn to cure the mice with drugs, then cautiously try with humans.

There are only about 10,000 people with CF in the United States. But the number **6.** of people dependent on research is much larger. Walk with me through Children's Hospital at Stanford University: here are the youngsters fighting cancer, rare genetic illnesses, immunological diseases. Amid their laughter and desperate attempts to retain a semblance of childhood, there is suffering.

Human Suffering

I think the motivation of animal-rights activists is to cut down on the suffering in this **7.** world, but I have yet to hear them acknowledge that people—young and old—suffer, too. Why is a laboratory rat's fate more poignant that that of an incurably ill child?

There are advocates for animals who only seek to cut down on "unnecessary **8.** research." They don't specify how to decide what is unnecessary, but they do create an atmosphere in which doing medical research is seen as distasteful work. I think that's wrong. Researchers should be thanked, not hassled.

Every time I see a bumper sticker that says "Lab animals never have a nice **9.** day," a fantasy plays in my brain. I get out of my car, tap on the driver's window and ask to talk. In my fantasy, the other driver gets out, we find a coffee shop and I show her photos of my kids. I ask her if she has ever visited Children's Hospital. I am so eloquent that her eyes fill with tears and she promises to think of the children who are wasting away as she considers the whole complicated issue of suffering.

I have other fantasies, too, that a cure is found for what ails my daughter, that **10.** she marries and gives us some grandchildren, and does great work in her chosen profession, which at this moment appears to be cartooning or computer programming. We can still hope—as long as the research continues.

WORKING WITH THE TEXT

Cultural and Historical References

In this section, the numbers at the margin refer to the numbered paragraphs in the selection itself.

1. Cystic fibrosis is a congenital disease of the mucous glands. It usually develops during childhood and slowly destroys the pancreas and the pulmonary system.

Writing Assignments: The Paragraph

Be sure to provide an introduction for each of the following paragraph writing assignments. That is, begin each paragraph with a phrase like this: "Thomas Brickle claims that. . . ." When it is relevant, you might also want to identify the expertise of the author ("Thomas Brickle, a New Testament scholar, claims that. . . ."), the name of the book or article, the century and country in which the work appeared, or any other circumstances that your readers might find significant. For more on this, see pp. 11–13 in Chapter 2.

1. Write a paragraph in which you summarize the contributions of animal research to individuals like Claire McCabe.
2. Write a paragraph in which you take issue with McCabe's rhetorical question, "Why is a laboratory rat's fate more poignant than that of an incurably ill child?"

Writing Assignments: The Short Essay

Use informal documentation for these short essays. That is, don't use footnotes or a Works Cited page to document your sources. Instead, cite only relevant information about your source, and keep that information *within* your text. Then follow the summary or quote with a page number in parenthe-

ses. (Use the page numbers that you find in this book to represent the page numbers of the source.) Thus, your informal documentation will look something like this:

> In *Animal Liberation*, Peter Singer asks an intriguing question, ". . . if people are not prepared to give up tobacco, can it be right to make animals suffer the cost of their decision to continue smoking" (p. 328)?

1. Develop an essay in favor of animal research with your own personal equivalent of Claire McCabe as your prime example. Surely you too know someone who is a victim of a crippling disease and whose progress depends heavily upon medical advancements made through animal research.

2. Develop a paper in which you take issue with McCabe's rhetorical question, "Why is a laboratory rat's fate more poignant than that of an incurably ill child?"

ETHICS AND ANIMALS

Steven Zak

Steven Zak, a court attorney for the California Superior Court in Los Angeles, has written about animals and the law for numerous publications, including *The Los Angeles Times, The New York Times*, and *The Chicago Tribune*. Zak makes a low-key philosophical and practical argument for the inherent rights of animals. You will find, we think, that this essay complements the Singer excerpt at the outset of this chapter.

1. In December of 1986 members of an "animal-liberation" group called True Friends broke into the Sema, Inc., laboratories in Rockville, Maryland, and took four baby chimpanzees from among the facility's 600 primates. The four animals, part of a group of thirty being used in hepatitis research, had been housed individually in "isolettes"—small stainless-steel chambers with sealed glass doors. A videotape produced by True Friends shows other primates that remained behind. Some sit behind glass on wire floors, staring blankly. One rocks endlessly, banging violently against the side of his cage. Another lies dead on his cage's floor.

2. The "liberation" action attracted widespread media attention to Sema, which is a contractor for the National Institutes of Health, the federal agency that funds most of the animal research in this country. Subsequently the NIH conducted an investigation into conditions at the lab and concluded that the use of isolettes is justified to prevent the spread of diseases among infected animals. For members of True Friends and other animals-rights groups, however, such a scientific justification is irrelevant to what they see as a moral wrong; these activists remain frustrated over conditions at the laboratory. This conflict between the NIH and animals-rights groups mirrors the tension between animal researchers and animal-rights advocates generally. The researchers' position is

Source: Steven Zak, "Ethics and Animals," *Atlantic*. March 1989: 69–74.

that their use of animals is necessary to advance human health care and that liberation actions waste precious resources and impede the progress of science and medicine. The animal-rights advocates' position is that animal research is an ethical travesty that justifies extraordinary, and even illegal, measures.

The Sema action is part of a series that numbers some six dozen to date and that **3.** began, in 1979, with a raid on the New York University Medical Center, in which members of a group known as the Animal Liberation Front (ALF) took a cat and two guinea pigs. The trend toward civil disobedience is growing. For example, last April members of animal-rights groups demonstrated at research institutions across the country (and in other countries, including Great Britain and Japan), sometimes blocking entrances to them by forming human chains. In the United States more than 130 activists were arrested, for offenses ranging from blocking a doorway and trespassing to burglary.

To judge by everything from talk-show programs to booming membership **4.** enrollment in animal-rights groups (U.S. membership in all groups is estimated at 10 million), the American public is increasingly receptive to the animal-rights position. Even some researchers admit that raids by groups like True Friends and the ALF have exposed egregious conditions in particular labs and have been the catalyst for needed reforms in the law. But many members of animal-rights groups feel that the recent reforms do not go nearly far enough. Through dramatic animal-liberation actions and similar tactics, they hope to force what they fear is a complacent public to confront a difficult philosophical issue: whether animals, who are known to have feelings and psychological lives, ought to be treated as mere instruments of science and other human endeavors.

The ALF is probably the most active of the world's underground animal-rights **5.** groups. It originated in England, where the animal-protection movement itself began, in 1824, with the founding of the Royal Society for the Prevention of Cruelty to Animals. The ALF evolved from a group called the Band of Mercy, whose members sabotaged the vehicles of hunters and destroyed guns used on bird shoots. It now has members across Europe, and in Australia, New Zealand, Africa, and Canada, as well as the United States. It does not, however, constitute a unified global network. The American wing of the ALF was formed in 1979. The number of its members is unknown, but their ages range from eighteen to over sixty. Some are students, some are blue-collar workers, and many belong to the suburban middle class.

Animal-rights activists feel acute frustration over a number of issues, including **6.** hunting and trapping, the destruction of animals' natural habits, and the raising of animals for food. But for now the ALF considers animal research the most powerful symbol of human dominion over and exploitation of animals, and it devotes most of its energies to that issue. The public has been ambivalent, sometimes cheering the ALF on, at other times denouncing the group as "hooligans." However one chooses to characterize the ALF, it and other groups like it hold an uncompromising "rights view" of ethics toward animals. The rights view distinguishes the animal-protection movement of today from that of the past and is the source of the movement's radicalism.

Early animal-protection advocates and groups, like the RSPCA, seldom talked **7.** about rights. They condemned cruelty—that is, acts that produce or reveal bad character. In early-nineteenth-century England campaigners against the popular sport of bull-baiting argued that it "fostered every bad and barbarous principle of our nature." Modern activists have abandoned the argument that cruelty is demeaning to human character ("virtue thought") in favor of the idea that the lives of animals have intrinsic value ("rights thought"). Rights thought doesn't necessarily preclude the consideraton of virtue, but it mandates that the measure of virtue be the foreseeable consequences to others of one's acts.

"Michele" is thirty-five and works in a bank in the East. She has participated **8.** in many of the major ALF actions in the United States. One of the missions involved freeing rats, and she is scornful of the idea that rats aren't worth the effort. "That attitude is rather pathetic, really," she says. "These animals feel pain just like dogs, but abusing them doesn't arouse constituents' ire, so they don't get the same consideration. They all have a right to live their lives. Cuteness should not be a factor."

While most people would agree that animals should not be tortured, there is no **9.** consensus about animals' right to live (or, more precisely, their right not to be killed). Even if one can argue, as the British cleric Humphrey Primatt did in 1776, that "pain is pain, whether it be inflicted on man or on beast," it is more difficult to argue that the life of, say, a dog is qualitatively the same as that of a human being. To this, many animal-rights activists would say that every morally relevant characteristic that is lacking in all animals (rationality might be one, according to some ways of defining that term) is also lacking in some "marginal" human beings, such as infants, or the senile, or the severely retarded. Therefore, the activists argue, if marginal human beings have the right to live, it is arbitrary to hold that animals do not. Opponents of this point of view often focus on the differences between animals and "normal" human beings, asserting, for instance, that unlike most human adults, animals do not live by moral rules and therefore are not part of the human "moral community."

The credibility of the animal-rights viewpoint, however, need not stand or fall **10.** with the "marginal human beings" argument. Lives don't have to be qualitatively the same to be worthy of equal respect. One's pereception that another life has value comes as much from an appreciation of its uniqueness as from the recognition that it has characteristics that are shared by one's own life. (Who would compare the life of a whale to that of a marginal human being?) One can imagine that the lives of various kinds of animals differ radically, even as a result of having dissimilar bodies and environments—that being an octopus feels different from being an orangutan or an oriole. The orangutan cannot be redescribed as the octopus minus, or plus, this or that mental characteristic; conceptually, nothing could be added to or taken from the octopus that would make it the equivalent òf the oriole. Likewise, animals are not simply rudimentary human beings, God's false steps, made before He finally got it right with us.

Recognizing differences, however, puts one on tentative moral ground. It is easy **11.** to argue that likes ought to be treated alike. Differences bring problems: How do we think about things that are unlike? Against what do we measure and evaluate them? What combinations of likeness and difference lead to what sorts of moral consideration? Such problems may seem unmanageable, and yet in a human context we routinely face ones similar in kind if not quite in degree: our ethics must account for dissimilarities between men and women, citizens and aliens, the autonomous and the helpless, the fully developed and the merely potential, such as children or fetuses. We never solve these problems with finality, but we confront them.

One might be tempted to say that the problems are complicated enough without **12.**

bringing animals into them. There is a certain attractiveness to the idea that animals—lacking membership in the human and moral communities, and unable to reciprocate moral concern—deserve little consideration from us. After all, doesn't one have obligations toward members of one's family and community that do not apply to outsiders? Yet this appeal to a sense of community fails to take into account certain people who likewise lack membership and yet have moral claims against us. Consider future people, particularly those who will live in the distant future. Suppose that our dumping of certain toxic wastes could be predicted to cause widespread cancer among people five hundred years in the future. Would we not have a heavy moral burden to refrain from such dumping? Probably most of us would say that we would. Yet in what meaningful sense can it be said that people we will never meet, who will never do anything for us, and whose cultures and ethical systems will likely be profoundly different from our own, are members of our community? Membership may count for something, but it is clearly not a necessary condition for moral entitlement. Also, some animals—my dog, for instance—may more sensibly be characterized as members of our community than may some human beings, such as those of the distant future.

Both advocates and opponents of animal rights also invoke utilitarianism in **13.** support of their points of view. Utilitarianism holds that an act or practice is measured by adding up the good and the bad consequences—classically, pleasure and pain—and seeing which come out ahead. There are those who would exclude animals from moral consideration on the grounds that the benefits of exploiting them outweigh the harm. Ironically, though, it was utilitarianism, first formulated by Jeremy Bentham in the eighteenth century, that brought animals squarely into the realm of moral consideration. If an act or practice has good and bad consequences for animals, then these must be entered into the moral arithmetic. And the calculation must be genuinely disinterested. One may not baldly assert that one's own interests count for more. Animal researchers may truly believe that they are impartially weighing all interests when they conclude that human interests overwhelm those of animals. But a skeptical reader will seldom be persuaded that they are in fact doing so. For instance, a spokesperson for a research institution that was raided by the ALF wrote in the *Los Angeles Times* that we should not be "more concerned with the fate of these few dogs than with the millions of people who are cancer victims." Note the apparent weighing: "few" versus "millions." But her lack of impartiality was soon revealed by this rhetorical question: "Would they [the ALF] really save an animal in exchange for the life of a child?"

Even true utilitarianism is incomplete, though, without taking account of rights. **14.** For example, suppose a small group of aboriginal tribespeople were captured and bred for experiments that would benefit millions of other people by, say, resulting in more crash-worthy cars. Would the use of such people be morally acceptable? Surely it would not, and that point illustrates an important function of rights thought: to put limits on what can be done to individuals, even for the good of the many. Rights thought dictates that we cannot kill one rights-holder to save another—or even more than one other—whether or not the life of the former is "different" from that of the latter.

Those who seek to justify the exploitation of animals often claim that it comes **15.** down to a choice: kill an animal or allow a human being to die. But this claim is misleading, because a choice so posed has already been made. The very act of considering the taking of life X to save life Y reduces X to the status of a mere instrument. Consider the problem in a purely human context. Imagine that if Joe doesn't get a new kidney he will die. Sam, the only known potential donor with a properly matching kidney, himself has only one kidney and has not consented to give it—and his life—up for Joe. Is there really a choice? If the only way to save Joe is to kill Sam, then we would be unable to do so—and no one would say that we chose Sam over Joe. Such a choice would never even be contemplated.

In another kind of situation there *is* a choice. Imagine that Joe and Sam both **16.** need a kidney to survive, but we have only one in our kidney bank. It may be that we should give the kidney to Joe, a member of our community, rather than to Sam, who lives in some distant country (though this is far from clear—maybe flipping a coin would be more fair). Sam (or the loser of the coin flip) could not complain that his rights had been violated, because moral claims to some resource—positive claims—must always be dependent on the availability of that resource. But the right not to be treated as if one were a mere resource or instrument—negative, defensive claims—is most fundamentally what it means to say that one has rights. And this is what members of the ALF have in mind when they declare that animals, like human beings, have rights.

Where, one might wonder, should the line be drawn? Must we treat dragonflies **17.** the same as dolphins? Surely not. Distinctions must be made, though to judge definitively which animals must be ruled out as holders of rights may be impossible even in principle. In legal or moral discourse we are virtually never able to draw clear lines. This does not mean that drawing a line anywhere, arbitrarily, is as good as drawing one anywhere else.

The line-drawing metaphor, though, implies classifying entities in a binary way: **18.** as either above the line, and so entitled to moral consideration, or not. Binary thinking misses nuances of our moral intuition. Entities without rights may still deserve oral consideration on other grounds: one may think that a dragonfly doesn't quite qualify for rights yet believe that it would be wrong to crush one without good reason. And not all entities with rights need be treated in precisely the same way. This is apparent when one compares animals over whom we have assumed custody with wild animals. The former, I think, have rights to our affirmative aid, while the latter have such rights only in certain circumstances. Similar distinctions can be made among human beings, and also between human beings and particular animals. For example, I recently spent $1,000 on medical care for my dog, and I think he had a right to that care, but I have never given such an amount to a needy person on the street. Rights thought, then, implies neither that moral consideration ought to be extended only to the holders of rights nor that all rights-holders must be treated with a rigid equality. It implies only that rights-holders should never be treated as if they, or their kind, didn't matter.

Animals, Refrigerators, and Can Openers

The question of man's relationship with animals goes back at least to Aristotle, **19.** who granted that animals have certain senses—hunger, thirst, a sense of touch—but who held that they lack rationality and therefore as "the lower sort [they] are by nature slaves, and . . . should be under the rule of a master." Seven centuries later Saint Augustine added the authority of the Church, arguing the "Christ himself [teaches] that to refrain from the killing of animals . . . is the height of superstition, for there are no common rights between us and the beasts. . . ." Early in the seventeenth century

René Descartes argued that, lacking language, animals cannot have thoughts or souls and thus are machines.

One may be inclined to dismiss such beliefs as archaic oddities, but even today **20.** some people act as if animals were unfeeling things. I worked in a research lab for several summers during college, and I remember that it was a natural tendency to lose all empathy with one's animal subjects. My supervisor seemed actually to delight in swinging rats around by their tails and flinging them against a concrete wall as a way of stunning the animals before killing them. Rats and rabbits, to those who injected, weighed, and dissected them, were little different from cultures in a petri dish: they were just things to manipulate and observe. Feelings of what may have been moral revulsion were taken for squeamishness, and for most of my lab mates those feelings subsided with time.

The first animal-welfare law in the United States, passed in New York State in **21.** 1828, emphasized the protection of animals useful in agriculture. It also promoted human virtue with a ban on ''maliciously and cruelly'' beating or torturing horses, sheep, or cattle. Today courts still tend to focus on human character, ruling against human beings only for perpetrating the most shocking and senseless abuse of animals. Indeed, courts sometimes have difficulty taking animal-abuse cases seriously. For instance, in 1986 a California man who had been convicted of allowing a fifty-year-old tortoise, Rocky, in his petting zoo to suffer untreated from maladies including infected eyes, labored breathing, and dehydration appealed the lower court's order removing the animal from his custody. The state argued that the defendant's rights to Rocky should be terminated just as parental rights might be terminated for abusing a child. The court, in rejecting this analogy, quipped that while ''a child preparing for homework or cleaning a bedroom may exhibit turtle-like qualities or creep toward school in turtle pace, we decline to equate title to a tortoise to the relationship between a parent and a child.'' Not to be outdone, another judge wrote, in a concurring opinion, that ''hopefully our decision will forestall the same problem should we be faced with Rocky II.''

Most states leave the regulation of medical research to Washington. In 1966 **22.** Congress passed the Laboratory Animal Welfare Act, whose stated purpose was not only to provide humane care for animals but also to protect the owners of dogs and cats from theft by proscribing the use of stolen animals. (Note the vocabulary of property law; animals have long been legally classified as property.) Congress then passed the Animal Welfare Act of 1970, which expanded the provisions of the 1966 act to include more species of animals and to regulate more people who handle animals. The AWA was further amended in 1976 and in 1985.

The current version of the AWA mandates that research institutions meet certain **23.** minimum requirements for the handling and the housing of animals, and requires the ''appropriate'' use of pain-killers. But the act does not regulate research or experimentation itself, and allows researchers to withhold anesthetics or tranquilizers ''when scientifically necessary.'' Further, while the act purports to regulate dealers who buy animals at auctions and other markets to sell to laboratories, it does little to protect those animals. For instance, dealers often buy animals at ''trade days,'' or outdoor bazaars of dogs and cats; some people bring cats by the sackful, and, according to one activist, ''sometimes you see the blood coming through.''

The 1985 amendments to the AWA were an attempt to improve the treatment of animals in laboratories, to improve enforcement, to encourage the consideration of alternative research methods that use fewer or no animals, and to minimize duplication in experiments. One notable change is that for the first time, research institutions using primates must keep them in environments conducive to their psychological well-being; however, some animal-rights activists have expressed skepticism, since the social and psychological needs of primates are complex, and the primary concern of researchers is not the interests of their animal subjects. Last September a symposium on the psychological well-being of captive primates was held at Harvard University. Some participants contended that we lack data on the needs of the thirty to forty species of primates now used in laboratories. Others suggested that the benefits of companionship and social life are obvious.

The U.S. Department of Agriculture is responsible for promulgating regulations **24.** under the AWA and enforcing the law. Under current USDA regulations the cages of primates need only have floor space equal to three times the area occupied by the animal "when standing on four feet"—in the words of the USDA, which has apparently forgotten that primates have hands. The 1985 amendments required the USDA to publish final revised regulations, including regulations on the well-being of primates, by December of 1986. At this writing the department has yet to comply, and some activists charge that the NIH and the Office of Management and Budget have delayed the publication of the new regulations and attempted to undermine them.

One may believe that virtue thought—which underlies current law—and rights **25.** thought should protect animals equally. After all, wouldn't a virtuous person or society respect the interests of animals? But virtue thought allows the law to disregard these interests, because virtue can be measured by at least two yardsticks: by the foreseeable effects of an act on the interests of an animal or by the social utility of the act. The latter standard was applied in a 1983 case in Maryland in which a researcher appealed his conviction for cruelty to animals after he had performed experiments that resulted in monkeys' mutilating their hands. Overturning the conviction, the Maryland Court of Appeals wrote that "there are certain normal human activities to which the infliction of pain to an animal is purely incidental"—thus the actor is not a sadist—and that the state legislature had intended for these activities to be exempt from the law protecting animals.

The law, of course, is not monolithic. Some judges have expressed great sympathy **26.** for animals. On the whole, though, the law doesn't recognize animal rights. Under the Uniform Commercial Code, for instance, animals—along with refrigerators and can openers—constitute "goods."

Alternatives to Us-Versus-Them

Estimates of the number of animals used each year in laboratories in the United **27.** States range from 17 million to 100 million: 200,000 dogs, 50,000 cats, 60,000 primates, 1.5 million guinea pigs, hamsters, and rabbits, 200,000 wild animals, thousands of farm animals and birds, and millions of rats and mice. The conditions in general—lack of exercise, isolation from other animals, lengthy confinement in tiny cages—are stressful. Many experiments are painful or produce fear, anxiety, or depression. For instance, in 1987 research at the Armed Forces Radiobiology Research Institute reported that nine monkeys were subjected to whole-body irradiation; as a result, within two hours six of the monkeys were vomiting and hypersalivating. In a proposed experiment at the University of Washington pregnant monkeys, kept in isolation, will be infected with the simian AIDS virus; their offspring, infected or not, will be separated from the mothers at birth.

Not all animals in laboratories, of course, are subjects of medical research. In **28.** the United States each year some 10 million animals are used in testing products and for other commercial purposes. For instance, the United States Surgical Corporation, in Norwalk, Connecticut, uses hundreds of dogs each year to train salesmen in the use of the company's surgical staple gun. In 1981 and 1982 a group called Friends of Animals brought two lawsuits against United States Surgical to halt these practices. The company successfully argued in court that Friends of Animals lacked "standing" to sue, since no member of the organization had been injured by the practice; after some further legal maneuvering by Friends of Animals both suits were dropped. Last November a New York City animal-rights advocate was arrested as she planted a bomb outside United States Surgical's headquarters.

In 1987, according to the USDA, 130,373 animals were subjected to pain or **29.** distress unrelieved by drugs for "the purpose of research or testing." This figure, which represents nearly seven percent of the 1,969,123 animals reported to the USDA that year as having been "used in experimentation," ignores members of species not protected by the AWA (cold-blooded animals, mice, rats, birds, and farm animals). Moreover, there is reason to believe that the USDA's figures are low. For example, according to the USDA, no primates were subjected to distress in the state of Maryland, the home of Sema, in any year from 1980 to 1987, the last year for which data are available.

Steps seemingly favorable to animals have been taken in recent years. In addition **30.** to the passage of the 1985 amendments to the AWA, the Public Health Service, which includes the NIH, has revised its "Policy on Humane Care and Use of Laboratory Animals," and new legislation has given legal force to much of this policy. Under the revised policy, institutions receiving NIH or other PHS funds for animal research must have an "institutional animal care and use committee" consisting of at least five members, including one nonscientist and one person not affiliated with the institution.

Many activists are pessimistic about these changes, however. They argue that **31.** the NIH has suspended funds at noncompliant research institutions only in response to political pressure, and assert that the suspensions are intended as a token gesture, to help the NIH regain lost credibility. They note that Sema, which continues to keep primates in isolation cages (as regulations permit), is an NIH contractor whose principal investigators are NIH employees. As to the makeup of the animal-care committees, animal-rights advocates say that researchers control who is appointed to them. In the words of one activist, "The brethren get to choose."

However one interprets these changes, much remains the same. For example, the **32.** AWA authorizes the USDA to confiscate animals from laboratories not in compliance with regulations, but only if the animal "is no longer required . . . to carry out the research, test or experiment"; the PHS policy mandates pain relief "unless the procedure is justified for scientific reasons." Fundamentally, the underlying attitude that animals may appropriately be used and discarded persists.

If the law is ever to reflect the idea that animals have rights, more-drastic **33.**

steps—such as extending the protection of the Constitution to animals—must be taken. Constitutional protection for animals is not an outlandish proposition. The late U.S. Supreme Court Justice William O. Douglas wrote once, in a dissenting opinion, that the day should come when ''all of the forms of life . . . will stand before the court—the pileated woodpecker as well as the coyote and bear, the lemmings as well as the trout in the streams.''

Suppose, just suppose, that the AWA were replaced by an animal-rights act, **34.** which would prohibit the use by human beings of any animals to their detriment. What would be the effect on medical research, education, and product testing? Microorganisms; tissue, organ, and cell cultures; physical and chemical systems that mimic biological functions; computer programs and mathematical models that simulate biological interactions; epidemiologic data bases; and clinical studies have all been used to reduce the number of animals used in experiments, demonstrations, and tests. A 1988 study by the National Research Council, while finding that researchers lack the means to replace all animals in labs, did conclude that current and prospective alternative techniques could reduce the number of animals—particularly mammals —used in research.

Perhaps the report would have been more optimistic if scientists were as zealous **35.** about conducting research to find alternatives as they are about animal research. But we should not be misled by discussion of alternatives into thinking that the issue is merely empirical. It is broader than just whether subject A and procedure X can be replaced by surrogates B and Y. We could undergo a shift in world view: instead of imagining that we have a divine mandate to dominate and make use of everything else in the universe, we could have a sense of belonging to the world and of kinship with the other creatures in it. The us-versus-them thinking that weighs animal suffering against human gain could give way to an appreciation that ''us'' includes ''them.'' That's an alternative too.

Some researchers may insist that scientists should not be constrained in their **36.** quest for knowledge, but this is a romantic notion of scientific freedom that never was and should not be. Science is always constrained, by economic and social priorities and by ethics. Sometimes, paradoxically, it is also freed by these constraints, because a barrier in one direction forces it to cut another path, in an area that might have remained unexplored.

Barriers against the exploitation of animals ought to be erected in the law, because **37.** law not only enforces morality but defines it. Until the law protects the interests of animals, the animal-rights movement will by definition be radical. And whether or not one approves of breaking the law to remedy its shortcomings, one can expect such activities to continue. ''I believe that you should do for others as you would have done for you,'' one member of the ALF says. ''If you were being used in painful experiments, you'd want someone to come to your rescue.''

WORKING WITH THE TEXT

Cultural and Historical References

In this section, the numbers at the margin refer to the numbered paragraphs in the selection itself.

9. What does Zak mean by "marginal" human beings? You should be able to define this term from the context.

13. Jeremy Bentham, born in 1748, was a philosopher, lawyer, and political theorist. He is usually considered to be the father of utilitarianism, which influenced modern social democracies.

13. Does Zak really demonstrate the spokesperson's "lack of impartiality" with the quote at the end of the paragraph? Could Zak have made his point more clearly here?

Writing Assignments: The Paragraph

Be sure to provide an introduction for each of the following paragraph writing assignments. That is, begin each paragraph with a phrase like this: "Thomas Brickle claims that. . . ." When it is relevant, you might also want to identify the expertise of the author ("Thomas Brickle, a New Testament scholar, claims that. . . ."), the name of the book or article, the century and country in which the work appeared, or any other circumstances that your readers might find significant. For more on this, see pp. 11–13 in Chapter 2.

1. Write a paragraph in which you briefly describe the history of animal rights movements (paragraphs 9 to 12).

2. Describe the animal rights argument involving "marginal human beings" (paragraphs 9 to 12).

3. Describe Zak's assertion that recognizing inherent animal rights involves "recognizing differences"—not merely similarities—between humans and other individual species (paragraphs 10 to 12).

4. Write a paragraph in which you explain the difference between "virtue thought" and "rights thought" (paragraph 25). At the same time, demonstate the inadequacy of "virtue thought" as far as animal rights advocates are concerned.

Writing Assignments: The Short Essay

Use informal documentation for these short essays. That is, don't use footnotes or a Works Cited page to document your sources. Instead, cite only relevant information about your source, and keep that information *within* your text. Then follow the summary or quote with a page number in parentheses. (Use the page numbers that you find in this book to represent the page numbers of the source.) Thus, your informal documentation will look something like this:

> In *Animal Liberation,* Peter Singer asks an intriguing question, ". . . if people are not prepared to give up tobacco, can it be right to make animals suffer the cost of their decision to continue smoking" (p. 328)?

1. Discuss and describe Zak's assertion that "law not only enforces morality but defines it" (paragraph 37). Be sure to illustrate this idea with at

least one example from this essay as well as several examples from your own experience.

2. Write an essay in which you paraphrase Zak's definition of utilitarianism. Also, discuss Zak's insistence that the utilitarian ethic must be qualified with a concern for the rights of an individual organism or species (paragraphs 13 to 18).

3. Describe and discuss the inadequacies which Zak sees in the Animal Welfare Act of 1970 (paragraphs 22 to 26).

4. Describe and discuss Zak's assertion that "instead of imagining that we have a divine mandate to dominate and make use of everything else in the universe, we could have a sense of belonging to the world and of kinship with the other creatures in it" (paragraph 35). Be sure to support this assertion with ideas and examples from throughout Zak's essay, as well as those from your own personal experience.

Essays on *Animal Rights*

Short Essays

Use informal documentation for these short essays. That is, don't use foot-notes or a Works Cited page to document your sources. Instead, cite only relevant information about your source, and keep that information *within* your text. Then follow the summary or quote with a page number in parentheses. (Use the page numbers that you find in this book to represent the page numbers of the source.) Thus, your informal documentation will look something like this:

> In *The Romance of Medicine,* Benjamin Gordon, a history professor, says that it was once believed that red wine replenished a person's depleted blood supply (p. 121).

1. Write a report in which you contrast the two extremes within the animal rights controversy (that is, the two extremes represented by the essays in this chapter).
2. Using ideas from two or three essays from this chapter, argue that it's both the *kind* of animal that is used and the *kind* of experimentation that determines whether experimentation on animals is ethical.
3. Contrast one essay that plays down the significance of animal research with one that magnifies the significance.
4. Contrast an essay that emphasizes how badly laboratory animals are treated with one that emphasizes how well they're treated.
5. Argue for or against the use of animals in cosmetic research.
6. Argue for or against the use of animals in psychology research.

Long Essays

For rules governing formal documentation, see Chapter 6.

1. Using the essays in this chapter, write on one side or the other of the animals rights controversy. Use some essays to support your argument and some to refute the opposing arguments.
2. Take a position somewhere in the middle of the animal rights controversy. You'll have to discover exactly where that middle is. Argue against both sides. Use a variety of essays from this chapter.
3. Take into account a number of essays from this chapter, and argue that it is ethical to experiment on the lower animals but not ethical to experiment on the higher ones. At some point, of course, you will have to draw a line between higher and lower animals. In other words, you will have to differentiate, through definition, between a higher and lower animal. You may also have to admit that no certain line can be drawn but a fuzzy line is better than no line at all. You may have to do a bit of outside research for this.

— 11 —

Sexist Language:
Is the Cure Worse Than the Disease?

INTRODUCTION

In 1976 Casey Miller and Kate Swift raised what proved to be an extremely controversial issue in the women's liberation movement. In *Words and Women,* Miller and Swift argued that the English language itself—the medium that influences the way we perceive the world--was sexist.

Miller and Swift, and many other feminists as well, are troubled by such time-hallowed language conventions as the use of the third-person singular pronoun "he" for both men and women and the use of the term "man" to refer to humans of both sexes. They argue that the shop fore*man*'s announcement that "Each employee is responsible for his own time card" is confusing and, more important, demeaning to female employees. They contend that anyone who marvels "What a piece of work is man" is simply refusing to acknowledge the identity of one-half of the human species. Such conventions, according to feminists, condition females from birth to think of themselves as second-class citizens.

Perhaps the most insidious influence on sex-biased language, feminists say, is the language of the Bible. God is depicted as a masculine being in both the Old and the New Testaments. Never mind that the male gender of Jesus is historically affirmed fact; his titles of "Lord" or "the Son of God," or, for that matter, "the Son of Man" reflect a male bias which excludes half of God's children.

Such sentiment has become sufficiently widespread to prompt the National Council of Churches to form a committee of religious scholars to remove "sexist" words from the scriptures when these words appear in congregational readings. This committee's deliberations have to date resulted in two volumes of *An Inclusive Language Lectionary* (1983, 1984), in which the editors have replaced numerous male-oriented biblical expressions with more sex-neutral ones. For instance, "Lord" becomes "Sovereign One"; "Son of God" becomes "Child of God"; "God, our Father" becomes "God, our Father [and Mother]"; and "Son of Man" becomes "Human One."

"Ahem, ahem," the traditionalists counter. The use of "man" and "he" as universal terms for humankind, they argue, has always allowed us to express ideas involving both sexes clearly and without syntactic awkwardness. "Mailpersons," "cowpersons," "firepersons," "milkpersons," and other similarly awkward expressions may be devoid of sexual bias, the traditionalists argue, but they are also silly and fatuously trendy. The traditionalists also argue that there is no other third-person singular pronoun besides "he" which can serve when that pronoun's antecedent can be of either sex. Substituting "he or she" or "he/she" simply clogs the syntax of the sentence. And shifting the pronoun's antecedent from singular to plural in order to substitute "they" for "he" is often impossible. "Don't fix what ain't broke merely to be politically hip," language traditionalists growl.

Even those traditionalists who can smile condescendingly at feminists' attempts to persuade the rest of us to change our language ways are annoyed when they contemplate federal regulations that coerce the federal bureaucracy into writing and rewriting documents to suit the tastes of feminists. And even those traditionalists who have no argument with reformation of the secular language bridle at attempts to excise the masculine element from the Bible. Changing God to a neutered being, they say, transforms the Bible into a trendy social document and obscures its divine origin.

The issue promises to animate our linguistic, political, and religious thinking for a long time to come. The feminists have political and social idealism on their side. Their opponents have verbal practicality and religious tradition on theirs. We can only guess at the impact that this furor will have on language or religion in the twenty-first century.

WORDS AND WOMEN

Casey Miller and Kate Swift

Casey Miller and Kate Swift are the authors of *Words and Women* (1976), the book from which our selection is taken, and *The Handbook of Nonsexist Writing* (1980). *Words and Women* is probably the most influential writing on sexist language. The following excerpts from this book come from its concluding chapter, "Language and Liberation," and an epilogue, "Let the Meaning Choose the Word."

Language expressing the struggle to break with cultural patterns of the past must **1.** sometimes precede language expressing newly sensed possibilities for the future. What is happening today with respect to women and words was described in principle by Edward Sapir in 1921:

Source: Casey Miller and Kate Swift, *Words and Women*. Garden City, New York: Doubleday, 1976. 142–153, 157–164.

> The birth of a new concept is invariably foreshadowed by a more or
> less strained or extended use of old linguistic material; the concept
> does not attain to individual and independent life until it has found a
> distinctive linguistic embodiment. . . . As soon as the word is at hand,
> we instinctively feel, with something of a sigh of relief, that the con-
> cept is ours for the handling. Not until we own the symbol do we feel
> that we hold a key to the immediate knowledge or understanding of the
> concept.[1]

Even in the mid-1970s the sexism deeply ingrained in Western culture is largely **2.**
nonconscious. As psychologists Sandra and Daryl Bem point out, we remain unaware
of the pervasive ideology that sees females as inferior beings "because alternative
beliefs and attitudes about women go unimagined."[2] We have lacked a vocabulary
even to formulate such alternatives.

Words that affirm positive qualities in women and girls mainly describe their **3.**
functions (real or assigned) as females, or like *masculine* in the phrase "She has a
masculine mind," or *tomboy,* they take away what they purport to give. "Is there no
word for women's *strength?*" asked Sophie Drinker,[3] and what makes her question
remarkable is that so few people have thought to ask it.

Among those who did were the editors of the American Heritage School **4.**
Dictionary. They began their work in 1969 by amassing data for a computerized study
of five million words found in a thousand representative books used by children in
grades three through nine throughout the United States. The purpose of the study was
to help the editors define the words children encounter most frequently in their school
work, and to this end the computer produced 700,000 alphabetized citation slips, each
showing a word in three lines of context and ranked by the frequency of its occurrence.

What the computer also, and unexpectedly, provided was impeccable evidence **5.**
that the language of American school books mirrors the sexist assumptions of society.
The school-book world, it turned out, was inhabited by twice as many boys as girls
and seven times as many men as women. More damaging than this demographic
improbability was the social conditioning of young readers through the sex-stereotyped
roles and character traits of females and males as the school books portrayed them.
Alma Graham, one of the editors of the school dictionary, wrote: "If this new dictionary
were to serve elementary students without showing favoritism to one sex or the other,
an effort would have to be made to restore the gender balance. We would need more
examples featuring females, and the examples would have to ascribe to girls and
women the active, inventive, and adventurous human traits traditionally reserved for
men and boys."[4]

Thus the dictionary, published in 1972, became the first in which editors made **6.**
a conscious effort to correct sexist biases through examples and through the wording
of definitions. At the word *daunt,* for instance, the illustration reads, "The difficulty
did not daunt her"; at *sole* it is "She took sole command of the ship." Numerous
examples in which *he* is also strong or brave are balanced by others in which the
pressure on boys always to be in control of a situation was eased: "His resolve began
to waver" and "Tears welled up in his eyes." No doubt most children would like to
be indomitable, but girls are not the only ones who waver or whose emotions of

gratitude or loss find release in tears. Similarly, in writing definitions the editors consciously dropped some of the sexist assumptions perpetuated by other definers. They defined a *sage,* for example, as "A very wise person, usually old and highly respected," in contrast to the "mature or venerable man sound in judgment" of a widely used college dictionary.

By 1975 many major textbook publishers had adopted or were preparing to adopt **7.** nonsexist guidelines for their authors and editors. The purpose of these guidelines is to give practical examples of how language can be used to liberate and expand thought. Scott, Foresman and Company suggests, for instance, that "When man invented the wheel . . ." can become "When people invented the wheel"; "congressmen" are more inclusively "members of Congress"; and "the typical American . . . he" can be "typical Americans . . . they." A sentence like "In New England, the typical farm was so small that the owner and his sons could take care of it by themselves" can more accurately be phrased, "In New England, the typical farm was so small that the family members could take care of it by themselves."[5] Amplifying this kind of distinction in more comprehensive guidelines based on an analysis of social studies textbooks, Elizabeth Burr, Susan Dunn, and Norma Farquhar wrote, "phrases such as 'the farmer's wife' clearly convey the idea that the female was merely a possession of the farmer and was not herself a farmer, when in fact the wives of most small farmers were themselves farmers *in every sense of the word.*"[6]

McGraw-Hill's guidelines received unusually extensive publicity and were widely **8.** distributed. Requests for the document came from government agencies, corporations, communications media, religious organizations, schools and universities, as well as thousands of individuals. One author who writes on business management and who had always assumed that his readership was overwhelmingly male, reported doing a turnabout after reading the guidelines. "I've been talking to a lot of business women," he said, "and find they *would* like to find books that included them and did not pretend they never existed in the business world. . . . There are 35 million women in the U.S. work force today."[7]

Some authors whose subjects have traditionally been considered male domains **9.** did not need guidelines to tell them that women resent being excluded. A few years ago a woman who had bought an old farmhouse in Maine and was remodeling it on her own wrote to Hubbard H. Cobb, author of *How to Buy and Remodel the Older House:* "My heartfelt thanks for using the words 'people' and 'a man or woman' in reference to homebuyers, builders, architects, etc. I've acquired a small library of how-to books ranging from masonry to heating, and the authors invariably use only the word 'man.' It's strange to admit but they make me feel so left out, especially when they add in passing that 'the little woman' might like such and such a style! . . . After all, I paid for the place myself, and I'm doing a large part of the work myself."[8]

Library cataloguers are carrying out a widespread campaign to revise the **10.** traditional use of subsuming and sexist language in subject headings and card catalogue descriptions as well as in the terminology of cataloguing instructions. "Women, children, the mentally and physically handicapped, and racial, sexual, and other minorities . . . fall outside the assumed norm and therefore qualify for separate and unequal categorization," Elizabeth Dickinson wrote in 1974 of the Library of Congress subject headings used in libraries throughout the country.[9] Dickinson is a cataloguer at the Hennepin County Library in Minnesota where a group under the leadership of Sanford Berman, head cataloguer, is coordinating nationwide efforts to bring pressure for reform on the Library of Congress and the American Library Association. As part of this effort, the chief cataloguer at the Brooklyn College Library prepared a position paper in which she makes the point that "language, if permitted to change only at its own pace and that of the mass mind, is conservative if not reactionary." But, Joan K. Marshall says, "Women have decided, quite simply, that that pace is not fast enough. We know that any genuine change in our status in society is inextricably tied to change in our language. And with that knowledge comes the conviction that we can increase the rate of change."[10]

11. The council of the American Library Association acknowledged in 1975 that many of its official documents and publications "use nouns and pronouns with strictly male connotations" and further that "consistent and exclusive use of the masculine gender perpetuates the traditional language of society which discriminates against women." The council therefore resolved: "That future publications and official documents of the American Library Association avoid terminology which perpetuates sex stereotypes, and existing publications and official documents, as they are revised, be changed to avoid such terminology."[11]

12. Another gain in eliminating separate and unequal categorization was made when the United States Department of Labor revised its list of occupational classifications to drop sex-stereotyped job titles. For the most part the changes were accomplished by replacing the suffix -man with common gender terms such as operator or worker. Carmen R. Maymi, director of the Women's Bureau of the department, called the new job titles a welcome step toward ending sex discrimination in employment. "It is not realistic to expect that women will apply for job openings advertised for foremen, salesmen or credit men," she said. "Nor will men apply for job vacancies calling for laundresses, maids, or airline stewardesses."[12] On the same grounds Mary M. Fuller, a management education specialist who advises government and private organizations, points out that the generic *he* covertly promotes economic discrimination and is inappropriate for use in job descriptions. In a position paper published in the *Training and Development Journal* she wrote, "Categorizing . . . by characteristics other than the ability to get the job done is now illegal as well as economically foolish for the total society."[13]

13. Legislation enforcing equal job opportunities has helped to expose and eradicate employment terminology prejudicial to women. In one case a federal court found a major airline guilty of discrimination against its female flight attendants: by calling women "stewardesses" and calling men performing the identical job "pursers," the company had camouflaged widely unequal pay and promotion schedules.[14]

14. The response of different religious bodies to linguistic change has varied widely, as might be expected. Whether ignored or acknowledged, however, the issue has theological implications. In fundamentalist sects like the one led by the Reverend Bill Gothard, who teaches that in families a chain of command exists from God to the husband to the wife to the children,[15] male domination in language is presumably accepted as divinely ordained. Other religious groups recognize the linguistic exclusion of females as a scandal that must be resolved, and a few have gone beyond lip service. Notable is the United Church of Christ, which by action of its General Synod in 1973 committed itself "to the elimination of sex and race discrimination in every area of its life." To implement that affirmation the constitution and by-laws of the United Church, as well as all its printed materials, including worship books and services, hymnals, curricula, journals, magazines, and personnel documents, are being written or revised "to make all language deliberately inclusive."[16]

Gates of Prayer, a revision of the Union Prayerbook published in 1975 by the **15.** Central Conference of American Rabbis, contains a number of references to the great women of Hebrew history, including "God of our mothers, God of Sarah, Rebekah, Leah, and Rachel, Deborah, Hannah, and Ruth" as a parallel to "God of our fathers, God of Abraham, Isaac, and Jacob, Amos, Isaiah, and Micah." Elsewhere Rachel and Leah are identified as "the Mothers of this people Israel" and the phrase "God of all generations" has been substituted for "God of our fathers." In their introduction the editors noted that "while our themes are the ageless ones of our tradition, the manner of their expression reflects our own day. . . . Our commitment in the Reform movement to the equality of the sexes is of long standing. In this book, it takes the form of avoiding the use of masculine terminology exclusively, when we are referring to the human race in general."[17]

The implications of these and similar revisions[18] were spelled out at some length **16.** in guidelines published in 1974 by the editors of the interfaith publication, the *Journal of Ecumenical Studies:*

> From the time of the Genesis story, human beings have been aware of the power involved in being able to name something or someone. If anything, men and women have become even more aware of the importance of language in the creation of their world, externally as well as internally, with the advent of modern linguistic analysis. Every significant human movement, social, political, economic—and religious—develops its own special language which helps form its adherents and project an influential image of itself to outsiders. . . .
>
> One of the most significant human movements of our day is feminism, i.e., the movement to acquire justice for women equally with men. One result of this movement is a growing awareness of sexism in our language, which most often takes the form of assuming that the male is the true human ideal. Such male dominance in language can be called linguistic sexism.[19]

Specifically, the editors of the journal asked that anyone submitting material to **17.** them for publication avoid, except in direct quotations or for other special reasons, all sex-based generic terminology, including references to God by masculine pronouns and the use of feminine pronouns "to refer to entities such as the Church of Israel." Of the latter they said:

> Such usage normally reflects the assumption that the feminine is inferior to the masculine, as with the feminine Church, or Israel, vis-à-vis a masculine God. It is clear that Israel, the Church, etc., are subordinate to God. But, upon reflection, it should also be clear that the feminine-masculine imagery used in the Jewish, Christian, Muslim, and other tra-

ditions is an attempt to express that inferior-superior, human-divine relationship in language that reflected the then (and often, still) existing
inferior-superior, female-male societal relationship. But once the position that "all humans are created equal" is accepted, such language is
no longer acceptable.[20]

Religious and secular guidelines are often greeted with dismay by alarmists who **18.**
jump to the conclusion that the Bible or the classics are going to be rewritten along
the lines George Orwell suggested in *Nineteen Eighty-Four*. No such suggestion has
ever been made, except in ridicule, but the question remains, if *man* becomes an
unequivocal symbol for the human male—the complement and companion of woman—
how will future generations understand the writings of past authors who intended (or
thought they intended) to include both sexes when they used the word? What will
readers in the twenty-first century make of the question phrased in sixteenth-century
English, "What is man that thou art mindful of him?"

What do we make of it now? Is not the man of whom the psalmist writes the **19.**
same man to whom Moses delivered the commandment "Thou shalt not covet thy
neighbor's wife"? Our descendants will know, just as we know, that our tongue has
for centuries mirrored the myth of the male as the true human ideal, and much of what
was written in the screened light of that myth will remain part of their heritage. But
our greatest literature is not bound by half-visioned myths, and it will survive the
semantic narrowing of masculine terms just as it has survived semantic changes in the
past.

When Chaucer wrote of one of the Canterbury pilgrims, "He was a gentle harlot **20.**
and a kind, a better fellow should men not find," he was not calling that gentle
pilgrim a whore. In the fourteenth century, *harlot* simply meant "good fellow."[21] In
Shakespeare's time *child* was ambiguous in much the same way *man* has become: a
child was a young person of either sex, but especially a female. *Bearn,* the Old English
word for "son," had become *barne* and widened its meaning to "child" in the sense
we use the word child today. So in *The Winter's Tale* a shepherd who finds an
abandoned baby says, "What have we here? Mercy on 's, a barne; a very pretty barne!
A boy or a child, I wonder?"[22] The word girl used to mean a young person of either
sex, but by the sixteen hundreds it had begun to be narrowed and was in the process
of replacing the special feminine-gender meaning of child. Eventually, of course, child
replaced barne and girl was restricted to young females. Just as glossaries are helpful
to a twentieth-century reader of Chaucer and Shakespeare, so they can be expected to
help readers of a future age interpret words whose meanings have changed in the
inevitable process of continuing linguistic evolution.

Sometimes the process of change involves a return to earlier uses. *Fellow,* for **21.**
example, is an ancient word with a history of varied and conflicting meanings, but it
is being used today with much of its Old English meaning intact: "One who shares
with another in a possession, official dignity, or in the performance of any work; a
partner, colleague, co-worker. Also one united with another in a covenant for common
ends; an ally." The Oxford English Dictionary, noting that this earliest meaning is
obsolete, goes on to give twelve other definitions of the noun, including a spouse of
either sex (Shakespeare used it to mean wife in *The Tempest*), a servant, one of the

common people, and a person who holds an academic award or membership in a learned society.[23] Yet we still recognize the Old English sense when we speak of fellowship or use a combination term like fellow student. Although *fellow* alone is applied colloquially more often to a boy or man than to a girl or woman, one can also say without constraint, "She's a good fellow," as one cannot say, "She's a good man."

22. The most far-reaching revolutions have been inspired by nothing more (or less) than seeing the obvious from a new perspective. The knowledge that the earth is not the center of the universe seemed at first to shatter the collective ego of the Western world. The recognition that man is not the species is also revolutionary, and in its way equally frightening. For as in the Copernican Revolution, the challenge is to an article of faith, an accepted dogma sanctified by Church and State, protected by tradition, and embedded in language.

23. Until 1543 when the Copernican theory was published, the word revolution referred primarily to the motion of a body in orbit; after that time it also came to mean, especially in the adjective revolutionary, a fundamental change in thought or organization. The revolution we are living through challenges the dominance of patriarchal structures.

24. In a time of change it is not enough to hang on to the old ways of seeing the universe or society. Not to look ahead is to be left behind. Alexander Korda put it this way: "Women are thinking out their roles; men are merely clinging desperately to theirs, hoping that they will survive the coming storm, searching for the means to prevent its happening."[24] Perhaps the distinction is overstated, but it touches on the real pain involved in efforts to imagine the new options we need to pursue if our perverse journey toward destruction is to be altered. For one thing, it is time we looked more carefully at where the thoughtless use of sexual stereotypes is taking us. Man as leader, woman as follower; man as producer, woman as consumer; man as strength, woman as weakness—this is the cosmography that has brought us to man as aggressor, humanity as victim.

25. In a discussion of the loss that can result when an activity is artificially limited to one sex, Margaret Mead once used this example:

> There are societies that wished to achieve the full beauty of a chorus which spanned the possibilities of the human voice, but in linking religion and music together also wished to ban women, as unsuited for an active rôle in the church, from the choir. Boys' voices provide an apparently good substitute. So also do eunuchs, and so in the end we may have music modelled on a perfect orchestration of men and women's voices, but at the price of the exclusion of women and the castration of men.[25]

It is an apt example.

26. Exclusion is another form of castration. For *castration,* in addition to its literal meaning—to remove the gonads of either sex—also means a depriving of vigor. One dictionary defines "castration complex" as "the often unconscious fear or feeling of bodily injury or loss of power at the hands of authority."[26] Why, then, is castration more often associated with male loss of power than female? Why do we not refer to

"castrating males" in connection with the losses women have suffered under a system that renders them impotent? Can it be because Authority is male? Because the Establishment is male? To admit women to full human membership is a threat to male prerogatives, and women who challenge this "natural" order are called castrating women. We forget, or refuse to acknowledge, the reality that men are more often the castraters of each other and of women. Used carelessly, the word assumes the warp our culture imposes, just as, used carelessly, language castrates thought.

27. Sexist expressions like "castrating women," "the man in the street," "bitch goddess Success," and "the weaker sex" are ready made. Ready-made phrases, as George Orwell said in his essay "Politics and the English Language," are the prefabricated strips of words and mixed metaphors that come crowding in when you do not want to take the trouble to think through what you are saying. "They will construct your sentences for you," he said, "—even think your thoughts for you, to a certain extent—and at need they will perform the important service of partially concealing your meaning even from yourself."[27]

28. To whom does one refer these days when invoking "the man in the street"? Why does the metaphor "bitch goddess" hang on? The Reverend Harvey Cox may have provided a clue to that when he came up with this assortment of images not long ago in an article on women priests. "What the conservatives fear, I welcome: a Christian sacrament enriched by the presence at the altar of the Great Mother, the Scarlet Woman, the Whore of Babylon and the Virgin Queen." Counterparts, perhaps, of the Great White Father, Jack the Ripper, Casanova, and King Henry the Eighth? What else can one conclude, since the point Cox was making was that women should become priests "not because they are no different from men, but because they are different."[28] And what, exactly, does *weaker* mean in "the weaker sex"? Or *fair*? Is that still a reference to beauty? Or complexion? Or does it now refer to fairness in sports or politics or everyday dealings in the shop, office, or home?

29. "The whole tendency of modern prose is away from concreteness," Orwell lamented. He urged the "scrapping of every word or idiom that has outgrown its usefulness. . . . What is above all needed is to let the meaning choose the word, and not the other way about. In prose, the worst thing one can do with words is surrender to them."[29]

30. When sexist language is deliberate, writers and speakers have a rich store of words to choose from. More often sexist language is not deliberate: it is either subconscious or lazy. It is easier to talk about all doctors and hospital patients as *he* and all nurses as *she*. Much easier to accept the masculine/feminine stereotypes than to think them through in relation to real people. Simpler by far to speak of the next President of the United States or the next chancellor of the university or the next head of the local school board as though, inevitably, they will be male.

31. Eliminating sexism need not result in graceless language, as many people fear. Sensitive speakers, writers, and editors have been doing it consciously and well for years. Language that does not depend on abstraction is superior, for it is forced to be specific. The number of people who are refusing to surrender to linguistic sexism is relatively small, but it will grow. When that happens, the faults of those less sensitive will become even more apparent.

32. Our vocabulary is already being affected by the increasing equality of women

and men under the law. As women continue to gain recognition in commerce, government, the professions, the arts, and higher education, the process will be accelerated. Most important, children acquiring language in their formative years will be free to imagine and explore the full range of their human potential. Significant gains have been made in many areas, but the transformation of English in response to the movement for human liberation has scarcely begun.

Epilogue

The "rules" that govern the "correct" use of a language have much in common with **33.** other social rules. They are not immutable, ordained to last forever; they evolved to meet social needs, and they are sensitive to social change. Some serve a useful purpose. Others are oppressive or have become outmoded: they are, in Shakespeare's phrase, "more honored in the breach than the observance."

The question is, how do you know when to abandon a word or phrase or **34.** grammatical rule that is still cited by language authorities as correct? We think the answer depends on a simple test: does the term or usage contribute to clarity and accuracy, or does it fudge them?

When you are faced with a particular problem of usage, this approach also helps **35.** to produce an alternative that avoids the original difficulty. For example, if it is your understanding that male human beings were solely responsible for the domestication of animals, then a sentence beginning "When man first domesticated animals . . ." conveys your meaning, even if its accuracy is highly suspect. If the possibility exists that women played some part in the process, however, then in the English we speak today the phrase "When man first domesticated animals" conveys misinformation. "When human beings first domesticated animals" or "our ancestors" or "early people" does a more accurate job.

A problem of incongruity may remain. At what point do you make the transition **36.** from an outmoded old usage to an awkward-sounding new one? The kind of person who tries to be open to change has an easier time moving with linguistic evolution than those who habitually react to change as unpleasant or frightening. But even the latter have given up whalebone corsets and starched wing collars without assuming they have to switch to miniskirts or tank tops. To address someone's great-grandmother as Ms. could be insensitive, but to speak of her only in terms of her late husband's life and achievements is rather like saying that she should always wear widow's weeds.

We have not attempted in what follows to present a comprehensive set of **37.** guidelines. We have tried, instead, to isolate the chief areas where unconscious, sexist assumptions get in the way of accurate and felicitous writing and speech. Most of the sexist offenses committed through language are not deliberate. They creep in as a result of laziness, habit, or overreliance on what the rule books say is correct, and they yield to the test of exactness. Although some solutions cannot be applied across the board, since their appropriateness varies with the circumstances, most involve nothing more than a healthy respect for fairness and precision. What's sauce for the goose is sauce for the gander, and the other way about.

Animals

Animals, with the exception of some of the lower forms, are either female or male. **38.**
This is true of the rabbit devastating the lettuce crop, the turtle crossing the road, the
cockroach scuttling under the baseboard, the sea gull riding an updraft. Yet many
people, including some who pride themselves on their knowledge of natural history,
habitually refer to the rabbit, the turtle, the cockroach, and the gull as "he." Why, is
a mystery, especially since the pronoun *it* provides an acceptable way to avoid a 50
per cent chance of error. Evidence is mounting that children are confused by this use
of *he*, and that the grammatical convention condoning it is one source of a prevalent
subconscious assumption that maleness is the norm.

Babies (and by Extension Muslims, Medical Students, Americans, Politicians, Etc.)

All babies are not alike, and all babies are not male, despite the impression most baby- **39.**
care books give to the contrary. What makes authors who write about babies especially
prone to using the masculine generic pronoun is that all mothers, unlike their offspring,
really are female, and referring to a mother as "she" leaves *he* as the handiest tag for
a child. One solution, when talking or writing about babies in general, is to use the
plural, especially since "most babies," "some babies," "babies are usually . . ." have
the advantage of being more accurate than sweeping generalizations about "the baby."
When it is desirable to generalize in the singular, it is usually possible to keep a
particular baby in mind, perhaps even to give it a name. Since particular babies are
either female or male, they obligingly provide their own sets of pronouns. Eliminating
the generic *he* avoids the suggestion that males are more important or more typical
than females, and it also frees the parents of a girl-baby from having to figure out
whether in a given instance the author is talking about boys only or both boys and
girls.

      The temptation to use *he* when generalizing about the people babies grow into **40.**
can also lead to oversimplification: again, avoiding sentences that refer to them with
singular third person pronouns is one way to reflect demographic realities.

-*Ess* Endings

Since authors, poets, Negroes, sculptors, Jews, actors, etc., may be either female or **41.**
male, the significance of a word like authoress is not that it identifies a female but that
it indicates deviation from what is consciously or unconsciously considered the standard.
Tacking an -ess ending onto a common gender English word because the person
referred to is a woman is reasonably resented by most people so identified. When it
is relevant to make a special point of someone's sex, pronouns are useful and so are
the adjectives male and female.

-*Ette* Endings

The suffix -ette indicates feminine gender in French words and frequently has nothing **42.**
to do with sex, as in *bicyclette*, which means "bicycle." In English the suffix has three

functions: to indicate imitation, as in *flannelette*; to denote small size, as in *dinette*; and to suggest that females need not be taken seriously, as in *farmerette* and *astronette*. By implication an usherette is a frivolous little woman hired to replace a bona fide usher.

      Except in grammar and rhyme, the terms feminine and masculine and their noun **43.** forms, femininity and masculinity, are so protean that they always warrant careful examination. They do not refer to femaleness and maleness but to arbitrary categories of appearance, personality, behavior, and activity that a given society or individual holds to be suitable. Since what is considered "masculine" or "feminine" will be different tomorrow from what it was yesterday, using either word carelessly may reinforce arbitrary double standards that suppress spontaneity and individuality in people of both sexes.

Forms of Address

The purpose of a social title (or courtesy title, or honorific) is to indicate respect for **44.** the person addressed. Ironically, one often conveys more respect for a woman by avoiding the conventional courtesy titles than by using them, since the distinction they make is related to a woman's marital state rather than to the person herself. In addition, the term chosen may be based on an erroneous assumption. Therefore, unless a woman's preference in titles is known, courtesy and honor may be better served by addressing her, in either speech or writing, by her first and last names together.

      One reason people are uneasy about using *Ms.*, an obvious solution to the Miss/ **45.** Mrs. dilemma, is that it is still so new it makes them self-conscious, with the result that they end up emphasizing the title rather than the name: "Good morning, *Mr.* Smithers," sounds sarcastic, and so does "Good morning, *Ms.* Smithers." As the title becomes more widely used the difficulty will disappear.

He as a Common Gender Pronoun

The use of masculine pronouns to include female referents, as in "the average reader **46.** . . . he," is part of the linguistic male-as-norm syndrome. Since English lacks a truly generic third-person singular pronoun, those who want to avoid both exclusiveness and ambiguity sometimes feel obliged to use "he or she" and sometimes "she or he." This device works unless the phrase must be repeated frequently, in which case it can become ludicrous. Another approach is to recast the sentence to omit third-person pronouns entirely: "If a student is unable to complete the course, he may apply for a refund" can be said more succinctly, "A student who is unable to complete the course may apply for a refund." Or the sentence can be phrased in the plural. "The visitor is invited to familiarize himself with the map before entering the park" is less cold when cast in the plural, and more to the point—unless, of course, the park is reserved for men and boys.

Job Titles

When a job is open to members of both sexes, describing it by a common gender term **47.** is more accurate and more conducive to effective recruiting than using one title for men and another for women. The same is true for elective offices that acquired male designations because—like congressman, alderman, and vestryman—they were held only by men in the past. Even since Jeannette Rankin broke the congressional sex barrier in 1917, referring to "members of Congress," "the men and women in Congress," or "U.S. representatives" has been more exact than using "congressmen" as a collective. Once an individual assumes an office or job, titles like congresswoman or congressman, newspaperwoman or newspaperman, forewoman or foreman are obvious choices.

Male as Norm

Who knows when a reference to "our forefathers" is intended to include "our **48.** foremothers" or when an evocation of "brotherhood" is meant to exclude the ladies' auxiliary? Words like forebears and ancestors are more accurate when inclusiveness is the aim, and a phrase that brings to mind the humanity common to both sexes leaves the words brotherhood and sisterhood to describe the special bonds that members of each sex feel for one another.

Man as the Species

The use of *man* to represent the human species reinforces the erroneous notion that the **49.** species is male or at least that the male is more representative than the female. A sentence like "Man is a tool-using animal" is misleading, since women also use tools. "Human beings are tool-using animals" says what it means. "Man is slowly destroying himself by polluting his environment" is doubly fuzzy. Even if one argues that most of the people responsible for industrial pollution are men, the results affect the health of females as well as males. "Humans are slowly destroying themselves by polluting their environment" gets around both faults and suggests that everyone will have to become involved in solving the problem.

Man as Typical

"The man who pays taxes," "the working man," "one man, one vote," all imply **50.** that the typical person who pays taxes, works, or votes is male. "Taxpayers," "workers" or "working people," "one person, one vote," do not. "Men of good will" number approximately half of all people of good will, give or take a few thousand.

Order

In pairs like male and female, men and women, husbands and wives, sons and daughters, **51.** boys and girls, Adam and Eve, males need not always come first. Occasionally reversing the order has two advantages: it counters the implication that members of the male sex rate a priority, and it helps to jog attention by avoiding the habitual. "Ladies and gentlemen" is a polite but empty form of address people use when talking to a group that includes women and men. Once the amenities have been taken care of and the speaker gets down to matters of substance, however, women are again relegated to second place or lose out altogether to broad-stroke generalizations about ''man.'' Specifically including women and making a conscious effort to avoid the hackneyed order can have the effect of bringing real people to mind instead of clichés.

-Person Compounds

Salesperson is a word that doesn't seem to throw anyone into a tizzy. This acceptance **52.** probably came about because *salesman* and *saleswoman* had already been used for many years as parallel sex-designating terms when the need was felt for a common gender term that could refer to either. As more women serve in posts once exclusively held by males, -person compounds will come to seem more natural. They are especially useful when candidates for a job or elective office are being considered without regard to sex.

Plural Constructions

Plural constructions help to avoid the built-in male-as-norm quality English has **53.** acquired, and they also provide a useful way to escape the trap of generalizing in the singular. ''The Indian . . . he'' omits half the Indian population. It implies in addition that all Indians can be described in terms of one Indian. Plurals do not automatically solve either problem, but they invite a certain amount of healthy qualification that the singular construction does not.

They as a Singular Pronoun

For more than four hundred years, reputable writers and speakers of English have used **54.** *they*, *their*, *them*, and *themselves* as singular pronouns for indefinite antecedents.

Womanly

This word is not parallel to *manly* because instead of describing human attributes, as **55.** manly does, it is limited to qualities assumed to be appropriate to or characteristic of females—and inappropriate to or uncharacteristic of males. A woman who is coura-geous, strong, and resolute cannot be called either manly or womanly. The only solution at present seems to be to call her courageous, strong, and resolute.

Notes

[1] Edward Sapir, *Language: An Introduction to the Study of Speech*, New York, Harcourt, Brace & World, Harvest Books, 1949, p. 17. (First published in 1921.)

[2] Sandra L. and Daryl J. Bem, ''Women's Role in American Society: Retrospect and Prospect,'' as reprinted in *Women's Role in Contemporary Society: The Report of the New York City Commission on Human Rights, September 21–25, 1970*, New York, Avon Books, Discus Edition, 1972, p. 102.

[3] Sophie Drinker, *Music and Women: The Story of Women in Their Relation to Music*, New York, Coward-McCann, 1948, p. 266.

[4] The material on the American Heritage School Dictionary is from Alma Graham, ''The Making of a Nonsexist Dictionary,'' *Ms.*, December 1973.

[5] ''Guidelines for Improving the Image of Women in Textbooks,'' Scott, Foresman, pp. 5, 8.

[6] Elizabeth Burr, Susan Dunn, and Norma Farquhar, "Equal Treatment of the Sexes in Social Studies Textbooks: Guidelines for Author and Editors," photocopy of typescript, 1972, p. 6.

[7] "Imprint," magazine for McGraw-Hill authors published by McGraw-Hill, Spring 1975, p. 2.

[8] Personal correspondence of Hubbard H. Cobb.

[9] Elizabeth Dickinson, "The Word Game," *Canadian Library Journal*, August 1974, p. 339.

[10] The position paper by Joan K. Marshall was reprinted in the Hennepin County Library's *Cataloging Bulletin 11/12/13*, March 15, 1975, pp. 10–11.

[11] The American Library Association resolution was reported in *Media Report to Women*, May 1, 1975, p. 10.

[12] U. S. Department of Labor, Office of Information, news release for November 9, 1973: "52 Job Titles Revised to Eliminate Sex-Stereotyping."

[13] Mary M. Fuller, "In Business, the Generic Pronoun 'He' Is Non-Job Related and Discriminatory," *Training and Development Journal*, May 1973, p. 10.

[14] Linda Charlton, "Rights Scoreboard," New York *Times*, November 18, 1973, the "Week in Review" section.

[15] "Obey Thy Husband," *Time* magazine, May 20, 1974, p. 64.

[16] Minutes of the Ninth General Synod, United Church of Christ, St. Louis, Mo., June 22–26, 1973.

[17] *Gates of Prayer: The New Union Prayerbook*, New York, Central Conference of American Rabbis, 1975, pp. xii, 229, 254–55, 257, and 265.

[18] In addition to the several religious bodies and communities in the process of revising their printed materials, the Division of Education and Ministries of the National Council of Churches has scheduled publication of "The Liberating Word: A Guide to Non-Sexist Interpretation of the Bible," edited by Letty M. Russell, assistant professor of theology at Yale Divinity School.

[19] "Linguistic Sexism," editorial, *Journal of Ecumenical Studies*, Vol. XI, No. 2, Spring 1974.

[20] Ibid.

[21] Oxford English Dictionary, under the entry *harlot*.

[22] William Shakespeare, *The Winter's Tale*, Act III, Scene 3.

[23] Oxford English Dictionary, under the entry *fellow*.

[24] Quoted from Alexander Korda, *Male Chauvinism!* New York, Random House, 1973, by Jo Ann Levine, "Male Chauvinism—As a Male Analyzes It," *Christian Science Monitor*, July 29, 1973.

[25] Margaret Mead, *Male and Female: A Study of the Sexes in a Changing World*, New York, Dell Publishing Company, Laurel Edition, 1968, p. 351. (First published in 1949.)

[26] Webster's Third New International Dictionary of the English Language, 1966, under the entry *castration complex*.

[27] Orwell, "Politics and the English Language," pp. 109, 110–11.

[28] Harvey Cox, "Of Witches and Pagans, Female," *New York Times*, October 1, 1973, p. 35.

[29] Orwell, "Politics and the English Language," pp. 109, 114.

WORKING WITH THE TEXT

Cultural and Historical References

In this section, the numbers at the margin refer to the numbered paragraphs in the selection itself.

18, 27, 29. In the novel *Nineteen Eighty-Four* and in the widely read essay, "Politics and the English Language," the British writer George Orwell parodies and discusses the efforts of totalitarian governments to control the way their citizens perceive reality by manipulating and prescribing the language these citizens use. Ironically, both those who advocate eliminating sexually biased terms from the language and those who express reservations about some of these efforts cite Orwell in an effort to make their cases.

21. *The Oxford English Dictionary*, a monumental work of scholarship completed between 1850 and 1920, lists all of the words which have

ever appeared in written form in the language and traces the evolution of each word's meaning, from its earliest appearance in writing to the present day.

22. If you don't know who Copernicus was, you can find out by reading this paragraph with some care. Why do Miller and Swift bring Copernicus up here? What point are they trying to make?

Writing Assignments: The Paragraph

Be sure to provide an introduction for each of the following paragraph writing assignments. That is, begin each paragraph with a phrase like this: "Thomas Brickle claims that . . . ." When it is relevant, you might also want to identify the expertise of the author ("Thomas Brickle, a New Testament scholar, claims that . . . ."), the name of the book or article, the century and country in which the work appeared, or any other circumstances that your readers might find significant. For more on this, see pp. 11–13 in Chapter 2.

1. After reading paragraphs 4 to 6, sample some of the definition illustrations in your own dictionary and discuss the presence or absence of sexually biased language in that dictionary. Support your conclusions with several examples.

2. After reading paragraph 9, discuss examples of books that you have read which made you feel excluded because of the writers' sexually biased language.

3. If you have reservations about the authors' point in paragraph 12, discuss them. Can you think of a number of job titles for which there are really no suitable nonsexist substitutes?

4. Choose one of the manifestations of sexually biased language which Miller and Swift discuss in paragraphs 39 to 55 which you emphatically would or would not like to see eliminated. Develop your opinion.

Writing Assignments: The Short Essay

Use informal documentation for these short essays. That is, don't use footnotes or a Works Cited page to document your sources. Instead, cite only relevant information about your source, and keep that information *within* your text. Then follow the summary or quote with a page number in parentheses. (Use the page numbers that you find in this book to represent the page numbers of the source.) Thus, your informal documentation will look something like this:

> In "In Defense of Gender," Cyra McFadden needles those who ostentatiously use a double last name: "Two surnames, to me," she says, "still bring to mind the female writers of bad romances and Julia Ward Howe" (p. 410).

1. Write an essay based on your own personal experience in response to Alexander Korda's observation in paragraph 24: "Women are thinking out their roles; men are merely clinging desperately to theirs."

2. In paragraph 29, Miller and Swift quote George Orwell: "What is above all needed is to let the meaning choose the word, and not the other way about." Relying upon this essay and upon your own personal experience, discuss efforts to eliminate sexually biased language which consist of letting "the meaning choose the word." (Or, you might want to discuss examples of such efforts which do not really comply with this principle.)

3. Miller and Swift insist in paragraph 31 that "eliminating sexism need not result in graceless language, as many people fear." This particular concern pervades most of the arguments which defenders of traditional language usage raise. Without reading beyond this piece, write an essay in which you agree with the authors' assertion. Support your opinion with examples from this essay or from your own personal experience.

HOW YOUR DAUGHTER GROWS UP TO BE A MAN

Gina Allen

Gina Allen, who has served as the vice president of the American Humanist Association and has chaired its women's caucus, makes the most comprehensive argument that appears in this chapter for the need to eliminate what she sees as sexist language (or "manglish"). Allen contends that there are many easy ways to eliminate sexist language and she offers up a number of them in her essay. Her argument has even wider implications, as you can see from her quotation from Benjamin Whorf: "The limits of my language are the limits of my thought."

1. It seems impossible, doesn't it? That the baby girl in the pink booties should grow up to be a man? But it happens to every little girl in the English-speaking world, courtesy of the English language—labeled *Manglish* by California critic Varda One.

2. Little girls, learning to speak, learning who they are, identify with *me—she—her—hers*. And they know that litle boys are *he* and *him*. Also most animals are *he's*, except, perhaps, kittens and ladybugs. In life and in picture books children are introduced to the puppy—"Isn't *he* cute?" And the elephant at the circus. "Isn't *he* big?" And the monkey in the zoo. "Isn't *he* funny?"

3. Being surrounded by a world of male animals doesn't interfere with a little girl's sense of identify. However, becoming a *he*—sometimes, and sometimes not, in the interests of grammar—can do just that. What is she to think when the instructions say that if a child wants to go on the field trip he should bring written permission from his parents? Is she a *he* in this instance, or is the field trip, like many other privileges, for boys only?

Source: Gina Allen, "How Your Daughter Grows Up to Be a Man," *The Humanist.* March/April 1980: 34–38, 62.

Expanding their language to include *she's* isn't hard for little boys. They never   **4**
have to change gender. They are never excluded. They only have to enlarge their word
world in general situations, knowing that the inclusion of females sometimes doesn't
apply in the real world, where the sexes are often carefully segregated. For little girls,
the lesson is much more difficult. Little girls have to switch back and forth, now
accepting a new identify as *he*, for reasons they don't understand, and then becoming
she again, no longer welcome in the masculine world.

Lexicographer Alma Graham, who, with Peter Davies, deleted Manglish from   **5.**
the American Heritage Dictionary, explains it this way: "If you have a group,
half of whose members are A's and half of whose members are B's and if you call the
group C, then A's and B's may be equal members of group C. But if you call the group
A, there is no way that B's can be equal to A's within it. The A's will always be the
rule and the B's will always be the exception—the subgroup, the subspecies, the
outsiders.

She might have added *invisible*, which women become with use of the masculine   **6.**
singular pronoun and with the generic terms *man* and *men*. Girls, growing up, learn
about the accomplishments of man, man's needs, man's ideals. They learn about
"Prehistoric Man," "Primitive Man," "Civilized Man," "Man In Space," "The
Future of Man."

They read and hear about "Courageous Men," "Frontiersmen," "Men of   **7.**
Science," "Famous Men," "Statesmen." They learn about their "forefathers," those
wise, intrepid architects of civilization. But what do they learn about their foremothers?
Not much, and little that is positive. Eve, the first woman according to the Hebrews,
was also the first sinner, who caused "mankind' to be banished from a paradise on
earth into a harsh world of toil and pain. Pandora, the first woman according to the
Greeks, opened her dowry box and unleashed among "men" the evils that plague them
still.

From then until today women have been remembered and recorded more often   **8.**
as treacherous temptresses than as accomplishing humans worthy of respect. Helen of
Troy was blamed for the ten-year Trojan War and the deaths of many Greek heroes.
The Greek Island of Lesbos is known, not as the home of Sappho the great poet, but
as the home of the seductress of young women, Sappho the Lesbian. Aspasla, teacher
of Socrates, is remembered, not as a wise philosopher, but as the courtesan who
destroyed Pericles.

According to the records, the Romans were beset by female treachery, from   **9.**
Cleopatra and Zenobia without to the likes of Fulvia, Livia, Agrippina, and Messalina
within. To have their works judged on merit, rather than disparaged, women have had
to disguise themselves as men and perform deeds of masculine valor. Even then, as
in the case of Joan of Arc, brilliant military victories could be attributed to the devil
who possessed her and she could be burned at the stake to exorcise him.

In order to have their writings published and accepted by readers many women,   **10.**
including the Brontë sisters and some modern mystery writers, have used male
pseudonyms (George Eliot, George Sand). Paintings and musical compositions of
women have been attributed to teachers, husbands, fathers, and brothers. And scores
of creative women are known to us only as "Anonymous." Female scholars are now
bringing these forgotten women to our attention, something male historians, writing

the story of "mankind," have never done. They thought they were writing the history of generic "man." They were, in fact, writing *his* story. *Her* story is only now being told.

I

In "Words and Women," authors Casey Miller and Kate Swift observed: "Man in the **11.** sense of male so overshadows man in the sense of human being as to make the latter use inaccurate and misleading for the purposes both of conceptualizing and communicating."

Consider the confusion: **12.**

> Abraham Maslow, writing about empathetic man, admits that man can't really know what it's like to be a different sort of animal. "He can't even know what it's like to be a woman."
> After an hour-long program on BBC, Jacob Bronowski's "The Ascent of Man," the host and a guest chat casually about what women might have been doing while man ascended from the apes.
> Erich Fromm: "Man's vital interests are life, food, and access to females."
> Sign on a New York subway: "Give a kid a job and mold a man."
> Television commentator: "People won't give up power. They'll give up anything else first—money, home, wife, children."
> Sociologist: "Americans of higher status have more years of higher education . . . and less chance of a fat wife."
> History text: "This ancient civilization allowed women to inherit property."

Benjamin Lee Whorf once said: "The limits of my language are the limits of **13.** my thought." We have been proving him right before and since. From the primary grades through college, students asked to illustrate concepts such as "Primitive Man," "Industrial Man," "Economic Man," have done so by drawing men. They add women only when the instructions are changed so that they are illustrating "Primitive Men and Women" or "Primitive Society," and so forth. There are never as many women as men. But at least when the term *man* or *men* isn't guarding the door women are allowed to appear in small numbers. Never enough, however, to make it seem that they had anything to do with human progress or are an important part of civilization.

The confusion between generic *man* and *man* as male is constant in English and **14.** sometimes troublesome in other languages. Frenchmen were outraged at women demonstrators, and had the women arrested, for carrying signs that stated: "One Frenchman in two is a woman." The men thought that half of them were being accused of homosexuality.

And then there's the Loch Ness monster, who has never been seen and therefore, **15.** gender unknown, is called "he." One group, wanting to draw him close enough for observation, got caught up in their semantics and created a synthetic female to lure the generic "he" into the open.

If we as adults can be so contradictory in our attempts to deal with a masculine **16.** gender that denotes both "male" and "male and female," how can we teach it intelligently to our children? The fact is that we can't, and don't.

Alma Graham, who has put children's texts through a computer, tells us that **17.** children learn their lessons from books in which there are twice as many boys as girls and seven times as many men as women. So much for the generic male gender's impartiality.

To add to the erasure of little girls as legitimate persons, most of the women in **18.** the books they read are mothers who have given birth to sons, not daughters. And, in these books, the sons are referred to as the sons of their fathers—not of their mothers. Little girls not only have no existence in their storybooks—they have no future.

A lot of linguists and ordinary citizens think this isn't important. An increasing **19.** number of educators and pediatricians, including Benjamin Spock and Lee Salk, think it is.

When he was president of Mills College, then for women only, Lynn T. White **20.** said: "The grammar of English dictates that when a referent is either of indeterminate sex or both sexes, it shall be considered masculine. The penetration of this habit of language into the minds of little girls as they grow up to be women is more profound than most people, including most women, have recognized: for it implies that personality is really a male attribute, and that women are a human subspecies. . . . It would be a miracle if a girl baby, learning to use the symbols of our tongue, could escape some wound to her self-respect: whereas a boy baby's ego is bolstered by the pattern of our language."

II

How did our English language get so mixed up that women have to tread carefully **21.** through it, learning, only with practice, when they are men and when they aren't? Other Indo-European languages of the Teutonic branch, of which ours is one, don't have this problem. German, Danish, Norwegian, and Swedish still have a word that represents "human," with separate words that denote men as males and women as females. When languages have masculine, feminine, and neuter genders, these don't put down one sex in favor of the other. Gender is usually quite random. Mark Twain complained bitterly, and comically, about German because it makes a turnip feminine while a young woman is neuter—"it."

English, too, once had a word for human beings of both genders. It was *mann*, **22.** derived from the Indo-European root meaning "earthling." In Early English *mann* meant a human being. *Wif* meant an adult female. And *wer* meant an adult male. In the ninth century, when Alfred the Great encouraged the use of English instead of Latin, women came and went as men did. They worked at the same trades and had equal rights.

Then in six centuries, under English common law, women's rights declined, and **23.** so did their position in the language. *Wer*, for man, all but disappeared (though retained in werewolf), and men, male, appropriated *man* and *men*, dropping the second *n*. *Wif* became *wife*, she who belongs to a man. *Wifman* became *woman*. And English lost its word for a human being. *Man* was expected to do double duty.

Up to that time it was possible to say that "his mother was a goodly man" or **24.** "the Lord had but one pair of men in Paradise." Can you imagine a child, now, making either statement (or making sense out of either one)? If it were to happen, parents, teachers, doctors would give up all allegiance to generic *man* and have the child treated for a severe identity crisis.

No one has measured, or done anything about, the identity crisis little girls **25.** experience as they learn that they are "he" and half of "mankind." For most it happens at too early an age for remembering. But there are things, along the way from girlhood to womanhood, that many women remember and wish they could forget.

Since women are defined not only as men, but by men, in the language, men go **26.** on defining, says social scientist Arthur Berger of San Francisco State University. And they define women as less than human:

as a different species: chicks, pussies, bitches, cows, pigs.
as something to eat: cookie, tart, tomato.
as mindless sex objects or parts of the body: piece, tease, sex pot, or worse.
as lesser or nonpeople: hags, broads, dolls.
as people who never grow up: babies, gals, girls.

When a woman marries, the couple is pronounced "man (the human being) and **27.** wife (the possession of the man)." And this is supposed to be the bride's day! When a woman goes to work she is part of "man-power." If she is injured on the job she is entitled to "workmen's compensation." If she is physically abused she is "manhandled." If she falls off a ship she is "man overboard!" If she is killed by another, the crime is "manslaughter."

Daily, women open letters addressed to "Dear Sir." They are called "gals" or **28.** "girls" by their employers and others until they are in their eighties. In nightclubs and on television they are ridiculed by stand-up comics as wives and mothers-in-law. If they aren't wives they are ridiculed as spinsters, too unattractive to catch a man. If they do something dumb, they are told they behaved "just like a woman." If they say something intelligent, they are told they "think just like a man."

III

Looking up a word in the dictionary (the final authority on the use of language) can **29.** be a traumatic experience for a woman. H. Lee Gershuny, of the Department of English, Manhattan Community College, City University of New York, hoped for improvement in the Random House Dictionary, which was the first new unabridged dictionary to be published after the resurgence of the women's movement in this country in 1966. It was widely distributed, inexpensively, by a major book club and thus became the first and only unabridged dictionary to be used in many households throughout the country.

In a preface to the dictionary, written in Manglish, Editor-In-Chief Jess Stein **30.** states: "The Random House Dictionary of the English Language . . . is an entirely new dictionary, written in midcentury for twentieth-century users. Because it is fully up to date and thoroughly reliable, the RHD will provide the user with all the information he is likely to need about . . . language matters."

Stein also says: "We have been guided by the premise that a dictionary editor **31.** must not only record, he must also teach. . . . We have often added illustrative examples after definitions in order to give the reader as much help in understanding the meaning and use of the word as possible."

32. In her study of the Random House Dictionary, Gershuny examined the illustrative sentences, two thousand of them, which accompanied nine hundred entry words, randomly selected. She found that "masculine-gender sentences appear almost three times as often as feminine-gender sentences in RHD," and that "where feminine-gender words occur, the reader will find 'her' stereotyped in nearly seven out of ten sentences."

33. The stereotypes are negative and unnecessary for illustrating the entry words. True, they teach—one of the purposes of the dictionary in Editor Stein's opinion. But what they teach is scarcely "fully up to date" or "reliable" for "twentieth-century users," more than half of whom are women and all of whom are living in a world in which sexual stereotypes and assumptions are being questioned and revised or else discarded entirely.

34. Let's look at illustrative sentences for the words *bargain, tremble, shrill, hypnotize.*

His mother-in-law was no bargain.
She trembled at his voice.
Women with shrill voices get on his nerves.
He really hypnotizes the women; they believe anything he tells them.

35. The lessons taught in such descriptive sentences are clear. They reinforce the injustices of the tongue we speak. Says Berger: "Women are subjected to an insidious, almost invisible domination in the very language they use to think about themselves and argue for their rights . . . Women are a subordinate sex and it shows in our everyday language as well as in our social life, and the language probably helps determine the social structure."

36. Indeed it does, and has. Asks Dan Lacy, senior vice-president of McGraw-Hill, Inc.: "Would the Declaration of Independence have meant the same thing if it said '. . . all men and women are created equal'? Indeed, would the signers have signed it? . . . *Man* and its compounds when used generically have an ambiguity useful to writers who want to be slippery with their meanings. They can decide for themselves when it will be offered as noble universality and when and by how much its meaning will be restricted."

37. The slippery universal *man* and the grammatically imposed masculine singular pronoun in our language serve nobody well. They turn women into invisible and/or lesser men. They reinforce men's low opinion of women and women's low opinion of themselves. They turn men and women into adversaries instead of partners. And they start their insidious work in the early years of childhood when children are gulping down uncritically the knowledge that we give them as if it were life-sustaining and enriching, which it should be.

IV

38. The problems posed by our male-dominated language are not insoluble, given determination and imagination. It takes only awareness to substitute *person* or *human* or *people* for generic *man* and *men*. And certainly *humanity* and *humankind* are more descriptive of all people than *mankind*. Miller and Swift have suggested another choice—*gen* and *genkind.* as in *genesis* and *generic.*

As far back as 1859 the American composer, Charles Converse, proposed *thon,* **39.** a contraction of *that one* as a substitute for the enveloping masculine singular pronoun. The suggestion found its way into two dictionaries. More recently, Mary Orovan's *co,* which she used in a 1973 book published by Harper and Row, has been adopted by several communes and the magazine *Community* addressed to communes.

It is possible that a new pronoun isn't needed. Once upon a time *you* was plural, **40.** used in the singular only to address a superior person one wished to honor. As the ideas of democracy made everyone worthy of honor, *you* was universally used and the singular *thee* and *thou* dropped from the language. Today an increasing number of teachers of English are allowing students to use *they* and *them* instead of *he* and *him,* placing equality of the sexes above arbitrary rules of grammar.

Writers, speakers, and once-strict grammarians are also training themselves to **41.** use and accept *they* and *them* as more realistic than *he, him, she,* and *her,* even when the referent is singular. In that they are in the best company. Including Shakespeare, Lord Chesterfield, George Bernard Shaw, F. Scott Fitzgerald, and John F. Kennedy, all of whom, at times, substituted the plural for the singular pronoun without apology.

There is another solution, proposed by columnist Gena Corea: "From now on, **42.** let's use *she* to refer to the standard human being. The word *she* includes *he* so that would be fair. Anyway, we've used *he* for the past several thousand years and we'll use *she* for the next few thousand; we're just taking turns."

It's one way to keep your daughter from growing up to be a man.   **43.**

WORKING WITH THE TEXT

Cultural and Historical References

In this section, the numbers at the margin refer to the numbered paragraphs in the selection itself.

5. Peter Davies and Alma Graham are lexicographers, or people who collect and define words in order to put together a dictionary. Allen's reference to them seems to reveal a small sexist bias on her part. If there is a bias, explain it.

9. According to Allen, Cleopatra, Zenobia, Fulvia, Livia, Agrippina, and Messalina are frequently cited historical examples of female treachery. If you were writing an essay in which you were trying to show that females are also treated generously by history, what examples could you come up with?

10. George Eliot and George Sand are pseudonyms for famous female authors. Why, according to Allen, did these women take on men's names?

12. Erich Fromm, a German-American psychoanalyst, believed that we are products of our environment and alienated, largely because we live in

an industrial society, even from ourselves. Allen uses Fromm as an example of a male writer who is making a generalization about humans, despite the fact that his last point concerning "access to females" suggests that he has forgotten that females make up half of the human race. Now, can you express Fromm's idea in a way that would clear up Fromm's apparent confusion and thereby satisfy Allen?

22. "Indo-European" is the name given to the contemporary family of languages to which English belongs, but the term also refers to an ancient language spoken in Eastern Europe around 2500 B.C. First, to which is Allen referring, the modern language family or the ancient language? Second, what point is Allen making when she brings up the word for "earthling" in Indo-European?

Writing Assignments: The Paragraph

Be sure to provide an introduction for each of the following paragraph writing assignments. That is, begin each paragraph with a phrase like this: "Thomas Brickle claims that. . . ." When it is relevant, you might also want to identify the expertise of the author ("Thomas Brickle, a New Testament scholar, claims that. . . ."), the name of the book or article, the century and country in which the work appeared, or any other circumstances that your readers might find significant. For more on this, see pp. 11–13 in Chapter 2.

1. In a paragraph, summarize Allen's discussion (paragraphs 1 to 37) of the sexism built into the English language. Before you begin, you might want to pay careful attention to her title and introductory paragraphs.

2. Summarize paragraph 26 and salt your summary with a few of the negative words for females from the list that Allen provides. You'll have to set up this question carefully so that your reader will be able to understand what Allen is doing in that paragraph.

3. Allen's arguments rely heavily upon directly quoted examples of verbal sexism. Summarize one of her arguments and then demonstrate it by quoting a few of her supporting examples.

Writing Assignments: The Short Essay

Use informal documentation for these short essays. That is, don't use footnotes or a Works Cited page to document your sources. Instead, cite only relevant information about your source, and keep that information *within* your text. Then follow the summary or quote with a page number in parentheses. (Use the page numbers that you find in this book to represent the page numbers of the source.) Thus, your informal documentation will look something like this:

> In "In Defense of Gender," Cyra McFadden needles those who ostentatiously use a double last name: "Two surnames, to me," she

says, "still bring to mind the female writers of bad romances and Julia Ward Howe" (p. 410).

1. Write a paper in which you use the same argument that Allen uses, but use the example of males rather than females. Cite examples of demeaning words that are often applied to males. Refer to Allen's argument and a few of her examples somewhere in your essay.

2. In a short paper, argue with Allen's idea that "sexist" language that describes women is demeaning and changes the way women see themselves. Summarize and quote from Allen as you develop your paper.

3. In paragraph 15, Allen uses the Loch Ness monster to reinforce her idea that sexism is rampant even in Scotland. Can you use the Loch Ness monster to show that the male pronoun is not always used positively? Using Allen's essay as your starting point, write a short paper to make your case.

4. How do paragraphs 8 to 10 relate to Allen's concern with sexism in English? Has the author simply wandered from her purpose here? Write a paper discussing the matter.

THE NON-SEXIST ASSAULT ON LANGUAGE, OR, A MEMORANDUM TO THE NATIONAL COUNCIL OF TEACHERS OF ENGLISH

Robert L. Spaeth

Robert Spaeth is dean of the College of Arts and Sciences at St. John's University in Collegeville, Minnesota. In 1981 the National Council of Teachers of English wrote an eight-page brochure showing its members how to avoid sexist language and replace it with sexually neutral language. Evidently the brochure was sent to Robert Spaeth and other educational administrators to encourage, or coerce, teachers in their colleges and departments to avoid what the NCTE considered sexist language. This is Spaeth's response.

1. A couple of years ago when Gloria Steinem accepted a fellowship from the Woodrow Wilson International Center for Scholars and became a fellow, I concluded that the feminist movement, or at least that part of it concerned with sexist language, had achieved a new state of maturity or peace. But now that "Guidelines for Nonsexist Use of Language in NCTE Publications" has appeared in my office mailbox, accompanied by a suggestion that I urge the contents of these guidelines on faculty members, I fear that some radical fringe of the movement has come into power—enough power to convince as large and responsible an organization as the National Council of Teachers of English (NCTE) to advocate changes in English usage that would do considerable violence to the language.

2. Both the spirit and the substance of the NCTE guidelines are objectionable.

Source: Robert L. Spaeth, "The Non-Sexist Assault on Language, or, a Memorandum to the National Council of Teachers of English," *Change.* July/August 1981: 12–13.

Altogether the guidelines treat the language like an innocent puppy waiting to be neutered for the convenience of his human masters. Evidently every word, prefix, or suffix suspected of maleness is to be emasculated. The ultimate goal of the operation—praiseworthy in so many other manifestations—is the banishment of sexism; the unintended result will be a disfigured English language.

3. The little brochure, just eight pages long, lacks sensitivity to the very language taught by thousands of members of the NCTE. Ordinary speakers and writers of English automatically turn to English teachers for professional assistance in understanding and protecting the language. One naturally wonders how the unnamed English teachers who wrote these guidelines could have such an advanced social conscience and yet fail to defend the very language they profess to love.

4. In our colleges, corporations, churches, and bureaucracies, power over the language is today in the hands of those who are committed to "nonsexist language." But the powerful, who get what they want, have always been free from facing up to the implications of what they want. Thus, by decree, the pronoun *he* will be replaced by *he or she* or by *he/she* or by some even more awkward expression. Perhaps the free use of power is appropriate in political circles, but we do not normally look to politicians for guidance in language.

5. We expect better from the NCTE, but in "Guidelines for Nonsexist Use of Language" we are not getting what we expect and deserve.

6. The first innocent victim of the authors of the guidelines is the little set of letters, *man*, which is introduced as follows:

> Although *man* in its original sense carried the dual meaning of adult
> human and adult male, its meaning has come to be so closely identified
> with adult male that the generic use of *man* and other words with
> masculine markers should be avoided whenever possible.

7. This premise is not only offensive but false. *Man* remains a word of two meanings, despite what these guidelines say. We need to know enough about its use in particular contexts to tell the difference. Bergen Evans, in *A Dictionary of Contemporary American Usage*, explains the ambiguity and provides some telling examples along the way:

> The words *man* and *men*, when used generically, may be ambiguous.
> Either word may be used to mean the human race as in . . . *the best
> laid schemes of mice and men*. But they may also be used to mean the
> males only, as in *man is destined to be a prey to woman*. . . . The
> singular *man* is used more often to mean the race, and the plural *men*,
> to mean the males. But this rule is not followed consistently.

8. Building fearlessly on its false premise, the NCTE recommends the avoidance of not only *man* but also *mankind, manmade, the common man, chairman, mailman,* and *policeman*. No mention is made—for good and sufficient reason, I suspect—of *horseman, penman, manhole, manslaughter, maneater, manhandle, manikin,* or *man-of-war*. If the NCTE can suggest, with a straight face, the use of *chair* for *chairman* and *synthetic* for *man-made*, who knows what horrors would appear as the equivalents of *manhole* and *horseman*?

"Guidelines" makes another error as it assults the pronoun *he:*   **9.**

> When we constantly personify "the judge," "the critic," "the execu-
> tive," "the author," as male by using the pronoun *he*, we are subtly
> conditioning ourselves against the idea of a female judge, critic, execu-
> tive, or author.

Here, NCTE does not commit an error in language, though it may well be an **10.**
error in psychology. The linguistic error appears in the sentence immediately preceding
the above in "Guidelines": ". . . English has no generic singular—or common-
sex—pronoun. . . ." Oh, but it has—*he*. The word *he*, like many other English words,
simply serves two purposes, and we English speakers and writers have to know enough
about our language to make the distinction.

Compounding its error, the NCTE next recommends plain illiteracy: ". . . plural **11.**
pronouns have become acceptable substitutes for the masculine singular." In other
words, *they* can mean *he*. Are we to thank our English teachers for this?

If one followed only the examples offered in the NCTE guidelines; if one **12.**
scrupulously avoided following out the logical extensions of its premises—then one
might keep his blood pressure down and his standards of English up. But the end,
unfortunately, is not in sight. In a recent book, *Words and Women: New Language in
New Times*, authors Casey Miller and Kate Swift propose the replacement of the word
mankind with *genkind*.

On this incendiary topic, it is easy to be misunderstood to be treating social **13.**
mores and problems when one is only treating problems of language. As the critic John
Simon pointed out in his book, *Paradigms Lost*,

> Doubtless, women are entitled to the process of getting the rights and
> freedom granted to men; once these goals are achieved, however,
> and even before that, they can leave the language alone.

The importance of language should not be denigrated even in the face of the **14.**
great importance of the women's movement itself. Joseph Epstein is certainly correct
in reporting that, for educated people, "standards of literacy have fallen below the
permissible" (*Commentary*, February, 1981). Let us hope, however—may I include
the NCTE in this hope?—that Mr. Epstein is wrong in the fear that "precision, elegance,
good sense, all must fall before the feminist juggernaut."

WORKING WITH THE TEXT

Cultural and Historical References

In this section the numbers at the margin refer to the numbered paragraphs
in the selection itself.

1. Gloria Steinem is one of the founders of *Ms.* magazine and an important
   figure in the women's liberation movement. What point is Spaeth
   making when he brings up Steinem?

2. Can you locate a word in this paragraph that the NCTE guidelines might object to?

2. There is a metaphor that runs through the last three sentences of paragraph 2. What is that metaphor, and where is it reflected in the three sentences?

4. Why does Spaeth use quotes for the word "nonsexist" in this paragraph?

10. What does "generic singular" mean when applied to language?

14. What does the word "juggernaut" suggest when applied to the NCTE?

Writing Assignments: The Paragraph

Be sure to provide an introduction for each of the following writing assignments. That is, begin each paragraph with a phrase like this: "Thomas Brickle claims that. . . ." When it is relevant, you might also want to identify the expertise of the author ("Thomas Brickle, a New Testament scholar, claims that. . . ."), the name of the book or article, the century and country in which the work appeared, or any other circumstances that your readers might find significant. For more on this, see pp. 11–13 in Chapter 2.

1. Summarize Spaeth's article in a paragraph. In the introduction to your summary, use a shortened version of Spaeth's title. The title of the article will tell you a lot about its slant. You might want to look over "An Essay's Title," pp. 3–4 in Chapter 1.

2. Write a single paragraph that begins with these words: "The angry tone of Spaeth's essay is reflected in his diction." Support that topic sentence with quoted examples.

3. Write a paragraph or two on the puppy metaphor in paragraph 2. What, for instance, is being compared to what? Why does Spaeth use a puppy? Quote a word or phrase to communicate the flavor of the image.

Writing Assignments: The Short Essay

Use informal documentation for these short essays. That is, don't use footnotes or a Works Cited page to document your sources. Instead, cite only relevant information about your source, and keep that information *within* your text. Then follow the summary or quote with a page number in parentheses. (Use the page numbers that you find in this book to represent the page numbers of the source.) Thus, your informal documentation will look something like this:

> In "In Defense of Gender," Cyra McFadden needles those who ostentatiously use a double last name: "Two surnames, to me," she says, "still bring to mind the female writers of bad romances and Julia Ward Howe" (p. 410).

1. Argue with Spaeth's central contention. That is, defend the NCTE. Be sure to summarize and quote Spaeth as you develop your argument.

2. In a short paper, analyze the puppy neutering metaphor that runs through paragraph 2. Show what is being compared to what. Also show what Spaeth is suggesting about the authors of the NCTE guidelines through his use of the puppy metaphor.

3. Analyze the basis for Spaeth's attack on the NCTE guidelines. That is, look hard at his arguments and try to decide what it is that serves as the basis for his attack. Don't get psychological here. Perhaps he's defending clarity or tradition or "sensitivity to language," or something else. What *is* it that bothers Spaeth?

IN DEFENSE OF GENDER

Cyra McFadden

Cyra McFadden, a free-lance writer from the San Francisco Bay area, is a former supporter of eliminating sexist language (or Manglish, as she terms it) from the language, but she has soured on her cause. Notice how heavily she relies upon specific examples to develop her points.

So pervasive is the neutering of the English language on the progressive West **1.** Coast, we no longer have people here, only persons: male persons and female persons, chairpersons and doorpersons, waitpersons, mailpersons—who may be either male or female mailpersons—and refuse-collection persons. In the classified ads, working mothers seek childcare persons, though one wonders how many men (archaic for "male person") take care of child persons as a full-time occupation. One such ad, fusing nonsexist language and the most popular word in the California growth movement, solicits a "nurtureperson."

Dear gents and ladies, as I might have addressed you in less troubled times, this **2.** female person knows firsthand the reasons for scourging sexist bias from the language. God knows what damage was done me, at 15, when I worked in my first job—as what is now known as a newspaper copyperson—and came running to the voices of men barking, "Boy!"

No aspirant to the job of refuse-collection person myself, I nonetheless take off **3.** my hat (a little feathered number, with a veil) to those of my own sex who may want both the job and a genderless title with it. I argue only that there must be a better way, and I wish person or persons unknown would come up with one.

Defend it on any grounds you choose; the neutering of spoken and written **4.** English, with its attendant self-consciousness, remains ludicrous. In print, those "person" suffixes and "he/she's" jump out from the page, as distracting as a cloud of gnats, demanding that the reader note the writer's virtue. "Look what a nonsexist writer person I am, avoiding the use of masculine forms for the generic."

Spoken, they leave conversation fit only for the Coneheads on "Saturday Night **5.**

Source: Cyra McFadden, "In Defense of Gender," *The New York Times Magazine.* August 2. 1981: 9–10.

Live." "They have a daily special," a woman at the next table told her male companion in Perry's, a San Francisco restaurant. "Ask your waitperson." In a Steig cartoon the words would have marched from her mouth in the form of a computer printout.

6. In Berkeley, Calif., the church to which a friend belongs is busy stripping its liturgy of sexist references. "They've gone berserk," she writes, citing a reading from the pulpit of a verse from I Corinthians. Neutered, the once glorious passage becomes "Though I speak with the tongue of persons and of angels . . ." So much for sounding brass and tinkling cymbals.

7. The parson person of the same church is now referring to God as "He/She" and changing all references accordingly—no easy undertaking if he intends to be consistent. In the following, the first pronoun would remain because at this primitive stage of human evolution, male persons do not give birth to babies: "And she brought forth her firstborn son/daughter, and wrapped him/her in swaddling clothes, and laid him/her in a manger; because there was no room for them in the inn. . . ."

8. As the after-dinner speaker at a recent professional conference, I heard a text replete with "he/she's" and "his/her's" read aloud for the first time. The hapless program female chairperson stuck with the job chose to render these orally as "he-slash-she" and "his-slash-her," turning the following day's schedule for conference participants into what sounded like a replay of the Manson killings.

9. Redress may be due those of us who, though female, have answered to masculine references all these years, but slashing is not the answer, violence never is. Perhaps we could right matters by using feminine forms as the generic for a few centuries, or simply agree on a per-woman lump-sum payment.

10. Still, we would be left with the problem of referring, without bias, to transpersons. These are not bus drivers or Amtrak conductors but persons in transit from one gender to the other—or so I interpret a fund-drive appeal asking me to defend their civil rights, along with those of female and male homosexuals.

11. Without wishing to step on anyone's civil rights, I hope transpersons are not the next politically significant pressure group. If they are, count on it, they will soon want their own pronouns.

12. In the tradition of the West, meanwhile, feminists out here wrestle the language to the ground, plant a foot on its neck and remove its masculine appendages. Take the local art critic Beverly Terwoman.

13. She is married to a man surnamed Terman. She writes under "Terwoman," presumably in the spirit of *vive la différence*. As a letter to the editor of the paper for which she writes noted, however, "Terwoman" is not ideologically pure. It still contains "man," a syllable reeking of all that is piggy and hairy-chested.

14. Why not Beverly Terperson? Or better, since "Terperson" contains "son," "Terdaughter"? Or a final refinement, Beverly Ter?

15. Beverly Terwoman did not dignify this sexist assault with a reply. The writer of the letter was a male person, after all, probably the kind who leaves his smelly sweat socks scattered around the bedroom floor.

16. No one wins these battles anyway. In another letter to the same local weekly, J. Selbert, female, lets fire at the printing of an interview with Phyllis Schlafly. Not only was the piece "an offense to everything that Marin County stands for," but "it is even more amusing that your interview was conducted by a male.

''This indicates your obvious assumption that men understand women's issues **17.** better than women since men are obviously more intelligent (as no doubt Phyllis would agree).''

A sigh suffuses the editor's note that follows: ''The author of the article, Sydney **18.** Weisman, is a female.''

So the war of the pronouns and suffixes rages, taking no prisoners except writers. **19.** Neuter your prose with all those clanking ''he/she's,'' and no one will read you except Alan Alda. Use masculine forms as the generic, and you have joined the ranks of the oppressor. None of this does much to encourage friendly relations between persons, transpersons or—if there are any left—people.

I also have little patience with the hyphenated names more and more California **20.** female persons adopt when they marry, in the interests of retaining their own personhood. These accomplish their intention of declaring the husband separate but equal. They are hell on those of us who have trouble remembering one name, much less two. They defeat answering machines, which can't handle ''Please call Gwendolyn Grunt-Messerschmidt.'' And in this culture, they retain overtones of false gentility.

Two surnames, to me, still bring to mind the female writers of bad romances and **21.** Julia Ward Howe.

It's a mug's game, friends, this neutering of a language already fat, bland and **22.** lethargic, and it's time we decide not to play it. This female person is currently writing a book about rodeo. I'll be dragged behind a saddle bronc before I will neuter the text with ''cowpersons.''

WORKING WITH THE TEXT

Historical and Cultural References

In this section, the numbers at the margin refer to the numbered paragraphs in the selection itself.

5. What characteristics of the Coneheads on *Saturday Night Live* does the author have in mind when she asserts that only such people could find neutered language satisfactory?

8. Why might McFadden find the Manson murders an appropriate simile for the ''he-slash-she'' construction favored by some advocates of a nonsexist language?

16–18. Phyllis Schlafly has worked on the national level to stop the Equal Rights Amendment.

16–18. McFadden's sarcasm in these paragraphs is more biting when you realize that Marin County, California, is often seen as a superficially hip and trendy community, full of BMWs and quiche.

19. Why would McFadden exclude Alan Alda from the legions of Americans who won't read writers who consistently neuter the language they use?

Writing Assignments: The Paragraph

Be sure to provide an introduction for each of the following paragraph writing assignments. That is, begin each paragraph with a phrase like this: "Thomas Brickle claims that. . . ." When it is relevant, you might also want to identify the expertise of the author ("Thomas Brickle, a New Testament scholar, claims that. . . ."), the name of the book or article, the century and country in which the work appeared, or any other circumstances that your readers might find significant. For more on this, see pp. 11–13 in Chapter 2.

1. Summarize the incident which McFadden relates regarding the Phyllis Schlafly interview in Marin County (paragraphs 16 to 18).

2. Summarize the controversy sparked by art critic Beverly Terwoman (paragraphs 12 to 15).

3. McFadden suggests the purpose of her essay in her title, but you can, nevertheless, state her intentions in more detail? Write a paragraph in which you summarize her article.

Writing Assignments: The Essay

Use informal documentation for these short essays. That is, don't use footnotes or a Works Cited page to document your sources. Instead, cite only relevant information about your source, and keep that information *within* your text. Then follow the summary or quote with a page number in parentheses. (Use the page numbers that you find in this book to represent the page numbers of the source.) Thus, your informal documentation will look something like this:

> In "In Defense of Gender," Cyra McFadden needles those who ostentatiously use a double last name: "Two surnames, to me," she says, "still bring to mind the female writers of bad romances and Julia Ward Howe" (p. 410).

1. Write a paper in which you agree or disagree with McFadden. Paraphrase and quote from her essay as you develop your thesis.

2. Write a paper in which you analyze the organization of McFadden's essay. Somewhere in your first paragraph, state her thesis clearly. In the body of your paper explain how she develops that thesis.

3. Write a paper in which you describe, and occasionally analyze, the humor in McFadden's essay.

O GOD, OUR [MOTHER AND] FATHER

Richard Ostling

> Richard Ostling, a *Time* reporter, summarizes the efforts of the National Council of Churches (NCC) to purge sexist language from the biblical scriptures which

Source: Richard N. Ostling, " 'O God, Our [Mother and] Father,' " *Time.* October 24 1983: 56–57.

appear in its book of congregational readings—*An Inclusive Language Lectionary.*
The scriptural revisions in this document have triggered a heated controversy, which
has been joined by several other writers in this chapter.

> *Then the LORD God said, "It is not good that the man should
> be alone. I will make him a helper fit for him."* . . . *and the rib
> which the LORD God had taken from the man he made into a
> woman and brought her to the man.*
>
> —Genesis 2:18,22 (Old)

> *Then God the SOVEREIGN ONE said, "It is not good that
> the human being should be alone. I will make a companion
> corresponding to the creature."* . . . *and God the SOVEREIGN
> ONE built the rib which God took from the human being into
> woman and brought her to the man.*
>
> —Genesis 2:18,22 (New)

> *For God so loved the world that he gave his only Son, that
> whoever believes in him should not perish but have eternal life.
> For God sent the Son into the world, not to condemn the world,
> but that the world might be saved through him.*
>
> —John 3:16,17 (Old)

> *For God so loved the world that God gave God's only Child,
> that whoever believes in that Child should not perish but have
> eternal life. For God sent that Child into the world, not to
> condemn the world, but that through that Child the world might
> be saved.*
>
> —John 3:16,17 (New)

1. For millions of Americans, no publication is awaited more eagerly than a fresh
translation of the biblical texts that are so important to their practice of religion. In the
past, even relatively minor changes have caused an uproar, but they pale beside the
revisions in a radical new version of scriptural readings that was released last week.
The translations alter or eradicate beloved phrases that have stood for millenniums.
God in heaven is no longer just the Father but the ''Father [and Mother]'' (or ''[Mother
and] Father''). The Deity is addressed as ''Sovereign One,'' but never as the ''Lord.''
Jesus Christ is no longer designated as either the Son of God or the Son of man.

2. These unconventional translations are not the product of some eccentric scholar
or self-appointed caucus, but of the National Council of Churches, supported by 32
Protestant and Orthodox denominations with 40 million members. The N.C.C. sought
to provide Bible readings for worship services that were free of the ''male bias'' in
Scripture that militant feminists have been complaining about for nearly a decade. To
proponents, the book is an advance toward equal treatment. To opponents, the
translations are tasteless, if not heretical.

3. The N.C.C. book of readings, offered for ''experimental and voluntary use in churches,'' remarkably affects the imagery and impact of many of the best-known Bible passages. Additions to the original text are set off in brackets. For instance, ''All things have been delivered to me by my Father; and no one knows the Son except the Father, and no one knows the Father except the Son and any one to whom the Son chooses to reveal him,'' *(Matthew 11:27)* becomes ''All things have been delivered to me by [God] my Father [and Mother]; and no one knows the Child except God, and no one knows God except the Child and any one to whom the Child chooses to reveal God.''

Drastic changes like these immediately started a strident debate. A Methodist **4.** agency dealing with the role of women in the church called on the 38,000 congregations and 9.5 million members of the denomination to employ the new translations. But the heads of two major N.C.C. churches disowned the book. Said Archbishop Iakovos of the Greek Orthodox Archdiocese (2 million members): ''It does not reflect the traditions and reverence of the Holy Scriptures.'' Bishop James R. Crumley Jr. of the Lutheran Church in America (2.9 million members) advised congregations not to read the book during worship services.

The task of taking the male orientation out of the Scriptures began in the 1970s, **5.** when women's caucuses in several Protestant denominations persuaded the N.C.C. to establish a Task Force on Sexism in the Bible. In 1980, the N.C.C. decided to form an Inclusive Language Lectionary Committee to prepare new Bible translations for reading during worship. Even before work began, the idea provoked the fiercest reaction in N.C.C. annals: nearly 10,000 letters attacking the project flooded into the organization's New York City headquarters.

To do the rewriting, the N.C.C. named a committee, headed by the Rev. Victor **6.** Roland Gold of California's Pacific Lutheran Theological Seminary, a minister in the I.C.A., whose leaders were to reject the book. Gold's group includes four other male and six female scholars, one of them a Roman Catholic nun. All are sympathetic to the feminist cause. Another participant dropped out midway, in part because he felt that the project was going too far.

The panel's new book, *An Inclusive Language Lectionary: Readings for Year A* **7.** ($7.95), rewrites 209 passages from the Revised Standard Version (RSV) of the Bible, which is also sponsored by the N.C.C. A lectionary is a list of Bible readings for services in congregations that follow liturgical worship. The N.C.C. book covers one year of readings often used by Protestant churches. Two other volumes are scheduled for 1984 and 1985.

The N.C.C. committee contends in its introduction that chauvinism characterizes **8.** not just English translations but the Old and New Testament manuscripts as written in Hebrew and Greek. The committee believes Scripture readings from standard Bibles ''exclude half of those who hear'' readings on Sunday—the women. The committee also complains that old Bible language about God the Father ''has been used to support the excessive authority of earthly fathers.''

It was the concept of God the Father that posed the toughest problem. The radical **9.** feminists' suggestion of ''God ess'' was unthinkable, and ''Parent'' seemed too impersonal. The solution is ''God our Father [and Mother],'' alternated with ''[Mother and] Father.'' Motherhood's rise is most striking in passages in which Jesus prays to ''my [Mother and] Father.'' Other N.C.C. innovations:

Son of God—in place of this New Testament designation for Jesus Christ, the **10.** texts use a unisex "Child of God." To critics, this has connotations of immaturity.

Son of Man—instead of this phrase Jesus used to refer to himself, the N.C.C. **11.** panel employs "Human One."

Lord—this masculine term, repeatedly used for God and the most frequent **12.** biblical title for Jesus Christ, is replaced with "Sovereign" or "Sovereign One."

The N.C.C. translators made insertions to change the emphasis of some parts of **13.** the Bible. In verses that mention Abraham alone, for example, the committee brings in Sarah, his wife, and even his concubine, Hagar. This kind of alteration especially infuriates critics of the N.C.C. work. "They want to rewrite history, just like the Russians," remarks the Rev. Elizabeth Achtemeier of Union Theological Seminary in Virginia.

In its zeal to achieve sexual equality, the N.C.C. Committee converted some of **14.** the most lyrical passages of the Bible into jolting newspeak. Pronouns turned out to be immovable obstacles. He, his, and him are minimized in references to male human beings, including the earthly Jesus, and no male pronouns at all are used to refer to God or to Jesus Christ before he came to earth and after he had risen from the dead. A sample of the resulting disaster: "For God so loved the world that he gave his only Son" *(John 3:16)* becomes "For God so loved the world that God gave God's only Child." Aversion to the pronoun himself is carried to a ludicrous extreme: "Christ humbled self."

Aesthetic problems aside, the N.C.C. is provoking fundamental theological **15.** disputes. The committee defends "Mother" as a metaphor for God that is just as acceptable as the traditional "Father." Indeed, it points out, the Bible contains numerous motherly metaphors to describe the Deity. If "Father" is taken to mean that God is literally male, the translators argue, the view is "idolatry."

But traditionalists like Vernard Eller of California's La Verne College believe **16.** God purposely revealed himself as masculine. "Whatever he may be in himself, *for us* he is Husband, Father and King." Achtemeier believes the N.C.C. version reflects the concepts of a pre-Christian, pre-Jewish paganism that worshipped goddesses. Theologian Donald Bloesch thinks the orthodox doctrine of the Trinity (Father, Son and Holy Spirit) is at stake, and that the Mother-Father God sounds like two deities in a "dyad."

Protestants who believe that God inspired the Bible word for word will, of course, **17.** be irate, as will moderates and liberals who think the Bible must be preserved as a historical text, however it might be interpreted today. Asks Lucetta Mowry, a New Testament scholar: "Is it the role of the translator to be a leader in social action? This seems to make the Bible into a manifesto for feminism."

The dispute even flares within the N.C.C. The council is now sponsoring a new **18.** edition of its bestselling Revised Standard Version of the Bible. The RSV translators plan to make modest use of inclusive language, such as "humanity" instead of "man." But they will have nothing to do with the approach of Gold's panel. Says the Rev. Bruce Metzger, a New Testament professor at Princeton Theological Seminary and the head of the RSV committee: "The changes introduced in language relating to the Deity are tantamount to rewriting the Bible. As a Christian, and as a scholar, I find this altogether unacceptable. It will divide the church, rather than work for ecumenical understanding."

The N.C.C. insists that it has no plans to publish a de-sexed version of the Bible. **19.**

Still, by the time it completes its next two lectionaries, Gold's panel will have renovated about 95% of the New Testament and 60% of the Old. Gold believes that, inevitably, such translations are "a first step in a process" leading, perhaps in a generation, to a complete Bible free of what the committee considers to be male bias. That could produce a Bible that would be more ideologically pure than other versions, but less read.

WORKING WITH THE TEXT

Cultural and Historical References

In this section, the numbers at the margin refer to the numbered paragraphs in the selection itself.

13. The Reverend Elizabeth Achtemeier is suggesting that, like the Communists, the NCC is rewriting history, to serve their own political agenda.

14. The term "newspeak" first appeared in George Orwell's novel *Nineteen Eighty-Four*.

16. Perhaps you can give a rough definition of "dyad" merely by looking at its context.

18. Perhaps you can define "ecumenical" merely by looking at its context.

Writing Assignments: The Paragraph

Be sure to provide an introduction for each of the following paragraph writing assignments. That is, begin each paragraph with a phrase like this: "Thomas Brickle claims that . . . ." When it is relevant, you might also want to identify the expertise of the author ("Thomas Brickle, a New Testament scholar, claims that . . . ."), the name of the book or article, the century and country in which the work appeared, or any other circumstances that your readers might find significant. For more on this, see pp. 11–13 in Chapter 2.

1. Explain the difference between a lectionary and a Bible. Quote or summarize from Ostling's essay.

2. Summarize the criticisms which have been leveled at the NCC's lectionary (paragraphs 2, 8, 15, 19).

Writing Assignments: The Short Essay

Use informal documentation for these short essays. That is, don't use footnotes or a Works Cited page to document your sources. Instead, cite only relevant information about your source, and keep that information *within* your text. Then follow the summary or quote with a page number in parentheses. (Use the page numbers that you find in this book to represent the page numbers of the source.) Thus, your informal documentation will look something like this:

In "In Defense of Gender," Cyra McFadden needles those who ostentatiously use a double last name: "Two surnames, to me," she says, "still bring to mind the female writers of bad romances and Julia Ward Howe" (p. 410).

1. Use Ostling's description of the purpose and content of the lectionary as the basis for your disagreement with the lectionary.

2. Discuss the changes in the Bible text which the lectionary entails by summarizing these changes. Use examples to illustrate your summary.

3. In a short paper, summarize the arguments of the creators and defenders of the NCC's lectionary (paragraphs 4, 13 to 18). In your first paragraph, carefully set the background of the controversy.

THE GOD OF THE NCC LECTIONARY IS NOT THE GOD OF THE BIBLE

Ben Patterson

This article by Ben Patterson, the pastor of a California Presbyterian church, appeared as a guest editorial in *Christianity Today*, a journal that describes itself as a magazine of "evangelical conviction." Patterson was inspired to write his article by the publication of the National Council of Churches' controversial lectionary, which excised references to the maleness of God and Jesus. In effect, the NCC was claiming, through their lectionary, that the Bible was a sexist document and needed to be revised, at least for the purposes of their religious services. Patterson thinks that the NCC's lectionary is, at the least, a pernicious document. In the following article, you'll read his reasons for that judgment.

Nations have a way of rewriting history to make their past look good, and to **1.** undergird what they are doing in the present. So do political parties and ethnic groups, universities and church councils: particularly church councils, it would seem, as in National Council of Churches. In October the council published a lectionary designed to rectify what it terms a "male bias" in Holy Scripture. (A lectionary is a compilation of Bible passages to be read in public worship.) This new age publication, *Inclusive Language Lectionary: Readings for Year A*, promises to enable Christians to offer their praise to God in nonsexist language. For the generic "man" it substitutes the more generic "humankind" or "human race." Better yet, no masculine pronouns refer to God; as a matter of fact, no pronouns at all refer to God, since all personal pronouns are specific in terms of gender. God will be called God. Jesus, his "Son," is now Jesus, his "Child." The title "Lord" has been replaced with the title "Sovereign." The "kingdom of God" is now the "realm of God." Where God was once called "King," he is now called "Ruler," or "Monarch."

But I save the best for last. In its zeal to declare its solidarity with its feminist **2.** sisters everywhere, the National Council of Churches' lectionary will no longer call God "Father" but rather "Father and Mother." It should be pointed out, however,

Source: Ben Patterson, "The God of the Lectionary Is Not the God of the Bible," *Christianity Today.* February 3, 1984: 12–13.

that the lectionary has not yet begun the Lord's Prayer with "Our Father and Mother in heaven." Acknowledging that that may be a bit too much for pious ears to bear, it will delay such a move, if it makes it at all, until the 1984 or 1985 volumes in this expanding series of lectionaries.

Well, brothers and sisters, what are we to make of all this? As I read the new **3.** lectionary, a slogan kept coming to mind. It appears under the masthead of *Rolling Stone* magazine, and it says, "All the news that fits." Presumably this means that *Rolling Stone* prints only the news that fits the themes of concern to the magazine. The rest of the news is omitted. The National Council of Churches has done *Rolling Stone* one better. Since God is referred to in the Bible in almost exclusively masculine terms, and it would not work to eliminate him from the Book altogether, the council, in a brilliant stroke, has just changed his name.

When I was in seminary I was taught to do exegesis and to avoid eisegesis. **4.** Exegesis is the science of reading *out of* the Bible its meaning; eisegesis is the practice of reading *into* the Bible our own meanings. The new lectionary has now introduced metagesis. If the text or term simply will not allow us to read into it our foregone conclusions, then change it! If the Bible is "patriarchal to the core," as some of the more radical religious feminists insist, then let us change the Bible, by all means.

When a person does something I deeply disagree with, it may win from me a kind **5.** of perverse admiration because of its sheer audacity. It has *chutzpah*: a characteristic a child would display if he murdered his parents and then threw himself on the mercy of the court because he was an orphan. My hat is off to you this time, National Council of Churches! You have pulled off a real coup.

My perverse admiration aside, let's get back to the issue. It is not just the National **6.** Council's cavalier revision of the Bible that should grieve us. It is what their revision has done to God. I realize, of course, that we mere mortals can do nothing to God. Thanks be to him, he will survive even our most monumental foul-ups. But when we distort what he has revealed to us about himself, we do great damage to ourselves. The God we believe in will determine the people we become.

What kind of God do we get when we change the terms in which he has chosen **7.** to reveal himself? To begin, we obviously get a god other than the God revealed in Jesus Christ. The real question is not whether the Bible is sexist, but whether Jesus was sexist. He is Lord and Savior. Our Lord and Savior has revealed God decisively and definitively as Father, not Father and Mother. The National Council of Churches officially confesses Christ as Savior and Lord. How does it reconcile its actions with that confession? Could it be that it uses the terms "Lord" and "Savior" as historic orthodoxy always has, but with a different dictionary? It has been accused of such, and its most recent publishing venture has done little to answer that accusation, and much to confirm it.

It will simply not do to explain Jesus' reference to God as Father by saying it **8.** is an accommodation to his culture. This view claims he was forced to speak of God's sovereignty in terms of "king" and "father" because his culture was patriarchal and would understand and respond to no alternative terms. Yet the pagan cultures surrounding Israel abounded in female deities. The head of the Canaanite pantheon, Baal, had his consort Astarte. The male and female were fully represented in the deities of paganism, and in cultures that made Israel's patriarchalism pale by comparison. Jesus had that option, but he refused it. The scribes and Pharisees took up rocks to stone him because he placed himself on equal footing with God. They would have been justified if they had. The new lectionary may not, as they say, play well in Peoria, but it would have done even worse in first-century Jerusalem.

But Jesus did not call God "Father and Mother" for fear of being stoned. He **9.** called God "Father" because it said it best about who God is toward us. It preserves the truth that God is over and above us in a way that maternal designations cannot. Karl Barth and Hendrikus Berkhof and Donald Bloesch have argued effectively that the word "Father" contends for the transcendence and spirituality of God over against a god of the fertility cults and Earth Mother, or a creative process within history. Bloesch says that when God is "Mother," the tendency has been irresistible "to look for God within the depths of the soul or of nature rather than in the particular events in history where God in his sovereign freedom has chosen to reveal himself."

We agree that God has maternal, nurturing qualities. We know it because **10.** Scripture says so. The point of "Father" is that toward us he is Father, and we are his children. He is Husband and we are his wife. This is not to say that because God is masculine, therefore being a male human is to be more godlike. The Bible teaches that all of us, male and female, comprise one humanity that is both male and female, and that humanity is to be related to God as female to his male, wife to his husband, and child to his father.

Let the new lectionary restrict its revisionism to humans. Perhaps there is **11.** nothing wrong with doing away with the generic "mankind" in favor of the generic "humankind." As for the personal pronoun, there is nothing wrong with making changes there too, I guess. I sometimes wonder, though, if there is all that much right in doing so. Will feminism do away with the personal pronoun altogether? Or will it introduce new words into our language? Will he or she and him or her become he/she, him/her and finally 'heshe" and "him'er"?

I know a language has its political dimension and can be pervasive in its influence **12.** on how we think. But does the use of personal pronouns have all that much influence on how we think about male and female roles and power? I have been impressed how concern over their use can trivialize great passages of Scripture and liturgy. I have seen persons in my congregation all but miss the beauty and truth of something said or read or sung in worship because the use of personal pronouns did not pay proper homage to their feminist convictions.

Martin Luther said the world's reforms are like trying to get a drunk peasant on **13.** a mule. Push him up one side and he falls off the other side. In that sense, the National Council of Churches' new lectionary is the worldliest of reforms. Whatever abuses it has set out to correct have been totally outweighed by the new abuses it has introduced. To borrow from one of our Lord's parables, the council may have driven out one demon, but it has made room for ten more.

WORKING WITH THE TEXT

Cultural and Historical References

In this section, the numbers at the margin refer to the numbered paragraphs in the selection itself.

1. At one time, to "gird one's loins" meant to wrap cloth—usually a man's skirt—around a person's upper legs. This leant support to the man's thighs and allowed him to move about more freely, especially in battle. Knowing that, what did Patterson mean when he wrote, "Nations have a way of rewriting history to make their past look good, and to undergird what they are doing in the present." What word could you substitute for "undergird"?

1. "New age" music is often said to be mushy and bland. "New age" ideas—astrology, reincarnation, and the like—strike some people as trendy and kooky. What is Patterson's purpose, then, when he calls the NCC's lectionary a "new age" publication.

1. A generic laundry soap is one that's merely called "laundry soap." What, then, does Patterson mean when he writes, "For the generic "man" it [the lectionary] substitutes the more generic "humankind" or "human race?"

5. "*Chutzpah*" is a Yiddish word with an interesting pronunciation and definition. Look it up in the dictionary.

8. The New Testament Pharisees were one of the sectarian groups that often opposed Jesus.

8. Something that "plays well in Peoria" is something that is acceptable to Middle America. Read the passage in which that phrase occurs. What is Patterson saying about the probable response to the NCC Lectionary in first-century Jerusalem?

13. Martin Luther is the man whose actions began the Protestant Reformation. He opposed abuses within the Catholic Church.

Writing Assignments: The Paragraph

Be sure to provide an introduction for each of the following paragraph writing assignments. That is, begin each paragraph with a phrase like this: "Thomas Brickle claims that. . . ." When it is relevant, you might also want to identify the expertise of the author ("Thomas Brickle, a New Testament scholar, claims that. . . ."), the name of the book or article, the century and country in which the work appeared, or any other circumstances that your readers might find significant. For more on this, see pp. 11–13 in Chapter 2.

1. Paraphrase paragraph 4. Be sure to let your reader know that Patterson uses three ways of reading a text to make his point, and that one of those ways is an ironic suggestion.

2. Instead of summarizing Patterson's thesis, quote his clearest and most forceful statement of it. Begin with these words: "The heart of Ben Patterson's argument is contained in his statement that . . . " Then fill out a paragraph by elaborating on that quote.

3. Paraphrase paragraph 6. Begin your paraphrase not with Patterson's initial sentence but with a sentence that sums up the paragraph. In other words, begin your summary with a topic sentence.

Writing Assignments: The Short Essay

Use informal documentation for these short essays. That is, don't use foot-notes or a Works Cited page to document your sources. Instead, cite only relevant information about your source, and keep that information *within* your text. Then follow the summary or quote with a page number in parenthe-ses. (Use the page numbers that you find in this book to represent the page numbers of the source.) Thus, your informal documentation will look something like this:

> In "In Defense of Gender," Cyra McFadden needles those who os-tentatiously use a double last name: "Two surnames, to me," she says, "still bring to mind the female writers of bad romances and Julia Ward Howe" (p. 410).

1. Essayists who argue often use irony, which is the use of words that convey the opposite of their literal meaning. When you tell your mom that you'll be back at 8 P.M., and she replies, "Sure you will," your mother is using irony. That is, she actually means, "I'm sure you won't be." Patterson uses irony throughout his essay. Look at the first sentence in the second paragraph. That's irony. There are two phrases in the third paragraph that are ironic. In a short essay, analyze the use of irony in Patterson's essay.

2. *The New York Times* claims that it is a newspaper that runs "all the news that's fit to print." *Rolling Stone* says it is a magazine that runs "all the news that fits." Write a paper that begins with Patterson's suggestion that the NCC lectionary does *Rolling Stone* one better.

3. Write a paper in which you take the side of the NCC lectionary. That is, argue that the language of the Bible is offensively male-oriented and therefore needs to be changed in church readings so that it won't offend, or exclude, the church's female members. Inform your argument by reading the next essay in this chapter.

4. Write a short paper that analyzes the connection between Patterson's concluding paragraph and his thesis. Be sure to consider the connection between Martin Luther's story of the drunk peasant on the mule and Patterson's thesis. Set this up carefully in your first sentence.

WHY THE INCLUSIVE LANGUAGE LECTIONARY?

Burton H. Throckmorton, Jr.

Burton Throckmorton, Jr., is a New Testament professor at Bangor Theological Seminary in Bangor, Maine. As Throckmorton tells us in his first paragraph, he was one of the experts who decided on language changes in the National Council

Source: Burton H. Throckmorton, Jr., "Why the Inclusive Language Lectionary?" *The Christian Century.* Vol. 101 (1984): 742–744.

of Church's lectionary. He wasn't surprised, he tells us, at the virulent responses to the lectionary by "anti-feminists" and fundamentalist Christian groups. But he was surprised at the negative reactions from "liberals" (his quotes). Throckmorton's essay, written for *The Christian Century*, is one of the harder pieces in this book. It is hard because it is filled with subtle reasoning, difficult words, and technical religious language. To surmount these difficulties, you'll have to read slowly, look up a few words, stop to think every now and then, and keep in mind the author's thesis. To begin, read the title and look up the word "inclusive."

The initial reactions to *An Inclusive Language Lectionary: Readings for Year A,* **1.** published in October 1983, have run the gamut from great joy to bitter hostility. All of us who worked on it expected both. We knew that countless men and women across this country would welcome a version of Scripture readings for worship in the church that were not sexist but inclusive of the whole congregation. We also knew that many fundamentalists, antifeminists and the more conservative Christian groups would respond negatively. But two other reactions were less expected: first, the enormous interest in the *Lectionary* on the part of the "secular" press—its general appreciation of the complex issues involved in the *Lectionary*'s preparation and its generally fair and balanced early assessment of the *Lectionary*'s significance (on the day following publication more than 90 newspapers gave the *Lectionary* front-page coverage); second, the extent of negative reaction coming from "liberal" religious journals and from "liberal" Christians.

The acrimonious rhetoric emanating from nonconservative quarters has shown **2.** that the *Lectionary* touched a raw nerve. Deep-seated fears that cut across the theological spectrum have been exposed. Much more is at stake than the elimination of some pronouns and the loss of some cherished appellations. The anxiety and the virulent clamor are caused, I have no doubt, by the recognition that the *Lectionary* has put the theological foundations of the status quo under siege, and that traditional perceptions of God, and of the power arrangements of men and women that are sanctioned and confirmed by those perceptions, have been threatened. A quiet revolution is under way all around us, the *Lectionary* is lending it strong support in the church, and Christians of all stripes are perplexed about what tactics to use to prevent its further advance.

Even before the *Lectionary*'s publication, and before its contents were known, **3.** it was mocked and attempts were made to discredit it. Since then it has been ridiculed as a misguided piece of fluff, easily to be blown away by the "scholarly community." Another occasion has been provided to attack the National Council of Churches, and some have even suggested that in light of the totally "disastrous" *Lectionary for Year A*, any further work on Years B and C surely ought to be abandoned.

From the very beginning, the lectionary committee made it known that it **4.** welcomes constructive responses and will take them all seriously in its future work. A number of people have made very helpful critiques, and the committee hopes that they will be joined by many others in our common task. I write at this juncture not to defend any particular judgments we have made in the *Lectionary for Year A*, but rather to talk about what I believe to be an absolute necessity for the church—namely, that Christians hear their Scriptures in language that includes them all equally.

There are, of course, many different reasons for reading the Bible. A biblical **5.**

scholar, professional or otherwise, will read or study it only in the languages in which it was written, and will not make a judgment about the meaning of a text on the basis of any English translation, no matter how good it is purported to be. Any translation is always one giant step away from what was written, as one who has read Shakespeare in German or French will readily testify.

But most people who read the Bible are not adept at Hebrew or Greek and, in **6.** this country, they will read it in an English translation. Of course, the King James Version may well be read primarily for its literary beauty and its significance in the history of the English language, quite aside from the fact that it is a translation. That translation has its own inherent value. Nevertheless, English translations are read mostly out of necessity, by those wanting to find out something about the history of Israel, or about the historical Jesus or about the theology of Paul. In order to facilitate all such investigations by both Christians and non-Christians, translations as accurate as it is possible to make them must be provided. For such purposes the Revised Standard Version is an excellent tool.

The Bible is also read in the church, by believers and to believers, as the medium **7.** through which the Word of God may be heard. When we say "Word of God" we do not mean English words and sentences into which the Bible, or part of it, has been translated more than 100 times already in this century alone. We do not even mean Hebrew and Greek words from which the English has been rendered. If such words were the "Word of God," then one could burn it or tear it to shreds. No, the Word of God, as the Prologue to the Gospel of John says, "became flesh." It is that Word, made flesh in Jesus Christ, that was God's communication of God's self to humanity. But subsequent to the crucifixion of the historical person Jesus, the church believed from the very beginning that Jesus was still present, as *Kyrios*, as the Spirit, as the Paraclete, as Jesus' words. Those words of Jesus were incorporated into the apostolic preaching of the church—the preaching of the church's first witnesses to Christ, recorded in the New Testament. It is that preaching, that witness, that became for the church the "Word of God," the vehicle by and through which God addresses those who believe. The Bible is the Word of God to those believers who hear it as Word of God, and only to them.

When the Bible is read and heard as the Word of God, it is not read or heard **8.** primarily for either literary or historical reasons, but in order that it may be appropriated. However, impediments may inhibit or destroy the possibility of hearing the Word—for example, great physical pain on the part of the hearer, or the pain of recognizing that one is not being addressed by the words one is hearing, or the pain of realizing that one's beloved is not being addressed. In order to hear the Word of God, one must understand *oneself* to be addressed by that Word, and one must also feel that the whole community is being addressed equally. This is not required when the Bible is studied for historical or literary reasons.

If the Word of God is not hearable by those who do not understand themselves **9.** to be addressed by the biblical language through which that Word is communicated, does it follow that the Word of God cannot any longer be heard by women who feel excluded by patriarchal language, or by men who feel themselves excluded by language that does not include women on an equal basis with them? Is the patriarchalism of the biblical languages, and of biblical faith as originally formulated, *inherent* in the faith? That is the fundamental question with which the church must wrestle in our day.

From the time of the earliest versions of biblical writing the church has believed **10.**

that the Bible *in translation*, and not simply the original Hebrew and Greek texts, is hearable as the Word of God. But if, in translating, one translates patriarchalism out, do we still have the Bible? Or is Scripture so distorted by the deletion of patriarchalism that it can no longer function as the vehicle for hearing and receiving the Word of God? Or, to put it another way, is it true that the God revealed in Jesus Christ and worshiped in the Christian church addresses humanity only in patriarchal language and with patriarchal assumptions about both the deity and the human race?

11. I am not willing to concede that humanity's understanding of itself has now outgrown and left behind the Bible's capacity to function as the vehicle for hearing the Word of God. If I am right, then it appears that what the *Lectionary* attempts to do is, in principle, justified.

12. Some argue that what I identify as "humanity's understanding of itself" pertains only to a small minority of men and women in this country and in Europe who represent a feminist ideology that, with time, will go the way of all ideologies. It is further argued that in any case, the church cannot let itself be influenced by ideologies. But I am convinced that the feminist movement represents a broad-based revolution in our culture which is slowly gathering momentum from many quarters and whose tide will not be turned back.

13. The lectionary committee has been chastised for producing a distortion of Scripture that is simply propaganda for a particular ideology, and that opens the door for all kinds of special-interest groups to make changes in the biblical text to support their points of view. It has been suggested, for example, that a group representing Alcoholics Anonymous would be justified in changing a well-known text to read, "Use a little orange juice for your stomach's sake." It seems to me, however, that this fear has no foundation, for the simple reason that interest in the equality of male and female members of the human race can hardly be said to represent a particular ideology or a special-interest group. Rather, the insistence that women are the full equals of men and must be valued as men are in their personhood represents nothing less than a cry for human equality and human justice. An inclusive-language version of the Bible in no way opens the door for every particular special-interest group to change the biblical text to suit its own concerns.

14. In sum, then, it seems clear that the church must provide its members with a version of its Scriptures that opens the way for congregations of women and men at worship to hear and appropriate the Word of God.

15. The Bible is the church's book. The church has always read the Old Testament from the point of view of the gospel, and the New Testament and the church have been in a dialectical relationship with each other. The church both produced the kerygma and was brought into being by it. The New Testament was created by and for the church, so that we may say that in some sense the Bible brought the church into being, and in some sense the church brought the Bible into being. The relationship between them was and remains reciprocal.

16. It was the whole church, however, and not ecclesiastical authorities that established the unquestioned, authoritative role the Bible plays in its life. As Bishop Brooke Foss Westcott has said: "The written Rule of Christendom must rest finally on the general confession of the Church, and not on the independent opinions of its members. . . . The extent of the Canon . . . was settled by common usage, and thus the testimony of Christians becomes the testimony of the church" (*A General Survey of the History of the Canon of the New Testament* [Macmillan, 1881], pp. 12, 13).

The Canon belongs to the *whole* church, and although for most of the church's **17.**
history the male portion of its membership has usurped the responsibility for translating
and interpreting that canon, the time is long past due for the *whole* church, including
its female members, to assert the right to its translation and interpretation. Patriarchal
assumptions not only pervade the various writings of the Bible, but they have also
controlled and determined both the form those writings take when rendered in another
language and the way in which that rendering is to be interpreted. The argument one
hears now presented with some vehemence—that the Bible is an unalterable given to
which the church is to be subservient, because it is unambiguously antecedent to the
church in chronology and precedent to the church in authority—clearly has the effect
of stifling all opposition to the patriarchal status quo. What has always been is to take
precedence—and what has been most of the time is universal patriarchalism. The Bible
just as it is, and just as it has been traditionally translated and interpreted, is appealed
to with great sanctimoniousness; but the early church certainly never understood itself
to be servile to biblical writings, and the church today is no less justified in appealing
to its dialectical relation to Scripture, and in reading and hearing that Scripture in such
a way as to allow the whole congregation to hear itself addressed equally.

We might note in passing that while the patriarchalism staunchly defended in **18.**
our day has been decisive throughout the history of the church, it is also true that the
struggle *against* it is likewise as old as the church—a fact documented by much recent
research.

We must now address the change that accompanies alterations of one's self- **19.**
perception—namely, the change in one's perception of God. That there is a relation
between one's perception of God and one's perception of oneself hardly needs
demonstration. The same correlation exists even in individual Christians' perceptions
of the historical Jesus, about whom we know many details. To a Marxist, Jesus looks
Marxist; to a pacifist, he seems a pacifist, and so on. And what is true in the case of
perceptions of the historical person Jesus is certainly true in the case of one's perception
of God. A patriarchal society will think about God in ways influenced by and compatible
with patriarchy. This is not to imply that one's understanding of God is entirely
"subjective"; it is simply to affirm that one's understanding of God is dialectical, that
what one believes about God and what one believes about oneself influence each other.

Many voices, however, affirm that God is a given, no way contingent on who **20.**
one *perceives* God to be. This view is very congenial to defenders of the status quo,
who announce to those of a feminist perspective that who God is is a matter
of record—a record written, transmitted, translated and interpreted by patriarchal
communities. To interpret revelation as the communication of information about God
which is transmitted from one generation to another is, of course, to sew up patriarchy.
So we are told that God is what "he revealed himself to be," and that is male.

It has also been argued that although God is "beyond sex, he revealed himself **21.**
to be male." But *which* revelation of God is referred to? God's self-revelation in the
Old Testament? (But are the images of God always male in the Old Testament?) Or
God's self-revelation in Jesus? (Then it must be assumed that Jesus' maleness was a
substantive aspect of God's self-revelation in "the Word made flesh." Is this, however,
an indisputable theological fact?) Or is it the fact that Jesus called God "Father"?
Then those who say that God transcends sex but that God reveals God's self to be male

would have to argue that when Jesus called God "Father," he was not addressing God but only what God revealed God's self to be. What profundity! One becomes engulfed in such sophistry when one assumes that biblical language is propositional and that theology is basically informational.

If the statement "God is Father" is a proposition, then, of course, God cannot **22.** be "Mother." But if "God is Father" is a metaphor, then one may also say "God is Mother" without being contradictory. For metaphors do not exhaust meaning, and a single metaphor does not make all others superfluous. Thus I can say, "Life is a dream," and I can also say, "Life is a bed of roses," and one who reads both statements as metaphors and not as propositions will not think that they disagree. Likewise, God may be called "Rock" as well as "Father," and Jesus may be spoken of as "Lion" as well as "Lamb." All such appellations are metaphors. Of course God *is* not a mother, any more than God *is* a father; and Jesus *is* neither a lion nor a lamb. But just as surely as Jesus may be spoken of as a "Lion" and a "Lamb," God may be addressed as "Father" and "Mother," without any damage being done to the brain. Why, then, the strong resistance to speaking of God as "Mother"? Because of many people's deep-rooted conviction that the God they worship is male—even though they will also proffer the opinion that God transcends sex.

It has been said that in the *Lectionary* the word "Father" takes on a sexual **23.** connotation it does not have "in the Bible." I find that statement curious, and possibly (depending on its presuppositions) very naïve. What is most notable about it, however, is its utterly patriarchal assumption that such images and metaphors as "Father" and "King," as well as the pronouns "he," "his" and "him," have no sexual connotation whatever and are, therefore, completely compatible with the belief that God transcends sex—but that such metaphors as "Mother" and "Queen" and the pronouns "she" and "her" are, on the contrary, *sexual* terms which, when used in the same contexts as their "nonsexual" counterparts, do give them sexual connotations. So the *Lectionary* is accused of "imposing sexuality" on God. This is a very good illustration of the dictum that "Words mean what I say they mean," and not what the community has always understood them to mean.

The *Lectionary* takes seriously the view that indeed God does transcend sex—that **24.** God is neither male nor female—but it also assumes that words like "father" and "king" have the same male connotations in the Bible that they have elsewhere, as do the pronouns "he," "his" and "him." So when it is insisted that only masculine pronouns be used for God, and that it is good to address God as Father but pagan and baalistic to address God as Mother, one begins to suspect that God is not believed to transcend sexuality at all but that, on the contrary, God is being used to legitimize patriarchalism. There is in the church an enormous vested interest in assuring that no one seriously tamper with the perception that God is the great Protector and Preserver of Patriarchy.

An Inclusive Language Lectionary is a serious attempt to meet a deeply felt need **25.** in the Christian community. While many of the specifics decided on for Year A are open to continuing thought and discussion, inclusive-language renderings of Scripture are needed and are here to stay. This lectionary is not, of course, the first attempt to render Scripture in inclusive language, but it is the most conspicuous attempt, and could not be ignored. No amount of belittling or abuse will dissuade uncounted numbers of women and men in the church from pursuing their course of working for mutuality and justice in the body of Christ. They will continue to bear testimony to the God to whom they believe the Bible bears witness: God who anointed Christ to let the oppressed go free.

WORKING WITH THE TEXT

Cultural and Historical References

In this section, the numbers at the margin refer to the numbered paragraphs in the selection itself.

1. What does the word "inclusive" in *An Inclusive Language Lectionary* mean?

2. Throckmorton takes a risk when he uses a rather large and sometimes technical vocabulary. For instance, in a single paragraph (2), he uses the words "acrimonious," "appellations," "virulent," "status quo," and "sanctioned." The diction that a writer uses is partly determined by his expectations of the educational and professional level of his audience. What kind of audience do you suppose he was writing for? What does he lose, even for that audience, when he uses such high language? What does he gain?

6. The King James version of the Bible was first published in 1611. The Revised Standard Version, a twentieth-century translation, is more accurate, but its language is thought not to be as inspiring and felicitous as the language of the King James Version.

7. You may not be able to locate "*kyrios*" in your dictionary. Can you define it through context? "Paraclete" is the third part of the Trinity, the Holy Ghost, or spirit.

9. What does Throckmorton mean when he says that biblical languages evidence "patriarchalism"?

15. "Kerygma" means "the preaching." In this case, Throckmorton seems to be using it as a synonym for the early church writings that became the books of the New Testament.

16. "Canon" comes from a Latin word meaning a "ruler" or "measuring rod." Knowing that, what do you suppose is meant by the "canonical" works of the Bible?

21. To understand this paragraph, you'll probably have to look up "substantive," "sophistry," and "propositional." Do it.

24. "Baalistic" is the adjective for Baal, a Caananite god.

Writing Assignments: The Paragraph

Be sure to provide an introduction for each of the following paragraph writing assignments. That is, begin each paragraph with a phrase like this: "Thomas

Brickle claims that. . . ." When it is relevant, you might also want to identify the expertise of the author ("Thomas Brickle, a New Testament scholar, claims that. . . ."), the name of the book or article, the century and country in which the work appeared, or any other circumstances that your readers might find significant. For more on this, see pp. 11–13 in Chapter 2.

1. Paraphrase paragraph 11. Remember that in paraphrases you'll usually want to follow the same order that your source used originally—with one exception: Don't begin without a clear topic sentence, even if your source lacks one (or provides one that only makes sense when it is read in context).

2. Closely examine Throckmorton's diction in paragraph 2. In a paragraph, argue whether or not it is appropriate for his audience.

3. In paragraph 6, Throckmorton prefers beauty over accuracy in Biblical translations. Why? How does that help his argument? Write a paragraph or two on these questions.

Writing Assignments: The Short Essay

Use informal documentation for these short essays. That is, don't use footnotes or a Works Cited page to document your sources. Instead, cite only relevant information about your source, and keep that information *within* your text. Then follow the summary or quote with a page number in parentheses. (Use the page numbers that you find in this book to represent the page numbers of the source.) Thus, your informal documentation will look something like this:

> In "In Defense of Gender," Cyra McFadden needles those who ostentatiously use a double last name: "Two surnames, to me," she says, "still bring to mind the female writers of bad romances and Julia Ward Howe" (p. 410).

1. Write a short paper in which you use Ben Patterson's statement that "Nations have a way of rewriting history to . . . undergird what they are doing in the present." Use that statement to begin a critique of the main thrust of Throckmorton's article. Identify "what they are doing in the present" as Throckmorton's "quiet support" of the feminist movement.

2. Analyze paragraphs 5 and 6. What is Throckmorton saying in those paragraphs? Is what he is saying central to or ancillary to his thesis? What is the purpose of paragraphs 5 and 6?

3. Analyze Throckmorton's attempt, in his first two paragraphs, to discredit his opponents. Is this an effective tactic? Quote some of the words that Throckmorton uses to characterize his opponents' arguments. You'll probably need to begin with a rather detailed introduction in

which you outline the background of the controversy and provide a clear thesis for your analysis.

HYPERSEXISM AND THE FEDS

William Safire

In this essay William Safire, a widely read conservative columnist for *The New York Times,* insists that he is not bothered by the angry criticisms of those who disagree with his defense of the traditional usage of gender in language. On the contrary he enjoys a heated exchange of opinions. He is not amused, however, when a federal bureaucracy joins the argument with opinions which have been galvanized into regulations.

1. Some people take sexism in language very seriously.

2. A few weeks ago, it was pointed out here that it was O.K. to say "Everyone should watch his pronoun agreement," that it was not necessary to say "Everyone should watch his *or her* pronoun agreement." Nor was it required that, in the name of equality, we drop *mankind* and substitute *humankind;* historically, the male usage has embraced the female, and such expressions as "the family of man" are no putdown of women. I don't get worked up over Mother Earth and don't expect women to get worked up over Father Time.

3. "It seems to me that inequality is so morally unacceptable," writes Iva E. Deutchman, assistant professor of political science at Vassar College, "that one cannot be 'too excited' about inequality." She believes that using the pronoun *their* would be better than *his* in referring back to the singular-construed *everyone,* despite the lack of agreement in number.

4. "Perhaps, however, you provide an inadvertent autobiographical clue to this," adds Professor Deutchman, "in your empirically incorrect and grossly sexist observation that 'male always embraces the female,' rather than the reverse. Having never known (I surmise) the warmth of a female-initiated embrace, you no doubt came to the astounding conclusion that women were socially and linguistically inferior."

5. Wow! I have frequently been engaged in *ad hominem* exchanges, but have never before come under *ad muherten* attack. "Such nonsense as sexism masquerading simply as concern for linguistic purity," snaps the professor, "must stop at once."

6. My first reaction to that is disappointment that anyone would surmise that I, a lifelong member of the Sadie Hawkins Day committee, have never known the warmth— nay, the all-consuming passion—of a female-initiated embrace. My second reaction is ungrudging admiration: as a professional polemicist who draws vitality from vituperation, I not only respect but also enjoy the sight and sound of a straight, hard shot, delivered with zest and good-natured venom, by an opponent who knows where they stand. (Somehow, the sexless pronoun *they* doesn't sound right as a substitute for *he* or *she* in that sentence, but I'll try anything once.) In my view, the professor goes overboard, but I like the form of her dive.

Source: William Safire, "Hypersexism and the Feds," *The New York Times Magazine.* May 26, 1985: 10, 12.

Academics and journalists can merrily, or even savagely, joust about language: **7.** it's a fair field and no favor, with nobody coerced. Not so when a government official enters the fray in his official capacity.

A couple of weeks ago, a seemingly sex-crazed agency that Ronald Reagan long **8.** ago promised to abolish—the United States Department of Education—leaned on a university for daring to use such sexist terms as *man-made* in one of its catalogues.

Paul D. Grossman, chief regional attorney for the department's office for civil **9.** rights, first called the office of the chancellor of the University of California to report a complaint that the school was using sexist language in course descriptions. . . . When university officials asked him to be specific, the Government lawyer then sent a hit list of words, which Mr. Grossman contended may be perceived by some persons as subtly discouraging female student interest in the courses to which the phrases pertain.'' Alongside each word to be deleted by Federal diktat was what the lawyer called ''a viable alternative.''

I have the departmental hit list. In the business-administration courses, the phrase **10.** *manpower development* was deemed outside the pale: in the Government's sexless-speak, the acceptable version is *human resource development.*

In the education section of the catalogue, the lawyer zeroed in on the colloquial **11.** term ''Grantsmanship'' in a course called ''The Role of Experts in Social Services.'' The word *grantsmanship* is an extension of Stephen Potter's *one-upmanship* and *gamesmanship;* it is a mocking coinage, meaning ''one who plays the game of getting Federal or foundation money.'' No matter; it has the word *man* in it, and the power of the Federal Government, wielded by one earnest lawyer, demands that the substitute be *grant acquisition* or *grantwriting;* for no apparent reason, he eschewed *grantpersonship.*

In other courses, the university was directed—''informally,'' as the lawyer put **12.** it—to scrap *mankind,* substituting *the human species, humankind* or *humanity.* In biochemistry, ''Of Molecules and Man: A View for the Layman,'' the school was told to kill the two mentions of ''man'' and change the course title to ''Of Molecules and Human Beings: A View for the Lay Person.'' In the history department, a reference to *Man on Horseback*—a phrase about the heroic ''solitary horseman'' who often led to military rule—was ordered watered down by our Federal bureaucrat to a meaning-less *combatant.* (Try this for size: ''Gaullists are seeking a new Combatant on Horse-back. . . .'')

To its credit, and to the relief of believers in academic freedom, the university **13.** told the Federal attorney to get lost. Vice Chancellor Roderic B. Park bucked the matter to Prof. David Littlejohn of the journalism school, who shrewdly circulated the lawyer's objections to 15 journalists for comment before answering. Highlights of his report:

On *mankind:* ''The argument against the long-accepted universal use of *man* and **14.** *mankind* is political, not linguistic or logical. It may be compared to the mandated universal use of *comrade* . . . in 'classless' societies. . . . Pretending, or asserting, that the syllable *man* signifies males exclusively can lead one into such barbarisms as *ombudsperson* or *freshperson.*''

On pronouns: ''*His* as the appropriate (and neutral) pronoun to follow *one* or **15.** *a person* is an English usage of similar longstanding acceptance, although some writers—especially in state institutions—have lately taken to substituting the cumbersome and unnecessary *his or her.*'' (Person-oh-person, are they going to hear from Vassar, which is not even a state institution.)

On hypersensitivity: "In no case should good English words, which are a part **16.** of our common history and heritage, simply be legislated in and out of usage according to the whims of persons or groups who suddenly declare themselves 'offended.' '' Mr. Littlejohn, who calls himself *chairman* and not *chair,* accepts some changes in the name of clarity, as in changing *workman's compensation to worker's compensation.*

On freedom: "In no case should the University accept the idea that the office **17.** for civil rights is a better judge of appropriate language in its publications, or descriptions of its courses, than the University itself.''

I tried to reach Mr. Grossman, the taxpayer's new Anti-Sexist Language Czar **18.** (which includes *czarina*), but was told gruffly that he was "in travel status," which is Federalese for junketing or vacationing. The Department of Education's regional director in San Francisco, John Palomino, won't come to the phone: presumably, he has dived under his desk and barricaded himself with blotters until the storm passes.

The Secretary of Education in Washington, William J. Bennett, did return my **19.** call: "The minute I saw this story in The Times," he said, referring to Wallace Turner's account of the brouhaha, "I said 'Good grief—I want to know how this happens.' '' And how would he characterize the action of his attorney in San Francisco, presently on travel status in Japan? "Intrusive, meddlesome, unwarranted and wrong. My assistant secretary has counseled the regional directors that this should not happen again.''

We then discussed the synonymy of his adjectives: *intrusive* implies forcing **20.** entrance without right, and *meddlesome* suggests a milder interposition without right; another adjective in this vein is *officious,* connoting authority where none exists. *Unwarranted* is stronger than *unapproved* and both more disapproving than and closer in meaning to *uncalled-for; wrong* imputes a moral or ethical error or, in this case, a big fat mistake. Sexism is *wrong;* the imposition of language change by Government fiat, rather than by spirited private debate, is—as the Secretary of Education likes to say—intrusive, meddlesome, unwarranted and wrong.

WORKING WITH THE TEXT

Cultural and Historical References

In this section, the numbers at the margin refer to the numbered paragraphs in the selection itself.

6. What does Safire mean when he claims to be "a lifelong member of the Sadie Hawkins Day committee"? What do people do on Sadie Hawkins Day? Do Pappy Yokum and his son Abner ring a bell?

9. Note that Safire uses the word "diktat," rather than a word that retains connotations of its ancestor, a German word meaning "command." Why would Safire use the German word rather than a more common one like "regulation"?

18. Safire informs us that the phrase "in travel status" is "Federalese for junketing or vacationing." How does it serve Safire's purpose to satirize this kind of stiff bureaucratic language?

20. "Fiat" is an arbitrary order or decree. Here the focus of Safire's attention is on the word "arbitrary."

Writing Assignments: The Paragraph

Be sure to provide an introduction for each of the following paragraph writing assignments. That is, begin each paragraph with a phrase like this: "Thomas Brickle claims that. . . ." When it is relevant, you might also want to identify the expertise of the author ("Thomas Brickle, a New Testament scholar, claims that. . . ."), the name of the book or article, the century and country in which the work appeared, or any other circumstances that your readers might find significant. For more on this, see pp. 11–13 in Chapter 2.

1. Summarize the reservations which Paul D. Grossman of the U.S. Department of Education expressed about the diction used in the University of California's course offerings. You'll have to take great care in setting this up. Otherwise your reader will not be able to understand the context of your summary.

2. Paraphrase one of the three letters which Safire cites in his essay: the Deutchman letter, the Grossman letter written to the University of California, or the Littlejohn letter written to Grossman. Set up your paraphrase in such a way that your reader will understand the context of the letter.

Writing Assignments: The Short Essay

Use informal documentation for these short essays. That is, don't use footnotes or a Works Cited page to document your sources. Instead, cite only relevant information about your source, and keep that information *within* your text. Then follow the summary or quote with a page number in parentheses. (Use the page numbers that you find in this book to represent the page numbers of the source.) Thus, your informal documentation will look something like this:

> In "In Defense of Gender," Cyra McFadden needles those who ostentatiously use a double last name: "Two surnames, to me," she says, "still bring to mind the female writers of bad romances and Julia Ward Howe" (p. 410).

1. Defend the government's actions against Safire's criticism. For background, read a couple of essays in this chapter by feminists that object to sexist language.

2. Analyze the structure of Safire's essay by explaining why he shifts from a discussion of a reader's hostile reaction to one of his previous columns

to a discussion of a correspondence between a representative of the University of California and a U.S. Department of Education attorney.

3. What *is* Safire upset about. That is, what is his *essential* gripe. Write an essay in which you recall a similar gripe, and combine your experiences with those of Safire.

MY SAY

Ron Durham

Ron Durham is director of Writing Services and ethnic director of a ministers book club at Word Inc., Waco, Texas. His article originally appeared in *Publishers Weekly*, a trade magazine for the publishing industry.

1. Being somewhat the religious type, I've always been slow to hurl a lot of accusations at God. I figure most of us are naughty enough to deserve most of the ills that befall us, and not nearly good enough to deserve the blessings we enjoy. In recent years, however, I've had the uneasy feeling that God may have been caught in a Catch-22 bind that poses a new problem in theodicy. It's a potential roadblock to faith, ranking with "Why did God create earthquakes?"

2. The question for me is: If God really created us male and female, why didn't he create English pronouns adequate for the occasion?

3. My fundamentalist friends can keep the problem at the level of propriety. If it's literally true that God created a man and a woman there in Eden, then the segregation of "he-him-her" from "she-her" talk seems quite appropriate. But, alas, scholars say that even a conservative reading of Genesis indicates that "adam" simply means "humankind." Apparently male and female were unceremoniously lumped together from the very first lump of clay. Why, then, did God give those who speak English discrete, gender-specific, singular personal pronouns?

4. Everyone is familiar with current ploys used by writers and editors to be less gender-specific than God. But none of them work. And I am faced with the blunt possibility that creation has a built-in flaw.

5. One trick every editor has tried is to change everyone to plurals. We might say, "The problem is as old as Adam: What kind of God would do that to them?" If the scholars are right, there's really nothing wrong with that sentence; but does it really *read*?

6. Many authors try to deal with the problem by filling their sentences with extra clauses. These are highly dependent clauses—depending upon ambivalence to communicate gender inclusion. For example: "The trouble with a person asking such questions is that he or she is soon met with other issues which she or he would rather postpone, but which he or she finds impinge on the issue of the Adam question of who he or she is." At least that settles one theological question. There must be a hell in which to burn such cumbersome attempts at egalitarianism.

7. It is equally awkward, and even cowardly, to flee from pronouns to safe (but repetitious) antecedents, as in: "A person should stand up for a person's point of view while not being rude to a person's friends."

Source: Ron Durham, "My Say," *Publishers Weekly.* June 28, 1985: 70.

Others would import the gender-neutral "one" to avoid the problem. But like **8.** many imported items, this tends to sound snobbish. One simply cannot write down-home prose (can one?) with such sentences as: "Abe, what'n damnation should one do with a consarned mule that kicks one like he or she'd et a bellyful-a red peppers?"

Then there are writers who slash their lines with diagonals, as in *he/she* and **9.** *s/he*. This poses problems for proofreaders, who have been known to waste hours looking for a word or letter above the line which they (observe the skillful plural) think a / must point to.

Other authors try to make a statement against sexism by simply changing him **10.** to her or he to she in the same sentence, hoping by sheer unpredictable variation, or some literary Heisenberg principle of indeterminacy, to show their disdain for meaning either sex in particular. One ms. recently had something like "He fell but she wasn't hurt." I spent an hour searching for a female antecedent, but s/he wasn't there. I wondered if *he* fell on *her*, but the words were opaque.

Some authors are given to elaborate apologies in the prefaces of their books, **11.** explaining why they have chosen their particular (unsatisfactory) way of handling gender pronouns. But it is not winsome to begin a book by saying, "I understand that over half my readers, being women, will be offended by my insistence on 'he,' but I can think of nothing better."

All this weighs so heavily on me that I have been tempted to campaign for **12.** desexing all pronouns in favor of the neuter, "it." We could write, "Bob turned away from Jenny and dived into the pool when it was empty, but it wasn't hurt." But the difficulties here are obvious. Was Jenny unhurt because Bob turned away? Did the pool or Bob survive the experience?

Several years ago someone suggested that we invent new pronouns. We could **13.** concoct a word like "hes" to mean both "his" and "her." When I first considered this proposal, I dismissed it, thinking it wouldn't catch on. I still don't think it would work; and the fact that I wonder if we should revive the notion anyway indicates the depths of my Catch-22 mindset.

My only hope may lie in the fact that I affirm that justification—in print, no less **14.** than in religion—is *sola fide*, by faith, not by sight. An author may simply have to win the reader's trust by more meaningful ways than how _____ (fill in the blank; I give up) uses pronouns.

Although I cannot see a solution to the God problem, I must trust that Hes way **15.** is best. The time saved by agents and publishers could be enormous, the reduction of writers' multiple submissions monumental. And every book writer could expect an impartial comment by the screening group. Thus in one small way we would advance "Toward a Reading Society."

WORKING WITH THE TEXT

Cultural and Historical References

In this section, the numbers at the margin refer to the numbered paragraphs in the selection itself.

1. "Catch-22" comes from Joseph Heller's novel *Catch 22*, where his main character keeps coming up against bureaucratic regulations contrived

to serve the bureaucracy's interests. That is, they are "heads I win, tails you lose" situations.

1. "Theo" is the Greek root for "God." Knowing that, what do you suppose "theodicy" means?

3. Don't be misled by Durham's gentle irony. If he doesn't really believe that "creation has a built-in flow," why does he say it?

10. Werner Heisenburg was a German scientist who concluded that at the atomic level, matter is unpredictable.

Writing Assignments: The Paragraph

Be sure to provide an introduction for each of the following paragraph writing assignments. That is, begin each paragraph with a phrase like this: "Thomas Brickle claims that . . . ." When it is relevant, you might also want to identify the expertise of the author ("Thomas Brickle, a New Testament scholar, claims that. . . ."), the name of the book or article, the century and country in which the work appeared, or any other circumstances that your readers might find significant. For more on this, see pp. 11–13 in Chapter 2.

1. Summarize Durham's thesis. To do this, you'll have to see through his ironic thesis to his real one. Then fill out a paragraph by elaborating on that thesis.

2. Indicate the tone of Durham's essay by quoting a few words and phrases.

3. Make this point: Durham brings up a number of solutions to the problem of how to sooth everyone's feelings about "exclusive" language. Quote a word or phrase to substantiate that point.

Writing Assignments: The Short Essay

Use informal documentation for these short essays. That is, don't use footnotes or a Works Cited page to document your sources. Instead, cite only relevant information about your source, and keep that information *within* your text. Then follow the summary or quote with a page number in parentheses. (Use the page numbers that you find in this book to represent the page numbers of the source.) Thus, your informal documentation will look something like this:

> In "In Defense of Gender," Cyra McFadden needles those who ostentatiously use a double last name: "Two surnames, to me," she says, "still bring to mind the female writers of bad romances and Julia Ward Howe" (p. 410).

1. Write a paragraph on the structure of Durham's essay. Answer questions like these: Where does the introduction stop and the body begin? Why the lengthy introduction? What does the body consist of?

2. Write a short paper on the tone of Durham's essay. (Tone is the

author's attitude toward his or her subject.) How serious is he about his conclusion? Is he wry, comical, ironic, grave, moralizing, venomous, gushing, sentimental, or what? Quote examples of Durham's ironic diction and exaggerated ideas to substantiate your points. (Look at the word "cowardly" in paragraph 7.)

3. Durham's conclusion in paragraph 15 is exceedingly hard to follow. Explain, as best you can, what it means. What, for instance, is "the God problem"? How serious is Durham about his solution?

SKIRTING SEXISM

Pearl G. Aldrich

This article originally appeared in *The Nation's Business*. The author, Pearl Aldrich, is a writing consultant who conducts writing workshops for business executives. Aldrich describes ways that writers can avoid sexist language. She also suggests that using sexually neutral language is not only good public relations but is a good business practice as well.

1. "But 'the manager . . . he' is correct grammar," the woman insisted. Several classmates had suggested that she should have used "the manager . . . he or she" in her presentation. "You're a manager, aren't you?" challenged one man. " 'The manager . . . he' isn't accurate."

2. Both were right. English-speaking people have been taught for 150 years that "the manager . . . he" is correct grammar, but in the business and professional world today, "the manager . . . he" is no longer accurate, any more than "the teacher . . . she."

3. Language reflects our attitudes. As we change our attitudes, we change our language. But change never comes smoothly either in life or in language. This discussion among managers attending a workshop to improve their writing abilities illustrates the confused state of linguistic affairs two decades after efforts to eliminate sexism in language began as part of the women's movement.

4. Though nonsexist language has not yet come of age, important changes have entered the mainstream of day-to-day business writing and speaking. Women executives still receive invitations to professional meetings containing assurances that shopping trips will be planned for their wives, but in the main, we see and hear *spouses* (sometimes it is *mate*—but not often; it is too suggestive of Tarzan swinging from tree to tree with Jane on his hip).

5. Generally, *supervisor* has replaced *foreman. Workmen's compensation* has become *workers' compensation, messenger* has replaced *errand boy, server* is slowly overtaking *waiter* and *waitress,* and *my girl* (meaning my secretary or my assistant) is seldom heard.

6. *Business people*, for the plural, is replacing reliance solely on *businessmen*, while

Source: Pearl G. Aldrich, "Skirting Sexism," *The Nation's Business.* December 1985: 34, 36.

businessman and *businesswoman* are being used when appropriate. As more women enter sales forces, options for *salesman* already in the language are being used more frequently: *sales rep., sales associate, seller.*

Many people dislike *salesperson* and *chairperson*. *Person* is used as a suffix **7.** primarily for women. A *chairman* is still a *chairman*, while a *chairperson* is a woman. In many organizations, *chair* or *head* is used.

Ms., commonly used now in both speech and correspondence, has entered English **8.** textbooks. So have women's names as illustrations for such rules as use of degrees after proper names (Alice Jones, M.D.). And a few recently published reference books for business writers include sections on nonsexist language.

Work hours and *work force* are still struggling to replace *man-hours* and *manpower* **9.** in costing jobs and writing proposals. Substitutes for *man* in such expressions as *man-made* (artificial), a *man-sized job* (a big job) and *the common man* (the average person) are hard to find.

However, the most pervasive problem, and the hardest to solve, is the pronoun **10.** problem. Using the single number masculine, *he* and *his*, as the inclusive pronoun when some of the people meant are women is a lesson in traditional grammar that we learn early and thoroughly. The double pronoun, *he/she, his/her*, is now used fairly generally to achieve nonsexist language, but many find it awkward.

And what about this type of awkwardness? Said the regional manager as he **11.** distributed a questionnaire at a sales meeting: "I'm asking every man and woman to answer all questions as accurately as he can."

Lindsy Van Gelder made the suggestion in *Ms.* magazine that the simplest way **12.** around the problem was to give "he" a rest and use "she" as the general pronoun. "Instead of having to ponder over the intricacies of 'Congressman' versus 'Representative,' we can simplify by calling them all 'Congresswoman.' And don't be upset by the business letter that begins 'Dear Madam,' fellas. It means you, too."

Well, we need not go that far to solve the pronoun problem. There are several **13.** ways to get around it without being absurd or awkward, or wrenching the language into impossible constructions.

Eliminate the pronoun.   A woman consultant recently received a contract from **14.** a corporation in which she was referred to as *he* and *his* throughout, despite being identified in the first paragraph by the obviously female name of her firm. She says, "Of course it's boilerplate and run off automatically even though the corporation's vendors are male, female and groups of both, but it makes me uncomfortable, and it certainly doesn't do the corporation's image any good."

Eliminating *his* in the following excerpt will cover all vendors without damaging **15.** the contract's intent or legality: "The independent contractor shall furnish *his* professional consulting services and advice as specified by purchase orders."

In another example, from an investment company letter, eliminating *himself* **16.** changes a sexist sentence to nonsexist quickly and easily without changing the meaning: "The investor has in fact reaped more than a dollar of deductions for each dollar invested, often moving *himself* to a lower tax bracket."

Make the sentence plural.   The sentence from the investment letter also could **17.** have been made plural: "Investors have in fact reaped more than a dollar of deductions for each dollar invested, often moving *themselves* to a lower tax bracket."

The sentence, for an employes' manual, "Each employe completes his time sheet **18.** at the end of his shift," would have been better in the plural: "All employes complete their time sheets at the end of their shifts."

Address the reader directly. The employes' manual would have been even **19.** better if the writer had said: "Complete your time sheet at the end of your shift."

And the regional sales manager quoted above could have avoided trouble by **20.** saying, "I'm asking you to answer all questions as accurately as you can."

The second-hardest problem is deciding on terms of address. **21.**

General use of *Ms.* has created awareness of other baffling situations. What can **22.** you do when you don't know if your addressee is a man, woman or computer, and the old reliable, Dear Sir, is obsolete? What term of address can you use in your reply when the original correspondence contains initials rather than a first name before a last name, a unisex name such as Loren Hadley, Blair Rogers or Page Paxton, or no name at all?

For the first two, if you want to be completely accurate, call the organization and **23.** ask the telephone operator or receptionist if Loren Hadley or L. J. Thompson is a man or a woman. If that is impossible or impractical, here are five solutions to choose from.

1. Use the complete name as provided: Dear Loren Hadley or L. J. Thompson.
2. Cover both bases: Dear Ms. or Mr. Thompson.
3. Use his or her title and last name: Dear Vice President Hadley or Dear Purchasing Agent Thompson.
4. Set up your letter in the form of a memo:
   To: L. J. Thompson
   From: Lindley Mercer
5. Ignore tradition, eliminate the salutation and start the first paragraph of your letter.

If your correspondence contains no name at all, chances are you are talking to **24.** a computer. Even if the computer is user friendly, it is the reference numbers or code that it responds to. Write the company address and the reference. Then start the first paragraph of your letter.

If the hand of tradition is heavy upon you and eliminating the salutation makes **25.** you uncomfortable, address the whole company (Dear Massachusetts General Insurance Company), To Whom It May Concern or Dear Friends.

Deciding terms of address in writing is infinitely easier than deciding how to **26.** speak to people when you can see their gender but don't know their rank. Men grow up learning how to operate in a male hierarchical system and usually can determine with reasonable accuracy which man to address formally and which informally.

Women usually address all men in business suits as Mr., but they have no easier **27.** time of it than men in deciding how to address a woman in a professional setting.

The automatic, trivializing use of a woman's first name is on its way out, but **28.** incidents like this still abound:

Bill's attempts to interest XYZ Company in his products had finally paid off. **29.**

He was invited to make a presentation and was offered the use of a conference **30.** room in a letter signed John Liveridge, assistant to the president.

When Bill signaled that he was set up, a woman and a man entered the room. **31.**

The woman said to Bill, "I'm Virginia Hancock, and this is John Liveridge, **32.**
my . . .''

Bill enthusiastically broke in, drowning her last word, "I'm delighted to meet **33.**
you, Mr. Liveridge, and you, too, Ginny.''

Ms. Hancock owned the company, Mr. Liveridge was her assistant, and Bill lost **34.**
a customer.

One rule fits all: Use Ms. until you are told something different. Do not address **35.**
women by their first names unless you are on well-established, friendly terms or you
have clear-cut signals that it is O.K.

And don't assume a Ph.D. or M.D. is a man.   **36.**

A sexually inclusive language is slowly evolving, and we can achieve it by **37.**
continuing to work on problem areas.

WORKING WITH THE TEXT

Cultural and Historical References

In this section, the numbers at the margin refer to the numbered paragraphs
in the selection itself.

12. *Ms.* is America's most widely read feminist magazine.

38. What does "inclusive" mean when it occurs in the phrase "sexually
    inclusive language"?

Writing Assignments: The Paragraph

Be sure to provide an introduction for each of the following paragraph writing
assignments. That is, begin each paragraph with a phrase like this: "Thomas
Brickle claims that. . . ." When it is relevant, you might also want to identify
the expertise of the author ("Thomas Brickle, a New Testament scholar,
claims that. . . ."), the name of the book or article, the century and country
in which the work appeared, or any other circumstances that your readers
might find significant. For more on this, see pp. 11–13 in Chapter 2.

1. Good introductions to summaries use appropriate verbs like "argues,"
   "compares," "claims," "describes," "shows," and "gives reasons" to
   indicate what the source is doing. Use an appropriate verb in the
   introduction to a brief summary of "Skirting Sexism."

2. In a paragraph, summarize and quote from Aldrich's essay. In an
   introduction to your quotation, show that Aldrich's article is basically
   a how-to piece and is filled with examples. Then quote from Aldrich
   to substantiate what you have said in your introduction.

3. Paraphrase paragraph 12. In your topic sentence, you'll have to do a
   good job of explaining Aldrich's use of Van Gelder's ideas.

Writing Assignments: The Short Essay

Use informal documentation for these short essays. That is, don't use foot-notes or a Works Cited page to document your sources. Instead, cite only relevant information about your source, and keep that information *within* your text. Then follow the summary or quote with a page number in parenthe-ses. (Use the page numbers that you find in this book to represent the page numbers of the source.) Thus, your informal documentation will look something like this:

> In "In Defense of Gender," Cyra McFadden needles those who os-tentatiously use a double last name: "Two surnames, to me," she says, "still bring to mind the female writers of bad romances and Julia Ward Howe" (p. 410).

1. There are several indications that Aldrich is not sympathetic to the more radical language innovators. Discuss this in a short paper.

2. Write a short paper in which you show that Aldrich believes that using sexually neutral language is a good business practice.

3. Write a short paper in which you argue the case that people should put ideals ahead of material considerations. Use Aldrich as your opponent.

REAL MEN DON'T: ANTI-MALE BIAS IN ENGLISH

Eugene R. August

August, an English professor at the University of Dayton, contends that women are not alone in being burdened by language that restricts, excludes, and stereotypes. For instance, August notes that newspapers often report that "innocent women and children" are killed in a war, but never refer to "innocent" men. The author quotes Herb Goldberg: "Men may very well be the last remaining subgroup in our society that can be blatantly, negatively and vilely stereotyped with little objection or resistance."

Despite numerous studies of sex bias in language during the past fifteen years, **1.** only rarely has anti-male bias been examined. In part, this neglect occurs because many of these studies have been based upon assumptions which are questionable at best and which at worst exhibit their own form of sex bias. Whether explicitly or implicitly many of these studies reduce human history to a tale of male oppressors and female victims or rebels. In this view of things, all societies become *patriarchal societies*, a familiar term used to suggest that for centuries males have conspired to exploit and demean females. Accordingly, it is alleged in many of these studies that men control language and that they use it to define women and women's roles as inferior.

Despite the popularity of such a view, it has received scant support from leading **2.** social scientists, including one of the giants of modern anthropology, Margaret Mead.

Source: Eugene R. August, "Real Men Don't: Anti-Male Bias in English," *University of Dayton Review.* Vol. 18 (1987): 115–124.

Anticipating current ideology, Mead in *Male and Female* firmly rejected the notion of a "male conspiracy to keep women in their place," arguing instead that

> the historical trend that listed women among the abused minorities . . .
> lingers on to obscure the issue and gives apparent point to the con-
> tention that this is a man-made world in which women have always
> been abused and must always fight for their rights.
>
> It takes considerable effort on the part of both men and women
> to reorient ourselves to thinking—when we think basically—that this is
> a world not made by men alone, in which women are unwilling and
> helpless dupes and fools or else powerful schemers hiding their power
> under their ruffled petticoats, but a world made by mankind for human
> beings of both sexes. (298, 299–300)

The model described by Mead and other social scientists shows a world in which women and men have lived together throughout history in a symbiotic relationship, often mutually agreeing upon the definition of gender roles and the distribution of various powers and duties.

More importantly for the subject of bias in speech and writing, women—as well **3.** as men—have shaped language. As Walter J. Ong reminds us,

> Women talk and think as much as men do, and with few exceptions we
> all . . . learn to talk and think in the first instance largely from women,
> usually and predominantly our mothers. Our first tongue is called our
> "mother tongue" in English and in many other languages. . . . There
> are no father tongues. . . . (36)

Feminists like Dorothy Dinnerstein agree: "There seems no reason to doubt that the baby-tending sex contributed at least equally with the history-making one to the most fundamental of all human inventions: language" (22). Because gender roles and language are shaped by society in general—that is, by both men and women—anti-male bias in language is as possible as anti-female bias.

To say this, however, is emphatically not to blame women alone, or even **4.** primarily, for anti-male usage. If guilt must be assigned, it would have to be placed upon sexist people, both male and female, who use language to manipulate gender role behavior and to create negative social attitudes towards males. But often it is difficult to point a finger of blame: except where prejudiced gender stereotypes are deliberately fostered, most people evidently use sex-biased terminology without clearly understand-ing its import. In the long run, it is wiser to concentrate not on fixing blame, but on heightening public awareness of anti-male language and on discouraging its use. In particular, teachers and writers need to become aware of and to question language which denigrates or stereotypes males.

In modern English, three kinds of anti-male usage are evident: first, gender- **5.** exclusive language which omits males from certain kinds of consideration; second, gender-restrictive language which attempts to restrict males to an accepted gender role, some aspects of which may be out-moded, burdensome, or destructive; and third, negative stereotypes of males which are insulting, dehumanizing, and potentially dangerous.

Although gender-exclusive language which excludes females has often been **6.** studied, few students of language have noted usage which excludes males. Those academics, for example, who have protested *alumnus* and *alumni* as gender-exclusive terms to describe a university's male and female graduates have failed to notice that, by the same logic, *alma mater* (nourishing mother) is an equally gender-exclusive term to describe the university itself. Those who have protested *man* and *mankind* as generic terms have not begun to question *mammal* as a term of biological classification, but by categorizing animals according to the female's ability to suckle the young through her mammary glands, *mammal* clearly omits the male of the species. Consequently, it is as suspect as generic *man*.

In general, gender-exclusive usage in English excludes males as parents and as **7.** victims. Until recently, the equating of *mother* with *parent* in the social sciences was notorious: a major sociological study published in 1958 with the title *The Changing American Parent* was based upon interviews with 582 mothers and no fathers (Roman and Haddad 87). Although no longer prevalent in the social sciences, the interchangeability of *mother* and *parent* is still common, except for *noncustodial parent* which is almost always a synonym for *father*. A recent ad for *Parents* magazine begins: "To be the best mother you can be, you want practical, reliable answers to the questions a mother must face." Despite the large number of men now seen pushing shopping carts, advertisers still insist that "Choosy mothers choose Jif" and "My Mom's a Butternut Mom." Frequently, children are regarded as belonging solely to the mother, as in phrases like *women and their children*. The idea of the mother as primary parent can be glimpsed in such expressions as *mother tongue, mother wit, mother lode, mother of invention*, and *mothering* as a synonym for *parenting*.

The male as victim is ignored in such familiar expressions as *innocent women* **8.** *and children*. In June 1985, when President Reagan rejected a bombing strike to counter terrorist activities, newspapers reported that the decision had been made to prevent "the deaths of many innocent women and children in strife-torn Lebanon" (Glass). Presumably, strife-torn Lebanon contained no innocent men. Likewise, *rape victim* means females only, an assumption made explicit in the opening sentences of this newspaper article on rape: "Crime knows no gender. Yet, there is one offense that only women are prey to: rape" (Mougey). The thousands of males raped annually, in addition to the sexual assaults regularly inflicted upon males in prison, are here entirely overlooked. (That these males have been victimized mostly by other males does not disqualify them as victims of sexual violence, as some people assume.) Similarly, the term *wife and child abuse* conceals the existence of an estimated 282,000 husbands who are battered annually (O'Reilly et al. 23). According to many expressions in English, males are not parents and they are never victimized.

Unlike gender-exclusive language, gender-restrictive language is usually applied **9.** to males only, often to keep them within the confines of a socially prescribed gender role. When considering gender-restrictive language, one must keep in mind that—as Ruth E. Hartley has pointed out—the masculine gender role is enforced earlier and more harshly than the feminine role in (235). In addition, because the boy is often raised primarily by females in the virtual absence of close adult males, his grasp of what is required of him to *be a man* is often unsure. Likewise, prescriptions for male behavior are usually given in the negative, leading to the "Real Men Don't" syndrome, a process which further confuses the boy. Such circumstances leave many males extremely vulnerable to language which questions their sense of masculinity.

Furthermore, during the past twenty years an increasing number of men and **10.** women have been arguing that aspects of our society's masculine gender role are emotionally constrictive, unnecessarily stressful, and potentially lethal. Rejecting "the myth of masculine privilege," psychologist Herb Goldberg reports in *The Hazards of Being Male* that "every critical statistic in the area of [early death], disease, suicide, crime, accidents, childhood emotional disorders, alcoholism, and drug addiction shows a disproportionately higher male rate" (5). But changes in the masculine role are so disturbing to so many people that the male who attempts to break out of familiar gender patterns often finds himself facing hostile opposition which can be readily and powerfully expressed in a formidable array of sex-biased terms.

To see how the process works, let us begin early in the male life cycle. A boy **11.** quickly learns that, while it is usually acceptable for girls to be *tomboys*, God forbid that he should be a *sissy*. In *Sexual Signatures: On Being a Man or a Woman* John Money and Patricia Tucker note:

> The current feminine stereotype in our culture is flexible enough to let a girl behave "boyishly" if she wants to without bringing her feminini-ty into question, but any boy who exhibits "girlish" behavior is promptly suspected of being queer. There isn't even a word corres-ponding to "tomboy" to describe such a boy. "Sissy" perhaps comes closest, or "artistic" and "sensitive," but unlike "tomboy," such terms are burdened with unfavorable connotations. (72)

Lacking a favorable or even neutral term to describe the boy who is quiet, gentle, and emotional, the English language has long had a rich vocabulary to insult and ridicule such boys—*mamma's boy, mollycoddle, milksop, muff, twit, softy, creampuff, painty-waist, weenie, Miss Nancy*, and so on. Although sometimes used playfully, the currently popular *wimp* can be used to insult males from childhood right into adulthood.

Discussion of words like *sissy* as insults have been often one-sided: most **12.** commentators are content to argue that the female, not the male, is being insulted by such usage. "The implicit sexism" in such terms, writes one commentator, "disparages the woman, not the man" (Sorrels 87). Although the female is being slurred indirectly by these terms, a moment's reflection will show that the primary force of the insult is being directed against the male, specifically the male who cannot differentiate himself from the feminine. Ong argues in *Fighting for Life* that most societies place heavy pressure on males to differentiate themselves from females because the prevailing environment of human society is feminine (70–71). In English-speaking societies, terms like *sissy* and *weak sister*, which have been used by both females and males, are usually perceived not as insults to females but as ridicule of males who have allegedly failed to differentiate themselves from the feminine.

Being *all boy* carries penalties, however: for one thing, it means being less **13.** lovable. As the nursery rhyme tells children, little girls are made of "sugar and spice and all that's nice," while little boys are made of "frogs and snails and puppy-dogs' tails." Or, as an American version of the rhyme puts it:

Girls are dandy,
Made of candy—
That's what little girls are made of.
Boys are rotten,
Made of cotton—
That's what little boys are made of.   (Baring-Gould 176–116)

When not enjoined to *be all boy*, our young lad will be urged to *be a big boy, be a brave soldier*, and (the ultimate appeal) *be a man*. These expressions almost invariably mean that the boy is about to suffer something painful or humiliating. The variant—*take it like a man*—provides the clue. As Paul Theroux defines it, *be a man* means: "Be stupid, be unfeeling, obedient and soldierly, and stop thinking."

Following our boy further into the life cycle, we discover that in school he will **14.** find himself in a cruel bind: girls his age will be biologically and socially more mature than he is, at least until around age eighteen. Until then, any ineptness in his social role will be castigated by a host of terms which are reserved almost entirely for males. "For all practical purposes," John Gordon remarks, "the word 'turkey' (or whatever the equivalent is now) can be translated as 'a boy spurned by influential girls' " (141). The equivalents of *turkey* are many: *jerk, nerd, clod, klutz, schmuck, dummy, goon, dork, square, dweeb, jackass, meathead, geek, zero, reject, goofball, drip*, and numerous others, including many obscene terms. Recently, a Michigan high school decided to do away with a scheduled "Nerd Day" after a fourteen-year-old male student, who apparently had been so harassed as a nerd by other students, committed suicide (" 'Nerd' day"). In this case, the ability of language to devastate the emotionally vulnerable young male is powerfully and pathetically dramatized.

As our boy grows, he faces threats and taunts if he does not take risks or endure **15.** pain to prove his manhood. *Coward*, for example, is a word applied almost exclusively to males in our society, as are its numerous variants—*chicken, chickenshit, yellow, yellow-bellied, lily-livered, weak-kneed, spineless, squirrelly, fraidy cat, gutless wonder, weakling, butterfly, jellyfish*, and so on. If our young man walks away from a stupid quarrel or prefers to settle differences more rationally than with a swift jab to the jaw, the English language is richly supplied with these and other expressions to call his masculinity into question.

Chief among the other expressions that question masculinity is a lengthy list of **16.** homophobic terms such as *queer, pansy, fag, faggot, queen, queeny, pervert, bugger, deviant, fairy, tinkerbell, puss, priss, flamer, feller, sweet, precious, fruit, sodomite*, and numerous others, many obscene. For many people, *gay* is an all-purpose word of ridicule and condemnation. Once again, although homosexuals are being insulted by these terms, the primary target is more often the heterosexual male who fails or refuses to live up to someone else's idea of masculinity. In "Homophobia Among Men" Gregory Lehne explains, "Homophobia is used as a technique of social control . . . to enforce the norms of male sex-role behavior. . . . [H]omosexuality is not the real threat, the real threat is change in the male sex-role'' (77).

Nowhere is this threat more apparent than in challenges to our society's male- **17.** only military obligation. When a young man and a young woman reach the age of eighteen, both may register to vote; only the young man is required by law to register for military service. For the next decade at least, he must stand ready to be called into military service and even into combat duty in wars, ''police actions,'' ''peace-keeping missions,'' and ''rescue missions,'' often initiated by legally dubious means. Should he resist this obligation, he may be called a *draft dodger, deserter, peacenik, traitor, shirker, slacker, malingerer,* and similar terms. Should he declare himself a conscientious objector, he may be labeled a *conchy* or any of the variants of *coward.*

In his relationships with women, he will find that the age of equality has not yet **18.** arrived. Usually, he will be expected to take the initiative, do the driving, pick up the tab, and in general show a deferential respect for women that is a leftover from the chivalric code. Should he behave in an *ungentlemanly* fashion, a host of words—which are applied almost always to males alone—can be used to tell him so: *louse, rat, creep, sleaze, scum, stain, worm, fink, heel, stinker, animal, savage, bounder, cad, wolf, gigolo, womanizer, Don Juan, pig, rotter, boor,* and so on.

In sexual matters he will usually be expected to take the initiative and to *perform.* **19.** If he does not, he will be labeled *impotent.* This word, writes Goldberg, ''is clearly sexist because it implies a standard of acceptable masculine sexual performance that makes a man abnormal if he can't live up to it'' (*New Male* 248). Metaphorically, *impotent* can be used to demean any male whose efforts in any area are deemed unacceptable. Even if our young man succeeds at his sexual performance, the sex manuals are ready to warn him that if he reaches orgasm before a specified time he is guilty of *premature ejaculation.*

When our young man marries, he will be required by law and social custom to **20.** support his wife and children. Should he not succeed as bread-winner or should he relax in his efforts, the language offers numerous terms to revile him: *loser, deadbeat, bum, freeloader, leech, parasite, goldbrick, sponch, mooch, ne'er-do-well, good for nothing,* and so on. If women in our society have been regarded as sex objects, men have been regarded as success objects, that is, judged by their ability to provide a standard of living. The title of a recent book—*How to Marry a Winner*—reveals immediately that the intended audience is female (Collier).

When he becomes a father, our young man will discover that he is a second- **21.** class parent, as the traditional interchangeability of *mother* and *parent* indicates. The law has been particularly obtuse in recognizing fathers as parents, as evidenced by the awarding of child custody to mothers in ninety percent of divorce cases. In 1975 a father's petition for custody of his four-year-old son was denied because, as the family court judge said, ''Fathers don't make good mothers'' (qtd. in Levine 21). The judge apparently never considered whether *fathers* make good *parents.*

And so it goes throughout our young man's life: if he deviates from society's **22.** gender role norm, he will be penalized and he will hear about it.

The final form of anti-male bias to be considered here is negative stereotyping. **23.** Sometimes this stereotyping is indirectly embedded in the language, sometimes it resides in people's assumptions about males and shapes their response to seemingly neutral words, and sometimes it is overtly created for political reasons. It is one thing to say that some aspects of the traditional masculine gender role are limiting and hurtful; it is quite another to gratuitously suspect males in general of being criminal and evil or to denounce them in wholesale fashion as oppressors, exploiters, and rapists. In *The New Male* Goldberg writes, "Men may very well be the last remaining subgroup in our society that can be blatantly, negatively and vilely stereotyped with little objection or resistance" (103). As our language demonstrates, such sexist stereotyping, whether unintentional or deliberate, is not only familiar but fashionable.

In English, crime and evil are usually attributed to the male. As an experiment **24.** I have compiled lists of nouns which I read to my composition students, asking them to check whether the words suggest "primarily females," "primarily males," or "could be either." Nearly all the words for law-breakers suggest males rather than females to most students. These words include *murderer, swindler, crook, criminal, burglar, thief, gangster, mobster, hood, hitman, killer, pickpocket, mugger,* and *terrorist.* Accounting for this phenomenon is not always easy. *Hitman* may obviously suggest "primarily males," and the *-er* in *murderer* may do the same, especially if it reminds students of the word's feminine form, *murderess.* Likewise, students may be aware that most murders are committed by males. Other words—like *criminal* and *thief*—are more clearly gender-neutral in form, and it is less clear why they should be so closely linked with "primarily males." Although the dynamics of the association may be unclear, English usage somehow conveys a subtle suggestion that males are to be regarded as guilty in matters of law-breaking.

This hint of male guilt extends to a term like *suspect.* When the person's gender **25.** is unknown, the suspect is usually presumed to be a male. For example, even before a definite suspect had been identified, the perpetrator of the 1980–1981 Atlanta child murders was popularly known as *The Man.* When a male and female are suspected of a crime, the male is usually presumed the guilty party. In a recent murder case, when two suspects—Debra Brown and Alton Coleman—were apprehended, police discovered *Brown*'s fingerprint in a victim's car and interpreted this as evidence of *Coleman*'s guilt. As the Associated Press reported:

> Authorities say for the first time they have evidence linking Alton
> Coleman with the death of an Indianapolis man.
> A fingerprint found in the car of Eugene Scott has been identified as
> that of Debra Brown, Coleman's traveling companion . . ." ("Police")

Nowhere does the article suggest that Brown's fingerprint found in the victim's car linked Brown with the death: the male suspect was presumed the guilty party, while the female was only a "traveling companion." Even after Brown had been convicted of two murders, the Associated Press was still describing her as "the accused accomplice of convicted killer Alton Coleman" ("Indiana").

In some cases, this presumption of male guilt extends to crimes in which males **26.** are not the principal offenders. As noted earlier, a term like *wife and child abuse* ignores battered husbands, but it does more: it suggests that males alone abuse children. In reality most child abuse is committed by mothers (Straus, Gelles, Steinmetz 71). Despite this fact, a 1978 study of child abuse bears the title *Sins of the Fathers* (Inglis).

The term *rape* creates special problems. While the majority of rapes are committed **27.**

by males and the number of female rape victims outdistances the number of male rape victims, it is widely assumed—as evidenced by the newspaper article cited above—that rape is a crime committed only by males in which only females are victims. Consequently, the word *rape* is often used as a brush to tar all males. In *Against Our Will* Susan Brownmiller writes: "From prehistoric times to the present, I believe, rape . . . is nothing more or less than a conscious process of intimidation by which *all men* keep *all women* in a state of fear" (15; italics in original). Making the point explicitly, Marilyn French states, "All men are rapists and that's all they are" (qtd. in Jenness 33). Given this kind of smear tactic, *rape* can be used metaphorically to indict males alone and to exonerate females, as in this sentence: "The rape of nature—and the ecological disaster it presages—is part and parcel of a dominating masculinity gone out of control" (Hoch 137). The statement neatly blames males alone even when the damage to the environment has been caused in part by females like Anne Gorsuch Burford and Rita Lavelle.

Not only crimes but vices of all sorts have been typically attributed to males. As **28.** Muriel R. Schulz points out, "The synonyms for *inebriate* . . . seem to be coded primarily 'male': for example, *boozer, drunkard, tippler, toper, swiller, tosspot, guzzler, barfly, drunk, lush, boozehound, souse, tank, stew, rummy,* and *bum*" (126). Likewise, someone may be *drunk as a lord* but never *drunk as a lady.*

Sex bias or sexism itself is widely held to be a male-only fault. When *sexism* is **29.** defined as "contempt for women"—as if there were no such thing as contempt for men—the definition of *sexism* is itself sexist (Bardwick 34).

Part of the reason for this masculinization of evil may be that in the Western **30.** world the source of evil has long been depicted in male terms. In the Bible the Evil One is consistently referred to as *he*, whether the reference is to the serpent in the Garden of Eden, Satan as Adversary in Job, Lucifer and Beelzebub in the gospels, Jesus' tempter in the desert, or the dragon in Revelations. *Beelzebub*, incidentally, is often translated as *lord of the flies*, a term designating the demon as masculine. So masculine is the word *devil* that the female prefix is needed, as in *she-devil*, to make a feminine noun of it. The masculinization of evil is so unconsciously accepted that writers often attest to it even while attempting to deny it, as in this passage:

> From the very beginning, the Judeo-Christian tradition has linked
> women and evil. When second-century theologians struggled to explain
> the Devil's origins, they surmised that Satan and his various devils had
> once been angels. (Gerzon 224)

If the Judeo-Christian tradition has linked women and evil so closely, why is the writer using the masculine pronoun *his* to refer to Satan, the source of evil according to that tradition? Critics of sex-bias in religious language seldom notice or mention its masculinization of evil: of those objecting to *God the Father* as sexist, no one—to my knowledge—has suggested that designating Satan as the *Father of Lies* is equally sexist. Few theologians talk about Satan and her legions.

The tendency to blame nearly everything on men has climaxed in recent times **31.** with the popularity of such terms as *patriarchy, patriarchal society,* and *male-dominated society.* More political than descriptive, these terms are rapidly becoming meaningless, used as all-purpose smear words to conjure up images of male oppressors and female victims. They are a linguistic sleight of hand which obscures the point that, as Mead has observed (299–300), societies are largely created by both sexes for both sexes. By using a swift reference to *patriarchal structures* or *patriarchal attitudes*, a writer can absolve females of all blame for society's flaws while fixing the onus solely on males. The give-away of this ploy can be detected when *patriarchy* and its related terms are never used in a positive or neutral context, but are always used to assign blame to males alone.

Wholesale denunciations of males as oppressors, exploiters, rapists, Nazis, and **32.** slave-drivers have become all too familiar during the past fifteen years. Too often the academic community, rather than opposing this sexism, has been encouraging it. All too many scholars and teachers have hopped on the male-bashing bandwagon to disseminate what John Gordon calls "the myth of the monstrous male." With increasing frequency, this academically fashionable sexism can also be heard echoing from our students. "A white upper-middle-class straight male should seriously consider another college," declares a midwestern college student in *The New York Times Selective Guide to Colleges.* "You [the white male] are the bane of the world. . . . Ten generations of social ills can and will be strapped upon your shoulders" (qtd. in Fiske 12). It would be comforting to dismiss this student's compound of misinformation, sexism, racism, and self-righteousness as an extreme example, but similar yahooisms go unchallenged almost everywhere in modern academia.

Surely it is time for men and women of good will to reject and protest such **33.** bigotry. For teachers and writers, the first task is to recognize and condemn forms of anti-male bias in language, whether they are used to exclude males from equal consideration with females, to reinforce restrictive aspects of the masculine gender role, or to stereotype males callously. For whether males are told that *fathers don't make good mothers*, that *real men don't cry*, or that *all men are rapists*, the results are potentially dangerous: like any other group, males can be subtly shaped into what society keeps telling them they are. In *Why Men Are the Way They Are* Warren Farrell puts the matter succinctly: "The more we make men the enemy, the more they will have to behave like the enemy" (357).

Works Cited

Bardwick, Judith. *In Transition: How Feminism, Sexual Liberation, and the Search for Self-Fulfillment Have Altered Our Lives.* NY: Holt, 1979.

Baring-Gould, William S., and Ceil Baring-Gould. *The Annotated Mother Goose: Nursery Rhymes Old and New, Arranged and Explained.* NY: Clarkson N. Potter, 1962.

Brownmiller, Susan. *Against Our Will: Men, Women and Rape.* NY: Simon, 1975.

Collier, Phyllis K. *How to Marry a Winner.* Englewood Cliffs, NJ: Prentice, 1982.

Dinnerstein, Dorothy. *The Mermaid and the Minotaur: Sexual Arrangements and Human Malaise.* NY: Harper, 1976.

Farrell, Warren. *Why Men Are the Way They Are: The Male-Female Dynamic.* NY: McGraw-Hill, 1986.

Fiske, Edward B. *The New York Times Selective Guide to Colleges.* NY: Times Books, 1982.

Gerzon, Mark. *A Choice of Heroes: The Changing Faces of American Manhood.* Boston: Houghton, 1982.

Glass, Andrew J. "President wants to unleash military power, but cannot." *Dayton Daily News* 18 June 1985: 1.

Goldberg, Herb. *The Hazards of Being Male: Surviving the Myth of Masculine Privilege.* 1976. NY: NAL, 1977.

———. *The New Male: From Self-Destruction to Self-Care.* 1979. NY: NAL, 1980.

Gordon, John. *The Myth of the Monstrous Male, and Other Feminist Fables.* NY: Playboy P, 1982.

Hartley, Ruth E. "Sex-Role Pressures and the Socialization of the Male Child." *The Forty-Nine Percent Majority: The Male Sex Role.* Ed. Deborah S. David and Robert Brannon. Reading, MA: Addison-Wesley, 1976. 235–44.

Hoch, Paul. *White Hero, Black Beast: Racism, Sexism and the Mask of Masculinity.* London: Pluto P, 1979.

"Indiana jury finds Brown guilty of murder, molesting." *Dayton Daily News* 18 May 1986: 7A.

Inglis, Ruth. *Sins of the Fathers: A Study of the Physical and Emotional Abuse of Children.* NY: St. Martin's, 1978.

Jennes, Gail. "All Men Are Rapists." *People* 20 Feb. 1978: 33–34.

Lehne, Gregory. "Homophobia Among Men." *The Forty-Nine Percent Majority: The Male Sex Role.* Ed. Deborah S. David and Robert Brannon. Reading, MA: Addison-Wesley, 1976. 66–88.

Levine, James A. *Who Will Raise the Children? New Options for Fathers (and Mothers).* Philadelphia: Lippincott, 1976.

Mead, Margaret. *Male and Female: A Study of the Sexes in a Changing World.* NY: Morrow, 1949, 1967.

Money, John, and Patricia Tucker. *Sexual Signatures: On Being a Man or a Woman.* Boston: Little, 1976.

Mougey, Kate. "An act of confiscation: Rape." *Kettering-Oakwood* [OH] *Times* 4 Feb. 1981: 1b.

" 'Nerd' day gets a boot after suicide." *Dayton Daily News* 34 Jan. 1986: 38.

Ong, Walter J. *Fighting for Life: Contest, Sexuality, and Consciousness.* Ithaca, NY: Cornell UP, 1981.

O'Reilly, Jane, et al. "Wife-Beating: The Silent Crime." *Time* 5 Sept. 1983: 23–4, 26.

"Police: Print links Coleman, death." *Dayton Daily News* 31 Aug. 1984: 26.

Roman, Mel, and William Haddad. *The Disposable Parent: The Case for Joint Custody.* 1978. NY: Penguin, 1979.

Schulz, Muriel R. "Is the English Language Anybody's Enemy:" *Speaking of Words: A Language Reader.* Ed. James MacKillop and Donna Woolfolk Cross. 3rd. ed. NY: Holt, 1986. 125–27.

Sorrels, Bobbye D. *The Nonsexist Communicator: Solving the Problems of Gender and Awkwardness in Modern English.* Englewood Cliffs, NJ: Prentice, 1983.

Straus, Murray A., Richard J. Gelles, and Suzanne K. Steinmetz. *Behind Closed Doors: Violence in the American Family.* 1980. Garden City, NY: Doubleday, 1981.

Theroux, Paul. "The Male Myth." *New York Times Magazine* 27 Nov. 1983: 116.

WORKING WITH THE TEXT

Cultural and Historical References

In this section, the numbers at the margin refer to the numbered paragraphs in the selection itself.

2. "Symbiotic" has become a contemporary buzzword. Can you suggest a less pretentious, clearer term here?

6. Has "alumni" ever struck you as being a gender-biased term? Look up the plural for "alumna" (the female singular term). Is our usage of "alumni" another manifestation of sexist language, or is it an example of a word that has evolved in meaning in recent history?

27. Anne Gorsuch Burford was director of the Environmental Protection Agency during the first half of the Reagan Administration. Rita Lavelle was one of Burford's top administrative assistants. Both were forced to resign under the pressure of widespread allegations of improper negligent enforcement of environmental statutes in various industrial waste disposal cases across the nation.

Writing Assignments: The Paragraph

Be sure to provide an introduction for each of the following paragraph writing assignments. That is, begin each paragraph with a phrase like this: "Thomas Brickle claims that. . . ." When it is relevant, you might also want to identify the expertise of the author ("Thomas Brickle, a New Testament scholar, claims that. . . ."), the name of the book or article, the century and country in which the work appeared, or any other circumstances that your readers might find significant. For more on this, see pp. 11–13 in Chapter 2.

1. After reviewing paragraphs 5 to 13, explain the difference between "gender-exclusive language" and "gender-restrictive language," and illustrate your explanation with specific examples from the essay.

2. After perusing paragraph 5 and then reviewing the remainder of the essay, explain the difference between "gender-restrictive language" and "negative stereotypes of males." Illustrate your explanation with specific examples from the essay. (You may, incidentally, want to conclude that the distinction isn't always clear.)

3. Disagree with one of the points which August makes in this essay, and support your argument with specific examples drawn from your own experience or from other essays in this chapter. (You might want to argue, for example, that in paragraphs 24 and 25, terms for lawbreakers imply males rather than females because, even in the late twentieth century, males continue to commit nearly 90 percent of all violent crimes.)

Writing Assignments: The Short Essay

Use informal documentation for these short essays. That is, don't use footnotes or a Works Cited page to document your sources. Instead, cite only relevant information about your source, and keep that information *within* your text. Then follow the summary or quote with a page number in parenthe-

ses. (Use the page numbers that you find in this book to represent the page numbers of the source.) Thus, your informal documentation will look something like this:

> In "In Defense of Gender," Cyra McFadden needles those who ostentatiously use a double last name: "Two surnames, to me," she says, "still bring to mind the female writers of bad romances and Julia Ward Howe" (p. 410).

1. After reviewing paragraphs 9 to 20, write an essay in which you argue that males aren't the only victims of gender-restrictive terms. Illustrate your argument with your own examples of gender-restrictive terms which victimize women. (You may want to make the point here that many of the gender-restrictive terms victimizing females don't surface in printed essays because the terms are often obscene.) ·

2. Write an essay in which you argue that August's essay is a self-pitying overreaction to antimale language. (Your argument here would be strengthened if you happened to be a male and you can think of few situations in which you have felt victimized by such language.)

3. Write an essay in which you relate how you have at times felt victimized by gender-exclusive or gender-restrictive language. Support your discussion with points and examples from this essay. If you have never felt victimized, you might want to write an essay in which you argue that writers like August or others in this chapter exaggerate the effect of gender-exclusive or gender-restrictive language.

4. Write an essay in which you disagree with two or three points which August makes in this article. (See item 3 above for a specific example.)

5. Contrast two or three points about antimale language which August makes in this essay with two or three points which Allen makes about antifemale language in the second essay in this chapter.

ESSAYS IN *SEXIST LANGUAGE*

Short Essays

Use informal documentation for these short essays. That is, don't use foot-notes or a Works Cited page to document your sources. Instead, cite only relevant information about your source, and keep that information *within* your text. Then follow the summary or quote with a page number in parenthe-ses. (Use the page numbers that you find in this book to represent the page numbers of the source.) Thus, your informal documentation will look something like this:

> In *The Romance of Medicine*, Benjamin Gordon, a history professor, claims that it was once believed that red wine replenished a per-son's depleted blood supply (p. 121).

1. In a short paper, relate an experience you've had with sexist language. During the course of your paper, summarize or quote from one or two of the essays in this chapter.

2. In a short paper, summarize Robert Spaeth's major objection to the desexing of people (see paragraph 14 in particular) and Ben Patterson's main objection to desexing God (see paragraph 7 in particular). Provide an appropriate transitional sentence when you move from one to an-other.

3. Summarize Gina Allen's suggested language reforms, and then discuss how you think William Safire would react to her proposals. In other words, at what point might these reforms become objectionable to Safire? (Pay close attention to paragraphs 1 to 7 in Safire's essay.)

4. Use Pearl Aldrich's statement in paragraph 3 that "change never comes smoothly" as an introduction to a comment about the tone of Robert Spaeth's article.

5. Contrast Ron Durham's dismissal of the *he*/she construction with Pearl Aldrich's recommendation of it.

Long Essays

For rules governing formal documentation, see Chapter 6.

1. Write a paper in which you clarify both sides of the secular (nonrelig-ious) controversy concerning sexist language. Your purpose is to clarify the issues, not to argue.

2. Write a paper in which you take a side in the secular controversy concerning sexist language. As you write your paper, summarize and quote from the other side.

3. Write a paper in which you take a side in the controversy involving the

NCC's lectionary. As you write your paper, summarize and quote from the other side.

4. Write a paper in which you clarify both sides of the controversy involving the NCC lectionary.

.

— 12 —

Hiroshima and Nagasaki:
Did We Have to Drop the Bomb?

INTRODUCTION

"The only real news is the history you don't know." That little bit of wisdom
appeared in a television advertisement for *American Heritage* magazine, but
it might serve just as well as a lead-in for this chapter on the atomic bomb
attack on Hiroshima and Nagasaki.

The news that most of us *do* know is the bare outlines of the story: In
August of 1945, with World War II winding down—Germany had surrendered
and Japan was on its knees—the United States, by order of President Harry
S. Truman, dropped the newly invented atomic bomb on two Japanese cities,
Hiroshima and Nagasaki. Those bombs killed over 150,000 civilians.

But the news we don't know is what lay behind Truman's decision. Oh,
we may have an opinion on that decision. Who could not? On August 6 each
year, the anniversary of the dropping of the bomb, we listen to the familiar
outlines of the story again. Dan Rather tells us all about it. We read editorials
in the newspapers. Perhaps we even get an interview with a Japanese woman,
now in her sixties who was 15 or so when she survived the bombing attack.

The dropping of the A-bomb on Japanese civilians is the kind of
historical event that is impossible *not* to have an opinion about. It's like other
enduring historical questions: What was the effect of the French Revolution?
What were the causes of the Civil War? Why were we in Vietnam?

Should we have dropped the bomb?

For most of us, our answer to that question is based on little more than
a paragraph in a high school history text, or perhaps something someone
said to us once. This chapter will change all that. What we have done is
assemble a variety of viewpoints on that decision, from infantrymen who

awaited the signal to invade Japan when the bomb was dropped to professional historians with 20/20 vision hindsight.

The soldier's view: Paul Fussell's essay, "Hiroshima: A Soldier's View," no doubt represents the view of the vast majority of the soldiers who were still fighting in the Pacific. The A-bomb attacks on Hiroshima and Nagasaki, argues Fussell, stopped the war and saved the lives of thousands of American GIs who were being assembled for an infantry assault on Japan—and only they can truly understand why the bomb was dropped. "Understanding the past," Fussell says, "means feeling its pressure on your pulses. . . ." Fussell's final say on the matter: "Thank God for the atomic bomb."

The orthodox view: The orthodox view is much like the soldier's view, but without the personal notes and the *ad hominem* argument that no one who wasn't there can legitimately argue against the dropping of the bomb. In "Did America Have to Drop the Bomb?" Chalmers Roberts represents the orthodox view: Truman was right when he made that fateful decision. He shows that Japan was digging in for an American invasion, and that invasion would have cost tens of thousands of American and Japanese lives.

The revisionist view: Gar Alperovitz's essay "Did America Have to Drop the Bomb?" argues two positions: the United States dropped the bomb to intimidate Russia, and Japan was prepared to surrender anyway. Kai Erikson argues that Americans should have "demonstrated" the power of the A-bomb by dropping it on an uninhabited area. That demonstration, Erikson argues, would have convinced the Japanese, already demoralized by the inevitability of ultimate defeat, that there was no reason to continue to fight. Erikson also argues that once we had the bomb, dropping it was inevitable. No country would sacrifice thousands of their men on an invasion when they were capable of preventing that invasion.

The antirevisionist view: André Ryerson's "The Cult of Hiroshima" represents the backlash to the revisionist's view. Ryerson claims that the revisionists have made something of a religion out of their antinuclear stands and that each year, on the anniversary of the attack on Hiroshima, the antinuclear crowd and pacifists bring out the photographs, the icons, the interviews. What they have forgotten, says Ryerson, were Japanese fascism and militarism, concentration camps, imperialism, and the heavily defended island of Japan. According to Ryerson, the evil of World War II is not found in the dropping of the A-bomb, but in the "mad and aggressive myths of superiority on which the German and Japanese people were too long fed."

The Japanese view: While we do not have an argument by a Japanese historian, what we do have is a ground-level description from John Toland's *The Rising Sun*. Toland describes the Japanese civilians who were in Hiroshima when the bomb dropped. "On Yorozuyo Bridge,"

Toland writes, "ten people left permanent outlines of themselves on the railing and the tar-paved surface." That image, one of many equally as compelling by Toland, serves as an unspoken argument against the dropping of the bomb.

Soon you're going to know a lot about the bomb, and there is always a danger connected with knowing a lot about something: Knowledge undermines easy, dogmatic responses. But that's a chance we all have to take.

"LITTLE BOY'S" LONG, LONG JOURNEY

Hanson W. Baldwin

At the time he wrote this essay, Hanson Baldwin was military editor for *The New York Times*. He had witnessed and written about most of the nuclear test explosions open to press coverage in the decades following World War II. Baldwin provides in clear detail the historical background leading to the decision to develop and finally to drop the atomic bombs on Hiroshima and Nagasaki. He concludes with a balanced evaluation of the arguments over whether or not the bombs should have been used. This essay will provide you with the kind of historical framework you will need as you analyze the arguments of the sources which follow in this chapter.

"Now, I am become death, destroyer of worlds." **1.**

Out of the darkness of the New Mexico desert on July 16, 1945, had risen a **2.** gigantic "sun," a "huge ball of fire," a "strange violet light," "a mighty thunder," the "nearest thing to doomsday," the "end of the world."

Robert Oppenheimer, then a little-known physicist, recalled the above line from **3.** the Bhagavad-Gita as he watched what he had helped to create—the world's first atomic explosion at Alamogordo.

"We knew the world would not be the same," he said. **4.**

It was the sixth year of the war. Germany—in smoking ruins—was finished, but **5.** Japan still fought on. Yet, by the spring of 1945 her position was hopeless. She was beleaguered; United States submarines, mines and carriers severed her shipping lanes. She was bereft; shortages of machines, spare parts, planes, food slowed the pulse of war. She was bombarded; almost 125,000 Japanese died, were wounded or burned in a single fire-bomb raid on Tokyo on March 10, 1945—until then the greatest man-made holocaust in history. And Gen. Curtis LeMay, chomping a cigar, said that his bombers were returning Japan to the Stone Age.

There had been many clear indications that Japan was approaching the end of **6.** the road long before Alamogordo. More than a year earlier, a few perceptive Japanese had concluded privately that their country's cause was lost, their only course to make the best peace possible.

But the hold of fanatic militarists was still strong throughout the land; even in **7.** the agonies of suffering, the half-mystic belief in *Bushido*, or the feudal warrior code.

Source: Hanson Baldwin, " 'Little Boy's' Long, Long Journey," *The New York Times Magazine.* August 1, 1965: 6–7, 44–47, 49–51.

in *Nippon seishin*—the "mind, the soul, the spirit of Japan"—was evoked as the way to victory.

The first Japanese attempts to make peace were tenuous, unofficial, even half- **8.** hearted. The loss of Saipan, and disastrous defeats in Burma and elsewhere, encouraged the defections of Cabinet members and increased the pressure of Japan's *jushin*, or senior statesmen, for a Japanese Government more amenable to peace terms.

In September, 1944, after the fall of Premier Hideki Tojo's Government, Bunshuri **9.** Suzuki, director of the newspaper Asahi, told the Swedish Minister to Japan that he was acting as go-between for a small group that "was prepared to surrender the conquered territories . . . " if peace could be arranged. The Swedes were asked to communicate this feeler to London where, the Japanese thought, it might receive a more sympathetic reception than in Washington. The Japanese-Swedish contacts continued intermittently for months in Japan and in Sweden but they were never formally acknowledged by Tokyo. Officials in Stockholm gathered that one major obstacle to peace was the Allied demand for "unconditional surrender."

In February and March, 1945, Premier Kuniaki Koiso, desperate for peace but **10.** inhibited by the militarists, made a curious maneuver to end the war. He enlisted the aid of one Miao Pin, a dubious renegade Chinese, in an attempt to make peace with Chiang Kai-shek's Government in Chungking. The attempt was futile. Miao Pin was unreliable; he was not a bona fide representative of Chiang.

On Easter Sunday, 1945, U. S. Marines and soldiers landed on Okinawa on **11.** Japan's doorstep, and a few days later the Koiso Cabinet fell. Its fall, like Tojo's, was the result of impossible pressures: the military insistence upon a fight to the finish, and the elder statesmen's growing awareness of the necessity for peace.

An old, retired admiral, Kantaro Suzuki, became Japan's last wartime Premier. **12.** Suzuki thought he had an unstated mandate from the Emperor to make peace as quickly as possible, but this was far easier thought than done. The military leaders, anticipating the day the hated Americans would attempt to invade the sacred soil of the homeland, clung to a sanguine strategy. They argued that huge losses inflicted upon the enemy during the invasion would force peace on terms Japan could live with.

But crosscurrents beneath the surface of Japanese leadership produced a strange **13.** ambivalence, which led to one of diplomacy's most Alice-in-Wonderland ventures.

Tokyo, ally of Germany, natural rival of Russia in the Far East, undertook to **14.** procure Soviet aid in the war, or failing that, to get Moscow to act as a friendly mediator in arranging peace terms. And Tokyo, which without declaration of war had attacked the Russians at Port Arthur and the United States at Pearl Harbor, believed—as provided for in the Russo-Japanese neutrality pact just denounced by Moscow—that she had a legal year of grace before the denunciation would be in effect!

The new Foreign Minister, Shigenori Togo, knew there had been a meeting at **15.** Yalta in the Crimea in February, 1945, of Stalin, President Roosevelt and Prime Minister Churchill. He was shrewd enough to guess that some arrangement relating to the Pacific War had been reached there. But Togo could not know and did not know how specific it was: that "in two or three months after Germany has surrendered . . . the Soviet Union shall enter into the war against Japan." Nor did he know that Russia had been promised in return territory and concessions that Japan could never match, ". . . the southern part of Sakhalin, as well as all the islands adjacent to it . . . the

Kurile islands'' and restoration to Russia of ''rights'' in Manchuria which she enjoyed prior to the Russo-Japanese war.

Togo was highly skeptical of Russia as a mediator. Nevertheless, the Japanese **16.** Army insisted that he approach Moscow with the deal. He did, and at the Gora Hotel, in the Hakone Mountains near Tokyo, Togo's emissary met with Soviet Ambassador Jacob A. Malik in early June, 1945.

Japanese diplomacy, seemingly eager for peace, tried to tempt Moscow: ''If the **17.** Soviet Army and the Japanese Navy were to join forces,'' Tokyo suggested, ''Japan and the Soviet Union together would become the strongest powers in the world.''

But Malik, inscrutable and cold, was noncommittal. Finally, weeks later, the **18.** discussions died as the Russian pleaded illness and refused repeatedly to receive Togo's representative.

Meanwhile, half a world away, in Switzerland, another Japanese, acting on his **19.** own initiative, started a series of feelers which were to end with similar failure. Commander Yoshiro Fujimura, the naval attaché at Bern, undertook a one-man effort to achieve peace in May, 1945.

Through an intermediary, Fujimura approached the U.S. Office of Strategic **20.** Services in Switzerland, headed by Allen Dulles, with a suggestion for direct negotiations between Japan and the United States. At the same time, he sent carefully phrased cables to Tokyo which made it appear that Washington had taken the initiative toward peace. He received temporizing and unencouraging answers; meanwhile, time was running out.

Unknown to Fujimura, still another peacemaking effort was initiated in Switzer- **21.** land by Japan's military attaché, Lieut. Gen. Seigo Okamoto, and Japanese officials of the Bank for International Settlement at Basel. An official of the bank acted as go-between with Allen Dulles, but the negotiations dragged on to a dead end. (When Japan surrendered, Okamoto committed suicide.)

Yet, in plain fact, all the Japanese peace feelers had strings attached; none **22.** offered capitulation and some were not even recognized by the Japanese Government. Moreover, the U.S., which was quite aware of the fumbling Japanese peace efforts, was in no mood after Pearl Harbor and four years of war to concede conditions to the enemy. Washington thought in terms of ''maximum force with maximum speed.'' As Secretary of War Henry L. Stimson later recorded: ''. . . reports of a weakening will to resist and of 'feelers' for peace terms . . . merely stimulated the American leaders . . . to press home on all Japanese leaders the hopelessness of their cause. . . .''

So the summer of 1945 opened with no real disposition on either side for **23.** concessions. The military in Japan planned to defend the home islands to the last man—with kamikaze planes, midget submarines, human torpedoes, suicide motor boats and ''human explosives'' who would throw themselves beneath U.S. tanks.

And in Washington, plans for Operation Olympic—the invasion of the Japanese **24.** home island of Kyushu—were approved by the White House. D-Day was to be Nov. 1, 1945. Some strategists opposed the plan. Adm. William D. Leahy, the President's Chief of Staff, believed that blockade and bombardment had already defeated Japan; invasion would mean an unnecessary blood bath, he thought.

No one mentioned the atomic bomb. Secretary Stimson simply said he ''hoped **25.** for some fruitful accomplishment through other means.''

The A-bomb, in June of 1945, was an unknown factor. Even the 125,000 em- **26.** ployes who worked on a $2¹/₂ billion enterprise called the Manhattan Project were hazy, or dubious, or uncertain.

This secret project had originated with a letter on Aug. 2, 1939, from Dr. Albert **27.** Einstein to President Roosevelt, suggesting the possibility of building a fission bomb of tremendous power. By September 1942, with the United States fighting in World War II and about to send its troops to invade North Africa, Einstein's suggestion had grown into a formalized program to develop such a bomb. During the war years the Manhattan Project had expanded at a fantastic rate—harnessing the efforts of British, United States and refugee scientists, engineers and technicians.

Its sense of mission and urgency was well-founded; Washington knew that Nazi **28.** scientists were working on the principle of fissionable explosives. If the Germans got the A-bomb first the world might be threatened with Hitlerian hegemony. Germany—not Japan—was the original target of the Manhattan Project.

Still, despite the massive U.S. investment in the project and the dedication of its **29.** workers, there was no certainty in early 1945 that an A-bomb could be developed. Indeed, there were many doubters. Leahy believed the bomb would never work. Some scientists who understood the frightful implication of success hoped it wouldn't.

Until April, even the Vice President of the United States knew nothing of the **30.** gigantic project headed by Maj. Gen. Leslie R. Groves of the Army Engineers. It was about 5:30 P.M. on April 12 that Harry Truman was told that Franklin Delano Roosevelt was dead.

"Is there anything I can do for you?" Mr. Truman, stunned and tearful, asked **31.** Mrs. Roosevelt.

"Is there anything *we* can do for *you*?" she replied. "For you are the one in **32.** trouble now."

Only after he became President was Mr. Truman briefed by Secretary of War **33.** Stimson on the nuclear project, which was expected to produce the world's first atomic bomb in another few months.

At the end of April, at Stimson's urging, the President established an "Interim **34.** Committee" to advise him about the problems of nuclear weaponry. Stimson headed it, and its members were George L. Harrison, president of the New York Life Insurance Company and a special assistant to Mr. Stimson; James F. Byrnes, then a private citizen and later Secretary of State; Ralph A. Bard, Under Secretary of the Navy; William L. Clayton, Assistant Secretary of State; Dr. Vannevar Bush, Director, Office of Scientific Research and Development; Dr. Karl T. Compton, president of M.I.T., and Dr. James B. Conant, president of Harvard. An advisory panel of scientists included Oppenheimer, Arthur H. Compton, E. O. Lawrence and Enrico Fermi.

The fighting on Okinawa was still raging and the Japanese peace feelers remained **35.** tentative and unconvincing when the Interim Committee and the scientists met at the end of May. Germany had surrendered and the question to decide was whether the bomb should be used against the Japanese, and if so, how. Gen. George C. Marshall and Groves met with them.

On June 1, the Interim Committee recommended unanimously that the "S-1 **36.** bomb" (the A-bomb's code name) should be dropped on Japan as soon as it was ready. With the same unanimity, the committee favored its use without prior warning to the

Japanese. The target, said the committee, should be of military importance, with adjacent built-up areas that would clearly show its "devastating strength." The scientific advisers later specifically reported that "we can propose no technical demonstration likely to bring an end to the war; we see no acceptable alternative to direct military use" of the atomic bomb.

And so the decision was made. President Truman had no qualms about it. Later **37.** he wrote that he "regarded the bomb as a military weapon and never had any doubt that it should be used."

But still to be decided was what the U.S. meant by unconditional surrender. On **38.** June 18, Under Secretary of State Joseph C. Grew, former Ambassador to Japan, won a favorable reaction from the President when he suggested a statement urging Tokyo to surrender, but "holding out the possibility that the Emperor might be allowed to remain in power." Grew was urgent but Mr. Truman deferred action until he could talk to his Allies at the forthcoming conference at Potsdam.

Long before Potsdam or the Interim Committee's decision, an Army Air Corps **39.** colonel named Paul W. Tibbets Jr., "a superb pilot with a distinguished record . . . ," had assembled a picked outfit, the 509th Composite Group, at Wendover Field, Utah. None except Tibbets knew the group's mission; they were told they were training to drop "the gimmick"—a special kind of bomb. The group was activated in December, 1944; by May, 1945, it had completed training. It was equipped with modified Boeing Superfortresses, with lengthened bomb bays and—to save weight—all guns and turrets removed except twin tail guns.

The 509th was ready to move overseas when, in the spring, Groves proposed to **40.** Marshall that detailed plans be made for the use of the atomic bomb.

"I don't like to bring too many people into this matter," Marshall replied. "Is **41.** there any reason why you can't take this over and do it yourself?"

Even before Groves got this tacit directive, he recalled, a military policy **42.** committee (including Oppenheimer and mathematician John Von Neumann) of the Manhattan Project had discussed target criteria "over and over again."

The criteria were then submitted to a seven-man special committee established **43.** by Groves, consisting of one Air Corps colonel and six civilians, among them William G. Penney, a member of the British scientific team at Los Alamos.

After several meetings the target committee drew up a "black list" of four **44.** Japanese cities: Kokura, Hiroshima, Niigata and Kyoto. The inclusion of Kyoto, the Japanese "city of temples," so affected a young professor who was serving in Army intelligence that he burst into tears in the office of his chief. The tears were shed by Edwin O. Reischauer, now U.S. Ambassador to Japan, and they may have saved Kyoto. In any case, Secretary of War Stimson later deleted Kyoto and substituted Nagasaki on the "black list."

The spade work was done, the crew trained and the targets selected, and by early **45.** June the Interim Committee had recommended use of the bomb—a recommendation that might, in Secretary Stimson's words, "turn the course of civilization."

On June 26, the "brave new world" was born. The United Nations Charter was **46.** signed in San Francisco, while throughout the Pacific the legions and armadas of the United States and its Allies were marshaled for the death blow against Japan.

But the colorful ceremonies, the bright hopes of a morrow freed from war were **47.**

gilt and tinsel; the most powerful weapon in the history of mankind was about to be born in a New Mexico desert. Not without pangs, forebodings and apprehension.

Seven scientists (including James Franck, Glenn Seaborg and Leo Szilard) who **48.** had worked in the Metallurgical Laboratory in Chicago as part of the Manhattan Project had already urged, in early June, a "demonstration in an appropriately uninhabited area. . . ."

It was the first of many afterthoughts. On June 17, Ralph Bard, the Navy **49.** member of the high-level Interim Committee, wrote a short memorandum urging some preliminary warning to Japan, perhaps two or three days before dropping the bomb.

"The position of the United States as a great humanitarian nation and the fair- **50.** play attitude of our people generally is responsible in the main for this feeling," Bard wrote. "During recent weeks I have also had the feeling very definitely that the Japanese Government may be searching for some opportunity which they could use as a medium for surrender.

"Following the three-power conference [scheduled for Potsdam in July], emis- **51.** saries from his country could contact representatives from Japan somewhere on the China coast and make representation with regard to Russia's position and at the same time give them some information regarding the proposed use of atomic power, together with whatever assurances the President might care to make with regard to the Emperor of Japan and the treatment of the Japanese nation following unconditional surrender. It seems quite possible to me that this presents the opportunity which the Japanese are looking for. . . ."

Thoughtful words, but written on water. The great wheels of government were **52.** turning and nothing could reverse them.

July 4—An Anglo-American agreement to use the A-bomb against Japan was **53.** formalized in the Pentagon.

July 5—President Truman approved the text of a public statement to be released **54.** after the bomb was dropped on Japan, then boarded the cruiser Augusta for the Potsdam conference.

July 12—The Japanese Ambassador in Moscow was instructed by his Government **55.** to inform Foreign Minister Molotov that "the Emperor wanted the war ended immediately and wished to send Prince Fumimaro Konoye to Moscow as a special envoy."

And, also on July 12, Arthur Compton asked for a poll of the scientists at the **56.** Manhattan Project's Metallurgical Laboratory in Chicago on the bomb's use. Of the 150 scientists, 69 voted for "a military demonstration in Japan to be followed by renewed opportunity for surrender before full use of the weapon is employed."

But no one knew clearly what was meant by a "military demonstration in Japan," **57.** and the wheels kept turning.

At 5:30 A.M., July 16, in a bleak and arid desert near Alamogordo, N.M., a **58.** "sunrise such as the world had never seen" spread across the land. The earth shook and the heavens trembled. A 100-foot steel tower supporting the test bomb was vaporized, and the flash from the explosion was seen hundreds of miles away. But an explanation had already been prepared, and The Associated Press reported:

"An ammunition magazine exploded early today in a remote area of the **59.** Alamogordo Air Base. . . ."

To Stimson in Potsdam went a top-secret message in prearranged code: "Operated **60.** on this morning. Diagnosis not yet complete but results seem satisfactory and already exceed expectations . . . Dr. Groves pleased. . . ."

Five days later, Groves's complete report on the test at Alamogordo reached **61.**
President Truman in Germany by courier. Winston Churchill, informed of the results,
agreed with Truman that the bomb should be dropped as soon as possible to save Allied
lives. In addition, Churchill pointed out that the bomb might result in a Japanese
surrender without the 11th-hour entry of Russia into the war.

The decision already reached was reaffirmed, and it was agreed that no mention **62.**
of the bomb should be made in the ultimatum to be directed to Japan.

In Washington, on July 23, where some doubts still persisted, Groves asked for **63.**
the poll tabulation of the Chicago scientists. Then he asked Arthur Compton for his
personal opinion. Compton said he believed the bomb should be used, but only to force
the surrender of Japan.

Another message to the Japanese Ambassador in Moscow arrived from Tokyo **64.**
on July 24; he was instructed to tell the Russians that the proposed visit by Prince
Konoye was specifically to seek "the good offices of the Soviet Union in order to bring
the war to an end."

That same day, a draft directive to Gen. Carl Spaatz, Commanding General, **65.**
United States Army Strategic Air Forces, was typed out in Washington. General Spaatz
had wanted a "piece of paper" instructing him to drop the superbomb. The directive
read: "1. The 509th Composite Group, 20th Air Force will deliver its first special
bomb as soon as weather will permit visual bombing after about 3 August 1945, on
one of the targets: Hiroshima, Kokura, Niigata and Nagasaki. . . .

"2. Additional bombs will be delivered on the above targets as soon as made **66.**
ready by the project staff. . . ."

In Potsdam, as the order to Spaatz was being written, President Truman "sauntered **67.**
over to Stalin," and "casually mentioned" to him that "we had a new weapon of
unusual destructive force."

"The Russian Premier showed no special interest," reported Mr. Truman. "All **68.**
he said was that he was glad to hear it and hoped we would make 'good use of it
against the Japanese.' "

Secretary of State Byrnes was later to record that he was glad that Stalin **69.**
apparently did not comprehend the bomb's importance.

"I would have been satisfied had the Russians determined not to enter the war. **70.**
Notwithstanding Japan's persistent refusal to surrender unconditionally, I believed the
atomic bomb would be successful and would force the Japanese to surrender on our
terms."

But Byrnes did not know—nor did anyone in the United States Government—that **71.**
the Soviet espionage apparatus in the United States, with the help of British scientists
Dr. Alan Nunn May, Klaus Fuchs and others, had been making regular reports to
Moscow about the progress of the Manhattan Project.

On July 24, in the dangerous Pacific, the cruiser Indianapolis, with a heavily **72.**
guarded secret cargo, was en route from San Francisco to the island of Tinian at high
speed. She carried a little lump of U-235, the powerful core of the A-bomb. Additional
packets of U-235, boxed and guarded, were shipped by air; by the end of July enough
had reached Tinian to create the "critical mass" of the weapon; more fissionable
material arrived for a second bomb.

And the 509th was ready; the crew selected for the bomb delivery had already **73.**
made a day run with a dummy bomb.

But the course of history still focused on Potsdam.   **74.**

On July 24 in Potsdam, Secretary Stimson told the President that he believed the **75.**
Japanese should be reassured on the continuance of their Emperor. Stimson said it
might spell the difference between their acceptance or rejection of the surrender terms.

It was already too late, Secretary of State Byrnes had opposed specific reference **76.**
to the Emperor and the text of the proposed Potsdam Declaration, to be signed by
Truman, Churchill and Chiang Kai-shek, already had been cabled to Chiang, who did
not come to Potsdam.

On July 25 the directive to Spaatz on dropping the bomb was approved by **77.**
President Truman. "I had made the decision," Truman later wrote. "I also instructed
Stimson that the order would stand unless I notified him that the Japanese reply to our
ultimatum was acceptable."

Next day (the day the Indianapolis reached Tinian), the Potsdam Declaration was **78.**
issued, and its terms disseminated to the Japanese Government. The statement left the
status of the Emperor ambiguous, but there was no doubt that Japan would be stripped
of all her conquests.

The declaration specifically said: "We call upon the Government of Japan to **79.**
proclaim now the unconditional surrender of all Japanese armed forces, and to provide
proper and adequate assurances of their good faith in such action. The alternative for
Japan is prompt and utter destruction."

No mention was made of the atomic bomb.   **80.**

July 27 was a day of decision. Japanese radio stations picked up the text of the **81.**
Potsdam Declaration and American planes—cruising the skies above Japan virtually
unchallenged—dropped thousands of leaflets demanding surrender or warning of
destruction. The Cabinet met in crisis session, but the majority of long-suffering
Japanese people knew nothing of the Allied proclamation until an expurgated version
was published the next day.

The Potsdam Declaration, with its demand for the "unconditional surrender of **82.**
all Japanese armed forces" and its vagueness about the status of the Emperor, faced
the desperate Japanese Government with the "necessity of determining exactly where
unconditional surrender ended and conditional surrender began," as Stanford historian
Robert J. C. Butow has noted.

It produced a sharpened, though customary, split between the military and the **83.**
Foreign Office—the military still opting for a fight to the death, the politicians still
believing Japan must end the war. The compromise result of the Cabinet meeting was
a determination to treat the declaration with silence.

Premier Suzuki, the man who had taken office with the unexpressed mandate **84.**
from the Emperor to end the war, and who had initiated peace feelers in various
countries, pronounced the official line at a press conference on July 28. Japan, he said,
"does not regard it [the Potsdam Declaration] as a thing of any great value; the
Government will just ignore it."

But privately Suzuki urgently wired his Ambassador in Moscow to press for **85.**
Russian acceptance of the Japanese peace mission led by Prince Konoye.

That night in Potsdam, Stalin told President Truman and Britain's newly elected **86.**
Prime Minister, Clement Attlee, attending his first summit session, about the Japanese
overtures. They thanked him politely. This time it was Mr. Truman's turn to play cat
and mouse. He had known for weeks all about the Japanese cables to Moscow; the
U.S. had broken the Japanese code but had not informed the Soviets.

The same day in Potsdam, Secretary of State Byrnes told James V. Forrestal, **87.**

Secretary of the Navy, that he was most "anxious to get the Japanese affair over with before the Russians get in."

On Monday morning, July 30, The New York Times carried Premier Suzuki's **88.** decision: JAPAN OFFICIALLY TURNS DOWN ALLIED SURRENDER ULTIMATUM.

Three days later, on Aug. 2, the Potsdam Conference ended. There were the usual **89.** toasts and a great display of conviviality, but beneath the surface simmered feelings of weariness and distrust.

Back in the U.S., among some of the scientists who developed the bomb, **90.** uneasiness was growing, too. Despite the tightest security, details of the Alamogordo test had leaked to scientists who were not there. Disturbed by the soul-searching of the scientific community, Groves, Stimson and others met to discuss what should be done about it.

On Guam, where Japanese soldiers still roamed the jungles, the headquarters of **91.** the 20th Air Force prepared a top-secret order: "20th Air Force attacks targets in Japan on 6 August. Primary target: Hiroshima urban industrial area."

On Aug. 4 on Tinian, Capt. "Deac" Parsons, the Navy scientist and Manhattan **92.** Project engineer who was to arm the weapon, showed motion pictures of the test at Alamogordo. Now the bomb crews knew why they had practiced steep, breakaway turns at high altitude.

Parsons told them no one knew what to expect when the bomb was dropped. **93.** Even though the proximity fuse was set to detonate the "new weapon"—Parsons did not use the term "atomic"—at 1,850 feet, some thought the mighty detonation might crack the earth's crust.

On Aug. 5, a Sunday, Paul Tibbets, the pilot chosen to make the first atomic **94.** flight in history, christened his plane for his mother—Enola Gay, a gentle lady from Glidden, Iowa. A painter lettered the name under the pilot's window.

That same day the "gimmick" that was to change the world was eased into the **95.** Enola Gay's bomb bay. The scientists and technicians called it "Little Boy," or "Thin Man." It was about 10 feet long and weighed 9,000 pounds. Only a tiny part of the weapon was U-235. It was a "guntype" bomb. When the proximity fuse indicated the correct height above the ground, a conventional explosive charge in the tail would hurl a small bit of U-235 down the gun barrel to mesh in the nose of the bomb with another chunk of U-235.

The casing of "Little Boy" was scrawled with crayoned slogans as it was stowed **96.** in the bomb bay. Maj. John F. Moynahan, a onetime reporter on The Newark Evening News and now public relations officer for an operation shrouded in the deepest secrecy, scrawled the note: "No white cross for Stevie"—a reference to his little son at home.

All day Sunday, Aug. 5, Parsons worked in the bomb bay of the Enola Gay, **97.** practicing arming the bomb in flight. It would not be armed until the B-29 was airborne to prevent blowing up a chunk of the island in case of a crash on take-off.

Four lieutenants installed a black box in the plane to monitor the weapon during **98.** flight and check that all its complex parts were in perfect working condition.

Meanwhile, many of the men of the 509th played softball in the closely guarded **99.** compound. At 11 P.M. on Aug. 5, a hot and humid night, the final briefing began.

"We are going on a mission," Tibbets said, "to drop a bomb different from any **100.** you have ever seen or heard about. This bomb contains a destructive force equivalent to 20,000 tons of TNT."

Chaplain William B. Downey of the 509th stood before the podium: "We pray **101.**

Thee that the end of the war may come soon, and that once more we may know peace on earth. . . .''

A few hours later, on Monday, Aug. 6, at 2:45 A.M., the Enola Gay, with a nine-man crew, Parsons and two other passengers from the Manhattan Project, ''Little Boy'' and the black box, roared down the runway at Tinian, beginning the long flight to Japan. **102.**

At 8:15 A.M. Aug. 6 (Aug. 5, Washington time), the Enola Gay was 31,600 feet above the unsuspecting city of Hiroshima. The great plane lurched as the 9,000-pound ''Little Boy'' left the bomb bay, and immediately Tibbets put the plane into a violent bank and turn. **103.**

''Make sure those goggles are on,'' Tibbets said over the intercom. ''Caron [the tail-gunner], keep watching and tell us what you see. . . .'' **104.**

''. . . the world went purple in a flash before Caron's eyes.'' **105.**

Hiroshima was obscured in a violent fireball and convulsive smoke; the Enola Gay and her accompanying observation ships were shaken as if they were being ''beaten with a telegraph pole.'' **106.**

The bomber's crew, looking back on what they had wrought, saw only boiling dust and dancing flame—a perfect mushroom cloud. **107.**

''My God, what have we done?'' **108.**

President Truman was aboard the Augusta, returning from the Potsdam conference. He was eating dinner with the crew when an Army aide brought him the message. **109.**

''I was greatly moved,'' the President later recalled. ''I telephoned Byrnes aboard ship to give him the news and then said to the group of sailors around me: 'This is the greatest thing in history. . . .' '' **110.**

Not until the next day, Aug. 7, did the smoke and flames over Hiroshima subside to permit adequate photo-reconnaissance; it showed that about 60 percent of the city had been destroyed. An estimated 70,000 to 80,000 people were dead or missing; an equal number were injured. **111.**

At 5 P.M. in Moscow on Aug. 8 (Aug. 9 in Tokyo), Russia declared war against Japan, and her Siberian armies moved across the Manchurian frontiers, brushing aside weak resistance. **112.**

At 11 A.M. Aug. 9, Tokyo time, ''Fat Man,'' an implosion bomb of plutonium, devastated Nagasaki, killing some 40,000 Japanese and wounding 60,000 others. **113.**

On Aug. 10 Tokyo announced its acceptance of the Potsdam Declaration ''with the understanding that the said declaration does not comprise any demand which prejudices the prerogative of His Majesty as a sovereign Ruler.'' **114.**

On Aug. 11, Byrnes replied that the ''ultimate form of government of Japan shall . . . be established by the freely expressed will of the Japanese people,'' adding that ''from the moment of surrender the authority of the Emperor and the Japanese Government to rule the state shall be subject to the Supreme Commander of the Allied Powers. . . .'' **115.**

On Aug. 14, the Japanese Government accepted the terms of the victors, but it was not until about noon on Aug. 15 that a stunned nation learned, in the Emperor's words, that it must ''endure the unendurable.'' **116.**

''Fat Man'' was the last A-bomb in the U.S. stockpile, but a third atomic weapon, Groves informed the President, would have been ready in three or four days. **117.**

History will long debate whether it was necessary to drop the bomb. **118.**

Obviously, the pressures for using it were tremendous. Huge amounts had been **119.**

spent on it; a vast machinery was dedicated solely to its development and employment. In fact, it was always assumed in Washington that the bomb *would* be used, and the entire mechanism of government had been geared accordingly. The "decision" to use it—actually made and reaffirmed again and again—was more a tacit confirmation of a *de facto* policy than an actual decision. Churchill later wrote that at Potsdam "the decision whether or not to use the atomic bomb was never an issue. . . . [The] unanimous, automatic, unquestioned agreement" represented a foregone conclusion.

The conclusion rested on military as well as political considerations. Following **120.** the bloody struggle for Okinawa, the U.S. could expect even more fanatic, costly resistance to an invasion of the Japanese home island of Kyushu. At the same time, mutual suspicion between Communist Russia and its Western allies—so close to the surface at Potsdam—helped shape the decision, since some U.S. policy-makers felt strongly that it would be greatly to the West's advantage to force a Japanese surrender *before* Russia could enter the Pacific war.

And Tokyo's inept peace overtures—always undermined by the diehard mili- **121.** tarists—also weakened the position of those Americans who opposed using the bomb or questioned the necessity of dropping it.

Yet there is little doubt that chances were missed. As Secretary Stimson later **122.** wrote, it was "possible that a clearer and earlier exposition of American willingness to retain the Emperor" might have resulted in an earlier surrender. But those who knew the Japanese mentality best—Under Secretary of State Grew, Eugene H. Dooman, a now-retired State Department official, and Capt. Ellis M. Zacharias of Naval Intelligence, among others—failed to persuade Secretary Byrnes and the top echelons of the United States Government.

The recriminations and regrets, the sense of guilt which germinated among some **123.** scientists and others in Government in early 1945 and which grew quickly after Alamogordo, blossomed fully after the war.

Adm. William Leahy, who had opposed both an invasion of Japan and the use **124.** of the bomb as militarily unnecessary, wrote later of this "barbarous" weapon. He condemned the bomb as taking us back "to the days of Genghis Khan."

There were many second thoughts about the slogan, "unconditional surrender." **125.** As a phrase, it may have been a great wartime rallying cry, but it was no substitute for a positive peacemaking program. It was not a practical political policy. In fact from June, 1945—even earlier at lower levels of government—the key problem in both Washington and Tokyo was determining "exactly where unconditional surrender ended and conditional surrender began," as Stanford historian Butow has observed. Washington and its allies thundered "unconditional surrender" at Potsdam, then accepted conditional terms after more than 100,000 died at Hiroshima and Nagasaki.

But would the war have ended when it did unless the fireballs had vaporized the **126.** bones and marrow of two cities? Might not the bloodshed have been long drawn out?

The Strategic Bombing Survey concluded that defeat had been hastened by only **127.** a few days or weeks or—at the most—a few months. The Japanese would have surrendered soon without the bomb, Russia's entry into the war, or invasion of the home islands. But the bomb did "foreshorten the war and expedite the peace," the survey declared.

The Russians still claim their entry into the war—not the A-bomb—caused **128.** Japan's capitulation.

The Japanese themselves, wrote Toshikazu Kase in "Journey to the Missouri," **129.**

believe that surrender would have come "in due time . . . even without the terrific chastisement of the bomb or the terrible shock of the Russian attack." But both events "facilitated . . . surrender."

Yet no man can ever be sure about the might-have-been. Not the statistics of **130.** defeat but the human imponderables—the code of *Bushido*, the vestiges of the age of feudalism, the profound Japanese belief that death in battle meant life in heaven—hung in the balance as the Enola Gay made her bombing run.

It was the human heart and the human mind that carried Japan to early triumph **131.** and ultimate destruction; it was the human heart and the human mind that broke the secret of the atom and devised and used the weapon that ushered in a new era for man.

WORKING WITH THE TEXT

Cultural and Historical References

In this section, the numbers at the margin refer to the numbered paragraphs in the selection itself.

1. This quotation comes from the *Bhagavad Gita*, a Hindu holy book. As Baldwin will tell us later, it was spoken by Robert Oppenheimer at the explosion of the first atomic bomb at Alamogordo, New Mexico, on July 16, 1945.

2. These quotes illustrate the confusion that can occur when the writer does not tag a quotation with its author. Whose words are these in quotation marks? See the same problem in paragraphs 105 and 108.

38. Potsdam, a city in Germany, is where leaders of the Allied Forces met to decide how the world was to be divided after World War II.

46. *Brave New World* is Aldous Huxley's novel of a dystopian world of the future.

105. Once again, notice the problem of unattributed quotations. Who is saying this?

108. And who is saying this?

124. Genghis Khan was a twelfth-century Mongol leader who conquered Asia and the Middle East, and invaded Russia.

Writing Assignments: The Paragraph

Be sure to provide an introduction for each of the following paragraph writing assignments. That is, begin each paragraph with a phrase like this: "Thomas Brickle claims that. . . ." When it is relevant, you might also want to identify the expertise of the author ("Thomas Brickle, a New Testament scholar, claims that. . . ."), the name of the book or article, the century and country in which the work appeared, or any other circumstances that your readers might find significant. For more on this, see pp. 11–13 in Chapter 2.

1. The author fails to identify his quotation in this paragraph. What is the result when writers fail to identify their sources?

2. Write a single paragraph in which you marshal evidence that Japanese fanaticism and a willingness to die wouldn't allow them to surrender.

3. Write a paragraph describing scientists' feelings about their own creation, the A-bomb.

Writing Assignments: The Short Essay

Use informal documentation for these short essays. That is, use footnotes or a Works Cited page to document your sources. Instead, cite only relevant information about your source, and keep that information *within* your text. Then follow the summary or quote with a page number in parentheses. (Use the page numbers that you find in this book to represent the page numbers of the source.) Thus, your informal documentation will look something like this:

> In *The Rising Sun*, John Toland says that in the instant after the A-bomb attack on Hiroshima, "All over the center of the city numerous silhouettes were imprinted on walls" (p. 468).

1. Argue from the facts in this essay that the United States should or should not have dropped the A-bomb.

2. Write a paper on the forces that pushed the United States to drop the bomb.

3. Write a paper on facets of Japanese tradition that would have prevented them from surrendering.

THE RISING SUN

John Toland

John Toland has written extensively on World War II. His books include *The Last 100 Days* (1966), *Adolf Hitler* (1976), and *Infamy: Pearl Harbor and Its Aftermath* (1982). In the following excerpts from *The Rising Sun*, Toland gives a grim, graphic account of what happened at the ground level during the Hiroshima and Nagasaki bombings. His description is based on the accounts of several Japanese citizens who survived the blasts.

Their primary target was Hiroshima on the southeast coast of Honshu, Japan's principal **1.** island. From this, the empire's eighth largest city, 120,000 civilians had been evacuated to the countryside, but 245,000 still remained. The city was almost unscarred by the war. Like the people of Dresden before them, the citizens of Hiroshima felt that their city was to be spared, though it was headquarters of 2nd General Army and was an important military port of embarkation. Their reasons for hope of immunity ranged

Source: John Toland, *The Rising Sun.* New York: Random House, 1970. 780, 782–785, 787–790, 793, 794.

from the naïve to the preposterous: they were exempt because they had numerous relatives in the United States; their city, like Kyoto, was so beautiful that the Americans wanted it as a residential area after the war; President Truman's mother lived nearby. They had taken little notice of 720,000 leaflets fluttering from the sky two days before, warning them that their city among others would be obliterated unless Japan surrendered at once. At 7:09 A.M. (an hour earlier than Tinian time), sirens blasted for a long minute. It was the third air-raid warning since midnight and few took to the shelters. . . .

Hiroshima was serene and so was the sky above it as the people continued on **2.** their daily routine. Those who noticed the three parachutes imagined that the plane had been hit and that the crew was bailing out or that more propaganda leaflets had been jettisoned. One man, remembering how the last leaflets had shimmered down in the sun, thought, The Americans have brought us some more beautiful things.

Several hundred yards north of Aioi Bridge . . . Private Shigeru Shimoyama, a **3.** recent draftee, looked up and idly peered through his thick glasses at one of the drifting chutes. He was standing outside his barracks, a huge wooden structure once a warehouse. He had been in Hiroshima four days and was already "bored to death." He wished he were back in Tokyo making school notebooks. All at once a pinkish light burst in the sky like a cosmic flash bulb.

Clocks all over Hiroshima were fixed forever at 8:15. **4.**

The bomb exploded 660 yards from the ground into a fireball almost 110 yards **5.** in diameter. Those directly below heard nothing, nor could they later agree what color the *pika* (lightning) flash was—blue, pink, reddish, dark-brown, yellow or purple.

The heat emanating from the fireball lasted a fraction of a second but was so **6.** intense (almost 300,000 degrees Centigrade) that it melted the surface of granite within a thousand yards of the hypocenter, or ground zero—directly under the burst. Roof tiles softened and changed in color from black to olive or brown. All over the center of the city numerous silhouettes were imprinted on walls. On Yorozuyo Bridge ten people left permanent outlines of themselves on the railing and the tar-paved surface.

Moments later came an unearthly concussion that obliterated all but a few solid, **7.** earthquake-proof buildings within two miles. Ferebee had been almost on target, little more than 300 yards off the intended drop point.

Private Shimoyama was 550 yards north of ground zero. He was not directly **8.** exposed to the *pika* flash or his life would have been puffed out, but the blast hurled him into the vast barnlike warehouse, driving him into the collapsing roof beam where five long nails in his back held him suspended several feet off the ground. His glasses were still intact.

Five hundred yards farther north Captain Hideo Sematoo, a company commander, **9.** had just cantered up to his office and was removing his riding boots. The building fell on top of him and ignited. He thought of the seven years he had fought in Manchuria, China, Singapore, Malaya and New Guinea. How miserable to be burned to death rather than die in battle! *"Tenno Heika banzai!"* he shouted. As the flames reached for him, the wreckage above him was pulled away and he wrenched himself free. Nauseated, he looked at an eerie yellow sky. The ground was flat as far as he could see. Everything was gone—towering Hiroshima Castle and 2nd General Army headquarters. Instinctively he stumbled and crawled toward the main branch of the Ota

River. There, crowded along the banks, were hundreds of dazed patients and nurses from the Army Hospital. Their hair was burned off, their skin charred a dark brown. He felt chilly.

A thousand yards on the other side of the hypocenter, Mrs. Yasuko Nukushina **10.** was trapped in the ruins of the family *sake* store. Her first thought was of her four-year-old daughter, Ikuko, who was playing outside somewhere. Unaccountably, she heard Ikuko's voice beside her: "I'm afraid, Mama." She told the child they were buried and would die there. Her own words made her claw desperately at the wreckage. She was a slight woman, four feet six inches tall, but in her frenzy she broke free into the yard. All around was devastation. She somehow felt responsible; "her" bomb had also destroyed the neighborhood. People drifted by expressionless and silent like sleepwalkers in tattered, smoldering clothing. It was a parade of wraiths, an evocation of a Buddhist hell. She watched mesmerized until someone touched her. Grasping Ikuko's hand, she joined the procession. In her confusion she had the illusion that vast numbers of planes were roaring over the city, dropping bomb after bomb without cessation.

Fourteen hundred yards east of ground zero at the presbytery of the only Catholic **11.** church in the city, Father Superior Hugo Lassalle, a German, had heard a plane overhead. He went to the window. The empty sky glared yellow—and the ceiling dropped. Cut and bleeding, Father Lassalle found his way to the street. It was dark. The entire city was covered by a blanket of dust. With another German priest he began searching through the rubble for residents of the mission.

Half a dozen blocks south, fifteen-year-old Michiko Yamaoka had just left home **12.** for work at the telephone office. She remembered "a magnesium flash," then a faraway voice calling "Michiko!" Her mother. "I'm here," she answered but didn't know where that was. She couldn't see—she must be blind! She heard her mother shout, "My daughter is buried under there!" Another voice, a man's, advised the mother to escape the flames sweeping down the street. Michiko begged her mother to save herself and heard running steps diminish to silence. She was going to die. Then came a shaft of light as concrete blocks were pushed aside by soldiers. Her mother was bleeding profusely, one arm skewered by a piece of wood. She ordered Michiko to escape. She herself was staying to rescue two relatives under the ruins of their house.

Michiko moved through a nightmare world—past charred bodies—a crying baby **13.** sealed behind the twisted iron bars of a collapsed reinforced-concrete building. She saw someone she knew and called out.

"Who are you?" the other girl asked.   **14.**

"Michiko."   **15.**

The friend stared at her. "Your nose and eyebrows are gone!"   **16.**

Michiko felt her face. It was so swollen that her nose seemed to have disappeared. **17.**

In the same area, 350 young girls from the Girls Commercial School had been **18.** working in an empty lot, clearing an evacuated area. They wore blue *mompei* and jackets but no hats or fire hoods, and those who turned, curious, toward the *pika*—almost 300 of them—were instantly doomed. Twelve-year-old Miyoko Matsubara's instinct was to bury her face in her arms. She regained consciousness in unimaginable desolation—no people, no buildings—only limitless rubble. Where were her *mompei*? All she had around her waist was a white cloth belt and it was on fire. (Everyone wearing dark clothing who was exposed to the *pika* suffered primary thermal burns but the cruel flash reflected harmlessly off white material.) She started to beat out the flames with her right hand but to her horror she saw strips of skin, her skin, dangling from it.

Mrs. Tomita had given birth to a baby girl that morning. Together with her **19.** husband, Torao, she was admiring their newborn daughter, Hiroko, when an intense light filled the window. Mrs. Tomita remembered a whooshing noise before losing consciousness. She came to on the floor. Her husband was gone. The baby in her little red dress was lying on top of the sewing machine—alive but unnaturally silent. Mrs. Tomita wrapped diapers tightly around her distended stomach—the midwife had told her to move as little as possible—and walked out into the street with the baby. Torao was hysterically digging in the ruins for their other two children. He found the elder daughter still alive, but her brother was hopelessly buried somewhere under the mass. There was a shout that more planes were on the way and the family sought shelter in a ditch trickling with foul water.

Less than a mile south of ground zero the main building of Hiroshima University **20.** stood intact amid the devastation. The hands of its huge clock, which faced the campus, had stopped at 8:15. But the bomb, which had stilled so many other clocks and watches at that time, had nothing to do with it; several days previously it had stopped prophetically at that catastrophic moment.

Two student nurses, who were ill in bed at a wooden dormitory of the Red Cross **21.** Hospital across the street, neither saw nor heard the bomb. Their first sensation was that their lungs were collapsing. Kyoko Sato crawled out of the caved-in building into a maelstrom of dust. A muffled call, "Sato-*san!*" led her to her friend, whom she pried loose from the debris. Together they tried to cross the highway to report to the hospital but couldn't penetrate the solid stream of silent humanity moving away from the city, half naked and bleeding but without hysteria, not even tears. The unreality of it was terrifying.

Dr. Fumio Shigeto, head of internal medicine at the hospital, never reached his **22.** office that morning. On his way to work, he was waiting for a trolley at the end of a long line which bent around the corner of the Hiroshima railway station, 2,000 yards east of the hypocenter. The flash seemed to turn a group of girls ahead of him white, almost invisible. An incendiary bomb! As he dropped to the sidewalk, covering eyes and ears, a heavy slate slammed into his back. Whirls of smoke blotted out the sun. In the darkness he groped blindly to reach shelter before the next wave of attackers came on. Fearing poison gas, he covered his mouth with a handkerchief.

A breeze from the east gradually cleared the area as though it were dawn, **23.** revealing an incredible scene: the buildings in front of the station were collapsed, flattened; half-naked and smoldering bodies covered the ground. Of the people at the trolley stop he alone, the last one in line, was unhurt, protected by the corner of the station building. Dr. Shigeto started for the hospital but was stopped by an impenetrable wall of advancing flames. He turned and ran for open space—toward an Army drill ground behind the station. He saw scores of survivors milling around, crying hysterically, and to ease the pain of their burns they extended their arms from which dangled long curls of skin.

A nurse approached him; he must be a doctor because he carried a black bag and **24.**

had a trim little mustache. She begged him to help another doctor and his wife lying on the ground. His first thought was: What if this mob of desperate people discovers I am a physician? He couldn't help them all. "Please treat my wife first," said the injured doctor, who was bleeding profusely. Shigeto gave the woman a camphor shot for shock, followed by another injection to stop the bleeding. He rearranged the bandages the nurse had applied and then turned to the other wounded, treating them until he ran out of medicine and supplies. There was nothing else he could do. He fled toward the hills. . . .

25. Two and a half miles south of the hypocenter, former news photographer Gonichi Kimura was working outside a stable for the Army when he saw a strong flash to his left and simultaneously felt a searing blast of heat. At first he thought the Hiroshima Gas Company's tank had exploded, but since he soon discovered that it was still standing, he felt intuitively that some special bomb must have been dropped and decided to take pictures as soon as he could get to his camera, which was stored in the warehouse nearby. By the time he had crawled through the wreckage of the stable, the narrow white column of smoke from the bomb had changed to pink and the top started to swell, making it look like a mushroom, and it kept growing massively.

26. At the warehouse Kimura found all the windows shattered from the blast, and there was so much broken glass on the floor where his camera was kept that he could not even step inside, but he managed to stretch in and pull the drawer open. The trees outside the warehouse were in the way, so he returned to the stable to take his first pictures of the atomic cloud—"indeed, a gruesome sight"—which was now covering most of the sky. Fires which had broken out in the western part of the city were spreading rapidly, and he finished his roll of film from the roof of a factory. Kimura escaped the bomb without injury, but he never saw his wife again—he had left her at home after breakfast that morning.

27. Those near the hypocenter never heard the explosion of the bomb. With distance, the noise grew perceptible, then shattering. From three miles it sounded like the rumbling of unworldly thunder; at four miles it was a distant moan which grew into a jarring boom. Near the port of Kure, twelve miles to the southeast, Tadahiko Kitayama thought a nearby ammunition dump had detonated, and several miles offshore, salvagers attempting to raise the four-man submarine *Koryu*, which was stuck in the bottom mud, heard a deafening "thunderbolt" clap. Moments later they noticed a B-29 coming from the direction of Hiroshima.

28. For a quarter of an hour the atmosphere above Hiroshima was churned by cosmic forces. Then huge drops of rain began to plummet down. The rising cloud column had carried moisture sufficiently high for water vapor to condense, and stained by radioactive dust, fall in large drops. The "black rain," weird and almost supernatural, horrified the survivors. Was it some kind of poisonous oil that would stick to the skin and slowly kill them? It pelted down on the half-naked people, leaving gray streaks on their bodies, releasing in many of them a sense of awareness of the unimaginable disaster that had been visited on Hiroshima. Mrs. Tomita tried to protect her two-hour-old baby, but little Hiroko was soaked by the fallout. She still had not uttered a sound since the blast.

29. The deadly rain, which had changed into a foggy, yellowish drizzle, spread to the northwest. Almost none fell on the area to the east where the fires were more intense, and Dr. Yoshimasa Matsuzaka, a skin specialist and head of the city's civil

defense, was trying to bring some order out of chaos. Ignoring his own wounds, he put on his civil defense uniform which his wife had rescued from the wreckage of his office, and leaning on his son, marched toward the East District police station holding high a Rising Sun flag on a long stick. The sight of the determined little procession extending first-aid treatment—Mrs. Matsuzaka and three nurses brought up the rear—calmed the people. The group set up a first-aid station in front of the police head-quarters—it was 1,200 yards from the hypocenter—and long lines of injured and burned began to form outside the shell of the station house.

From his destroyed home less than half a mile away the police chief, Shiroku **30.** Tanabe, was desperately trying to get to the station. But he was impeded by thousands of refugees (they looked ''as if they had crawled out of a pool of blood'') streaming away from ground zero. By the time Tanabe reached the station house, it had caught fire. He took command and organized a bucket brigade to a nearby ''fire pool.'' Though half the building was ablaze, Dr. Matsuzaka and his indomitable first-aid team continued to treat the injured and to urge them to seek refuge outside the city.

All over town, charcoal braziers full of hot coals (housewives had been preparing **31.** breakfast) ignited the tinderbox rubble. These thousands of small fires were whipped into fury by a cyclonic wind that was sucked in toward the hypocenter with such force that large trees were uprooted. Blasts of flame—they could have come from monster blowtorches—erratically ripped off corrugated roofs as if they were cardboard, blasted houses apart and twisted metal bridges. Telephone poles ignited explosively.

Near the site of Hiroshima Castle four men staggered through the burning streets **32.** with a massive portrait of the Emperor; they had rescued it from the inferno of the 2nd General Army communications center and were trying to get it safely out of the city. At the sight of the picture, lines of apathetic refugees broke into cries of ''The Emperor's portrait!'' The burned and bleeding saluted or bowed low. Those unable to get to their feet clasped hands in prayer. As the picture was trundled through Asano Sentei Park to a waiting boat moored on the river, towering pine trees flamed into torches. Wounded soldiers on the banks, waiting to be rescued, struggled to attention and saluted as the boat headed upstream for safety through a shower of flaming debris.

Their commander, General Fujii, was incinerated in the first minutes at his **33.** quarters near the castle but Private Shigeru Shimoyama, who was closer to ground zero, was still alive even after being impaled on the spikes of a roof beam. He painfully pulled himself free from the spikes, and using his head as a battering ram, relentlessly slammed at the roof, blinded by streams of blood, until he broke through. Thick stifling clouds of dust swirled about him, but he could tell that some irresistible force had swept across the city like the hand of a vengeful giant. At the river he watched scores of wounded making the long frantic leap from its banks. What did they think they were doing? The surface of the water was covered with carmine scum. From blood? Shimoyama kept telling himself to remain calm. He was no stranger to disaster; he had almost been killed in the earthquake of '23, the Doolittle raid and the Tokyo fire bombing of April 13. He started up the river against the wind; it would help keep the fires behind him.

Directly in his path was a cavalry horse standing alone. It was pink; the blast **34.** had seared off its skin. It looked at him pleadingly and followed with a few faltering steps. The pitiful sight fascinated Shimoyama, and he had to force himself to press on (he would dream about the pink horse for years afterward). Half a dozen other soldiers were also purposefully following the bank north, but it was as if each man was solitary, preoccupied with his own survival. Civilians, some almost naked, tried to keep up with them, but as the dull rumble of flames behind grew louder, the soldiers quickened their pace, leaving the others far behind.

Several miles upstream Shimoyama forded the river where the water only came **35.** up to his neck. As he proceeded into the suburbs where the havoc of the bomb had not reached, he was obsessed by one thought—that it was an atomic bomb. He must get home and see his daughter before he died of the effects. In 1943 a brother-in-law of his had informed him that the Japanese were working on one and for the past few days, oddly, there had been so much talk in his barracks about such a bomb that if a man lost his temper someone would say, "He's like an atomic bomb." He passed scores of high school girls, horribly burned, sprawling on either side of the road. Long strips of skin hung in ribbons from their faces, arms and legs. The reached out in supplication for water. But what could he do? Farther up the road, villagers were laying sliced cucumbers on the burns of other survivors and carrying those most seriously hurt to first-aid stations in vegetable carts.

The first fragmentary reports that came into Tokyo indicated simply that Hiroshi- **36.** ma had suffered an unprecedented disaster. . . .

In the dying light of dusk the fires began to subside and from a distance Hiroshima **37.** looked peaceful, like the gigantic encampment of a quiescent army on the plain. And high overhead, stars appeared startlingly bright against the darkening sky. The flow out of the city had been reversed as the first trickle of help entered from the outside.

Dr. Shigeto of the Red Cross Hospital, who had fled the holocaust, was back. **38.** Going from one first-aid station to another, he was told that water was harmful for those suffering burns. On the contrary, he announced, it flushed the poison from burns out of the system. He had signs put up: YOU MAY GIVE WATER, DR. SHIGETO, VICE DIRECTOR, RED CROSS HOSPITAL.

As he penetrated deeper into the ravaged city, he found his way blocked by **39.** smoldering rubble. Although there seemed to be no passable road, he saw to his astonishment a large charcoal-burning truck come rumbling, out of the smoke, its cab crowded with men. He recognized the driver, a *sake* manufacturer from his suburb. He had braved the inferno to carry emergency food and *sake* to his customers, but found their stores burned down. Shigeto started past the truck. "There's not a living soul in there!" the driver called out. "Not an animal. What use is a doctor?" Shigeto was forcibly lifted into the truck.

The doctor had to borrow a bicycle to cover the last mile home. He came **40.** unexpectedly upon a woman, a baby on her back, wandering on the dark road. When she saw him she began to weep hysterically. It was his wife, and in his memory, she had already placed a burning candle on the family Buddhist shrine.

Outside the city, first-aid stations were powerless to help the hundreds dying **41.** every hour. Seven-year-old Shizuko Iura was close to death but no one had heard her cry or complain. She continually asked for water, which her mother gave her against the advice of attendants. Why not ease her dying? "Father [he was a sailor on some Pacific island] is far away from home in a dangerous place," Shizuko said as if she saw him in a vision. "Please stay alive, Mother. If both of us die, he will be very lonely.'' She mentioned the names of all her friends and relatives. When she came to her grandparents she added, ''They were good to me.'' She cried ''Papa, Papa!'' and died.

That day perhaps 100,000 human beings perished in Hiroshima, and an equal **42.** number were dying from burns, injuries and a disease of the atomic age, radiation poisoning . . .

In Hiroshima the mysterious effects of radiation were making themselves known **43.** at dawn on August 7. Shogo Nagaoka, formerly a geologist at the university, was trying to get through the rubble to the campus. A recent draftee, he had deserted his Army unit out of concern for the fate of the university and had been traveling for hours. He could hardly fathom the endless devastation. At the Gokoku Shrine near the hypocenter he slumped exhausted at the foot of a stone lantern. He felt a stinging sensation—it was radiation—and sprang to his feet. Then he noticed a strange silhouette on the lantern and that some of its surface was melted. An awful and sudden realization came to him: an atomic bomb! Japan had to surrender at once.

At scores of aid stations doctors were mystified. Their patients' symptoms were **44.** so bizarre that it was suspected an acrid poison gas had been used to spread bacillary dysentery. Some victims were scorched on just one side of the face; oddly, some had the shadow of a nose or ear stenciled on their cheek. Like Nagoaka, Dr. Shigeto of the Red Cross Hospital had heard of atomic energy and guessed that the victims were suffering from primary radiation. He checked the walls of the hospital with a simple X-ray indicator. The count was so low, however, that he concluded it was safe to remain.

The aftereffects were unpredictable. Private Shimoyama, one of those closest to **45.** ground zero, had been near-sighted before the *pika*. Now as he peered through his glasses everything seemed slightly blurred to him. Was he going blind? When he finally removed his glasses he discovered that he had regained perfect vision. But his hair was falling out and he was suffering from the same sickness that had struck thousands of others. First they felt nauseated and vomited; diarrhea and fever followed. Other reactions were erratic. Some victims were covered with brilliant spots—red, green-yellow, black and purple—and lived; others whose bodies had no apparent marks died abruptly. One man escaped with a slightly burned hand and ignored it until he began vomiting blood. He put his injured hand in water for relief and ''something strange and bluish came out of it, like smoke.''

Terror of the unknown, intensified by vague feelings of guilt and shame, swept **46.** over the survivors; they were alive because they had ignored pleas of relatives and neighbors for help and left them trapped in burning wreckage. The anguished voices of those who had died kept haunting them. Parents who had lost children blamed themselves, and children who had lost parents felt this was punishment for some wrongdoing. The tragedy had cruelly shattered the intricate and intimate structure of Japanese family life.

WORKING WITH THE TEXT

Cultural and Historical References

In this section, the numbers at the margin refer to the numbered paragraphs in the selection itself.

1. In 1944 Dresden, Germany, had suffered an incendiary bombing attack that had killed tens of thousands of people.

32. At this time the Japanese emperor was considered by many Japanese to be a deity.

Writing Assignments: The Paragraph

Be sure to provide an introduction for each of the following paragraph writing assignments. That is, begin each paragraph with a phrase like this: "Thomas Brickle claims that. . . ." When it is relevant, you might also want to identify the expertise of the author ("Thomas Brickle, a New Testament scholar, claims that. . . ."), the name of the book or article, the century and country in which the work appeared, or any other circumstances that your readers might find significant. For more on this, see pp. 11–13 in Chapter 2.

1. Write a paragraph on the effect of the A-bomb on family relationships. See paragraph 46.
2. Summarize the whole essay.
3. Summarize the effects of the A-bomb's heat.

Writing Assignments: The Short Essay

Use informal documentation for these short essays. That is, don't use footnotes or a Works Cited page to document your sources. Instead, cite only relevant information about your source, and keep that information *within* your text. Then follow the summary or quote with a page number in parentheses. (Use the page numbers that you find in this book to represent the page numbers of the source.) Thus, your informal documentation will look something like this:

> In *The Rising Sun*, John Toland says that in the instant after the A-bomb attack on Hiroshima, "All over the center of the city numerous silhouettes were imprinted on walls" (p. 468).

1. Write on what you think is the most pathetic description of the injured, dying, or dead. Analyze *why* that particular description is the most pathetic.
2. Write a report on the aftereffects of the bomb.
3. Analyze Toland's use of isolated details—the clocks, outlines on the wall, and so forth. What are the effects of those details? Could they be seen as suggesting anything about the author's attitude toward the bombing?

HIROSHIMA: A SOLDIER'S VIEW

Paul Fussell

Paul Fussell, a contributing editor for *The New Republic*, served in the infantry on the Pacific Front during World War II. Fussell argues that President Truman's

Source: Paul Fussell, "Hiroshima: A Soldier's View," *The New Republic.* Aug. 22–29, 1981: 26–30.

decision to drop the bomb was a godsend for the grunts who were actually fighting the war. Fussell is annoyed by those who, not having been in the war themselves, now indulge in moral indignation concerning the dropping of the bomb. In the course of his essay, Fussell also surveys several articles and books which have appeared on the issue in recent years.

Many years ago in New York I saw on the side of a bus a whiskey ad which I've **1.** remembered all this time, for it's been for me a model of the brief poem. Indeed, I've come upon few short poems subsequently that evinced more genuine poetic talent. The ad consisted of two lines of "free verse," thus:

In life, experience is the great teacher.
In Scotch, Teacher's is the great experience.

For present purposes we can jettison the second line (licking our lips ruefully as it disappears), leaving the first to encapsulate a principle whose banality suggests that it enshrines a most useful truth. I bring up the matter this August, the 36th anniversary of the A-bombing of Hiroshima and Nagasaki, to focus on something suggested by the long debate about the ethics, if any, of that affair: namely, the importance of experience, sheer vulgar experience, in influencing, if not determining, one's views about the first use of the bomb. And the experience I'm talking about is that of having come to grips, face to face, with an enemy who designs your death. The experience is common to those in the infantry and the Marines and even the line Navy, to those, in short, who fought the Second World War mindful always that their mission was, as they were repeatedly told, "to close with the enemy and destroy him." I think there's something to be learned about that war, as well as about the tendency of historical memory unwittingly to resolve ambiguity, by considering some of the ways testimonies emanating from experience complicate attitudes about the cruel ending of that cruel war.

"What did you do in the Great War, Daddy?" The recruiting poster deserves **2.** ridicule and contempt, of course, but its question is embarrassingly relevant here. The problem is one that touches on the matter of social class in America. Most of those with firsthand experience of the war at its worst were relatively inarticulate and have remained silent. Few of those destined to be destroyed if the main islands had had to be invaded went on to become our most eloquent men of letters or our most impressive ethical theorists or professors of history or international jurists. The testimony of experience has come largely from rough diamonds like James Jones and William Manchester, who experienced the war in the infantry and the Marine Corps. Both would agree with the point, if not perhaps the tone, of a remark about Hiroshima made by a naval officer menaced by the kamikazes off Okinawa: "Those were the best burned women and children I ever saw." Anticipating objection from the inexperienced, Jones, in his book *WWII*, is careful to precede his chapter on Hiroshima with one detailing the plans already in motion for the infantry assaults on the home islands of Kyushu, scheduled for November 1945, and ultimately Honshu. The forthcoming invasion of Kyushu, he notes, "was well into its collecting and stockpiling stages before the war ended." (The island of Saipan was designated a main ammunition and supply base for the invasion, and if you visit it today you can see some of the assembled stuff still sitting there.) "The assault troops were chosen and already in training," Jones reminds us, and he illuminates the situation by the light of experience:

> What it must have been like to some old-timer buck sergeant or staff sergeant who had been through Guadalcanal or Bouganville or the Philippines, to stand on some beach and watch this huge war machine beginning to stir and move all around him and know that he very likely had survived this far only to fall dead on the dirt of Japan's home islands, hardly bears thinking about.

On the other hand, John Kenneth Galbraith is persuaded that the Japanese would have surrendered by November without an invasion. He thinks the atom bombs were not decisive in bringing about the surrender and he implies that their use was unjustified. What did he do in the war? He was in the Office of Price Administration in Washington, and then he was director of the United States Strategic Bombing Survey. He was 37 in 1945, and I don't demand that he experience having his ass shot off. I just note that he didn't. In saying this I'm aware of its offensive implications *ad hominem*. But here I think that approach justified. What's at stake in an infantry assault is so entirely unthinkable to those without experience of one, even if they possess very wide-ranging imaginations and sympathies, that experience is crucial in this case.

A similar remoteness from experience, as well as a similar rationalistic abstrac- **3.** tion, seems to lie behind the reaction of an anonymous reviewer of William Manchester's *Goodbye Darkness: A Memoir of the Pacific War* for the *New York Review of Books*. First of all the reviewer dislikes Manchester's calling the enemy Nips and Japs, but what really shakes him (her?) is this passage:

> After Biak the enemy withdrew to deep caverns. Rooting them out became a bloody business which reached its ultimate horrors in the last months of the war. You think of the lives which would have been lost in an invasion of Japan's home islands—a staggering number of Americans but millions more of Japanese—and you thank God for the atomic bomb.

Thank God for the atomic bomb. From this, "one recoils," says the reviewer. One does, doesn't one?

In an interesting exchange last year in the *New York Review of Books*, Joseph **4.** Alsop and David Jarovsky set forth the by now familiar arguments on both sides of the debate. You'll be able to guess which sides they chose once you know that Alsop experienced capture by the Japanese at Hong Kong in 1942 and that Jarovsky made no mortal contact with the Japanese: a young soldier, he was on his way to the Pacific when the war ended. The editors of the *New York Review* have given their debate the tendentious title "Was the Hiroshima Bomb Necessary?"—surely an unanswerable question (unlike "Was It Effective?") and one suggesting the intellectual difficulties involved in imposing *ex post facto* a rational ethics on this event. Alsop focuses on the power and fanaticism of War Minister Anami, who insisted that Japan fight to the bitter end, defending the main islands with the same means and tenacity with which it had defended Iwo and Okinawa. He concludes: "Japanese surrender could never have been obtained, at any rate without the honor-satisfying bloodbath envisioned by . . . Anami, if the hideous destruction of Hiroshima and Nagasaki had not finally galvanized the peace advocates into tearing up the entire Japanese book of rules.'' The Japanese planned to deploy the undefeated bulk of their ground forces, over two million men, plus 10,000 kamikaze planes, in a suicidal defense. That fact, says Alsop, makes it absurd to ''hold the common view, by now hardly challenged by anyone, that the decision to drop the two bombs on Japan was wicked in itself, and that President Truman and all others who joined in making or who [like Oppenheimer] assented to this decision shared in the wickedness.'' And in explanation of ''the two bombs'' Alsop adds: ''The true climactic, and successful effort of the Japanese peace advocates . . . did not begin in deadly earnest until *after* the second bomb had destroyed Nagasaki. The Nagasaki bomb was thus the trigger to all the developments that led to peace.''

Jarovsky, now a professor of history at Northwestern, argues on the other hand **5.** that those who decided to use the bomb on cities betray defects of ''reason and self-restraint.'' It all needn't have happened, he asserts, ''if the US government had been willing to take a few more days and to be a bit more thoughtful in opening the age of nuclear warfare.'' But of course in its view it wasn't doing that: that's a historian's tidy hindsight. The government was ending the war conclusively, as well as irrationally remembering Pearl Harbor with a vengeance. It didn't know then what everyone knows now about leukemia and carcinoma and birth defects. History, as Eliot's ''Gerontion'' notes,

> . . . has many cunning passages, contrived corridors
> And issues, deceives with whispering ambitions,
> Guides us by vanities. . . .
> > Think
> Neither fear nor courage saves us.
> Unnatural vices
> Are fathered by our heroism. Virtues
> Are forced upon us by our impudent
> crimes.

Understanding the past means feeling its pressure on your pulses and that's harder than Jarovsky thinks.

The Alsop-Jarovsky debate, which can be seen as reducing finally to a collision **6.** between experience and theory, was conducted with a certain civilized respect for evidence. Not so the way the new scurrilous agitprop *New Statesman* conceives those favoring the bomb and those opposing. They are, on the one hand, says Bruce Page, ''the imperialist class-forces acting through Harry Truman,'' and, on the other, those representing ''the humane, democratic virtues''—in short, ''fascists'' opposed to ''populists.'' But ironically the bomb saved the lives not of any imperialists but only of the low and humble, the quintessentially democratic huddled masses—the conscripted enlisted men manning the fated invasion divisions. Bruce Page was nine years old when the war ended. For a man of that experience, phrases like ''imperialist class-forces'' come easily, and the issues look perfectly clear.

He's not the only one to have forgotten, if he ever knew, the savagery of the **7.** Pacific war. The dramatic postwar Japanese success at hustling and merchandising and tourism has (happily, in many ways) effaced for most people important elements of the assault context in which Hiroshima should be viewed. It is easy to forget what Japan was like before it was first destroyed and then humiliated, tamed, and constitution-alized by the West. "Implacable, treacherous, barbaric"—those were Admiral Halsey's characterizations of the enemy, and at the time few facing the Japanese would deny that they fit to a T. One remembers the captured American airmen locked for years in packing-crates, the prisoners decapitated, the gleeful use of bayonets on civilians. The degree to which Americans register shock and extraordinary shame about the Hiroshima bomb correlates closely with lack of information about the war.

And the savagery was not just on one side. There was much sadism and **8.** brutality—undeniably racist—on ours. No Marine was fully persuaded of his manly adequacy who didn't have a well-washed Japanese skull to caress and who didn't have a go at treating surrendering Japs as rifle targets. Herman Wouk remembers it correctly while analyzing Ensign Keith in *The Caine Mutiny:* "Like most of the naval executioners of Kwajalein, he seemed to regard the enemy as a species of animal pest." And the enemy felt the same way about us: "From the grim and desperate taciturnity with which the Japanese died, they seemed on their side to believe they were contending with an invasion of large armed ants." Hiroshima seems to follow in natural sequence: "This obliviousness on both sides to the fact that the opponents were human beings may perhaps be cited as the key of the many massacres of the Pacific war." Since the Japanese resisted so madly, let's pour gasoline into their emplacements and light it and shoot the people afire who try to get out. Why not? Why not blow them all up? Why not, indeed, drop a new kind of big bomb on them? Why allow one more American high school kid to see his intestines blown out of his body and spread before him in the dirt while he screams when we can end the whole thing just like that?

On Okinawa, only weeks before Hiroshima, 123,000 Japanese and Americans **9.** *killed* each other. "Just awful" was the comment not of some pacifist but of MacArthur. One million American casualties was his estimate of the cost of the forthcoming invasion. And that invasion was not just a hypothetical threat, as some theorists have argued. It was genuinely in train, as I know because I was to be in it. When the bomb ended the war I was in the 45th Infantry Division, which had been through the European war to the degree that it had needed to be reconstituted two or three times. We were in a staging area near Reims, ready to be shipped across the United States for final preparation in the Philippines. My division was to take part in the invasion of Honshu in March 1946. (The earlier invasion of Kyushu was to be carried out by 700,000 infantry already in the Pacific.) I was a 21-year-old second lieutenant leading a rifle platoon. Although still officially in one piece, in the German war I had already been wounded in the leg and back severely enough to be adjudged, after the war, 40 percent disabled. But even if my legs buckled whenever I jumped out of the back of the truck, my condition was held to be satisfactory for whatever lay ahead. When the bombs dropped and news began to circulate that "Operation Olympic" would not, after all, take place, that we would not be obliged to run up the beaches near Tokyo assault-firing while being mortared and shelled, for all the fake manliness of our facades we cried with relief and joy. We were going to live. We were going to grow up to adulthood after all. When the *Enola Gay* dropped its package, "There were cheers," says John Toland, "over the intercom; it meant the end of the war."

Those who cried and cheered are very different from high-minded, guilt-ridden **10.**

GIs we're told about by the late J. Glenn Gray in *The Warriors* (1959). During the war in Europe Gray was an interrogator in the Counter Intelligence Corps, and in that capacity he underwent the war at division level. After the war he became a professor of philosophy at Colorado College (never, I've thought, the venue of very much reality) and a distinguished editor of Heidegger. There's no doubt that Gray's outlook on everything was noble and elevated. But *The Warriors*, his meditation on modern soldiering, gives every sign of remoteness from experience. Division headquarters is miles behind the places where the soldiers experience terror and madness and relieve these pressures by sadism. "When the news of the atomic bombing of Hiroshima and Nagasaki came," Gray asks us to believe, "many an American soldier felt shocked and ashamed." But why, we ask? Because we'd bombed civilians? We'd been doing that for years and, besides the two bombs, wiped out 10,000 Japanese troops, not now often mentioned, John Hersey's kindly physicians and Jesuit priests being more touching. Were Gray's soldiers shocked and ashamed because we'd obliterated whole towns? We'd done that plenty of times. If at division headquarters some felt shocked and ashamed, down in the rifle companies none did, although Gray says they did:

> The combat soldier knew better than did Americans at home what
> those bombs meant in suffering and injustice. The man of conscience
> realized intuitively that the vast majority of Japanese in both cities
> were no more, if no less, guilty of the war than were his own parents,
> sisters, or brothers.

I find this canting nonsense: the purpose of dropping the bombs was not to "punish" people but to stop the war. To intensify the shame he insists we feel, Gray seems willing to fiddle the facts. The Hiroshima bomb, he says, was dropped "without any warning." But actually, two days before, 720,000 leaflets were dropped on the city urging everyone to get out and indicating that the place was going to be obliterated. Of course few left.

Experience whispers that the pity is not that we used the bomb to end the Japanese **11.** war but that it wasn't ready earlier to end the German one. If only it could have been rushed into production faster and dropped at the right moment on the Reich chancellery or Berchtesgaden or Hitler's military headquarters in East Prussia or—Wagnerian *coup de theatre*—at Rommel's phony state funeral, most of the Nazi hierarchy could have been pulverized immediately, saving not just the embarrassment of the Nuremburg trials but the lives of about four million Jews, Poles, Slavs, gypsies, and other "subhumans," not to mention the lives and limbs of millions of Allied and Axis soldiers. If the bomb could have been ready even as late as July 1944, it could have reinforced the Von Stauffenberg plot and ended the war then and there. If the bomb had only been ready in time, the men of my infantry platoon would not have been killed and maimed.

All this is not to deny that like the Russian revolution, the atomic bombing of **12.** Japan was a vast historical tragedy, and every passing year magnifies the dilemma into which it has thrown the contemporary world. As with the Russian revolution there are two sides—that's why it's a tragedy rather than a disaster—and unless we are simple-mindedly cruel, like Bruce Page, we need to be painfully aware of both at once. To observe that from the viewpoint of the war's victims-to-be the bomb was precisely the right thing to drop is to purchase no immunity from horror. See, for example, the new book *Unforgettable Fire: Pictures Drawn by Atomic Bomb Survivors*, issued by the Japan Broadcasting Corporation and distributed here by Pantheon Books. It presents a number of amateur colored-pencil, pastel, and water-color depictions of the scene of the Hiroshima bombing made by the middle-aged and elderly survivors for a peace exhibition in 1975. In addition to the heartrending pictures the book offers brief moments of memoir, not for the weak-stomached:

> While taking my severely wounded wife out to the riverbank . . . , I was horrified indeed at the sight of a stark naked man standing in the rain with his eyeball in his palm. He looked to be in great pain but there was nothing that I could do for him. I wonder what became of him. Even today, I vividly remember the sight. It was simply miserable.

The drawings and paintings, whose often childish style makes them doubly touching, are of skin hanging down, breasts torn off, people bleeding and burning, dying mothers nursing dead babies. A bloody woman holds a bloody child in the ruins of a house, and the artist remembers her calling, ''Please help this child! Someone, please help this child. Please help! Someone, please.'' As Samuel Johnson said of the smothering of the innocent Desdemona in another tragedy, ''It is not to be endured.'' Nor, we should notice, is an infantryman's account of having his arm blown off in the Arno Valley in Italy in 1944:

> I wanted to die and die fast. I wanted to forget this miserable world. I cursed the war, I cursed the people who were responsible for it, I cursed God for putting me here . . . to suffer for something I never did or knew anything about. For this was hell, and I never imagined anything or anyone could suffer so bitterly. I screamed and cursed. Why? Why? What had I done to deserve this? But no answer came. I yelled for medics, because subconsciously I wanted to live. I tried to apply my right hand over my bleeding stump, but I didn't have the strength to hold it. I looked to the left of me and saw the bloody mess that was once my left arm; its fingers and palm were turned upward, like a flower looking to the sun for its strength.

13. The future scholar-critic of rhetoric who writes *The History of Canting in the Twentieth Century* will find much to study in the utterances of those who dilate on the wickedness of the bomb-droppers. He will realize that such utterance can perform for the speaker a valuable double function. First, it can display the fineness of his moral weave. And second, by implication it can also inform the audience that during the war he was not socially so unfortunate as to find himself at the cutting edge of the ground forces, where he might have had to compromise the pure clarity of his moral vision by the experience of weighing his own life against other people's. Down there, which is where the other people were in the war, is the place where coarse self-interest is the rule. When the young soldier with the wild eyes comes at you firing, do you shoot him in the foot, hoping he'll be hurt badly enough to drop or mis-aim the gun with which he is going to kill you, or do you shoot him in the chest and make certain he stops

being your mortal enemy? It would be stupid to expect soldiers to be very sensitive humanitarians (''Moderation in war is imbecility''—Admiral of the Fleet Lord Fisher); actually, only the barest decencies can be expected of them. They didn't start the war, except in the terrible sense hinted in Frederic Manning's observation based on his experience in the Great War: ''War is waged by men; not by beasts, or by gods. It is a peculiarly human activity. To call it a crime against mankind is to miss at least half its significance; it is also the punishment of a crime.'' Knowing that fact by experience, soldiers have every motive for wanting a war stopped, by any means.

The predictable stupidity, parochialism, and greed in the postwar international **14.** mismanagement of the whole nuclear problem should not tempt us to mis-imagine the circumstances of the bomb's first ''use.'' Nor should our well-justified fears and suspicions occasioned by the capture of the nuclear business by the mendacious classes (cf. Three Mile Island) tempt us to infer retrospectively extraordinary corruption, cruelty, and swinishness in those who decided to drop the bomb. Times change. Harry Truman was not a fascist, but a democrat. He was as close to a real egalitarian as we've seen in high office for a very long time. He is the only president in my lifetime who ever had the experience of commanding a small unit of ground troops obliged to kill people. He knew better than his subsequent critics what he was doing. The past, which as always did not know the future, acted in ways that ask to be imagined before they are condemned. Or even before they are simplified.

WORKING WITH THE TEXT

Cultural and Historical References

In this section, the numbers at the margin refer to the numbered paragraphs in the selection itself.

1. The following difficult words from the first paragraph—''evinced,'' ''ruefully,'' ''encapsulate,'' ''banality,'' ''ethics,'' ''ambiguity,'' ''emanating''—suggest that improving one's vocabulary ought to be a reader's number one goal. Look at the magazine that Fussell was writing for. Judging from the vocabulary of this piece of Fussell, what kind of readers must that magazine have?

2. James Jones wrote a famous World War II novel, *From Here to Eternity*. William Manchester, who later became a well-known journalist, wrote a personal history of the war, *Goodbye Darkness: A Memoir of the Pacific War*.

2. John Kenneth Galbraith is a liberal economist and essayist.

4. Oppenheimer was one of the physicists and architects of the Manhattan Project, the group that put together the first A-bomb.

5. T. S. Eliot is a well-known poet who wrote *The Waste Land*, a poem critical of the ''emptiness'' of modern society.

6. ''Agitprop'' is a portmanteau word: agitation and propaganda. What is a portmanteau word? Where does it come from?

9. The *Enola Gay* was the name of the plane that dropped the A-bomb on Hiroshima.

10. Heidegger was a German metaphysicist. With that in mind, why do you think Fussell mentions the fact that J. Glenn Gray was a "distinguished editor of Heidegger"?

12. Samuel Johnson, an eighteenth-century author and dictionary maker, was a cynic and a realist.

Writing Assignments: The Paragraph

Be sure to provide an introduction for each of the following paragraph writing assignments. That is, begin each paragraph with a phrase like this: "Thomas Brickle claims that. . . ." When it is relevant, you might also want to identify the expertise of the author ("Thomas Brickle, a New Testament scholar, claims that. . . ."), the name of the book or article, the century and country in which the work appeared, or any other circumstances that your readers might find significant. For more on this, see pp. 11–13 in Chapter 2.

1. Write a paragraph on why so few justifications for the dropping of the bomb came from infantrymen.

2. Clarify this sentence, taken from paragraph 4: "The editors of the *New York Review* have given their debate the tendentious title 'Was the Hiroshima Bomb Necessary?'—surely an unanswerable question (unlike 'Was It Effective?') and one suggesting the intellectual difficulties involved in imposing *ex post facto* a rational ethics on this event." Can there be any justification for such a knotty and difficult sentence?

3. Clarify this sentence, taken from paragraph 14: "Nor should our well-justified fears and suspicions occasioned by the capture of the nuclear business by the mendacious classes (cf. Three Mile Island) tempt us to infer retrospectively extraordinary corruption, cruelty, and swinishness in those who decided to drop the bomb."

Writing Assignments: The Short Essay

Use informal documentation for these short essays. That is, don't use footnotes or a Works Cited page to document your sources. Instead, cite only relevant information about your source, and keep that information *within* your text. Then follow the summary or quote with a page number in parentheses. (Use the page numbers that you find in this book to represent the page numbers of the source.) Thus, your informal documentation will look something like this:

> In *The Rising Sun*, John Toland says that in the instant after the A-bomb attack on Hiroshima, "All over the center of the city numerous silhouettes were imprinted on walls" (p. 468).

1. Fussell says that the arguments against the dropping of the A-bomb by those who didn't fight in the war are empty. Is Fussell's position reasonable?

2. What does Fussell mean when he says, in paragraph 5, that "Understanding the past means feeling its pressure on your pulse"? Illustrate your answer by citing parts of Fussell's text.

3. Why does Fussell bring up, in paragraph 12, the discussion of the infantryman who has his arm blown off?

4. Comment on the use of statistics in Fussell's essay. How are they used? See in particular paragraph 9.

OF ACCIDENTAL JUDGEMENTS AND CASUAL SLAUGHTERS

Kai Erikson

Kai Erikson is editor of *The Yale Review* and a professor of sociology at Yale. He argues against the decision to drop the atomic bomb, asserting that the decision was a product of an inevitable wartime mentality. He contends that an American invasion of the Japanese mainland was unnecessary after the test bomb was exploded in July 1945 because a weakened Japan was incapable of mounting an offensive at that late point in the war—and because a demonstration to the Japanese of the bomb's capabilities would have produced the same results that actually dropping the bombs on civilian populations did.

The bombings of Hiroshima and Nagasaki, which took place forty years ago this **1.** month, are among the most thoroughly studied moments on human record. Together they constitute the only occasion in history when atomic weapons were dropped on living populations, and together they constitute the only occasion in history when a decision was made to employ them in that way.

I want to reflect here on the second of those points. The "decision to drop"— **2.** I will explain in a minute why quotation marks are useful here—is a fascinating historical episode. But it is also an exhibit of the most profound importance as we consider our prospects for the future. It is a case history well worth attending to. A compelling parable.

If one were to tell the story of that decision as historians normally do, the details **3.** arranged in an ordered narrative, one might begin in 1938 with the discovery of nuclear fission, or perhaps a year later with the delivery of Einstein's famous letter to President Roosevelt. No matter what its opening scene, though, the tale would then proceed along a string of events—a sequence of appointees named, committees formed, reports issued, orders signed, arguments won and lost, minds made up and changed—all of it coming to an end with a pair of tremendous blasts in the soft morning air over Japan.

The difficulty with that way of relating the story, as historians of the period all **4.** testify, is that the more closely one examines the record, the harder it is to make out

Source: Kai Erikson, "Of Accidental Judgements and Casual Slaughters," *The Nation.* August 3/10, 1985: 65, 80–85.

where in the flow of events something that could reasonably be called a decision was reached at all. To be sure, a kind of consensus emerged from the sprawl of ideas and happenings that made up the climate of wartime Washington, but looking back, it is hard to distinguish those pivotal moments in the story when the crucial issues were identified, debated, reasoned through, resolved. The decision, to the extent that one can even speak of such a thing, was shaped and seasoned by a force very like inertia.

Let's say, then, that a wind began to blow, ever so gently at first, down the **5.** corridors along which power flows. And as it gradually gathered momentum during the course of the war, the people caught up in it began to assume, without ever checking up on it, that it had a logic and a motive, that it had been set in motion by sure hands acting on the basis of wise counsel.

Harry Truman, in particular, remembered it as a time of tough and lonely choices, **6.** and titled his memoir of that period *Year of Decisions*. But the bulk of those choices can in all fairness be said to have involved confirmation of projects already under way or implementation of decisions made at other levels of command. Brig. Gen. Leslie R. Groves, military head of the Manhattan Project, was close to the mark when he described Truman's decision as "one of noninterference—basically, a decision not to upset the existing plans." And J. Robert Oppenheimer spoke equally to the point when he observed some twenty years later: "The decision was implicit in the project. I don't know whether it could have been stopped."

In September of 1944, when it became more and more evident that a bomb would **7.** be produced in time for combat use, Franklin Roosevelt and Winston Churchill met at Hyde Park and initialed a brief *aide-mémoire*, noting, among other things, that the new weapon "might, perhaps, after mature consideration, be used against the Japanese." This document does not appear to have had any effect on the conduct of the war, and Truman knew nothing at all about it. But it would not have made a real difference in any case, for neither chief of state did much to initiate the "mature consideration" they spoke of so glancingly, and Truman, in turn, could only suppose that such matters had been considered already. "Truman did not inherit the question," writes Martin J. Sherwin, "he inherited the answer."

What would "mature consideration" have meant in such a setting as that anyway? **8.**

First of all, presumably, it would have meant seriously asking whether the weapon **9.** should be employed at all. But we have it on the authority of virtually all the principal players that no one in a position to do anything about it ever really considered alternatives to combat use. Henry L. Stimson, Secretary of War:

> At no time, from 1941 to 1945, did I ever hear it suggested by the
> President, or by any other responsible member of the government, that
> atomic energy should not be used in the war.

Harry Truman:

> I regarded the bomb as a military weapon and never had any doubt that
> it should be used.

General Groves:

> Certainly, there was no question in my mind, or, as far as I was ever

aware, in the mind of either President Roosevelt or President Truman
or any other responsible person, but that we were developing a weapon
to be employed against the enemies of the United States.

Winston Churchill:

There never was a moment's discussion as to whether the atomic bomb
should be used or not.

And why should anyone be surprised? We were at war, after all, and with the most
resolute of enemies, so the unanimity of that feeling is wholly understandable. But it
was not, by any stretch of the imagination, a product of mature consideration.

"Combat use" meant a number of different things, however, and a second **10.**
question began to be raised with some frequency in the final months of the war, all the
more insistently after the defeat of Germany. Might a way be devised to demonstrate
the awesome power of the bomb in a convincing enough fashion to induce the surrender
of the Japanese without having to destroy huge numbers of civilians? Roosevelt may
have been pondering something of the sort. In September of 1944, for example, three
days after initialing the Hyde Park *aide-mémoire*, he asked Vannevar Bush, a trusted
science adviser, whether the bomb "should actually be used against the Japanese or
whether it should be used only as a threat." While that may have been little more than
idle musing, a number of different schemes were explored within both the government
and the scientific community in the months following.

One option involved a kind of *benign strike*: the dropping of a bomb on some **11.**
built-up area, but only after advance notice had been issued so that residents could
evacuate the area and leave an empty slate on which the bomb could write its terrifying
signature. This plan was full of difficulties. A dud under those dramatic circumstances
might do enormous damage to American credibility, and, moreover, to broadcast any
warning was to risk the endeavor in other ways. Weak as the Japanese were by this
time in the war, it was easy to imagine their finding a way to intercept an incoming
airplane if they knew where and when it was expected, and officials in Washington
were afraid that it would occur to the Japanese, as it had to them, that the venture
would come to an abrupt end if American prisoners of war were brought into the target
area.

The second option was a *tactical strike* against a purely military target—an **12.**
arsenal, railroad yard, depot, factory, harbor—without advance notice. Early in the
game, for example, someone had nominated the Japanese fleet concentration at Truk.
The problem with this notion, however—and there is more than a passing irony
here—was that no known military target had a wide enough compass to contain the
whole of the destructive capacity of the weapon and so display its full range and power.
The committee inquiring into likely targets wanted one "more than three miles in
diameter," because anything smaller would be too inadequate a canvas for the picture
it was supposed to hold.

The third option was to stage a kind of *dress rehearsal* by detonating a bomb **13.**
in some remote corner of the world—a desert or empty island, say—to exhibit to
international observers brought in for the purpose what the device could do. The idea
had been proposed by a group of scientists in what has since been called the Franck

Report, but it commanded no more than a moment's attention. It had the same problems as the benign strike: the risk of being embarrassed by a dud was more than most officials in a position to decide were willing to take, and there was a widespread feeling that any demonstration involving advance notice would give the enemy too much useful information.

14. The fourth option involved a kind of *warning shot*. The thought here was to drop a bomb without notice over a relatively uninhabited stretch of enemy land so that the Japanese high command might see at first hand what was in store for them if they failed to surrender soon. Edward Teller thought that an explosion at night high over Tokyo Bay would serve as a brilliant visual argument, and Adm. Lewis Strauss, soon to become a member (and later chair) of the Atomic Energy Commission, recommended a strike on a local forest, reasoning that the blast would "lay the trees out in windrows from the center of the explosion in all directions as though they were matchsticks," meanwhile igniting a fearsome firestorm at the epicenter. "It seemed to me," he added, "that a demonstration of this sort would prove to the Japanese that we could destroy any of their cities at will." The physicist Ernest O. Lawrence may have been speaking half in jest when he suggested that a bomb might be used to "blow the top off" Mount Fujiyama, but he was quite serious when he assured a friend early in the war: "The bomb will never be dropped on people. As soon as we get it, we'll use it only to dictate peace."

15. Now, hindsight is too easy a talent. But it seems evident on the face of it that the fourth of those options, the warning shot, was much to be preferred over the other three, and even more to be preferred over use on living targets. I do not want to argue the case here. I do want to ask, however, why that possibility was so easily dismissed.

16. The fact of the matter seems to have been that the notion of a demonstration was discussed on only a few occasions once the Manhattan Project neared completion, and most of those discussions were off the record. So a historian trying to reconstruct the drift of those conversations can only flatten an ear against the wall, as it were, and see if any sense can be made of the muffled voices next door. It seems very clear, for example, that the options involving advance notice were brought up so often and so early in official conversations that they came to *mean* demonstration in the minds of several important players. If a James Byrnes, say, soon to be named Secretary of State, were asked why one could not detonate a device in unoccupied territory, he might raise the problem posed by prisoners of war, and if the same question were asked of a James Bryant Conant, another science adviser, he might speak of the embarrassment that would follow a dud—thus, in both cases, joining ideas that had no logical relation to each other. Neither prisoners of war nor fear of failure, of course, posed any argument against a surprise demonstration.

17. There were two occasions, however, on which persons in a position to affect policy discussed the idea of a nonlethal demonstration. Those two conversations together consumed no more than a matter of minutes, so far as one can tell at this remove, and they, too, were off the record. But they seem to represent virtually the entire investment of the government of the United States in "mature consideration" of the subject.

18. The first discussion took place at a meeting of what was then called the Interim Committee, a striking gathering of military, scientific and government brass under the chairmanship of Secretary Stimson. This group, which included James Byrnes and Chief of Staff Gen. George C. Marshall, met on a number of occasions in May of 1945 to discuss policy issues raised by the new bomb, and Stimson recalled later that at one of their final meetings the members "carefully considered such alternatives as a detailed advance warning or a demonstration in some uninhabited area." But the minutes of the meeting, as well as the accounts of those present, suggest otherwise. The only exchange on the subject, in fact, took place during a luncheon break, and while we have no way of knowing what was actually said in that conversation, we do know what conclusion emerged from it. One participant, Arthur H. Compton, recalled later:

> Though the possibility of a demonstration that would not destroy
> human lives was attractive, no one could suggest a way in which it
> could be made so convincing that it would be likely to stop the war.

And the recording secretary of the meeting later recalled:

> Dr. Oppenheimer . . . said he doubted whether there could be devised
> any sufficiently startling demonstration that would convince the
> Japanese they ought to throw in the sponge.

19. Two weeks later, four physicists who served as advisers to the Interim Committee met in Los Alamos to consider once again the question of demonstration. They were Arthur Compton, Enrico Fermi, Ernest Lawrence and Robert Oppenheimer—as distinguished an assembly of scientific talent as could be imagined—and they concluded, after a discussion of which we have no record: "We can propose no technical demonstration likely to bring an end to the war; we see no acceptable alternative to direct military use." That, so far as anyone can tell, was the end of it.

20. We cannot be sure that a milder report would have made a difference, for the Manhattan Project was gathering momentum as it moved toward the more steeply pitched inclines of May and June, but we can be sure that the idea of a demonstration was at that point spent. The Los Alamos report ended with something of a disclaimer ("We have, however, no claim to special competence. . . ."), but its message was clear enough. When asked about that report nine years later in his security hearings, Oppenheimer said, with what might have been a somewhat defensive edge in his voice, "We did not think exploding one of those things as a firecracker over the desert was likely to be very impressive."

21. Perhaps not. But those fragments are telling for another reason. If you listen to them carefully for a moment or two, you realize that these are the voices of nuclear physicists trying to imagine how a strange and distant people will react to an atomic blast. These are the voices of nuclear physicists dealing with psychological and anthropological questions about Japanese culture, Japanese temperament, Japanese will to resist—topics, we must assume, about which they knew almost nothing. They did not know yet what the bomb could actually do, since its first test was not to take place for another month. But in principle, at least, Oppenheimer and Fermi reflecting on matters relating to the Japanese national character should have had about the same force as Ruth Benedict and Margaret Mead reflecting on matters relating to high-energy physics, the first difference being that Benedict and Mead would not have presumed

to do so, and the second being that no one in authority would have listened to them if they had.

The first of the two morals I want to draw from the foregoing—this being a 22. parable, after all—is that in moments of critical contemplation, it is often hard to know where the competencies of soldiers and scientists and all the rest of us begin and end. Many an accidental judgment can emerge from such confusions.

But what if the conclusions of the scientists had been correct? What if some kind 23. of demonstration had been staged in a lightly occupied part of Japan and it *had* been greeted as a firecracker in the desert? What then?

Let me shift gears for a moment and discuss the subject in another way. It is 24. standard wisdom for everyone in the United States old enough to remember the war, and for most of those to whom it is ancient history, that the bombings of Hiroshima and Nagasaki were the only alternative to an all-out invasion of the Japanese mainland involving hundreds of thousands and perhaps millions of casualties on both sides. Unless the Japanese came to understand the need to surrender quickly, we would have been drawn by an almost magnetic force toward those dreaded beaches. This has become an almost automatic pairing of ideas, an article of common lore. If you lament that so many civilians were incinerated or blown to bits in Hiroshima and Nagasaki, then somebody will remind you of the American lives thus saved. Truman was the person most frequently asked to account for the bombings, and his views were emphatic on the subject:

> It was a question of saving hundreds of thousands of American lives.
> I don't mind telling you that you don't feel normal when you have to
> plan hundreds of thousands of complete, final deaths of American boys
> who are alive and joking and having fun while you are doing your
> planning. You break your heart and your head trying to figure out a
> way to save one life. The name given to our invasion plan was "Olym-
> pic," but I saw nothing godly about the killing of all the people that
> would be necessary to make that invasion. I could not worry about
> what history would say about my personal morality. I made the only
> decision I ever knew how to make. I did what I thought was right.

Veterans of the war, and particularly those who had reason to suppose that they 25. would have been involved in an invasion, have drawn that same connection repeatedly, most recently Paul Fussell in the pages of *The New Republic*. Thank God for the bomb, the argument goes, it saved the lives of countless numbers of us. And so, in a sense, it may have.

But the destruction of Hiroshima and Nagasaki had nothing to do with it. It only 26. makes sense to assume, even if few people were well enough positioned in early August to see the situation whole, that there simply was not going to be an invasion. Not ever.

For what sane power, with the atomic weapon securely in its arsenal, would hurl 27. a million or more of its sturdiest young men on a heavily fortified mainland? To imagine anyone ordering an invasion when the means were at hand to blast Japan into a sea of gravel at virtually no cost in American lives is to imagine a madness beyond anything even the worst of war can induce. The invasion had not yet been called off, granted. But it surely would have been, and long before the November 1 deadline set for it.

The United States did not become a nuclear power on August 6, with the **28.** destruction of Hiroshima. It became a nuclear power on July 16, when the first test device was exploded in Alamogordo, New Mexico. Uncertainties remained, of course, many of them. But from that moment on, the United States knew how to produce a bomb, knew how to deliver it and knew it would work. Stimson said shortly after the war that the bombings of Hiroshima and Nagasaki ''ended the ghastly specter of a clash of great land armies,'' but he could have said, with greater justice, that the ghastly specter ended at Alamogordo. Churchill came close to making exactly that point when he first learned of the New Mexico test:

> To quell the Japanese resistance man by man and conquer the country
> yard by yard might well require the loss of a million American lives
> and half that number of British. . . . Now all the nightmare picture had
> vanished.

It *had* vanished. The age of inch-by-inch crawling over enemy territory, the age **29.** of Guadalcanal and Iwo Jima and Okinawa, was just plain over.

The point is that once we had the bomb and were committed to its use, the **30.** terrible weight of invasion no longer hung over our heads. The Japanese were incapable of mounting any kind of offensive, as every observer has agreed, and it was our option when to close with the enemy and thus risk casualties. So we could have easily afforded to hold for a moment, to think it over, to introduce what Dwight Eisenhower called ''that awful thing'' to the world on the basis of something closer to mature consideration. We could have afforded to detonate a bomb over some less lethal target and then pause to see what happened. And do it a second time, maybe a third. And if none of those demonstrations had made a difference, presumably we would have had to strike harder: Hiroshima and Nagasaki would still have been there a few weeks later for that purpose, silent and untouched—''unspoiled'' was the term Gen. H. H. Arnold used—for whatever came next. Common lore also has it that there were not bombs enough for such niceties, but that seems not to have been the case. The United States was ready to deliver a third bomb toward the end of August, and Groves had already informed Marshall and Stimson that three or four more bombs would be available in September, a like number in October, at least five in November, and seven in December, with substantial increases to follow in early 1946. Even if we assume that Groves was being too hopeful about the productive machinery he had set in motion, as one expert close to the matter has suggested, a formidable number of bombs would have been available by the date originally set for invasion.

Which brings us back to the matter of momentum. The best way to tell the story **31.** of those days is to say that the ''decision to drop'' had become a force like gravity. It had taken life. The fact that it existed supplied its meaning, its reason for being. Elting E. Morison, Stimson's biographer, put it well:

> Any process started by men toward a special end tends, for reasons log-
> ical, biological, aesthetic or whatever they may be, to carry forward, if
> other things remain equal, to its climax. [This is] the inertia developed

in a human system. . . . In a process where such a general tendency
has been set to work it is difficult to separate the moment when men
were still free to choose from the moment, if such there was, when
they were no longer free to choose.

I have said very little about Nagasaki so far because it was not the subject of any **32.**
thought at all. The orders of the bomber command were to attack Japan as soon as the
bombs were ready. One was ready on August 9. Boom. When Groves was later asked
why the attack on Nagasaki had come so soon after the attack on Hiroshima, leaving
so little time for the Japanese to consider what had happened to them, he simply said:
"Once you get your opponent reeling, you keep him reeling and never let him recover."
And that is the point, really. There is no law of nature that compels a winning side to
press its superiority, but it is hard to slow down, hard to relinquish an advantage, hard
to rein the fury. The impulse to charge ahead, to strike at the throat, is so strong a habit
of war that it almost ranks as a reflex, and if that thought does not frighten us when
we consider our present nuclear predicament, nothing will. Many a casual slaughter
can emerge from such moods.

If it is true, as I have suggested, that there were few military or logistic reasons **33.**
for striking as sharply as we did and that the decision to drop moved in on the crest
of an almost irreversible current, then it might be sensible to ask, on the fortieth
anniversary of the event, what some of the drifts were that became a part of that larger
current. An adequate accounting would have to consider a number of military, political
and other matters far beyond the reach of this brief essay, the most important of them
by far being the degree to which the huge shadow of the Soviet Union loomed over
both official meetings and private thoughts. It is nearly impossible to read the remaining
record without assuming that the wish to make a loud announcement to the Russians
was a persuasive factor in the minds of many of the principal participants. There were
other drifts as well, of course, and I would like to note a few of the sort that sometimes
occur to social scientists.

For one thing, an extraordinary amount of money and material had been invested **34.**
in the Manhattan Project—both of them in short supply in a wartime economy—and
many observers thought that so large a public expense would be all the more willingly
borne if it were followed by a striking display of what the money had been spent for.

And, too, extraordinary investments had been made in men and talent, both of **35.**
them in short supply in a wartime economy. The oldest of the people involved in the
Manhattan Project—soldiers, engineers and scientists—made sacrifices in the form of
separated families, interrupted careers and a variety of other discomforts, and it makes
a certain psychological sense that a decisive strike would serve as a kind of vindication
for all the trouble. The youngest of them, though, had been held out of combat, thus
avoiding the fate of so many men of their generation, by accidents of professional
training, personal skill and sheer timing. The project was their theater of war, and it
makes even more psychological sense that some of them would want the only shot
they fired to be a truly resonant one.

The dropping of such a bomb, moreover, could serve as an ending, something **36.**
sharp and distinct in a world that had become ever more blurred. The Grand Alliance

was breaking up, and with it all hope for a secure postwar world. Roosevelt was dead. The future was full of ambiguity. And, most important, everybody was profoundly tired. In circumstances like that, a resounding strike would serve to clarify things, to give them form, to tidy them up a bit.

37. There are other matters one might point to, some of them minor, some of them major, all of them strands in the larger weave. There was a feeling, expressed by scientists and government officials alike, that the world needed a rude and decisive shock to awaken it to the realities of the atomic age. There was a feeling, hard to convey in words but easy to sense once one has become immersed in some of the available material, that the bomb had so much power and majesty, was so compelling a force, that one was almost required to give it birth and a chance to mature. There was a feeling, born of war, that for all its ferocity the atomic bomb was nevertheless no more than a minor increment on a scale of horror that already included the firebombings of Tokyo and other Japanese cities. And there was a feeling, also born of war, that living creatures on the other side, even the children, had somehow lost title to the mercies that normally accompany the fact of being human.

38. The kinds of points I have been making need to be stated either very precisely or in some detail. I have not yet learned to do the former; I do not have space enough here for the latter. So let me just end with the observation that human decisions do not always emerge from reflective counsels where facts are arrayed in order and logic is the prevailing currency of thought. They emerge from complex fields of force, in which the vanities of leaders and the moods of constituencies and the inertias of bureaucracies play a critical part. That is as important a lesson as one can learn from the events of 1945—and as unnerving a one.

39. The bombings of Hiroshima and Nagasaki supply a rich case study for people who must live in times like ours. It is not important for us to apportion shares of responsibility to persons who played their parts so long ago, and I have not meant to do so here: these were unusually decent and compassionate people for the most part, operating with reflexes that had been tempered by war. We need to attend to such histories as this, however, because they provide the clearest illustrations we have of what human beings can do—this being the final moral to be drawn from our parable—when they find themselves in moments of crisis and literally have more destructive power at their disposal than they know what to do with. That is as good an argument for disarming as any that can be imagined.

WORKING WITH THE TEXT

Cultural and Historical References

In this section, the numbers at the margin refer to the numbered paragraphs in the selection itself.

3. Albert Einstein had written a letter to President Roosevelt that it was now feasible to build a fission bomb.

6. Robert Oppenheimer, a physicist, was one of the architects of the Manhattan Project.

12. Edward Teller was one of the physicists who worked on the Manhattan Project.

21. Ruth Benedict and Margaret Mead were cultural anthropologists—and thus experts in "exotic" human behavior.

Writing Assignments: The Paragraph

Be sure to provide an introduction for each of the following paragraph writing assignments. That is, begin each paragraph with a phrase like this: "Thomas Brickle claims that. . . ." When it is relevant, you might also want to identify the expertise of the author ("Thomas Brickle, a New Testament scholar, claims that. . . ."), the name of the book or article, the century and country in which the work appeared, or any other circumstances that your readers might find significant. For more on this, see pp. 11–13 in Chapter 2.

1. Metaphors usually clarify an abstraction. Support that statement by discussing the metaphor in paragraph 5.

2. How does the conclusion in the very last paragraph follow from what preceded it?

3. Explain the reason Erikson gives for the decision to bomb Nagasaki.

Writing Assignments: The Short Essay

Use informal documentation for these short essays. That is, don't use footnotes or a Works Cited page to document your sources. Instead, cite only relevant information about your source, and keep that information *within* your text. Then follow the summary or quote with a page number in parentheses. (Use the page numbers that you find in this book to represent the page numbers of the source.) Thus, your informal documentation will look something like this:

> In *The Rising Sun*, John Toland says that in the instant after the A-bomb attack on Hiroshima, "All over the center of the city numerous silhouettes were imprinted on walls" (p. 468).

1. Describe the options to dropping the bomb.

2. Erikson argues that there would never have been an invasion of the Japanese mainland. What is his major argument (in paragraph 27)? Is there a reasonable argument on the other side? Try to argue the other side.

3. In paragraph 30 Erikson rejects the frequently cited justification for dropping the atomic bombs by concluding that "once we had the bomb

and were committed to its use, the terrible weight of invasion no longer hung over our heads." Summarize and analyze Erikson's discussion (throughout the remainder of the essay) of the complex influences which led to the decision to bomb Japanese cities at the earliest opportunity, despite the fact that with such weapons in our arsenal, we could have afforded to be more patient with Japan.

DID AMERICA HAVE TO DROP THE BOMB?

Gar Alperovitz

Gar Alperovitz is the author of *Atomic Diplomacy: Hiroshima and Potsdam* (1965). One of the early revisionist historians of the Hiroshima issue, Alperovitz argues that President Truman's prime motive for dropping the bomb was to send a political message to Stalin in the aftermath of the Potsdam Treaty negotiations. Alperovitz quotes Truman administration memos and statements extensively in his effort to demonstrate his thesis.

The ambassador had just had a long private meeting with President Harry S 1. Truman, in office less than six weeks following the death of Franklin D. Roosevelt. Truman had told him two extraordinary things: First, if all went well, the United States would soon possess a weapon of awesome and hitherto unknown power.

Charging him with "utmost secrecy," Truman revealed something "which I 2. have not told anybody"—that he had decided to postpone negotiations with Stalin on the shape of the postwar world until he knew for sure whether the weapon really worked.

"I was startled, shocked and amazed," Joseph E. Davies, former U.S. envoy to 3. the Soviet Union, wrote in his diary on May 21, 1945 after the meeting. In an asterisked footnote he added: "Uranium—for reason of security I will have to fill this in later."

On July 16, the first atom bomb was tested successfully at Alamogordo, N.M. 4. On July 17, Truman sat down to talk with Stalin. And on Aug. 6, a bomb would fall on Hiroshima, ultimately killing an estimated 130,000 Japanese and changing the world.

Now, 40 years later, revelations based on privately held and previously classified 5. information continue to illuminate the complex decision-making that led to the destruction of Hiroshima and Nagasaki.

Most Americans assume the reason Hiroshima and Nagasaki were destroyed was 6. simply to prevent a costly invasion of Japan.

However, the newest documents have strengthened the theory that other consider- 7. ations—especially the new weapon's impact on diplomacy toward the Soviet Union—were involved.

The invasion of Japan—which President Truman claimed might cost up to a 8. million casualties—was scheduled to begin on Nov. 1 with a landing on the island of

Source: Gar Alperovitz, "Did America Have to Drop the Bomb?" *The Washington Post.* August 4, 1985, sec. B: 1, 4.

Kyushu, with a full invasion in the spring of 1946. (Documents of the time suggest that many planners foresaw far fewer casualties.)

But by the mid-summer of 1945 Japan was in a very bad way. How allied **9.** intelligence understood the situation at the time was detailed in a report to the American and British Combined Chiefs of Staff, made public in 1976:

"The increasing effects of sea blockade and cumulative devastation wrought by **10.** strategic bombing . . . has already rendered millions homeless and has destroyed from 25 percent to 50 percent of the built-up area of Japan's most important cities. . . . A conditional surrender . . . might be offered by them at any time. . . ."

The Japanese code had been broken early in the war. Faint peace feelers appeared **11.** as early as September 1944.

In July, Secretary of the Navy James V. Forrestal's diary described the latest **12.** cables as "real evidence of a Japanese desire to get out of the war. . . ."

Forrestal was referring to a message from Togo to his ambassador in Moscow **13.** instructing him to see Molotov before he and Stalin left to meet Truman at the Potsdam Conference. The Japanese envoy was "to lay before him the emperor's strong desire to secure a termination of the war."

Forrestal noted that "Togo said further that the unconditional surrender terms of **14.** the Allies was [sic] about the only thing in the way. . . ."

Discussion of surrender was also underway through a channel in Switzerland. In **15.** a recently discovered memo dated May 12, William J. Donovan, director of the Office of Strategic Services, told Truman that an OSS source had "talked with Shunichi Kase, the Japanese minister to Switzerland. . . . Kase expressed a wish to help arrange for a cessation of hostilities. . . ."

Donovan reported the same judgment as that contained in the intercepted **16.** cables—a slight change in the surrender formula seemed the only remaining issue: "One of the few provisions . . . would be the retention of the emperor. . . ."

Did top U.S. officials understand the import of the cables? There was, to be sure, **17.** the possibility that the initial feelers were without substance. However, Truman's diary, discovered in 1978, terms the key intercepted message "the telegram from Jap emperor asking for peace."

Adm. William D. Leahy, who served as chief of staff to the president and presided **18.** over the Joint Chiefs of Staff, wrote in his diary in mid-June that "at the present time . . . a surrender of Japan can be arranged with terms that can be accepted by Japan and that will make fully satisfactory provision for America's defense against future trans-Pacific aggression." Afterwards, Leahy would reflect that "the use of this barbarous weapon at Hiroshima and Nagasaki was of no material assistance in our war against Japan. . . ."

Likewise, Eisenhower would later state that "it wasn't necessary" to hit the **19.** Japanese "with that awful thing." On July 20, 1945, in front of Gen. Omar Bradley, he advised Truman of his objections.

There is some confusion as to precisely how other top military figures felt, **20.** particularly in the crucial last month before Hiroshima. There is no doubt, of course, that they approved planning for an invasion.

The important question is whether by July and early August military planners **21.** still believed an invasion would be required if the atomic bomb was not used.

Adm. Ernest J. King, commander in chief of the U.S. Fleet, had for much of the   **22.**
war argued that naval blockade would secure unconditional surrender without an
invasion.

The top Army air forces commander, Gen. H.H. "Hap" Arnold, said uncondition-   **23.**
al surrender could be won by October. He outlined the devastation that would hit the
Japanese population, with its enormous casualties.

"Japan, in fact, will become a nation without cities, with her transportation   **24.**
disrupted and will have tremendous difficulty in holding her people together for
continued resistance."

Precisely how the leading Army figure, Gen. George C. Marshall, felt is not   **25.**
entirely clear. On the one hand, Marshall pressed forward on invasion planning, but
he also urged changing the surrender formula and, as we shall see, advised of the
importance of a Russian declaration of war.

As for the troops in the field: "Every individual moving to the Pacific," Marshall   **26.**
said, "should be indoctrinated with a firm determination to see it through."

Once the new weapon had been proven, the military leaders went along with the   **27.**
president's decision to use it. But this fact has often led subsequent observers to confuse
approval with the question of whether, as Eisenhower put it, the weapon was still
deemed "mandatory as a measure to save American lives." Strategy for the bomb was
in any event largely handled outside the normal chain of command by the president
and his advisers.

Did the president understand the possibility that the atomic bomb was not required   **28.**
to prevent an invasion? On this question there is much dispute. However, the documents
now available make it very difficult to believe he did not.

First, Truman was repeatedly advised that a change in the unconditional surrender   **29.**
formula allowing Japan to keep the emperor seemed likely to end the war. There is
also documentation—from the diaries of Secretary of War Henry L. Stimson, acting
Secretary of State Joseph C. Grew and from British Prime Minister Winston Churchill—
confirming that the president did not regard such a change as major. And in the end,
of course, he did make such a change after the bomb was used.

It is sometimes argued that the Japanese military would have prevented a   **30.**
surrender had the atomic bomb not been used. But this argument usually assumes there
would have been no change in the surrender formula. Given the right terms, as Leahy
put it, "We were certain that the Mikado could stop the war with a royal word."

Of course, the president preferred not to alter the terms if possible.   **31.**

The idea that the atomic bomb had to be used to avoid an invasion turns on   **32.**
whether or not there were other options.

As early as September 1944, Churchill felt the Japanese might collapse when   **33.**
Russia entered the war. On May 21, 1945, Secretary of War Stimson advised of the
"profound military effect" of Soviet entry.

In mid-June, Marshall advised the president that "the impact of Russian entry   **34.**
on the already hopeless Japanese may well be the decisive action levering them into
capitulation at that time or shortly thereafter if we land in Japan."

A month later the Combined British-U.S. Joint Chiefs of Staff discussed the   **35.**
Russian option at Potsdam. Gen. Sir Hastings Ismay summarized the Combined
Intelligence Staffs' conclusion for Churchill: "If and when Russia came into the war

against Japan the Japanese would probably wish to get out on almost any terms short of the dethronement of the emperor.''

Did the president also understand the advice that the Russian declaration of war **36.** was likely to bring about capitulation?

After his first meeting with Stalin on July 17, 1945—three weeks before **37.** Hiroshima—the president noted in his diary:

"He'll be in the Jap war on August 15th. Fini Japs when that comes about.'' **38.**

It is clear that the president preferred to end the war without Russian help, but **39.** that does not mean that he had no alternative but to use the atomic bomb. We now know he rejected Russian help for political, not military, reasons.

The original planning date for Russian entry into the war was Aug. 8. Hiroshima **40.** was bombed on Aug. 6 and Nagasaki on Aug. 9.

The person for whom the linkage between the atomic bomb and strategy towards **41.** Russia was most direct was Secretary of State James F. Byrnes—Truman's chief adviser both on diplomacy and on the atomic bomb.

Byrnes was a complex, secretive, even devious politician. In his diary Truman **42.** refers to him at this time as ''conniving.''

There is unmistakable evidence that Byrnes tried to rewrite the historical record, **43.** in part by destroying documents, in part by literally rewriting the private diaries of his assistant, Warren Brown—and passing them off to official government archivists as authentic.

In any case, Forrestal's diaries show Byrnes ''most anxious to get the Japanese **44.** affair over with before the Russians got in. . . .'' It was also Byrnes who formally proposed that the bomb be targeted on a factory surrounded as closely as possible by workers' housing to achieve maximum psychological effect.

Ambassador Davies, who was ''shocked, startled and amazed'' when told of the **45.** decision to postpone talks with Stalin, was disturbed by ''Byrnes' attitude that the atomic bomb assured ultimate success in negotiations. . . .'' On July 28, 1945 Davies warned him that ''the threat wouldn't work, and might do irreparable harm.''

Byrnes was particularly worried that if the Russians entered the Japanese war **46.** they would get control of Manchuria and north China. He was also concerned about Eastern Europe. Roosevelt had selected Byrnes—his ''assistant president'' at the time—as the leading public advocate and defender of the famous Yalta agreement which promised democracy and free elections in Eastern Europe.

Though at Yalta Byrnes participated in cutting the teeth out of language that **47.** would have made the agreement more than a statement of general intentions, recent research indicates he hoped the atomic bomb would enforce in practice what had been signed away in principle.

According to atomic scientist Leo Szilard, who met with Byrnes on May 28, **48.** 1945—10 weeks before Hiroshima: ''Mr. Byrnes did not argue that it was necessary to use the bomb against the cities of Japan in order to win the war. . . .'' Byrnes ''was concerned about Russia's postwar behavior.

''Russian troops had moved into Hungary and Rumania; Byrnes thought it would **49.** be very difficult to persuade Russia to withdraw . . . and that Russia might be more manageable if impressed by American military might.

''I shared Byrnes's concern . . .'' Szilard observed, ''but I was completely **50.**

flabbergasted by the assumption that rattling the bomb might make Russia more manageable. . . .''

There is no evidence Byrnes used the atomic bomb as an explicit threat, but a **51.** month after the Potsdam meeting with Stalin, for example, Stimson talked with him at the White House, and noted in his diary: ''I found that Byrnes was very much against any attempt to cooperate with Russia. His mind is full of his problems with the coming meeting of foreign ministers, and he looks to having the presence of the bomb in his pocket, so to speak, as a great weapon. . . .''

Byrnes, who previously had been senator from South Carolina, was on very **52.** intimate terms with the president. He had, in fact, acted as Truman's mentor when he went to the Senate from Missouri. Roosevelt had also seemingly selected Byrnes to be vice president in 1944, switching only at the last minute to Truman.

One of the reasons Truman made Byrnes secretary of state was that this move **53.** put Byrnes next in line of succession for the presidency after Truman moved up from vice president.

On May 3, 1945, Truman also asked Byrnes to be his representative on the **54.** ''Interim Committee'' studying atomic strategy—and there were numerous meetings between the two men throughout the summer.

Truman and Byrnes left Washington together on July 7 to meet with Stalin at **55.** Potsdam, where Stimson complained that Byrnes was ''hugging matters pretty close to his bosom.''

Before the Potsdam conference Truman was also advised by Stimson: ''We shall **56.** probably hold more cards in our hands later than now.'' During the conference Truman was enormously bolstered by the successful atomic test. ''Now I know what happened to Truman yesterday,'' Churchill observed. ''I couldn't understand it. When he got to the meeting after having read this report [of the atomic test] he was a changed man.''

''He told the Russians just where they got on and off and generally bossed the **57.** whole meeting.''

He also told Stalin that America had developed a powerful new weapon, but did **58.** not specify that it was atomic.

There are still many unanswered questions about the decisions made during the **59.** month before Hiroshima. However, there is little doubt about some things. Had the United States so desired, either the forthcoming Russian declaration of war or a change in the surrender formula (or both together) seemed likely to end the war without the atomic bomb. There was also plenty of time to use the weapon if these options failed in the three months before the Kyushu landing.

''The historic fact remains, and must be judged in the aftertime,'' Churchill **60.** subsequently observed, ''that the decision whether or not to use the atomic bomb . . . was never even an issue.'' It is possible that top policy makers, especially the president, simply wanted to leave no stone unturned to end the war.

However, in the view of what we now know about Japan's attempt to surrender, **61.** military factors alone appear inadequate to explain the choice.

As historian Martin Sherwin put it, the idea the atomic bomb would help make **62.** Russia manageable both in Asia and in Europe was an important consideration—''inextricably involved.''

In mid-May America's leaders had postponed negotiations with Stalin, basing **63.**

their strategy on the assumption the bomb would strengthen their hand. Thereafter, some of those most intimately involved in diplomacy—unlike some of the top military figures—apparently were either unable or unwilling to understand the significance of the June and July information on Japan's collapse.

The evidence that diplomatic considerations were very important is especially **64.** clear in connection with the president's closest adviser, Byrnes. Nevertheless, 40 years after the fact some government documents still remain classified. It may be that when these are finally released—perhaps when still other diaries are discovered—we will know the full story.

WORKING WITH THE TEXT

Cultural and Historical References

In this section, the numbers at the margin refer to the numbered paragraphs in the selection itself.

13. Shigenori Togo was the foreign minister of Kantaro Suziki, Japan's last wartime Premier.

30. The Mikado is another name for the emperor of Japan, who was revered as a deity.

46. Churchill, Stalin, and Truman met at Yalta to decide what was to become of the defeated nations and their territories.

48. Leo Szilard was a physicist and one of the architects of the Manhattan Project that created the A-bomb.

55. Potsdam, a German city, was the site of a number of Allied meetings to discuss what was to happen after the war was over.

Writing Assignments: The Paragraph

Be sure to provide an introduction for each of the following paragraph writing assignments. That is, begin each paragraph with a phrase like this: "Thomas Brickle claims that. . . ." When it is relevant, you might also want to identify the expertise of the author ("Thomas Brickle, a New Testament scholar, claims that. . . ."), the name of the book or article, the century and country in which the work appeared, or any other circumstances that your readers might find significant. For more on this, see pp. 11–13 in Chapter 2.

1. Sum up the two reasons for Alperovitz's belief that the war could have been ended without the use of the A-bomb.

2. What is Alperovitz's reason for beginning with those particular first three paragraphs? That is, how do they serve his ultimate purpose? Write a paragraph.

3. Summarize the evidence which Alperovitz cites in his efforts to demon-

strate that by mid-1945 Japanese leaders were actively seeking to end the war.

Writing Assignments: The Short Essay

Use informal documentation for these short essays. That is, don't use footnotes or a Works Cited page to document your sources. Instead, cite only relevant information about your source, and keep that information *within* your text. Then follow the summary or quote with a page number in parentheses. (Use the page numbers that you find in this book to represent the page numbers of the source.) Thus, your informal documentation will look something like this:

> In *The Rising Sun*, John Toland says that in the instant after the A-bomb attack on Hiroshima, "All over the center of the city numerous silhouettes were imprinted on walls" (p. 468).

1. Alperovitz argues that Truman dropped the A-bomb to impress Russia. What evidence does he marshal to back up that idea?
2. Discuss James Byrnes's role in all this political maneuvering.
3. Sum up Alperovitz's essay.
4. Argue the other side. Use what you can find in Alperovitz's essay to support your argument.

DID AMERICA HAVE TO DROP THE BOMB?

Chalmers M. Roberts

Chalmers M. Roberts is a former diplomatic correspondent for *The Washington Post*. During World War II he was a Pentagon intelligence officer who, shortly after the war ended, flew over the island of Japan and saw the immense preparations the Japanese had made in order to defend their island.

For 40 years many Americans, and foreigners too, have been contending that the United **1.** States never should have dropped the bomb on Hiroshima, that Japan was so battered and beaten it was on the point of surrender. They reject the counter-argument that only use of that dreadful weapon forced the surrender and thus avoided the heavy loss of life inevitable if the planned invasion of Japan had taken place.

Because I played a small role in this matter and because, by sheer coincidence, **2.** I was flying over the initial invasion beach in Japan on Nov. 1, 1945, the day it was to begin, I want to cite the record as I've been able to accumulate it, including some from recent digging into the National Archives.

That record, to me, is overwhelming that Harry S Truman, president only four **3.** months when he made the decision, chose to drop the bomb essentially to end the war

Source: Chalmers M. Roberts, "Did America Have to Drop the Bomb?" *The Washington Post.* August 4, 1985, sec. B: 1, 4.

in a hurry and save American lives. In his 1955 memoirs, Truman wrote: "In all, it had been estimated that it would require until the late fall of 1946 to bring Japan to her knees." And: "Gen. Marshall told me that it might cost half a million American lives to force the enemy's surrender on his home grounds."

On July 18, 1945, when he was at the Potsdam Conference with Stalin and **4.** Churchill and just after he heard that the Alamogordo, N.M., test was a success and after Stalin had promised to join the war on Aug. 15, Truman wrote to his wife in a letter not disclosed until 1983: "I'll say that we'll end the war a year sooner now, and think of the kids who won't be killed! That is the important thing."

On June 15, 1945, Gen. George C. Marshall, Army chief of staff, sent a message, **5.** recently declassified, to Gen. Douglas MacArthur, then planning to lead the invasion: "The president is very much concerned as to the number of casualties we will receive in the Olympic operation [code name for the first phase of the invasion]. . . . This will be discussed with the president. . . ."

At a meeting that took place on June 18 Marshall inquired about a MacArthur **6.** staff report that "for planning purposes" had estimated "battle casualties" for the first 90 days at 105,050 plus non-battle casualties of 12,600. MacArthur's response was to brush this aside as an "academic and routine" estimate, adding: "I do not anticipate such a high rate of loss." He went on to argue that the invasion's decisive effect will eventually save lives by eliminating wasteful operations of non-decisive character," doubtless meaning those of his Navy rival, Adm. Chester W. Nimitz.

The general, who later would contend that by 1945 he had felt Russian intervention **7.** "had become superfluous," added that "the hazard and loss will be greatly lessened if an attack is launched from Siberia sufficiently ahead of our target date to commit the enemy to major combat."

At the June 18 meeting Marshall put the casualty estimate for the first 30 days **8.** at 31,000. MacArthur's staff estimate for the same initial phase had been 50,800.

Some revisionist historians have contended that Truman's bomb decision had an **9.** anti-Soviet cast, that it was designed to use the American monopoloy for atomic blackmail. The evidence to support such a view is certainly thin and scanty, although Truman was shortly to become a cold warrior. Others contend that the million casualties estimate was ridiculous, at best simply a typical Pentagon worst-case figure.

In a recent case study, for example, Roger Hilsman, a World War II military **10.** intelligence officer and later the State Department's intelligence chief, put it this way: "Although no one knows where he got his figures, Stimson also told Truman that an invasion . . . would cost a million American casualties, not to mention Japanese casualties." Hilsman contended that Marshall's estimate of the invasion cost was not 1 million but only 40,000. For this Hilsman relied on a 1968 book by Nuel Pharr Davis in which Davis, without giving any source, flatly stated that "Marshall estimated the cost at 40,000." I think this figure is in error.

Secretary of War Henry L. Stimson wrote in his 1947 memoirs, done in **11.** collaboration with McGeorge Bundy, that the invasion plans would involve military and naval forces "of the order of 5 million men" or more and that "we estimated that if we should be forced to carry this plan to its conclusion, the major fighting would not end until the latter part of 1946, at the earliest. I was informed that such operations might be expected to cost over a million casualties to American forces alone. . . ."

Stimson called use of the bomb "our least abhorrent choice" for ending the **12.**
American fire raids, lifting the blockade and avoiding the "the ghastly specter of a
clash of great land armies. . . ." In his public report at war's end, Marshall wrote that
"defending the homeland the enemy had an army of 2 million, a remaining air strength
of 8,000 planes of all types, training and combat."

After leaving the presidency, Truman in a television interview said "it was **13.**
estimated" that the initial invasion of the southernmost island of Kyushu, Operation
Olympic, "would cost 700,000 men—250,000 of our youngsters to be killed and
500,000 of them to be maimed for life." Those figures doubtless stretch any 1945
estimate. But Truman that day also referred to another key factor in his decision: the
murderous Okinawa campaign that had lasted from April 1 to June 21 and had cost
48,000 American casualties.

The key import of Okinawa in affecting the Truman decision was the mass **14.**
employment of so-called suicide aircraft, known in Japanese as *kamikaze*. The toll on
American ships by these one-way pilots had been the greatest in the Navy's history:
30 vessels sunk and 368 ships damaged including 10 battleships and 13 aircraft carriers.
At the June 18 White House meeting Truman had commented that he hoped to avoid "an
Okinawa from one end of Japan to the other." And on the TV program he recalled that
bloody Okinawa "gave us some idea of what we had to do in order to defeat the
Japanese. . . ."

A U.S. Fleet Headquarters estimate as of Aug. 9, the day the second bomb was **15.**
dropped on Nagasaki, totaled the Japanese army and navy aircraft still available in the
home islands as 3,669 and of these 1,115 were in western Japan, the Kyushu area.
During the Okinawa assault by *kamikazes* the Navy had begun to include in its estimate
of enemy aircraft both training and combat units because trainers were being used in
battle. However, the Navy said, "not included in this estimate is a substantial number
of training types which may be used for suicide attacks, especially at night."

By that time I was a military intelligence officer in the Pentagon, in charge of **16.**
tracking the *kamikaze* units in the Army Air Force on the basis of intercepted Japanese
military messages. And the reason I was flying, with three other officers, over that
initial invasion beach, at Miyazaki on Kyushu, was that at war's end I had gone to
Japan where I headed an eight-man team checking up on our intelligence estimates,
part of the U.S. Strategic Bomb Survey.

The Miyazaki beach, barely 30 miles long, looked like an ideal landing spot, **17.**
long and gently sloping to the sea, the biggest beach on the island. But it was terribly
shallow and behind it rose a range from which murderous fire on the beaches would
have been possible.

My notes show that at Oita, in northern Kyushu, we found Japanese biplane **18.**
trainers with bomb racks loaded for *kamikaze* pilots, that at Karasehara further south
the now meek Japanese officers furnished order-of-battle documents to show that at
war's end they had 56,000 troops dug in with another 70,000 in reserve and that there
were many planes, 850 regular planes plus 790 suicide planes, a total of 1,640 tucked
into the aircraft at air strips or hillsides.

A general told me "we were figuring on 1,000 planes, special attack *kamikaze* **19.**
type" for defense against allied landings on Kyushu. There was a gasoline shortage
but some ingenious substitutes already had been used. The Japanese told us they figured
we would land on Miyazaki beach—where else, they asked?

One Japanese general, once an assistant military attache in Washington, broke **20.**

down and cried as he told us how he had planned to go out with his men on a large scale suicide mission on Aug. 16. A few others actually did so after the surrender. A lieutenant colonel objected to the American use of the word ''suicide,'' calling it a ''misnomer.'' ''The pilot,'' he told me, ''did not start out on his mission with the intention of commiting suicide. He looked upon himself as a human bomb which would destroy a certain part of the enemy fleet for his country. They considered it a glorious thing, while a suicide may not be so glorious.''

I have no doubt that my Pentagon shop's estimates of *kamikaze* strength were **21.** fed into the weekly order-of-battle tables that worked their way up the chain of command to become a fragment of what was put before Marshall, Stimson and Truman. In 1948 Stimson obviously depended on such figures in writing that ''the air force had been reduced mainly to reliance upon *kamikaze*, or suicide, attacks. These latter, however, had already inflicted serious damage on our seagoing forces, and their possible effectiveness in a last ditch fight was a matter of real concern to our naval leaders.''

Stimson summarized: ''As we understood it in July, there was a very strong **22.** possibility that the Japanese government might determine upon resistance to the end, in all the areas of the Far East under its control. In such an event the Allies would be faced with the enormous task of destroying an armed force of 5 million men and 5,000 suicide aircraft, belonging to a race which had already amply demonstrated its ability to fight literally to the death.''

The last word should come from Marshall on whom the responsibility must **23.** ultimately rest for the estimates, however good or bad the intelligence work on which he had to depend. On June 11, 1947, not long after Stimson's initial account had appeared in Harper's magazine, the general, now secretary of state, ruminated with David Lilienthal, head of the Atomic Energy Commission, who recounted Marshall's comments in his diary:

''There has been a good deal of discussion about whether we were justified in **24.** using the atomic bomb. . . . One of the things that appalled me was the cost, in casualties, of an invasion. . . . Even an ill-equipped force can cost terrible losses to a landing party. To get to the plains [of eastern Japan] would have been a very costly operation, in lives. We knew the Japanese were determined and fanatical . . . and we would have to exterminate them, almost man by man. So we thought the bomb would be a wonderful weapon as a protection and preparation for landings. But we didn't realize its value to give the Japanese such a shock that that they could surrender without complete loss of face. . . . What he [Stimson] said as to the considerations that were weighed is entirely true. But we missed one of the most important consequences.''

It is easy now, 40 years later, to forget the passions, bitterness, hatred, the faulty **25.** intelligence, misjudgments and sheer stupidities of the war. Using the bomb, especially against non-whites, certainly has hurt the United States in the eyes of many worldwide. But even at such a cost and even at this remove, to one who had some small role in it all, it seems to have been the right choice.

WORKING WITH THE TEXT

Cultural and Historical References

In this section, the numbers at the margin refer to the numbered paragraphs in the selection itself.

4. The Potsdam Conference was a meeting of the leaders of the United States, England, and Russia about the makeup of the postwar world.

9. What is a "revisionist" history? Can you tell from the context?

9. Truman is said to be a cold warrior. What does that mean? Can you tell from the context?

13. Okinawa was a Japanese island in the Pacific where American forces took huge casualties from heavily entrenched Japanese forces.

Writing Assignments: The Paragraph

Be sure to provide an introduction for each of the following paragraph writing assignments. That is, begin each paragraph with a phrase like this: "Thomas Brickle claims that. . . ." When it is relevant, you might also want to identify the expertise of the author ("Thomas Brickle, a New Testament scholar, claims that. . . ."), the name of the book or article, the century and country in which the work appeared, or any other circumstances that your readers might find significant. For more on this, see pp. 11–13 in Chapter 2.

1. Summarize in a paragraph Roberts's comments on Japanese resolve to defend Japan to the last person.

2. Write a paragraph in which you show how Roberts's personal experience lends credibility to his account.

3. Summarize and very briefly discuss the possible influence of the bloody Okinawa campaign on Truman's decision to drop the bomb.

Writing Assignments: The Short Essay

Use informal documentation for these short essays. That is, don't use footnotes or a Works Cited page to document your sources. Instead, cite only relevant information about your source, and keep that information *within* your text. Then follow the summary or quote with a page number in parentheses. (Use the page numbers that you find in this book to represent the page numbers of the source.) Thus, your informal documentation will look something like this:

> In *The Rising Sun*, John Toland says that in the instant after the A-bomb attack on Hiroshima, "All over the center of the city numerous silhouettes were imprinted on walls" (p. 468).

1. Do you find Roberts's account persuasive? Why? Why not?

2. What is Roberts's purpose in discussing at such length the number of lives that would have been lost by invading the Japanese mainland? How does he persuade us that his are the correct figures? What is his most powerful argument?

3. Summarize and discuss the findings of Roberts's Pentagon intelligence team which visited Miyazaki Beach in early November, 1945 (the

scheduled starting time for the mainland invasion) to check on their earlier intelligence estimates (paragraphs 16 to 20), and then relate these findings to the earlier, somewhat contradictory, casualty estimates which he cites in paragraphs 6 to 13.

THE CULT OF HIROSHIMA

André Ryerson

André Ryerson, a free-lance writer and former professor of French, develops a strong attack on the "cult of Hiroshima," the members of which, he says, insist that Americans should wallow in guilt indefinitely over the Hiroshima bombing. During the course of this attack he makes a spirited justification for President Truman's decision to drop the bomb.

Even as the formal days of atonement in the Jewish and Christian calendar **1.** weaken, lose some of their traditional power, and attract fewer of the young to their rites, the age-old human impulse to critical self-scrutiny, with resulting acts of contrition to amend for past sins, takes on a new and secularized form. The date is August 6. Its icon is a mushroom cloud. The sin to be expiated is America's. And the event is Hiroshima.

I

The casual observer can witness year by year the transformation of history into myth. **2.** With the predictability of a religious sacrament, the familiar images are pulled from the film vaults and presented to the public for viewing yet again—a sort of passion play for our time, with a cast of thousands and gorier than any Spanish depiction of the Cross.

This year, to break the growing pall of anonymity, newsmagazines commemorated **3.** the fortieth anniversary of the dropping of the bomb by detailing the minute-by-minute agonies of specific individuals at Hiroshima in 1945, those who perished, and those who painfully survived. Television showed American children taken to the exhibits at Hiroshima, choking and weeping with remorse and shame, for belonging to the nation that committed this crime. Evidently, while we would not think it proper to impose on the youth of Japan pangs of guilt for a war launched by their forebears in 1941, advanced opinion now seems ready to impose on the youth of the U.S. a more searing guilt for the way in which our country ended it.

The four hours consecrated to Hiroshima by PBS television on the evening of **4.** the fortieth anniversary this year encapsulated the now-standard view. A black social scientist from Harvard assured us that the dropping of the bomb was motivated by "racism." None of the five other guests saw fit to challenge this interpretation. Kurt Vonnegut, Jr., the celebrated novelist, calmly declared that Hiroshima was an act of "genocide," and that by dropping the bomb the United States "went into the Auschwitz business." Only one of the six guests (William Manchester, the lone historian) saw

Source: André Ryerson, "The Cult of Hiroshima," *Commentary.* October 1985: 36–40.

reason to object to this. The next three hours were given over to films, interspersed with commentary by an MIT scientist who had worked on the bomb and in remorse has since devoted his spare time to "peace" activities.

The first film, *The Day After Trinity,* gave a fair and even eloquent account of **5.** the decision to build the atomic bomb. But as it headed to the finish, and Japan instead of Germany loomed as the designated target, a distant crunch of ideological gears was felt, guilt began to flower, interviews concentrated almost exclusively on the scientists who later decided Hiroshima was a profoundly wrong decision, and the film concluded with an outright historical falsehood: that the United States did nothing to try to control the power of the atom it had unleashed. (Somehow, the Baruch and Lilienthal proposals for the international control of atomic energy and weapons—which Bertrand Russell considered so generous he thought America should present it to the Soviets not as a proposal but as an ultimatum—managed to slip the minds of the film's producers.)

There followed an animated Japanese film which even more perfectly served the **6.** cause of "peace activists" determined to transform history into myth. The scene is Hiroshima on August 6, 1945. Japanese people are seen going about their own business, children are at play, a trolley tinkles gaily down the street, a mother bares her breast tenderly to nurse her babe, and the only hint that a war might be going on is vaguely suggested by a man in uniform going to his lookout post to scan the skies. Then a silver plane appears. A smiling little boy points to it. Suddenly a flash, and hell on earth is loosed—peeling flesh, dead babies, blood encased bodies, carbonized corpses in grotesque postures.

This was a fairy tale of malevolence as neat as any that could be conceived, and **7.** here we had in its purest form the contemporary myth of Hiroshima. People are pursuing their daily lives, and for no rhyme or reason are blasted out of existence by distant, cold, technologically diabolical Americans. Small wonder that Hiroshima, presented thus, impresses the young around the world as a monstrous crime for which Americans are commanded to feel an endless guilt.

That such feelings of guilt are the aim of Western commemorations of Hiroshima, **8.** certainly, is unmistakable to anyone who has attended them. Where once such ceremonies were limited to Quakers, today all manner of activist groups, political and religious, old leftists, young pacifists, environmentalists, mainline churches. Eastern cultists, the hopeful and the frightened, peppered with secular liberals long out of the habit of Yom Kippur or Lent, gather ecumenically to mark Hiroshima Day as a date worthy of our shame and obloquy. To ensure that those congregated express themselves beyond mere tears and symbolic grief they are invited henceforth to "work actively for peace" so as to expiate in a meaningful way their understandable feelings of anguish. Exactly what "working for peace" should consist of, the more subtle public speakers and pastors do not say. They teach by example, through their own support of "peace" groups, through the Catholic bishops' pastoral letter on nuclear war, through the nuclear-freeze campaign, and through acts of protest and even civil disobedience against defense spending, local military installations, and the Pentagon.

Increasingly they also teach, directly, through the schools. Now our children can **9.** be called on to stare at the icon of a mushroom cloud not just on August 6 but on any day of the year. Boards of education have been lobbied assiduously to approve the introduction of "peace education" into the school curriculum from kindergarten through grade 12, and small towns to big cities such as Pittsburgh, Baltimore, Milwaukee, San Francisco, and the two largest—New York and Los Angeles County—have given their imprimatur to what have invariably turned out to be highly politicized programs of instruction drawn up either by nuclear-freeze groups or out-and-out pacifists. The entire state of California is about to make such programs mandatory for the children of its 25 million people. (Oregon has already done so.) The powerful National Education Association has taken a leading role in this cause. Films, grisly photographs, and detailed descriptions of what the Hiroshima residents endured at American hands enjoy a premier place in the effort to trace on the minds of the young the stigmata of permanent remorse, disgust at the mad ''build-up'' by our country of weapons far worse than the Hiroshima bomb, and a metaphysical resolve to pursue nuclear disarmament at any cost.

II

That there is something not quite *right* about all this, seemed as clear to some Americans **10.** this past August as was the equally apparent impropriety of protesting it. Who would deny the suffering of the victims of Hiroshima? The ill-articulated reactions of popular irritation, the grumblings from American veterans of the Pacific, the angry letters to the networks for their failure to stress why it was we dropped the bomb, expressed what ''sophisticated'' people may consider crude emotions. On closer scrutiny, however, these crude emotions may constitute not just signs of basic health but a more accurate understanding of the moral complexities of forty years ago. Since August 6 is not going to disappear from our calendar, and since the evolution of Hiroshima into myth has been accomplished by isolating and removing it from the context of the war in which it occurred, the proper response is patiently, deliberately, and repeatedly to recontextualize it.

To begin with, if we wish yearly to remember the personal sufferings of those **11.** who died in World War II, surely one may ask why we ignore the millions of victims of Japanese fascism—Koreans, Manchurians, Chinese, Indochinese, Burmese, Malays, and Filipinos? After all, those who died at Hiroshima and Nagasaki were made to do so for a reason—to end the war—whereas the millions of people killed and wounded by the Japanese suffered for no reason at all, were *victims* in the root sense of being truly innocent. Yet thanks to contemporary revisionism, the primary victims—the victims of Japanese aggression across the Pacific—have been forgotten, allowed to slip down some black hole of cultural memory, while the secondary victims—the Japanese themselves—have been raised to a privileged public altar. It is as if the war in Europe were to be commemorated by yearly attention to German civilians who died in the bombing of Dresden and Hamburg, while the victims of Nazi aggression on the battlefield and in the death camps were to be consigned to oblivion.

When it comes to the decision taken by Truman and his advisers to drop the **12.** bomb, a similarly selective amnesia seems to operate, both with regard to the actual circumstances that existed at the time and with regard to other possible courses of action open to the U.S. Thus, many of those who denounce Truman for dropping the bomb cite an alternative option: the United States could have invited the Japanese to witness a demonstration of the new weapon on some empty atoll, and the spectacle would have sufficed to make them acknowledge defeat and accept surrender. It is a nice idea. Unfortunately, this scenario ignores two sets of facts. The first concerns the practicality of such a demonstration; the second concerns the philosophy of death and war that prevailed in Japan at the time and that dominated the thinking of the Japanese leadership until the very end.

It was Dr. Arthur Holly Compton, a scientist-adviser to the interim committee **13.** on the ultimate use of the new weapon, who explicitly proposed to Secretary of War Henry L. Stimson that the bomb first be shown the Japanese by way of demonstration. The committee then discussed the proposal. The objections were numerous.

First, if the test were done on neutral soil the Japanese might think it was a fake, **14.** accomplished with a massive amount of ordinary TNT.

Second, if it were to be dropped on an isolated spot in Japan, the need to notify **15.** the Japanese as to time and place would allow them to shoot down the plane carrying the bomb.

Third, the actual bomb devices were new and scarcely tested. Any number of **16.** things could malfunction. What would be the psychological effect on Japanese leaders of a flub?

Fourth, only two bombs were available at the time, and every day the war **17.** continued meant death for thousands.

Fifth, the very idea of demonstrating the bomb ran counter to its purpose—to **18.** shock the Japanese out of their faith that dying in war was a noble and heroic enterprise.

Nothing is more natural for a democracy at war than for its leader—elected by **19.** the people and answerable to them—to attempt to ensure that victory is attained with the minimum loss of soldiers' lives. For an industrial democracy, firepower is the means to that end. The almost extravagant use of material firepower in order to save young men's lives has been called, rightly, "the American way of war." Using the atom bomb against Japan was simply the ultimate step in an approach to war that marked the Pacific conflict from the moment Douglas MacArthur took command.

The Japanese view was close to the reverse of the American. Death in war was **20.** not to be avoided, but to be sought. The Shinto cult of radical self-sacrifice taught that suicide was glorious while surrender was unthinkable disgrace. So numerous were the suicide volunteers who spontaneously arose in the ranks of the Japanese armed forces that they were organized separately for routine training in the technique of air or naval *kamikaze,* the way other soldiers were taught to operate a radio or drive a jeep. One-man suicide submarines were specifically designed and manufactured for the purpose, and human torpedoes or *kaiten* followed, employed by the hundreds against Allied shipping.

But it was in the air that the *kamikaze* ethos proved most effective; at Okinawa **21.** alone the Special Attack Corps sent as many as 1,500 volunteers against American ships. In addition to the spiritual satisfactions of a glorious suicide, the Japanese considered this an effective means of countering the American advantage in materiel. A lone suicidal airman could sink a whole destroyer. The motto of the Special Attack Corps was, "one plane, one ship."

The peculiar disgrace that the Japanese attached to surrender was one of the **22.** causes of the despicable treatment American POW's suffered at the hands of the Japanese—far worse than their treatment by the Nazis. The reason lay in the very fact of surrender. For the Japanese this made the American POW's the equivalent of "subhumans," and in consequence there was no compunction about using them for experimental purposes, either to inject them with diseases or to observe the effects on them of weapons and exposure. All this was quite apart from the ordinary cruelty in warfare for which the Japanese made themselves notorious in all the nations of the Orient they conquered.

Japanese revulsion at the idea of surrender was seen throughout the war. The **23.** number of prisoners yielded was minimal. When U.S. troops succeeded in taking Okinawa not only did Japanese uniformed men commit suicide in droves to avoid the degradation of being captured, but thousands of ordinary Japanese civilians did so as well. Mothers with their babies in their arms leaped off cliffs to their deaths; student nurses, gathered in small groups, blew themselves up with a single hand grenade.

As American forces advanced closer to the Japanese mainland, this ferocity and **24.** refusal to surrender, clearly witnessed at Iwo Jima, did not diminish but increased. The Japanese military leaders used it to argue—quite logically—that a battle on the soil of Japan would result in a toll of American dead in numbers not yet seen and would certainly produce the most sensational and bloody climax to the Pacific war.

The American plan of invasion (until news of the successful Trinity test reached **25.** Truman at Potsdam) was to land three-quarters of a milion U.S. troops on Kyushu on November 1. (This would be the *initial* landing, already four times the troop level at Normandy.) The Japanese for their part had prepared KETSUGO or Operation Decision: 2,350,000 soldiers would crush the Americans as they landed on the beaches. They would be backed by four million army and navy civilian employees, a special garrison of a quarter-million, and a mammoth civil militia of 28 million men and women armed with everything from feudal muskets to bamboo spears.

The leadership repeatedly made clear its intention to fight to the last man, woman, **26.** child. As late as June, following the devastating incendiary bombing of Tokyo, the entire Cabinet issued this statement: "With a faith born of eternal loyalty as our inspiration, we shall—thanks to the advantages of our terrain and the unity of our nation—prosecute the war to the bitter end in order to uphold our national essence, protect the imperial land, and achieve our goals of conquest." Prime Minister Suzuki spelled it out more colloquially at a press conference: "If our hundred million people fight with the resolve to sacrifice their lives, I believe it is not at all impossible to attain the great goal of preserving the essence of Japan."

The slaughter that would have followed an American land invasion of Japan **27.** would have been unimaginable on both sides. Estimates of a half-million U.S. soldiers and one million Japanese killed are not high but low. Any American President deciding to undertake such a bloody exchange of lives while refusing to use the atom bomb once the option presented itself would almost certainly have been impeached by the American people and condemned at the bar of history.

If anything, Truman and his aides exaggerated the shock effect that atomic blasts **28.** would have on the Japanese leadership. Even *after* both Hiroshima and Nagasaki, the Japanese Cabinet was deadlocked and could not agree on the Allied terms of surrender. General Umezu expressed his confidence that future atomic attacks could be stemmed by anti-aircraft measures, while on land "we will be able to destroy the major part of an invading force." The War Minister, General Anami, told the Cabinet: "That we will inflict severe losses on the enemy when he invades Japan is certain, and it is not impossible to reverse the situation and pull victory out of defeat.'' When several civilian ministers timidly ventured that the people were tired and that food shortages threatened, the War Minister snapped: ''Everyone understands all that, but we must fight to the end no matter how great the odds against us!'' He concluded with finality, ''Our men will simply refuse to lay down their arms. They know they are forbidden to surrender. There is really no alternative for us but to continue the war.''

Despite two atomic bombs, then, the Cabinet could not accept the idea of **29.** conceding defeat. As John Toland reveals in his fascinating and monumental *The Rising Sun: The Decline and Fall of the Japanese Empire,* the surrender of Japan was finally the result of a bold initiative by Prince Kido. As Privy Seal, Kido was in a position to sound out the Emperor, who was constitutionally forbidden from initiating policy; Kido found he favored surrender. Prime Minister Suzuki now also inclined to surrender, so Kido proposed the unprecedented move of having Suzuki ask the Emperor—at an imperial conference with the full Cabinet present—what his opinion was. The Emperor would delicately indicate his preference, and the military would be confronted with a *fait accompli,* for how could they defy the Emperor's will?

Yet even though the imperial conference went just as Prince Kido planned, that **30.** too was not the end of it. Once out of the Emperor's presence, various military leaders began having second thoughts. Not just one but several plots were hatched for a palace coup to seize power, isolate the Emperor, and pursue the war. Admiral Onishi, the organizer of the *kamikaze* corps, said to conspirators of the Hatanaka group: ''We must throw ourselves headlong into the plan and make it come true. If we are prepared to sacrifice 20 million Japanese lives in a 'special attack' effort, victory will be ours!'' General Anami was disposed to sacrifice still more lives while holding out the hope of less tangible results: ''Even if we fail in the attempt, 100 million people are ready to die for honor, glorifying the deeds of the Japanese race in recorded history!''

To succeed in averting the surrender of Japan it was essential that the conspirators **31.** seize the recording the Emperor had made calling on his people to envisage ''enduring the unendurable and suffering what is insufferable.'' The insurgents narrowly failed in the attempt. Their leaders then duly and by various means committed *hara-kiri.*

As Japanese who were adults at the time later testified, the greatest shock of **32.** those days was not the news of Hiroshima and Nagasaki. It was hearing for the first time in their lives the voice of the Emperor, speaking the unspeakable, and instructing them to surrender. They could hardly believe it.

III

These facts, readily available to anyone interested, explode the claim that the Japanese **33.** were ready to surrender prior to the dropping of the atom bombs, and that Hiroshima and Nagasaki amounted to gratuitous acts of barbarism. Almost as foolish is the claim that the Soviet entry into the Pacific war was enough to make the Japanese surrender. The Germans, after all, had maintained two war fronts without seeing in this circumstance a reason to surrender, and only seven weeks before Hiroshima, Prime Minister Suzuki—a "moderate"—confessed himself astonished that the Germans had not fought to the last man.

It required, finally, the combination of all three events—Hiroshima, Nagasaki, **34.** and the August 9 declaration of war on Japan by the Soviets—to convince even the civilian leadership of the need for surrender. It then required the stratagem of Prince Kido to outfox the military leaders, a stratagem which in turn had to survive their attempts at a palace coup. The claim that the bomb was not a necessary element in this chain of events simply cannot withstand an examination of the historical record.

Neither can the outrageous and impertinent charge that the United States dropped **35.** the bomb on Hiroshima out of "racism." Proving this would require, first of all, showing that the bomb was not needed for reasons of war, and that the Japanese leadership was previously disposed to surrender—claims plainly contrary to fact. But even if the bomb had not been needed to compel surrender, end the war promptly, and thus save *Japanese* as well as American lives, the "racism" thesis would founder on the fact that the bomb had been developed in the first place with Nazi Germany—a white European nation—in mind. Nor had this supposed racial advantage preserved the Germans from Allied bombings quite as deadly as what befell Hiroshima, as those who survived Dresden and Hamburg can testify. Likewise impaled on these same humble points of fact is Gar Alperovitz's thesis, advanced in *Atomic Diplomacy: Hiroshima and Potsdam*, that Truman used the atom bomb simply to intimidate the Soviets, the Japanese being, so to speak, gratuitous victims of American cold-war malevolence (even before any conventionally accepted date for when the cold war actually began).

The real meaning of Hiroshima is that war is an extremely nasty business, and **36.** that we must do everything consonant with our freedom and our honor to assure that such terrible events do not recur. Modern warfare is particularly trying on the conscience of decent people because the tension between the need to save one's own men and the requirement indiscriminately to kill the enemy's rises with each "improvement" in the destructive capacity of the weapons, thereby narrowing the scope of moral choice into a series of increasingly grim alternatives. The decision to drop the bomb on Hiroshima was just such a choice. It was almost certainly the correct choice. But that does not make it any more pleasant in retrospect to contemplate. The evil, if evil there was, lay not in the dropping of the bomb but in the circumstances, i.e., the war itself, that compelled Truman and his advisers to make the choice they did.

Intelligent thinkers, were such unexpectedly to arise in the television business, **37.** would begin to grasp that the evil of World War II is not to be found by flying a crew to Hiroshima to record interviews, but by inquiring a little more studiously into the causes of that war. Those causes in the first instance lay in the mad and aggressive myths of superiority on which the German and Japanese people were too long fed but also in their perception of the Western democracies as decadent, hedonistic, and timorous societies that would be reluctant to fight.

Western pacifists of the 1930's were significantly responsible for creating and **38.** abetting the latter impression. Oblivious of history's lessons, and armed now with a powerful myth of guilt and shame, their descendants are spreading the selfsame notions today. The consequences then were death, suffering, and destruction on a hitherto unimaginable scale. If old follies are embraced anew, what will be the consequences tomorrow?

WORKING WITH THE TEXT

Cultural and Historical References

In this section, the numbers at the margin refer to the numbered paragraphs in the selection itself.

1. An "icon" is a religious image or object. Why might Ryerson want to call the A-bomb's mushroom cloud an icon?

2. A "passion play" is a drama of Jesus's trial, agonies, and death.

2. A "sacrament," in general terms, is something that has sacred significance. In specific terms it is one of the seven official rites of the Catholic church.

4. To "consecrate" something is to set it aside for religious purposes. Ryerson continues to use words with religious connotations. Why?

4. "Genocide" is the planned annihilation of a race or cultural group. What genocides can you think of in human history?

5. Bertrand Russell was a pacifist and constant critic of U.S. involvement in World War II, the Korean conflict, and the war in Vietnam.

8. On Yom Kippur, a Jewish holiday, and Lent, a Christian holiday, its celebrants fast and atone. Do you know what those two holidays commemorate?

20. Shinto is the ancient religion of Japan. It is characterized, in part, by worship of one's ancestors. Why does Ryerson bring it up?

29. A "*fait accompli*" is something that has already been accomplished—or is as good as accomplished. Why is it in italics?

Writing Assignments: The Paragraph

Be sure to provide an introduction for each of the following paragraph writing assignments. That is, begin each paragraph with a phrase like this: "Thomas Brickle claims that. . . ." When it is relevant, you might also want to identify the expertise of the author ("Thomas Brickle, a New Testament scholar, claims that. . . ."), the name of the book or article, the century and country in which the work appeared, or any other circumstances that your readers might find significant. For more on this, see pp. 11–13 in Chapter 2.

1. Begin by introducing Ryerson's phrase, "fairy tale of malevolence" (paragraph 7), and then paraphrase his support for that statement.

2. Summarize paragraph 10.

3. What does Ryerson mean when he says that we must "recontextualize" the war?

Writing Assignments: The Short Essay

Use informal documentation for these short essays. That is, don't use footnotes or a Works Cited page to document your sources. Instead, cite only relevant information about your source, and keep that information *within* your text. Then follow the summary or quote with a page number in parentheses. (Use the page numbers that you find in this book to represent the page numbers of the source.) Thus, your informal documentation will look something like this:

> In *The Rising Sun*, John Toland says that in the instant after the A-bomb attack on Hiroshima, "All over the center of the city numerous silhouettes were imprinted on walls" (p. 468).

1. Write a paper on the religious terminology in Ryerson's essay, particularly in paragraphs 1 and 2.

2. Argue with Ryerson's point in paragraph 11 that the victims of Hiroshima and Nagasaki were somehow different than the victims of Korea, Manchuria, and so on.

3. Paraphrase Ryerson's conclusion, which begins with paragraph 36.

4. Write an essay on Ryerson's arguments, and state why you did or did not find them to be persuasive.

ESSAYS ON *HIROSHIMA AND NAGASAKI*

Short Essays

Use informal documentation for these short essays. That is, don't use foot-notes or a Works Cited page to document your sources. Instead, cite only relevant information about your source, and keep that information *within* your text. Then follow the summary or quote with a page number in parentheses. (Use the page numbers that you find in this book to represent the page numbers of the source.) Thus, your informal documentation will look something like this:

> In *The Romance of Medicine*, Benjamin Gordon, a history professor, says that it was once believed that red wine replenished a person's depleted blood supply (p. 121).

1. Contrast Kai Erikson's analysis of the probable effectiveness of the demonstration of the A-bomb's power with André Ryerson's analysis of the same topic.
2. Contrast Gar Alperovitz's analysis of the Stalin factor with Kai Erikson's.
3. Contrast Gar Alperovitz's appraisal of Japanese strength on the eve of Hiroshima with André Ryerson's.
4. Contrast Gar Alperovitz's interpretation of Japanese willingness to sue for peace with Chalmers Roberts's interpretation.

Long Essays

For rules governing formal documentation, see Chapter 6.

1. Argue the case for dropping the A-bomb.
2. Argue the case for not dropping the A-bomb.
3. Write a report on the arguments on both sides.
4. Discuss the statistics in a number of the essays in this chapter. You might focus in particular on the estimates of the numbers of Americans who would be killed in an invasion attempt. We'll start you off by pointing you to paragraph 8 in Gar Alperovitz's essay, paragraph 27 in André Ryerson's essay, and most paragraphs in Chalmers Roberts's essay.

Acknowledgments

CHAPTER 1

Edmund Hillary. "Epitaph to the Elusive Abominable Snowman." *Life,* January 13, 1961.

Ernest Sackville Turner. *Call the Doctor.* New York: St. Martin's Press, 1959.

Aaron Copland. "How We Listen." From *What to Listen for in Music.* New York: McGraw-Hill, 1957.

Roul Tunley. "Can You Afford to Die?" *The Saturday Evening Post.* June 17, 1961.

John Madson. "On the Trail of the Curly Cows." *Outdoor Life.* April 1981.

William Zinsser. "Simplicity." From *On Writing Well: An Informal Guide to Writing Nonfiction.* New York: Harper and Row, 1976.

CHAPTER 2

Ernest Sackville Turner. *Call the Doctor.* New York: St. Martin's Press, 1959.

J. H. Plumb. "De Mortuis." *Horizon,* Spring 1967.

Barbara Tuchman. *A Distant Mirror. The Calamitous 14th Century.* New York: Alfred A. Knopf, 1978.

H. S. Glasscheib. *The March of Medicine.* Mervyn Savill (trans.). New York: G. P. Putman's Sons, 1964.

E. B. White. "Here Is New York." From *The Essays of E. B. White.* New York: Harper and Row, 1977.

Carla Herndandez. "Legs." [student essay].

Jacob Bronowski. "Man and the Grunion." From *The Ascent of Man.* New York: Little, Brown, 1973.

Kelli Burkeen. "Main Street: The Agora of Rural America" [student essay].
Judy Syfers. "Why I Want a Wife." *Ms.*, January 1972.
Marina Warner. "New-Born Mother." London, *Observer,* July 24, 1977.
Nat Hentoff. "When Nice People Burn Books." *The Progressive,* February 1983.

CHAPTER 3

Barbara Tuchman. *A Distant Mirror: The Calamitous 14th Century.* New York: Alfred A. Knopf, 1978.
Edward Sackville Turner. *The Court of St. James's.* London: Michael Joseph, Ltd., 1959.
Spenser Klaw. "Belly My Grizzle." *American Heritage,* June 1977.
H. S. Glasscheib. *The March of Medicine.* Mervyn Savill (trans.). New York: G. P. Putman's Sons, 1964.
Eric Gelman. "MTV's Message." *Newsweek,* December 30, 1985.
Richard Kuh. "Foolish Figleaves?" *Pornography in—and out of—Court.* New York: Macmillan, 1967.
D. Keith Mano. "Cruel Lib." *Newsweek,* September 8, 1975.
Paul Russell Cutright. "I gave him barks and saltpeter . . ." *American Heritage,* December 1963.
Barbara Ehrenreich and Deirdre English. "For Her Own Good—The Tyranny of the Experts." *Ms.,* December 1978.
Dalma Heyn. "Body Hate." *Ms.,* August 1989.

CHAPTER 4

Robert and Peggy Stinson. "On the Death of a Baby." *Atlantic,* July 1979.
Thomas Chalmers and Alfred Stern. "The Staggering Cost of Prolonging Life." *Business Week,* February 23, 1981.
Andrew H. Malcolm. "Test Case Is Shaped by Doctors' Ethics, One Man's Suffering." *The Courier-Journal,* October 22, 1984.
Terry Daniels. "Nurse's Tale." *New York,* April 30, 1971.
Arthur Caplan. "We're the Prisoners of Medical Technology." *USA Today,* September 20, 1984.
Matt Clark. "When Doctors Play God." *Newsweek,* August 31, 1981.
Nat Hentoff. "The Awful Privacy of Baby Doe." The *Atlantic Monthly,* January 1985.
Jiggs Gallagher. "Don't Pull the Plug, Even on the Terminally Ill." *USA Today,* November 27, 1984.
Steven Findlay. "It's a Costly Mistake That Just Denies Death." *USA Today,* November 27, 1984.
Judie Brown. "Best Medicine Is Love, Not Doses of Death." *USA Today,* January 11, 1985.

CHAPTER 5

Vance Packard. From *The Wastemakers.* New York: Pocket Books, 1965.
John Lee. "Has Anyone Here Seen My Old Friend Jimi?" [student essay].

Keith Mano. ''Cruel Lib.'' *Newsweek,* September 8, 1975.
Anne Roiphe. ''Confessions of a Female Chauvinist Sow.'' *New York Magazine,* October 30, 1972.

CHAPTER 6

Donna J. Habig. ''Tropical Rain Forests: An Endangered Species'' [student essay].

Index